THE GREAT RECESSION AND IMPORT PROTECTION

The Role of Temporary Trade Barriers

The Great Recession and Import Protection: The Role of Temporary Trade Barriers

ISBN: 978-1-907142-38-3

The sculpture on the cover of this book is *Bread Line* by George Segal, Franklin Delano Roosevelt Memorial, Washington, DC

Copyedited and typeset by T&T Productions Ltd, London

Published in association with the London Publishing Partnership
www.londonpublishingpartnership.co.uk

Centre for Economic Policy Research

The Centre for Economic Policy Research is a network of over 700 Research Fellows and Affiliates, based primarily in European universities. The Centre coordinates the research activities of its Fellows and Affiliates and communicates the results to the public and private sectors. CEPR is an entrepreneur, developing research initiatives with the producers, consumers and sponsors of research. Established in 1983, CEPR is a European economics research organization with uniquely wide-ranging scope and activities.

The Centre is pluralist and non-partisan, bringing economic research to bear on the analysis of medium- and long-run policy questions. CEPR research may include views on policy, but the Executive Committee of the Centre does not give prior review to its publications, and the Centre takes no institutional policy positions. The opinions expressed in this report are those of the authors and not those of the Centre for Economic Policy Research.

CEPR is a registered charity (No. 287287) and a company limited by guarantee and registered in England (No. 1727026).

The World Bank

The World Bank Group is a major source of financial and technical assistance to developing countries around the world, providing low-interest loans, interest-free credits and grants for investments and projects in areas such as education, health, public administration, infrastructure, trade, financial and private sector development, agriculture, and environmental and natural resource management. Established in 1944 and headquartered in Washington, DC, the Group has over 100 offices worldwide. The World Bank's mission is to fight poverty with passion and professionalism for lasting results and to help people help themselves and their environment by providing resources, sharing knowledge, building capacity and forging partnerships in the public and private sectors.

The Great Recession and Import Protection

The Role of Temporary Trade Barriers

edited by
CHAD P. BOWN

Contents

List of Figures

List of Tables

Acknowledgements

While it took the Great Recession of 2008-9 to incite the questions addressed by this volume, this research is part of a project that has been a number of years in the making. As such, I must gratefully acknowledge the contributions of many individuals; this research would not have been possible without them.

In 2004, Bernard Hoekman took me up on the idea of obtaining funding for the creation of the Global Antidumping Database. Without him, even the mere collection and public dissemination of the data would not have occurred. His support for the continued provision of this global public good has been unwavering.

Over the next seven years, many research assistants contributed tirelessly to the evolution and expansion of what has eventually turned into the World Bank's *Temporary Trade Barriers Database*. This began with the leadership of David Cheong in 2004, and, during the height of trade policy uncertainty of 2009 into 2010, it included the relentless data gathering and data improvement efforts of Milla Cieszkowsky, Yubing Cui, Paul Deng, Laura Gutowski, Sharon Kim and Aimi Yamamura.

One of the most important individuals behind this project was Aksel Erbahar, who led the data collection team throughout 2009–10, doggedly searching for new information, providing rigorous checking of facts and attention to even the most minute of details. He was also the fundamental organising force behind this book. Aksel deserves much of the credit for what can be learned from this body of research and none of the blame for any errors that remain.

Finally, the research in this book was supported by the generosity of the World Bank's Multi Donor Trust Fund for Trade and Development. Ongoing funding for data collection and dissemination of the *Temporary Trade Barriers Database* during 2009–10 was generously provided to the World Bank by the UK-funded Global Trade and Financial Architecture (GTFA) project.

Chad P. Bown, Editor

1

Introduction

CHAD P. BOWN[1]

The Great Recession of 2008–9 caused a negative shock to the global economy that is comparable with the Great Depression of the 1930s. The major advanced nations experienced painful economic contraction, severe dislocation to industrial production and sharp spikes in unemployment. Trade flows collapsed across all the regions of the world. Even the high-achieving emerging markets, seemingly isolated from the underlying financial-system mishaps that triggered the recessions in advanced economies, suffered a severe slowdown in their growth trajectories. The simultaneity and depth of this recession were new, and with them came an uncertainty that was especially endemic to the early periods of the crisis. There was uncertainty regarding the nadir to which global economic activity would ultimately plunge. There was uncertainty regarding the policies that governments were committed to implementing. There was particularly acute uncertainty regarding trade policy. Could the modern trading system withstand such a devastating economic blow? Specifically, would governments live up to their early-crisis pledge to refrain from protectionism?

In many ways, the 21st century world economy is very different from the 1930s. The possibility of a simultaneous and widespread economic calamity is greater given that trade volumes are larger, technology is more advanced, information flows more quickly, trade costs are lower, supply chains are extended across more countries, and nations are more economically and financially integrated with one another. And yet, cooperative international institutions—such as the World Trade Organization (WTO), World Bank, International Monetary Fund (IMF) and the Group of Twenty (G20)—have arisen since the 1930s to establish rules, norms and means of communicating and coordinating national policy decisions, especially during times of crisis, to help prevent calamity.

Ex post, one fundamental distinction between the Great Depression and the Great Recession is that the 2008–9 global economic contraction did *not* result in a massive wave of new protectionism. International trade was one of the

[1]Development Research Group, Trade and International Integration (DECTI), The World Bank, MSN MC3-303, 1818 H Street, NW Washington, DC 20433, USA. Email: cbown@worldbank.org. I gratefully acknowledge the research assistance of Aksel Erbahar. Caroline Freund and Cristina Neagu also shared useful data. All remaining errors are my own.

casualties of the 1930s as countries responded to recession by implementing policies designed either to isolate themselves from the global economy or to discriminate among potential trading partners as a form of retaliation (Irwin 2011). The 1930s policies contributed to the immediate disruption of international commerce and had the effect of impeding resumption of multilateral trade when underlying national economic conditions ultimately improved. In the midst of the 2008–9 global economic crisis, international trade flows also suffered a precipitous collapse. Nevertheless, international commerce quickly resumed on the path towards recovery. It is now unequivocal that the 2008–9 Great Recession did not lead to a set of catastrophic protectionist policies on anywhere near the scale of the 1930s Great Depression.

Comprehending *why* the 2008–9 economic crisis failed to trigger a downward spiral of 'beggar-thy-neighbour' policies is fundamental to understanding the resilience of the global economy and the 21st century multilateral trading system. The lack of a more potent protectionist response is still a puzzle, and the potential causes of the system's resilience will be investigated by researchers over the near and long term. Was it that the WTO architecture was impeccably constructed for the handling of the crisis? Or was it completely unrelated to WTO rules, and was the lack of a major protectionist response the result of a new political–economic order based on global supply chains? That is, because firms are exporters *and* importers, and lobbying for protection no longer happens, has the multilateral, rules-based WTO system become redundant? Was it the proliferation of preferential trade agreements (PTAs) that dampened the incentive to impose new trade barriers that would have ultimately only favoured PTA partners through trade diversion and not domestic industry? Was the policy discipline the result of developed economies' decisions to use fiscal stimulus as opposed to alternative (and arguably less efficient) trade policy to subsidise domestic industry and to address falling aggregate demand and political pressure? Or was it that the 'lessons learned' from earlier eras of economic calamity, including the Great Depression, created a stalwart resolve of the world's leaders this time around?

What is clear is that an ultimate understanding of how the multilateral trading system survived the crisis requires an accurate assessment of how the import protection landscape did change alongside the events of 2008–9. While there was not a large-scale resort to protectionism, the facts simply do not support the idea that countries did not adjust their trade policies during this period. Many countries were quite active with their trade policy during the crisis, and an understanding of the details of this activity is required in order to generate insight into how the trading system withstood the threat of collapse.

Policies like anti-dumping, safeguards and countervailing duties (CVDs)—what this volume refers to collectively as *temporary trade barriers* (TTBs)—played an important and perhaps even critical role during the 2008–9 crisis. Governments are authorised, under the rules of the WTO system, to have access in place to such policies and to implement new trade restrictions that temporarily limit imports if certain economic conditions are met. During the crisis, the media focused tremendous public attention on certain high profile TTB cases, such as European Union (EU) treatment of imported footwear from China, the US safeguard on imports of tyres from China, and China's retaliatory use of anti-dumping—in one instance on EU exports of steel fasteners and in another on US exports of autos and chicken parts. Nevertheless, TTBs arguably made substantial contributions to the *stability* of the trading system during 2008–9, although the channels through which this took place are complex. These channels include not only the ways in which TTBs were used, but how they were not used, and how their availability made it possible for governments to *avoid* using other, potentially more draconian protectionist measures. This volume offers a collection of research that begins to fill a major information gap by providing empirical details of many of the important changes taking place under these trade policies during 2008–9.

This volume focuses on 11 of the largest economies in the world.[2] By 2007, these 11 economies—including 4 developed and 7 emerging—collectively accounted for nearly three-quarters of world GDP and nearly two-thirds of world merchandise imports. Each of these economies is a member of the G20 and the WTO, and is thus subject to multilateral disciplines on TTB use. They each had substantial pre-crisis experience with TTB use, and collectively they account for 76% of total TTB investigations initiated by all WTO members between 1995 and 2007. The approach of each chapter in the volume is to establish facts on how one economy used TTBs in 2008–9 given the context of its historical use, how these TTBs relate to its other trade policies, and how the economy was affected by prevailing conditions during the crisis. Collectively, these facts improve our understanding of how the WTO system was able to withstand the crisis intact, and the facts contribute an insight into what policy and institutional challenges remained as a legacy of the crisis.

The rest of this introductory chapter proceeds as follows. Next, I provide a more detailed timeline and summary of events in the Great Recession, including its macroeconomic and trade impacts, the uncertainty over trade policy in 2008–9, and the response to calls for additional monitoring of trade policy. In particular, Section 1 highlights the real time monitoring efforts of the World Bank's Global Antidumping Database and subsequent *Temporary Trade Barriers Database*. These contributions have addressed some of the immediate concern about the unknown scale of protectionism taking place in 2008–9, but they have also revealed a lack of informational preparedness that has ultimately spurred this volume's research. In Section 2, I introduce a relatively simple methodological framework to improve intertemporal assessment of the scope of TTB use, an approach that many of the volume's chapters adopt or modify to construct better measures of the 'stock' and 'flow' of imported

---

[2]In particular, and in chapter order, these 11 economies are the USA, the EU, Canada, Korea, China, India, Brazil, Argentina, Mexico, Turkey and South Africa.

products that countries subject to TTBs. (A more technical description of the methodology is provided in the Appendix (Section 6), along with details of the many common data sources used across the subsequent chapters.)

What are the empirical results? Section 3 provides a simple application of this methodology and finds that, during the crisis, these economies collectively increased by 25% the imported products that they subjected to TTB import protection. Nevertheless, it turns out this collective expansion in TTB coverage during 2008–9 was dominated by *emerging* economies. Developing countries used TTBs to cover 39% more imported products by the end of 2009 compared with 2007, whereas recession-ravaged high-income economies surprisingly increased their coverage by only 4%. However, it is also clear from the data that understanding these crisis changes demands recognition of longer-term trends. Thus, given these high-level results, Section 4 turns to a number of common questions that the subsequent chapters investigate, on an economy-by-economy basis, in more detail. This section provides a short preview of how the volume's authors subsequently address these questions by placing the trade policy changes of 2008–9 into historical context. Section 5 then concludes.

1 A WALK THROUGH 2008–10

1.1 The Great Recession, Trade Collapse and Protectionist Uncertainty

The 2008–9 Great Recession resulted in a massive global economic contraction. The IMF has estimated that world output contracted by 0.2% in 2009, led by a developed economy decline of 3.2% and relatively anaemic emerging and developing economy growth of only 2.5% (IMF 2010).

Figure 1.1 illustrates the abrupt and simultaneous decline in economic activity during the Great Recession for the 11 economies studied in this volume. In the quarterly data, panel (a) illustrates that real US GDP began to decline in the first quarter (Q1) of 2008.[3] After a brief respite in Q2, US GDP fell sharply in Q3 (−4.0% at an annualised rate) and Q4 (−6.8%) and continued its decline into 2009 Q1 and Q2. Quarterly GDP for the EU and Canada followed a similar trend—each also experienced steady declines until the EU (respectively, Canada) shrank by a *stunning* 9.4% (respectively, 7.0%) at an annualised rate in 2009 Q1. Each of these three major developed economies did not achieve positive quarterly growth again until 2009 Q3.

Panels (b) and (c) of Figure 1.1 indicate similar trends on GDP growth for other major economies. Korea, Turkey, South Africa, Argentina, Brazil and Mexico had all been experiencing positive growth until 2008, when economic conditions sharply deteriorated and each of them witnessed at least one quar-

[3] The National Bureau of Economic Research's official Business Cycle Dating Committee marked the monthly beginning of the US recession as December 2007 and its conclusion as June 2009 (NBER 2010). In the full quarterly data, US GDP did not fall until 2008 Q1.

ter of economic contraction. The exceptions in Figure 1.1 are China and India, presented in panel (d), whose economies did not contract during 2008–9. Nevertheless, even China's and India's real GDP experienced sharp slowdowns to their growth trajectories in the second half of 2008 and the first half of 2009, coinciding with the timing of the economic contractions experienced in other economies.

In comparison, international trade flows collapsed shortly *after* the decline in real GDP growth in the major developed economies in early 2008. Figure 1.2 presents indices of nominal, seasonally adjusted merchandise imports by country on a quarterly basis for 2007–10. European Union imports began to decline sharply in 2008 Q3 and bottomed out in 2009 Q1. US and Canadian imports began to fall in 2008 Q4 and did not reach their lowest point until 2009 Q2. The sharp contraction in international trade flows beginning in 2008 Q4 is apparent for each of the other economies illustrated in Figure 1.2 as well. This includes China and India, countries that did not experience economic contraction. The peak-to-trough *decline* in nominal imports for these 11 economies during this period ranged from a low of 30% for the EU to a high of 49% for South Africa, with all of the others in between.[4]

The economic uncertainty beginning in late 2008 was palpable. Was this another Great Depression? How deep would the economic contraction get? Why were international trade flows falling so much faster than even GDP, which itself was contracting sharply? How much of the trade collapse was due to protectionism? Would a continued recession spark additional demands by injured industries and unemployed workers for isolationist trade policies? While it was difficult even for economic analysts to address these questions at the time given the delay in data reporting and the lack of comprehensive and up-to-date information, public attention quickly picked up on these themes.

Figure 1.3 illustrates some of this uncertainty and the associated public interest by plotting a Google Trends time series of data for two Internet searches. Internet searches for the term 'Great Depression' spiked sharply in 2008 Q4 (October), a timing that corresponds with the deepening contraction illustrated by the macroeconomic indicators of Figure 1.1.[5] In September,

[4]Freund (2009a,b) provides a thorough comparison of the 2008–9 trade collapse with other historical downturns. It is important to highlight that the indices in Figure 1.2 are presented in nominal terms by design. The collapse in *real* imports during this period was much smaller than the collapse in nominal imports, due to the sharp drop in import prices that accompanied the fall in volumes. (The sharp run-up in oil and other commodity prices reversed itself in the middle of 2008, the price decline moderating the impact on real imports.) Nevertheless, because this price decline was potentially not immediately understood by all market participants, the nominal figures are illustrated here.

[5]Figure 1.3 does not seasonally adjust the search terms. For example, it might be the case that Internet searches for 'Great Depression' tend to increase during the spring and fall, when students are writing term papers. For a discussion of uses of Google Trends in research, see Choi and Varian (2009).

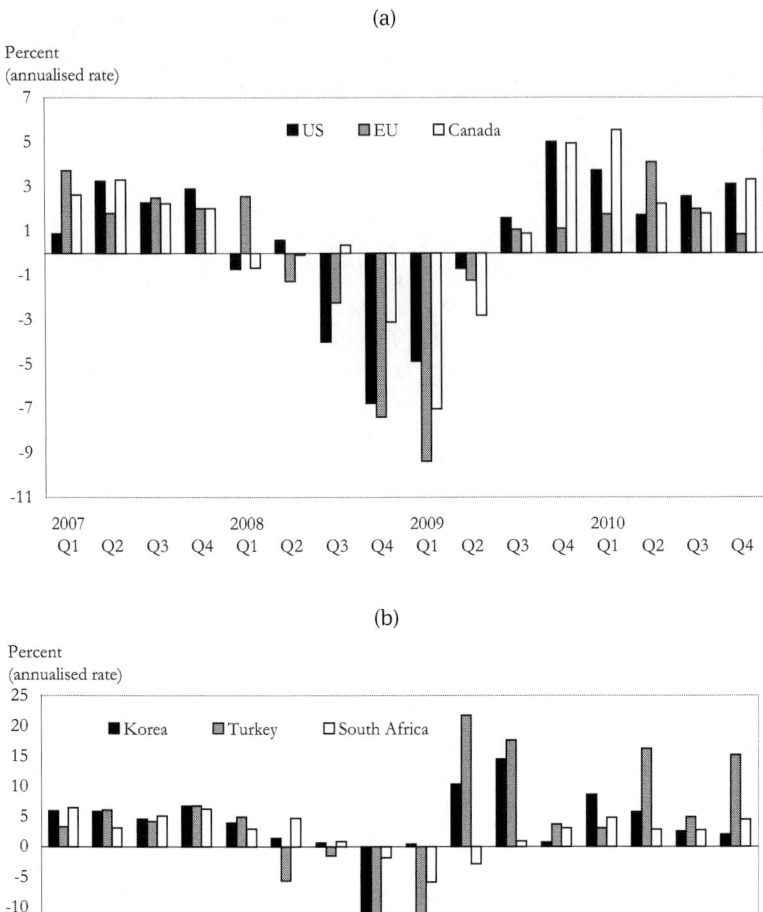

Figure 1.1: *The Great Recession: real GDP growth by quarter, 2007–10.*

the investment bank Lehman Brothers had filed for bankruptcy, setting off US government support for other major financial institutions that ultimately led to the US establishment of the Troubled Asset Relief Program in October.

The first G20 leaders' summit took place in Washington in November 2008, and world leaders announced the need for major policy coordination. One particularly important and oft-cited announcement was their call for self-

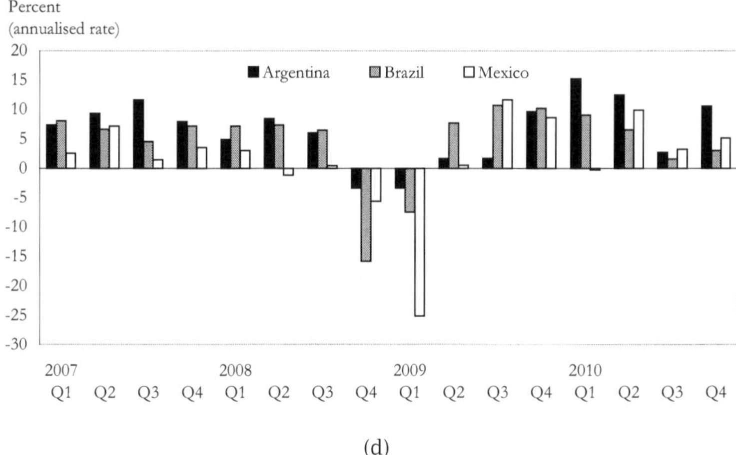

(d)

Percent
(annualised rate)
16
14
12
10
8
6
4
2
0
China
India
2007
2008
2009
2010
Q1 Q2 Q3 Q4 Q1 Q2 Q3 Q4 Q1 Q2 Q3 Q4 Q1 Q2 Q3 Q4

Figure 1.1: *Continued.*

Source: OECD (2011) for all countries except China and India, for which the data are World Bank estimates. Each figure presents the percentage change in quarterly real GDP growth at an annualised rate. Brazil's figures are estimates.

restraint on protectionist behaviour.[6] Nevertheless, the scope of new trade barriers that countries may have *already* imposed was, for data availability

[6]The G20 leaders' summit on 15 November 2008 included the following in its declaration (emphasis added): 'We underscore the critical importance of *rejecting protectionism* and not turning inwards in times of financial uncertainty. In this regard, within the next 12 months, we will refrain from raising new barriers to investment or to trade in goods and services, imposing new export restrictions, or implementing WTO-inconsistent measures to stimulate exports'.

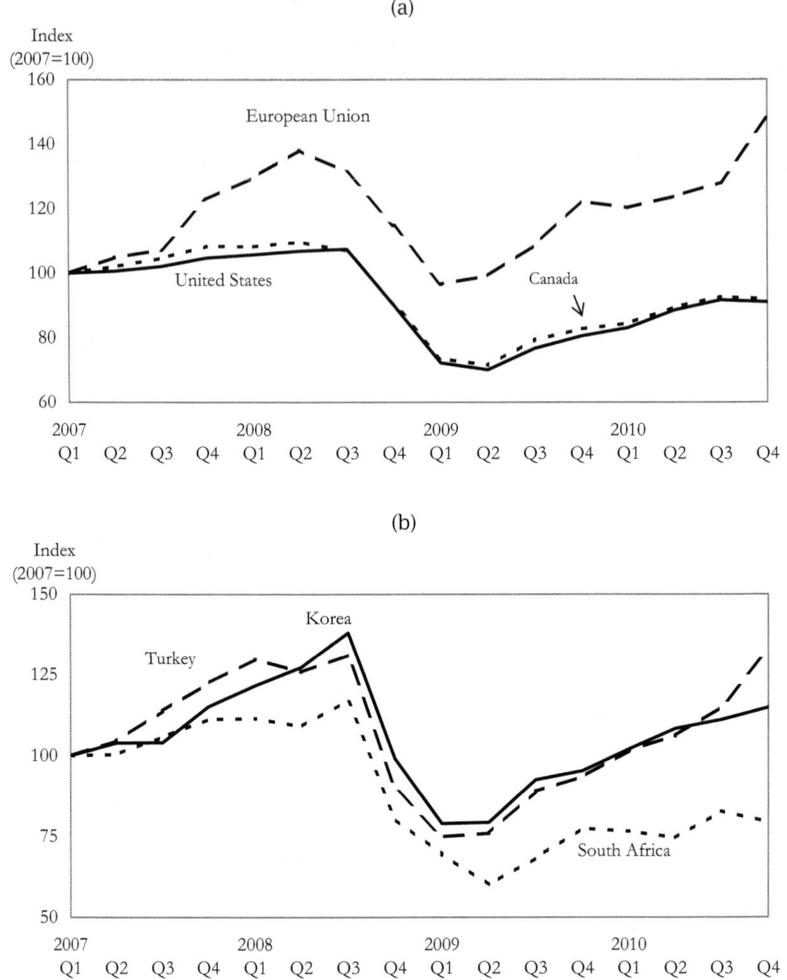

Figure 1.2: *The great trade collapse and recovery: merchandise imports by quarter, 2007–10.*

reasons, still largely unknown. The trade collapse that had begun in 2008 Q3 (see again Figure 1.2) was still in the early stages of being detected by the government statistical agencies charged with collecting and disseminating monthly trade data. The extent to which previously undetected protectionism may have somehow contributed to the deepening and ongoing trade collapse was unclear, but the idea that new trade barriers had been contributors was likely under suspicion. Furthermore, a second and increasing concern was that the deepening contraction to the global macroeconomy might stoke

(c)

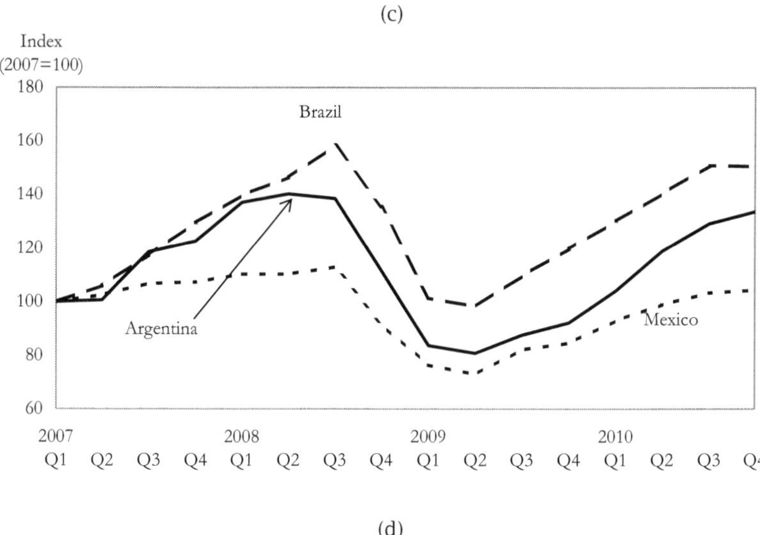

(d)

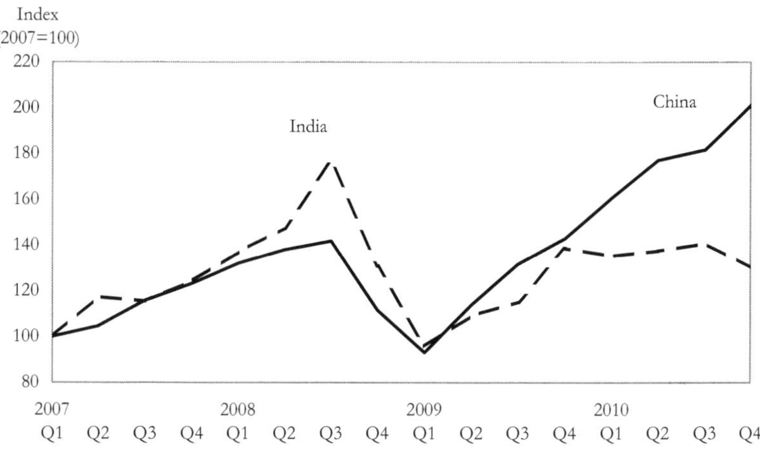

Figure 1.2: *Continued.*

Source: author's calculations based on data provided by World Bank's Trade Watch (Freund and Ngeau 2011). Each figure presents an index of seasonally adjusted, nominal merchandise trade flows.

nationalist sentiment and populist demands that governments impose *future* trade barriers in an attempt to isolate national economies from the events of the global economy.

Figure 1.3 documents this uncertainty over trade policy and the increased public interest during 2008–9 by plotting the Google Trends time series of data for an Internet search of the term 'Protectionism'. This search term tracked the increased search for 'Great Depression', with an accompanying

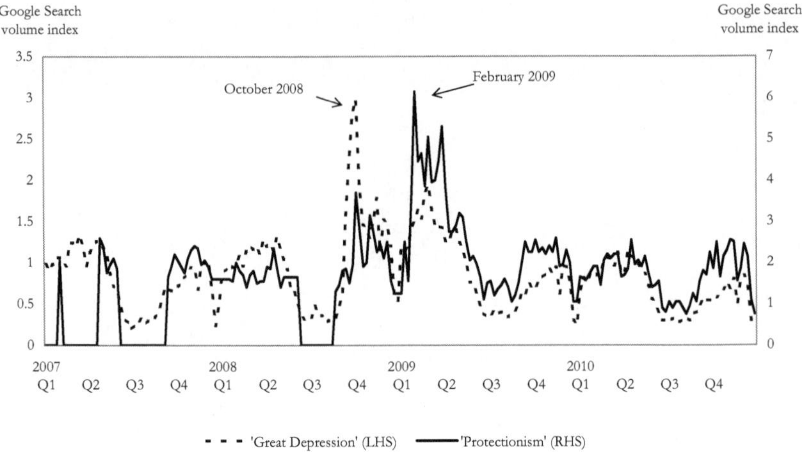

Figure 1.3: *Increased public interest in the Great Depression and Protectionism during 2008-9.*

Source: author's calculations from Google Trends based on Internet searches for 'Great Depression' and 'Protectionism'. Data reported weekly and each index averages a value of 1 for 2004–10.

uptick in November 2008, which was also likely to be due to public curiosity drawn by the attention of the Washington G20 summit. The public interest in 'Protectionism' continued to increase until it reached a peak in 2009 Q1 (February).

During the period of November 2008 to February 2009, what *facts* did the public and policymakers know about recently occurring changes to national trade policies? The answer is 'not much'. While there were anecdotal stories about events taking place, the next section describes how it was not until March 2009 that data *began* to emerge and facts began to be learned about how national governments had been adjusting their trade policies in 2008. Hence, March 2009 was the turning point at which sufficient information *began* to be revealed so that some of this public uncertainty on the scope and impact of any 'Protectionism' in 2008 could begin to be resolved.

1.2 The Trade Collapse and Great Recession Spur New Trade Policy Monitoring Initiatives

The spectre of potential protectionism and the uncertainty over how the major economies were utilising their trade policy inspired a number of monitoring initiatives in 2009 that were designed to improve transparency. Table 1.1 provides a timeline of three major initiatives and how their activities took shape over the course of the year. In January 2009, the WTO published a

Table 1.1: *Timeline of major new trade policy monitoring initiatives in 2009.*

Organisation	Date	Information and data provided
WTO Secretariat: report to the TPRB from director-general on the financial and economic crisis and trade-related developments	23 January	Identification of problem of potential of new crisis-induced trade barriers; no provision of any detailed lists of new trade or trade-related measures
World Bank: Global Antidumping Database	5 March	Provides public list *and* detailed data on anti-dumping use through December 2008
WTO Secretariat: report to the TPRB from the director-general on the financial and economic crisis and trade-related developments	20 April	Provides public list of trade and trade-related measures imposed from September 2008 to March 2009
World Bank: Global Antidumping Database	11 May	Provides public list *and* detailed data on anti-dumping, global safeguards, China-specific safeguards, and CVD use through March 2009
Global Trade Alert	8 June	Launch begins its *ongoing* and continuous provision of detailed and real-time information on state measures likely to affect foreign trading partners

report from the Trade Policy Review Body (TPRB) identifying the problem of new crisis-induced protectionist barriers. Nevertheless, the TPRB did not yet make public any new information on actual trade barriers that members had imposed.

In March 2009, a World Bank-sponsored initiative called the Global Anti-dumping Database provided its first crisis-era update. This database had published historical details of cross-country use of anti-dumping, CVDs and safeguard policies—with information dating back to the 1980s—and had been made freely available on the Internet since 2005.[7] The March 2009 release provided details on policy activity that had taken place through 2008 Q4, and it was accompanied by a brief monitoring report that examined simple

[7]Bown (2008) provides a first use of the Global Antidumping Database information to document the heterogeneous application of anti-dumping over time across developing countries. The database had been updated periodically since 2005, and the last complete update (prior to the crisis) was published in June 2007. In 2009–10, the Global Antidumping Database was folded into the World Bank's larger *Temporary Trade Barriers Database*, since it contains detailed policy data on other, increasingly used TTBs such as CVDs and safeguards in addition to anti-dumping. The *Temporary Trade Barriers Database* is the source of much of the detailed policy data used by the authors in the subsequent chapters to this volume.

Table 1.1: *Continued.*

Organisation	Date	Information and data provided
WTO Secretariat: report to the TPRB from the director-general on the financial and economic crisis and trade-related developments	15 July	Provides public list of trade and trade-related measures imposed from 1 March to 19 June 2009
World Bank: Global Antidumping Database	23 July	Provides public list *and* detailed data on anti-dumping, global safeguards, China-specific safeguards, and CVD use through June 2009
World Bank: Global Antidumping Database	21 October	Provides public list *and* detailed data on anti-dumping, global safeguards, China-specific safeguards, and CVD use through September 2009
WTO Secretariat: overview of developments in the international trading environment—annual report by the director-general	18 November	Provides public list of trade and trade-related measures imposed through October 2009

Source: reports to the WTO's Trade Policy Review Body (TPRB) were documents JOB(09)/2, WT/TPR/OV/W/1 and WT/TPR/OV/W/2 and the November annual report by the director-general was WT/TPR/OV/12. The monitoring reports for the Global Antidumping Database (now *Temporary Trade Barriers Database*) are all available online at http://econ.worldbank.org/ttbd/. Global Trade Alert's website is www.globaltradealert.org.

indicators on the newly collected policy data. It was this March 2009 release that provided the first public evidence on the relative increase in trade policy activity during 2008.[8] While this initial step was informative, it too was incomplete for a number of reasons that are addressed in more detail in the discussion below. However, and most importantly for transparency reasons, the data used in the analysis were made public immediately for other policy analysts to examine, verify and include in their own monitoring efforts. The World Bank continued to update this policy data publicly and promptly at the end of each of the nine quarters between 2008 Q4 and 2010 Q4. Public

[8]This monitoring report was published on the initial website of the Global Antidumping Database at www.brandeis.edu/~cbown/global_ad/monitoring/. The evidence from this report was also published in March 2009 as Bown (2009a) and was circulated most publicly as part of the information provided in Gamberoni and Newfarmer (2009a,b). Later in the crisis, the ongoing monitoring efforts were transferred to a new World Bank website for the *Temporary Trade Barriers Database*, http://econ.worldbank.org/ttbd/. The *Temporary Trade Barriers Database* website also provides examples of media dissemination beginning in March 2009 of the World Bank-sponsored monitoring through reporting featured in, among others, *Economist*, *Financial Times*, *Wall Street Journal*, *BusinessWeek*, *Reuters*, *Xinhua* and *VoxEU.org*.

monitoring reports that interpreted the newly arriving data were provided for those first six quarters from 2008 Q4 to 2010 Q1.

The other monitoring efforts also continued through 2009. In addition to the ongoing Global Antidumping Database monitoring reports and data releases, the WTO initiative came out with its first *list* in April of trade and trade-related measures that members had imposed between September 2008 and March 2009. The WTO followed up with additional, periodic lists in July and November. The third and final monitoring initiative—the Global Trade Alert (GTA)—was introduced through a public launch in June 2009. The GTA quickly became the most publicly visible and aggressive watchdog to report on trade policy changes during 2009–10.[9] While each of the initiatives provided useful information and served an important role during this period, the WTO and GTA efforts were somewhat limited by the fact that there existed no comparable historical (*ie* pre-crisis) data against which to evaluate the magnitude of the information on their lists. For comparative purposes, it was unclear whether the trade policy activity that these two initiatives identified was any larger or more frequent than what WTO members undertook during the 'normal' course of operation, *ie* even in the *absence* of a crisis.

1.3 New TTBs in 2008 Did Not Cause the 2008–9 Trade Collapse

While the collective monitoring efforts continued throughout the crisis, a first rough estimate of the *potential trade impact* and hence economic scale of the new, 2008-to-date protectionism was not published until July 2009. This first estimate in Bown (2009b) focused on the G20's new anti-dumping, global safeguard, China-specific safeguard and CVD activity for the five quarters between 2008 Q1 and 2009 Q1.[10] These estimates indicated that *at most* 0.45% of the major G20 economies' merchandise imports were being affected by newly imposed import restrictions under TTB policies. Hence, this evidence made clear for the first time that the massive, global trade collapse of 2008 Q4 to 2009 Q1 (see again Figure 1.2) had *not* been caused by new TTB activity during that particular time period.

---

[9]Many interpreted the GTA approach as an attempt to 'name and shame' governments and prevent countries from imposing, in an undetected way, a trade policy to successfully pawn off its domestic economic woes as a negative externality on its trading partners. Nevertheless, the GTA was also subject to criticism during the crisis; see, for example, Rodrik (2009) and the Reuters interview with Richard Eglin, Director of the WTO's Trade Policies Review Division (Lynn 2009).

[10]The Bown (2009b) approach was to match product-level, six-digit Harmonized System import data on pre-crisis trade flows to the TTB-affected product codes. A full description of the data and approach to the July 2009 estimates was later published in Bown (2009c). Kee *et al* (2010) provide later evidence broadly confirming the relative size of the initial estimates from Bown (2009b,c) through a more rigorous approach that relies on trade elasticities and the Overall Trade Restrictiveness Index (OTRI) methodology.

It is worth noting one additional caveat before returning to an examination of the escalating use of TTBs in 2009. First, and as the WTO and GTA information revealed, governments made many *other* policy adjustments beyond TTBs during 2008–9 in ways that also may have affected trade flows. This includes governments subsidising industries directly (including through bailouts), intervening in currency markets to affect relative exchange rates, inserting local content requirements into stimulus packages, and even changing applied tariff rates— both upwards and downwards—in selected instances. Nevertheless, most of the measures that these initiatives have identified were also imposed in 2009 or beyond and thus could not have been responsible for the global trade collapse that began in 2008 Q4.

Thus, a focused examination of the data and information provided in the World Bank's *Temporary Trade Barriers Database*—which admittedly only reported data on anti-dumping, CVD and safeguard use—does not provide a comprehensive assessment of all trade-impacting policies in use during the crisis. Where possible, the chapters in this volume attempt to complement TTB data with other information so as to begin to address the more complete picture. That being said, this volume is still a first step in the research literature with a primary aim of establishing clear facts on the use and role of TTBs during 2008–9.

1.4 Tracking Protectionism and Lessons Learned from Monitoring TTBs through 2009–10

The World Bank's ongoing contribution to the monitoring of TTBs continued throughout 2009 and into 2010 even though it had become clear by July 2009 that new TTBs in 2008 had not caused the trade collapse.[11] In addition to that initial, first-order concern about the contributing causes to the 2008–9 collapse, the impact of *future* TTBs on a potential 'V-shaped' trade recovery was still an unknown. To what extent would the industries and workers devastated by the global economic contraction increasingly petition their governments for additional TTBs? Would their governments respond favourably to domestic political pressure and impose such barriers?

Figure 1.4(a) presents quarterly data on anti-dumping use during 2007–10 in a manner consistent with the reporting approach of earlier prominent research on the global proliferation of the policy (Prusa 2001; Zanardi 2004). Though the figure breaks down the information into a higher frequency (quarterly) than anti-dumping use has traditionally been reported, this method of listing the counts of new investigations was also how such policy activ-

[11]For a collection of early research (published in November 2009) assessing the suspected causes of the 2008–9 trade collapse, including the contraction of global demand and supply-side credit constraints, see Baldwin (2009).

ity would typically be reported semi-annually by the WTO.[12] In March 2009, the Global Antidumping Database initially adopted this approach of counting anti-dumping investigations (and newly imposed final measures) as the 'headline' summary statistic for its first monitoring report that accompanied the public release of the full data for 2008. For the 11 major economies illustrated here, the number of new anti-dumping initiations in 2008 had grown by 33% relative to 2007.[13] Furthermore, the second half of 2008 experienced 38% more anti-dumping investigations than the first half of 2008. The 2008 Q4 data alone saw a 65% increase in anti-dumping investigations relative to the same period in 2007, and a 69% increase relative to 2008 Q3.

However, when the 2009 Q1 information in the Global Antidumping Database arrived, it became clear that basing the headline summary statistic on anti-dumping alone and simply counting the number of new investigations might not provide an accurate assessment of the demands that industries and workers were making for new trade barriers.[14] In particular, newly available information increasingly suggested that countries were using *other* TTB instruments, many of which were extremely close substitutes for anti-dumping in terms of the desired effect of shielding domestic industries from what was perceived as injurious imports. Figure 1.4(b) illustrates the newly initiated *CVD* investigations over this full period, including a bunching of cases that would occur later in 2009 Q3. Similarly, Figure 1.4(c) documents the counts of newly initiated *global safeguard* investigations, including a spike in 2009 Q2. Finally, Figure 1.4(d) shows the *China-specific safeguard* investigations, including the highly publicised US investigation of tyres that was initiated in 2009 Q2 (April).

To explain this potential concern most clearly, let us focus on the case of India. Consider the problem that arises when examining its anti-dumping use in isolation and ignoring the other TTB policies. In 2009 Q1, India initiated 7 new anti-dumping investigations, a sharp decline in industry demand for new

---

[12]The WTO reported information on new anti-dumping activity typically twice per year, and thus with a substantial delay relative to when the activity had occurred, due to the fact that it was constrained to obtain information from member economies' self-reporting to the Committee on Antidumping. The Global Antidumping Database approach was to gather its information directly from official, national government sources from their Internet websites. As such, it was able to update its data publicly and to disseminate quarterly monitoring reports relatively quickly.

[13]These figures are slightly different from the monitoring report published in March 2009 (which found a 31% increase) because that report covered a wider sample of countries than those covered by this volume.

[14]For ease of discussion, this section focuses only on the data released covering newly initiated TTB investigations. In reality, the monitoring efforts in 2009–10 also tracked (and provided detailed data on) the imposition of final measures and even preliminary measures. The text here focuses on newly initiated investigations as its leading indicator of domestic economy demands for new import protection. The discussion below also focuses in substantial detail on important other indicators including, of course, imposed measures.

(a) Anti-dumping

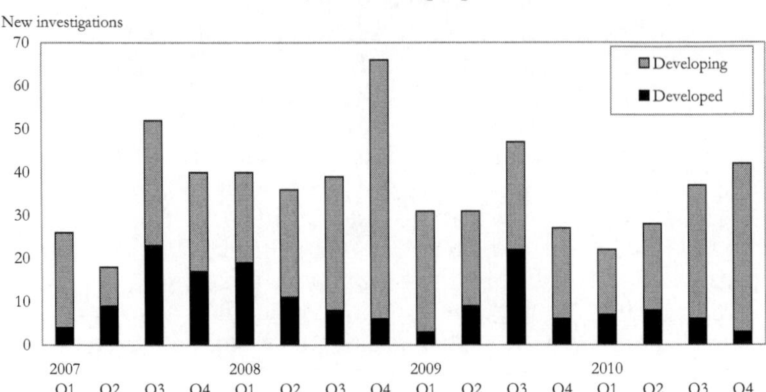

(b) Countervailing duties

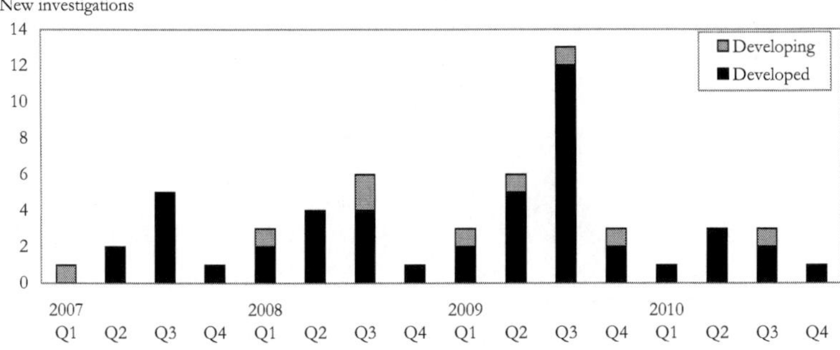

Figure 1.4: *Monitoring TTBs: initiations of new investigations by policy, by quarter, 2007–10.*

protection when compared with the 39 new anti-dumping investigations it had initiated in 2008 Q4. However, also in 2009 Q1, India initiated three different China-safeguard investigations, two different global safeguard investigations, and its first-ever CVD investigation. Furthermore, an examination of the prior period's Indian anti-dumping data (*ie* 39 new investigations, a major share of the aggregate spike for the 11 economies illustrated in Figure 1.4(a)) reveals that 29 of the 39 new investigations in 2008 Q4 were associated with only 3 products (cold-rolled flat stainless steel, hot-rolled steel and carbon black) that were imported from many foreign sources.[15] This example illustrates

[15]Put differently, because of the means of reporting the information inherent in Figure 1.4, the 2008 Q4 data presented in Figure 1.4 would have looked much different if India had initiated three global safeguard investigations (over cold-rolled flat stainless steel, hot-rolled steel and carbon black) instead of 29 anti-dumping investigations over those same products, even though the economic impacts might have been quite similar.

(c) Global safeguards

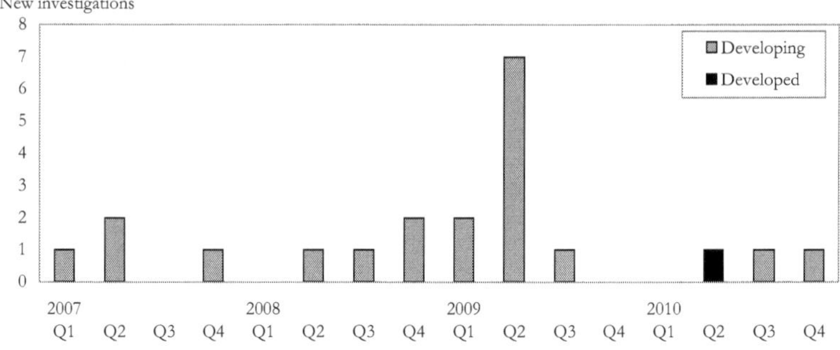

(d) China-specific safeguards

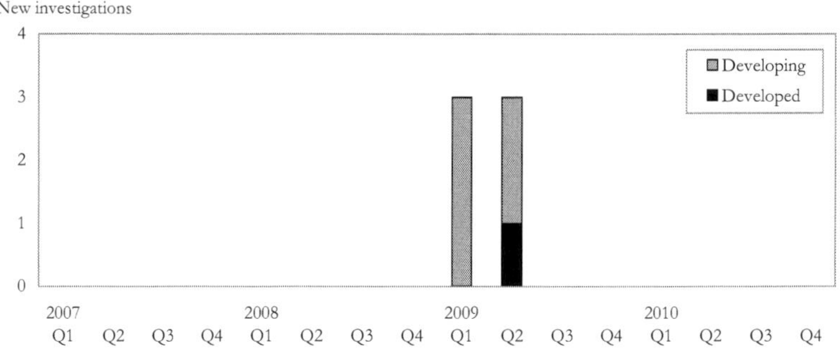

Figure 1.4: *Continued.*

Source: author's calculations from the *Temporary Trade Barriers Database* (Bown 2010a). Each panel includes data for the 11 policy-imposing economies in this volume: Argentina, Brazil, Canada, China, the EU, India, Mexico, South Africa, Korea, Turkey and the USA.

that, even when focusing on TTBs, an examination of anti-dumping alone had the potential to miss one important part of the new import protection and to overstate another. To be more comprehensive, reporting a headline statistic on protectionism through TTBs needed to capture more accurately the expanding use of these other policy instruments. Although more countries were beginning to expand use of CVDs, global safeguards and China-specific safeguards, the Indian 2008 Q4 data also revealed that focusing on anti-dumping based on the number of initiated investigations could potentially *overstate* a run-up in protectionism.

With these considerations in mind, beginning in 2009 Q1, the subsequent Global Antidumping Database monitoring reports presented an alternative headline summary statistic characterising the newly reported data on protectionism. Instead of focusing on anti-dumping alone, the headline for the 2009 Q1 report included all four TTB policies—anti-dumping, CVDs, global

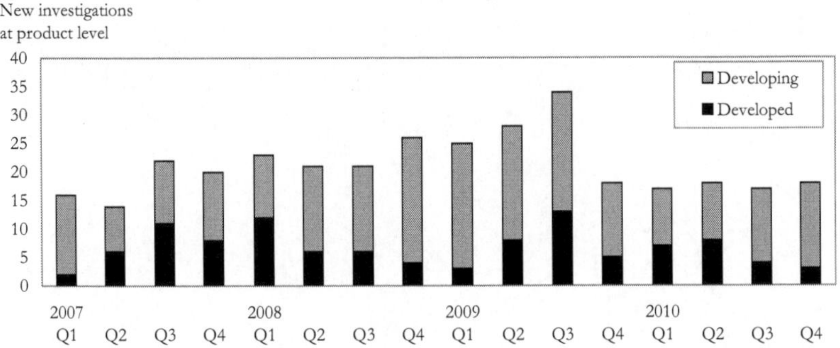

Figure 1.5: *Monitoring TTBs: combining data on TTB investigations over non-redundant products by quarter, 2007–10.*

Source: author's calculations from the *Temporary Trade Barriers Database* (Bown 2010a). Figure includes data for the 11 policy-imposing economies in this volume: Argentina, Brazil, Canada, China, EU, India, Mexico, South Africa, Korea, Turkey and the USA. This figure makes comparable the data on policy use across different (anti-dumping, CVD, safeguards, China-specific safeguards) TTBs by counting, for each policy-imposing economy, multiple investigations over the same product at most once, regardless of how many policy instruments (*eg* anti-dumping or CVDs) simultaneously investigate the product and regardless of how many foreign sources of imports of the product (*eg* anti-dumping versus safeguards) are investigated.

safeguards and China-specific safeguards. Furthermore, so as to make these policies more comparable, it also no longer simply counted up all investigations against all named foreign sources. Instead, in order to reduce the likelihood of double counting, the approach was to provide information on 'non-redundant' cases and the products behind those investigations—regardless of how many foreign trading partners were being investigated and how many different TTB policy instruments were being used against the same product.[16]

Figure 1.5 presents this alternative reporting approach and applies it to these 11 economies' TTB use over the period 2007–10. The figure shows that 2009 Q1 experienced 9% more of these non-redundant, product-level TTB investigations than a year earlier (2008 Q1), though there was a small decline from the spike of the previous quarter (2008 Q4). Under the approach illustrated in Figure 1.5, these 11 economies continued to show increases in newly initiated investigations in each of 2009 Q2 and 2009 Q3. Then in 2009 Q4, new investigations were cut nearly 50% from the previous quarter, and new initiations remained remarkably flat at this new, lower level through each quarter of 2010. This measure suggests 2009 Q3 as the clear end to at least the *initial*

[16]This was designed to address the issue that, increasingly, governments were simultaneously initiating CVD investigations over the same product and against the same foreign target as their anti-dumping investigations. For a discussion, see Bown (2011).

run-up in demands for new TTB activity associated with the 2008-9 global economic crisis.

While this reporting during the crisis provided useful information about the flows of new TTB investigations, and it made some improvement relative to earlier approaches, the information provided was nevertheless still incomplete for at least two additional reasons.

First, the monitoring still did not accurately reflect the concern that a 'product' was reported however an industry's TTB petition defined it, for which there was no standard. One petition's product could cover billions of dollars of trade, and another less than one million.

Second, reporting information on the flow of newly initiated investigations and newly imposed measures revealed insufficient information on the accumulating 'stock' of TTBs, because it ignored other potentially important elements of the TTB process. In particular, the ongoing TTB monitoring efforts ignored whether countries were *removing* on schedule what were supposed to be *temporary* trade barriers that had been imposed prior to the crisis. Indeed, one of the highest profile TTB cases captured by media attention did not involve the imposition of any *new* barriers, but whether, in 2008 and again in 2009, the EU would remove anti-dumping measures on imported footwear from China that had been imposed long before the crisis. Eventually, the EU decided to renew the TTB and keep it in place. While such an important policy decision prevented an anticipated decline in the stock of products covered by TTBs during 2008-9, this was not picked up by the monitoring approach at the time.

One of the lessons learned from the monitoring of TTBs during 2009-10 is that, despite even the prior data collection efforts through the Global Antidumping Database, the research community was still not well enough positioned to provide an immediate assessment on the scale and potential impact of new protection. Trade policy monitors can do better. The more formal approach described in the next section, as well as the results reported beginning in Section 3 that are developed in great depth throughout the chapters in this volume, should inspire much improved and responsive monitoring efforts earlier in the *next* crisis.

2 TRANSITIONING TO RESEARCH ON TEMPORARY TRADE BARRIERS: INSTITUTIONS, METHODOLOGICAL APPROACH AND DATA

2.1 *Institutional Aspects of Anti-Dumping, CVDs and Safeguards*

Anti-dumping, CVDs, global safeguards and China-specific safeguards—collectively referred to as TTBs—are the four policy instruments of central focus to this volume of research. This section briefly introduces some of the more formal institutional aspects of TTBs.[17] Collectively, TTBs are some of the primary means through which many governments have flexibility with respect to their trade policy. In particular, in the face of binding legal commitments on WTO members' most-favoured-nation (MFN) tariff rates as well as preferential tariff commitments, many economies are prevented from simply raising their applied tariff rates to respond to political-economic shocks. The WTO's legal agreements covering TTBs create conditions by which countries can impose new trade barriers in potentially WTO-consistent ways and thus achieve some trade policy flexibility in response to changes in domestic economic conditions.[18]

The four TTBs have a number of common elements, which, for domestic industry users and policymakers, implies some degree of substitutability. First, each can be permissible under the rules of the WTO, provided certain economic conditions are met and certain procedures are adhered to so as to justify new measures being imposed under their auspices. For example, a necessary condition required before implementation of a new trade barrier is evidence of injury (or threat thereof) to a domestic industry that competes with the imported products. Second, each of the trade barriers imposed under these TTB provisions is supposed to be *temporary*. While the relevant WTO agreements implemented after the Uruguay Round precisely define the legal requirements, anti-dumping and CVDs are typically supposed to be removed after five years after a sunset review investigation, and global safeguards are typically terminated after three (if no compensation is granted) or four years. The China-specific safeguard is a transitional policy introduced into the WTO under the terms of China's WTO accession in 2001, and other WTO members have the right to use the policy to address injurious import surges from China until the policy expires in 2013.

Despite a number of common characteristics, there are important distinctions between the TTB policies. Perhaps most importantly, triggering the safeguards provisions requires no evidence that trading partners have done anything 'unfair'. Broadly put, all that is required is evidence of injury that can

[17]This section does not attempt to provide a thorough legal analysis of the similarities and differences among the TTBs since the literature is vast in this area. Mavroidis *et al* (2008) is an accessible legal-economic assessment with a much more detailed discussion of the relevant WTO agreements on TTBs; see also Hoekman and Kostecki (2009). Blonigen and Prusa (2003) and Nelson (2006) provide extensive surveys of the economic research on anti-dumping, and Bown and Crowley (2005) survey the economic literature on safeguards. Reynolds (2008) discusses CVDs. Bown (2010b) describes early use of the China-specific safeguard. Bagwell and Staiger (2002) present a classic political-economic theory of the WTO, including one particular role for TTBs (Chapter 6).

[18]See, in particular, the WTO Agreement on Antidumping, Agreement on Safeguards, and the Agreement on Subsidies and Countervailing Measures. For the China-specific safeguard, see China's Accession Protocol.

be linked to proper evidence of changes to imports.[19] The other two TTBs—anti-dumping and CVDs—require a second piece of important evidence. In addition to demonstration of injury, use of anti-dumping requires evidence that the injury can be linked to imports that have been priced at a value that is 'too low'. Use of CVDs requires evidence that domestic injury can be linked to imports that have benefited from foreign subsidies. A final important distinction between the TTBs involves how they are applied. Global safeguards are supposed to be applied on a relatively non-discriminatory basis across all trading partners, regardless of the source of imports. On the other hand, anti-dumping and CVDs allow for much more discrimination between foreign sources of the same product. In fact, the imposed duties are often firm-specific, indicating the possibility of using trade policy to discriminate between firms within the same exporting country, let alone between firms in one country versus another. Finally, as indicated by its name, the China-specific safeguard is also discriminatory as it can only be applied against imports from China.

In a typical TTB case, a domestic industry petitions its government under one (or more) of these TTB laws. The government quickly makes the decision whether to initiate an investigation—in most instances choosing to do so—and then begins collecting information on whether the case has merit. Each WTO member has its own distinct domestic implementing legislation that generates some variation in timing of when new trade barriers would subsequently get imposed. Nevertheless, the government makes a preliminary determination, typically within 30–90 days, of whether the case has enough merit to impose a preliminary trade barrier and to continue to the final investigation. The final investigation then takes longer to complete. The investigation of whether to impose a final (definitive) measure can take as long as 14–18 months depending on the investigating country and the TTB policy being used.

Historically, anti-dumping has been the most frequently used TTB policy. As such, anti-dumping has also been the most thoroughly researched of the TTB policies, though until the late 2000s much of the detailed research in this area focused on developed economy use, mainly due to data availability reasons. With the spread of increased use to developing economies in the 1990s and the initial publication of detailed data in the Global Antidumping Database in 2005, additional research has emerged assessing the policy's use by other countries, including a number of major emerging economies.

---

[19]Nevertheless, the practical evidence necessary to impose a WTO-consistent safeguard is still relatively unsettled, given the evolving jurisprudence on this issue under the WTO's Dispute Settlement Understanding (see, for example, Sykes (2003) and Irwin (2003)). For a legal–economic assessment of the substantial number of WTO Panel and Appellate Body decisions regarding WTO consistency with regard to applied TTBs, see also the American Law Institute-sponsored research (Mavroidis and Horn 2004, 2005, 2006, 2008, 2009).

2.2 Methodological Approach and Data

As suggested in Section 1, the approach to monitoring new TTBs during the crisis so as to provide useful information on their *economic importance* amid fear of growing protectionism was still incomplete. First, simply counting cases relied on a domestic industry's own, self-reported characterisation of a 'product' subject to a newly initiated investigation or imposed barrier. There is no uniform definition of a 'product'—it results from the petition filed by the domestic industry and is designed so as to increase the likelihood that the petition will be accepted and that a new barrier will be imposed. If there is substantial heterogeneity in the amount of product coverage across TTB investigations, countries or time, relying on this measure may not accurately reflect the economic importance or unimportance of TTBs. Second, the information on the initiation of new investigations or even the imposition of newly imposed barriers only reports on 'flow' variables, and these variables may themselves be affected by the pre-existing 'stock' of TTBs already in place. However, examining the 'stock' build-up of such trade barriers not only requires information on past flows, but it also requires up-to-date information on *removals* of previously imposed barriers. Data on policy removals have typically been more difficult to obtain systematically. For example, during the crisis, reliable data on removals were obtained only after a substantial time lag relative to the flow data on newly initiated investigations and newly imposed barriers, thereby hindering the construction of stock measures.

Bown (2011) proposes two methodological approaches to move beyond previous accounting efforts that assess TTB proliferation. Each method addresses some of these concerns by constructing flow and stock measures of imported products and the share of a country's imports that are affected by its use of TTBs. The merits of such an approach include the ability to better assess the scope of TTB coverage in the face of heterogeneity in the timing of newly imposed barriers, the length of time that such barriers stay imposed, and the trading partners affected. The remainder of this section summarises and provides the intuition behind the Bown (2011) approaches. The technical details are explained in the Appendix (Section 6).

The first methodological approach of Bown (2011) constructs 'count' measures of the annual stock of Harmonized System products at the six-digit level (HS-06) subject to TTBs, measured as the share of the importing economy's total set of that year's imported HS-06 products from all sources. This count measure reflects information on the country's newly imposed trade barriers, previously imposed trade barriers, and the removal of previously imposed barriers. The methodology starts with the approach of Bown and Tovar (2011, Figure 1), which focused on India's use of anti-dumping over the 1992–2003 period, and modifies it along three important dimensions: first, by examining not only cumulative stocks but also flows; second, by examining not only anti-dumping, but also HS-06 products subject to other TTB policies such as

CVDs, global safeguards and China-specific safeguards to address the concern raised in Section 1.4 (when comparing Figure 1.4(a) with Figure 1.5); and third, by normalising the count of TTB-affected HS-06 products by the economy's stock of HS-06 products with positive imports in that year.

The second approach refines the 'count' measure by using data on import values to trade-weight the importance of TTBs at the HS-06 product level. Construction of this complementary 'value' measure is one way of investigating the possibility that there may be significant variation in the economic (trade) importance across HS-06 products affected by TTB use. Some TTBs are applied against multiple foreign sources and can affect more imports than a TTB used against a single foreign supplier. Furthermore, some HS-06 products may be larger contributors to the economy's overall level of imports than others; one product from one foreign source may cover only a few hundred thousand dollars of trade, while another may cover billions of dollars. The 'value' approach uses HS-06 import-value data from the United Nations Comtrade database to construct year-by-year trade-weighted coverage ratios of imports subject to TTBs. The results reported in this chapter construct the economy's TTB-affected imports as a share of the economies' *non-oil* imports. The Appendix (Section 6) provides a more detailed explanation of methodology and data.

The product-level TTB policy data are taken from the World Bank's *Temporary Trade Barriers Database* (Bown 2010a).

3 HIGH-LEVEL OVERVIEW OF RESULTS: CHANGES TO THE STOCKS OF IMPORTS SUBJECT TO TEMPORARY TRADE BARRIERS

This section applies the methods described in Section 2 and in the Appendix (Section 6) to provide a broad and suggestive overview of results. The added context then raises questions for the country-specific research in the subsequent chapters. In particular, this section reports the results from Bown (2011) and begins with evidence aggregated over the countries in this volume—so as to make comparisons with Figure 1.4(a) and Figure 1.5—before introducing some country-specific results. Note first that the results reported in this section are all based on *annual* data—as opposed to the quarterly information highlighted earlier—due to data availability constraints on policy *removals* and HS-06 imports.

Before turning to a discussion of results on TTB use over the longer period of 1997–2009, it is useful to first describe how Figure 1.6 *presents* four distinct pieces of information.[20] First, the *solid grey* line defines the TTB indi-

[20]The aggregated data in Figures 1.6 and 1.7 begin in 1997 because 1997 was the first year for which all of the economies in this volume were using TTBs. (China was the last of these economies to initiate use.) The economy-specific results of Figures 1.8, 1.9, 1.10 and 1.11 illustrate TTB use beginning in 1990. These four figures, discussed in more detail below, use the same visual approach as Figure 1.6 to present the results.

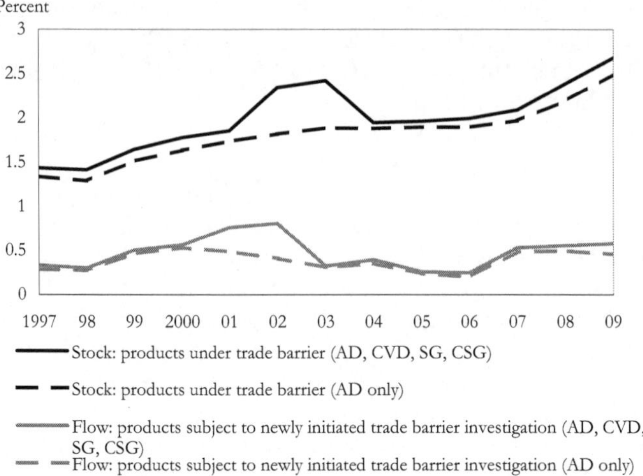

Figure 1.6: *The major economies' imported products collectively affected by TTBs, 1997–2009.*

Source: figure based on annual data, author's calculations using a modified version of Equation (1.1) from data in the *Temporary Trade Barriers Database* (Bown 2010a). Data are aggregated over the following ten policy-imposing economies: Argentina, Brazil, Canada, China, the EU, India, South Africa, Korea, Turkey and the USA. Of the economies analysed in this volume, Mexico is the only user of such policies not included in construction of the data for the figure, for reasons explained in Chapter 10 by Raymond Robertson (this volume). See also Figure 1.10.

cator based on imported products affected by newly initiated investigations under *any* TTB policy, and is thus a broad measure of the potential annual 'flow' of new barriers. Second, the *dashed grey* line defines the indicator similarly, but captures the flow of potential imported products affected by the *anti-dumping* policy alone. For countries that only used anti-dumping and did not have any CVD, global safeguard or China-specific safeguard investigations during this period, the solid grey line and the dashed grey line would overlap. Any divergence between these two lines represents the products subject to investigations under the countries' other (non-anti-dumping) TTB policies. For the reasons described in the last section, these two lines serve as more informative 'flow' indicators of new protectionism than the data presented in Figures 1.4(a) or even Figure 1.5. The *solid black* line in Figure 1.6 presents the third piece of information on the annual 'stock' of import products subject to *any* TTB policy. It defines the TTB indicator as taking on a value of 1 whenever the import was subject to some TTB that had been imposed in that year or a prior year (and had not yet been removed). Fourth, the *dashed black* line represents the stock of products subject to *anti-dumping* policy only.

3.1 These Economies Collectively Increased TTB Product Coverage by 25% During the Crisis

Figure 1.6 illustrates the data cumulated across the policy-imposing economies in this volume over the period 1997–2009. It uses the 'count' method described in Equation (1.1) (see the Appendix (Section 6)) and constructs measures of the aggregated stocks and flows of imported products subject to TTBs.[21] By the end of 2009, the solid black line indicates that these economies had collectively increased the stock of imported products they subjected to imposed TTBs by 25% relative to the pre-crisis levels of 2007. By 2009, 2.7% of HS-06 products that these economies imported were subject to a TTB, having increased from 2.4% of imported products prior to the crisis in 2007. Despite the potential concern over TTB policy substitutability raised in Section 1, the vast majority of the increase in TTB product coverage came through anti-dumping policy (dashed black line) and not through CVDs and global or China-specific safeguards. The figure reveals that this differs from the major TTB increase during 2001–3. During that period it turns out that *global safeguards* on steel products were a major contributor to increased TTB use.

Figure 1.7 further divides the black and grey lines of Figure 1.6, *ie* the stock and flow series based on *all TTBs*, according to whether the policy-imposing economy was developed or developing. The result shows that the main source of the overall increase in the stock of product coverage during the 2008–9 crisis was new TTBs imposed by *developing* economies. The developing economies in this volume combined to have 39% more products subject to a TTB by 2009 (2.9% of their imported HS-06 products) than before the crisis in 2007 (2.4% of their imported HS-06 products). On the other hand, the developed economies combined to have only 4% more products subject to a TTB in 2009 (2.4% of their imported HS-06 products) than before the crisis in 2007 (2.3% of their imported HS-06 products).

Did the 2008–9 crisis *cause* the observed changes in new TTB protection? The second main insight from Figure 1.7 is that, visually, it is difficult to rule out the possibility that the relative changes in the data between 2007 and 2009 are simply part of a longer-term trend in TTB use. In particular, the 39% increase for developing economy users may have taken place even under more 'normal' macroeconomic conditions had the 2008–9 crisis not occurred, given the pre-crisis upwards trend. Furthermore, the relatively small (4%) increase in TTB coverage between 2007 and 2009 for developed economies, while surprising in the face of a crisis, is consistent with the secular decline in the importance of TTB coverage for these economies since 2003.

[21] Of the economies analysed in this volume, Mexico is the only user of such policies that is not included in construction of the data for the aggregate Figure 1.6 and Figure 1.7. For reasons explained below (see also Figure 1.10) and in Chapter 10 by Raymond Robertson (this volume), Mexico coincidentally removed TTBs over imports of hundreds of products from China in late 2008 that had been in place since 1993.

Table 1.2: *The crisis: predicted versus realised economies' stocks of imposed TTBs in 2009.*

Imposing economy (ranked by column 1)	Percentage change in 2009 import share relative to pre-crisis 2007 level, by count (1)	2009 import share, by count (2)	Predicted 2009 share, by count (3)	Percentage change in 2009 import share relative to pre-crisis 2007 level, by value (4)	2009 import share, by value (5)	Predicted 2009 import share, by value (6)
Total	24.83	2.68	2.38	—	—	—
Developing economy total	39.29	2.87	2.44	—	—	—
India	69.69	6.09	4.28	39.14	2.94	2.62
Argentina	48.01	2.81	2.12	18.66	2.01	2.36
Turkey	34.39	5.31	4.36	−9.25	3.05	3.35
Brazil	20.03	1.53	1.27	−13.57	1.73	2.49
China	−10.03	0.87	1.65	−28.75	1.71	3.91
South Africa	−18.54	0.76	1.00	−60.57	0.25	0.51
Mexico	−287.94	1.09	18.98	−31.81	0.68	0.76
High-income economy total	3.93	2.40	2.28	—	—	—
Canada	15.68	1.27	1.19	21.04	0.64	0.59
USA	10.17	4.72	4.63	−0.11	2.33	1.80
European Union	−4.98	2.50	2.37	−58.04	1.59	2.66
Korea	−36.39	0.86	0.92	−14.33	0.39	0.45

The aggregate levels for 'Total' and 'Developing economy total' do not include Mexico, for reasons described in the text and in Chapter 10 by Raymond Robertson (this volume).

Source: Bown (2011, Table 2), and author's calculations. Columns 1, 2 and 3 are based on Equation (1.1) and columns 4, 5 and 6 are based on Equation (1.2).

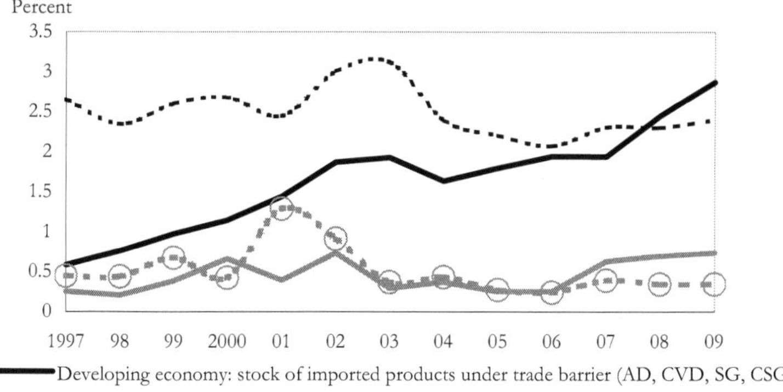

Figure 1.7: *Developed economy versus developing economy imported products collectively affected by TTBs, 1997–2009.*

Source: figure based on annual data, author's calculations using a modified version of Equation (1.1) from data in the *Temporary Trade Barriers Database* (Bown 2010a). Data are aggregated over the following ten policy-imposing economies: Argentina, Brazil, Canada, China, the EU, India, South Africa, Korea, Turkey and the USA. Of the economies analysed in this volume, Mexico is the only user of such policies not included in construction of the data for the figure, for reasons explained in Chapter 10 by Raymond Robertson (this volume). See also Figure 1.10.

One way to investigate this question more formally is to decompose these overall trends into economy-by-economy use of TTBs. Table 1.2 presents data on the percentage change in the stock of product coverage of TTBs between 2007 and 2009. The table reports both the count (column 1) and value (column 4) methods of Equations (1.1) and (1.2), respectively. First, the table summarises the data based on Figure 1.7 reported above: developed economies increased their count of products covered by 3.93% compared with the developing countries' combined increase of 39.29%. By category of country, the economies are then ordered according to which had the largest percentage change in TTB product coverage between 2007 and 2009 using the count method. Two major emerging economies—India and Argentina—lead the list with the largest percentage increases in the stocks of products covered by TTBs during this period.

Table 1.2 also provides simple, economy-by-economy forecasts of the 2009 level of TTB coverage based on predictions from each economy's historical data. (The economy-specific historical data are discussed in more detail below.) Motivated by Figure 1.7, results are reported from a simple regression of the 1997–2007 import share data on a linear time trend; the estimated coefficient from the regression is then used to predict the (out-of-sample) import share for 2009. Column 3 reports the prediction which uses the count measure, and column 6 reports the prediction that uses the value measure.

Compare the prediction for 2009 in Table 1.2 with the realised data. Regardless of whether one compares column 2 with column 3 or column 5 with column 6, there is hardly conclusive evidence that the change in TTB product coverage taking place between 2007 and 2009 is different from that predicted by the historical trend. According to the count measure, seven economies (four developing and three developed) had a larger share of 2009 imports becoming subject to TTBs than was predicted from the models. Four economies (China, South Africa, Mexico and Korea) had *less* product coverage by 2009 than was predicted. A comparison of column 5 with column 6, which uses the value measure, gives different results. Only three economies (one developing and two developed) had a higher-than-predicted share of imports become subject to TTBs by 2009. While these economies (India, Canada and the USA) did experience increases in the share of imported products subject to TTBs during the economic crisis (see column 4), the simple linear time-trend model predicted this. Thus, it is really only the small difference between the realised 2009 data and the 2009 forecast that would be the *unpredicted* component to the new import protection to be associated with the crisis. For a country such as Argentina, column 6 suggests that it actually experienced a *smaller* increase in imports covered by TTBs in 2009 than that predicted by the time-trend model.

3.2 The 4% TTB Increase: High-Income-Economy Use Before and During the Crisis

Figures 1.8 and 1.9 present the 'stock' and 'flow' TTB information (formatted in the same way as Figure 1.6) on an economy-by-economy basis for the developed economies. Figure 1.8 illustrates the time trend of product coverage using the 'count' measure of Equation (1.1), and Figure 1.9 illustrate the time trend of import coverage using the 'value' measure of Equation (1.2). For each economy, I examine TTB use dating back to either its inception or 1990, whichever is later.

First, consider the USA and the EU. Across developed economies, the USA and the EU have the first- and second-highest annual stock of products covered by TTBs on average, and their historical use tends to track (countercyclically) domestic macroeconomic indicators. The USA, for example, experienced a spike in TTB flows (and increases to stocks) during its 1990–1 recession, in response to the surge in imports during the 1997–8 Asian crisis, and during the 2001–2 recession. In terms of policy choice across TTBs, most US

Figure 1.8: *Developed economies' use of TTBs by economy, 1990–2009, using Equation (1.1): counts of products.*

Source: Bown (2011, Figure 1).

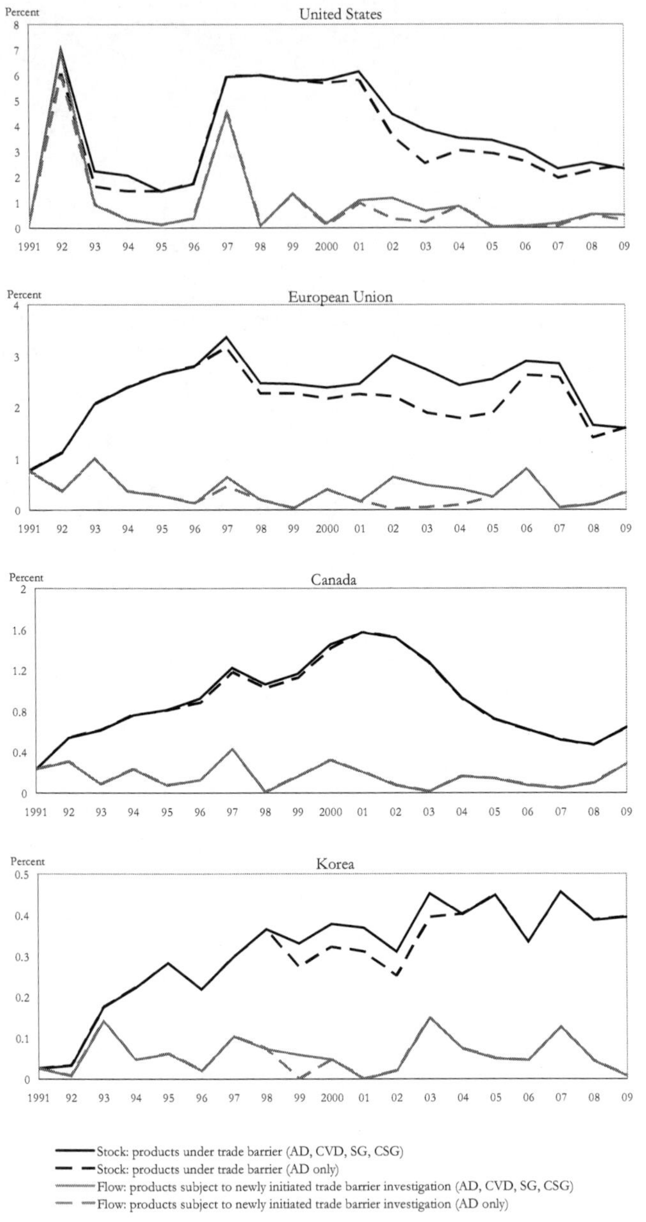

Figure 1.9: *Developed economies' use of TTBs by economy, 1990–2009, using Equation (1.2): share of value of imports.*

Source: Bown (2011, Figure 1).

and EU use involves anti-dumping policy during 1990–2009. The exception for both was 2001–3, during which the two economies used the *global safeguards* policy over a large share of imported steel products. Furthermore, in comparing Figure 1.8 with Figure 1.9, the 'count' and 'value' measures for these two economies tend to track fairly closely over time. Divergences between the two series reveal instances in which counts of products overstate or understate the trade-weighted importance of the TTBs. Finally, the time trend also suggests a relatively flat or declining importance attached to TTB use by these economies during 2005–9 in particular, lacking even a major uptick in import coverage in response to the 2008–9 crisis, as reported in Table 1.2.

The other panels of Figures 1.8 and 1.9 illustrate TTB use for Canada and Korea. While at a lower average level, the time series changes to Canada's TTB coverage also tracks US and EU changes; the one difference is a slightly larger increase in TTB use during 2008–9. Korea has the lowest average TTB coverage of these four developed economies, and the pattern to its time series is quite different as well.

3.3 The 39% TTB Increase: Emerging-Economy Use Before and During the Crisis

Developing economies' use of TTBs as presented in Figure 1.10 and Figure 1.11 indicates a different story. To highlight some of the distinctions from developed economy use during this period, consider the example of India. India only began using TTBs in 1992. While the flow of products under India's investigations spiked at various points in time (1999, 2002 and 2007), the stock of Indian imports affected by TTBs indicates a steady, *continual* increase over 1992–2009. By 2009, India had a stock of TTBs in place that covered 6% of its imported HS-06 product lines and 3% of the value of its imports. While India is now a user of each of the four TTB policy instruments—it initiated the most anti-dumping, global safeguard and China-specific safeguard investigations during 1995–2009, and it initiated its first CVD investigation in 2009—the divergences between the straight and dashed lines in Figure 1.10 and again in Figure 1.11 are relatively small. This reveals that anti-dumping has been the instrument that has affected most of the products impacted by India's total use of TTBs.

Each of the developing economies illustrated in Figures 1.10 and 1.11 has its own distinct history of TTB use, though many share characteristics with the Indian experience. Countries like Argentina, Brazil, China, Mexico and Turkey each experienced substantial increases in TTB coverage after they undertook transformative episodes of trade liberalisation. Some of them also witnessed a substantial increase in TTB coverage during the 2008–9 crisis. Other economies did not. Mexico even managed the astonishing result, despite being in the middle of the 2008 Q4 trade collapse, of following through with the planned removal of TTBs that had covered 20% of its imported products

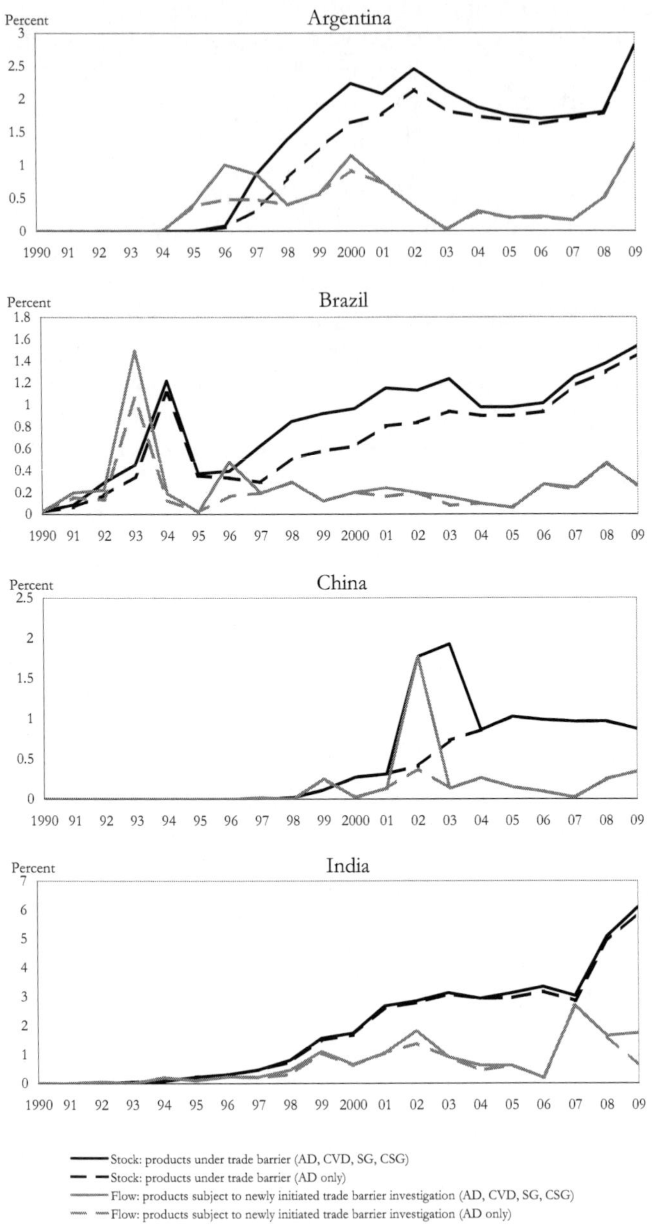

Figure 1.10: *Developing economies' use of TTBs by economy, 1990–2009, using Equation (1.1): counts of products.*

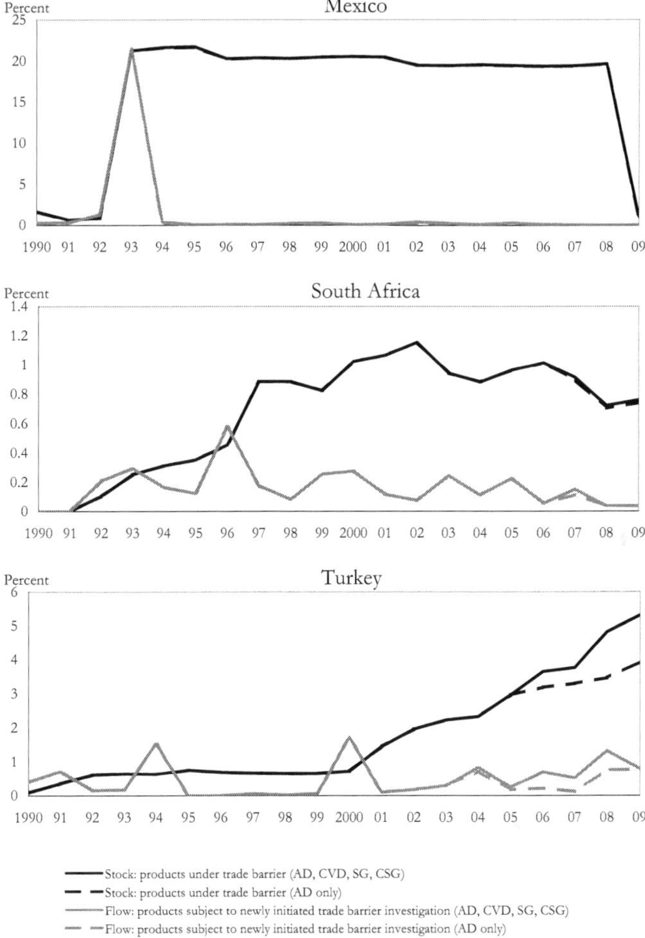

Figure 1.10: *Continued.*
Source: Bown (2011, Figure 2).

from China since 1993. For all of these economies, as well as South Africa, the chapters that follow document how TTB use relates to the countries' own macroeconomic conditions; paths towards trade liberalisation and use of other (*ie* non-TTB) trade barriers; political-economic relationships between industry, workers and government; comparative advantage; and trading relationships.

To summarise the results of this section, while there is an increase in TTB coverage alongside the 2008–9 crisis, this is mainly attributable to an increase

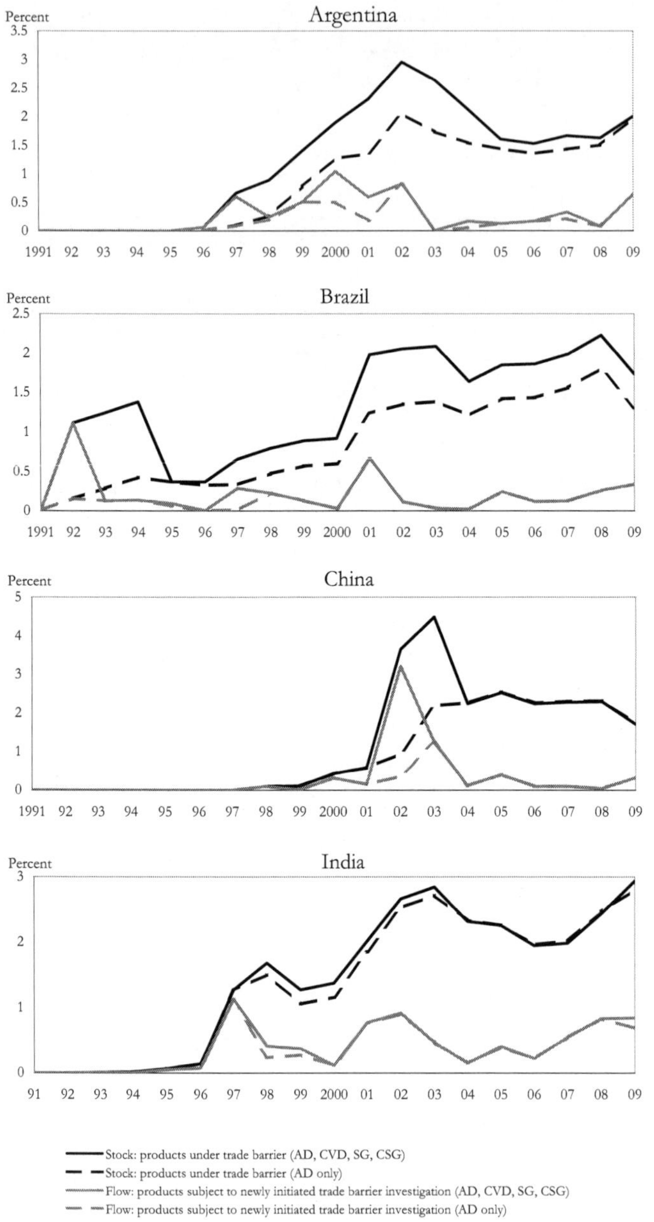

Figure 1.11: *Developing economies' use of TTBs by economy, 1990–2009, using Equation (1.2): share of value of imports.*

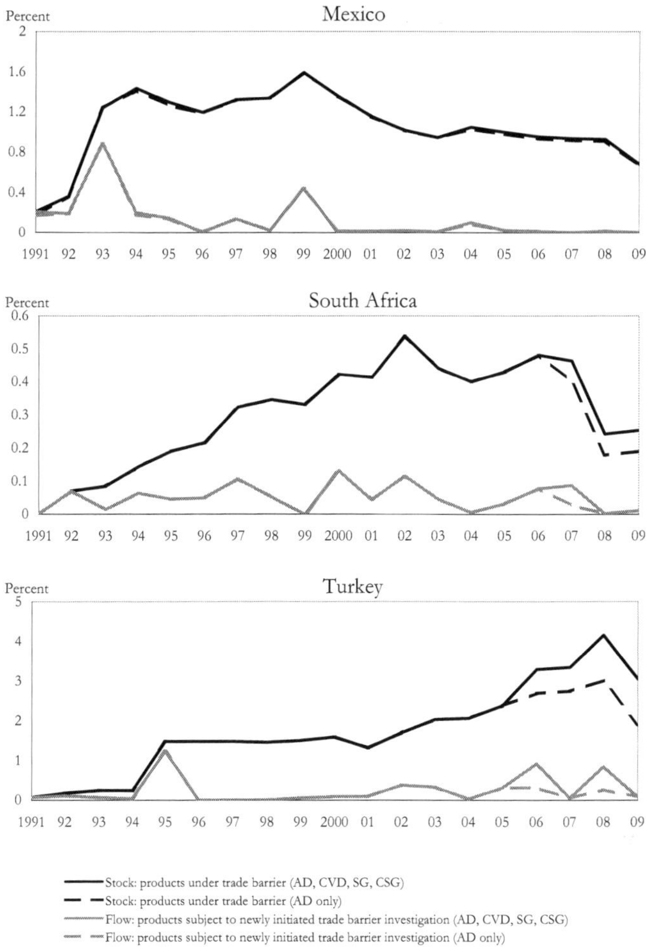

Figure 1.11: *Continued.*
Source: Bown (2011, Figure 2).

in usage by developing countries. For many of these emerging economies, TTB coverage was already increasing prior to the crisis. Thus, there is an evolving consensus that the response of the overall WTO system, and how it withstood the crisis, was positive—TTBs may have increased, but WTO members weathered the severe uncertainty and economic calamity of 2008–9 with the multilateral trading system intact. Nevertheless, even at this broad level, the import protection in place at the end of 2009 appears somewhat different from how it was before the crisis hit. The next section provides a preview of the details of trade policy changes taking place, economy by economy, in the chapters that follow. This research also begins to examine explanations for this policy response based on a more micro-orientated analysis as well as a more nuanced historical context that better reflects how each economy arrived at its *pre-crisis* trade policies by 2007.

4 COUNTRY-SPECIFIC QUESTIONS AND PREVIEW OF CHAPTERS' RESULTS

The flavour of the results presented in Figures 1.8, 1.9, 1.10 and 1.11 suggests heterogeneity in TTB use across these major economies over time. Indeed, the main purpose of this volume is to document the economic significance and details of 11 major economies' varied use of TTBs, in order to better understand the implications for the world trading system. These figures also make clear that understanding the trade policy changes of 2008–9 requires a recognition of prevailing, pre-crisis trends in the evolution of national trade policies.

4.1 Baseline Questions: Putting 2008–9 TTB Use into Historical Context

The authors of the subsequent chapters have been tasked with addressing a fundamental question. Each has been asked to shed light on how TTB policies were used during the global economic crisis of 2008–9, and how this use (and non-use) compares with *expected* use based on economic theory and pre-crisis experiences. To form those expectations, each chapter considers many additional questions and thus considers a much longer time horizon than 2008–9.

The formation of expectations of the economy's potential TTB use in response to the events of 2008–9 is likely to be fuelled by a number of factors from its political–economic history. How has the economy's TTB use been affected by prior macroeconomic shocks such as recessions and crises (Knetter and Prusa 2003)? Even in the absence of prior macroeconomic shocks, how has TTB use evolved alongside the economy's other fundamental trade policy changes, such as episodes of trade liberalisation and commitments to the multilateral system (Bown and Tovar 2011)? Is there a relationship between the economy's TTB use and its applied MFN tariffs, bound tariffs and PTA tariffs? Does the amount of 'water' in the economy's tariff structure (defined as the difference between its legally bound and the applied tariff rates) affect the economy's TTB use?

Table 1.3 provides a snapshot of these economies' trade policies immediately prior to the crisis. It reports information on their levels of tariff protection and the restrictiveness of their import regimes in 2007. Even at this extremely aggregated level, the table reveals substantial variation across policy-imposing economies based on a number of trade policy indicators that

Table 1.3: *Tariffs, trade restrictiveness and TTBs immediately before the crisis in 2007.*

Economy	Average applied MFN tariff	Average bound MFN tariff	MFN tariff binding coverage	Average applied tariff (including preferences)	OTRI	TTB coverage by value by 2007	Share of world merchandise imports in 2007
USA	3.5	3.5	100.0	1.3	6.3	2.3	19.6
EU	5.2	5.4	100.0	2.1	6.4	2.8	20.1
Canada	5.5	6.5	99.7	3.1	5.1	0.5	3.7
Korea	12.2	17.0	94.6	6.8	—	0.5	3.6
China	9.9	10.0	100.0	4.8	9.8	2.3	8.7
India	14.5	50.2	73.8	7.8	18.0	2.0	2.2
Brazil	12.2	31.4	100.0	7.0	20.3	2.0	1.2
Argentina	12.0	31.9	100.0	5.4	9.3	1.7	0.4
Mexico	12.6	36.1	100.0	11.1	18.0	0.9	2.8
Turkey	10.0	28.3	50.4	1.8	3.8	3.4	1.6
South Africa	7.8	19.1	96.6	4.9	6.3	0.5	0.7

Source: first three columns of data are from WTO (2008). The data on average applied tariff (including preferences) are trade-weighted. These data and the Overall Trade Restrictiveness Index (OTRI) are from the World Bank's World Trade Indicators. For data availability reasons, Mexico's and Turkey's OTRI are for 2006. Temporary trade barrier coverage by value by 2007 is calculated by the author according to Equation (1.2). The share of world merchandise imports in 2007 excludes intra-EU trade and is taken from Comtrade.

many of the individual chapters investigate further in detail. High-income economies, such as the USA, the EU and Canada, came into the crisis with relatively low applied and bound MFN tariff rates, nearly 100% of their tariffs being legally bound in the WTO, and also very little water in their tariff structure. Other measures of their import regimes in 2007—such as the trade-weighted applied tariffs inclusive of preferences, and the Overall Trade Restrictiveness Index (OTRI) developed by Kee *et al* (2009)—also indicate evidence of relative openness. For the major emerging economies, on the other hand, Table 1.3 indicates that they were not nearly as open by 2007. On average, emerging economies had much higher OTRIs, applied tariffs and bound tariffs, and they had much less tariff binding coverage.

Nevertheless, a number of the individual chapters highlight a major point that can be missed by focusing on the Table 1.3 snapshot of 2007 data, *ie* even these emerging economies were *much more open* by 2007 than they had been 15 years earlier. The chapters investigate the potential role of TTBs in those liberalisation processes, and how liberalisation forces may have also shaped the economy's TTB response to the events of the 2008–9 crisis.[22] Each chapter

[22]See Finger and Nogués (2005), for example, which provides an interesting collection of case studies describing the potential role that TTBs played during the major wave of Latin American trade liberalisation in the 1990s. Moore and Zanardi (2009) use relatively aggregated data to examine the cross-country relationship between average tariff cuts and previous resorting to anti-dumping for a number of developing economies.

also investigates the within-country, cross-product variation in TTB use relative to some of the other trade policies listed in Table 1.3 to better understand the interrelationship across instruments of import protection. An important research question is how these TTB policies interact, *ie* as substitutes, complements or independently, both with each other and with other important trade policy changes to the economy's applied MFN or preferential trade agreement tariffs.

Furthermore, many of the chapters address, in empirical detail, the important issue of the temporary nature of TTBs. The *time coverage* of the average TTB may be changing in addition to any changes in the scope of TTB product coverage. Moore (2006) and Cadot *et al* (2007) were among the first to examine the Uruguay Round's addition of a formal sunset review requirement for anti-dumping that attempted to limit the time duration of imposed measures. How have such innovations affected the impact of TTBs, and did this change systematically during the crisis?

Finally, consider the set of TTB-affected economy-wide imports. Are there changes across industries as to which sectors' imports are covered by TTBs? Can changes in this structure of TTB-affected industries be linked to the evolution of political-economic forces and changes to comparative advantage? Furthermore, the broad evidence aggregated across countries (Bown and Kee 2011) is that TTBs overall, but anti-dumping in particular, are increasingly targeting imports from *developing* countries. The practice of using TTBs to target imports from China is well known (Bown 2010b) but, for the chapters on TTB policy use by emerging economies in particular, is the targeting of developing countries specific to China's exports, or are there other emerging-country exporters increasingly and significantly impacted by TTB use, and was China simply the first casualty of TTBs affecting more south–south trade?

This section has raised a number of questions. While not all of the following chapters address each of these issues, each chapter addresses most of these questions. Furthermore, each chapter also pursues a number of more subtle, economy-specific questions that arise from the authors' examination of the details of the underlying events.

4.2 High-Income-Economy Use of TTBs

In Chapter 2, Thomas Prusa examines the USA's TTBs, finding a sharp decline in the flow of TTBs over the longer term (2000–2009) and only a modest uptick during 2008–9. Despite experiencing a macroeconomic slowdown that traditionally would have triggered a sharp increase in TTBs, the USA initiated relatively few investigations during the 2007–9 US recession. With respect to the targets of protection, he finds that US TTBs are increasingly directed at imports from developing countries in general, and China in particular. While the steel industry has long been the heaviest user of TTBs within the USA, other industries such as seafood and wood products display significant ebbs and flows in TTB protection. Surprisingly, the Uruguay Round mandatory sunset provisions have adversely affected developing countries as US TTBs brought against developing countries are at least 60% more likely to remain in place than those against developed countries. Finally, he briefly examines the widely publicised 2009 China safeguard on tyres, highlighting how the availability of many alternative tyre suppliers limited the likely impact of the discriminatory import restriction.

Hylke Vandenbussche and Christian Viegelahn examine the EU's use of TTBs in Chapter 3. They too fail to find clear signs of a major trade policy change since the outbreak of the crisis. Like many other economies, EU anti-dumping policy has increasingly focused on China as a target. The chapter provides an innovative method of analysis and finds that the EU is more likely to impose protection against countries and country-industry combinations the more similar they are to the EU in their product mix. Country-product combinations subject to a preferential tariff are also more likely to be targeted by the EU's TTBs. In terms of product characteristics, the shares of consumer goods and differentiated goods covered by EU anti-dumping measures have increased rapidly, and they have remained at a relatively high level during the crisis. These TTB patterns do not appear to be driven by a few outlying countries within the EU but are also similar when considering individual EU member states.

Canada's use of TTBs during 1989–2009 is the focus of the study by Rodney Ludema and Anna Maria Mayda in Chapter 4. Despite the retreat in the stock of products covered by TTB over the 2000s, they find signs of a rebound. The connection of anti-dumping protection to the business cycle remains strong as new Canadian anti-dumping cases have surged since the crisis, which portends a rise in anti-dumping stocks that could last for several years. They also provide evidence of a major structural shift occurring in terms of the products and countries on which Canada's TTBs are applied. The product scope of anti-dumping protection has narrowed, and increases in anti-dumping protection have taken place in sectors with relatively small reductions of MFN tariffs. China and, to a lesser extent, other developing countries are being targeted with far greater intensity than before 2000. Finally, the duration of anti-dumping remedies fell during the first half of the 2000s, though this seems to have been reversed in the later half of the decade.

Chapter 5 presents an examination of Korea. Moonsung Kang and Soonchan Park describe Korea's export-led growth strategy beginning in the 1970s, which led its exporters to become a major anti-dumping target in the 1980s and 1990s. As Korea has become more market-orientated and liberalised its import regime, it has slowly used TTBs with more regularity. In particular, Korea had a dramatic increase in usage during the Asian financial crisis of 1997–8, immediately before the recession of 2000, and a small increase during 2008–9. Korea's TTB use has most frequently targeted China, followed by Japan and the USA. Finally, evidence from Korea's anti-dumping use during

2008–9 suggests that its politically organised sectors tend to receive more protection than unorganised ones.

4.3 Emerging-Economy Use of TTBs

The last seven chapters of the volume focus on developing economies' emerging use of TTBs, beginning with Piyush Chandra's analysis of China in Chapter 6. While the flow of new Chinese anti-dumping investigations increased during 2008–9, the stock of China's imports subject to anti-dumping measures decreased as China terminated a number of previously imposed measures covering large numbers of products and shares of imports. Nevertheless, the 2008–9 crisis did lead to a number of changes in how China is using anti-dumping in particular. The increase in the flow of China's anti-dumping investigations was a reversal of the trend from the previous five years. Furthermore, whereas prior to the crisis almost all of China's anti-dumping use was confined to only five industrial sectors, during 2008–9 China initiated new, large-scale anti-dumping investigations in previously unaffected sectors—including the controversial cases against US autos and chicken parts that immediately followed the US-imposed China safeguard on tyres in 2009. Furthermore, China is similar to other countries in the large number of anti-dumping measures that last longer than five years, but it is different from other countries in that most of its anti-dumping targets high-income trading partners. Finally, Chandra also provides evidence that, despite anti-dumping affecting a relatively sizeable share of China's imports, very few Chinese firms have participated as petitioners in the process.

Patricia Tovar analyses India's increasing reliance on TTBs in Chapter 7. While India did not use anti-dumping, safeguards and countervailing measures prior to 1992, it has subsequently become the WTO system's dominant user of TTB policies. There has been an increase in the stock of Indian imports subject to anti-dumping measures during 1992–2009; in particular, the percentage of tariff-line products affected by an anti-dumping measure increased from 1.8% in 2007 to 4.0% by 2009. Another dimension along which India's anti-dumping protection increased during 2008–9 was via the failure to remove previously imposed policies that came up for review during the crisis. Furthermore, the incidence of India's anti-dumping policy has shifted over time towards China and other developing countries. Finally, while India increased its use of anti-dumping, global safeguards and China-specific safeguards during 2008–9, India's process of tariff liberalisation continued during the period. As such, it is possible that India's use of TTBs may have contributed to its sustained move towards greater openness.

Marcelo Olarreaga and Marcel Vaillant present the case of Brazil in Chapter 8. Brazil put a regime of TTB protection into place in the late 1980s, when it began its process of trade liberalisation. In the period 1990–2009, Brazil's TTBs were highly concentrated in a few sectors and its government relied most heavily on anti-dumping measures, as opposed to countervailing or safeguards measures. While Brazil's TTBs affect a relatively small share of its imports overall, 18% of imports within politically sensitive sectors are affected. The main historical targets of Brazil's TTBs are high-income and upper-middle-income countries, with imports from China and lower-middle-income countries increasingly targeted over the 2000s. There is some evidence of complementarity between Brazil's MFN tariffs and its use of TTBs, which could signal that politically strong sectors are able to obtain both forms of protection. Furthermore, although Brazil had a significant amount of 'water' in its MFN tariff structure during this period, the TTBs are twice as large as would be allowed by the water in the existing tariff structure. Interestingly, any acceleration of Brazilian TTBs during 2008–9 appears to be unrelated to the performance of the Brazilian real economy (which continued to grow in annual terms), relating instead to an appreciation of the *real* with respect to the currency of Brazil's trading partners.

In Chapter 9, Michael O. Moore investigates Argentina's use of TTBs. Argentina, once a prominent example of the 'Washington consensus', took dramatic steps to reduce its integration into the world economy in the aftermath of the peso crisis in 2001. Thus, while it would not have been unprecedented for Argentina to use TTBs aggressively in response to the 2008–9 crisis, the share of imports subject to ongoing Argentine TTBs increased from 1.2% of total imports in 2006 to only 2.7% by 2009. Considering a broader definition of suppressed imports allows the affected import share to rise to 5% by 2009. With respect to export targets, while Argentine anti-dumping continues to focus on developing countries, this focus has shifted from Brazil in earlier periods to almost all of the recent anti-dumping activity being narrowly focused on China.

Raymond Robertson documents Mexico's experience with TTBs in Chapter 10. Among developing economies, Mexico was one of the early liberalisers of its overall import regime. In the early 1990s, Mexico stood out as one of the largest users of TTBs—almost entirely in the form of anti-dumping measures—but consistent with its other trade barriers, Mexico has reduced the use of these measures over time. Mexico's two primary targets have been and remain China and the USA. Unlike many other developing countries, Mexico's increased use of TTBs during the 2008–9 crisis was slight (if at all), especially when compared with historical use. The most significant Mexican TTB activity during the crisis was the *removal* in 2008 of anti-dumping measures over hundreds of tariff lines that had been in place against China since 1993 (see Figure 1.10).

Turkey's use of TTBs is the subject of Baybars Karacaovali's study in Chapter 11. Turkey has been an active user of anti-dumping since the 1990s and more recently began using safeguards and CVDs. Turkey's use of TTBs during the 1990s took place at the same time that it was liberalising its import regime as a founding member of the WTO and through formation of a customs union with the EU in 1996. Turkey has also signed numerous PTAs that the EU has been involved in as part of its EU candidacy. The drastic intra-group and extra-group trade liberalisation brought on by the relations with the EU in particular is a likely contributing determinant to the rise of Turkey's use of TTBs during 2000–2009. Turkey continued to use TTBs aggressively during 2008–9 as it was significantly affected by the global economic crisis. Finally, Turkey has not targeted established EU members with TTBs but instead has targeted developing countries, and especially China, at rates that are disproportionate to their import market share.

Lawrence Edwards concludes with a detailed analysis of South Africa's use of TTBs in Chapter 12. South Africa's TTBs exhibit many similarities with other emerging economies: an increase in the use of anti-dumping measures during the 1990s and a shift in the incidence of anti-dumping policy towards China, India and other emerging economies in the 2000s. Yet there are important differences that reflect the unique domestic characteristics of South Africa's anti-dumping policy. While South Africa was a world leader in the use of anti-dumping measures during the 1990s, it had dramatically reduced the number of products subject to TTBs by the late 2000s. South Africa responded to the global economic crisis in 2008–9 by revoking over a third of all anti-dumping measures. This, however, was not a proactive response by the government to the crisis, but rather the consequence of a High Court ruling that various anti-dumping measures had exceeded the five-year period allowed under the WTO. South Africa's anti-dumping measures were not used to offset the 1990s multilateral tariff liberalisation but were more likely used to cover products that already had high tariffs and faced relatively low tariff reductions, suggesting common political economy determinants of South Africa's tariff and anti-dumping policy. Finally, there is little evidence that the political economy determinants of anti-dumping policy have changed, despite the integration of previously unrepresented economic interests after the demise of apartheid in 1994.

5 CONCLUSIONS

The chapters in this volume clarify a number of important facts on TTB policy changes during the 2008–9 crisis. These changes are presented in the context of a longer-term perspective; the trading system and global economy have undergone a significant evolution over the previous 20 years. Ultimately, these facts raise more questions for research than they answer. Recall the questions described earlier. What are the likely contributing causes to the resilience of the WTO system in the face of the 2008–9 global economic shock? How is this related to the evolving landscape of import protection through TTBs that, for some WTO members, forms an increasingly important portion of its overall portfolio of protection? What does the changing nature of TTB use mean for the future of a cooperative, multilateral WTO system?

The legacy of the TTB policy changes taking place during the crisis is far from decided. The 25% increase in product coverage by 2009 has established new barriers that are likely to remain in place for a number of years, before the battles begin for their removals under sunset reviews. Nevertheless, other battles over crisis-era TTBs have already been initiated. By 2010, a number of these TTBs were already subject to a formal dispute settlement challenge at the WTO—including the US-imposed China safeguard on tyres, China's anti-dumping and CVDs on US exports of grain-orientated electrical steel, the EU's decision to continue duties on Chinese exports of footwear, and China's imposed anti-dumping duties on steel fastener imports from the EU. This is also consistent with pre-crisis trends; the relative importance of TTBs is also accounted for by its increasingly significant role as a source of formal WTO legal challenges (Bown 2009d).

To conclude, it must stressed that, despite the contribution of the following chapters to economic research, it will be a long time before we can close the book on the 2008–9 crisis and its long-term implications for import protection.

6 APPENDIX

6.1 Technical Explanation of Methodological Approach

This description follows from Bown (2011). The first methodological approach takes an importing economy's set of HS-06 products as the unit of observation and builds from Bown and Tovar (2011, Figure 1). More formally, let k be the policy-imposing (importing) economy and let $m^k_{i,t} \in \{0, 1\}$ be an indicator for whether the economy had non-zero imports of product i in year t. The HS-06 product i is in the economy's time-varying set of HS-06 products with non-zero imports, defined as I^k_t. Next, let $b^k_{i,t} \in \{0, 1\}$ be an indicator for whether the importing economy k 'applies' a TTB on imports of product i in year t. Thus, define the first 'count' measure of the share of annual stock of economy k imported products subject to a TTB as

$$\frac{\sum_{I^k_t} b^k_{i,t} m^k_{i,t}}{\sum_{I^k_t} m^k_{i,t}}. \tag{1.1}$$

The approach can rely on a variety of definitions for the TTB indicator $b^k_{i,t}$ depending on the application. Sometimes it may be defined as an indicator of the initiation of a TTB *investigation* of product i in year t; alternatively, $b^k_{i,t}$ may be defined as the actual application of a barrier (*eg* import duty, quantitative restriction, price undertaking) imposed over product i in year t. Note that, when referring to applied barriers, the approach adopted in the text is to take the year of imposition as the first year that the barrier was imposed, even if it was only a preliminary barrier and even if that preliminary barrier was subsequently removed after completion of the full investigation. The application, even of preliminary barriers, can affect trade both directly (raising costs to exporters) and indirectly (increasing uncertainty about future policy); see Staiger and Wolak (1994).

The second approach refines Equation (1.1) by replacing the binary indicator variable for imports, $m_{i,t}^{k}$, with import-value data at the product level and thus *trade-weighting* the $b_{i,t}^{k}$ indicator by the HS-06 product-level value of imports from country j, $v_{i,j,t}^{k}$. While this approach builds from Equation (1.1), it is adapted in two ways.

First, redefine the product-specific, time-varying TTB indicator to now be at the *bilateral* level: let $b_{i,j,t}^{k} \in \{0, 1\}$ be an indicator for whether a TTB applies to the economy k imports of product i from exporter j in year t. This modification allows the approach to address the possibility of heterogeneity across foreign sources in terms of which trading partners are negatively affected by the TTB and which are not.

The second adaptation requires a slightly more detailed explanation. In order, ultimately, to create coverage ratios that are comparable within a country *over time*, an assumption is required for the counterfactual level of economy k imports in t (as well as $t + 1$, *etc*) from a supplier j whose exports had been subject to a TTB imposed in an earlier year (*eg* $t - 1$, $t - 2$, *etc*) and thus did not grow at a 'normal' rate in later years (*eg* t, $t + 1$, *etc*). To determine the counterfactual level of imports for such products, the approach in the text is to make the simple and conservative assumption that, beginning in year t, yearly imports of TTB-impacted products would have grown *at the same rate* as the economy's non-TTB impacted products.[23] To make this clear, decompose the set of economy k imported products I^{k} into two subsets. Define the first subset as $\hat{I}^{k}$ and allow it to contain those HS-06 products i subject to a TTB imposed during the sample and for which there is a need to construct *counterfactual* import values, defined as $\hat{v}_{i,j,t}^{k}$, for all years that the TTB is in effect. Define the second subset of products as I^{*k} and allow it to contain all (other) imported HS-06 products i that were never subject to an imposed TTB and for which there is *not* a need to construct counterfactual import val-

[23] There are arguments to suggest that such products may grow at a rate that is different from other products in the economy. For example, these are products that typically had been growing at rates faster than the average rate of import growth, perhaps because of a technological innovation or productivity improvement, and thus one might expect that to have continued. On the other hand, if the imports were growing at faster rates because they were dumped or subsidised (and if the dumping or subsidisation had terminated), one might expect the rate of growth to fall (if the dumping or subsidising stopped), even in the absence of the TTB. While acknowledging the range of theoretical arguments for counterfactual import growth, to construct these measures the approach adopted here is to rely on the conservative assumption of TTB-impacted imports growing at the same rate as imports not impacted by TTBs.

ues, and thus for which only the observable import data $v^k_{i,j,t}$ is required.[24] This modification also addresses the well-known concern that any TTB policy imposed in year t may reduce the (contemporaneous) year t value of imports, and this would underweight the economic importance of the trade barrier in the averaging.

The second measure of the share of annual stock of economy k imported products subject to a TTB in year t, reflecting the three modifications to Equation (1.1) and thus weighted by the 'value' of imports, is defined as[25]

$$\frac{\sum_{I^k_t} b^k_{i,j,t}\hat{v}^k_{i,j,t}}{\sum_{\hat{I}^k_t}\hat{v}^k_{i,j,t} + \sum_{I^{*k}_t} v^k_{i,j,t}}. \tag{1.2}$$

There are at least three other, more subtle transmission mechanisms through which Equations (1.1) and (1.2) can diverge beyond ways through which trade-weighting the HS-06 products leads to differences between the two series that have already been identified. First, defining the series according to the stock of covered HS-06 products prevents the case of a product already subject to a TTB in $t - 1$ from being double counted if a new TTB is imposed over the same product in subsequent years (*eg* in year t). For example, suppose a HS-06 product from a given foreign trading partner became subject to an anti-dumping barrier in $t - 1$ and then a CVD in t. Since the approach is to measure the 'stock' of products affected by TTBs, this would not result in a change to series (1.1) or (1.2) between $t - 1$ and t. On the other hand, if there is a *new* trading partner being subject to the TTB between $t - 1$ and t, even if the underlying product is unchanged, there can be a change in series (1.2). A change in trading partner coverage could occur because either the second partner was targeted under a different underlying TTB policy instrument (*eg* anti-dumping versus CVD) or because of differences in the timing under the same policy instrument (*eg* the first anti-dumping imposed over the HS-06 product was imposed against country A in $t - 1$ and not against country B until t). Third, the stock series can also be affected through differential timing in the *removal* of a previously imposed TTB over the same HS-06 product. For example, if the TTB on trading partner A is removed in $t - 1$ but the TTB on trading partner B is not removed until t, this differential timing in the removal will affect series (1.2). However, there will be no change in series (1.2) until *all* previously imposed TTBs affecting this product are removed.

---

[24]The approach in the text adopts the mean annual growth rate of products from the set I^{*k} in t to construct the counterfactual import levels for the products in $\hat{I}^k$ in t, which are denoted $\hat{v}^k_{i,j,t}$.

[25]The 'value' share measures presented throughout the Introduction are based on non-oil import data only. In the country-specific chapters of this volume, the authors have made alternative applications of this and related methodological approaches to different samples of trade data.

Before concluding this section, consider five remaining caveats to these approaches.

First, some economies impose TTBs at a level of product disaggregation (*eg* HS-08, HS-10) that is finer than the HS-06 level that is the focus here. Nevertheless, examination at the HS-06 level is desirable for the context of this chapter, since HS-06 is the finest level of disaggregation that is both comparable across countries and that has available import-value data back to the early 1990s. While the application of measures using HS-06 data will overstate the trade impact (in the level) for any economy that typically does not cover all subproducts within an HS-06 category, because these measures are defined consistently over time and across trading partners, measurement error is much less of a concern for two questions of interest to this and the subsequent chapters in the volume: *intertemporal changes* (*ie* whether the scope of imported products subject to a country's use of TTBs is increasing or decreasing over time) and the *relative exporter incidence* (*ie* whether certain exporters are relatively more or less frequently targeted than others by the stock of imposed TTBs).

Second, these approaches concentrate entirely on the potential first-order impact of TTBs on trade. There is a substantial theoretical and empirical literature from case studies that identifies potentially important second-order effects of TTBs (especially anti-dumping) on trade flows. Some accentuate the potential negative trade effects identified here, while others are offsetting and reduce the overall size of the trade effects. Examples of accentuating effects include downstream impacts, tariff-jumping foreign direct investment, and retaliation, while examples of offsetting effects include trade diversion. For an excellent survey of the anti-dumping literature, see Blonigen and Prusa (2003). Furthermore, alternative approaches to measuring the economic importance of anti-dumping in particular include Egger and Nelson (forthcoming) and Vandenbussche and Zanardi (2010) for gravity-model-style assessments and Gallaway *et al* (1999) for a computable general equilibrium style assessment.

Third, even trade-weighting the incidence of TTBs does nothing to address heterogeneity in the size of the imposed trade barriers. Bown (2010b), for example, notes substantial heterogeneity in the size of duties imposed across both policy-imposing economies and across targeted exporters by (within) a policy-imposing country, especially with respect to barriers imposed on imports from China.

Fourth, these approaches do not address potential heterogeneity in the *form* of the applied TTBs. For example, some economies apply anti-dumping as *ad valorem* duties, whereas others may be more likely (or against certain trading partners or over certain imported products) to apply it as a specific duty or a 'price undertaking' in which the exporter voluntarily raises its price above some threshold under the threat of an imposed duty. Global safeguards,

Table 1.4: *Industry classification in the Harmonized System.*

Section	Two-digit HS codes	Description
I	01–05	Live animals, animal products
II	06–14	Vegetable products
Iii	15	Animal or vegetable fats and oils
IV	16–24	Prepared foodstuffs
V	25–27	Mineral products
VI	28–39	Chemicals
VII	39–40	Plastics and rubber
VIII	41–43	Leather, raw hides and skins
IX	44–46	Woods and articles of wood
X	47–49	Pulp of wood
XI	50–63	Textiles
XII	64–67	Footwear
XIII	68–70	Stone
XIV	71	Pearls
XV	72–83	Metals
XVI	84–85	Machinery and electrical
XVII	86–89	Vehicles
XVIII	90–92	Optical instruments
XIX	93	Arms and ammunition
XX	94–96	Miscellaneous manufacturing
XXI	97–98	Works of art

on the other hand, are frequently applied as quantitative restrictions such as tariff rate quotas.

Fifth, these approaches do not address the issue of the likely import demand or export supply responses to the imposed TTBs because they do not control for import demand or export supply elasticities. For an application of the OTRI approach to the global economic crisis of 2008–9, see Kee *et al* (2010).

6.2 Data

Detailed data on anti-dumping, CVDs, global safeguards and China-specific safeguards are available from the World Bank's *Temporary Trade Barriers Database* (Bown 2010a). For anti-dumping and CVD policies, the data in Bown (2010a) are derived from original government source documents. Each government reports tariff-line product codes that are subject to the investigations, the dates and countries from whom imports are being investigated, and the decisions regarding whether to impose preliminary and final trade barriers, as well as when they are removed. The data on the use of global safeguards and China-specific safeguards are derived from both original government source documents and what governments report to the WTO's Committee on Safeguards. Bown (2010a) provides a complete discussion of the data sources, as well as the other information contained in the database that is not used in the analysis here.

The tariff-line product codes from Bown (2010a) are then matched to bilateral import data at the product level taken from UN Comtrade via the World Bank's Internet-based, freely available World Integrated Trade Solution (WITS).[26] Comtrade has two levels of disaggregation available: at the HS-06 level and at the tariff-line level, which may be at the 8-, 10- or 12-digit level, depending on the economy. Only the HS-06 data are publicly available. Chapter authors also have access to the tariff-line import data, though they differ on which of the different import series they chose to apply given tradeoffs associated with each. For example, whereas the tariff-line level import data provide more granularity, they are generally not available in as long a time series as the HS-06-level data (which date back at least to the early 1990s), and they also may be more susceptible to classification changes of products over the sample.

This volume also takes advantage of data on tariff-line MFN applied tariff rates and PTA rates, as well as information on tariff-line WTO bindings from the WTO's Consolidated Tariff Schedules. While there are many years of tariff data available for these economies, most countries are missing at least one or two years' worth of tariff data.

The chapter authors then further supplemented the data on TTBs, trade and tariff policies with data on the macroeconomy, industries or national features of the domestic political economy from a number of other sources. Additional details are provided within each chapter where appropriate.

Finally, many of the chapters in this volume use a common approach to defining 'industries' so as to examine more detailed data on TTB policy use and trade flows. In many instances, the authors refer to industries based on the two-digit Harmonized System 'sections' that are documented in Table 1.4.

Chad P. Bown is Senior Economist at the World Bank in the Development Research Group, Trade and International Integration Team (DECTI).

REFERENCES

Bagwell, K., and R. W. Staiger (2002). *The Economics of the World Trading System.* Cambridge, MA: MIT Press.

Baldwin, R. (ed.) (2009). *The Great Trade Collapse: Causes, Consequences and Prospects.* VoxEU e-book (November).

---

[26]These data are publicly available from the World Bank via WITS at http://wits.worldbank.org/.

Blonigen, B. A., and T. J. Prusa (2003). Antidumping. In *Handbook of International Trade* (ed. E. K. Choi and J. Harrigan). Oxford, UK: Blackwell.

Bown, C. P. (2011). Taking stock of anti-dumping, safeguards, and countervailing duties, 1990–2009. *The World Economy*, forthcoming.

Bown, C. P. (2010a). *Temporary Trade Barriers Database*. World Bank (July). URL: http://econ.worldbank.org/ttbd/.

Bown, C. P. (2010b). China's WTO entry: anti-dumping, safeguards, and dispute settlement. In *China's Growing Role in World Trade* (ed. R. Feenstra and S. Wei). Chicago, IL: University of Chicago Press for NBER.

Bown, C. P. (2009a). Protectionism is on the rise: antidumping investigations. In *The Collapse of Global Trade, Murky Protectionism, and the Crisis: Recommendations for the G20* (ed. R. Baldwin and S. J. Evenett). London: CEPR/VoxEU.org (March).

Bown, C. P. (2009b). Antidumping, safeguards, and other trade remedies. In *The Fateful Allure of Protectionism: Taking Stock for the G8* (ed. S. J. Evenett, B. M. Hoekman, and O. Cattaneo). London: CEPR/World Bank (July).

Bown, C. P. (2009c). The global resort to antidumping, safeguards, and other trade remedies amidst the economic crisis. In *Effective Crisis Response and Openness: Implications for the Trading System* (ed. S. J. Evenett, B. M. Hoekman, and O. Cattaneo). London: CEPR/World Bank (December).

Bown, C. P. (2009d). *Self-Enforcing Trade: Developing Countries and WTO Dispute Settlement*. Washington, DC: Brookings Institution Press.

Bown, C. P. (2008). The WTO and antidumping in developing countries. *Economics and Politics* **20**(2), 255–288.

Bown, C. P., and M. A. Crowley (2005). Safeguards. In *The World Trade Organization: Legal, Economic and Political Analysis* (ed. P. F. J. Macrory, A. E. Appleton, and M. G. Plummer). New York: Springer.

Bown, C. P., and H. L. Kee (2011). Trade barriers, developing countries, and the global economic crisis. In *Managing Openness: Trade and Outward-Oriented Growth After the Crisis* (ed. M. Haddad and B. Shepherd). Washington, DC: World Bank.

Bown, C. P., and P. Tovar (2011). Trade liberalization, antidumping, and safeguards: evidence from India's tariff reform. *Journal of Development Economics* **96**(1), 115–125.

Cadot, O., J. de Melo, and B. Tumurchudur (2007). Anti-dumping sunset reviews: the uneven reach of WTO disciplines. CEPR Working Paper 6502 (September).

Choi, H., and H. Varian (2009). Predicting the present with Google Trends. Google, Inc. Working Paper (April).

Egger, P., and D. Nelson (forthcoming). How bad is antidumping? evidence from panel data. *The Review of Economics and Statistics*.

Finger, J. M., and J. J. Nogués (eds) (2005). *Safeguards and Antidumping in Latin American Trade Liberalization: Fighting Fire with Fire*. New York: World Bank/Palgrave.

Freund, C. (2009a). The trade response to global downturns. In *The Great Trade Collapse: Causes, Consequences and Prospects* (ed. R. Baldwin). VoxEU.org e-book (November).

Freund, C. (2009b). The trade response to global crises: historical evidence. World Bank Working Paper 5015 (August).

Freund, C., and I. C. Neagu (2011). Trade watch: 4th quarter 2010. World Bank. URL: http://go.worldbank.org/PPOQADSA70.

Gallaway, M. P., B. A. Blonigen, and J. E. Flynn (1999). Welfare cost of the US antidumping and countervailing duty law. *Journal of International Economics* **49**(2), 211–244.

Gamberoni, E., and R. Newfarmer (2009a). Trade protection: incipient but worrisome trends. World Bank Trade Notes 37 (March).

Gamberoni, E., and R. Newfarmer (2009b). Trade protection: incipient but worrisome trends. Online Article, VoxEu.org (March). URL: www.voxeu.org/index.php?q=node/3183.

Hoekman, B. M., and M. M. Kostecki (2009). *The Political Economy of the World Trading System* (3rd edition). Oxford University Press.

Irwin, D. A. (2011). *Peddling Protectionism: Smoot-Hawley and the Great Depression.* Princeton University Press.

Irwin, D. A. (2003). Causing problems? The WTO review of causation and injury attribution in US Section 201 cases. *World Trade Review* **2**(3), 297–325.

Horn, H., and P. C. Mavroidis (eds) (2009). *The WTO Case Law of 2006–2007.* Cambridge University Press.

Horn, H., and P. C. Mavroidis (eds) (2008). *The WTO Case Law of 2004–2005.* Cambridge University Press.

Horn, H., and P. C. Mavroidis (eds) (2006). *The WTO Case Law of 2003.* Cambridge University Press.

Horn, H., and P. C. Mavroidis (eds) (2005). *The WTO Case Law of 2002.* Cambridge University Press.

Horn, H., and P. C. Mavroidis (eds) (2004). *The WTO Case Law of 2001.* Cambridge University Press.

International Monetary Fund (2010). *World Economic Outlook: Recovery, Risk and Rebalancing.* Washington, DC: IMF.

Kee, H. L., I. C. Neagu, and A. Nicita (2010). Is protectionism on the rise? Assessing national trade policies during the crisis of 2008. World Bank Working Paper 5274 (April).

Kee, H. L., A. Nicita, and M. Olarreaga (2009). Estimating trade restrictiveness indices. *The Economic Journal* **119**(534), 172–199.

Knetter, M. M., and T. J. Prusa (2003). Macroeconomic factors and antidumping filings: evidence from four countries. *Journal of International Economics* **61**(1), 1–17.

Lynn, J. (2009). WTO warns on protectionism scare-mongering. *Reuters* (18 December).

Mavroidis, P., P. Messerlin, and J. Wauters (2008). *The Law and Economics of Contingent Protection in the WTO.* Cheltenham, UK: Edward Elgar.

Moore, M. O. (2006). An econometric analysis of US antidumping sunset review decisions. *Weltwirtschaftliches Archiv* **142**(1), 122–150.

Moore, M. O., and M. Zanardi (2009). Does antidumping use contribute to trade liberalization in developing countries? *Canadian Journal of Economics* **42**(2), 469–495.

National Bureau of Economic Research (2010). The NBER's business cycle dating committee. URL: www.nber.org/cycles/recessions.html.

Nelson, D. R. (2006). The political economy of antidumping. *European Journal of Political Economy* **22**(3), 554–590.

Organisation for Economic Co-operation and Development (2011). Quarterly national accounts. URL: http://stats.oecd.org/Index.aspx.

Prusa, T. J. (2001). On the spread and impact of antidumping. *Canadian Journal of Economics* **34**(3), 591–611.

Reynolds, K. M. (2008). Countervailing duties. In *The Princeton Encyclopedia of the World Economy* (ed. K. A. Reinert and R. S. Rajan). Princeton University Press.

Rodrik, D. (2009). The myth of rising protectionism. Project Syndicate Opinion Editorial (October).

Staiger, R. W., and F. A. Wolak (1994). Measuring industry-specific protection: antidumping in the United States. *Brookings Papers on Economic Activity (Microeconomics)* 51–118.

Sykes, A. O. (2003). The safeguards mess: a critique of WTO jurisprudence. *World Trade Review* **2**(3), 261–295.

Vandenbussche, H., and M. Zanardi (2010). The chilling trade effects of antidumping proliferation. *European Economic Review* **54**(6) 760–777.

World Trade Organization (2008). *World Tariff Profiles 2008*. Geneva: WTO.

Zanardi, M. (2004). Antidumping: what are the numbers to discuss at Doha? *The World Economy* **27**(3), 403–433.

2

USA: Evolving Trends in Temporary Trade Barriers

THOMAS J. PRUSA[1]

1 INTRODUCTION

The USA has long been among the most active seekers of contingent protection. This was true in the 1980s and 1990s and remains true in the first decade of the 2000s. While other policies such as 'buy American' provisions and domestic content rules have received considerably more press attention during the economic crisis of 2007–9, the simple truth is that contingent trade policies remain the primary means of changing the relative cost and/or availability of imports. Under WTO rules, contingent protection policies like antidumping, CVDs, China safeguards and global safeguards should be applied for a limited duration.[2] Consequently, the term 'temporary trade barriers' (TTBs) is a particularly apt description of the policies.

In this chapter the trends in US TTB activity since 1990 are discussed. In order to provide a broad perspective on the issue, the trends are examined using several different metrics. We begin with the traditional case metric. However, Bown (2011b) argues that, for many questions, a product metric provides more insight into the trends and thus both unweighted and trade-weighted product metrics will be used.

These findings indicate that US use of TTBs is evolving. Some of the stylised facts of the past are no longer true. Although the USA continues to be a heavy user of TTBs (as compared with other countries), the number of new TTBs sought by US industries has fallen markedly since 2004. Over 2005–9, the number of new requests for TTBs (case metric) by US industries has fallen by about 60% compared with the late 1990s.

This decrease is especially noteworthy in light of the sharp decline in US economic activity in 2007–9, a development that one would have expected to

[1]Department of Economics, New Jersey Hall, Rutgers University, 75 Hamilton St, New Brunswick, NJ 08901-1248, USA. Email: prusa@econ.rutgers.edu.

[2]I discuss what is meant by 'limited duration' later in the chapter.

produce increased calls for protection.[3] Interestingly, using any of the three metrics for TTB activity, little evidence is found that the 2007–9 recession spurred a surge in US protectionism, or at least protectionism in the form of TTBs (Evenett (2010) presents evidence that other forms of protection have increased).

The current level of TTB activity for the USA is even more striking from a longer-run perspective. During 2006–10, the US initiated fewer cases than during any five-year span since 1960.[4] In fact, the two years with the fewest new TTB petitions, 2006 and 2010, have both occurred in this period.

The decline in new TTB activity, however, does not indicate that the USA has turned its back on TTBs. The USA continues to have a large stock of products under existing TTB orders. It seems that the USA is now far more reluctant to remove existing orders than in the pre-Uruguay Round period. In this sense, US TTBs are more onerous than those imposed previously. For example, this study finds that 75% (respectively, 90%) of US TTB orders were removed in the 1980s within five (respectively, ten) years; since 1995 only about 25% (respectively, 50%) of TTB orders were removed within five (respectively, ten) years.

This trend in longer duration is seen in both anti-dumping and CVD orders. Temporary trade barrier measures are far less likely to be removed (or 'sunset' as it is often termed) now than in the past. These trends are particularly noteworthy since the Uruguay Round agreement included a mandatory sunset provision for TTBs. Clearly, what was negotiated and what has happened in practice are two different things.[5] The findings suggest that, in the USA, the term *temporary* trade barrier means something different today from what it did previously. Perhaps the term 'semipermanent' trade barrier is a more accurate description. It is certainly debatable whether the term 'temporary' is an accurate description when a trade barrier is imposed for 20 years.

At least equally as concerning is the discovery that the increased duration of TTBs is especially felt by developing countries. In the post-Uruguay Round period, at the initial sunset review stage, approximately 40% of anti-dumping measures against developed countries are revoked as compared with fewer than 25% of measures against developing countries. The difference between developed and developing countries is even starker for CVD measures. About 10% of CVD measures against developing countries are revoked at the initial review versus 40% of CVD measures against developed countries.

What do these trends mean for the stock of TTBs? The reduced flow of new TTBs should result in a smaller stock of TTBs. On the other hand, longer

[3]Levchenko *et al* (2010) provide evidence that the reduction in trade relative to overall economic activity in the 2007–9 period was far larger than in previous downturns. Their findings might partially explain why there was not a surge in contingent protection.

[4]Comprehensive data on worldwide use of anti-dumping prior to 1980 are not available (Bown 2010a; WTO 2010). The statistics presented in Irwin (2005) suggest that the USA has probably been a leading anti-dumping user since the 1950s.

[5]These findings are consistent with those in Moore (1999, 2002).

duration of existing TTBs means less attrition in existing TTBs and this, in turn, should increase the stock of TTBs. Using either the unweighted measure or trade-weighted measure, the two effects are found to essentially offset each other; as a result, the stock of US TTBs is far more stable than the flow.

There have also been striking developments to the pattern of who is targeted by US TTBs. In the 1980s and 1990s, the majority of TTBs was directed against imports from developed countries. Historically, somewhere between one-half to two-thirds of both the flow and the stock of TTBs were against developed countries. This is no longer the case. By 2009, only about one-third of the US *stock* of TTBs was against developed countries. The change in the flow of TTBs is even more noticeable: more than 80% of the *flow* of TTBs is against developing countries.

While China is the main reason for the shift, China alone does not explain the changing pattern. Even if China were excluded, there would still be a marked increase in the share of US TTBs directed against developing countries. Non-China developing countries accounted for about half of US TTBs by 2009; in comparison, in the mid-1990s, non-China developing countries accounted for about one-third of US TTBs.

Although developing countries are getting greater attention, China is easily the major target of US TTBs. As is the case for many US trade policy issues, China looms large in US TTB activity. With respect to the stock of TTBs, the USA now has more TTBs in effect against China than against all developed countries taken together. China also dominates the flow of new TTBs.

When one accounts for the fact that anti-dumping and CVD protection is often sought against multiple suppliers in a single investigation (*ie* the US industry alleges unfair behaviour against more than one import supplier), it becomes apparent that the attention paid to China is even more intense. In 2006–10, China was involved in about 85% of anti-dumping and CVD investigations. In contrast, in the late 1990s, only about one-quarter of anti-dumping investigations involved China.

The distribution of TTBs by industry is also examined. Not surprisingly, the steel industry dominates US activity throughout the period, consistently accounting for 30–50% of TTBs. The value of the trade-weighted measure of TTB protection is most apparent when examining the pattern of TTBs by industry. When the long-standing Canadian softwood lumber dispute was resolved, the wood product industry went from roughly 20% of all imports subject to TTBs to having less than 5% subject to TTBs. By contrast, when duties were imposed on over $1 billion of warm-water shrimp, the share of all seafood imports covered increased dramatically.

The final section of the chapter considers the impact of the one instance in which the USA levied protection under the China safeguard provision—the 2009 dispute involving Chinese exports of passenger and truck tyres. This has been one of the most widely publicised TTB during 2005–9, garnering significant press attention both in the USA and in China. While Chinese volume

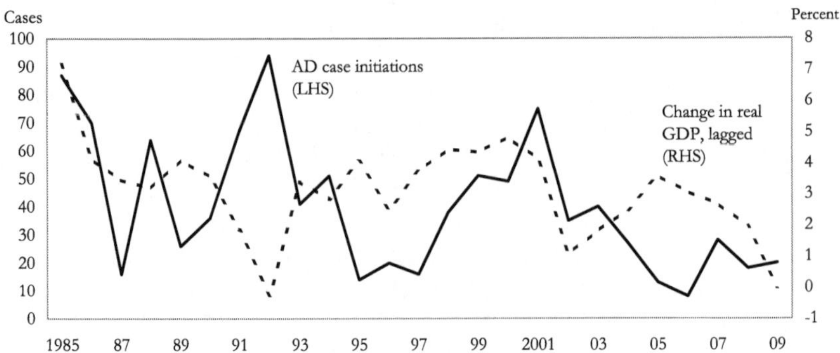

Figure 2.1: *US anti-dumping cases initiated and change in real GDP.*
Source: author's calculations using *Temporary Trade Barriers Database* (Bown 2010a) and US Bureau of Economic Analysis (2010).

and market share had grown in the years prior to the case, China was just one of many countries supplying tyres to the USA. In such circumstances, the country-specific nature of the China safeguard provision is likely to hinder any real change in overall trade flow.

Due to space limitations and because it is rarely invoked, global safeguards are not discussed here.[6] Readers interested in US use of global safeguards should consult Bown (2004, 2011b).

2 CONTEXT FOR CURRENT TRENDS: THE 2007–9 RECESSION

The recent US recession was quite severe by historical standards. The 4.1% peak-to-trough fall in US GDP was greater than any recession since the end of World War II. The 2007–9 recession was certainly far larger than any recession since accurate statistics have been kept on TTBs. For instance, peak-to-trough GDP fell by about 2.7% in the early 1980s recession, by about 1.4% during the early 1990s recession, and by about 0.3% in the 2001 recession.

Knetter and Prusa (2003) show that the flow of new TTB cases is counter-cyclical; typically, TTB activity increases (respectively, decreases) during economic downturns (respectively, expansions). Figure 2.1 depicts this general relationship using anti-dumping cases. In the figure, the number of new anti-dumping cases (solid line) initiated in each year is plotted along with the

[6]The USA did not initiate any global safeguards during the 2008–9 economic crisis. In fact, in the first decade of the 2000s there was only a single global safeguard case and that was in 2001. While that case (steel) was broad, received heavy press coverage and resulted in a WTO dispute, the trade impact was muted for several reasons: the largest volume products and suppliers were already covered by existing anti-dumping and countervailing orders; the order was only in place for 18 months; and over 700 product exemptions were granted (Bown 2004).

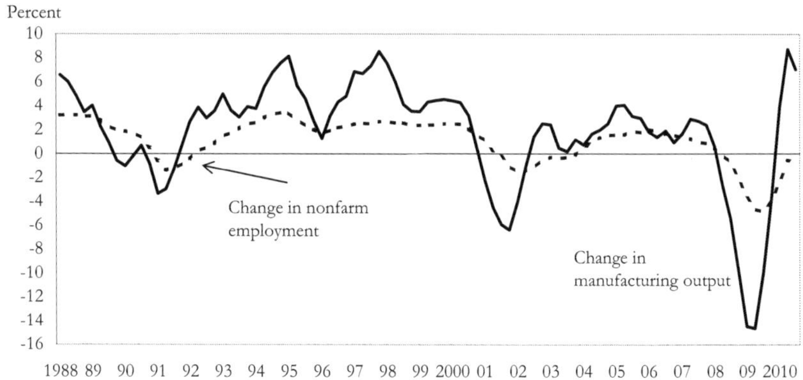

Figure 2.2: *Percentage change in US manufacturing output and non-farm employment.*
Source: US Bureau of Economic Analysis (2010).

lagged change in real GDP (dashed line). The negative correlation between economic activity and the flow of anti-dumping cases is most clearly seen during the recessions in the early 1980s, early 1990s and early 2000s, during which there were large increases in TTB activity (the global safeguard cases triggered by the recessions in the early 1980s and 2000s is not captured in the figure). By contrast, the significant decrease in GDP in 2007–9 was met with only a modest increase in US TTB activity.

Other measures of economic activity reinforce the finding that the level of TTB activity during 2008–9 is quite modest. Figure 2.2 depicts two common measures of US macroeconomic performance, the annual percentage change in manufacturing output and the percentage change in non-farm employment. As can be seen from the figure, the drop during 2008–9 in both measures was deeper than the declines during the 1991 and 2001 downturns. The fall in manufacturing output during the 2007–9 recession was more than twice as large as the 2001 recession and more than three times as large as the early 1990s recession. Only during the recession of the early 1980s has the unemployment level approached the 2007–9 recession's 10%+ level; notably, during the early 1980s recession, there was a large surge in anti-dumping and CVD investigations.

The performance of the steel sector, perennially the heaviest TTB-using industry, further buttresses the view that conditions in 2007–9 were ripe for a surge in TTB activity. In Figure 2.3, steel industry production is shown. Steel output fell by more than 50% during the 2007–9 recession, from a monthly output of over 9 million tons to about 4 million tons. Given a drop of this magnitude, it is not surprising that numerous steel-making facilities were shuttered or operated at unprofitably low rates (Uchitelle 2009). In the previous three downturns, 1982–3, 1991, and 2001, the steel industry used the

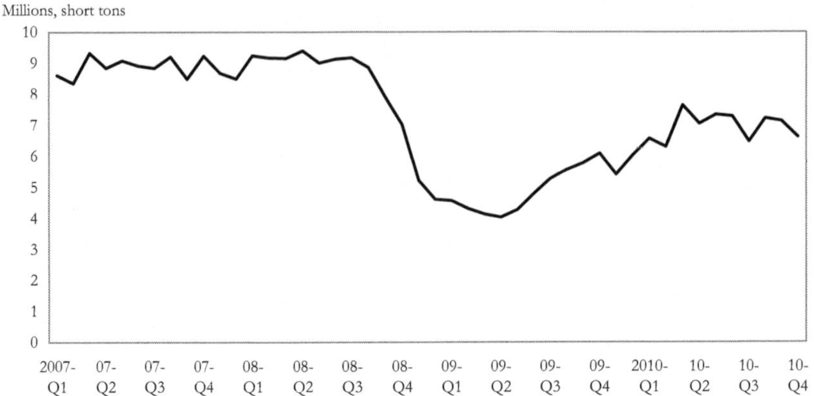

Figure 2.3: *US raw steel production (quarterly).*
Source: American Iron and Steel Institute (2010).

recession to justify their need for TTBs. Yet that is not what occurred in the 2007–9 recession.

Given historical TTB trends, one would have expected the 2007–9 recession to have spurred a significant increase in US TTB activity in 2008–9. US anti-dumping and CVD activity did increase—from 8 anti-dumping initiations in 2006 to 20 in 2009, and from 3 CVD initiations in 2006 to 14 in 2009. Yet this level of activity is quite modest by historical standards. In 1992 there were 94 anti-dumping initiations and in 2001 there were 75 anti-dumping initiations. In fact, the current level of TTB is more akin to the level of activity during previous periods of robust economic activity. Given the severity of the 2007–9 recession, the modest increase in TTB activity is surprising and one of the major findings of this chapter.

This finding will be returned to at various times in the chapter. The fact that US TTBs did not return to previous recessionary levels is important. No matter whether TTBs are measured using a case metric, product metric or trade-weighted metric, there is little evidence that the 2007–9 recession spurred a significant increase in TTB activity. In the final section of the chapter some possible explanations are offered as to why TTBs did not surge during the 2007–9 recession.

3 PATTERNS IN US TEMPORARY TRADE BARRIERS: CASE METRIC

3.1 General Discussion

With this backdrop, let us take an extended look at US TTB activity. In this section, the traditional case metric is used. This metric has several advantages.

First, it is consistent with how the USA and the WTO report TTB activity. Second, it is the most convenient metric for a long-run perspective on TTB activity; given changes in product code definitions, it is quite difficult to construct long time series using the product metric. On the other hand, as discussed in the next section, the case metric also has some weaknesses: most notably, the case metric treats a relatively small case (*eg* plastic shopping bags) the same as a very large case (*eg* warm-water shrimp). If the type and size of cases vary over time, the case metric will not adequately capture the changing impact of TTBs on imports.

Tables 2.1 and 2.2 give statistics on anti-dumping and CVD activity since 1990 using the case metric. The data are drawn from Bown (2010a). The tables report activity against developed countries, developing countries, China, and, finally, all targets (total cases). The number of cases initiated each year from 1990 to 2009 is listed.[7] The tables also report the number of measures taken, which are the cases that result in duties being levied. Finally, in the last column of each table, the number of conducted investigations is reported. The term 'case' refers to each individual country involved (*eg* warm-water shrimp from Thailand, warm-water shrimp from China) and 'investigation' refers to the set of countries involved (*eg* warm-water shrimp from all source countries). A single investigation often involves multiple countries. On average, a typical anti-dumping or CVD investigation involves two or three countries.[8]

As shown in Table 2.1, between 1990 and 2009 there were 741 anti-dumping cases. Of these, 346 resulted in imposed measures. Table 2.2 gives similar statistics for CVD disputes: there were 187 CVD cases, 82 of which resulted in measures. Put differently, over the entire period, about 45% of anti-dumping and CVD cases resulted in measures.

Figure 2.4 depicts the flow of new anti-dumping and CVD activity (petitions) using the case metric and provides visual evidence of the cyclical nature of TTB filing patterns. Both anti-dumping and CVD cases increased significantly during the economic slowdown in 1991–2 and 2001–2. As discussed above, there was only a modest uptick in activity in the 2007–9 recession.

Tables 2.1 and 2.2 also list the number of measures in effect during each year. If more measures are revoked than imposed in a given year, then the aggregate number of measures in effect will fall. For example, as shown in Table 2.1, the USA had 269 anti-dumping measures in effect during 2000 and 248 measures in effect during 2001. The USA imposed 28 new anti-dumping

---

[7]One caveat when looking at the annual numbers is that investigations typically take 11–14 months, so usually the measure will not be taken until the following calendar year. This makes it quite possible that more measures can be imposed in a given year than new cases initiated.

[8]Distinguishing between a case and an investigation has little impact on the later discussion in this chapter. Nevertheless, it can be important for other questions, such as, for example, Hansen and Prusa's (1996) study of cumulation and Bown and Crowley's (2007) study of trade depression, diversion and deflection.

Table 2.1: *US anti-dumping activity (by case), 1990–2009.*

	Developed			Developing			China			Total cases			
		Measures			Measures			Measures			Measures		
	Cases initiated	Taken	In effect	Cases initiated	Taken	In effect	Cases initiated	Taken	In effect	Cases initiated	Taken	In effect	Total number of investigations
1990	16	11	100	12	3	47	8	7	11	36	21	158	18
1991	30	6	110	31	9	50	6	3	19	67	18	179	24
1992	62	24	116	27	12	57	5	3	21	94	39	194	25
1993	16	6	140	18	7	70	7	4	24	41	17	234	20
1994	17	7	144	22	13	75	12	7	28	51	27	247	23
1995	7	5	141	5	2	86	2	1	33	14	8	260	9
1996	5	2	140	9	4	85	6	6	34	20	12	259	13
1997	12	5	138	4	3	88	0	0	39	16	8	265	7
1998	19	11	139	18	9	92	1	1	39	38	21	270	12
1999	22	11	145	22	6	97	7	4	40	51	21	282	19
2000	19	9	139	23	17	88	7	5	42	49	31	269	12
2001	31	11	110	36	13	93	8	4	45	75	28	248	21
2002	11	3	118	15	2	104	9	7	46	35	12	268	15
2003	12	2	119	18	7	102	10	7	53	40	16	274	20
2004	7	4	120	14	7	108	6	5	59	27	16	287	12
2005	5	2	115	4	3	110	4	3	62	13	8	287	8
2006	1	0	87	3	0	102	4	2	59	8	2	248	5
2007	10	5	75	6	4	93	12	12	61	28	21	229	14
2008	2	1	71	5	4	94	11	10	72	18	15	237	12
2009	0	0	72	8	3	96	12	2	81	20	5	249	13
Total	304	125	—	300	128	—	137	93	—	741	346	—	302
Share (average)	41%	36%	29%	40%	37%	39%	18%	27%	33%	—	—	—	—
Success rate	—	41%	—	—	43%	—	—	68%	—	—	47%	—	—

‘Share’ denotes average end-of-period share for ‘measures in effect’.

Source: author’s calculations using *Temporary Trade Barriers Database* (Bown 2010a).

Table 2.2: *US countervailing activity (by case), 1990–2009.*

	Developed			Developing			China			Total cases			
		Measures			Measures			Measures			Measures		
	Cases initiated	Taken	In effect	Cases initiated	Taken	In effect	Cases initiated	Taken	In effect	Cases initiated	Taken	In effect	Total number of investigations
1990	2	0	18	5	2	46	0	0	0	7	2	64	4
1991	3	2	17	8	3	46	1	0	0	12	5	63	9
1992	32	13	17	12	6	46	1	0	0	45	19	63	9
1993	2	1	30	4	0	52	0	0	0	6	1	82	3
1994	5	2	30	2	0	51	0	0	0	7	2	81	5
1995	1	1	30	1	1	51	0	0	0	2	2	81	1
1996	1	0	27	0	0	23	0	0	0	1	0	50	1
1997	4	1	26	2	0	22	0	0	0	6	1	48	3
1998	9	5	27	4	1	20	0	0	0	13	6	47	7
1999	5	4	32	10	2	17	0	0	0	15	6	49	5
2000	5	4	31	6	6	15	0	0	0	11	10	46	4
2001	9	4	23	6	2	20	0	0	0	15	6	43	8
2002	5	2	30	0	0	22	0	0	0	5	2	52	5
2003	0	0	32	6	2	22	0	0	0	6	2	54	5
2004	1	0	32	3	0	24	0	0	0	4	0	56	3
2005	0	0	29	2	2	24	0	0	0	2	2	53	1
2006	1	0	20	1	0	21	1	0	0	3	0	41	1
2007	0	0	12	0	0	19	7	7	0	7	7	31	7
2008	0	0	10	1	1	19	5	5	7	6	6	36	6
2009	1	0	9	3	1	20	10	2	12	14	3	41	12
Total	86	39	—	76	29	—	25	14	—	187	82	—	99
Share (average)	46%	48%	22%	41%	35%	49%	13%	17%	29%	—	—	—	—
Success rate	—	45%	—	—	38%	—	—	56%	—	—	44%	—	—

'Share' denotes average end-of-period share for 'measures in effect'.

Source: author's calculations using *Temporary Trade Barriers Database* (Bown 2010a).

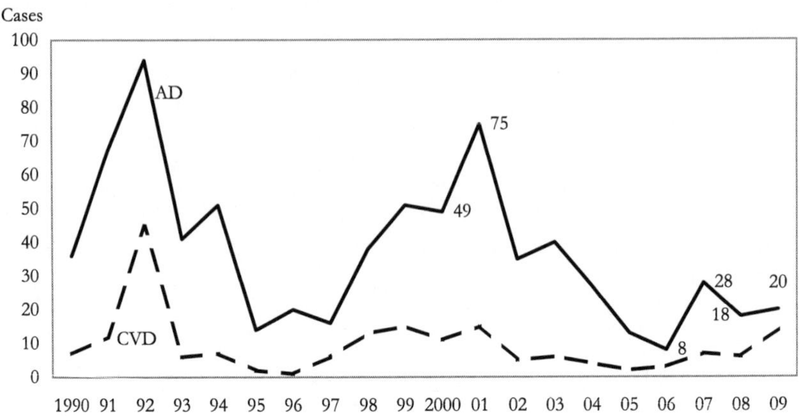

Figure 2.4: *US anti-dumping and CVD case initiations.*
Source: author's calculations using *Temporary Trade Barriers Database* (Bown 2010a).

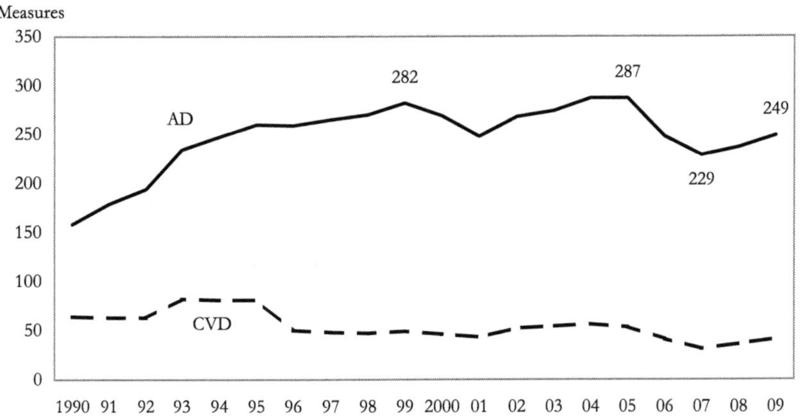

Figure 2.5: *US anti-dumping and CVD measures in effect.*
Source: author's calculations using *Temporary Trade Barriers Database* (Bown 2010a).

measures in 2001. This implies that 49 anti-dumping measures were 'sunsetted' in 2001.

When using the case metric, 'measures in effect' give the stock of TTB activity. The trends are depicted in Figure 2.5. As can be seen from the figure, there have always been far more anti-dumping measures than CVD measures, but the differential has grown since 1990. Countervailing duty measures have declined modestly, while anti-dumping measures have grown significantly over the period, and, consequently, the relative importance of the two TTBs has widened: in 1990 the ratio of anti-dumping to CVD measures was 3:1 and by 2009 it was 5:1.

Figure 2.5 also provides some evidence of the impact of the inclusion of the mandatory sunset provision in the Uruguay Round. In the first two years of its use (1999–2000), mandatory sunset reviews had an appreciable impact on measures in effect; the USA revoked almost 100 orders.[9] Since that initial trove of sunset cases, however, the USA has been disinclined to remove orders (Moore 1999, 2002). This issue will be returned to in Section 6.

The number of CVD measures in effect has been relatively stable. As seen in Figure 2.5, CVD measures declined in the mid-1990s but have since remained nearly constant at 40–50 measures in effect. The impact, if any, of mandatory sunset reviews is not seen in the stock of CVD measures. Table 2.2 reveals that the main development with respect to CVDs is the decrease in the flow. About one-tenth as many CVD cases were initiated during 2000–2009 as during the 1980s.

3.2 *Target Countries*

It is also interesting to examine TTB patterns after dividing the target countries into development groupings: developed, developing (not including China), and China. China is separated from other developing countries because of the intense trade scrutiny to which it is subject within the USA. There are several important insights gleaned by looking at the targets by development status.

First, developed countries were targeted far less frequently by either anti-dumping or CVD actions over the 2000s relative to the preceding two decades. In the 1980s, about two-thirds of US anti-dumping and CVD cases targeted developed countries. The share of cases targeting developed countries fell throughout the 1990s and even more dramatically over the first decade of the 2000s. Since 2004, the number of cases brought against developed countries has dropped sharply; during 2005–9, fewer than ten cases in any year were aimed at developed countries. Averaging over the 1990–2009 period, 42% of the initiated cases targeted developed countries, but over 2005–9, only 20% of the cases targeted developed countries. The decline in cases brought against developed countries is even sharper for CVDs. Over 2003–9, only three CVD cases involved developed countries and none resulted in measures. By the end of 2009, only nine CVD measures were in effect against developed countries.

Second, the trends against developing countries are more stable. For most of the period, about 40% of US anti-dumping and CVD cases have targeted developing countries.[10] The total number of anti-dumping and CVD measures

[9]Moore (1999) points out that the majority of the initial trove of sunset orders involved measures that had been in place for more than 10 years.

[10]There is more volatility in the CVD trends due to the relatively small number of cases in any one year.

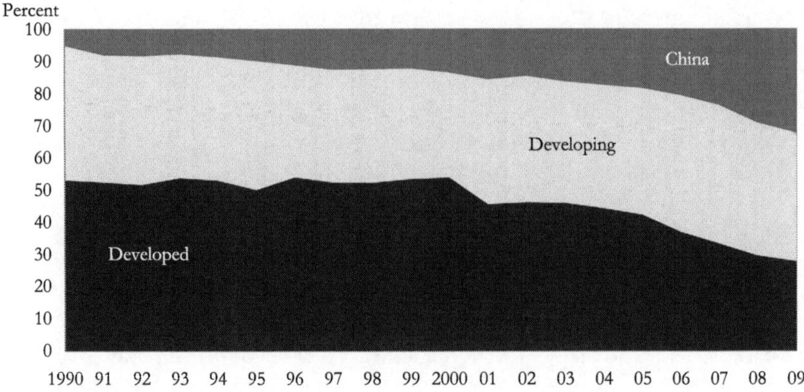

Figure 2.6: *Share of US anti-dumping and CVD measures, by development status (and China).*

Source: author's calculations using *Temporary Trade Barriers Database* (Bown 2010a).

in effect against developing countries has also remained fairly stable during the 1995–2009 period, with 90–100 anti-dumping measures and 20–25 CVD measures in effect in most years.

Third, and very importantly, China has emerged as the single most prominent target of US TTBs over the 2000s. Table 2.1 indicates that the absolute number of anti-dumping cases brought against China is about the same over the 2000s as during the 1990–1995 period. However, given that the number of TTBs targeting all other countries has fallen so sharply, China has emerged as the leading target. In a sense, other targets have taken two steps back while China stood still.

Perhaps the most startling statistic is the growth in the number of measures in effect against China. Over the first decade of the 2000s, the number of US anti-dumping measures in effect against China's exporters increased from 40 to 81. As a result, as of 2009, a full one-third of all US anti-dumping measures in effect are against China.

In addition, China now finds itself under unprecedented CVD scrutiny. Prior to 2007, no US CVD case against China had ever successfully resulted in a measure. This is largely because the US rules made it impossible to levy a CVD against a non-market economy. In 2007, the USA changed its rules and broadened its interpretation of CVDs. Under the new rules, CVDs could be levied on non-market economies like China. Subsequent to this rule change, a remarkable 23 of 30 US CVD cases have involved China.

Figure 2.6 depicts the yearly share of anti-dumping and CVD measures in effect, grouped by development status. The figure highlights the growing importance of China. As can be seen from the figure, over 1990–2009, developing countries accounted for about 40% of all measures. The big difference

Table 2.3: *US contingent protection against China (number of cases).*

	Cases initiated (%)	China involved (%)	Only China (%)
(a) China's share of US anti-dumping actions			
1980s	4	7	4
1990–94	13	34	16
1995–99	12	27	15
2000–04	18	50	21
2005–09	49	83	42
	Cases initiated (%)	China involved (%)	Only China (%)
(b) China's share of US CVD actions			
1980s	0	1	0
1990–94	3	7	7
1995–99	0	0	0
2000–04	0	0	0
2005–09	72	85	78

Source: author's calculations using *Temporary Trade Barriers Database* (Bown 2010a).

is the diminished role of developed countries and the growing role of China. By the end of the sample period, China accounts for almost one-third of all TTB measures in effect.

While the above trends indicate the growing prominence of China for US TTBs, the focus on China is arguably even greater. As mentioned above, often domestic industries initiate cases against multiple import sources and these cases are almost always considered within a single investigation. While China accounts for a large share of cases, its influence on investigations is even greater. Consider the information in Table 2.3. In panel (a), information for anti-dumping cases is tallied and, in panel (b), CVD cases are considered.

In the first column of panel (a), China's share of anti-dumping cases is reported. China accounted for less than 20% of anti-dumping cases up until 2004. During 2005–9, however, China's share jumped to almost 50% of all cases. Yet, as is argued by Bown (2010b) and Prusa (2010), this statistic does not capture the true extent to which China dominates the action. In the second column, the fraction of *investigations* where China was involved is given. China has been a major target since the early 1990s. From 1990–1999, China was involved in no more than one-third of all anti-dumping investigations. During 2000–2004, China's anti-dumping participation rate jumped to 50%. A remarkable 82% of anti-dumping investigations have involved China since 2005. In the final column, the fraction of investigations that involve only China is reported. Amazingly, over 40% of US investigations target only China. The ascent of China is even more startling for CVDs (panel (b) in Table 2.3). China went from zero CVD activity prior to 2005 to account for 85% of all CVD investigations in 2005–9. To a large extent, US TTB policies have become 'stop China' policies.

4 PATTERNS IN US TEMPORARY TRADE BARRIERS: PRODUCT (HS-06) METRIC

4.1 General Discussion

An issue with the case metric is that it treats each case the same. It does not allow the scope to vary by case. For example, under the case metric, five small cases would be considered to have five times the impact of one large case, even if the one large case covered billions in imports and the small cases involved a few million dollars of imports. Thus, it may be desirable to use a metric that captures the size of each case. Bown (2011b) argues that this 'better' measure can be computed using information on the products involved.[11] For more than 20 years the USA has used the Harmonized System to classify imports. These codes are reported for every TTB case and define the products involved in each dispute.

The advantages of the product measure are two-fold. First, cases rarely involve a single-tariff-line item. A case almost always involves a number of tariff lines. As a result, the scope of a case can be measured by the number of HS products involved (*ie* an unweighted measure of products). Second, the dollar value of trade varies by product. Therefore, the breadth of trade affected by a case may be more accurately measured by the value of trade involved (*ie* a weighted measure of products).

As discussed in Chapter 1 by Bown, constructing a trade-weighted metric is not a trivial task since subject imports fall as a result of the measures. Suppose, for example, that US TTBs completely eliminate subject imports. Since no trade value is measured, a trade-weighted measure of TTBs would imply that no trade is covered by TTBs; given what actually happened, this would be an odd interpretation of TTBs. Instead, here we follow Bown's (2011b) approach and create a measure that adjusts for the trade distortion created by the TTB. Interested readers should consult Chapter 1 for a full discussion of how the trade-weighted product measure is computed.

Despite the product metric's advantages, there are two drawbacks. Both highlight the difficulty in creating accurate time-series trends with the product metric. First, the Harmonized System was only implemented in 1989. While attempts have been made to concord the Harmonized System with the old

[11] Until relatively recently, such product information was not available but this information is now publicly available in Bown (2010a).

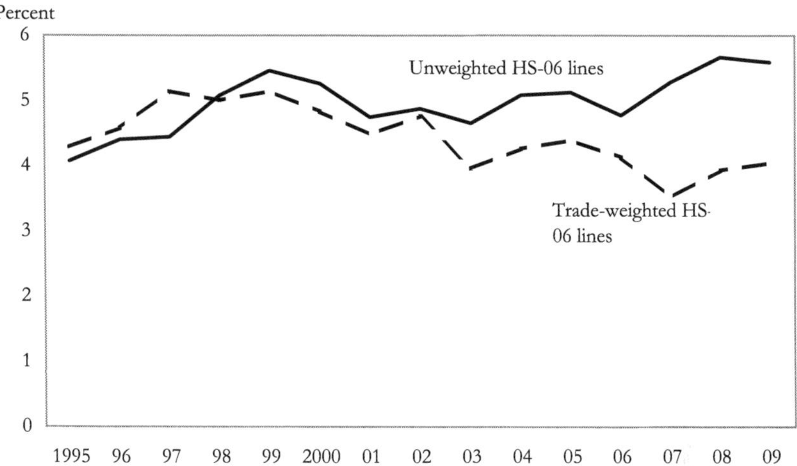

Figure 2.7: *Percentage of HS-06 lines under US anti-dumping/CVD measures (all suppliers).*

Source: author's calculations using *Temporary Trade Barriers Database* (Bown 2010a) and Comtrade.

tariff system, the reality is that measurement error becomes a serious concern if the product measure uses pre-1989 cases. As a result, only measures since 1989 are considered. Consequentially, because TTBs prior to 1989 have been excluded, my product metric will understate the true trade coverage of TTBs. This is likely to be especially problematic prior to the mid-1990s. It becomes less of a concern by the mid-to-late-1990s as more and more of these pre-1989 TTBs were revoked. Consequently, in an attempt to reduce the impact of these pre-1989 codes, results are reported using HS-06 metrics only from 1995. Second, the Harmonized System has undergone regular revisions since it was instituted. As a result, the codes for about one-third of the products have changed since 1990. While an attempt is made to control for these product code changes, some lost coverage is inevitable. In an attempt to balance the desire to use disaggregated data with a desire to minimise the number of code changes, the decision was made to use the HS-06 level to measure products.[12]

With these caveats in mind, let us now turn to examination of TTBs using the product metric. In Figures 2.7–2.9, unweighted and trade-weighted measures are presented. Figure 2.7 summarises the overall trends. In this figure,

[12]In most cases the products are identified at the eight-digit or ten-digit level. I opt to do my analysis at the six-digit level because doing so reduces the number of product code changes over time. Code changes occur more frequently at more disaggregated levels. Given that I report the fraction of imports subject to TTBs rather than the absolute level of imports subject to TTBs, I believe the cost of performing my analysis at the higher level of aggregation to be small.

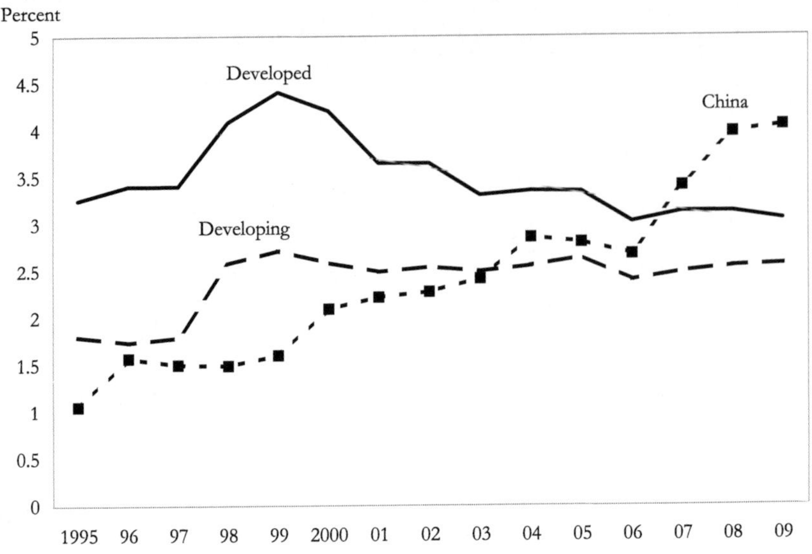

Figure 2.8: *Percentage of HS-06 lines under US anti-dumping/CVD measures by development status (and China).*

Source: author's calculations using *Temporary Trade Barriers Database* (Bown 2010a) and Comtrade.

the dashed line depicts the fraction of HS-06 products (unweighted) subject to anti-dumping/CVD orders; the solid line illustrates the fraction of HS-06 import *value* subject to anti-dumping/CVD orders. In terms of the overall picture, the two measures are broadly consistent: both measures indicate that 4–6% of all US imports are subject to TTBs. However, the two metrics differ when it comes to the trends in TTB coverage. The unweighted metric indicates that TTB coverage has increased fairly consistently over 2003–9, and especially over 2006–9. On the other hand, the weighted metric implies that TTB protection has fallen since 2003 and has only risen modestly in 2007–9. The difference in the trends reflects the impact of the removal of TTBs on several large import-value products such as galvanized sheet steel and softwood lumber.

4.2 Unweighted Measure

Figure 2.8 partitions the subject countries by development status. In Figure 2.8, the products covered are measured relative to the entire universe of products (*eg* the number of Chinese products subject to TTBs relative to all US imports of all products from China, the number of developed country products subject to TTBs relative to all US imports from developed countries, *etc*).

Figure 2.9: *Percentage of import value under US anti-dumping/CVD measures by development status (and China).*

Source: author's calculations using *Temporary Trade Barriers Database* (Bown 2010a) and Comtrade.

Figure 2.8 echoes the trends found using the case metric. First, TTBs against developed countries peaked in about 1998 (solid line) and declined thereafter. At the peak, about 4.5% of imported products from developed countries were subject to US TTBs. Beginning in 1998, the USA conducted its initial trove of sunset determinations, and these early sunset reviews involved a large share of products from developed countries. As is shown by the figure, these revocations resulted in a big decline in TTB coverage. The reduced flow of new TTBs over the 2000s resulted in the coverage ratio steadily declining to about 3% by 2009. Second, TTBs against developing countries (dashed line) rose in the mid-1990s but have remained quite stable at about 2.5% for more than a decade. Third, TTB coverage against China has nearly quadrupled over the 1995–2009 period. In 1995 about 1% of China's products were subject to TTBs; by 2009 China's TTB coverage had risen to more than 4%. As can also be seen when using the case metric, when it comes to TTBs, China is 'wearing the bull's-eye'.

4.3 Trade-Weighted Measure

Figure 2.9 is similar to the previous figure but relies on the trade-weighted metric. While the trends are consistent across the two metrics, the changing incidence of TTBs is much starker under the trade-weighted metric. Using the unweighted metric (Figure 2.8), developed countries' TTB coverage fell from about 4.5% to 3% by 2009. Using the trade-weighted metric (Figure 2.9), developed countries' TTB coverage fell substantially faster, from about 6%

Table 2.4: *Distribution of new US anti-dumping/CVD TTB initiations (case basis, flow).*

	1990–1994 (%)	1995–1999 (%)	2000–2004 (%)	2005–2009 (%)	2007–2009 (%)
Animal and animal products	0.7	4.9	5.3	0.0	0.0
Vegetable products	1.3	3.5	3.3	0.0	0.0
Foodstuffs	1.6	8.3	4.1	3.2	0.0
Mineral products	5.9	0.0	1.2	0.0	0.0
Chemicals and allied industries	17.4	4.9	16.3	24.2	27.0
Plastics/rubbers	1.3	11.1	9.0	8.4	10.8
Wood and wood products	3.0	0.0	1.6	11.6	6.8
Textiles	5.3	2.1	0.0	6.3	5.4
Stone/glass	0.0	0.0	0.8	2.1	2.7
Metals	48.4	55.6	50.6	30.5	29.7
Machinery/electrical	4.9	6.3	3.7	8.4	10.8
Transportation	6.3	1.4	0.8	0.0	0.0
Miscellaneous	3.9	2.1	3.3	5.3	6.8

Source: author's calculations using *Temporary Trade Barriers Database* (Bown 2010a).

to under 3%. The difference is even more pronounced for China. Using the unweighted metric, China's TTB coverage rose from about 1% to 4% by 2009. Under the trade-weighted metric, China's TTB coverage rose from about 1.5% to about 9%.

Taking the two figures together, not only are a very large number of products from China under TTB protection, but as compared with other countries, the TTBs against China (on average) involve larger trade volume than those against other countries.

5 INDUSTRY PATTERNS

Next, let us turn to the question of whether the US industries seeking TTB protection have changed over 1990–2009. We begin by examining the flow of TTBs. In Table 2.4, I use the case metric and report each industry's share of new cases as five-year averages.[13] What is remarkable is how TTB activity is dominated by just a few industries. Very few cases involve food, vegetables, minerals and textiles.

As can be seen from the table, in every subperiod the US steel industry has been the leading seeker of TTB protection. The steel industry was a particularly heavy user during the 1995–2004 period when a large number of

[13]Reporting annual filings would produce extremely volatile patterns from year to year.

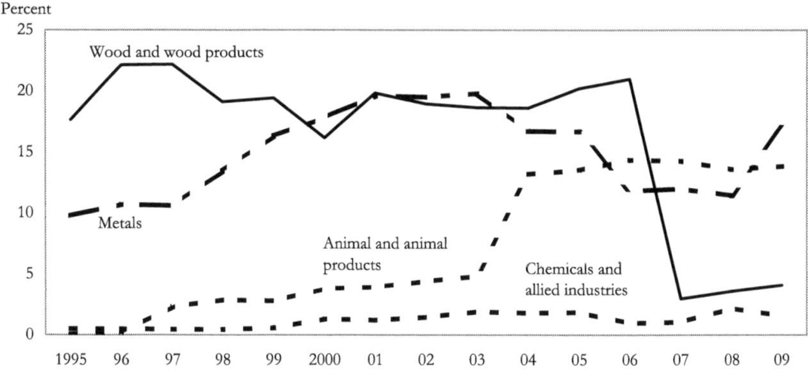

Figure 2.10: *Percentage of import value under US anti-dumping/CVD measures by industry.*

Source: author's calculations using *Temporary Trade Barriers Database* (Bown 2010a) and Comtrade.

firms went through bankruptcy and restructuring. In this ten-year period the industry accounted for more than half of all TTB cases. Throughout the entire 1990–2009 period, chemicals and plastics were the second and third most active industries, respectively.

Filings during the 2007–9 period are also reported in order to examine whether there is any evidence that the recession spurred a significant change in the industry filing patterns. The short-answer is 'no'. The same handful of industries that account for most US TTB activity prior to the crisis are the same industries that account for most TTB activity during the recession.

The stock of TTBs is probably a more revealing metric when considering industry patterns of protection. The lack of new TTB requests (small flow) for a given industry may simply reflect that it already has a large fraction of its import competition subject to TTBs; this pre-existing coverage will be evident when looking at the stock measure. When examining the stock of TTBs by industry, the trade-weighted product metric is used to compute the fraction of each industry's trade value subject to TTBs. The results are given in Figure 2.10 and Table 2.5.

First, consider that, across all industries and suppliers, the USA has about 4–5% of total imports subject to TTBs (see Figure 2.7 and Table 2.5). The average misrepresents the impact at an industry level. For example, the steel industry's persistent use of TTBs has resulted in large coverage. For much of the period, the steel industry had more than 15% of all competing imports subject to TTBs. The industry's coverage peaked at almost 20% during the steel crisis of 1999–2002.[14] It should be noted that a large fraction of steel

[14]Temporary trade barrier coverage would be even larger in 2002–3 if the trade effects of the steel safeguard action had been included.

Table 2.5: *Trade impact of US anti-dumping/CVD measures in effect (trade-weighted).*

	1995–99 (%)	2000–2004 (%)	2005–2009 (%)	2007–2009 (%)
All suppliers	4.9	4.5	4.0	3.8
By development status				
Developed	6.1	5.1	3.6	2.8
Developing	2.9	3.3	2.1	2.1
China	1.5	4.1	7.5	8.4
By industry				
Animal and animal products	1.7	6.2	13.9	13.9
Vegetable products	0.7	1.2	0.9	0.4
Foodstuffs	2.6	3.8	6.5	6.5
Mineral products	3.1	2.8	2.5	2.6
Chemicals and allied industries	0.5	1.6	1.5	1.6
Plastics/rubbers	5.3	3.1	3.9	5.1
Wood and wood products	20.1	18.4	11.7	3.5
Metals	12.3	18.5	13.4	13.0
Machinery/electrical	6.8	4.2	2.5	2.6
Transportation	3.9	3.6	4.6	4.9

Source: author's calculations using *Temporary Trade Barriers Database* (Bown 2010a) and Comtrade.

trade is intra-firm trade; one would not expect this trade to be threatened with TTBs. Hence, the industry's TTB coverage on non-affiliated trade is even more impressive. For instance, if one-third of US steel imports is intra-firm trade, then 30% of all unaffiliated imports are covered by TTBs.

Second, other industries have experienced large changes in their stock of imports subject to TTBs. Until 2006, the wood and wood products industry had about 20% of its import competition subject to TTBs. Despite the fact that this industry filed few cases over the period (Table 2.4) it was able to maintain TTBs on a large share of its competition. This was possible because softwood lumber dominates US wood imports and Canada accounts for nearly all of US softwood lumber imports. For this industry, a single dispute against a single supplier can create high coverage. The USA and Canada litigated this dispute for over 20 years. Given the amount of trade involved, neither side was willing to compromise. Finally, after numerous North American Free Trade Agreement (NAFTA) panel and WTO appellate body decisions, the US and Canada agreed to settle the dispute in 2006. The USA revoked the CVDs on softwood lumber and Canada agreed to limit how much softwood lumber it would export to the USA. As can be seen from Table 2.4, the removal of this order reduced the coverage ratio from over 20% to below 5%.

The 'animal products' industry makes for an interesting comparison with the wood industry. Akin to the wood products industry, the animal and animal products industry has not filed a large number of TTB cases (Table 2.4). However, the cases that have been pursued have been large. Most notably, in 2004 the USA imposed anti-dumping duties on shrimp from six developing country suppliers, resulting in over $2 billion of trade to be covered in a single TTB. This single case increased industry coverage from about 5% to about 14%.

6 DURATION OF TEMPORARY TRADE BARRIERS

The length of the period that measures remain in effect is vital for understanding the protection afforded by US TTBs. A mandatory sunset provision for anti-dumping and CVD measures was included in the Uruguay Round because developing countries were frustrated by the challenge involved in getting orders removed.[15] As part of the grand bargain to conclude the Uruguay Round, developing countries were able to insert language that required a mandatory sunset review for each TTB every five years. As Moore (1999, 2002) discusses, some users interpreted the language to mean that TTBs were to be removed after five years, while others, including the USA, interpreted the provision to mean that only a mandatory sunset *review* was required. Under US law, the presumption is that the order will be removed unless doing so would lead to a resumption of unfair trade and injury.

The extent to which the new provision matters depends on the basis for determining the likelihood of resumed unfair trade and injury. Moore (1999, 2002) documents that the US procedures make revocation via the sunset review a difficult proposition. With respect to the question of whether there would be a resumption of unfair trade if the order was removed, Moore documents that the USA has *always* found that there would be a return to unfair trading. In every case, no matter how long the order has been in effect, no matter how much evidence administrative reviews have revealed about the changed pricing, the USA always concludes that the affected countries will trade unfairly. With respect to the recurrence of injury, the USA has become far more hesitant to remove orders as it has gained more experience with sunset reviews. In the initial set of reviews covering measures that were in place prior to the 1995, the USA revoked about 50% of the orders.[16] Once these transition orders were finished, the USA adopted a much harder line towards revocation. Only about one-third of the post-Uruguay Round cases have been revoked.

---

[15]While a higher proportion of cases were brought against developed countries pre-1990, developing countries pushed the sunset provision. To begin with, many of the TTB cases brought against developed countries in the 1980s were 'settled'. Second, the accounting requirements to obtain TTBs were particularly difficult for developing countries to master. Hence, developing countries felt that there was a lot to gain by mandatory sunset reviews.

[16]Some of these transition orders were so old that there was no domestic interest in continuing them.

The duration of TTBs is quantified by computing the number of measures that are revoked as a fraction of the total number of measures that are in effect each month/year. Each measure's key calendar dates (date the measure went into effect and date of revocation) are converted into a duration basis. For instance, a measure that went into effect in January 2000 and was revoked in January 2005 would have a duration of 60 months.

Statistically, duration is estimated using the non-parametric Kaplan–Meier survival function. In Figures 2.11 and 2.12, the survival estimates for anti-dumping and CVD measures, respectively, are reported. Both figures are based on the case metric. First, considering panel (a) of each figure, three lines have been graphed: the grey dashed line is the survival experience for cases filed pre-mandatory sunset, the black dashed line is the survival experience for transition cases, and the solid line is the survival experience for cases initiated post-mandatory sunset reviews. Note that these figures use TTB information on cases prior to 1990. Because the case metric is used for the duration analysis, we are not hindered by the fact that the Harmonized System codes are unavailable for these early cases.

The lines depict the fraction of cases that survive through a given time period. As seen, within 36 months, more than half of both anti-dumping and CVD cases during the pre-Uruguay Round period were revoked (grey dashed line). By contrast, in the post-Uruguay Round period, less than 10% were revoked (*ie* more than 90% were still in effect). In the pre-mandatory sunset era, cases ended more or less continuously. In the post-Uruguay Round period, the survival curve is almost constant until the sunset review, and then it drops sharply. About 25–33% of initial sunset reviews result in the order being revoked.[17] In the post-Uruguay Round period, almost all revocations occur during the sunset review.

Mandatory sunset reviews appear to have had two effects on the removal of orders. First, it appears that foreign firms do not seek to have the orders removed via demonstrating multiple years of zero margins. This is not that surprising given the large expense associated with each administrative review. Also, given that the probability of revocation is small (zero unless several prior reviews already demonstrated zero margins), foreign firms seem to have decided to preserve resources for the sunset review.[18]

To get a sense of why they might do so, suppose a TTB was imposed on three firms exporting from a given target country. Each administrative review can cost *each* firm over $1 million. Thus, if all three firms were to pursue an administrative review sunset, they could jointly spend $9 million. By contrast,

[17]Due to the time required for the sunset review investigation, the initial sunset review often occurs between 60 and 72 months after the initial order is imposed.

[18]The foreign firms' reluctance to pursue administrative reviews is also possibly due to the 'zeroing' procedures used by the Department of Commerce. We could see more effort on administrative reviews once the USA changes its zeroing policy (Bown and Prusa 2011).

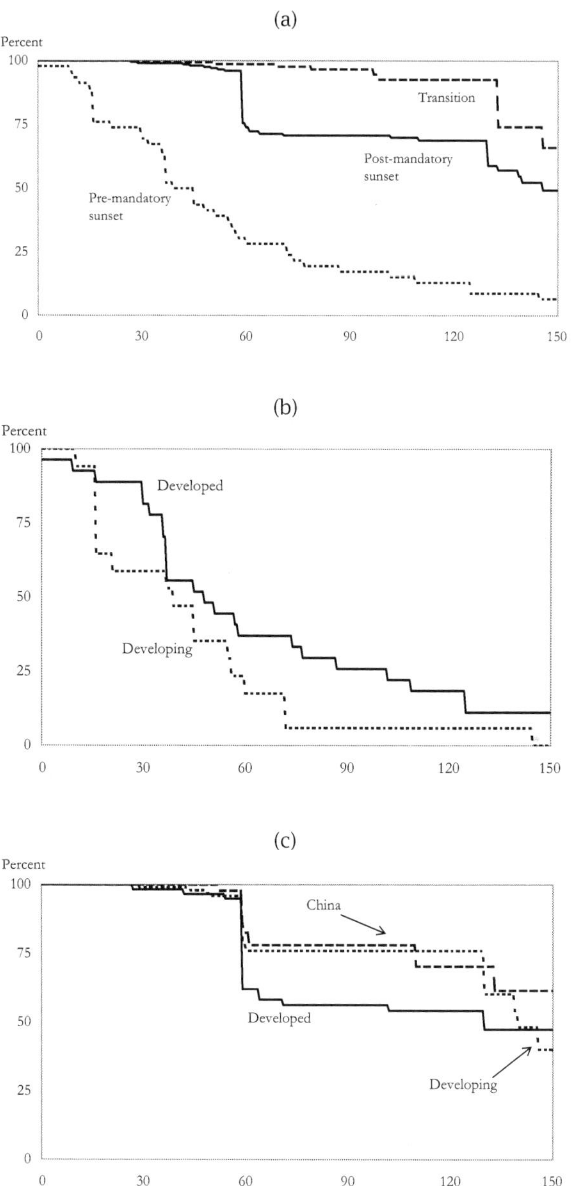

Figure 2.11: *Percentage of US anti-dumping measures in effect by duration (in months): (a) pre- versus post-mandatory sunset review clause; (b) developed versus developing countries (pre-mandatory sunset); (c) developed versus developing countries and China (post-mandatory sunset).*

Source: author's calculations using *Temporary Trade Barriers Database* (Bown 2010a).

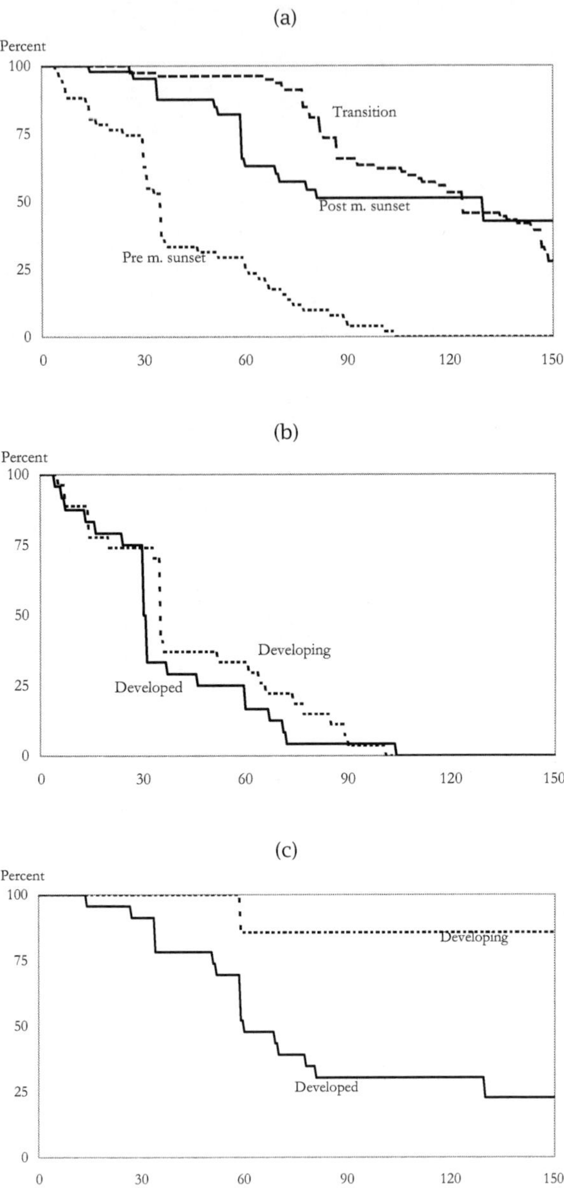

Figure 2.12: *Percentage of US CVD measures in effect by duration (in months): (a) pre- versus post-mandatory sunset review clause; (b) developed versus developing countries (pre-mandatory sunset); (c) developed versus developing countries (post-mandatory sunset).*

Source: author's calculations using *Temporary Trade Barriers Database* (Bown 2010a).

pursuing a sunset review is a decision common to all three firms and would likely be jointly funded. A sunset review might cost a total of $1 million, about one-ninth the cost of the sunset via the administrative review process.

Second, if countries thought the Uruguay Round's sunset review language would appreciably lower the duration of anti-dumping and CVD orders, they were mistaken. The US implementation of sunset review has produced the opposite effect—measures are now in place longer than they were pre-Uruguay Round. That is, the fraction of measures revoked in two, three, four and five years in the pre-Uruguay Round era far exceed the fraction of measures revoked by four years in the post-Uruguay Round era.

In panels (b) and (c) of Figures 2.11 and 2.12, developed and developing countries' sunset experiences are compared. In panel (b), the duration of orders prior to mandatory sunset is examined. In this period there were sufficiently few cases brought against China that the decision was made not to report China separately. Both Figure 2.11 (anti-dumping) and Figure 2.12 (CVDs) show that, in this early period, developed and developing countries had very similar experiences. The two survival curves are very similar. A log-rank test of equality of the curves cannot reject that they have the same survival experience.

A very different story emerges for the post-Uruguay Round period. Temporary trade barriers against developing countries are far longer lived than those against developed countries. With anti-dumping, developed and developing countries have a similar experience during the first five years. However, at the initial sunset review stage about 40% of measures against developed countries are revoked as compared with less than 25% of measures against developing countries. Moreover, the difference persists for years. About as many cases are revoked against developing countries after 11 years as are against developed countries after 5 years. This is a remarkable result that is especially surprising given that it was developing countries that pushed hardest for mandatory sunset. This observation can be made from Figure 2.11(c), where China is separated from other developing countries as the activity against China becomes significant in the mid-1990s.

The difference between developed and developing countries is even starker when CVDs are considered. As can be seen from the figure, US CVDs imposed against developing countries are rarely revoked. The data indicate that more than 90% of measures against developing countries remain in effect after the initial review. By contrast, measures against developed countries have been removed fairly consistently throughout the period. By year five about 40% of the orders have been removed, and by year ten about 75% of the orders have been removed. The gap in duration is large.

The difference in duration is a serious issue for developing countries. The data indicate that the USA is much more likely to keep an order in place against a developing country than it is against a developed country. This policy issue certainly warrants further analysis.

7 CHINA SAFEGUARD ON PASSENGER AND TRUCK TYRES

Arguably the most publicised TTB during the 2008–9 crisis involved automobile and light-truck tyres imported from China under the 'China safeguard' statute. Prior to the tyre case, US industries had filed six China safeguard petitions between 2002 and 2009. None had resulted in measures being taken. In each case the USA decided that either the imports from China were not a cause of injury to the US industry or that the costs of protection (greater tensions with China, consumer costs) exceeded the benefits (increases in output and/or employment for the domestic industry). In September 2009, the USA announced that it would impose tariffs on tyres from China for three years: 35% tariff in year one, 30% in year two and 25% in year three. The decision not only provoked public criticism and a WTO complaint by China but it was likely a contributing factor in China initiating TTBs on US exports of automotive products and chicken parts. What made this case different from others? Was all the attention warranted?

The primary explanation for the press attention is size: the passenger and truck tyre case involved considerably more trade than any prior China safeguard case. In the last year before the safeguard case was initiated, the USA imported $6.9 billion of tyres—$1.8 billion from China alone. The next biggest China safeguard case involved welded steel piping in 2005. In the last year before the steel piping case was initiated, the USA imported $725 million of steel piping, of which $154 million was sourced from China. Thus, in terms of trade value, the tyres case was about ten times the size of the next largest case.

Yet, there are at least two reasons to believe that too much was made of the involved trade value. First, while the case was easily the biggest China safeguard case, it was not extraordinarily large as far as TTBs go. Figure 2.13 gives information on trade value for other TTB cases in 2009. Trade values for three significant cases initiated earlier in the decade are also included. As can be seen from the figure, the tyre case was not even the biggest TTB case in 2009; the anti-dumping/CVD dispute involving oil-country tubular goods affected almost a billion dollars more of imports (from China alone). The China safeguard on tyres also involved less trade value than earlier TTB cases on shrimp, furniture or dynamic random-access memory, none of which garnered as much of the spotlight as the tyre case. Second, while tyre imports from China were indeed large, the USA also imported almost $5 billion in tyres from other suppliers. The availability of significant alternative suppliers likely diminished the chance that US consumers would experience shortages or significantly higher prices.

Another reason why the tyre case drew so much press was that it was *not* initiated by domestic producers of tyres. In fact, the public record indicates that domestic producers were opposed to the safeguard action. The case was initiated by tyre workers. The argument was that injury from imported tyres

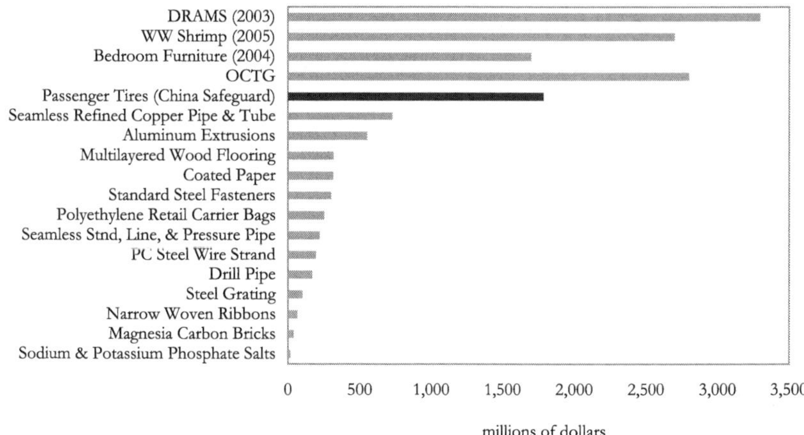

Figure 2.13: *Annual import values of selected products subject to US measures (annual import value corresponds to the year before the case was initiated).*

Source: author's calculations using *Temporary Trade Barriers Database* (Bown 2010a) and Comtrade.

was accruing to workers, not the firms. It might seem surprising that the firms and workers viewed imports so differently before it is understood that the firms accounting for nearly all US domestic production also accounted for most of the tyres imported from China (see United States International Trade Commission (2009, Table II-3)). The vast majority of tyres are produced by large global multinational firms and US tyre facilities are just one part of their global manufacturing base. A trade policy focusing exclusively on China overlooked the many other developing countries who, but for China, would export more tyres to the US market.

Despite the availability of other suppliers, the trade data show that China had indeed gained market share during the late 2000s. Figure 2.14 illustrates imports of tyres, showing both total imports and imports from China alone. As can be seen from the figure, China was selling more than twice as many tyres to the USA in early 2008 than it had just a few years earlier.

The case also highlighted the problem of discerning injury caused by the recession from injury caused by subject imports. Given the lack of support from domestic producers, injury essentially boiled down to evidence of job losses. Nevertheless, blaming imports from China for the losses was confounded by the fact that, during the 12 months prior to the filing of the case, tyre imports from China had fallen. Overall imports were falling, imports from China were receding, tyre demand was plummeting and tyre workers were being laid off, all at the same time. China felt that the case was a prime

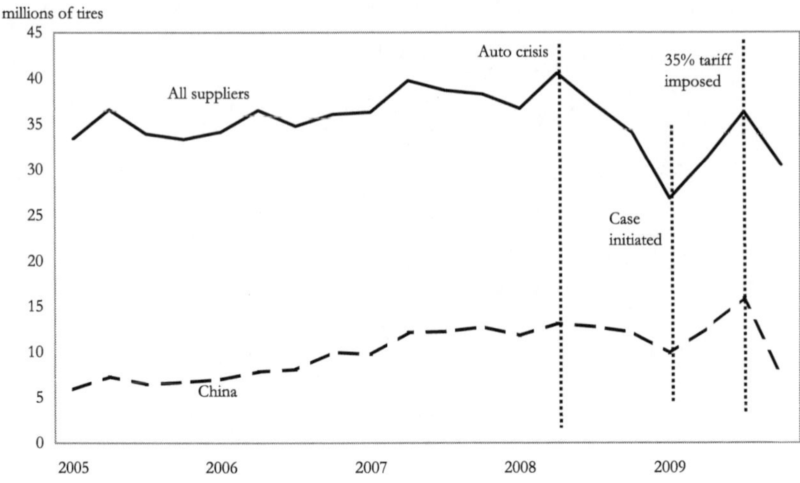

Figure 2.14: *US tyre imports (quarterly).*

Source: author's calculations using *Temporary Trade Barriers Database* (Bown 2010a) and Comtrade.

example of it being made the scapegoat for woes caused by the worldwide recession.

8 CONCLUSION

This review of US TTB activity has yielded a number of interesting insights. One important finding is methodological—most key insights are not sensitive to the metric used to measure TTBs. The different metrics (case, unweighted product, trade-weighted product) are all found to portray similar qualitative results with respect to the flow of new activity. However, the stock of TTBs is sensitive to choice of metric. While the merits of each metric can be debated, it is clear that the weighted metric reveals details on the scope and depth of TTBs that the easier-to-use metrics miss. Exploring these differences is something future research should investigate.

A second key finding is the extraordinary extent to which US TTBs are focused on a single supplier (China). Depending on exactly how the question is framed, the data show that China now accounts for 50–85% of new US TTB activity. China now has a higher fraction of its trade under US TTB measures than all developing countries put together and all developed countries put together. This would be remarkable under any circumstances, but it is even more striking when one realises that China was subject to very few TTBs just a decade ago.

The relative lack of TTB surge during (and following) the 2007–9 recession is also a key finding. While anti-dumping and CVD filings did increase, the overall level of activity was modest by historical standards. The recession also seemed to have influenced the first (and only) China safeguard measure, but one action cannot reasonably be called a surge.

Why wasn't there a sharp increase in new petition filings in the 2007–9 recession that has been typical in past recessions? Here, four contributing explanations are given. First, the single biggest user of TTBs in the US—the steel industry—already had TTB measures on most of its key products. The efforts by the steel industry to pressurise US authorities into not sunsetting cases meant that most of the usual suspects were already subject to large TTB tariffs. For example, key products such as hot-rolled steel, plate, ball bearings and piping fuelled the surge in TTB activity in the early 1980s, early 1990s, and early 2000s.[19] In the 2007–9 recession, the key foreign suppliers of each of these products (and many other steel products) were already subject to TTBs.

Second, in earlier recessions, the decline in imports appears to have been roughly proportional to the decline in US manufacturing activity. In the 2007–9 recession, imports fell by a greater amount than the decline in US manufacturing activity (Levchenko *et al* 2010). US imports declined by more than 25% in 2009. In earlier recessions, imports declined by about one-quarter that amount. This unusually severe contraction meant that there were not a lot of products where imports were *increasing*, either absolutely or relative to domestic production or consumption. On average, the fall in import market share makes it more difficult to allege that imports 'cause' the domestic industry's injury. In such circumstances, the recession is a more apparent cause of the downturn.

Despite the evidence, it must be stressed that the role of the decline in imports is speculative. Trade cases are filed on specific products that usually make up a very small share of total industry imports, so extrapolating from industry-wide data to a conclusion as to why a particular product within that industry did not seek TTB protection involves a leap of faith that may or may not be warranted. In addition, there is clear evidence that cases were filed and received TTB protection despite large falls in import volume and market share. At least some industries were able to take advantage of the demand fall. Three cases adjudicated in 2010—oil-country tubular goods, drill piping and coated paper—all experienced huge declines in imports. Moreover, in each case the domestic industry was able to remain profitable despite the recession. Consequently, in each case the domestic industry claimed the recession made it vulnerable to imports. The USA was apparently sympathetic to this claim. In each case the US imposed the TTB measure not because the industry was injured but because it was threatened with injury.

---

[19]Moore (1996) discusses the steel industry's surge of cases during the recessions of the early 1980s and early 1990s.

Third, the changing role of manufacturing in the US economy might also be influencing trends. Trade remedy laws like anti-dumping and CVD only apply to goods, not to services. Yet the US economy continues to shift from manufacturing to services. Moreover, an increasing portion of that manufacturing takes place in segments where there is some unique US advantage, or where the industry is highly globalised so that intra-industry trade occurs and each involved country is necessary to the overall functioning. The traditional users of trade remedy laws—industries with large capital costs, and large investments in fixed assets—are becoming a smaller and smaller part of the overall economy.

Fourth, as documented by Knetter and Prusa (2003), the exchange rate plays an even larger role in driving new TTBs than changes in GDP. Since 2001, the US dollar has depreciated relative to other currencies (except the Chinese yuan). This tends to put a damper on import levels, as stronger foreign currencies makes exports to the USA less competitive in US dollar terms. Similarly, China's fixed exchange rate is likely a key contributing factor behind many US TTBs targeting Chinese exporters.

Thomas J. Prusa is Professor at Rutgers, The State University of New Jersey, and Research Associate at The National Bureau of Economic Research.

REFERENCES

American Iron and Steel Institute (2010). Online steel industry resource. URL: www.steel.org.

Bown, C. P. (2011a). Introduction. In *The Great Recession and Import Protection: The Role of Temporary Trade Barriers* (ed. C. P. Bown). London: CEPR/World Bank. (Chapter 1 of this volume.)

Bown, C. P. (2011b). Taking stock of anti-dumping, safeguards, and countervailing duties, 1990–2009. *The World Economy*, forthcoming.

Bown, C. P. (2010a). *Temporary Trade Barriers Database*. World Bank (July). URL: http://econ.worldbank.org/ttbd/.

Bown, C. P. (2010b). China's WTO entry: anti-dumping, safeguards, and dispute settlement. In *China's Growing Role in World Trade* (ed. R. Feenstra and S. Wei). Chicago, IL: University of Chicago Press for NBER.

Bown, C. P. (2004). How different are safeguards from anti-dumping? Evidence from US trade policies toward steel. Econometric Society Report 434 (July).

Bown, C. P., and M. A. Crowley (2007). Trade deflection and trade depression. *Journal of International Economics* **72**(1), 176–201.

Bown, C. P., and T. J. Prusa (2011). US anti-dumping: much ado about zeroing. In *Waiting on Doha* (ed. A. Mattoo and W. J. Martin). Washington, DC: World Bank, forthcoming.

Evenett, S. (ed.) (2010). *Tensions Contained...For Now: The 8th GTA Report*. London: Centre for Economic Policy Research.

Hansen, W., and T. J. Prusa (1996). Cumulation and ITC decision-making: the sum of the parts is greater than the whole. *Economic Inquiry* **34**, 746–769.

Irwin, D. A. (2005). The rise of US anti-dumping activity in historical perspective. *World Economy* **28**, 651–668.

Knetter, M. M., and T. J. Prusa (2003). Macroeconomic factors and anti-dumping filings. *Journal of International Economics* **61**(1), 1–18.

Levchenko, A. A., L. T. Lewis, and L. L. Tesar (2010). The collapse of international trade during the 2008–2009 crisis: in search of the smoking gun. *IMF Economic Review* **58**(2), 214–253.

Moore, M. O. (2002). Commerce department anti-dumping sunset reviews: a first assessment. *Journal of World Trade* **36**(2), 675–698.

Moore, M. O. (1999). Anti-dumping reform in the US: a faded sunset. *Journal of World Trade* **33**(4), 1–28.

Moore, M. O. (1996). The rise and fall of big steel's influence on US trade policy. In *The Political Economy of Trade Protection* (ed. A. Kreuger). University of Chicago Press.

Prusa, T. J. (2010). Comments on 'China's WTO entry: anti-dumping, safeguards, and dispute settlement', by C. P. Bown. In *China's Growing Role in World Trade* (ed. R. Feenstra and S. Wei). Chicago, IL: University of Chicago Press for NBER.

Uchitelle, L. (2009). Steel industry, in slump, looks to federal stimulus. *New York Times*, 1 January 2009. URL: www.nytimes.com/2009/01/02/business/02steel.html.

US Bureau of Economic Analysis (2010). US Department of Commerce. URL: www.bea.gov/national/index.htm#gdp.

United States International Trade Commission (2009). Certain passenger vehicle and light truck tires from China. Investigation no. TA-421-7. Publication 4085.

World Trade Organization (2010). Anti-dumping statistics. URL: www.wto.org/english/tratop_e/adp_e/adp_e.htm.

3

European Union: No Protectionist Surprises

HYLKE VANDENBUSSCHE AND CHRISTIAN VIEGELAHN[1]

1 INTRODUCTION

On 3 October 2008, the EU launched a review of anti-dumping duties on leather shoes from China and Vietnam. In December 2009, the EU decided to extend duties on the imports of leather shoes from China and Vietnam for another 15 months.[2] This affirmative decision was taken despite heavy protests from consumers, importers and outsourcing firms, and it overruled the negative advice that had been formulated earlier by the EU Anti-Dumping Advisory Committee.[3] The review procedure was launched just a few days after the collapse of Lehman Brothers, which marked the outbreak of the Great Recession and fuelled the fear that the EU would engage in a 'protectionist spiral'. In such a spiral, some countries would raise protection in order to counter the negative spillovers from the financial sector on the real economy. Other countries would become adversely affected by this protection and then start to retaliate. The question is whether this review marked the beginning of a more protectionist attitude in the EU in the face of the global recession.

Though the impact of the crisis varied considerably across EU member states, the EU as a whole has been strongly hit, indicating that protectionist pressure was likely to be high after the outbreak of the crisis at the end of 2008. The macroeconomic indicators in Figure 3.1 show that, for the EU27 as a whole, GDP growth plunged from 3.0% in 2007 to 0.5% in 2008 and turned into a negative growth of −4.2% in 2009. Export and import growth slowed down

[1]Hylke Vandenbussche: Department of Economics, Université catholique de Louvain, Place Montesquieu 3, 1348 Louvain-la-Neuve, Belgium. Email: hylke.vandenbussche@uclouvain.be. Christian Viegelahn: Department of Economics, Université catholique de Louvain, Place Montesquieu 3, 1348 Louvain-la-Neuve, Belgium. Email: christian.viegelahn@uclouvain.be

[2]See Council Implementing Regulation No. 1294/2009 of 22 December 2009, available from EUR-Lex website (http://eur-lex.europa.eu/en/index.htm), and press release from European Commission of 2 October 2008, available on the website of the Directorate General for Trade of the European Commission.

[3]See International Centre for Trade and Sustainable Development (2010).

(a)

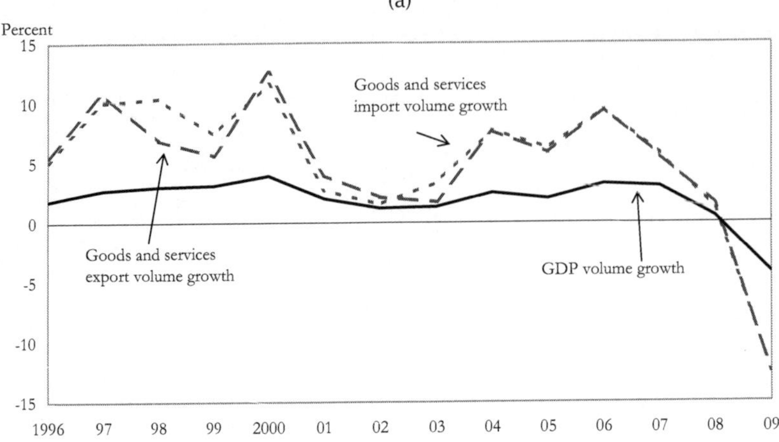

(b)

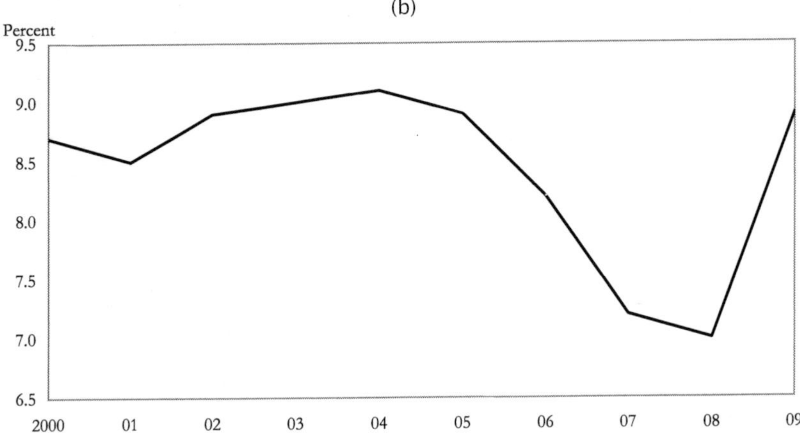

Figure 3.1: *EU macroeconomic conditions: (a) real export, import and GDP growth (EU27); (b) unemployment rate (EU27).*

Source: Eurostat.

dramatically in 2008, before falling roughly by 12.5% in 2009. The unemployment rate, shown in Figure 3.1(b), jumped from 7% in 2008 to 9% in 2009 after having decreased continuously since 2004.

Deviation from free trade is tempting for any country in times of economic downturn and trade protection is regarded as a quick and easy way of safeguarding jobs and replacing imports by domestic production. Trade protection is often perceived as being a far less painful remedy than fiscal austerity and budget cuts since it is likely to raise tariff revenue for the protecting

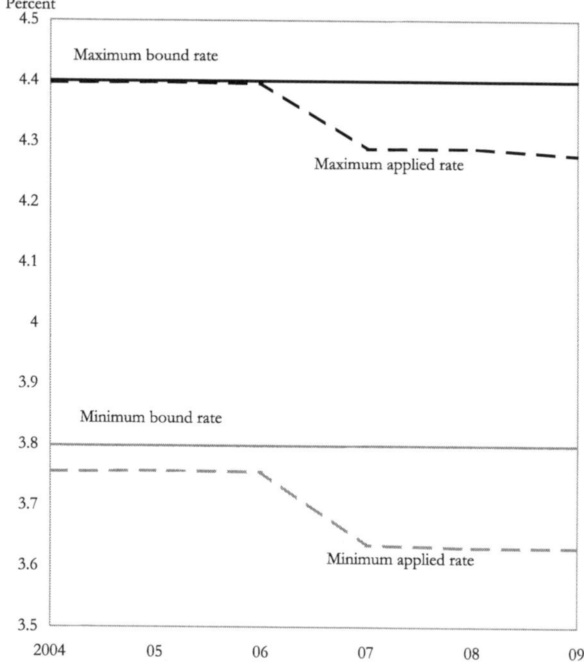

Figure 3.2: *EU average MFN tariff, bound and applied rates.*

Source: authors' calculations based on UN TRAINS and the WTO's consolidated tariff schedule. Maximum and minimum rate correspond to maximum and minimum tariff at the tariff line level for each HS-06 product (HS revision 1996). Average is calculated as simple average over all HS-06 products. Only HS-06 products for which applied and bound rates are *ad valorem* duties are included. Only HS-06 products with 1:1 match between HS revisions 1996, 2002 and 2007 are included.

country. However, if all countries start applying protectionist measures, trade between countries will dry up. With no more benefits to reap unilaterally, individual country welfare will be much lower than in the case of free trade, and countries will revert to a state of relative autarky, thereby forgoing the benefits from trade. For members of the WTO like the EU, there are generally three ways to raise import protection.

First, countries can pull their applied MFN tariff rates up to the level of their WTO-committed bound rates. In Figure 3.2, we show the tariff overhang, *ie* the difference between bound and applied MFN rates for the EU. Average applied MFN rates have remained roughly constant, suggesting that the EU has not used this channel to raise protection during the crisis. Average tariff overhang was in fact close to zero throughout 2004–9 and a more detailed look at the underlying data reveals that tariff overhang actually equalled zero

Table 3.1: *'Doing Business' indicators on importing, EU27.*

Year	Mean: number of documents to import	Mean: time to import in days
2005	6.25	14.75
2006	5.54	13.46
2007	5.46	13.25
2008	5.33	13.29
2009	5.33	13.25

All EU27 countries are included except Cyprus, Luxembourg and Malta.
Source: authors' calculations based on 'Doing Business' indicators from World Bank.

for 97% of all products or more, implying that the EU's scope for using this channel has been quite limited.

Second, countries may increase protection through the imposition of technical trade barriers such as an increase in administrative obligations related to a shipment or the technical clearance time at the border.[4] Table 3.1 illustrates that EU member states generally seem to have refrained from doing so. The 'Doing Business' indicators from the World Bank measure business regulations for local firms around the world and also include information on the procedural requirements related to importing.[5] Table 3.1 indicates that the EU average of both the number of documents that are required to fill out and the number of days needed to import a standardised cargo of goods have largely remained unchanged in 2008–9, suggesting that there has not been an increase of technical trade barriers during the crisis.[6]

Third, countries can use temporary trade barriers (TTBs) that are exceptions to the WTO's overall goal to promote free trade and to abstain from imposing unilateral tariffs.

The purpose of this chapter is to identify major trends in the EU's application of TTBs and to verify whether there has been any sign of a change in the use of TTBs during the 2008–9 crisis. There are three TTBs available to countries: safeguard, countervailing and anti-dumping measures. Since, for

[4]The extent to which this is legal is determined by the WTO Agreement on Technical Barriers to Trade.

[5]See Doing Business (2011) for methodological details. A third indicator related to importing measures the fees (in dollars) levied on a 20-foot container. However, since this indicator has to be deflated and converted into euros to make a comparison and is therefore largely dependent on the inflation and exchange rate, we exclude this indicator from our analysis.

[6]The only EU member state for which we observe an increase in any of these indicators in 2008 or 2009 is Czech Republic, where it took 17 days in 2008 instead of 16 days in 2007 to import a standardised cargo of goods.

the EU, as in many other countries, the use of TTBs mainly coincides with the use of anti-dumping measures (with almost 90% of TTB cases consisting of anti-dumping cases), we predominantly focus on the EU's use of anti-dumping policy. We match data on anti-dumping cases from the World Bank's Temporary Trade Barrier Database (Bown 2010) with UN Comtrade data, which detail product-level trade at the HS-06 (HS six-digit) level by country of origin. Our period of analysis runs from 1995 until 2009. To facilitate the comparison over time, we construct a set of 'count' and 'value' indicators. These indicators will be used to examine anti-dumping policy with respect to product coverage, country coverage, product–country coverage and import-value coverage. We will distinguish between anti-dumping case initiations and anti-dumping measures in force. The methodology we use primarily consists of a graphical examination of these indicators over time.

We carry out our analysis not only for aggregate imports (so as to identify overall trends in the use of anti-dumping policy) but also for targeted countries in specific income groups and analyse behaviour by industry. Furthermore, we investigate the link between anti-dumping policy and more 'traditional' forms of protection such as applied MFN and preferential tariffs. We also reveal new insights regarding the link between product-mix similarity of a country to the EU and EU anti-dumping policy. Another novelty that we introduce is the link between anti-dumping policy and product characteristics using the well-known Rauch (1999) classification of homogeneous versus differentiated goods and a distinction between industrial, consumer, and capital goods based on the Broad Economic Categories (BEC) classification. Finally, by engaging in an analysis at the individual EU member state level, we examine the extent to which results for the EU as a whole are driven by a few outlying member states or whether they reflect an EU-wide pattern.

The remainder of the chapter is organised as follows. In Section 2 we briefly discuss anti-dumping law and the features of it that are specific to the EU. Section 3 introduces the methodology that we apply. In Section 4 the main results on product, country, product–country combination and import-value coverage are presented. Section 5 examines the link between 'traditional' forms of protection, product-mix similarity and product characteristics, respectively, and anti-dumping policy. Section 6 presents results for individual EU member states and, finally, Section 7 concludes.

2 ANTI-DUMPING POLICY: THE RULES IN THE EU

The WTO regulates the use of anti-dumping policy in the General Agreement on Tariffs and Trade (GATT) Article VI and the Anti-Dumping Agreement, which are currently implemented in the EU by Council Regulation 1225/2009. By and large, the EU's anti-dumping law specifies three conditions that must be met before the EU can impose import protection in the form of anti-dumping measures on imported products.

The first condition is the presence of *dumping* by a foreign firm into the EU market. Interestingly, there appears to be a divide between the legal definition of dumping and a more economic one. From a legal point of view, any form of price discrimination by a foreign firm, where the ex-factory price in the foreign firm's own home market is higher than the price for export markets, is regarded as international dumping. From an economic point of view, however, there are very few instances where dumping also implies 'unfair' behaviour. Mainstream economics suggests that predatory dumping is an instance where there is room for government intervention. However, a predatory pricing strategy only works under very specific circumstances. First, predation can only be successful in industries with high entry barriers to prevent easy entry after exit from a market. Second, the foreign trading partner must have very deep pockets to wait for domestic competitors to exit the market. Third, predatory pricing only works in concentrated markets with few domestic firms. When it comes to the establishment of dumping, it is important to note that none of these issues are considered in the anti-dumping legislation.

The second condition specified in Article VI of the GATT is that only dumping that *causes domestic injury* is a reason for protection. The WTO rules do not clearly define what is meant by 'injury'. The Anti-Dumping Agreement mentions a list of injury indicators including the decline of domestic sales, profits, output, employment and stocks, amongst others. However, in the EU's practical application of this agreement, injury is very often regarded to be present whenever the foreign good is sold at a price that is lower than that of a similar domestic product in the EU market. Put differently, this simple price comparison often decides a positive or negative injury ruling (Vandenbussche 1996; Vermulst and Waer 1991).

The third condition embedded in the EU's anti-dumping regulations is that imposed anti-dumping measures have to be in the EU's *community interest.* The existence of this 'community interest clause' marks an important difference from, for example, the anti-dumping law in the USA and many other countries. This clause implies that protection should be in the interest of the EU as a whole and not just in the interest of EU producers. This requires EU officials to at least consider whether prices on the EU market are likely to rise dramatically after the imposition of a duty, as this would be against the interest of consumers. The EU's anti-dumping case on leather shoes imported from Vietnam and China described earlier is an illustrative example. In this case, the European Commission justified the imposition of anti-dumping duties by claiming that the price of European shoes would increase by at most €1.50 a pair. This is in contrast to the USA, where welfare issues need not be taken into account in the evaluation of whether or not to impose protection.

On the whole, many economists have expressed doubts as to whether anti-dumping rules are sufficiently well equipped to discriminate between 'fair' and 'unfair' foreign imports. However, some economists have recently argued that their existence generates an equilibrium that is more desirable in terms of worldwide welfare than pure free trade (Martin and Vergote 2008; Hartigan and Vandenbussche 2010). If governments act as welfare-maximisers, this could explain the WTO members' apparent reluctance to change anti-dumping rules fundamentally or even to get rid of them.

The purpose of this chapter is not to resolve this debate but merely to point out that the use of anti-dumping duties driven by industrial policy motives cannot be ruled out. The current anti-dumping rules cannot discriminate well whether domestic injury from import competition is due to 'unfair' imports or an 'uncompetitive' domestic industry suffering from tough but fair competition from a more efficient foreign supplier. This implies that a rise in anti-dumping measures need not necessarily reflect an increase in 'unfair' behaviour but could simply stem from an increasing use of anti-dumping policy to shelter domestic firms from import competition, in which case anti-dumping policy would be nothing more than a 'beggar-thy-neighbour' policy. It is important to make that distinction to interpret any changes in anti-dumping policy in the course of the 2008–9 crisis.

3 DATA AND METHODOLOGY

In order to compare the EU's use of TTBs before and during the crisis, we construct a broad set of indicators that will allow us to analyse the coverage of TTBs over time in several dimensions. We will then use these indicators to examine the main trends in the EU's use of TTBs, enabling us to detect whether any major policy changes occurred during the Great Recession.

We use information from the World Bank's *Temporary Trade Barriers Database* (Bown 2010), which contains detailed data on anti-dumping, countervailing and safeguard cases initiated by the EU. We overcome the problem of changes in the HS product classification over time by using concordance tables from the United Nations Statistics Division.[7] From this database we extract data on initiations and measures in force.[8] We will refer to the former as the *flow* of TTBs, while the latter will be referred to as the *stock* of TTBs. Since we are interested in the 2008–9 crisis period, it is important to consider more than just the stock of TTBs, as it can usually take up to a year or more from the initiation of a case to the imposition of a measure. Changes in the

[7]Results are based on the 1992 revision of HS-06.

[8]The *Temporary Trade Barriers Database* was complemented with additional information from original EU notifications, taken from the EUR-Lex webpage. For a few anti-dumping measures, information on the revocation date is missing in the TTB database. In these cases, we assume that anti-dumping measures were in place for five years as foreseen by EU anti-dumping law. We do a robustness check in which we exclude these anti-dumping measures from our whole analysis and find that results are generally very similar.

use of TTBs during the crisis would therefore be observed 'in real time' only when looking at the flow of TTBs.

Table 3.2 gives an overview of the number of case initiations for the three types of TTBs used by the EU in the period before and during the crisis. For anti-dumping policy and countervailing duties, which are trading partner specific, we use two distinct case definitions. One is to consider a case by targeted country (panel (a)), while the other is to consider a case by country and product (panel (c)). For global safeguard measures, which do not discriminate between trading partners, we count the total number of initiations (panel (b)) and measure a case by product (panel (d)). Whatever definition we use and whichever way we count cases, Table 3.2 does not suggest a major change in the EU's use of TTBs during the crisis. Based on the numbers provided in Table 3.2, we find that the EU's TTB policy largely coincides with anti-dumping policy. Since, in addition, the EU initiated relatively few countervailing cases and no safeguard cases in 2008 and 2009, we focus our subsequent analysis on anti-dumping policy only. Also, since the number of cases does not provide any information on the number of products and countries affected nor on the extent to which the EU's value of imports is affected, we will define a finer set of indicators.

For this purpose we match data on EU anti-dumping policy to UN Comtrade data on import values for each EU member state over a period from 1995 to 2009, provided at the HS-06 product level and by EU trading partner.[9] One issue that we face is the changing EU composition over time, which has some implications for our methodological approach.[10] First, since previously targeted countries have become members of the EU customs union and can no longer be targeted with anti-dumping measures, we only consider extra-EU27 imports.[11] Second, the results reported for the EU as a whole are based on imports of ten EU member states that have always been EU members between 1995 and 2009 and for which data coverage is typically the best: Austria, Denmark, Finland, France, Germany, Ireland, Italy, Portugal, Sweden and United Kingdom. These ten member states represented around 64% of all extra-EU27 imports in 2008. However, for robustness, we also verify our results for alter-

[9]Import data for some EU member states are missing, particularly before 1995, which is why we opt for our period of analysis to start in 1995. For more detailed information on the data sources described in this section, please see Chapter 1.

[10]In 2004, Cyprus, Czech Republic, Estonia, Hungary, Latvia, Lithuania, Malta, Poland, Slovakia and Slovenia joined the EU15. In 2007, Bulgaria and Romania became EU member states.

[11]Extra-EU27 imports do not comprise imports from Réunion, French Guiana, Martinique, Guadeloupe, Isle of Man, Jersey, Guernsey and the Åland Islands that are current members of the EU customs area and, thus, cannot be targeted with anti-dumping measures. We also exclude imports of commodities 'not elsewhere specified' in the data.

native EU definitions.[12] Results are always very similar and all of our main findings are equally valid across other EU definitions.

With the database at hand, we construct four indicators that we will refer to extensively in the following sections. In the baseline specification, we use actual import values in order to compute these indicators.

Indicator 1 assesses the *product coverage* of anti-dumping. This indicator counts the number of products under anti-dumping protection that are imported into the EU from at least one country targeted with anti-dumping measures. In order to control for variations in the product scope of the EU's imports, we divide the resulting number by the total number of products imported by the EU.

Indicator 2 measures *country coverage* of anti-dumping. It counts the number of countries targeted with anti-dumping measures and importing at least one product under anti-dumping protection into the EU. We divide this number by the total number of countries importing into the EU.

Indicator 3 combines indicator 1 and indicator 2 and looks into product-country combinations covered by anti-dumping. This *product-country coverage* counts the number of product-country combinations for which imports are positive and anti-dumping measures are imposed as a share of all combinations for which imports are observed.

The three indicators described thus far are all 'count' measures but do not reflect the importance of anti-dumping protection in terms of import values. To address this issue we introduce a fourth indicator (indicator 4). This is a 'value' measure corresponding to the *import value covered* by anti-dumping measures as a share of the EU's total import value.

One limitation of the above approach is that it does not take into account the impact of anti-dumping measures on imports. For example, Vandenbussche and Zanardi (2010) find strong evidence for a substantial decrease of imports in response to anti-dumping policy. For this reason, indicator 4 is likely to underestimate the 'true' impact of anti-dumping policy on imports. For indicators 1-3, such an underestimation can equally occur, but only in the extreme cases in which anti-dumping measures are prohibitive, *ie* when the anti-dumping causes a disruption of imports for some product-country combinations.

We therefore carry out several robustness checks and recalculate our indicators using import counterfactuals instead of actual import values for those imports that are under anti-dumping protection. First, we follow a relatively simple approach and assume that import values do not change when anti-dumping protection is set in place, *ie* we assume that the import values in the year before an anti-dumping measure is imposed are the ones that prevail in the years under anti-dumping protection. Second, we construct the

[12]This includes an analysis for EU15, EU27, and a 'current' EU that follows the changes in EU composition over time.

Table 3.2: *Use of TTBs by the EU.*

	1995	'96	'97	'98	'99	2000	'01	'02	'03	'04	'05	'06	'07	'08	'09	Total	Relative (%)
(a) Number of anti-dumping, countervailing and China-specific safeguard case initiations, counted by trading partner																	
Anti-dumping	33	23	42	21	66	31	27	20	7	29	24	35	9	18	14	399	87.89
Countervailing	0	1	4	8	20	0	6	3	1	0	2	1	0	2	6	54	11.89
China-specific safeguard	0	0	0	0	0	0	0	0	1	0	0	0	0	0	0	1	0.22
(b) Total number of global safeguard case initiations																	
	1995	'96	'97	'98	'99	2000	'01	'02	'03	'04	'05	'06	'07	'08	'09	Total	Relative (%)
Global safeguard	0	0	0	0	0	0	0	1	1	1	1	0	0	0	0	4	100

Table 3.2: *Continued.*

	1995	'96	'97	'98	'99	2000	'01	'02	'03	'04	'05	'06	'07	'08	'09	Total	Relative (%)
(c) Number of anti-dumping, countervailing and China-specific safeguard case initiations, counted by trading partner and HS-06 product																	
Anti-dumping	55	94	99	27	123	33	76	42	8	72	90	65	22	62	25	892	89.03
Countervailing	0	4	6	8	55	0	6	9	2	0	4	1	0	5	10	110	10.97
China-specific safeguard	0	0	0	0	0	0	0	0	1	0	0	0	0	0	0	1	0.01
(d) Number of global safeguard case initiations, counted by HS-06 product																	
	1995	'96	'97	'98	'99	2000	'01	'02	'03	'04	'05	'06	'07	'08	'09	Total	Relative (%)
Global safeguard	0	0	0	0	0	0	0	120	1	6	1	0	0	0	0	128	100

Anti-dumping case initiations with HS code missing in the *Temporary Trade Barriers Database* (Bown 2010) are excluded. Global safeguard measures are non-discriminatory, *ie* they apply to all trading partners.

import counterfactual for products under anti-dumping on the basis of industry import growth rates for products that are never subject to anti-dumping throughout our data period.[13] Due to import data restrictions, we restrict the use of counterfactuals to anti-dumping cases for which measures were imposed after 1995 and stick to actual import values otherwise.

For indicators 1–3, the two robustness checks are in fact methodologically identical and yield results that are very similar to those in our baseline specification. This allows us to conclude that anti-dumping measures are generally non-prohibitive in nature. For indicator 4, results from the robustness analysis also support our findings from the baseline specification. Though we find that coverage shares are indeed frequently higher when using counterfactuals instead of actual import values, the difference is relatively small. Additionally, trends in coverage are very similar to the baseline specification. Thus, we report our results only for the baseline specification.

Though our findings are robust to using import counterfactuals, it is important to note a couple of other caveats. First, the indicators defined above only capture the 'direct effects' of anti-dumping. There may also be a number of 'indirect effects' such as import diversion, downstream effects, tariff-jumping foreign direct investment, domestic market entry, and retaliation or strategic behaviour. We do not attempt to capture such effects, though research literature has shown that they exist.[14] Second, we do not consider the size of measures or the type of measures applied. Third, in the absence of firm-level data, it was not possible to engage in an evaluation of the impact of anti-dumping on EU firm performance. Finally, while EU anti-dumping measures are imposed at the eight-digit product level, we performed our analysis at the six-digit product level due to import data limitations.[15]

One final remark is in order before turning to the results. While we have defined the four different coverage indicators above in terms of stocks, we also compute them for the flows of anti-dumping (*ie* for case initiations), and

---

[13]Note that this methodology is directly related to Equation (1.2) in Chapter 1 and Bown (2011b). Equation (1.2) is the formal description of the application of our second counterfactual to indicator 4, except for two differences. First, we calculate the counterfactual on the basis of industry-specific import growth rates for non-anti-dumping products rather than economy-wide import growth rates for non-anti-dumping products. Second, only final anti-dumping measures are taken into account. According to EU anti-dumping law, preliminary duties can only be imposed for a maximum period of nine months and, since we use annual data, are likely to be negligible.

[14]See Vandenbussche and Zanardi (2010) for a comprehensive overview of these 'indirect effects'.

[15]The EU usually imposes anti-dumping measures at the eight-digit Combined Nomenclature (CN) level. The first six digits of the CN code actually correspond with the first six digits of HS, allowing us to base our study on HS-06.

for subsamples of products, countries, product-country combinations and imports.[16] All results are reported in the following results sections.

4 GENERAL TRENDS IN THE USE OF EU ANTI-DUMPING POLICY

4.1 *Overall Trends*

We start by showing the trends in EU anti-dumping initiations during 1995-2009 in Figure 3.3. Figure 3.3(a) shows the flow of new cases and Figure 3.3(b) shows the stock of cases, *ie* the number of anti-dumping measures in force in a particular year.[17]

Two alternative definitions of a 'case' are applied in Figure 3.3. The first one is 'by target country' and the second one is 'by target country and HS-06 product'.[18] To illustrate the difference, consider the following example. In May 2008, the EU initiated an anti-dumping case against China, Moldova and Turkey, each involving 7 HS-06 products. Using the first definition, we count 3 anti-dumping cases. Using the second definition, we count 21 cases involved in the investigation.[19] Since an anti-dumping measure was imposed only against China for the 7 HS-06 products in August 2009, we count this as one anti-dumping measure in force against China according to the first definition. Using the second definition, we count this as 7 anti-dumping measures in force against China.

Whatever definition we apply, the crisis period does not look unusual. In terms of anti-dumping initiations in panel (a), we observe about five peaks between 1995 and 2009. There is also one in 2008, but it seems a stretch to attribute this peak to increased protectionism at the outbreak of the financial crisis. First, the magnitude of the peak suggests that this can still be regarded in the range of 'normal' fluctuations. Second, only 44% of cases initiated in 2008 resulted in protection due to a considerable share of cases withdrawn by EU firms or terminated by the EU authority, compared with 58% for 1995-2007.

The stock of anti-dumping measures in force, shown in panel (b), shows a clear downward trend in the 2000s according to the 'traditional' count

[16]Note that the use of counterfactuals is redundant for the calculation of coverage shares for flows of anti-dumping policy assuming that the mere initiation of an anti-dumping case does not have an impact on imports.

[17]Note that, for some cases initiated in 2009, the outcomes were not yet known at the time of writing. The number of initiations that result in measures is therefore not reported for 2009 in Figure 3.3(a).

[18]Previous literature has predominantly used the 'by target country' definition of a case. See, for example, Prusa (2001) and Zanardi (2004).

[19]Note that if the EU had initiated another anti-dumping investigation in the same year against one of the same countries and on one of the same HS-06 products, this anti-dumping investigation would have been counted as a separate case.

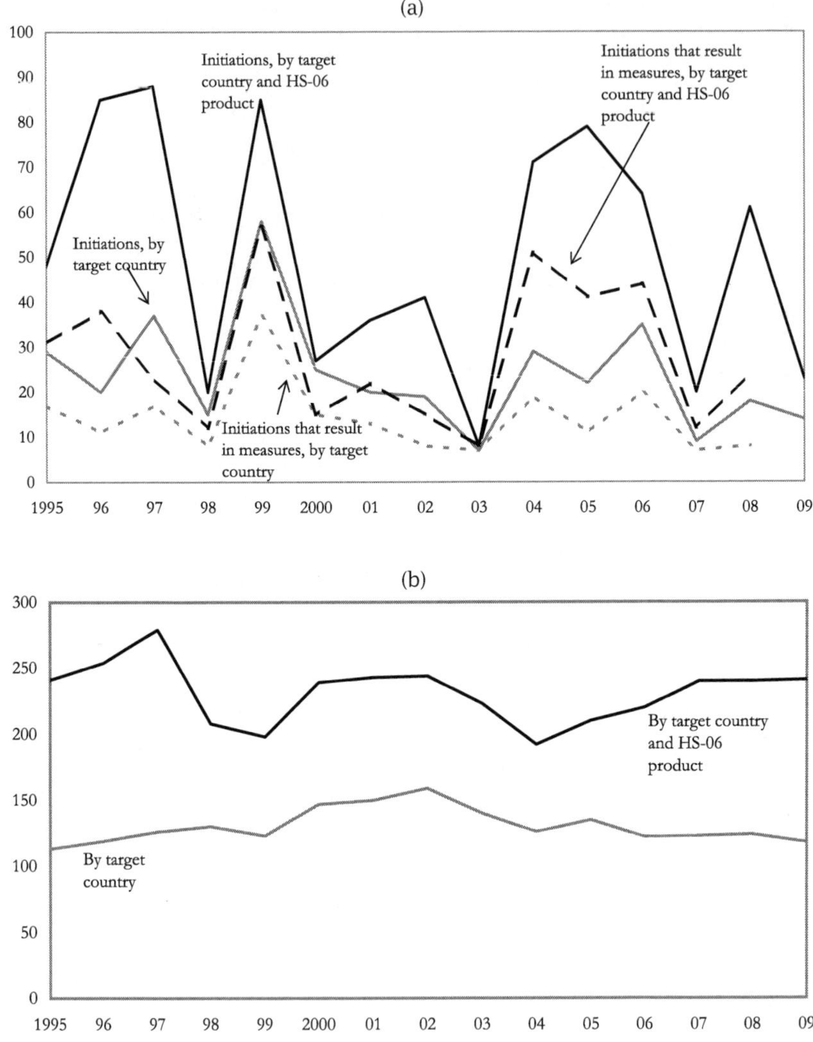

Figure 3.3: *EU anti-dumping policy. (a) Flow: total number of anti-dumping initiations and number of anti-dumping initiations that result in measures. (b) Stock: number of anti-dumping measures in force.*

Source: authors' calculations based on *Temporary Trade Barriers Database* (Bown 2010). For the number of anti-dumping initiations that result in protection, the 2009 value was not yet available at the time of writing. For anti-dumping measures with a missing revocation date, we assume that anti-dumping protection was in place for five years. Anti-dumping cases that have missing HS codes in the database are excluded. Cases against EU27 member states before their EU accession are excluded.

of anti-dumping cases by target country. However, when we define an anti-dumping case by target country and HS-06 product, we observe a clear upward trend beginning in 2004. This suggests that the average number of products involved in an anti-dumping investigation against a certain trading partner has increased over time. Indeed, aggregating anti-dumping case initiations over time, we find an average of 1.9 products per case for 1995–2003, while for 2004–9 this number is 2.5 products per case.

Due to the sunset clause in EU anti-dumping law, the usual duration of an anti-dumping measure is five years. However, the duration can be shorter or longer if accompanied by a justified decision from the trade authority. Figure 3.4 provides some descriptive statistics on the duration of EU anti-dumping measures defined by target country and HS-06 product. Panel (a) counts the number of anti-dumping measures, expired before the end of 2009, by their duration.[20] The duration varies between 1 and 18 years, and the most frequent duration is 5 years, accounting for 62.9% of all measures. The duration exceeds 5 years for 23.7% of all measures and is smaller than 5 years for 13.4%. Panel (b) considers those anti-dumping measures that are still in force by the end of 2009. Roughly 74.2% of measures were in force for less than 5 years before the end of 2009, while 25.8% were in force for more than 5 years.

Figure 3.4(c) examines whether the EU has increased protection during the crisis through a prolongation of existing anti-dumping measures in force. For this purpose, we calculate the share of those anti-dumping measures that were supposed to expire due to the sunset clause but were still in force after a sunset review. To state this more precisely, we calculate the share of measures that are still in place despite having being imposed more than five but less than six years ago. This share exhibits substantial variation over time and was at its peak in 1995, when none of the anti-dumping measures imposed five to six years before were removed. It has been decreasing since 2007, which suggests that there has not been an increase in protection during the crisis through the channel of prolonging the duration of existing measures.

Next, we compute indicators 1–4 on product coverage, target-country coverage, product-country coverage, and import-value coverage for both anti-dumping initiations and measures in each year. For the count indicators 1–3, in addition to calculating anti-dumping coverage for all products, countries and product-country combinations, we also separately show the coverage in the respective top quartile by import value. To establish the top quartile of products, we aggregate imports by product over 1995–2009 and then keep the highest 25% of products by import value. We take an equivalent approach to obtain the top 25% trading partners and the top 25% product-country combinations. For indicator 3, we additionally calculate the anti-dumping coverage

[20]We exclude a few cases for which information on HS code or revocation date is missing in the *Temporary Trade Barriers Database* (Bown 2010).

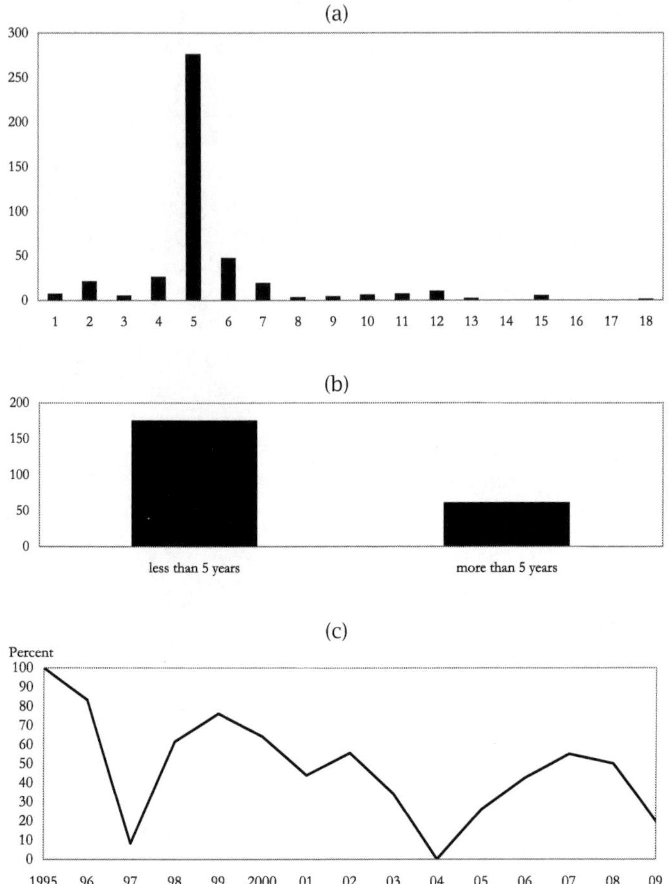

Figure 3.4: *Duration of EU anti-dumping measures: (a) number of anti-dumping measures expired before 31 December 2009 by duration in years; (b) number of anti-dumping measures in force on 31 December 2009 by duration in years; (c) percentage of anti-dumping measures imposed more than five and less than six years and still in force.*

Source: authors' calculations based on *Temporary Trade Barriers Database* (Bown 2010). Measures counted by target country and HS-06 product. Anti-dumping measures with revocation date or HS code missing in the database are excluded. In panel (a), duration of x years on the horizontal axis implies a duration of between $x - 0.5$ and $x + 0.5$ years. In panel (b), duration calculated referring to 31 December 2009, the end of the data period. In panel (c), percentage of total anti-dumping measures not removed by 30 June of the year on the horizontal axis despite being imposed more than five and less than six years ago.

after excluding '*de minimis*' trading partners that are defined as those countries that account for less than 1% of EU imports of a certain product in a certain year. Results are shown in Figure 3.5.

The first observation that stands out from Figure 3.5 is that products, countries and product–country combinations that are 'important' in terms of import value are more frequently subject to anti-dumping protection.

Figure 3.5(a) illustrates that product coverage of anti-dumping measures has clearly increased since 2004, with many products covered by new anti-dumping initiations especially in 2004–6. Panel (b) suggests that target-country coverage did not change much over time. If anything, we observe a weak inverse-U-shape, suggesting a slight decrease in country coverage of anti-dumping measures after 2004. For the share of product–country combinations that fall under anti-dumping protection (shown in panel (c)) we expect to see the combined effect of product and country coverage. Indeed, we observe an upward trend since 2004, which is likely driven by the increase in the share of products covered by anti-dumping measures. All three 'count' indicators for the stock and the flow of anti-dumping policy in panels (a)–(c) indicate that the EU approximately followed its pre-crisis path during 2008–9.

Figure 3.5(d) illustrates our results for the 'value' indicator, *ie* the import share covered by anti-dumping initiations and measures. No clear patterns stand out. The only noticeable patterns are a sharp decrease in the import share covered by anti-dumping measures until 1998, and a relatively larger import share covered in 2006 and 2007. During the crisis, however, coverage shares of both stock and flow of protection remain at a relatively modest level.

In unreported results, we have also calculated indicators 1–4 with information on coverage shares of newly imposed anti-dumping measures being in place in year t but not in year $t-1$, and expired anti-dumping measures being in place in year $t-1$ but removed by year t. This allows us to investigate whether, due to expired measures, Figure 3.5 hides a substantial increase in new anti-dumping coverage during the crisis. Indeed, we find an increase in the share of products, product–country combinations and imports covered by anti-dumping measures newly imposed in 2009. However, to say that this pattern represents a major change in the application of anti-dumping policy would be too strong a conclusion since the increase is still in the range of pre-crisis fluctuations for all three indicators.

In the aggregate, there is no evidence of any major shift in EU anti-dumping policy around the time of the global crisis in 2008–9. The EU appears to have applied its policies during the crisis the way it did before.

4.2 By Country Income Group

We next categorise targeted countries according to broad income groups. Our data confirm earlier studies (Rovegno and Vandenbussche 2011) and show that China has increased its importance as an anti-dumping target both in

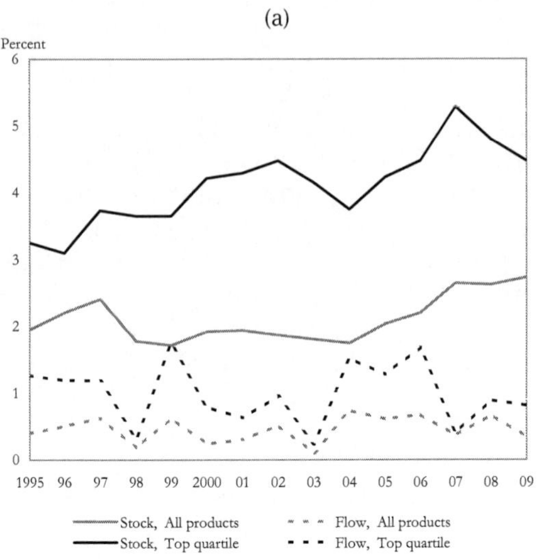

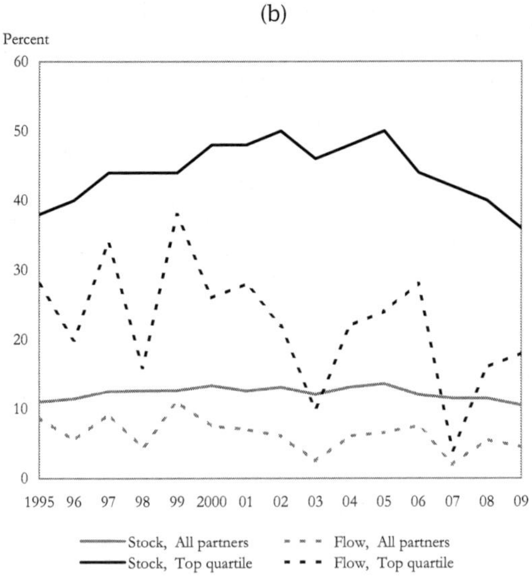

Figure 3.5: *Total coverage shares of EU anti-dumping policy. (a) Stock/flow: share of products covered. (b) Stock/flow: share of countries covered.*

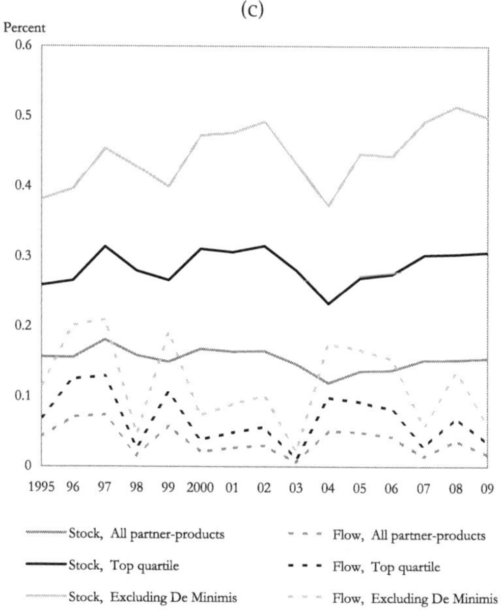

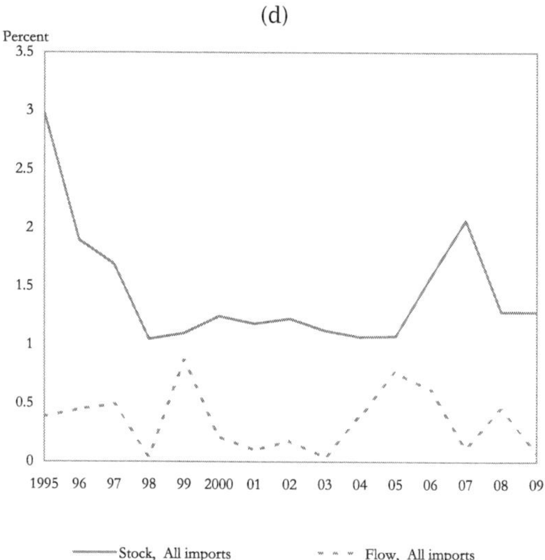

Figure 3.5: *Continued: (c) Stock/flow: share of product-country combinations covered. (d) Stock/flow: share of imports covered.*

Source: panels (a), (b), (c) and (d) calculated using indicators 1, 2, 3 and 4, respectively. All figures based on EU definition that includes Austria, Denmark, Finland, France, Germany, Ireland, Italy, Portugal, Sweden and United Kingdom. For definitions of 'top quartile' and '*de minimis*', see Section 4.1.

terms of initiations and imposed measures. The number of anti-dumping initiations against China as a share of the total has increased dramatically from around 15% in 1995–2003 to about 40% in 2004–9.

When constructing different income categories of countries we follow the latest World Bank classification but take into account the special status of China as a main EU anti-dumping target.[21] This results in four groups of countries: high-income countries, upper-middle-income countries, lower-middle-and-low-income countries (excluding China), and China. For each of these four groups, we compute indicator 1 to measure product coverage and indicator 4 to measure import-value coverage.

The share of products coming from China and falling under EU protection has been increasing rapidly since 2004, as illustrated in Figure 3.6(a), which reports the product coverage of the stock of protection by country income group. Products from other lower-middle-and-low-income countries have also been increasingly falling under anti-dumping protection.[22] This is not the case for countries in the high-income group, for which the share of products affected by EU anti-dumping measures has remained roughly stable over time. The product coverage of flows of anti-dumping policy shown in panel (b) is largely consistent with our observations for the stock values. The share of products imported from China and covered by anti-dumping case initiations is relatively high throughout 1995–2009, but initiations against other lower-middle-and-low-income countries also cover many products, especially in 2005–6.

The import-value indicator for the stock of protection, shown in Figure 3.6(c), reveals that while a large share of China's imports is subject to EU anti-dumping measures, this share decreased during the 2008–9 crisis. Nevertheless, China clearly remains the dominant target country during the crisis, followed by other lower-middle-and-low-income countries. Panel (d) reports a peak in import-value coverage of initiations against China and other lower-middle-and-low-income countries around 2005. The leather shoe case against China and Vietnam described earlier likely plays an important role in explaining this pattern since this case was initiated in 2005.

Figure 3.6 suggests that anti-dumping coverage has remained relatively low in all country income groups during the crisis, compared with pre-crisis levels of protection. Furthermore, we find some evidence for the increasing 'north-south' divide in anti-dumping policy, with the EU targeting the 'south' more and more, at least in terms of product coverage. Given the recent proliferation of anti-dumping laws, particularly in the 'south', an important question is to what extent the retaliatory power of the 'south' may shift the future targeting

[21] This classification contains all World Bank member economies and all other economies with a population of more than 30,000.

[22] In fact, positive anti-dumping coverage for lower-middle-and-low-income countries results exclusively from anti-dumping measures against lower-middle-income countries.

pattern. Miyagiwa *et al* (2010) suggest that, in a global world with multilateral trading relations, market size may be the key to understanding these patterns.

4.3 By Industry

In this section we analyse anti-dumping coverage by industry, defined according to the 21 sections of the Harmonized System. The EU's anti-dumping policy is not equally applied across industries and, in fact, a simple count of case initiations between 1995 and 2009 suggests that anti-dumping policy is concentrated in a few sectors. 'Base metals', 'chemicals', 'textiles', 'machinery and electrical appliances' and 'plastics and rubber' accounted for 82% of all EU anti-dumping initiations during the data period. However, these figures do not account for industry size or product scope per industry. A few cases could have a large impact in industries where the import value and the number of products imported are low. Hence, to simply focus our analysis on the five industries that have the highest number of anti-dumping cases over time is not sufficient.

We compute indicators 1 and 4 for the stock of protection across *all* industries. One way to visualise the breadth and depth of anti-dumping policy at the industry level is to examine an industry–year matrix in which cells are shaded according to the degree of protection: darker cells indicate higher levels of protection. Table 3.3 illustrates the matrices and provides an overview of the industries under anti-dumping protection for each year in 1995–2009, both in terms of product coverage (panel (a)) and import-value coverage (panel (b)). The table shows how anti-dumping does not only affect the 'usual suspect' industries listed above, as coverage reaches high values for other industries as well.

For example, the EU mineral products industry was intensively protected by anti-dumping between 1996 and 2001, attaining product coverage ratios of up to 8%. The animal products industry had 15–16% of the total import value covered by anti-dumping between 2006 and 2008. Within 'animal products', EU anti-dumping measures on rainbow trout and farmed salmon were the main underlying cause of the relatively high coverage. The breakdown of protection by industry also reveals that the EU footwear industry had substantial anti-dumping protection with an annual import-value coverage of 15–22% between 2006 and 2009, mainly due to the imposed anti-dumping measures on certain footwear from China and Vietnam.

An important observation on coverage *across* industries is that the number of industries protected under anti-dumping increased, a trend that began around 2004 and that may partially explain the increased product coverage over time. Only industries like arms and ammunition, art, and precious stones are not covered by anti-dumping. The EU's new user industries of anti-dumping policy are animal products, vegetable products, fats and oils, and foods and beverages. As only fats and oils started to be a user industry in

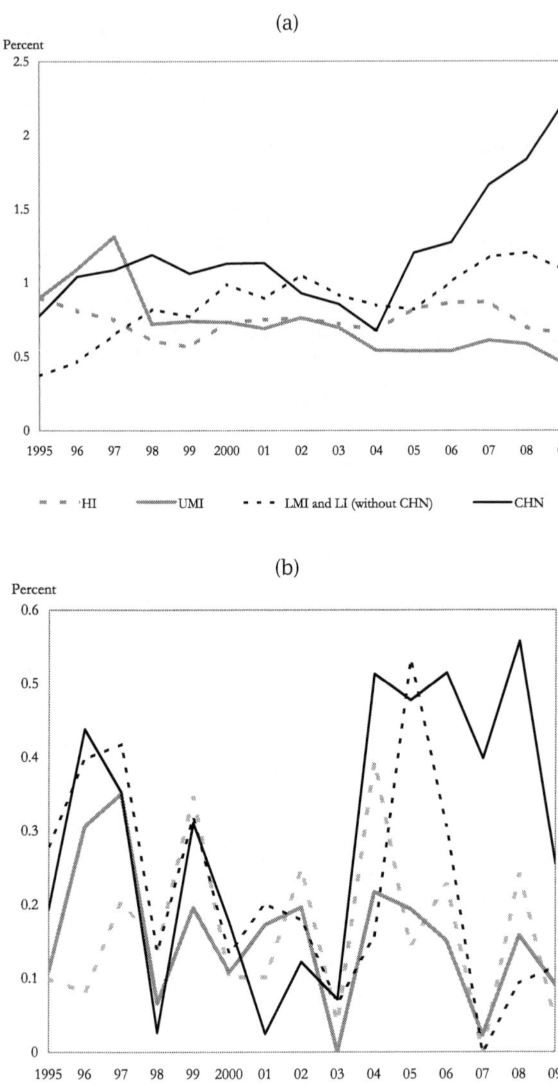

Figure 3.6: *Coverage shares of EU anti-dumping policy by country income group. (a) Stock (share of products covered). (b) Flow (share of products covered).*

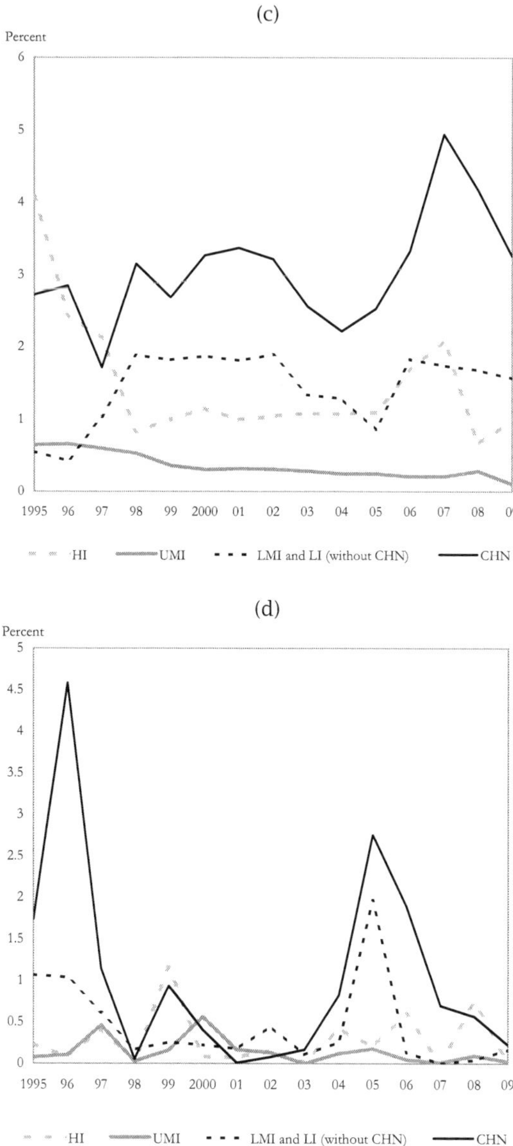

Figure 3.6: *Continued: (c) Stock (share of imports covered). (d) Flow (share of imports covered).*

Source: panels (a) and (b) calculated using indicator 1. Panels (c) and (d) calculated using indicator 4. All figures are based on an EU definition that includes Austria, Denmark, Finland, France, Germany, Ireland, Italy, Portugal, Sweden and United Kingdom. HI: high-income. UMI: upper-middle-income. LMI and LI (without CHN): lower-middle-and-low-income (without China). CHN: China.

Table 3.3: *Coverage shares of EU anti-dumping measures in force across industries.*

HS	Name of industry	Year														
		'95	'96	'97	'98	'99	'00	'01	'02	'03	'04	'05	'06	'07	'08	'09
(a) Share of products covered																
01	Animal products															
02	Vegetable products															
03	Fats and oils															
04	Food, beverages															
05	Mineral products															
06	Chemicals															
07	Plastics and rubber															
08	Leather															
09	Wood															
10	Pulp and paper															
11	Textiles															

Table 3.3: *Continued.*

HS	Name of industry	Year														
		'95	'96	'97	'98	'99	'00	'01	'02	'03	'04	'05	'06	'07	'08	'09
		(a) Share of products covered														
12	Footwear															
13	Stones and glass															
14	Precious stones															
15	Base metals															
16	Machinery															
17	Transport															
18	Instruments															
19	Arms, ammunition															
20	Miscellaneous															
21	Art															

Table 3.3: *Continued.*

HS	Name of industry	Year														
		'95	'96	'97	'98	'99	'00	'01	'02	'03	'04	'05	'06	'07	'08	'09
(b) Share of imports covered																
01	Animal products															
02	Vegetable products															
03	Fats and oils															
04	Food, beverages															
05	Mineral products															
06	Chemicals															
07	Plastics and rubber															
08	Leather															
09	Wood															
10	Pulp and paper															
11	Textiles															

Table 3.3: *Continued.*

HS	Name of industry	Year '95	'96	'97	'98	'99	'00	'01	'02	'03	'04	'05	'06	'07	'08	'09
		(b) Share of imports covered														
12	Footwear															
13	Stones and glass															
14	Precious stones															
15	Base metals															
16	Machinery															
17	Transport															
18	Instruments															
19	Arms, ammunition															
20	Miscellaneous															
21	Art															

Coverage rate of 0% denoted by blank entries; coverage rate of 0–2% denoted by light grey box; coverage rate of 2–4% denoted by medium grey box; coverage rate > 4% denoted by dark grey box. Panel (a) is based on calculation of indicator 1. Panel (b) is based on calculation of indicator 4. Both panels are based on an EU definition that includes Austria, Denmark, Finland, France, Germany, Ireland, Italy, Portugal, Sweden and United Kingdom.

2009 during the crisis, the evidence seems too weak to suggest an increased coverage across industries related to the crisis.

With few exceptions, the pre-crisis levels of anti-dumping protection *within* industries prevailed during the crisis. The base metals industry is one exception, where anti-dumping protection increased tremendously and attained an unprecedented high in 2009 both in terms of product and import-value coverage.

To summarise Section 4, we have not found any significant overall change in the EU's use of anti-dumping policy in 2008–9. While product and industry coverage of anti-dumping have increased since 2004, country coverage remains at a roughly constant level over the period of analysis, with a slight decrease in the set of targeted countries after 2004. Anti-dumping measures are increasingly imposed on products coming from lower-middle-and-low-income countries, especially from China, which has been an ongoing trend since 2004.

5 WHAT MAKES PRODUCTS AND TRADING PARTNERS PRONE TO ANTI-DUMPING PROTECTION?

5.1 'Traditional' Trade Protection

According to the 'substitution hypothesis', trade liberalisation efforts in the form of tariff reductions have gone hand in hand with increased trade protection through other means such as anti-dumping policy. The existing evidence that examines the extent to which anti-dumping substitutes for eliminated tariff protection has not resulted in uniform patterns across countries.[23] For the EU, the average applied MFN tariff plotted in Figure 3.2 and our data on MFN and preferential tariffs suggest that tariffs have not changed much in the 2000s. Therefore, it is difficult to examine the 'substitution hypothesis' and to relate the use of EU anti-dumping policy to *changes* in 'traditional' trade protection. We can, however, explore the relationship between EU anti-dumping policy and the *level* of 'traditional' protection. If the EU grants import preferences to some countries or sets a low applied MFN tariff on a certain product, the level of 'traditional' protection is rather low. One interesting question is whether these products and trading partners are more prone to EU anti-dumping protection.

We start by investigating the relationship between anti-dumping policy and preference margins, *ie* the differences between applied MFN tariffs and preferential rates of the EU *vis-à-vis* its preferential trading partners in the WTO. With numerous multilateral and bilateral PTAs in place, the question for the

---

[23]See, for example, Feinberg and Reynolds (2007), Moore and Zanardi (2009) and Bown and Tovar (2011).

EU is whether anti-dumping policy has focused on product-country combinations subject to a preferential regime.

We calculate preference margins as the difference between applied MFN tariffs and preferential tariffs, using data from UN TRAINS.[24] Then we divide product-country combinations into two categories distinguishing between those for which preference margins are zero and those for which they are positive. We calculate indicators 3 and 4 on product-country combinations and import-value coverage, respectively, for each of the two groups, basing indicators for year t on the preference margins granted in $t-1$. The results are shown in Figure 3.7.

Figures 3.7(a) and 3.7(c) show that the share of product-country combinations and imports subject to anti-dumping measures are considerably higher among those with a preference margin greater than zero. Similarly, the coverage shares of anti-dumping case initiations reported in panels (b) and (d) of Figure 3.7 predominantly involve product-country combinations subject to a preferential EU regime. This suggests that anti-dumping policy is largely used for product-country combinations subject to preferential tariffs and tends to be a substitute for the lower import tariffs granted under preferential regimes.

Next, we investigate the link between applied MFN tariff rates and anti-dumping policy. We are interested in whether anti-dumping measures are most frequently imposed on products with high or low applied MFN tariffs. For this purpose, we calculate indicator 1 on product coverage and indicator 4 on import coverage for subsets of products that differ in the size of applied MFN duty. No clear pattern stands out from the data. If anything, the EU is imposing more anti-dumping on products with intermediate levels of MFN tariffs, but less on products subject to very high or low tariff levels. We conclude that there is no evidence for a clear link between anti-dumping policy and the level of applied MFN tariffs in the EU.[25]

5.2 *Product-Mix Similarity*

An interesting question that has not been explored in the earlier literature is the extent to which countries with an export product mix that is similar to the EU are a focus of EU anti-dumping policy. For reasons related to direct competition, exporting countries that overlap in their product mix with the EU would be more likely to be targeted by protection (Facchini *et al* 2010). For this purpose, we develop a 'similarity index' first introduced by Finger and Kreinin (1979) and used by Schott (2008). To create the similarity index, we use detailed data on exports for all exporting countries in the following way:

$$\sum_{i \in J} \min(\mathrm{sh}_{ipt}, \mathrm{sh}_{i\,\mathrm{EU}\,t})$$

[24]For each product-country combination, we calculate the preference margin as the maximum of all preference margins at the more disaggregated tariff-line level.

[25]Corresponding figures can be obtained from the authors upon request.

(a)

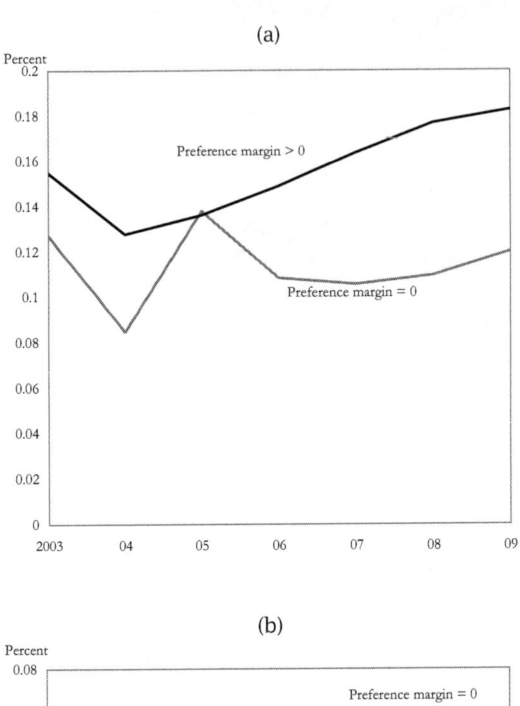

(b)

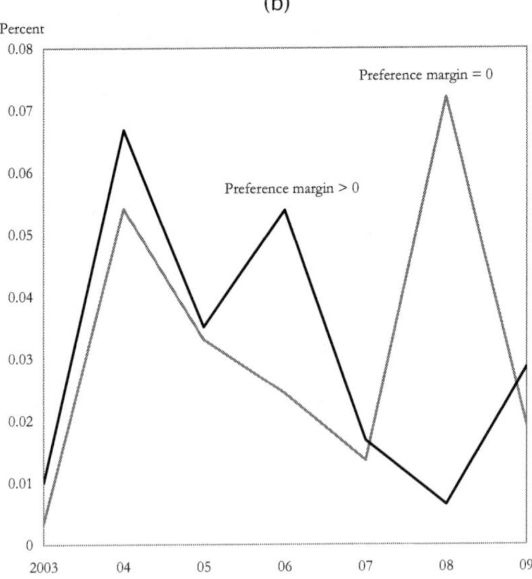

Figure 3.7: *Coverage shares of EU anti-dumping policy by preference margin. (a) Stock: share of product–country combinations covered. (b) Flow: share of product–country combinations covered.*

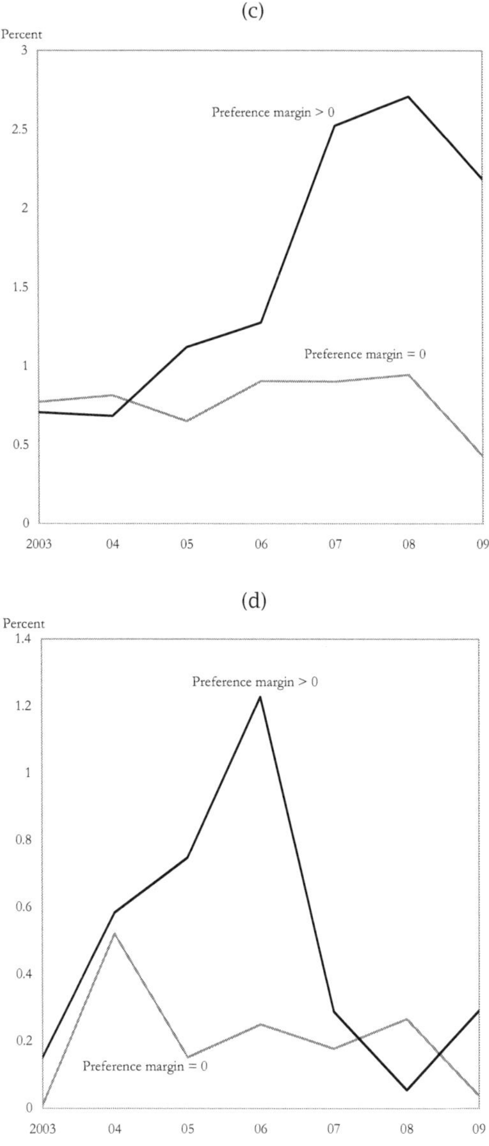

Figure 3.7: *Continued: (c) Stock: share of imports covered. (d) Flow: share of imports covered.*

Source: panels (a) and (b) calculated using indicator 3. Panels (c) and (d) calculated using indicator 4. All figures are based on an EU definition that includes Austria, Denmark, Finland, France, Germany, Ireland, Italy, Portugal, Sweden and United Kingdom. Preference margin corresponds to the difference of applied MFN and preferential tariff as described in Section 5.1.

with sh_{ipt} being the exports of product i, which is an element of the total set of products J, from country p in year t as a share of total exports from country p in year t. The variable $sh_{i\,EU\,t}$ is defined as the exports of product i from the EU in year t as a share of total exports from the EU in year t.

We first calculate the index for each exporting country by comparing its shares with respect to total exports to those of the EU across all products. This will eventually give us an indicator of product-mix similarity by *country*. Second, we calculate the index by *industry-country* combination and compare the shares with respect to total exports of the specific industry to those of the EU across products in the industry. In this case, the indicator yields an industry-country specific measure by assessing the similarity of, say, China's textile industry to EU's textile industry. In both cases the indicator lies between 0 and 1. Values closer to 1 indicate a more similar product mix of the country or the industry-country combination with the EU.[26] Ideally, we would use product-level production data rather than export data to assess the product mix of countries. However, these data are not available and we approximate product mix with export data at the HS-06 level from UN Comtrade.

To assess whether product-mix similarity by country and by industry-country combination result in greater anti-dumping incidence, we assign observations into quartiles depending on their index value.[27] For country observations in the same quartile in year $t-1$, we determine the country and import-value coverage ratios of anti-dumping policy in year t, *ie* indicators 2 and 4. For industry-country observations, we do the same to determine product-country and import-value coverage ratios, *ie* indicators 3 and 4.

Figure 3.8 shows the coverage ratios (indicators 2 and 4) for the quartiles of country-specific product-mix similarity calculated in this way. Panels (a) and (b) of Figure 3.8 illustrate that, for both stock and flow measures of anti-dumping policy, countries most similar to the EU are targeted relatively more frequently with anti-dumping than less similar countries. One explanation could be that the trade volume between similar trading partners is also larger and that this may be driving the higher incidence of anti-dumping cases in that group. Hence, we are not able to distinguish between product-mix similarity and volume of imports as drivers of anti-dumping incidence. To overcome this, panels (c) and (d) of Figure 3.8 illustrate the relative import value covered by anti-dumping policy, *ie* indicator 4, which should account for the larger

---

[26] In case the exports of a country to the world are zero in an industry for a certain year, we set product-mix similarity index by industry-country combination equal to zero.

[27] In order to avoid any dependency of results on changing data availability over time, we only include those countries into our analysis for which export data are available for all years between 2000 and 2009. This drops mostly small developing economies that have never been subject to EU anti-dumping measures. We end up with a balanced panel of 77 countries containing the main EU anti-dumping targets.

trade between similar partners. Here, we still find that similar trading partners appear more often in EU anti-dumping policy than others.[28]

In unreported results, we have also calculated indicators 3 and 4 for quartiles of the industry-country-specific similarity index. Here, we also conclude that foreign industries that are similar to the EU are targeted relatively more by its anti-dumping policy.

5.3 Product Characteristics

We introduce a further novelty to the literature by linking anti-dumping policy to certain product characteristics. To see whether anti-dumping policy is more orientated towards homogeneous or differentiated products, we apply the Rauch (1999) indicator of product differentiation. Also, we analyse whether EU anti-dumping focuses primarily on products for industrial purposes (referred to as industrial goods), products for household consumption (referred to as consumer goods) or capital goods, for which we use the BEC classification.[29]

The Rauch (1999) indicator classifies products into three categories: differentiated goods, homogeneous goods quoted on an organised exchange, and homogeneous goods whose reference prices are quoted in trade publications. For our purposes, we merge the latter two categories into one broad category of homogeneous products. Imports are then split into homogeneous versus differentiated goods.[30] Our methodology consists of assessing indicators 1 and 4 involving the share of products and imports covered by anti-dumping and computing them for each class of products. Figure 3.9 illustrates our results.

In terms of Rauch (1999) product types, anti-dumping policy is used both on homogeneous and differentiated products. The main difference appears to be that indicator 1, the count measure, always takes on higher values for homogenous products than for differentiated products (panel (a)), while the reverse is true for indicator 4, the value measure (panel (c)). This suggests that the number of differentiated products under anti-dumping appears to be relatively low, while their import value is relatively large.

---

[28]Doing so generates an unexpected outcome in the quartile of trading partners that are least similar to the EU. Panel (d) shows a somewhat unexpected spike in 2002 of the import value covered by anti-dumping initiations against the trading partners least similar to the EU, contributing to considerable coverage shares of anti-dumping measures, as can be seen in panel (c). A closer look at the data suggests that this is mainly due to one outlier case, 'large rainbow trout' imported from Faroe Islands, initiated in 2002, such that our general results remain valid.

[29]In order to match Rauch (1999) and BEC classification to HS-06, we use concordance tables provided by the United Nations Statistics Division.

[30]Rauch (1999) defines a 'liberal' and a 'conservative' classification, the latter defining some products as 'differentiated' that are 'homogeneous' according to the former classification. Our results are reported for the 'conservative' classification, but a robustness check shows that they are very similar when using the 'liberal' classification.

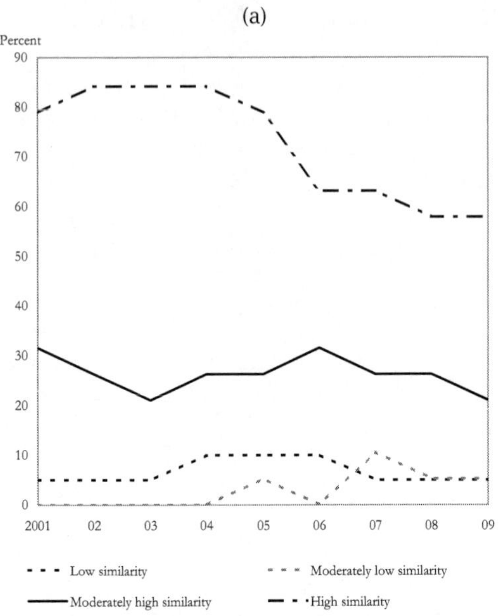

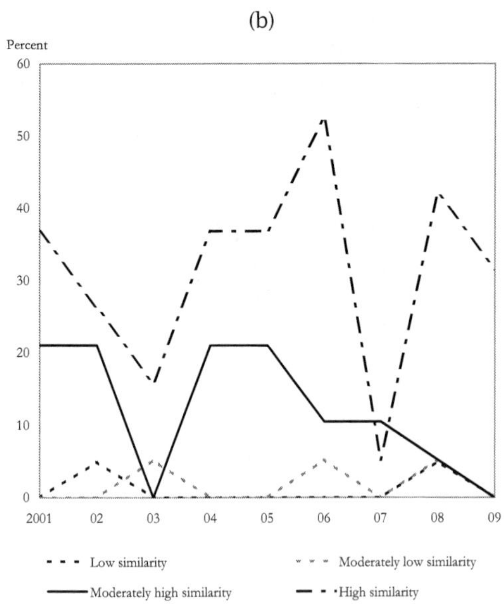

Figure 3.8: *Coverage shares of EU anti-dumping policy by product-mix similarity at country level. (a) Stock: share of countries covered. (b) Flow: share of countries covered.*

(c)

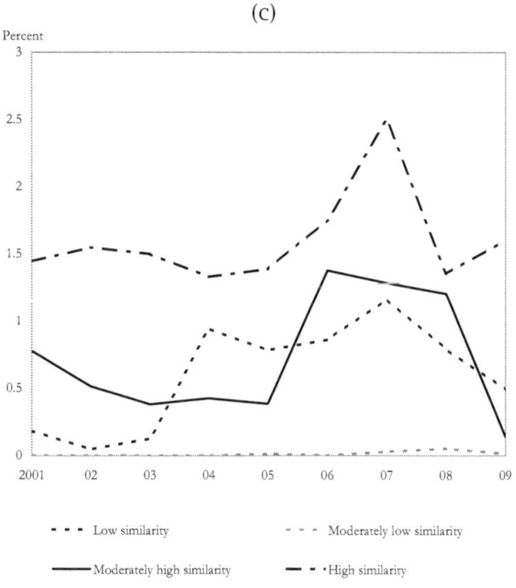

(d)

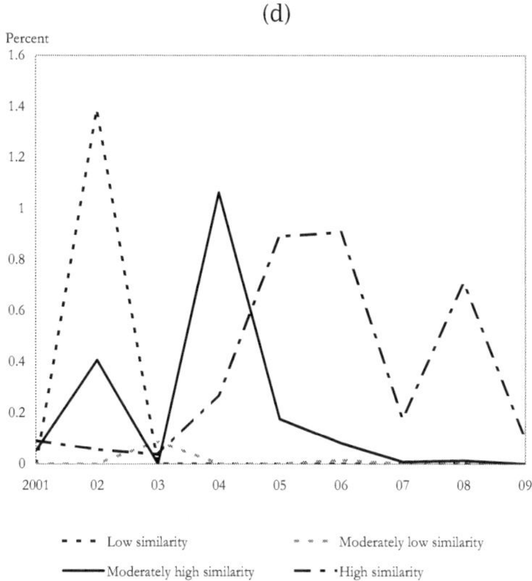

Figure 3.8: *Continued: (c) Stock: share of imports covered. (d) Flow: share of imports covered.*

Source: panels (a) and (b) calculated using indicator 2. Panels (c) and (d) calculated using indicator 4. All figures based on EU definition that includes Austria, Denmark, Finland, France, Germany, Ireland, Italy, Portugal, Sweden and United Kingdom. Index for product-mix similarity by country calculated following Finger and Kreinin (1979). Degree of product-mix similarity is based on assignment of index value to corresponding quartile as described in Section 5.2.

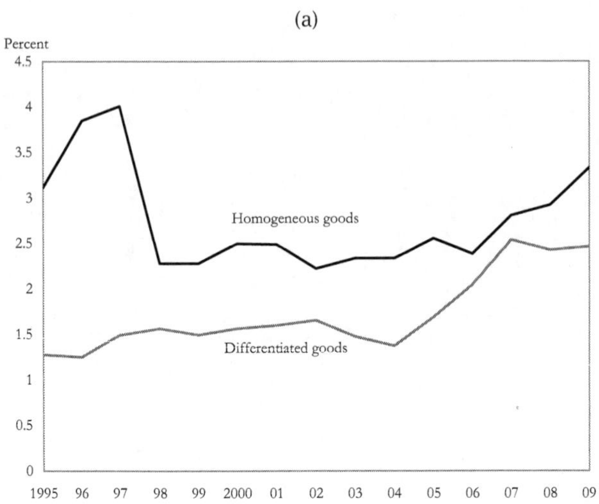

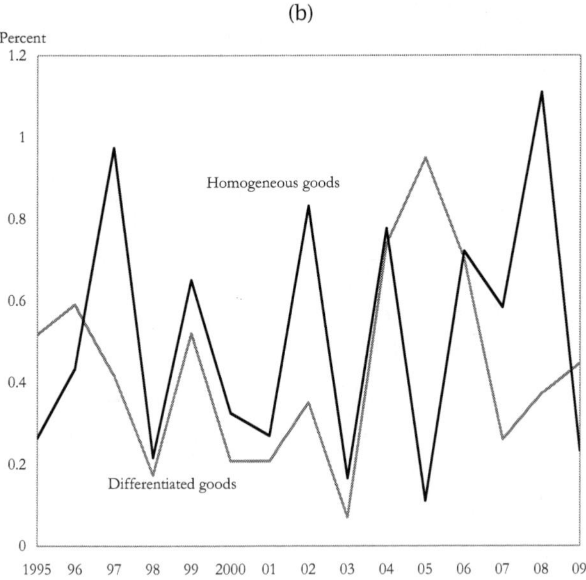

Figure 3.9: *Coverage shares of EU anti-dumping policy for homogeneous and differentiated goods. (a) Stock: share of products covered. (b) Flow: share of products covered.*

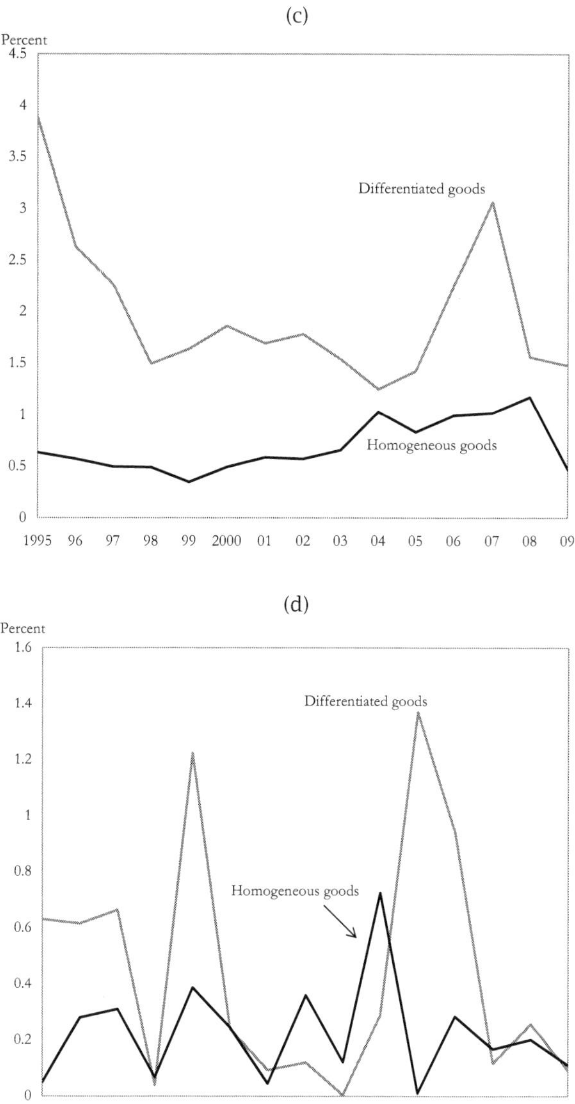

Figure 3.9: *Continued: (c) Stock: share of imports covered. (d) Flow: share of imports covered.*

Source: panels (a) and (b) calculated using indicator 1. Panels (c) and (d) calculated using indicator 4. All figures are based on EU definition that includes Austria, Denmark, Finland, France, Germany, Ireland, Italy, Portugal, Sweden and United Kingdom. Definition of differentiated and homogeneous goods follows 'conservative' Rauch (1999) classification.

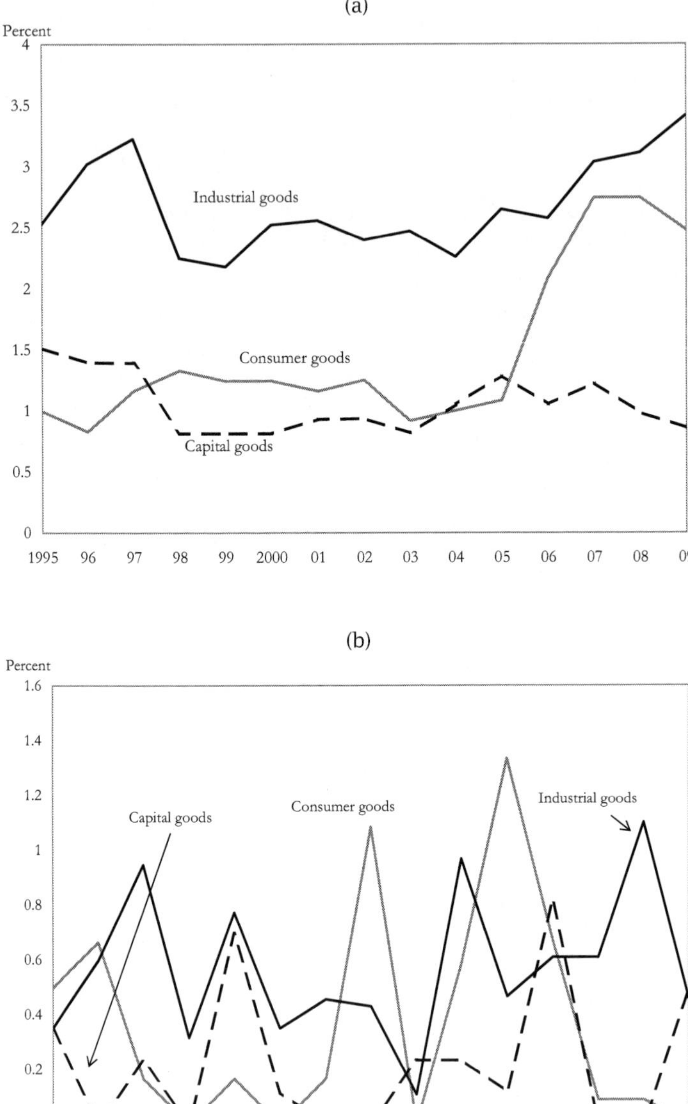

Figure 3.10: *Coverage shares of EU anti-dumping policy for consumer, industrial and capital goods. (a) Stock: share of products covered. (b) Flow: share of products covered.*

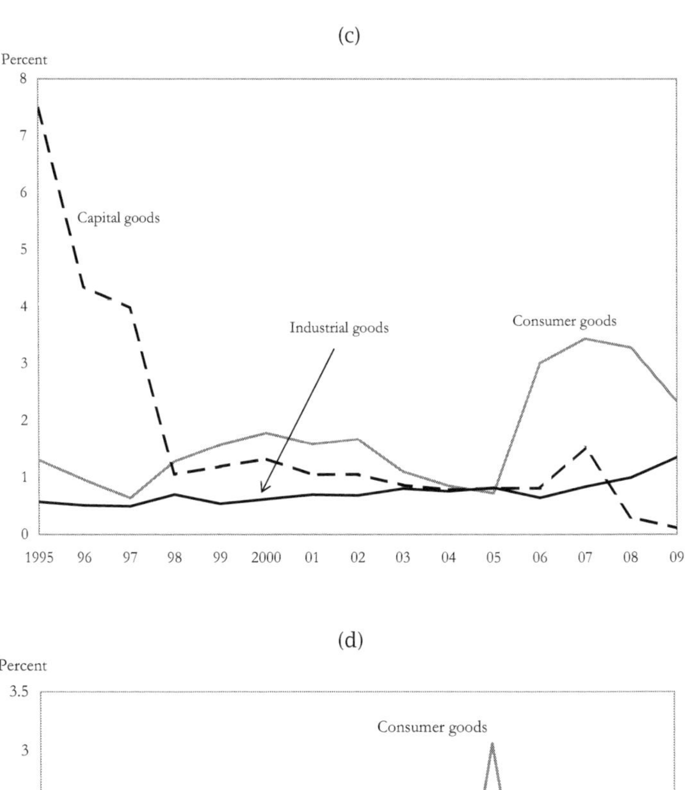

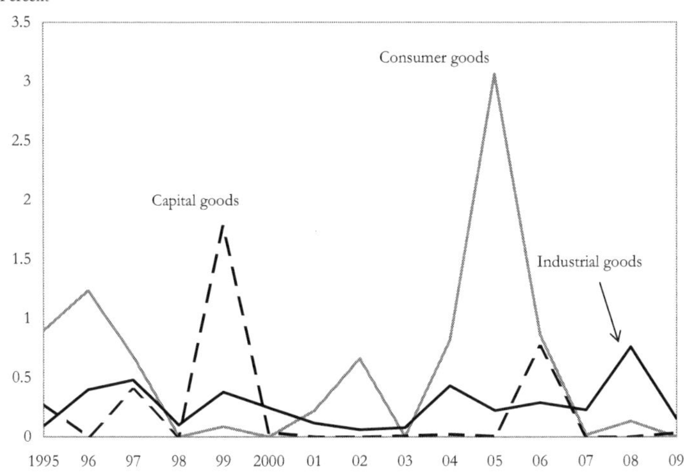

Figure 3.10: *Continued: (c) Stock: share of imports covered. (d) Flow: share of imports covered.*

Source: panels (a) and (b) calculated using indicator 1. Panels (c) and (d) calculated using indicator 4. All figures based on EU definition that includes Austria, Denmark, Finland, France, Germany, Ireland, Italy, Portugal, Sweden and United Kingdom. The exact link between the definition of consumer goods, industrial goods and capital goods and BEC is available from the authors of this chapter upon request.

Figure 3.9(a) illustrates that the share of differentiated products covered by anti-dumping measures increased between 2004 and 2007. This suggests that the onset of the increase in product coverage that we noted earlier is mainly driven by differentiated products. The coverage share of anti-dumping initiations (depicted in panels (b) and (d)) points at such a conclusion as well. Case initiations cover a large share of differentiated products and imports, particularly after 2004. We find that not one, but several industries account for this peak, including footwear, base metals and machinery and electronic equipment. The share of homogeneous products under anti-dumping protection also rises, but a few years after 2004.

Another product classification for which we verify the link to anti-dumping policy is the BEC that we aggregate to three broad categories: capital goods, industrial goods and consumer goods.[31] For each group of products, we again compute indicators 1 and 4 on product and import-value coverage, respectively. The indicators are plotted in Figure 3.10.

Panels (a) and (c) of Figure 3.10 indicate that both the share of consumer goods and the import share of consumer goods subject to anti-dumping measures increased tremendously shortly after 2004. Although there is a weak reversal trend during the crisis with anti-dumping initiations focusing on industrial goods as shown in panels (b) and (d), consumer goods continue to play a more important role in anti-dumping policy than before. The increased importance of consumer goods is a general tendency, not driven by a few peculiar cases. It is also in line with the increase in the number of industries covered by anti-dumping documented earlier, where the new users of anti-dumping policy include animal products, food and beverages and vegetables, *ie* all final consumer goods industries.[32] Capital goods played a minor role in EU anti-dumping policy in the first decade of the 2000s.

One potential explanation for a shift in the relative importance of anti-dumping policy from industrial products to consumer products could be related to the fragmentation of production across countries. European Union firms that offshore the production of intermediates they used to produce domestically may be less prone to formulating dumping complaints against imported intermediates when these intermediates are shipped back to the EU. This is because anti-dumping measures may raise the prices of imported intermediates and are then likely to have a negative impact on firms' sales, as shown by Konings and Vandenbussche (2009).

[31] The BEC classification is available on the website of the United Nations Statistics Division. The link between BEC and the categorisation into consumer, capital and industrial products is available from the authors upon request.

[32] A closer look at the data indeed shows that the newly covered products that led to this jump include farmed salmon, preserved sweet corn and frozen strawberries. Also, refrigerators, leather footwear, ironing boards and bike saddles are consumer products on which anti-dumping measures were imposed.

6 IS THERE EU MEMBER STATE HETEROGENEITY?

This section inspects individual EU member states' imports more closely in order to verify the results regarding the coverage of anti-dumping measures in terms of products, countries, product-country combinations and import values. For each individual member state in the EU, we calculate product and country coverage as well as import-value ratios 1–4 using extra-EU27 imports only. Results could differ across EU member states because the import composition of each member state is different. This approach gives us a measure of the exposure to anti-dumping protection for each EU member state. Since results are quite similar for indicators 2–4, we focus on indicator 1, which measures product coverage. Results are shown in Table 3.4.

With respect to product coverage of anti-dumping measures, the results for most individual EU member states are consistent with the results obtained for the EU as a whole. Product coverage has increased for all countries and is at a similar level across countries. There are relatively few member states that are outliers. Luxembourg is an outlier as product coverage is somewhat smaller than in other member states, which may be due to its small country size and heavy specialisation in banking and finance. However, an alternative explanation could be that Luxembourg imports those products that are under anti-dumping protection only indirectly via other EU member states, something that would not show up in our coverage ratios.

The relatively homogeneous response across member states is reassuring. Not only does it show that aggregate EU trends are not driven by a few outlying countries, but it also reflects a similar pattern across most individual member states. Moreover, it suggests that trade policy shocks in the EU affect member states in a similar manner. From the outset of the European integration and the creation of the eurozone, EU policies have been aimed at convergence since symmetric shocks in an optimum currency area constitute a necessary condition for eurozone survival.

7 CONCLUSION

One of the most important conclusions arising from this chapter is that there is no evidence of a major change in the EU's trade policy since the outbreak of the crisis. After failing to find evidence that applied MFN tariff rates or technical trade barriers have increased, we examine EU anti-dumping protection. The detailed descriptive evidence on EU anti-dumping policy patterns suggests that there was no major change in the EU's policy regime through 2008–9. The EU seems to have largely remained on its pre-crisis path of anti-dumping policy.

Our analysis is based on several newly constructed indicators. In terms of the 'value' indicator, the analysis shows that the value of imports covered by

Table 3.4: *Coverage shares of EU anti-dumping measures in force across EU member states: share of products covered.*

	Year														
Member state	'95	'96	'97	'98	'99	'00	'01	'02	'03	'04	'05	'06	'07	'08	'09
Austria	medium	medium	medium	medium	medium	medium	medium	medium	medium	medium	dark	black	black	black	black
Belgium					medium	dark	dark	dark	medium	medium	dark	black	black	black	black
Germany	dark	dark	black	dark	dark	dark	dark	dark	dark	dark	dark	black	black	black	black
Denmark	medium	light	medium	medium	medium	medium	medium	medium	medium	light	dark	dark	black	black	black
Spain	medium	medium	dark	medium	medium	dark	dark	dark	dark	dark	dark	black	black	black	
Finland	medium	medium	medium	medium	medium	medium	medium	medium	medium	medium	dark	black	black	black	black
France	dark	dark	dark	dark	medium	dark	dark	dark	dark	dark	dark	black	black	black	black
Greece	medium	medium	medium	medium	medium	medium	medium	medium	medium	medium	dark	dark	black	black	
Ireland	medium	light	light	light	light	medium	medium	medium	light	light	medium	dark	black	dark	black
Italy	dark	dark	black	medium	medium	dark	dark	dark	dark	medium	dark	dark	black	black	black
Luxembourg					light	light	light	light	light	light	light	light	medium	light	light
Netherlands	medium	medium	dark	dark	medium	medium	dark	dark	dark	medium	dark	dark	black	black	
Portugal	medium	medium	medium	medium	light	light	medium	medium	medium	light	medium	dark	black	black	black
Sweden	medium	light	medium	medium	medium	medium	medium	medium	light	light	medium	medium	black	black	black
UK	medium	dark	dark	dark	medium	dark	dark	dark	medium	medium	dark	black	black	black	black
Cyprus										medium	medium	dark	black	black	black
Czech Rep.										medium	dark	dark	black	black	black
Estonia										medium	dark	dark	black	black	black
Hungary										medium	dark	black	black	black	
Lithuania										medium	medium	dark	black	black	black
Latvia										light	medium	dark	black	black	black
Malta										light	dark	dark	black	dark	black
Poland										dark	dark	black	black	black	
Slovakia										dark	dark	black	black	black	
Slovenia										light	medium	dark	dark	dark	black
Bulgaria													black	black	black
Romania													black	black	black

Missing share denoted by blank entries; coverage rate of 0–1.2% denoted by light grey box; coverage rate of 1.2–1.6% denoted by medium grey box; coverage rate of 1.6–2.0% denoted by dark grey box; coverage rate > 2.0% denoted by black box. Based on calculation of indicator 1.

EU anti-dumping measures as a share of total import value remained at a relatively modest level during the crisis. Results arising from 'count' indicators point at a turnaround in EU's trade policy beginning in 2004. The interesting pattern arising from the analysis is that the share of products under EU anti-dumping protection has been on an upward trend since 2004. At the same time, we detect a small decrease in the number of countries targeted by anti-dumping that started after 2004. Product-country coverage under anti-dumping as a share of total product-country combinations, with positive imports, has gone up. This confirms that the increase in product coverage is the stronger pattern. The higher product coverage does not seem to come from the EU initiating a higher number of anti-dumping investigations with a constant number of products. Rather, it reflects that the number of products per investigation has increased.

Another trend is an increasing EU focus on China as a target for anti-dumping cases, with cases brought against China representing around 40% of EU anti-dumping initiations between 2004 and 2009. To a lesser extent, other lower-middle-and-low-income countries have also become more frequent targets of EU anti-dumping measures, suggesting a clearer 'north–south' divide in trade policy with the EU targeting developing countries more frequently over time. At the industry level, anti-dumping policy now affects nearly every industry, so industry coverage has gone up. Again, this is not a crisis phenomenon but a trend that started earlier.

When analysing the relationship between EU anti-dumping policy and its preferential tariffs, evidence suggests that anti-dumping measures are imposed relatively more often on products and against countries subject to a preferential import regime. However, when analysing the relationship between anti-dumping policy and the levels of applied MFN tariffs, we do not find any clear pattern of substitution. In addition, we assess the relationship between product-mix similarity of trading partners and the EU's use of anti-dumping policy. We find that anti-dumping measures are more often imposed against country and country–industry combinations that are similar to the EU. In terms of product characteristics, we observe that, in particular, the shares of consumer goods and differentiated goods covered by EU anti-dumping measures have increased rapidly after 2004. Although there is a weak reversal trend during the crisis, consumer goods and differentiated goods continue to play an important role in anti-dumping policy. Finally, we also verify that the results we obtain for the EU as a whole are not driven by any outlying pattern in the import composition at the level of the individual EU member states. We find that general patterns surrounding anti-dumping policy mostly hold up, even when results are considered at the level of individual EU member states.

The EU's anti-dumping policy through the late 2000s is mainly characterised by trends that had already started by 2004. While there are a number of events that coincide with this date and that could provide an explanation, it is hard to pinpoint a single one for the change in the trend. One possible explanation is that a new European Commission entered office in 2004 with the arrival of a new trade commissioner.[33] Another potential explanation is that, in 2004, ten new EU member states joined the EU, which may have altered the policy mix and the decision-making. Alternatively, it could just be that European firms, the ultimate initiators of anti-dumping cases, have been subject to new

[33]The trade commissioner taking office in 2004 was Peter Mandelson, a UK national.

globalisation forces that may have affected the demand for protection and some of its characteristics.

More importantly for this chapter is the fact that we have not found any evidence that points at a major turnaround in EU trade policy during the crisis. Nevertheless, it remains to be seen whether governments such as the EU can continue to resist the use of anti-dumping as a 'beggar-thy-neighbour' policy in the aftermath of the crisis. Research by Reinhart and Rogoff (2009) suggests that negative effects of financial crises, in terms of unemployment and other output related variables, tend to linger much longer, which could make trade protection a tempting option in the coming years.

Hylke Vandenbussche is the Chaire Jacquemin Professor in International Economics at the Université catholique de Louvain (IRES and CORE), and a research fellow at CEPR and LICOS-KULeuven.

Christian Viegelahn is a PhD candidate at the Université catholique de Louvain in Belgium, and a researcher at IRES.

REFERENCES

Bown, C. P. (2011a). Introduction. In *The Great Recession and Import Protection: The Role of Temporary Trade Barriers* (ed. C. P. Bown). London: CEPR/World Bank. (Chapter 1 of this volume.)

Bown, C. P. (2011b). Taking stock of anti-dumping, safeguards, and countervailing duties, 1990–2009. *The World Economy*, forthcoming.

Bown, C. P. (2010). *Temporary Trade Barriers Database.* World Bank (July). URL: http://econ.worldbank.org/ttbd/.

Bown, C. P., and P. Tovar (2011). Trade liberalization, anti-dumping and safeguards: evidence from India's tariff reform. *Journal of Development Economics* **96**(1), 115–125.

Doing Business (2011). World Bank/IFC resource. URL: www.doingbusiness.org.

Facchini G., M. Olarreaga, P. A. da Silva, and G. Willmann (2010). Substitutability and protectionism: Latin America's trade policy and imports from China and India. *World Bank Economic Review* **24**, 446–473.

Feinberg, R. M., and K. M. Reynolds (2007). Tariff liberalization and increased administrative protection: is there a quid pro quo? *The World Economy* **30**, 948–961.

Finger, J. M., and M. E. Kreinin (1979). A measure of 'export similarity' and its possible uses. *Economic Journal* **89**, 905–912.

Hartigan, J. C., and H. Vandenbussche (2010). Why does the WTO have an anti-dumping agreement? LICOS Discussion Paper 25310, LICOS Centre for Institutions and Economic Performance, Leuven.

International Centre for Trade and Sustainable Development (2010). China brings anti-dumping case against EU in shoe dispute. *Bridges Weekly Trade News Digest* **14**(5), 8–9.

Konings, J., and H. Vandenbussche (2009). Anti-dumping protection hurts exporters: firm-level evidence from France. CEPR Discussion Paper 7330, Centre for European Policy Research, London.

Martin, A., and W. Vergote (2008). On the role of retaliation in trade agreements. *Journal of International Economics* **76**, 61–77.

Miyagiwa, K., H. Song, and H. Vandenbussche (2010). Innovation, anti-dumping and retaliation. CORE Discussion Paper 2010/64, Center for Operations Research and Econometrics, Louvain-la-Neuve.

Moore, M. O., and M. Zanardi (2009). Does anti-dumping use contribute to trade liberalization in developing countries? *Canadian Journal of Economics* **42**, 469–495.

Prusa, T. J. (2001). On the spread and impact of anti-dumping. *Canadian Journal of Economics* **34**, 591–611.

Rauch, J. E. (1999). Networks versus markets in international trade. *Journal of International Economics* **48**, 7–35.

Reinhart, C. M., and K. S. Rogoff (2009). The aftermath of financial crises. *American Economic Review* **99**, 466–472.

Rovegno, L., and H. Vandenbussche (2011). Anti-dumping practices in the European Union: a comparative analysis of rules and application in WTO context. In *Liberalising Trade in the EU and the WTO: Comparative Perspectives* (ed. S. Gaines, B. E. Olsen and K. E. Sørensen). Cambridge University Press, forthcoming.

Schott, P. K. (2008). The relative sophistication of Chinese exports. *Economic Policy* **23**, 5–49.

Vandenbussche, H. (1996). Is European anti-dumping protection against Central Europe too high? *Review of World Economics* **132**, 116–138.

Vandenbussche, H., and M. Zanardi (2010). The chilling trade effects of anti-dumping proliferation. *European Economic Review* **54**, 760–777.

Vermulst, E., and P. Waer (1991). The calculation of injury margins in EC anti-dumping proceedings. *Journal of World Trade* **25**, 5–42.

Zanardi, M. (2004). Anti-dumping: what are the numbers to discuss at Doha? *World Economy* **27**, 403–433.

4

Canada: No Place Like Home for Anti-Dumping

RODNEY D. LUDEMA AND ANNA MARIA MAYDA[1]

1 INTRODUCTION

Canada is the ancestral home of anti-dumping law. In 1904, it became the first country to adopt an anti-dumping law; other industrialised countries quickly followed suit. Anti-dumping provisions were later incorporated into the GATT in 1947. Today, virtually all members of the WTO have anti-dumping laws in operation.

Despite its prominent (some would say infamous) place in anti-dumping history, Canada has not been among the major users of anti-dumping or other TTBs since 1989. At their two-decade peak in 2000, Canadian anti-dumping duties covered around 2% of all HS-06 products and less than 1% of total Canadian imports by value. While this is roughly average for industrialised countries, it lags well behind the USA, the EU and several developing countries (*eg* India, China, Argentina, Brazil and Mexico). Moreover, anti-dumping coverage has retreated substantially since the peak, despite the 2008–9 global economic crisis. Thus, neither the aggregate level nor the aggregate trend of Canadian TTB usage seems to indicate a strong protectionist tendency. Could it be that anti-dumping policy is no longer welcome in its home and native land, or will it return in the wake of the global economic crisis to stand on guard for Canada once again? In what follows, we explore this question in greater detail.

The main finding is that, despite the retreat in TTB stocks in the first decade of the 2000s, there are signs of a rebound. New anti-dumping cases surged during the crisis, which portends a rise in anti-dumping stocks that could last for several years. Thus, the connection of anti-dumping protection to the business cycle remains strong. A second finding is that there appears to be

[1]Rodney D. Ludema: Department of Economics, Georgetown University, 37th and O Streets, NW, Washington, DC USA 20057. Email: ludemar@georgetown.edu. Anna Maria Mayda: Department of Economics, Georgetown University, 37th and O Streets, NW, Washington, DC USA 20057. Email: amm223@georgetown.edu.

a major structural shift underway in terms of the products and countries on which TTBs are applied. China and, to a lesser extent, other developing countries are being targeted with far greater intensity than ever before, and sectors that compete against Chinese imports are the ones seeking protection. Indeed, although China accounts for less than 10% of Canada's imports, seven out of the ten anti-dumping cases initiated during the 2008–9 crisis were against China. Moreover, as the typical anti-dumping duty against China remains in effect for over ten years (nearly twice as long as against the rest of the world), the anti-dumping surge during the 2008–9 crisis could be unprecedented in its duration.

1.1 Aggregate Trends in Canadian TTBs

All Canadian TTBs during the sample period 1989–2009 were in the form of either anti-dumping or CVDs. Only four safeguard cases—three general and one special case against China—were initiated, but none resulted in duties. Of the CVDs imposed, almost all were imposed on the same products covered by existing anti-dumping remedies (anti-dumping duties or price undertakings). Thus, CVDs add virtually nothing to the TTB coverage ratios. For this reason, we focus our analysis on anti-dumping remedies.

Tables 4.1 and 4.2 (and the corresponding Figures 4.1 and 4.2) show the overall stocks and flows of anti-dumping remedies at the HS-06 level.[2] Table 4.1, which shows count measures, is based on Equation (1.1) of Chapter 1. For the stock, the count measure refers to the fraction of all six-digit HS codes (with positive imports) in which an anti-dumping remedy was in force in a given year. For the flow, the count measure refers to the fraction of all six-digit HS codes (with positive imports) in which an anti-dumping case was initiated in that year. Table 4.2, which shows value measures, is based on Equation (1.2) of Chapter 1. Value measures provide information on the share of total imports affected by an anti-dumping remedy (stock) or an initiation (flow).

Anti-Dumping Initiations

Figure 4.1 shows three distinct spikes in the count measure of anti-dumping initiations. The first was 1992, the second was the period from 1997 to 2001,

[2] Ideally, we would like to construct these measures at the ten-digit HS level, which is the level of disaggregation of Canadian data in the World Bank's *Temporary Trade Barriers Database* (Bown 2010). The problem is that the HS classification was modified four separate times during this period. The TTB database records only the ten-digit code of the affected product at the time of the initiation, which means that a TTB in force for multiple years could get lost if the ten-digit code of the affected product is modified. The only way to track TTBs accurately over time is to use a ten-digit concordance for each modification. However, the Canadian Border Services Agency provides a concordance only for the most recent modification (Canadian Border Services Agency 2007).

Table 4.1: *Canada's count measure by year (anti-dumping only).*

	Count measure	
Year	Stock	Flow
1989	1.11	0.32
1990	1.30	0.12
1991	1.07	0.26
1992	1.22	0.69
1993	1.52	0.22
1994	1.53	0.04
1995	1.52	0.16
1996	1.44	0.12
1997	1.62	0.39
1998	1.53	0.45
1999	1.92	0.39
2000	2.15	0.55
2001	2.11	0.66
2002	2.09	0.25
2003	1.95	0.17
2004	1.72	0.17
2005	1.43	0.04
2006	1.29	0.12
2007	1.18	0.02
2008	1.10	0.22
2009	1.45	0.44

Source: authors' calculations using *Temporary Trade Barriers Database* (Bown 2010) and Comtrade.

and the third was 2009.[3] When measured in value (Figure 4.2), we see spikes in 1992, 1997 and 2009. A discrepancy between the two series occurs in 2001, where a surge is present in the count measure that does not appear in the value measure, suggesting that cases initiated in 2001 targeted numerous products with relatively small import value.

Theory suggests that anti-dumping initiations should increase during periods of weak domestic demand, weak foreign demand and an appreciating real exchange rate (see Knetter and Prusa (2003) and Hallworth and Piracha (2006) for further discussion and evidence regarding the macroeconomic determinants of anti-dumping filings). The reason has to do with the material injury test that is the main determinant of the success or failure of an anti-dumping filing. In practice, there are two parts to the test. The first requires showing that the domestic industry is suffering injury, based on indicators such as profits, employment, prices, or capacity utilisation. The second requires showing that the injury is due to the dumped imports, which normally requires establishing that imports have increased. When an industry experiences a decline in domestic demand, as would normally occur during a recession at

[3]While our data only go back to 1989, Malhotra and Rus (2009) document earlier surges in initiations in 1985 and 1987.

Table 4.2: *Canada's value measure by year (anti-dumping only).*

	Value measure	
Year	Stock	Flow
1989	0.20	0.08
1990	0.27	0.05
1991	0.36	0.12
1992	0.46	0.19
1993	0.48	0.11
1994	0.51	0.04
1995	0.52	0.09
1996	0.53	0.01
1997	0.65	0.22
1998	0.58	0.05
1999	0.62	0.09
2000	0.76	0.10
2001	0.82	0.10
2002	0.78	0.01
2003	0.67	0.02
2004	0.49	0.09
2005	0.39	0.02
2006	0.31	0.04
2007	0.29	0.03
2008	0.28	0.05
2009	0.35	0.12

Source: authors' calculations using *Temporary Trade Barriers Database* (Bown 2010) and Comtrade.

home, the industry has an easier time convincing the government (specifically, the Canadian International Trade Tribunal) of injury. A decline in demand for the same product in foreign markets causes firms in those countries to export more to Canada, thereby increasing Canadian imports. Similarly, an appreciation in the real exchange rate increases Canadian imports. Thus, recessions both in Canada and abroad and an appreciating Canadian dollar tend to increase the likelihood of satisfying the material injury test.[4] Anticipating this greater likelihood, industries should increase their initiations.

The response of initiations to the macroeconomic experience of Canada appears reasonably consistent with the theory. Figure 4.3 shows real GDP

[4]The other half of an anti-dumping investigation involves estimation of dumping margins, which is conducted by the Canadian Border Services Agency. Like injury, dumping margins may also be affected by macroeconomic conditions. For example, foreign firms may respond to an appreciation in Canada's real exchange rate by raising prices charged to Canadian importers, thus reducing the dumping margin. This suggests a theoretically ambiguous effect of real exchange rates on initiations. Empirical work by Knetter and Prusa (2003) shows that currency appreciations significantly increase anti-dumping filings in a sample consisting of Canada, Australia, the EU and the USA for 1980–1998, suggesting that the material injury effect is dominant.

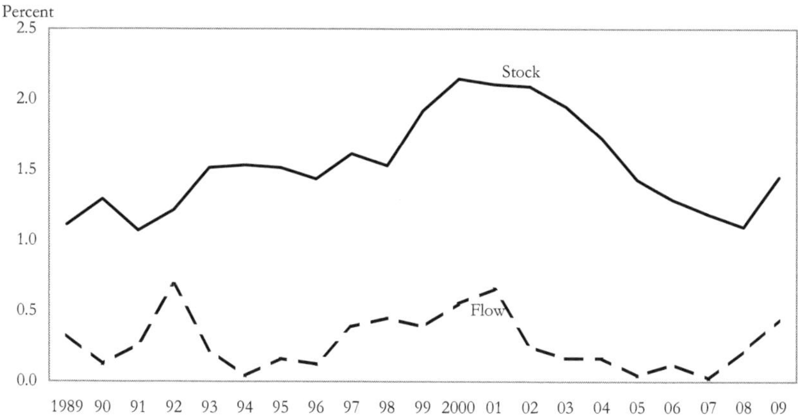

Figure 4.1: *Canada's count measure by year (anti-dumping only).*
Source: authors' calculations using *Temporary Trade Barriers Database* (Bown 2010) and Comtrade.

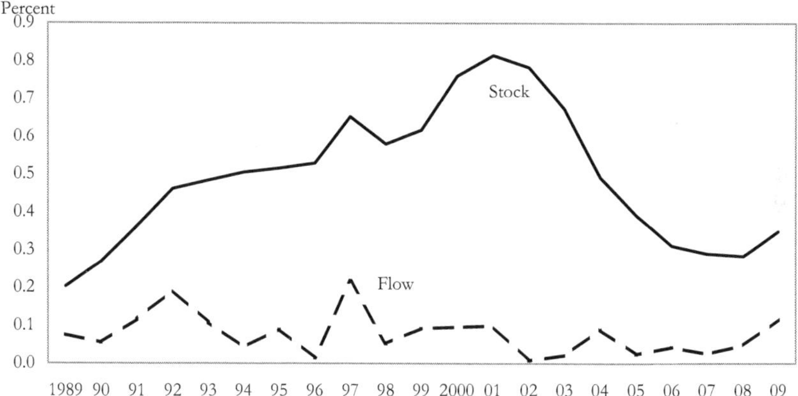

Figure 4.2: *Canada's value measure by year (anti-dumping only).*
Source: authors' calculations using *Temporary Trade Barriers Database* (Bown 2010) and Comtrade.

growth, unemployment, the real exchange rate (US dollars per Canadian dollar, adjusted for inflation), and the current account. Canada experienced deep recessions in 1991 and 2009 in parallel with the global recessions of those time periods. These episodes were accompanied by current account deficits and relatively high real exchange rates. All of these factors predict a surge in anti-dumping initiations.

(a)

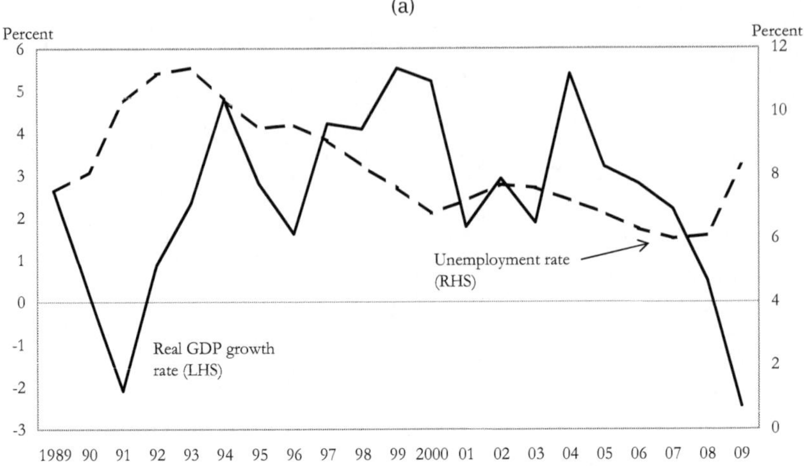

(b)

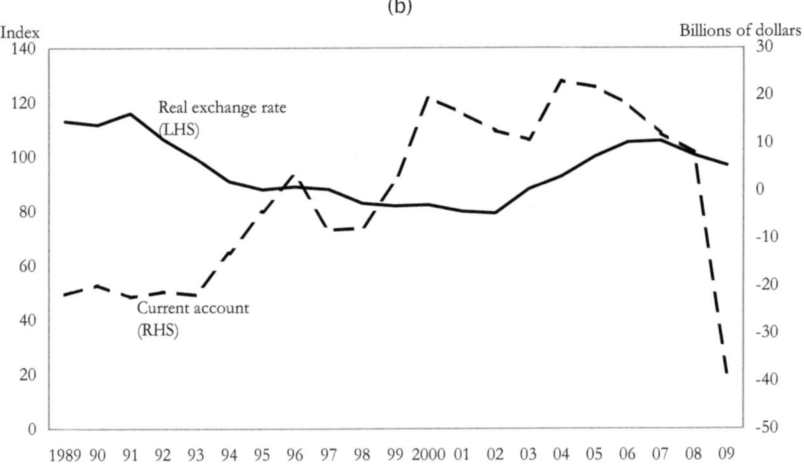

Figure 4.3: *Canada's macroeconomic indicators, 1989–2009: (a) real GDP growth rate and unemployment rate; (b) real exchange rate and current account.*

Source: authors' calculations using World Development Indicators (2010).

The macroeconomic basis for initiations during the 1997–2001 period is less obvious. Neither the Asian financial crisis of 1997 nor the US recession of 2001 caused major disruptions in Canadian GDP growth or unemployment. Furthermore, the real exchange rate was at a historic low. The only indication of impact of the foreign shocks on Canada was a short-lived current account deficit corresponding to the Asian financial crisis. It could be that the foreign shocks alone were sufficient to drive the surge in initiations that occurred. However, as a more disaggregated analysis will reveal in subsequent sections, the reality is more complex. Part of the rise in initiations is due to sectors renewing protection obtained in the earlier surge. Furthermore, while the Asian financial crisis did coincide with a strong shift in anti-dumping actions towards Asian countries, this shift appears to have had long-lasting effects.

Anti-Dumping Stocks

Turning to the stock measures, the average stock over the sample period by the count measure is 1.5%, with a maximum of 2.1% in 2000 and a minimum of 1.1% in 1991. The average stock by value is 0.5%, with a maximum of 0.78% in 2001 and a minimum of 0.2% in 1989. Figures 4.1 and 4.2 also show that stocks display a very clear hump-shaped pattern with a peak between 2000 (count) and 2001 (value). Compared with this peak, the increases in stocks associated with the recessions were quite minor. Furthermore, the stock of TTBs rose steadily during the 1990s and fell rather dramatically during the 2000s. If anything, these trends in TTB stocks appear to be procyclical. The correlation between the anti-dumping stock count measure and Canadian GDP growth is 0.5 (while the correlation with real exchange rate is −0.86).[5]

At first glance, the finding that TTB stocks are procyclical seems puzzling. After all, why would a system that is arguably designed to provide protection to industries under stress give more protection in good times? It is also somewhat troubling, because it would imply that TTB stocks are likely to continue to rise as Canada emerges from the aftermath of the global recession of 2008–9.

One explanation for the procyclical pattern in TTB stocks has to do with the persistence of anti-dumping remedies. Once in effect, an anti-dumping remedy typically remains in place for five or more years, which means that a surge in initiations during a recession will lead to an accumulation of anti-dumping stocks lasting well into the recovery. That is, it could be that the bulge in anti-dumping stocks in the late 1990s is simply the lagged result of the recession-driven flurry of initiations in the early 1990s. If this is correct, then the future will indeed feature more protection, as the 2009 surge in initiations works its way through.

A more optimistic possibility is that the Canadian government has changed its policy. Specifically, it could be that the decline in TTB stocks that began in 2001 is the result of a permanent change in Canadian government's likelihood of awarding or revoking anti-dumping remedies.

Can we detect whether the Canadian government has changed its anti-dumping policy? One way to get at this question is to assume that it has

[5]The correlation with GDP growth is statistically significant at the 5% level, while the correlation with real exchange rate is significant at the 1% level.

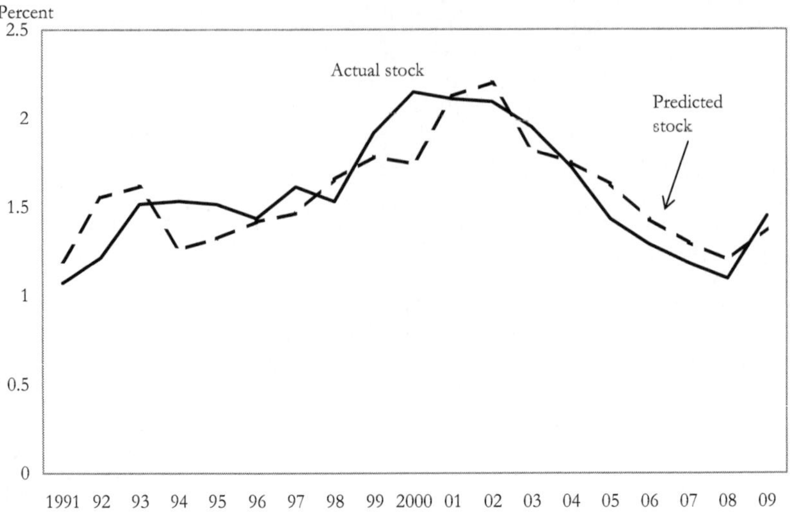

Figure 4.4: *Canada's predicted versus actual stock (count) measure (anti-dumping only).*

Source: authors' calculations using *Temporary Trade Barriers Database* (Bown 2010) and Comtrade.

not—that is, assume constant award and revoke rates—and ask to what extent initiations alone can explain the pattern of anti-dumping stocks. If initiations do a poor job of explaining anti-dumping stocks, we would take this as an indication that award and revoke rates are changing over time. This would then warrant further investigation into the source of such changes.

By definition, the stock of anti-dumping remedies is equal to the sum of all past successful initiations (*ie* initiations that result in a remedy) minus remedies revoked. There are three key rates that determine the motion of the stock: the rate at which initiations receive preliminary anti-dumping remedies, the rate at which preliminary remedies are converted into final remedies, and the rate at which final remedies are revoked. Assuming these rates are constant, we can estimate a simplified version of this model as follows:

$$S_t = \alpha + \beta_1 F_t + \beta_2 F_{t-1} + \beta_3 S_{t-2} + \varepsilon_t,$$

where S_t and F_t are our stock and flow measures in year t, respectively. The coefficient β_1 is the rate at which initiations in year t are awarded duties in year t. The coefficient β_2 is the rate at which initiations in year $t-1$ are awarded duties in year t, either because of delayed preliminary duties or final duties being imposed. The coefficient β_3 measures the rate of carry-over from earlier stocks.

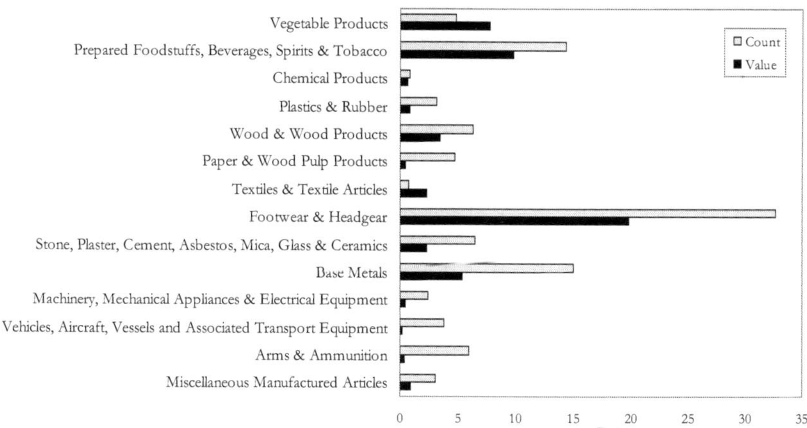

Figure 4.5: *Canada's count and value (stock) measures by HS section (anti-dumping only).*

Source: authors' calculations using *Temporary Trade Barriers Database* (Bown 2010) and Comtrade.

Figure 4.4 shows that the estimated model is reasonably good at predicting the actual stocks, based on past flow and stock data. In fact, the model explains 70% of the variation in anti-dumping stocks. The estimated coefficients are also plausible: $\beta_1 = 0.33$, $\beta_2 = 0.8$ and $\beta_3 = 0.56$. Thus, we expect that the upswing in anti-dumping stocks in 2009 will continue for several more years.

On the other hand, the model does have a tendency to under-predict the stocks during the late 1990s and to over-predict them after 2000. This is indicative of either the success rates being greater, or the revoke rates being smaller, in the 1990s than in the 2000s. Indeed, the raw success rate of initiations in the data (percentage of initiations that result in final anti-dumping remedies) is 70% in the 1990s and 53% in the 2000s. This may reflect a change in policy or a change in the quality of cases. We discuss several possibilities in later sections.

1.2 Canadian TTBs by Industry

In this section we break down the count and value measures (both stock and flow) according to product category. We use the 21 sections of the Harmonized System as our product categories. Figure 4.5 shows the shares of HS-06 codes within each section that have been affected by an anti-dumping remedy (stock) *at any time* during the 1989–2009 period, both in count and in value terms. Of the 21 sections, 14 have experienced at least one anti-dumping remedy during the sample period.

Canadian anti-dumping activity tends to be concentrated in a few product categories. The most active is footwear and headgear. Some 33% of products and 20% of the value of imports in this category have been subject to an anti-dumping remedy. The second most active by count is base metals, which includes steel. About 15% of products and 5% of the value of imports in this category have been subject to an anti-dumping remedy. Close behind is prepared foodstuffs, beverages, spirits and tobacco, with 14% (count) and 10% (value), and vegetable products, with 5% (count) and 8% (value). It is worth noting that, except for steel, this list of most active users of anti-dumping is quite different from the rest of the world. Worldwide, the chemical industry is the most active, followed by steel, machinery and textiles (Stevenson 2007).

Figures 4.6 and 4.7 show stocks and flows of anti-dumping remedies over time across industries. Figure 4.6 shows the count measure, while Figure 4.7 shows the value measure. A few conclusions are evident immediately. First, the number of sectors active in seeking anti-dumping remedies seems to have declined with each wave of anti-dumping initiations. All sectors were active in seeking anti-dumping protection during the recession of the 1990s. The majority of sectors initiated anti-dumping investigations during 1997 and 2001, though fewer than in the previous wave. Only five sectors initiated anti-dumping investigations in 2009: plastics, footwear, steel, machinery and miscellaneous manufactures. For two of these (machinery and miscellaneous manufactures), only a tiny fraction of imports by value were targeted, as can be seen in Figure 4.7. Thus, there is a clear narrowing of the product scope of Canadian anti-dumping investigations.

Second, many of the anti-dumping initiations in the second and third waves are immediately preceded by declines in the anti-dumping stock, suggesting that industries sought to replace recently revoked protection. Examples include base metals, vegetable products and wood products in 1998 and footwear, plastics and machinery in 2009.

Finally, the two most active sectors, footwear and base metals, exhibit high stocks of anti-dumping protection throughout the period.

Footwear

Canada's footwear industry has been in steady decline since the 1950s. In 1950 the industry employed over 20,000 workers. By 1985 this was down to 14,000, and in 2008 there were only 2,700 employees (Canadian Industry Statistics 2010). Most footwear produced in Canada is in the form of winter boots.

Figures 4.6 and 4.7 show that the footwear industry petitioned for the initiation of anti-dumping cases in 1989, 1992, 2000–2002 and 2009, resulting in substantial count rates of anti-dumping protection for all years after 1989, except 2008. For some reason, the footwear industry allowed its protection to lapse in 2008 but quickly reapplied and was awarded a preliminary duty in

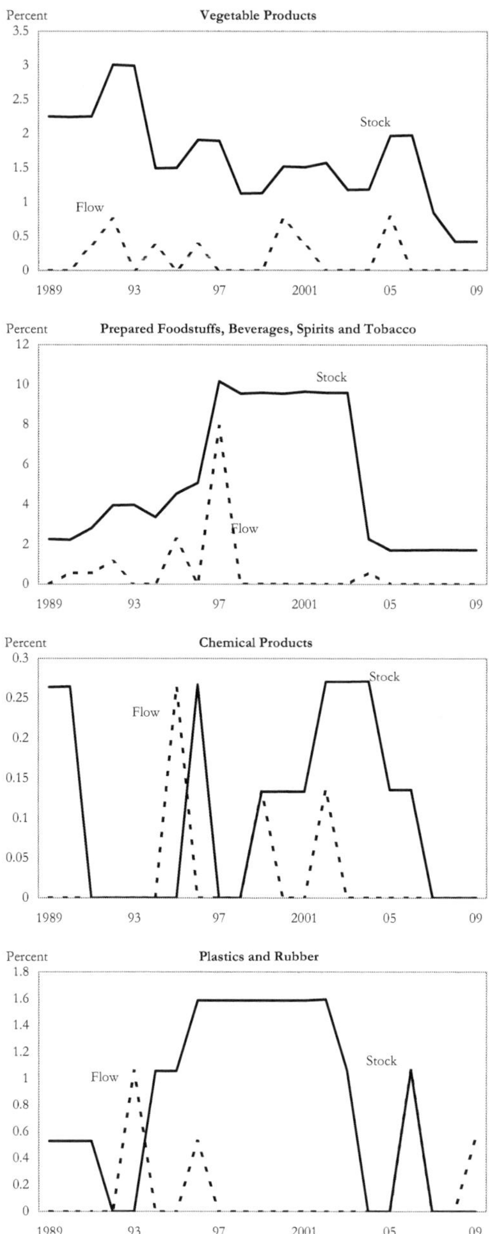

Figure 4.6: *Canada's count measure (stock and flow) by HS section and by year (anti-dumping only).*

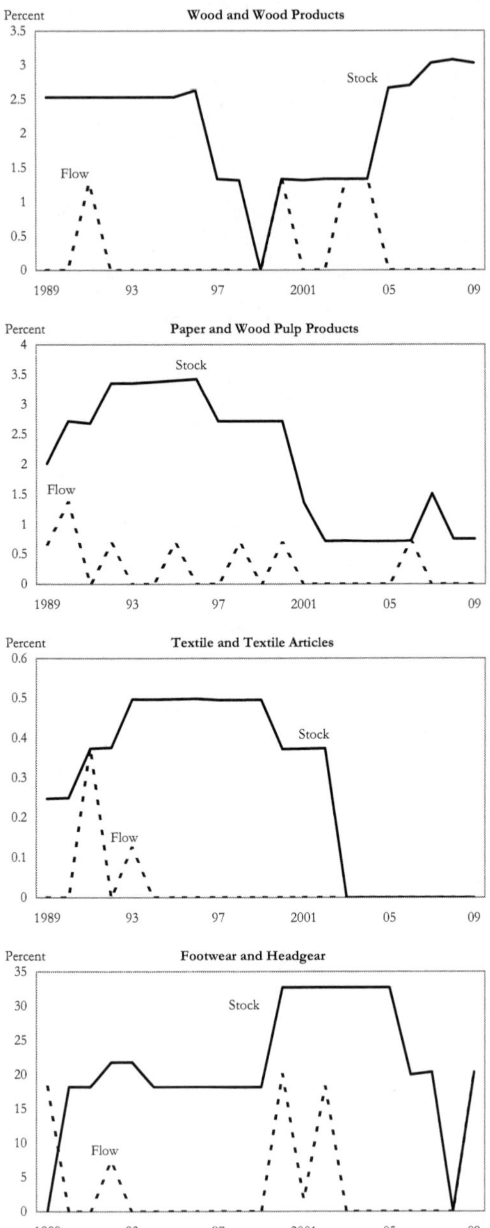

Figure 4.6: *Continued.*

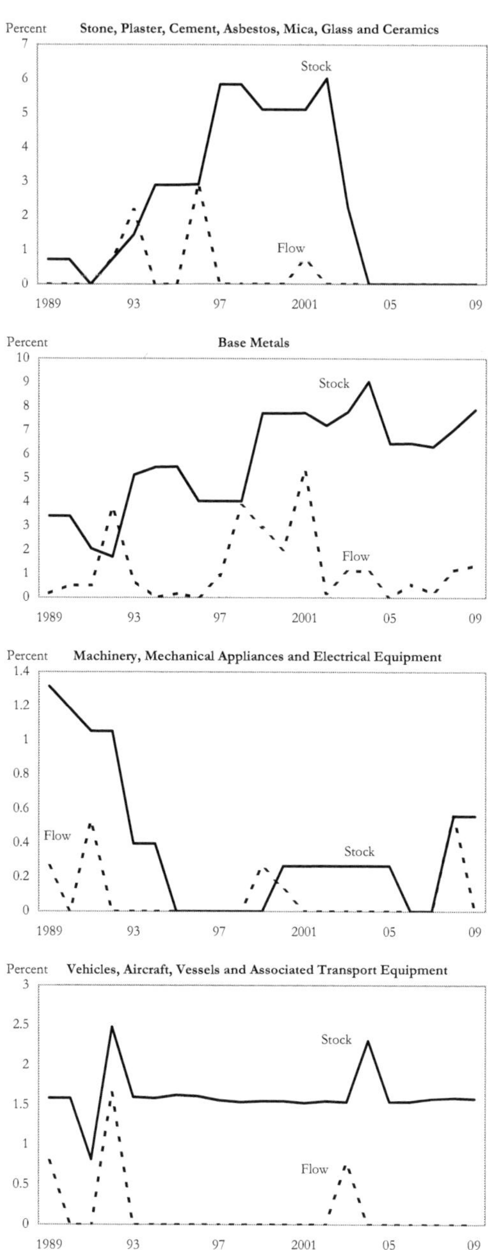

Figure 4.6: *Continued.*

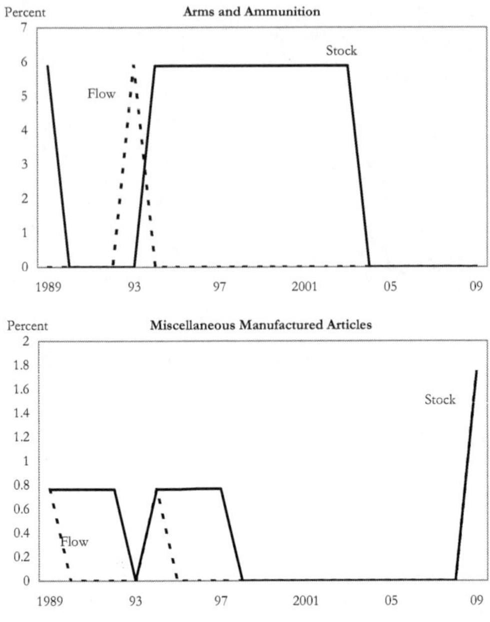

Figure 4.6: *Continued.*

Source: authors' calculations using *Temporary Trade Barriers Database* (Bown 2010) and Comtrade.

2009. The 2008 drop in anti-dumping stock on footwear helps to explain the dip in overall anti-dumping stock that occurred that year.

Steel

The Canadian steel industry is a frequent user of anti-dumping. Figure 4.6 illustrates that in only 3 of the past 20 years has the industry *not* initiated an anti-dumping case. The most active periods of anti-dumping initiation were 1992 and 1998–2001. These time periods correspond to historic low points in world steel prices. Low world steel prices make it easier for the industry to qualify for anti-dumping protection, both because positive dumping margins, based on the gap between average cost and price, and material injury, based on the 'price suppression' argument, become easier to establish. It should also be noted that 2001 saw the initiation of a major steel safeguard case in the USA. While Canadian exports were exempt from the safeguard duties by virtue of the NAFTA, it may be that firms sought to protect themselves from the trade deflection that protection of the US steel industry would cause (see Bown and Crowley (2007) for discussion and evidence on trade deflection). During the 2009 recession, Canadian anti-dumping initiations on steel rose

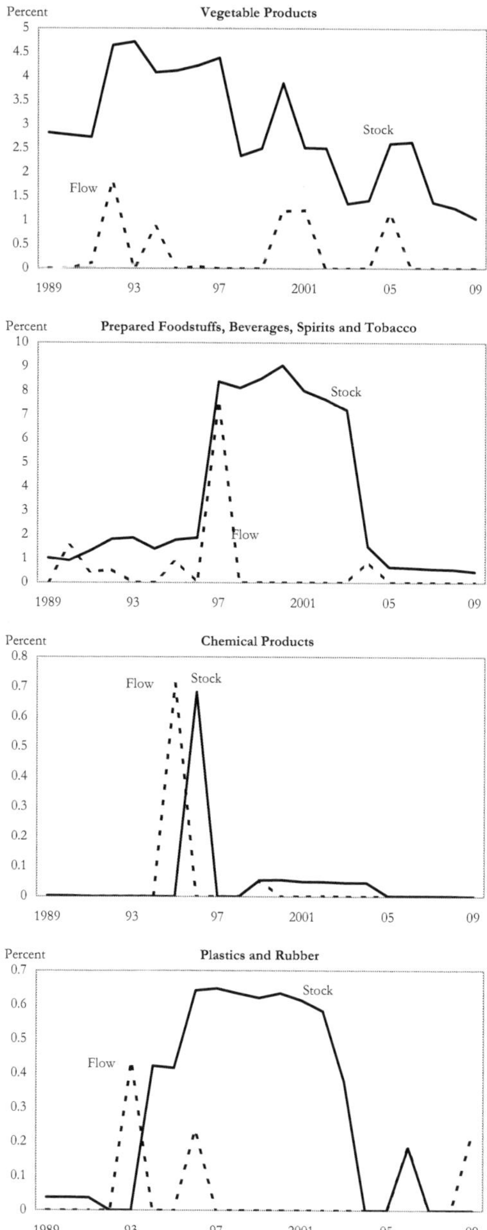

Figure 4.7: *Canada's value measure (stock and flow) by HS section and by year (anti-dumping only).*

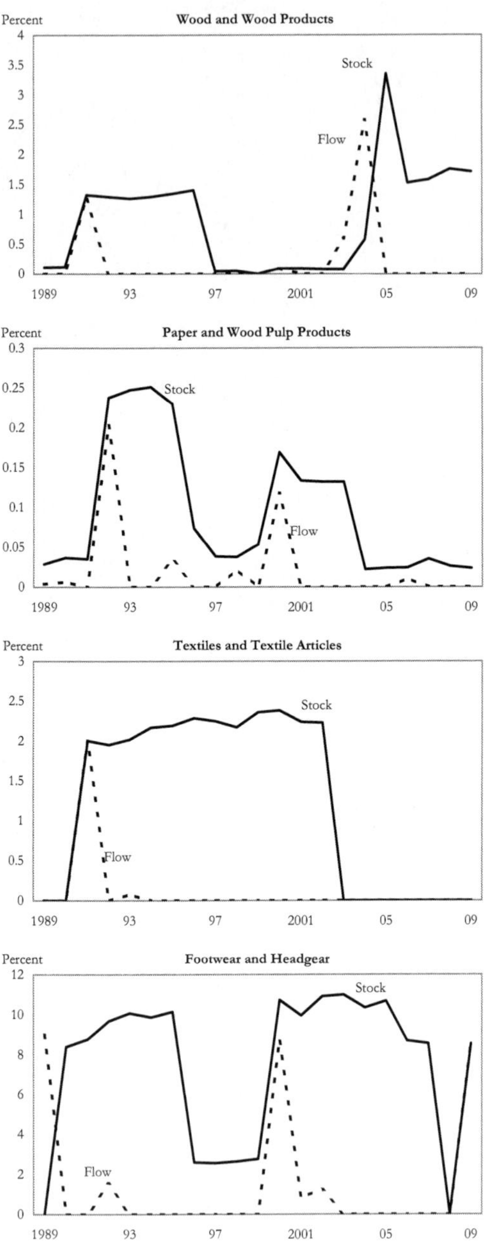

Figure 4.7: *Continued.*

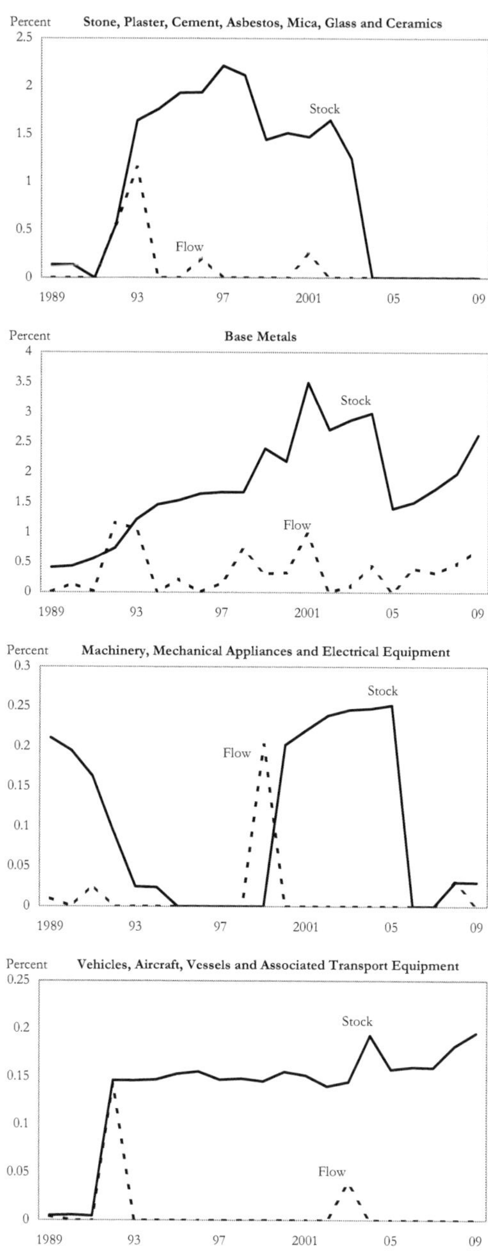

Figure 4.7: *Continued.*

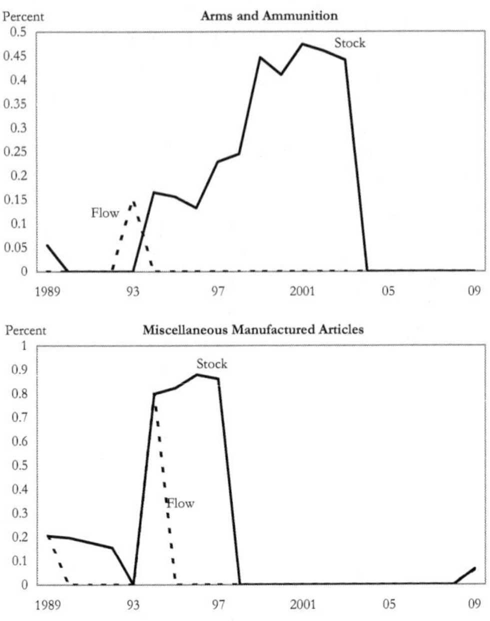

Figure 4.7: *Continued.*

Source: authors' calculations using *Temporary Trade Barriers Database* (Bown 2010) and Comtrade.

again, despite the fact that world steel prices had rebounded strongly from the 2001 lows and did not fall appreciably in the downturn.

The stock of anti-dumping remedies in the steel sector has been mostly rising throughout the sample period. It reached a peak in 2005 according to the count measure, though the 2005 peak was slightly lower than 2001 in value terms. Nevertheless, the overall pattern of anti-dumping remedies in the steel sector runs counter to the pattern observed in the aggregate. Whereas aggregate TTBs dropped off sharply after 2001, steel protection has remained high.

1.3 Uruguay Round Tariff Cuts

The sectoral trends in Canadian anti-dumping must be seen in light of other changes taking place in the structure of Canadian trade policy at the same time. For example, it is worth noting that the rise of anti-dumping stocks in the late 1990s coincides with the implementation of the tariff cuts negotiated in the Uruguay Round.

The connection between tariff cuts and the growth of anti-dumping is theoretically ambiguous. On the one hand, sectors that are politically powerful

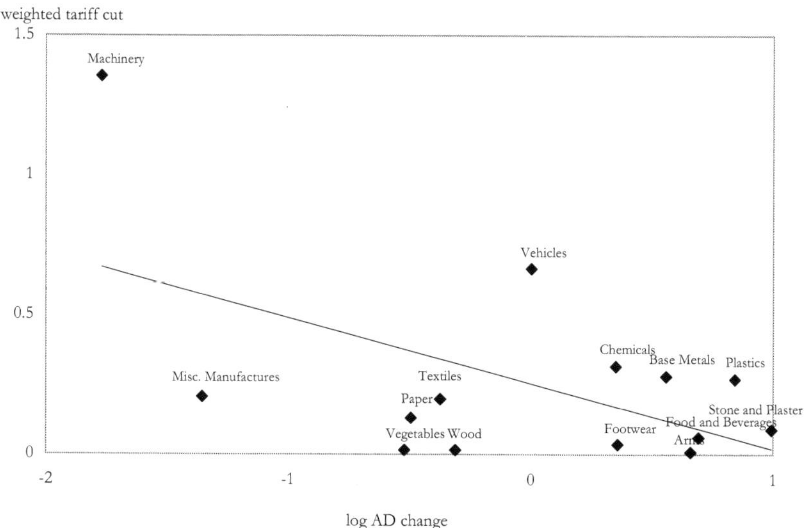

Figure 4.8: *Canada's tariff cuts versus growth in anti-dumping stocks by sector, 1989–2009.*

Source: authors' calculations using *Temporary Trade Barriers Database* (Bown 2010), Comtrade and TRAINS.

to prevent tariff reductions may also be able to expand, or prevent reductions in, anti-dumping protection. This suggests a negative relationship between tariff cuts and anti-dumping growth. On the other hand, it may be that tariff cuts themselves cause producers to seek anti-dumping remedies as a replacement, suggesting a positive relationship between tariff cuts and anti-dumping growth.

Figure 4.8 shows the relationship between Uruguay Round tariff cuts and changes in average annual anti-dumping stocks (in logs) before and after 1995, for each sector with positive anti-dumping activity. The change in stock is measured by count; however, the value measure produces a qualitatively similar picture. The tariff cuts are measured as the trade-weighted average of absolute cuts of MFN applied tariffs between 1993 and 2000, and the trade weights are from 1993. There is a negative correlation of −0.54 between the two measures that is significant at the 5% level. This suggests that while there may be cases in which anti-dumping remedies replace MFN tariffs, the tariff replacement effect is swamped by the ability of certain sectors to sustain both tariff and anti-dumping protection. The machinery sector was liberalised through both tariff cuts and a retreat of anti-dumping stocks. Meanwhile, food and beverages, footwear, arms, stone and plaster were spared significant tariff cuts and were increasingly protected by anti-dumping duties. That the sectors with the greatest anti-dumping growth tend to be those with the

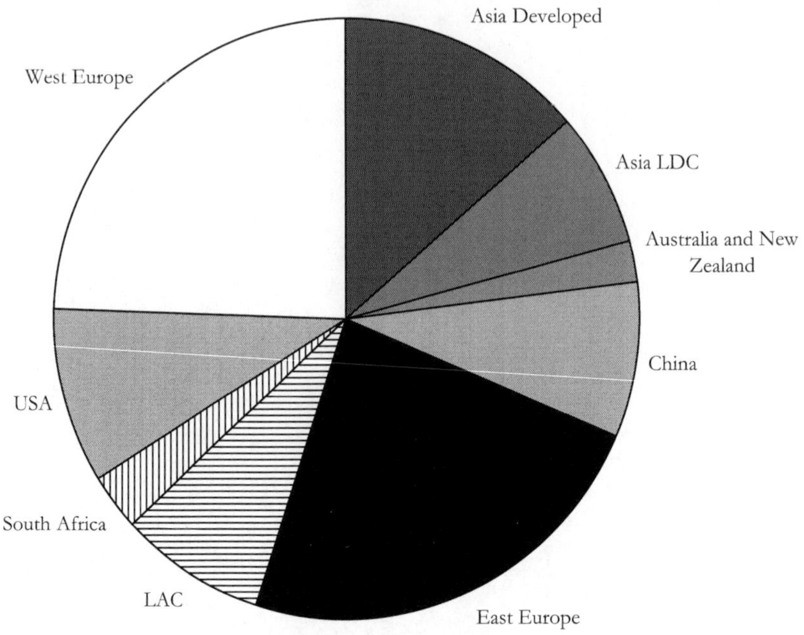

Figure 4.9: *Distribution of Canadian anti-dumping remedies by target exporter for 1989–2009 (percentage of product-target-country-year combinations).*

Source: authors' calculations using *Temporary Trade Barriers Database* (Bown 2010).

smallest Uruguay Round tariff cuts points to a growing divergence in total import protection between protected and liberalising sectors.

1.4 Targets of Canadian TTBs

Which exporting countries have been most targeted by Canadian anti-dumping remedies? Here we measure the distribution of anti-dumping remedies across exporting countries by counting the number of products from each exporting country that are subject to a Canadian anti-dumping remedy in each year. Summing over all years and dividing by the total number of product-year-target-country combinations produces an overall share of Canadian anti-dumping remedies by country. It turns out that the most frequently targeted country is the USA with 10% of the total, followed by China (8%), Brazil (7%), Germany (6%) and Taiwan (5%). Figure 4.9 illustrates the worldwide distribution of targets by grouping countries into regions. Europe and Asia are the most frequently targeted regions. Moreover, anti-dumping protection is roughly evenly distributed between developing and developed regions.

Moving Targets

Figure 4.10 shows the evolution of Canadian anti-dumping targeting by region over time. Here there are several striking patterns. First, anti-dumping stocks against the USA, Western Europe, Australia and New Zealand peaked in the mid-1990s and continued to fall through 2009. Second, anti-dumping protection against all other regions surged in 2001. For most regions, this surge was short-lived and protection returned to levels comparable with the early 1990s. For China and South Africa, however, this reversal did not occur, and for Asian less developed countries the reversal was only partial.[6] Finally, the 2009 surge in anti-dumping stocks was directed entirely at China and less developed countries in Asia.

Figure 4.11 documents more clearly the shift in targeting of anti-dumping protection from developed to developing countries and from west to east. This figure compares the number of product-years of protection across the two decades of the sample for all major target countries (*ie* target countries with more than 100 total product years of protection). Those countries above the 45-degree line are the ones against which anti-dumping protection has increased in frequency, while those below the line experienced a decrease. The vast majority of countries above the line are developing countries (indicated with a black diamond), while only two developing countries are below, though one of those two (Brazil) is virtually unchanged. Looking at the very largest targets, there is a major shift away from the USA and towards China.

Figure 4.12 shows the degree to which Canadian anti-dumping remedies are concentrated across different target exporters. The measure of concentration used is a Herfindahl index: the sum of squared shares of anti-dumping remedies by country. The figure shows that, from 1989 to 2003, Canada became steadily more diversified in its use of anti-dumping remedies, while this trend is sharply reversed from 2003 onwards. Although the total stock of anti-dumping remedies has not dramatically risen during the crisis, this suggests the imposed remedies are targeting an increasingly small group of (developing country) exporters. Combined with our earlier findings of the narrowing of the product scope of anti-dumping initiations and the coincidence between small tariff cuts and large anti-dumping increases across sectors, these findings point to a much more focused trade policy for Canada. Canada has increasingly turned away from protecting its manufacturing sector from imports from the USA and Europe. Instead, it is protecting itself from developing Asia and especially in those sectors where it is losing comparative advantage to China.

---

[6] 'Less developed countries' refers to non-high-income countries according to the World Bank definition.

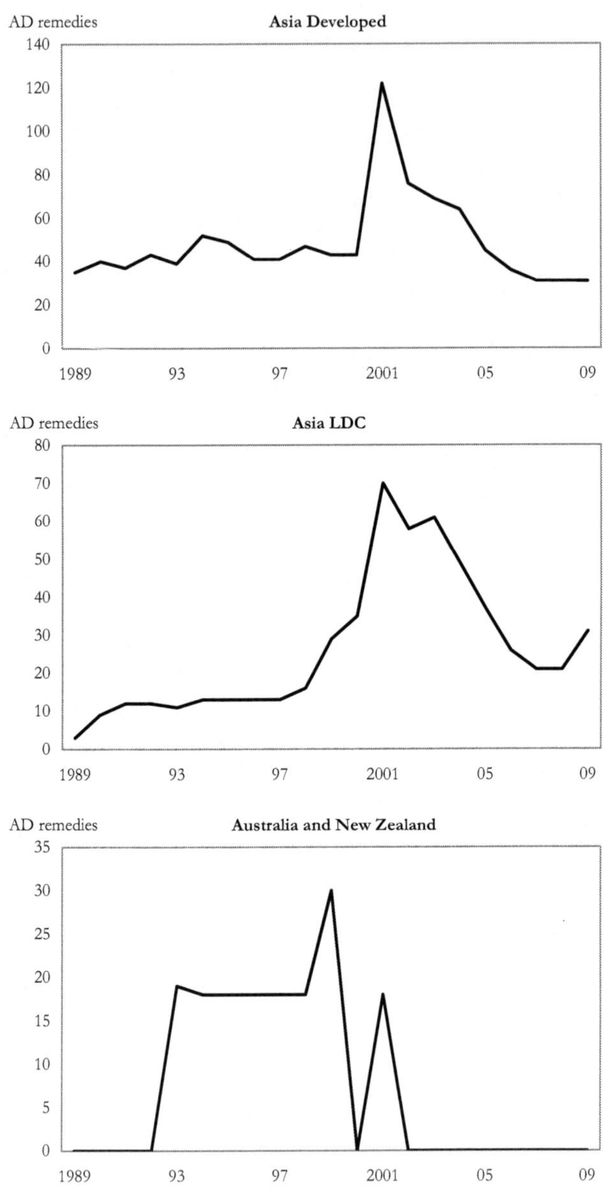

Figure 4.10: *Evolution of Canadian anti-dumping remedies by target exporter for the period 1989–2009 (number of product-target-country combinations).*

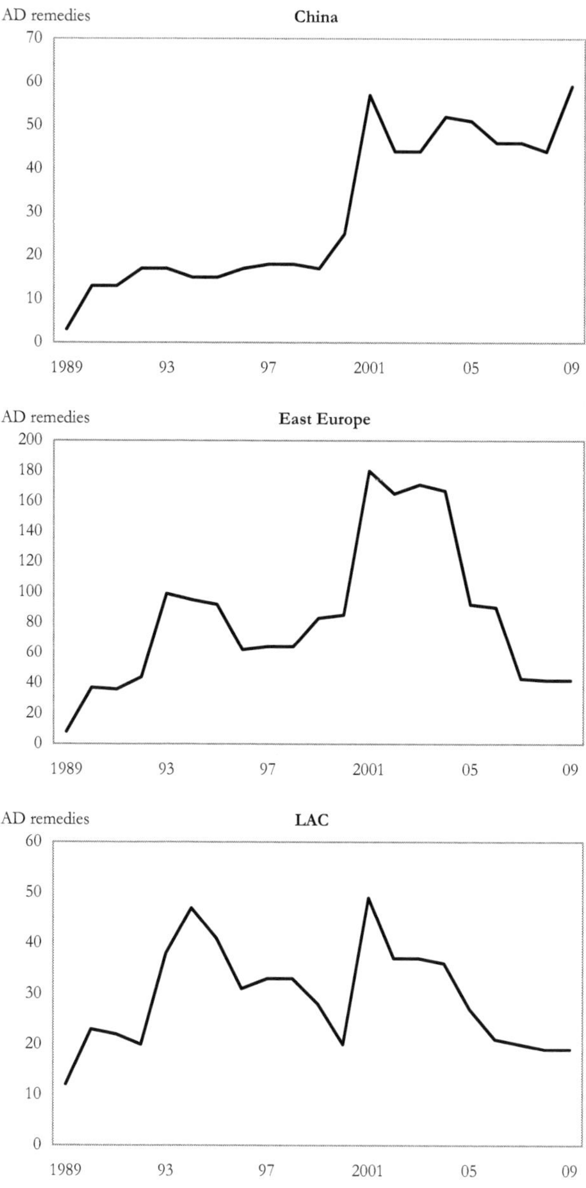

Figure 4.10: *Continued.*

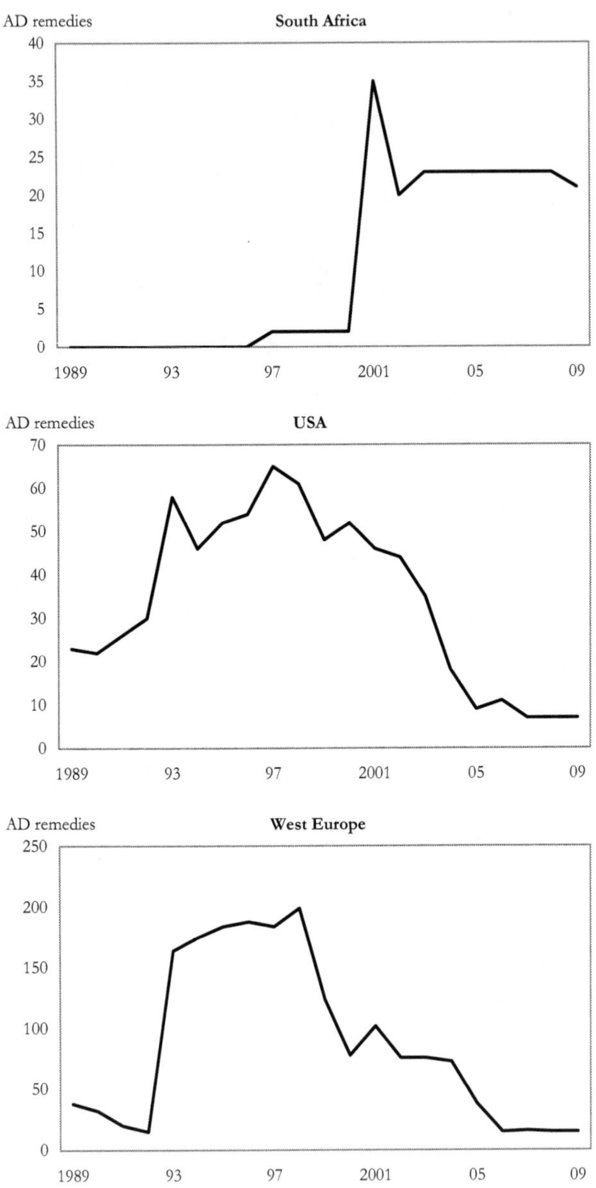

Figure 4.10: *Continued.*

Source: authors' calculations using *Temporary Trade Barriers Database* (Bown 2010).

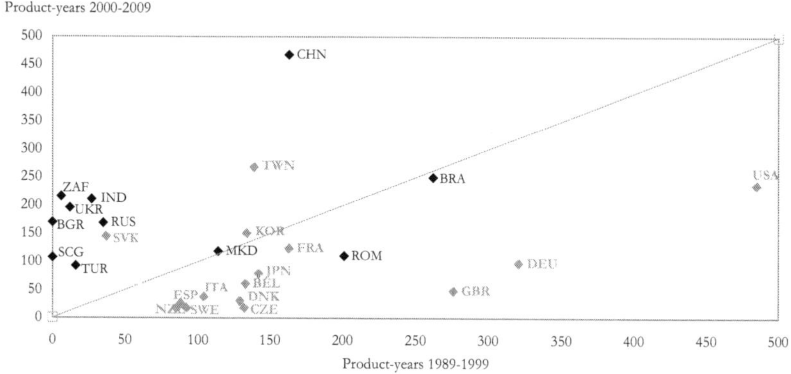

Figure 4.11: *The shift in Canadian targets of anti-dumping remedies.*
Source: authors' calculations using *Temporary Trade Barriers Database* (Bown 2010). Developing countries are shown in black while developed countries are shown in grey.

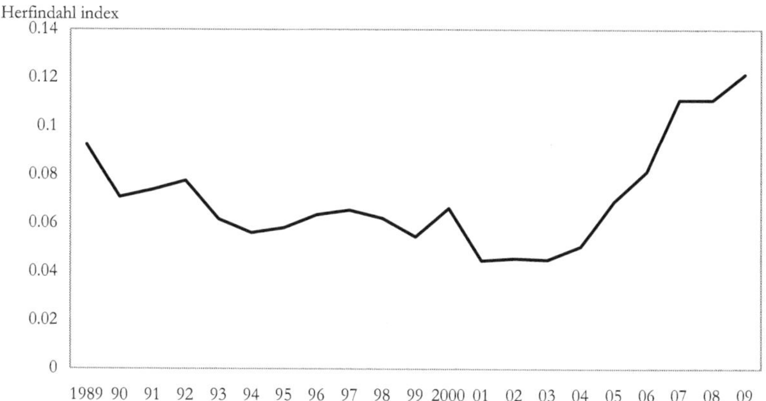

Figure 4.12: *Concentration of Canadian anti-dumping remedies across exporters.*
Source: authors' calculations using *Temporary Trade Barriers Database* (Bown 2010).

The NAFTA Effect

While USA was the biggest target of Canadian anti-dumping remedies, this should come as no surprise considering that USA accounts for the majority of Canadian imports. In 2007, for example, 55% of Canadian imports were from the USA, China was second with 9%, Germany was third with 3%, while Brazil and Taiwan accounted for less than 1% each.[7] Seen in this context, anti-dumping action against USA is in fact disproportionately low.

[7] Statistics Canada.

Bown (2007) argues that this feature of Canadian TTBs serves to reinforce the discrimination inherent in Canada's external trade policy, because of the tariff preferences already granted to the USA and Mexico through NAFTA. Whether this apparent NAFTA bias in Canadian anti-dumping is in fact a result of NAFTA or some other factor is unknown.

There are not sufficient data on Canada's use of anti-dumping towards the USA prior to the Canada–USA trade agreement in 1987, but it is likely that it was never commensurate with USA–Canada trade volumes. One possible explanation for this is the fear of retaliation. Being highly dependent on trade with the USA, Canada may restrain its anti-dumping against the US industries to avoid US retaliatory anti-dumping against Canadian exports. Blonigen and Bown (2003) provide empirical support for this mechanism.

Bhagwati and Panagariya (1996) were among the first to express concern about the selective use of anti-dumping as a means of reinforcing discrimination in free trade agreements (FTAs). Their hypothesis is confirmed by the empirical work of Prusa and Teh (2010). They estimate that anti-dumping provisions in PTAs decrease initiations of anti-dumping cases between partners by 33–55%, while increasing initiations of anti-dumping cases against non-PTA members by 10–30%.

In addition to NAFTA, which took effect in 1994, Canada entered into FTAs with Chile and Israel in 1997, Costa Rica in 2002, and several more countries in 2007–9 (European Free Trade Association (EFTA), Peru, Colombia, Jordan and Panama).

1.5 Duration of Canadian Anti-Dumping Remedies

Anti-dumping remedies generally do not last forever. Although there are extreme cases, such as whole potatoes from the USA, which have faced a 32% anti-dumping duty for the past 25 years, the average duration of Canadian anti-dumping is 7.5 years. The median duration is just under 6 years. These duration figures are measured from the initiation date, which typically precedes the imposition of final duties by several months. Looking at final duties only, the median duration is 5 years. This is consistent with the WTO's mandatory 'sunset' rule, which specifies that final duties should last no more than 5 years, unless an investigation prior to that date establishes that revocation would be likely to lead to continuation or recurrence of dumping and injury. An anti-dumping remedy may also be reviewed before or after the 5-year review at the request of an 'interested party' (*eg* an exporter), though the information an interested party must submit in support of such a review is considerable and costly.

Figure 4.13 shows the duration of anti-dumping remedies for cases initiated during three time periods (1989–1995, 1996–2001 and 2002–9) encompassing the three waves of initiations described in Section 1.1. The figure shows the percentage of cases on which anti-dumping remedies remained in effect after so many months from the date the case was initiated.

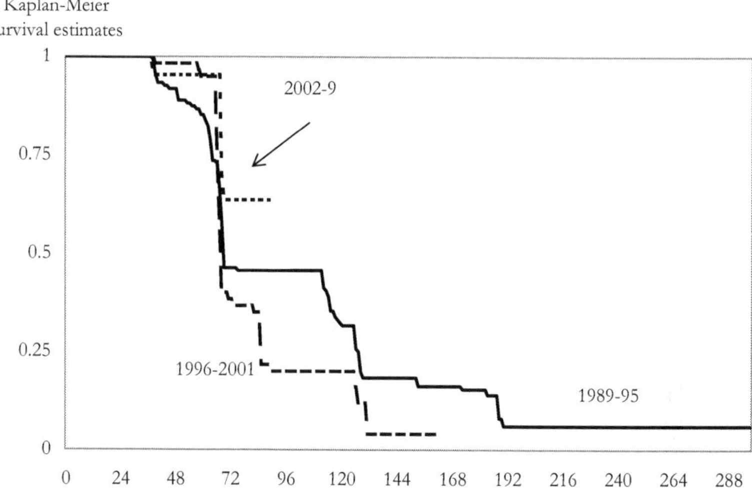

Figure 4.13: *Duration of Canadian anti-dumping remedies in three waves (in months). Source:* authors' calculations using *Temporary Trade Barriers Database* (Bown 2010).

In each of the three periods, there is a clear drop between five and six years. Interestingly, however, the decline is more gradual for cases initiated during 1989–1995. In particular, during this period there were a number of cases being revoked before the mandatory sunset review, whereas in the second and third periods almost all duties survived at least five years. While it is tempting to attribute this to the WTO sunset rule, which went into effect in 1995, Canada had already adopted a five-year sunset rule in 1984. It is possible that this is a spillover effect from the USA, which had no sunset provision prior to 1995. Before 1995, exporters subject to US duties requested reviews idiosyncratically. If these same exporters were also subject to Canadian duties, they may have chosen to synchronise their review requests to economise on legal costs. Alternatively, the gradualism of the 1989–1995 period may just be a function of the products (a wide variety) and countries (predominantly Western-developed countries) that were targeted.

The more striking aspect of Figure 4.13 is that the three periods feature very different survival rates beyond the five-year review. Compared with 1989–1995, initiations during 1996–2001 had fewer cases lasting beyond the review, whereas cases initiated after 2002 had more. The relatively short duration of 1996–2001 cases, combined with the relatively low success rate of cases initiated after 2000, probably accounts for the over-prediction of anti-dumping stocks emerging from our stock model of Section 1.1.

Figure 4.14 shows the duration of anti-dumping remedies from a target-country perspective. There is very little difference in patterns between devel-

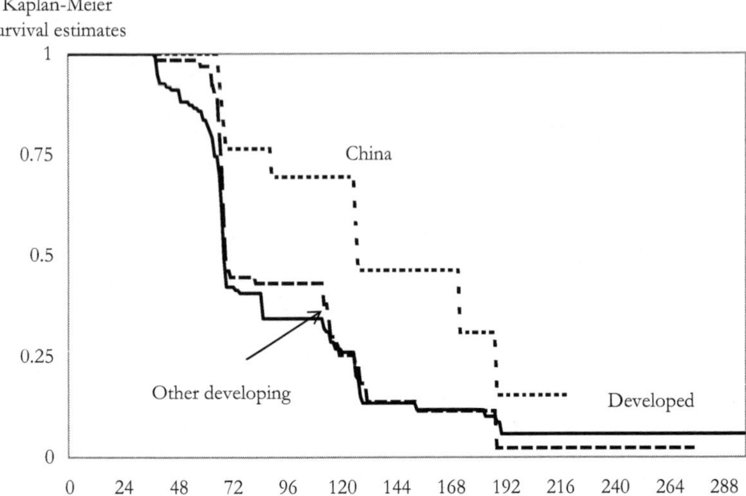

Figure 4.14: *Duration of Canadian anti-dumping remedies by target (in months).*
Source: authors' calculations using *Temporary Trade Barriers Database* (Bown 2010).

oped and other developing countries, other than the tendency for revocation prior to the five-year review for developed countries. Measures imposed on China, on the other hand, displays consistently greater duration. This is not simply the result of China emerging as the prominent target in the 2000s. Anti-dumping remedies against China lasted longer than average in all three waves.[8]

The general picture that emerges from both the target and duration analyses is that Canadian import-competing industries regard China as their number one threat. The Canadian government has responded by implementing more anti-dumping duties against China and keeping them in force for longer.

1.6 Canada in the WTO

Although macroeconomic fluctuations, TTB persistence and shifting comparative advantage go a long way towards explaining the behaviour of Canadian TTBs, the picture would not be complete without factoring in Canada's WTO membership. We have already discussed the effects of the tariff cuts and sunset provision introduced following the Uruguay Round. However, Canada continues to be involved in ongoing multilateral negotiations over anti-dumping rules and has been affected by WTO dispute settlement rulings.

---

[8]It is also not the case that China alone drives the higher duration seen in 2002–9 cases; Figure 4.13 changes very little when China is removed.

The Doha Round negotiations commenced in 2001 with reform of the anti-dumping agreement on the agenda. While calls for reform had long been resisted by the traditional users of anti-dumping, the rapid spread of anti-dumping use by non-traditional users after 1995 led to widespread support for including anti-dumping on the Doha agenda (though the USA remained reluctant). While not a member of the reform-minded 'Friends of Anti-Dumping' group, Canada became actively involved in the negotiations, accounting for nearly a third of the specific reform proposals tendered in 2002 and 2003 (Finger and Zlate 2005).[9] In half of its proposals, Canada has been joined by the Friends of Anti-Dumping group. The most notable recommendations among Canada's proposals are to 'avoid the unwarranted permanence of trade restrictions under the disguise of anti-dumping duties' and to 'take the broader public interest into account' when determining remedies. In 2005, it also proposed extensive revisions to the process of sunset reviews (WTO Negotiating Group on Rules 2005). While it is difficult to prove, it seems plausible that Canadian anti-dumping authorities chose to exercise a degree of self-restraint during the time Canada was making these proposals at the WTO. This may help to explain the high rate of revocations and the low rate of new duties in this period.

Further evidence of Canada's willingness to restrain its behaviour in light of the WTO is found in the 2005 decision by the Canadian Border Services Agency (CBSA) to discontinue the practice of 'zeroing' in the determination of dumping margins.

A dumping margin is defined as the difference between the 'fair' or 'normal' value of a product and the actual price charged by a foreign firm in the domestic market of the complaining industry. If prices vary over time or across different varieties of the product, then the dumping margins may vary as well and, in particular, they may be positive in some cases and negative in others. To establish a single dumping margin for the purposes of applying anti-dumping remedy, it is common practice to take the average of the margins over varieties and time periods. Zeroing is the practice of first converting all of the negative dumping margins to zero before taking the average. Its effect is to inflate the average dumping margin, thus providing higher protection to the complaining industry.

Zeroing is standard practice in the USA, but it has been challenged in several disputes in the WTO. The WTO Appellate Body has ruled that zeroing is contrary to member countries' commitments under the WTO Anti-Dumping Agreement, Article 2.4.2, on the grounds that it fails to take into account 'all comparable export transactions' in the calculation of dumping margins. It is likely that the CBSA discontinued zeroing to avoid being targeted in future

[9]The Friends of Anti-Dumping group consists of Brazil, Chile, Colombia, Costa Rica, Hong Kong, Israel, Japan, Norway, Singapore, South Korea, Switzerland, Taiwan, Thailand and Turkey.

disputes. It is interesting to note that the decision was announced one month after Canada joined the EU in sanctioning the USA over another WTO-illegal practice, known as the 'Byrd Amendment'.

The proximate effect of the CBSA rule change was the termination of an anti-dumping case on laminate flooring from Austria, Belgium, Germany and Poland. In its reasons for termination, the CBSA concluded that margins of dumping for these countries were insignificant. Two other countries, China and France, were ultimately hit with duties, and thus zeroing decision had no direct affect on our count measure of anti-dumping stocks. However, it did affect the value measure, reducing it by about 5% on average from 2005 onwards.

The long-term impact is more difficult to discern. While no further cases since 2005 have been terminated for insignificant dumping margins, the change could have deterred cases with small margins from being initiated. It also may have reduced dumping margins, and thus the anti-dumping duty rates, imposed in most cases.

1.7 Conclusions

Despite the retreat in Canadian TTB stocks in the first decade of the 2000s, there are signs of a rebound. New anti-dumping cases have surged during the 2008–9 crisis, which portends a rise in anti-dumping stocks that could last for several years. There is also evidence of a major structural shift underway in terms of the products and countries upon which Canadian TTBs are applied. The product scope of anti-dumping protection has narrowed, and increases in anti-dumping protection have coincided with relatively small reductions of MFN tariffs. China and, to a lesser extent, other developing countries are being targeted with far greater intensity by 2009 than they were at earlier points in the sample. The duration of Canadian anti-dumping remedies fell during the first half of the 2000s though this seems to have been reversed in the later half of the decade. While Canada has shown some willingness to reign in its anti-dumping policy during the Doha negotiations, whether this is temporary or permanent is difficult to discern. Its intense targeting of China and its lengthening of anti-dumping duty duration since 2002 raises doubts about its permanence.

Rodney D. Ludema is Associate Professor in the Edmund A. Walsh School of Foreign Service and the Department of Economics at Georgetown University.

Anna Maria Mayda is Associate Professor in the Edmund A. Walsh School of Foreign Service and the Department of Economics at Georgetown University, a CEPR Research Affiliate, an external fellow at CReAM and a research fellow at IZA.

REFERENCES

Bhagwati, J., and A. Panagariya (eds) (1996). *The Economics of Preferential Trade Agreements.* Washington, DC: AEI Press.

Blonigen, B. A., and C. P. Bown (2003). Antidumping and retaliation threats. *Journal of International Economics* **60**(2), 249–73.

Bown, C. P. (2011). Introduction. In *The Great Recession and Import Protection: The Role of Temporary Trade Barriers* (ed. C. P. Bown). London: CEPR/World Bank. (Chapter 1 of this volume.)

Bown, C. P. (2010). *Temporary Trade Barriers Database.* World Bank (July). URL: http://econ.worldbank.org/ttbd/.

Bown, C. P. (2007). Canada's antidumping and safeguard policies: overt and subtle forms of discrimination. *The World Economy* **30**(9), 1457–1476.

Bown, C. P., and M. A. Crowley (2007). Trade deflection and trade depression. *Journal of International Economics* **72**(1), 176–201.

Canadian Border Services Agency (2007). *Customs Tariff 2007 (Archive).* URL: http://cbsa-asfc.gc.ca/trade-commerce/tariff-tarif/2007/10-digit-concordance-07-06.pdf.

Canadian Industry Statistics (2010). Industry snapshot—footwear manufacturing: 2004–8. URL: www.ic.gc.ca/eic/site/footwear-chaussure.nsf/eng/fw03143.html.

Finger, J. M., and A. Zlate (2005). Antidumping: prospects for discipline from the Doha negotiations. *Journal of World Investment and Trade* **6**(4), 531–552.

Hallworth, T., and M. Piracha (2006). Macroeconomic fluctuations and anti-dumping filings: evidence from a new generation of protectionist countries. *Journal of World Trade* **40**, 407–423.

Knetter, M. M., and T. J. Prusa (2003). Macroeconomic factors and antidumping filings: evidence from four countries. *Journal of International Economics* **61**, 1–17.

Malhotra, N., and H. A. Rus (2009). The effectiveness of the Canadian antidumping regime. *Canadian Public Policy* **35**(2), 187–202.

Prusa, T. J., and R. Teh (2010). Protection reduction and diversion: PTAs and the incidence of antidumping disputes. NBER Working Paper 16276.

Stevenson, C. (2007). Global Trade Protection Report 2007. Report. URL: www.antidumpingpublishing.com/.

World Development Indicators (2010). World Bank reference data. URL: http://data.worldbank.org/data-catalog/world-development-indicators.

WTO Negotiating Group on Rules (2005). Sunset reviews. Communication from Canada, TN/RL/GEN/61 (15 September).

5

South Korea: Temporary Trade Barriers Before and During the Crisis

MOONSUNG KANG AND SOONCHAN PARK[1]

1 INTRODUCTION

International trade has severely declined alongside the global economic and financial crisis that originated in the USA in 2008. As described by the OECD (2010) and WTO (2010), world merchandise exports fell by 12% in 2009, and world GDP fell by 2.5%. Korea was no exception to this trend, exhibiting a 13.9% reduction in its exports, and a 25.8% reduction in its imports in 2009.[2] The Korean version of the *trade collapse* appears to be based in part on its profound dependence on exports to the markets of the USA and Europe.[3] Having adopted export promotion as part of its industrialisation strategy beginning in the 1960s, Korea has principally exported its commodities to the USA and Europe. Hence, the economic and financial crisis in the USA and Europe significantly reduced the demand for Korean products, thereby negatively affecting Korea's export performance. As shown in Figure 5.1, the real GDP growth rate in the fourth quarter of 2008 plummeted to −4.5%, the largest drop since the Asian financial crisis of 1997–8, as both exports and domestic sales shrank dramatically.

According to the OECD (2010), the *global* trade collapse occurring alongside the global economic and financial crisis can be explained by three main

---

[1]Moonsung Kang: Division of International Studies, Korea University, 5-1 Anam-dong, Sungbuk-gu, Seoul, 136-701, Republic of Korea. Email: mkang@korea.ac.kr. Soonchan Park: Department of International Trade and Commerce, Kongju National University, 182 Shinkwan-Dong, Kongju, Chungnam, Republic of Korea. Email: spark@kongju.ac.kr.

[2]In this chapter, 'Korea' refers to the Republic of Korea (South Korea).

[3]In particular, the US share of Korea's total exports was over 40% during the 1970s and it decreased in the 1990s. In 2009, the shares of USA and Europe were 10.4% and 15.4%, respectively, even though China was the top destination for Korea's exports. Additionally, global and regional production networks in East Asia have been regarded as additional channels of the trade collapse in Korea. For more information, see OECD (2010).

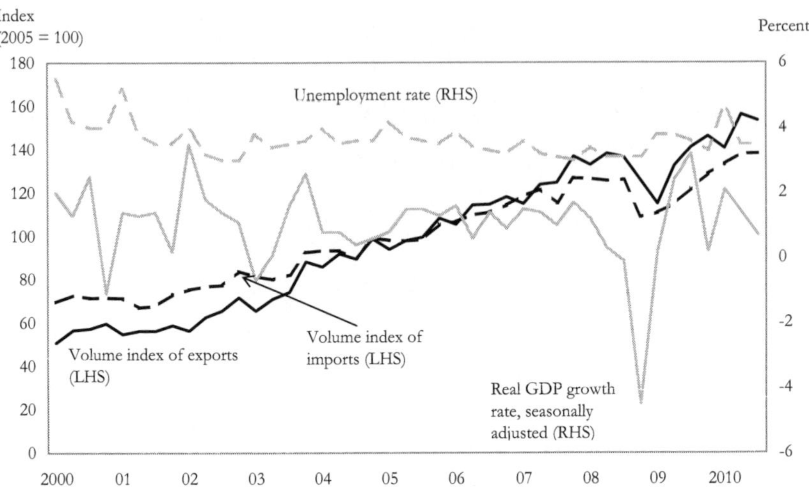

Figure 5.1: *Korea's macroeconomic indicators, 2000–2010 (quarterly).* *Source:* Bank of Korea (2010).

factors: a collapse in demand, the drying up of short-term trade finance, and structural factors associated with the global production network. The OECD also points out that there has been no evidence thus far to suggest that *protectionism* has been a major factor underlying the trade collapse. However, this does not imply that the risk of protectionism is of little concern.

Having established this background, this chapter attempts to elucidate the manner through which the global economic and financial crisis affected economic and political determinants of Korea's TTBs such as anti-dumping, countervailing measures, and safeguards. It also explores a Korea-specific institutional framework for the implementation of TTBs, including their coverage of imports, relevant policies towards regional trade agreement partners, and use of discretionary practices.

The Korea Trade Commission (KTC) is a quasi-judicial agency responsible for trade remedy measures against unfair trade practices, including dumping, illegally subsidised imports and a sudden increase in imports.[4] The KTC's most frequently implemented TTB is anti-dumping measures, as opposed to CVDs or safeguards. As shown in Table 5.1, the KTC has imposed safeguards

[4]Temporary trade barriers or trade remedy measures are used interchangeably in this chapter. Unlike most countries in the world, Korea includes any piracy of intellectual property rights in its trade remedy measures as well. However, this chapter focuses primarily on anti-dumping measures.

Table 5.1: *Korea's anti-dumping and safeguard initiations and outcomes: 1986–2010 (number of cases).*

	Initiations	Preliminary measures	Final measures	No dumping	No injury	Terminated or withdrawn	Missing
			(a) Anti-dumping				
1986	2	0	0	0	0	0	2
1987	0	0	0	0	0	0	0
1988	0	0	0	0	0	0	0
1989	1	0	0	0	0	1	0
1990	5	0	0	3	3	0	0
1991	0	0	2	0	0	0	0
1992	5	6	0	0	0	3	0
1993	6	2	4	0	0	0	0
1994	8	8	3	5	5	0	0
1995	1	4	0	4	4	1	0
1996	12	9	9	0	0	0	0
1997	15	6	4	1	1	5	0
1998	3	5	8	0	0	0	0
1999	7	1	2	0	0	3	0
2000	2	4	3	1	1	1	0
2001	4	1	0	0	0	5	0
2002	10	1	1	1	1	0	0
2003	18	3	4	1	1	4	0
2004	3	14	10	0	0	8	0
2005	4	2	3	0	0	0	0
2006	7	7	8	0	0	0	0
2007	15	5	0	0	3	3	0
2008	5	2	12	0	0	0	0
2009	0	0	4	2	2	0	0
2010	3	1	1	0	1	0	1
Total	136	81	78	16	21	34	3

relatively less frequently and has *never* imposed CVDs. As the number of countervailing measures and safeguards is negligible in terms of Korea's TTB experience, this chapter limits the scope of its analysis and discussion to anti-dumping.

2 KOREA'S UNILATERAL TRADE LIBERALISATION AND ANTI-DUMPING INSTITUTIONS

2.1 Industrialisation Strategy and Unilateral Trade Liberalisation in Korea

Historically, Korea has used active industrial policy to develop its own strategic industries, and its trade policy was designed to fulfill this objective.

Table 5.1: *Continued.*

	Initiations	Final measures	No injury	Terminated or withdrawn
(b) Safeguards				
1986	0	0	0	0
1987	0	0	0	0
1988	0	0	0	0
1989	0	0	0	0
1990	0	0	0	0
1991	0	0	0	0
1992	0	0	0	0
1993	0	0	0	0
1994	0	0	0	0
1995	1	0	0	0
1996	2	0	0	1
1997	0	1	0	1
1998	0	0	0	0
1999	1	0	0	0
2000	0	1	0	0
2001	0	0	0	0
2002	0	0	0	0
2003	0	0	0	0
2004	0	0	0	0
2005	0	0	0	0
2006	0	0	0	0
2007	0	0	0	0
2008	0	0	0	0
2009	0	0	0	0
2010	0	0	0	0
Total	4	2	0	2

The *Temporary Trade Barriers Database* (Bown 2010) identified 144 cases, but we excluded 3 cases for having neither information nor documentation from the KTC, and 5 cases for having no information on the date of investigation. Information on preliminary and final decisions for some of the anti-dumping initiations in 2010 is still not available.

Source: authors' calculations using *Temporary Trade Barriers Database* (Bown 2010) and KTC (2010).

Since the 1960s, Korea has transformed from an agrarian economy with very low productivity into one of the world's most rapidly growing industrialised economies.[5] While earning more foreign currency was crucial to foreign pay-

[5]During the period between the liberation from the Japanese colonial regime in 1910–45 and the end of the Korean War in 1953, the Korean economy, one of the poorest in the world, experienced extreme devastation, severe dislocation and poverty. Additionally, the Korean War destroyed roughly 42–44% of the production facilities in South Korea, but the Korean population has rapidly expanded since the Korean War. For more information, see Amsden (1989, pp 27–54).

ments in the 1960s, owing to a gradual decrease in US aid, the size and purchasing power of Korea's domestic market proved insufficient for sustainable growth.[6] In 1962, in the middle of the first Five-Year Economic Development Plan in 1962–66, the Park Administration abandoned its import substitution strategy and shifted its policy focus to an export-orientated growth strategy, even though some features of its import substitution strategy, *ie* setting high trade barriers in order to protect domestic producers, had been in force for a very long time. Korea's export promotion strategy was designed to use its comparative advantage in labour-intensive manufactured goods for exports such as textiles, apparel, clothing and footwear.

Korea initiated a variety of incentive programs for export promotion in the mid-1960s, which it maintained until the early 1980s. Among these programs were three key policies for export promotion: automatic export financing and tax breaks, tariff deductions on inputs for export manufacturing, and targeting the exchange rate at a stable level.[7]

In the 1970s, the Korean economy climbed the economic development ladder by promoting the chemical and heavy industries. After announcing the Heavy and Chemicals Industry (HCI) Development Plan, the Korean government designated specific industries and companies that would receive government financial support, and it directed commercial banks to financially support selected companies. During the early period of the HCI, there was a great deal of strong criticism from economists and the public, who believed that the development of the HCI would prove too difficult and too expensive. However, the Korean government strongly pushed its strategy and based it on security issues, the Japanese experience and theories of development, protectionism in developed countries, and current account deficits.[8]

---

[6]The annual flow of US aid accumulated to $2,537 million during 1945–61 before decreasing to $132 million in 1965.

[7]In automatic export financing and tax breaks, the government automatically granted bank loans at a very low interest rate when exporters submitted their export letter of credit. The preferential interest rate for exporters was roughly 20%, which is much lower than the market interest rate of the 1960s. The total amount of the interest support increased dramatically and reached a level of 139.5 billion Korean won ($288.2 million) in 1978. The Korean government deducted tariffs on raw material imports for export promotion and exempted tariffs on capital equipment for export production. The tariff deduction continued to be applied to most products of heavy industries throughout the 1970s, with the deducted amount recorded at over 20% of the tariff revenue. The exchange-rate system was also changed from the multiple-rate system to the unitary floating exchange-rate system. As discussed above, it was designed to ameliorate the complexity and uncertainty of the multiple-rate system and to enhance policy credibility in international financial markets.

[8]First, security issues were the most prominent reason for the sudden shift in Korea's industrial strategy. In 1969, US President Richard Nixon formulated the Nixon Doctrine, also known as the Guam Doctrine, stating that the USA henceforth expected its allies to take care of their own military defence, but that the USA would aid in defence as requested. In line with this doctrine but facing the militant army of North Korea, the US government

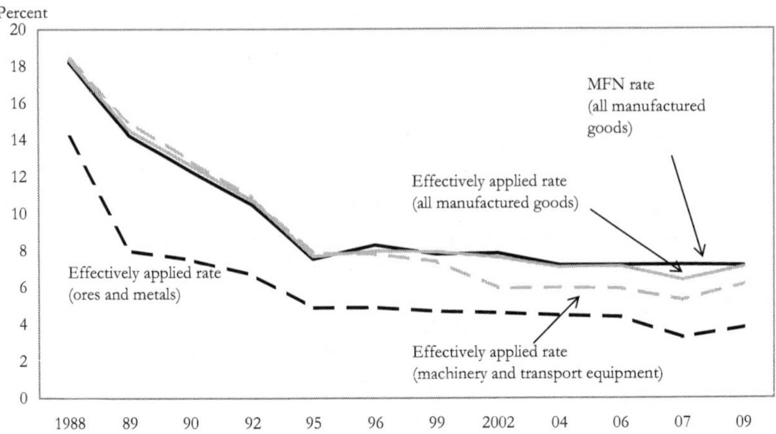

Figure 5.2: *Korea's simple average tariff rates: manufactured goods.*
Source: UNCTAD. All manufactured goods include 5, 6, 7, 8, 27 and 28 of Standard International Trade Classification (revision 3).

The Korean government began to liberalise its economy in the 1980s by adopting a more market-orientated system. In particular, Korea gradually opened its domestic markets to selective agricultural products, expecting that liberalisation would enhance the global competitiveness and economic efficiency of its domestic firms. As a component of its liberalisation policy, the Korean government altered its export support system from direct export subsidisation to indirect export incentive programs. While the export support system was predicated mainly on policy loan and tax benefit programs established in the 1970s, the Korean government designed a more advanced export support system that relied on duty drawbacks and export insurance.

---

attempted to reduce its troops in South Korea by 30%. Korea's sudden shift to HCI development from light manufacturing was motivated by the urgent need to improve national defence capabilities and to build up Korea's own defence industry. Second, the Korean government was motivated by the successful Japanese development experience. As such, the Korean government shifted its development strategy and upgraded its industrial structure ahead of newly emerging competitors such as Taiwan, Singapore and Hong Kong. Third, some developed economies—such as the USA and Europe, where the textile and apparel industries were politically sensitive—raised their trade barriers in the 1970s, specifically targeting labour-intensive goods from developing countries. The Korean government had a vital need to identify new export industries. Finally, in the 1960s, textile machinery was one of the top goods imported by Korea, because the textile industry was a key export industry but Korea's own machinery industry was not advanced. The Korean economy sought to develop its machinery industry in order to help solve its continued current account deficits.

After the formal launch of the WTO in 1995, *open and fair competition* became a new directional watchword in the formulation of Korea's industrial and trade policies. The Korean government felt new pressure to comply with the WTO rules and disciplines and to commit to liberalising the Korean trading regime. Korea has continued to aggressively reduce tariff rates since its accession to the multilateral trading system and the Uruguay Round.[9] As shown in Figure 5.2, the MFN and applied tariff rates were over 18% in 1988, but they were reduced to less than 8% by 2009. Nevertheless, Korea also suffers from tariff escalation, the phenomenon by which tariffs rise with increasing transformation of a product (*eg* in the production stages of basic metal products and non-metallic mineral products). However, Korea had phased out government intervention programs that sought to achieve the intended industrial structure, and export subsidies became prohibited under the WTO's Agreement on Subsidies and Countervailing Measures. Additionally, and so as to comply with WTO disciplines on anti-dumping measures, the Korean government established a more systemic institutional framework to impose anti-dumping duties.

2.2 Institutional Perspectives of Anti-Dumping Measures in Korea

The KTC is responsible for the implementation and administration of trade remedy measures. The KTC was founded in July 1987, in accordance with the Article of the Foreign Trade Act, which was enacted in December 1986. Initially, the KTC played an advisory role in reviewing and clarifying the impacts of imports on domestic industry, while the Ministry of Finance and Economy took care of anti-dumping initiations, conducted investigations, and made preliminary and final decisions. However, in December 1989, along with the revision of the Foreign Trade Act, the KTC changed its institutional identity into a consultative administration organisation. Its functions expanded so that it was put in charge of determining whether to initiate investigations, making determinations of 'injury' to domestic industries, and instituting anti-dumping measures. This responsibility was formally transferred from the Ministry of Finance to the KTC under the Ministry of Commerce and Industry (currently the Ministry of Knowledge Economy) in December 1993. Since the inception of the WTO, the laws and regulations related to the KTC and trade remedy measures had been revised to comply with WTO disciplines.

Temporary trade barriers have been a critical component of Korea's trade policy since the late 1980s. Not only was Korea a primary target of such a policy tool by its major trading partners in the 1980s and 1990s, but Korea has become increasingly active in imposing anti-dumping measures itself.

[9] Korea signed the GATT in 1967, incorporating its economy into the multilateral trading system.

Table 5.2: *Korea's Anti-dumping investigations and outcomes (number of cases).*

		Affirmative				Negative				
	Initiation	AVD	PU	AVD/PU	Subtotal	N	W	T	Subtotal	Other
1986	2	0	0	0	0	0	0	0	0	2
1987	0	0	0	0	0	0	0	0	0	0
1988	0	0	0	0	0	0	0	0	0	0
1989	1	0	0	0	0	0	1	0	1	0
1990	5	0	0	0	0	3	0	0	3	0
1991	0	2	0	0	2	0	0	0	0	0
1992	5	0	0	0	0	0	3	0	3	0
1993	6	4	0	0	4	0	0	0	0	0
1994	8	3	0	0	3	5	0	0	5	0
1995	1	0	0	0	0	4	1	0	5	0
1996	12	9	0	0	9	0	0	0	0	0
1997	15	4	0	0	4	1	2	3	6	0
1998	3	8	0	0	8	0	0	0	0	0
1999	7	0	2	0	2	0	3	0	3	0
2000	2	2	1	0	3	1	0	1	2	0
2001	4	0	0	0	0	0	3	2	5	0
2002	10	1	0	0	1	1	0	0	1	0
2003	18	3	0	1	4	1	0	4	5	0
2004	3	9	1	0	10	0	7	1	8	0
2005	4	2	0	1	3	0	0	0	0	0
2006	7	8	0	0	8	0	0	0	0	0
2007	15	0	0	0	0	3	3	0	6	0
2008	5	11	0	1	12	0	0	0	0	0
2009	0	4	0	0	4	2	0	0	2	0
2010	3	1	0	0	1	1	0	0	1	0
Total	136	71	4	3	78	22	23	11	56	2

'AVD' stands for *ad valorem* duty; 'PU' stands for price undertaking; 'N' stands for negative; 'W' stands for withdrawn; 'T' stands for terminated.

Source: authors' calculations using *Temporary Trade Barriers Database* (Bown 2010) and KTC (2010).

3 DEVELOPMENTS IN KOREA'S TEMPORARY TRADE BARRIERS

3.1 Flow and Stock of TTBs

Table 5.2 documents annual data on Korea's new anti-dumping cases between 1986 and 2010 by providing detailed information on their outcomes.[10] The *Temporary Trade Barriers Database* of Bown (2010) identified 139 anti-dumping cases, but we excluded 3 cases from our analysis that were missing information from the KTC. Therefore, this chapter explores these 136 cases to analyse Korea's use of TTBs. Korea's first anti-dumping investigation was carried out in 1986, and it only imposed its first anti-dumping duties in

[10]We updated the TTB database of Bown (2010) using information from the KTC and the Ministry of Strategy and Finance.

1991, targeting polyoxymethylene from Japan and the USA. Table 5.2 illustrates that Korea's anti-dumping initiations and final measures have been *counter-cyclical*; they increased dramatically during the Asian financial crisis of 1997–8 and immediately after the recession of 2000–2001. During the global economic crisis, there were only 5 new initiations in 2008 and none in 2009, but the KTC rendered an affirmative decision in 12 cases in 2008 that had been initiated earlier.[11]

Korea initiated 136 investigations during 1986–2009; 78 (57.4%) resulted in the imposition of new definitive trade barriers and 56 (41.2%) were withdrawn, terminated, or resulted in a negative determination.[12] Korea's 78 imposed anti-dumping measures consisted of 71 (91.0%) *ad valorem* duties, 4 (5.1%) price undertakings, and 3 (3.8%) *ad valorem*/price undertaking duties. The remaining cases did not result in final measures; 23 (41.1%) of these were withdrawn prior to rulings by the petitioning industry, 22 (39.3%) were negative in terms of anti-dumping practices or injury to domestic producers and 11 (19.6%) were terminated.

One implication of Table 5.2 is that Korea's anti-dumping initiations and final decisions have been counter-cyclical in nature. However, during the 2008–9 financial crisis, despite there being a relatively small number of initiations, the KTC actively engaged in other important anti-dumping-related activities. For example, Korea had 11 reviews of previously imposed anti-dumping measures come up in 2009. The KTC decided to continue imposing its anti-dumping duties in 9 of these 11 cases (81.8%) and price undertaking in 2 cases (18.2%) during the crisis, even though 5 previously imposed Korean anti-dumping measures were expired without review in this period.

Next we adopt the approach developed in Chapter 1 and Bown (2011b) to analyse the *stock* of imports subject to anti-dumping duties in Korea rather than the *flow* of imports. We measure *counts* of HS-06 products subject to anti-dumping duties between 1991 and 2009. As shown in Figure 5.3, the share of imported products subject to anti-dumping duties in Korea has increased moderately over time. In 1991, only one HS-06 product (polyoxymethylene) was subject to anti-dumping duties. However, during the 1997–8 Asian financial crisis, the count of HS-06 products subject to anti-dumping duties rose to 24 (by 1998), representing 0.51% of all tariff lines. Although Table 5.2 indicates a relatively small number of initiations during 1998–2001, Figure 5.3 shows how the share of HS-06 products subject to anti-dumping duties remained

[11] This may be attributable to the Declaration of Summit on Financial Markets and the World Economy in the G20 summit meeting in Washington DC on 15 November 2008 (G20 2008). According to this declaration, the leaders of the G20 countries agreed to 'refrain from raising new barriers...to trade in goods and services' (paragraph 13). In Korea, it was known that President Lee Myung-Bak proposed this idea during the summit meeting. Hence, domestic producers in Korea would be reluctant to petition against dumping practices.

[12] The two remaining cases have no information on their outcomes.

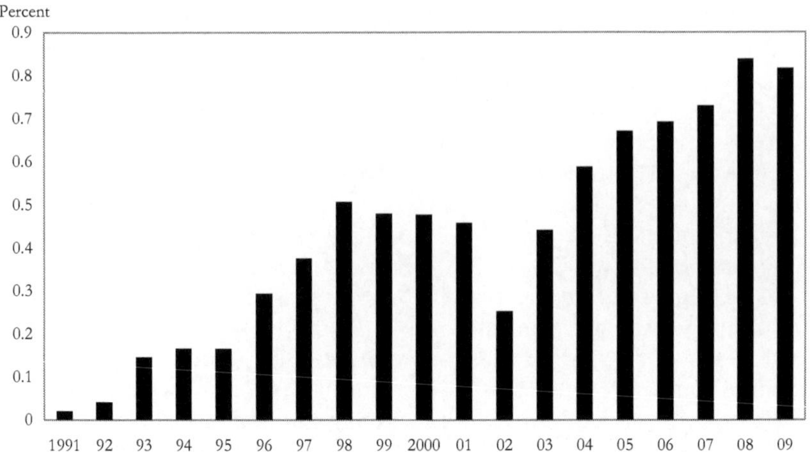

Figure 5.3: *Korea's use of anti-dumping measures: share of imported products, based on counts of HS-06 products subject to anti-dumping measures.*

Source: authors' calculations using *Temporary Trade Barriers Database* (Bown 2010).

constant at around 0.5%. Korea's anti-dumping duties imposed during the Asian financial crisis thus persisted for 3 or 4 years.[13] During the 2008–9 crisis, the count of HS-06 products subject to anti-dumping duties jumped to 38 in 2008 and 37 in 2009—more than double the average of 18.2 during the 1991–2007 period. Korea's share of anti-dumping-affected products in its total tariff lines rose to over 0.8% during the 2008–9 financial crisis.

Figure 5.4 shows the share of import products, based on values of HS-06 products subject to anti-dumping measures, including counterfactual imports calculated using the method described by Equation (1.2) of Chapter 1. The share increased moderately between 1992–2004, but it increased sharply beginning in 2005 and reached a peak of 0.37% in 2008. The sudden increase since 2005 could be explained by a cumulative effect of the stock of anti-dumping measures. As the number of products subject to anti-dumping measures continues to increase, the import values subject to anti-dumping measures continues to accumulate, causing their share to increase.

3.2 Tariffs and TTBs

Figure 5.2 illustrates how Korea has continued to aggressively reduce its tariff rates since its accession to the multilateral trading system and as a result of the Uruguay Round. Since 1999, Korea's average MFN and applied tariff rates have fallen to and remained lower than 8%. However, Figures 5.3 and 5.4 show that Korea's use of anti-dumping increased rapidly in the 2000s. Considering

[13] The duration of TTBs is discussed in Section 3.3.

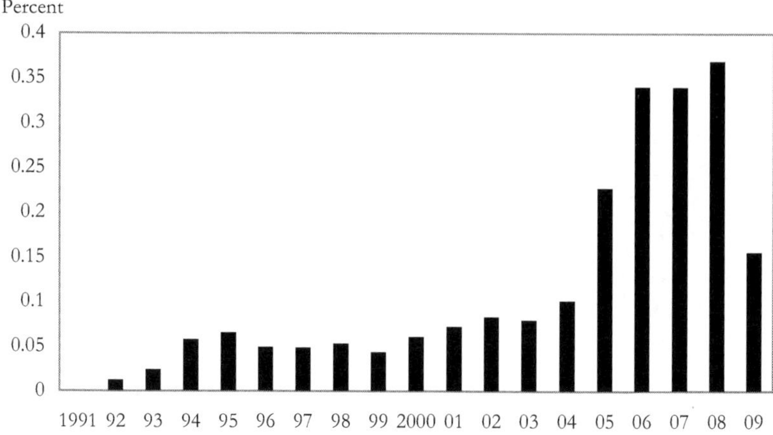

Figure 5.4: *Korea's use of anti-dumping measures: share of value of imports subject to anti-dumping measures.*

Source: authors' calculations using Bown (2011b, Equation (1.2)) and *Temporary Trade Barriers Database* (Bown 2010).

these figures together suggests that Korea's anti-dumping measures could be a substitute for tariff protection.

We begin to address this issue by using Figure 5.5 to compare tariff rates for anti-dumping-protected products with products not affected by anti-dumping. The simple and weighted tariff rates for non-anti-dumping products are higher than those for products protected by anti-dumping measures, *ie* domestic producers are more likely to file anti-dumping petitions over products receiving low tariff rates. This interpretation suggests that anti-dumping measures are likely to be a substitute for tariff protection in Korea.

Motivated by Bown and Tovar (2011), we next analyse the relationship between Korea's anti-dumping measures and 'tariff overhang', defined as the bound tariff level minus the applied tariff level. We consider only products that are subject to final anti-dumping measures and we focus on the 2002–9 period, since data on applied tariffs at the HS-08 level of disaggregation are only available from 2002 onwards. Since anti-dumping margins are generally reported as a range, Table 5.3 compares the tariff overhang with both the lowest and the highest anti-dumping margins. The lowest anti-dumping margins are greater than the tariff overhang in 98.5% (133 out of 135) of observations, and the highest anti-dumping margins are greater in 100% of observations. Table 5.3 also breaks down the period into two subperiods—2002–5 and 2006–9—and demonstrates no change in the trend; for almost all observations, Korea's anti-dumping margins are greater than the tariff overhang.

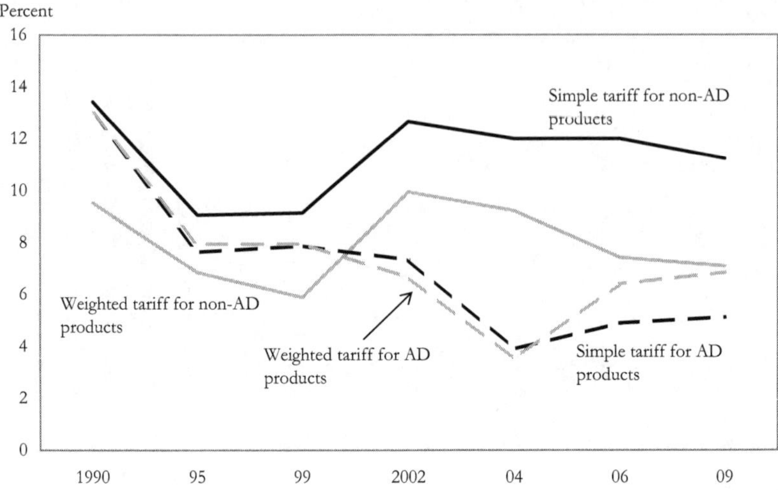

Figure 5.5: *Korea's tariffs for anti-dumping-protected and non-anti-dumping HS-06 products.*

Source: authors' calculations using WITS and *Temporary Trade Barriers Database* (Bown 2010).

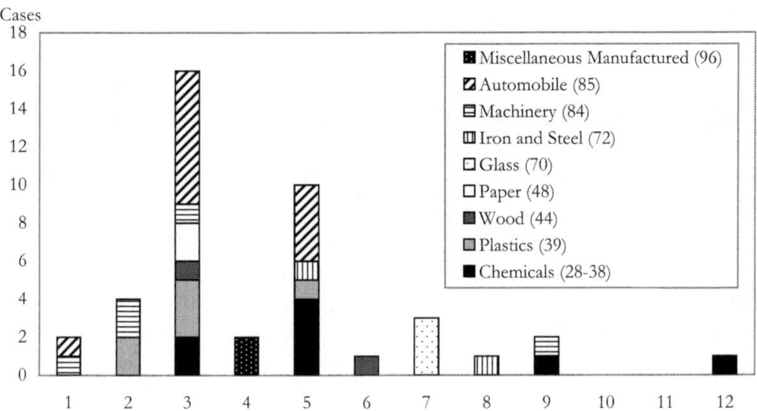

Figure 5.6: *Duration of anti-dumping duties in Korea (in years).*

Source: authors' calculations using *Temporary Trade Barriers Database* (Bown 2010).

3.3 Duration of TTBs

In this subsection, we explore the duration of Korea's anti-dumping duties. We ignore those products *currently subject to anti-dumping duties* and those with

Table 5.3: *Korea's anti-dumping measures and WTO tariff bindings: 2002–9.*

	2002–9		2002–5		2006–9	
	Lowest firm-specific anti-dumping margin	Highest firm-specific anti-dumping margin	Lowest firm-specific anti-dumping margin	Highest firm-specific anti-dumping margin	Lowest firm-specific anti-dumping margin	Highest firm-specific anti-dumping margin
Total number of HS-06 product observations	135	135	87	87	48	48
Number of observations with anti-dumping margin greater than tariff overhang (share)	133 (98.5)	135 (100.0)	87 (100.0)	87 (100.0)	46 (95.8)	48 (100.0)
Number of observations with anti-dumping margin less than tariff overhang (share)	2 (1.5)	0 (0.0)	0 (0.0)	0 (0.0)	2 (4.1)	0 (0.0)

Source: authors' calculations using *Temporary Trade Barriers Database* (Bown 2010).

missing information. Figure 5.6 shows the 42 cases during the sample in which anti-dumping measures were imposed and later revoked. Korea revoked 81.0% of its anti-dumping measures within 5 years, but 8 cases have been subject to anti-dumping duties for more than 5 years. The most frequent duration was 3 years (16 cases) followed by 5 years (10 cases), 2 years (4 cases), and 7 years (3 cases). The 8 cases that lasted more than 5 years include glass, chemicals, paper, iron and steel, and machinery. The glass industry had only 3 cases, but in each instance the anti-dumping duties persisted longer than 5 years.

As pointed out in the previous section, the KTC reviewed 11 anti-dumping cases in 2009. The KTC continued imposing its anti-dumping duties on 72.7% of the cases and price undertaking on 27.3%. None were terminated in the review process during the financial crisis of 2008–9, even though five measures were expired without review.

3.4 Sectoral Imposition of TTBs

Table 5.4 documents the industries that the Korean authorities targeted with anti-dumping during 1989–2009, using data on cases subject to anti-dumping initiations as reported by Bown (2011b).[14] Chemicals was the dominant focus

[14] We excluded 19 out of 136 cases because they lack information on HS codes and/or dates.

Table 5.4: *Sectoral division of Korea's anti-dumping initiations (number of cases).*

Section (HS code)	'89	'90	'91	'92	'93	'94	'95	'96	'97	'98	'99	'00	'01	'02	'03	'04	'05	'06	'07	'08	'09	'10	Total	Share (%)
Animal/ vegetable fats (15)	0	0	0	0	0	0	0	0	0	0	0	0	0	0	0	0	0	3	0	0	0	0	3	2.6
Mineral products (25–28)	1	0	0	1	1	4	0	2	0	0	0	0	0	0	1	1	0	0	0	0	0	0	11	9.4
Chemicals (29–38)	0	0	0	3	2	0	0	3	1	0	2	0	0	4	4	0	0	0	4	0	0	1	24	20.5
Plastics/ rubber (39–40)	0	2	0	0	0	0	0	0	2	0	0	0	0	0	0	1	0	3	2	0	0	0	10	8.5
Wood (44–46)	0	0	0	0	0	0	0	0	2	0	0	2	0	0	0	0	0	0	0	2	0	1	7	6.0
Pulp/ paper (47–49)	0	0	0	0	0	0	0	0	2	0	0	0	0	2	0	0	0	0	8	0	0	0	12	10.3
Textile (50–63)	0	0	0	0	0	0	0	0	0	0	0	0	3	0	0	0	3	0	0	2	0	0	8	6.8

Table 5.4: *Continued.*

Section (HS code)	'89	'90	'91	'92	'93	'94	'95	'96	'97	'98	'99	'00	'01	'02	'03	'04	'05	'06	'07	'08	'09	'10	Total	Share (%)
Footwear (64–67)	0	0	0	0	0	0	0	0	0	0	0	0	0	0	0	0	0	0	0	0	0	0	0	0.0
Stone/ glass (68–70)	0	0	0	0	3	0	0	0	0	0	0	0	0	0	0	0	1	0	1	0	0	0	5	4.3
Base metals (72–83)	0	0	0	0	0	4	1	1	1	0	1	0	0	0	3	0	0	0	0	0	0	1	12	10.3
Machinery (84–85)	0	0	0	2	0	0	0	7	4	0	4	0	1	0	2	1	0	1	0	0	0	0	22	18.8
Misc. (94–96)	0	0	0	0	0	0	0	0	1	0	0	0	0	2	0	0	0	0	0	0	0	0	3	2.6
Total	1	2	0	6	6	8	1	13	13	0	7	2	4	8	10	3	4	7	15	4	0	3	117	100.0

Source: authors' calculations using *Temporary Trade Barriers Database* (Bown 2010).

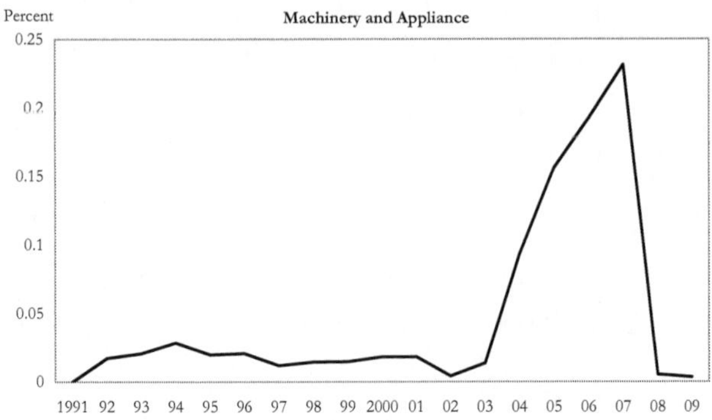

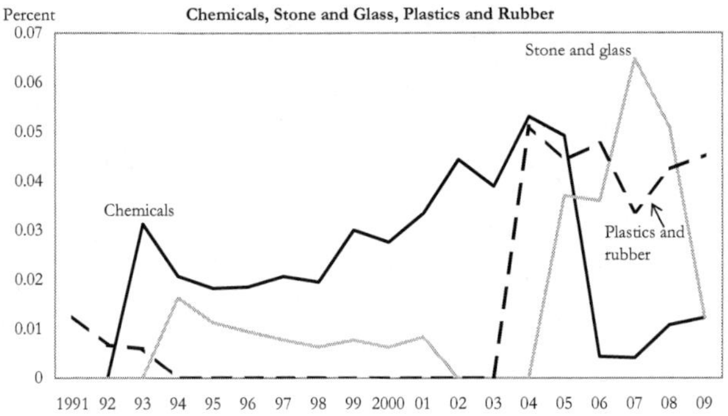

Figure 5.7: *Share of Korea's import value affected by anti-dumping measures, by sector, 1991-2009.*

of anti-dumping investigations with 24 cases (20.5%). Other frequent users were machinery (22 cases, 18.8%), pulp and paper (12 cases, 10.3%), base metals (12 cases, 10.3%), mineral products (11 cases, 9.4%), and plastics and rubber (10 cases, 8.5%). During the 2008–9 financial crisis, only 7 cases were under investigation, mainly in wood (3 cases), textiles (2 cases), chemicals (1 case), and base metals (1 case).

Next we consider the sectoral coverage of imports based on the *value* of each sector subject to anti-dumping duties rather than anti-dumping initiations. Here we focus on cases with final affirmative decisions, and we measure the value of HS-06 products of each case subject to anti-dumping duties. Figure 5.7 plots the shares of Korea's import value affected by anti-dumping measures relative to the total imports by sector. The machinery industry faced the largest share of its imports becoming subject to anti-dumping measures, reaching a peak of 0.23% in 2007. Prepared foodstuffs, textiles, and plastics and rubber exhibit an increasing trend in the stock of import value affected by anti-dumping measures during 2008–9. The wood and paper and

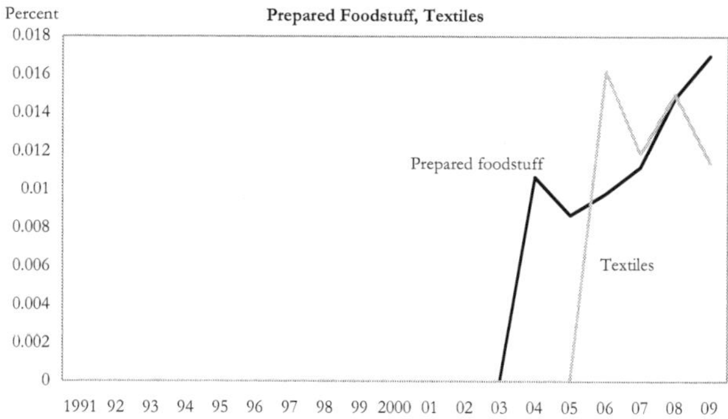

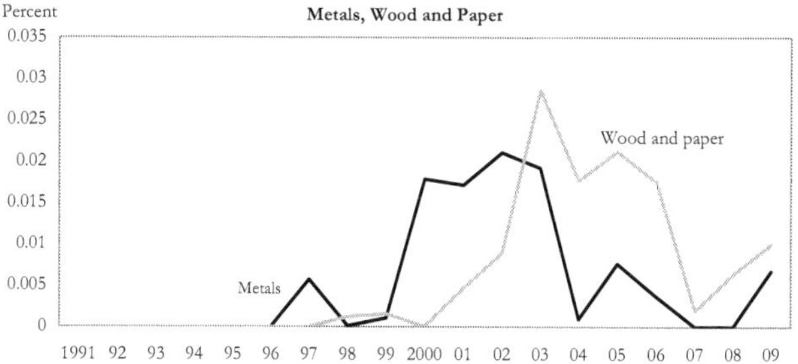

Figure 5.7: *Continued.*
Source: authors' calculations using *Temporary Trade Barriers Database* (Bown 2010).

metal industries had been protected heavily during the mid-2000s, while the chemical industry had the longest period of anti-dumping protection during 1993–2005.

Figure 5.8 reports each sector's share of total Korean imports subject to anti-dumping measures. Plastics and rubber was the only sector to be subjected to anti-dumping duties in 1991, showing a 100% share of the total value of imports subject to anti-dumping duties. Korean firms continued to target imports (mainly of plastics and rubber, machinery and chemicals) with anti-dumping duties in the early 1990s. However, by the mid-1990s, stone and glass also became key target sectors. Korea began targeting wood, pulp and paper in the early 2000s, and the share of stone and glass fell. Interestingly, during the global crisis of 2008–9, Korea targeted a wider set of sectors even though plastics and rubber as well as stone and glass had large shares of the total value of Korea's imports subject to anti-dumping duties. Four sectors had more than 8% of imports in 2008 and five sectors had more than 8% by 2009. Korea thus applied its anti-dumping use over a broader number of sectors during 2008–9.

(a)

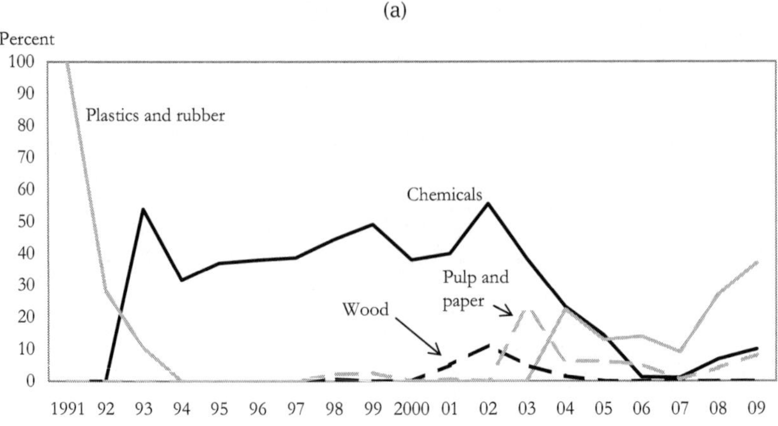

(b)

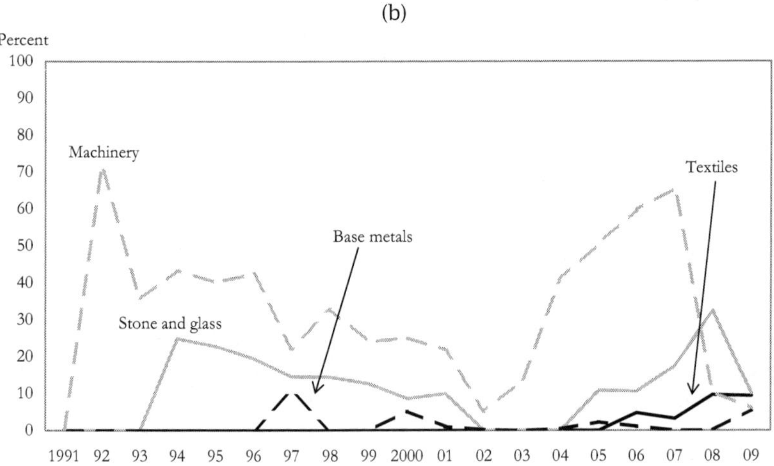

Figure 5.8: *Sectoral share of the total value of imports subject to anti-dumping measures, 1991–2009: (a) chemicals, plastics and rubber, wood, and pulp and paper; (b) textiles, stone and glass, base metals, and machinery.*

Source: authors' calculations using *Temporary Trade Barriers Database* (Bown 2010).

3.5 Target Countries

Table 5.5 decomposes Korea's anti-dumping investigations during the period 1986–2010 by target country. China was the most frequently targeted country with 27 cases (19.4%), followed by Japan (20 cases, 14.4%) and the USA (17 cases, 12.2%). As a number of other chapters in this volume have documented, Korea is not the only country that is particularly active in imposing anti-dumping measures against Chinese imports. Nevertheless, Korea has also used anti-dumping to target many high-income countries, with 65 cases brought against OECD members and 12 cases brought against non-OECD high-income countries.[15] One interpretation of these data is that Korea's domestic industries use anti-dumping to address competition from producers in high-income countries. Upper-middle-income countries were targeted in 14 (10.1%) cases and lower-middle-income countries (not including China) were targeted in only 21 cases (15.1%).

Table 5.6 documents Korea's 5 FTAs currently in force with 16 countries. As of December 2010, Korea had also completed negotiations of 3 FTAs with 29 countries; it was negotiating 7 FTAs with 12 countries, and it was considering 9 additional FTAs with 21 other countries.

Table 5.7 shows Korea's use of anti-dumping measures against preferential trading partners. There are mixed results regarding Korea's use of anti-dumping measures prior to and after each FTA enters into force. Korea never targeted Chile and the EFTA countries with anti-dumping measures even before their FTAs. However, Korea's anti-dumping against imports from Singapore and members of the Association of South East Asian Nations (ASEAN) increased after the implementation of their bilateral FTAs. Korea's anti-dumping measures among its FTA partners were concentrated on ASEAN countries; anti-dumping measures increased from coverage of 13 products in 2006 to 16 products by 2009. Additionally, Table 5.7 shows a slight increase in Korea's anti-dumping measures against its FTA partners, once again principally against Singapore and ASEAN countries, during the financial crisis of 2008–9.[16] Among ASEAN members, Korea's anti-dumping measures have concentrated on Indonesia (ten products each in 2008, 2009 and 2010), Malaysia (one, two and three products in 2008, 2009 and 2010, respectively), and Thailand (one product each in 2009 and 2010). With regard to its sectoral division, Korea's anti-dumping measures against its FTA partners during the 2008–9 crisis have focused primarily on the wood and paper industry, including craft paper, particle board and plywood. This trend is consistent with its use of anti-dumping measures against all trading partners, as is shown in Section 3.4.

One potential contributing explanation to Korea's differential anti-dumping use across its PTA partners may be found in the country's PTA rules. Table 5.8 documents legal disciplines on anti-dumping measures in Korea's FTAs. Even though all of Korea's FTAs allow members to maintain rights and obligations

---

[15] According to the World Bank's country classifications, Taiwan was not classified into any group due to its political status; however, we classified it into the group of non-OECD high-income countries.

[16] We calculated its share of total imports, using counterfactual estimates of the import value of products subject to anti-dumping measures, according to the approach described by Equation (1.1) of Chapter 1. However, this share is very low (0.01%), exhibiting few fluctuations and no significant changes during the 2008–9 crisis.

Table 5.5: *Country division of Korea's anti-dumping initiations (number of cases).*

Country	'86	'87	'88	'89	'90	'91	'92	'93	'94	'95	'96	'97	'98	'99	'00	'01	'02	'03	'04	'05	'06	'07	'08	'09	'10	Total
North America																										
Canada	0	0	0	0	0	0	0	0	0	0	0	0	0	0	0	0	0	2	0	0	0	2	0	0	0	4
USA	0	0	0	0	1	0	0	1	1	0	3	2	0	1	0	0	1	2	0	0	2	2	1	0	0	17
Latin America																										
Argentina	0	0	0	0	0	0	0	0	0	0	0	0	0	0	0	0	0	0	0	0	1	0	0	0	0	1
Brazil	0	0	0	0	0	0	0	0	0	0	0	0	0	0	0	0	0	0	0	0	1	0	0	0	0	1
Asia																										
China	0	0	0	0	0	0	2	1	2	0	2	4	0	1	0	0	2	3	1	2	1	5	1	0	0	27
India	0	0	0	0	0	0	1	0	0	0	0	0	0	0	0	1	0	2	2	0	0	1	0	0	0	7
Indonesia	0	0	0	0	0	0	0	0	0	0	0	0	1	0	1	1	3	0	0	0	0	1	0	0	0	7
Japan	1	0	0	0	1	0	2	2	0	1	2	1	0	2	0	0	1	3	0	0	1	1	0	0	2	20
Kazakhstan	0	0	0	0	0	0	0	0	1	0	0	0	0	0	0	0	0	0	0	0	0	0	0	0	0	1
Malaysia	0	0	0	0	0	0	0	0	0	0	0	1	1	0	0	0	0	0	0	1	0	0	1	0	1	5
Pakistan	0	0	0	0	0	0	0	0	0	0	0	0	0	0	0	1	0	0	0	0	0	0	0	0	0	1
Singapore	0	0	0	0	0	0	0	0	0	0	0	1	0	1	0	0	0	0	0	0	1	1	0	0	0	4
Taiwan	1	0	0	0	0	0	0	1	0	0	0	1	0	1	0	1	0	0	0	1	0	0	1	0	0	7
Thailand	0	0	0	0	0	0	1	0	0	0	0	0	1	0	1	0	0	0	0	0	0	0	1	0	0	4
Uzbekistan	0	0	0	0	0	0	0	0	1	0	0	0	0	0	0	0	0	0	0	0	0	0	0	0	0	1
Vietnam	0	0	0	0	0	0	0	0	0	0	0	0	0	0	0	0	1	0	0	0	0	0	0	0	0	1

Table 5.5: *Continued.*

Country	'86	'87	'88	'89	'90	'91	'92	'93	'94	'95	'96	'97	'98	'99	'00	'01	'02	'03	'04	'05	'06	'07	'08	'09	'10	Total
Europe																										
Belgium	0	0	0	0	0	0	0	0	1	0	0	0	0	0	0	0	0	2	0	0	0	0	0	0	0	3
Bulgaria	0	0	0	0	0	0	0	0	0	0	1	0	0	0	0	0	0	0	0	0	0	0	0	0	0	1
France	0	0	0	1	1	0	0	0	1	0	0	1	0	0	0	0	1	0	0	0	0	0	0	0	0	5
Germany	0	0	0	0	1	0	0	0	0	0	1	2	0	0	0	0	1	0	0	0	0	0	0	0	0	5
Italy	0	0	0	0	0	0	0	0	0	0	0	0	0	0	0	0	0	2	0	0	0	0	0	0	0	2
Liechtenstein	0	0	0	0	0	0	0	0	0	0	0	1	0	0	0	0	0	0	0	0	0	0	0	0	0	1
Netherlands	0	0	0	0	0	0	0	0	0	0	1	0	0	1	0	0	0	0	0	0	0	0	0	0	0	2
Poland	0	0	0	0	0	0	0	0	0	0	0	0	0	0	0	0	1	0	0	0	0	0	0	0	0	1
Russia	0	0	0	0	0	0	0	1	1	0	2	0	0	0	0	0	0	0	0	0	0	1	0	0	0	5
Spain	0	0	0	0	0	0	0	0	0	0	0	0	0	0	0	0	0	3	0	0	0	0	0	0	0	3
UK	0	0	0	0	1	0	0	0	0	0	0	1	0	0	0	0	0	0	0	0	0	0	0	0	0	2
Oceania																										
New Zealand	0	0	0	0	0	0	0	0	0	0	0	0	0	0	0	0	0	0	0	0	0	1	0	0	0	1
Total	2	0	0	1	5	0	6	6	8	1	12	15	3	7	2	4	11	19	3	4	7	15	5	0	3	139

Source: authors' calculations using *Temporary Trade Barriers Database* (Bown 2010) and KTC (2010).

Table 5.6: *Korea's current and potential FTA partners.*

Status	Countries
FTAs in force	Chile (April 2004); Singapore (March 2006); EFTA (Iceland, Liechtenstein, Norway, Switzerland; September 2006); ASEAN (Goods: June 2007, Services: May 2009, Investment: September 2009); and India (January 2010)
Talks completed	USA (December 2010); EU (October 2009); and Peru (January 2010)
Talks ongoing	Canada (since July 2005); Mexico (since February 2006); GCC (since July 2008); Australia (since May 2009); New Zealand (since June 2009); Columbia (since December 2009); and Turkey (since April 2010)
Consideration	Japan; China; Japan–China–Korea (trilateral); Mercosur; Russia; Israel; SACU; Vietnam; and Central America (SICA)

Korea had negotiated a bilateral FTA with Japan since December 2003, but the negotiation had been stalled since November 2004 due to conflicting views of agricultural market access in Japan. 'GCC' is the Gulf Cooperation Council including Saudi Arabia, Kuwait, United Arab Emirates, Qatar, Oman and Bahrain; Mercosur is a common market encompassing Brazil, Argentina, Paraguay and Uruguay; SACU (South African Customs Union) is a customs union including the Republic of South Africa, Botswana, Lesotho, Swaziland, and Namibia; and SICA (Central American Integration System) is an economic, cultural and political organisation convened among Guatemala, El Salvador, Honduras, Nicaragua, Costa Rica, Panama, Belize and Dominican Republic.

Source: Ministry of Foreign Affairs and Trade (2010).

under the WTO Agreement on Anti-Dumping, the FTA legal texts contain different rules. For example, Korea's bilateral FTA with the EFTA stipulates that the two parties shall review whether there is a need to maintain the possibility of carrying out anti-dumping measures between them (Article 2.10.2), with an eye towards deeper economic integration. With regard to the matter of zeroing, bilateral FTAs with Singapore and India prohibit zeroing practices, indicating that 'when anti-dumping margins are established on the weighted average basis, all individual margins, whether positive or negative, should be counted toward the average'.[17]

In addition, FTAs with Singapore, EFTA, India, the EU and Peru require members to 'apply a duty less than the margin of dumping where such lesser duty would be adequate to remove the injury to the domestic industry' (the so-called 'lesser duty rule').[18] Moreover, FTAs with India and the EU require

[17]See Article 6.2.3(a) of the Korea–Singapore FTA and, similarly, Article 2.18 in the Korea–India Comprehensive Economic Partnership Agreement. Zeroing is a methodology used principally by the USA for calculating dumping margins by setting the negative differences to zero, which occurs whenever the imported product's price is higher than the price in the USA.

[18]See Article 6.2.3(b) in the Korea–Singapore FTA, Article 2.10.1(b) in the Korea–EFTA FTA, Article 2.17 in the Korea–India Comprehensive Economic Partnership Agreement, Article 3.14 in the Korea–EU FTA, and Article 8.9.3 in the Korea–Peru FTA.

Table 5.7: *Korea's use of anti-dumping measures by preferential trading partner: stock of partner–HS-06 product combinations subject to anti-dumping duties.*

Year	Chile	Singapore	EFTA	ASEAN	India
1992	0	0	0	1	0
1993	0	0	0	1	0
1994	0	0	0	1	0
1995	0	0	0	1	0
1996	0	0	0	0	0
1997	0	0	0	0	0
1998	0	1	0	2	0
1999	0	1	0	2	0
2000	0	1	0	2	0
2001	0	1	0	2	0
2002	0	0	0	1	0
2003	0	0	0	11	0
2004	**0**	0	0	11	4
2005	**0**	0	0	10	4
2006	**0**	**2**	**0**	13	4
2007	**0**	**2**	**0**	**11**	4
2008	**0**	**3**	**0**	**14**	6
2009	**0**	**3**	**0**	**16**	6
2010	**0**	**1**	**0**	**16**	**6**

The bold values represent the count of PTA partner–HS-06 product combinations subject to anti-dumping investigations after each PTA entered into force. Since Singapore is also a member of ASEAN, the count for ASEAN includes Singaporean imports.

Source: authors' calculations using *Temporary Trade Barriers Database* (Bown 2010).

members not to initiate an investigation when anti-dumping measures are terminated as a result of the review process, unless the circumstances have changed.[19]

Overall, Korea's FTAs with India, EFTA, the EU and Singapore have been progressive in terms of the design of disciplines that limit the opportunity for governments to misuse anti-dumping measures. On the other hand, Korea's FTAs with Chile, the USA and ASEAN provide more freedom for participants to use anti-dumping measures. It is especially interesting that Korea's bilateral FTA with India appears relatively more aggressive in its attempts to limit the overuse of anti-dumping given that India is one of the most frequent users of anti-dumping in the world (Tovar, this volume).

Although all Korean FTAs have maintained and upheld all the rights and obligations under the WTO Anti-Dumping Agreement, modified models of anti-dumping administration in Korea's FTAs have begun to emerge. Ahn (2008) describes this 'rule diversification' in the anti-dumping disciplines as

---

[19]See Article 2.19 in the Korea–India Comprehensive Economic Partnership Agreement and Article 3.11 in the Korea–EU FTA.

Table 5.8: *Rules on anti-dumping measures of Korea's FTAs.*

FTA	Maintaining rights and obligations under the WTO Agreement	Prohibition of zeroing	Lesser duty rule	Future possibility of elimination of anti-dumping measures	Exemption from investigation after termination
Korea-Chile	Yes	No rules	No rules	No rules	No rules
Korea-Singapore	Yes	Prohibited	Yes	No rules	No rules
Korea-EFTA	Yes	No rules	Yes	Yes	No rules
Korea-ASEAN	Yes	No rules	No rules	No rules	No rules
Korea-India	Yes	Prohibited	Yes	No rules	Yes
Korea-USA	Yes	No rules	No rules	No rules	No rules
Korea-EU	Yes	No rules	Yes	No rules	Yes
Korea-Peru	Yes	No rules	Yes	No rules	No rules

Source: legal texts of each agreement from Korea's Ministry of Foreign Affairs and Trade (2010).

a phenomena that is likely linked to the 'spaghetti bowl' effect of preferential trade liberalisation.

4 DOMESTIC POLITICS OF KOREA'S TEMPORARY TRADE BARRIERS

4.1 Background and Econometric Model

To what extent are Korea's anti-dumping duties a function of its domestic political-economic considerations? To address this question, we apply the Grossman and Helpman (1994) model of trade protection to the Korean manufacturing industries, and we attempt to determine whether Korea uses anti-dumping to protect politically organised industries. In particular, we explore the impacts of political interest groups on the Korean use of anti-dumping measures in 2005 and in 2009, both before and during the global financial crisis, using import data at the HS-06 product level.

Based on Grossman and Helpman's (1994) model, Bown and Tovar (2011) formulate the following equation for the determinants of trade policy:

$$\tau_i = \frac{I_i - \alpha_L}{a + \alpha_L} \frac{z_i}{\varepsilon_i}, \tag{5.1}$$

where τ_i is the *ad valorem* tariff in sector i, where I_i is an indicator variable that takes a value of 1 if sector i is politically organised, and 0 otherwise. Additionally, α_L is the fraction of the population organised into lobbies, a is the weight placed on welfare by the government, z_i is the inverse of the import penetration ratio, and ε_i is a measure of the absolute value of the elasticity of import demand. In accordance with Bown and Tovar (2011), we establish the following estimation equation:

$$\tau_{it} = \beta_0 + \beta_1\left(I_i\frac{z_i}{\varepsilon_i}\right) + \beta_2\left(\frac{z_i}{\varepsilon_i}\right) + \mu_{it}, \tag{5.2}$$

where μ_{it} is the regression error term.

4.2 Data

Import data at the HS-06 level in 2005 and 2009 are available from UNCTAD/TRAINS. Data regarding import demand elasticities at the HS-06 level were obtained from Kee *et al* (2008). Data on production, total value added, employment, capital, and the number of firms at the Korean Standard Industrial Classification (KSIC) four-digit level were obtained from the Korean Statistical Information Service (The Statistics Korea 2010). We use Nicita and Olarreaga (2007) to concord the import data at the HS-06 product level to International Standard Industrial Classification (ISIC) industries, matching data from the KSIC (revision 9).

One difficulty in the estimation approach involves the construction of accurate data on political campaign contributions by Korean industries. Previous work for other countries, including Bown and Tovar (2011), Murrell (1984), Bischoff (2003) and Coates *et al* (2007) used data on the number of groups listed in the World Trade Associations publication as a measure of interest group activities. For the case of Korea, these data are somewhat outdated as they report a very small number of politically organised industries, which is inconsistent with increasing political contribution activity by Korean industries. Therefore, as an alternative approach, we searched websites to identify each Korean industry's own industrial associations at the HS-02 level. When an industry had more than one industrial association, we considered the industry to be politically organised.[20]

4.3 Empirical Results

Applied tariff rates in Korea between 2005 and 2009 have hardly changed, except for a small number of commodities such as crude oil. Thus, we did not employ applied tariff rates for the dependent variable. Rather, we employed anti-dumping duties at the HS-06 level in force in 2005 and 2009.

We adopt the methodology of Bown and Tovar (2011) by using an IV-Tobit estimation approach, as proposed by Kelejian (1971). We calculate two anti-dumping duties, measuring the duties weighted by the import share of the targeted countries in the total imports of the product at the HS-06 level. The variables used in the instrument for political organisation include the value added per firm, the number of employees by establishment, the capital–labour

---

[20]Using this methodology, we identified the following as politically organised industries: HS 17–23, 27–31, 33, 44, 48–49, 51–55, 62, 64, 68, 70, 72–73, 84–85, 87–90 and 94.

Table 5.9: *Estimation of Grossman and Helpman model's determinants of Korean use of anti-dumping duties in 2005 and 2009.*

	1	2	3	4
	2005		2009	
Dependent variables	AD_{min}	AD_{max}	AD_{min}	AD_{max}
$I\frac{z}{\varepsilon}$	0.003 (0.022)	0.005 (0.035)	0.054 (0.022)**	0.101 (0.042)**
$\frac{z}{\varepsilon}$	−0.024 (0.014)*	−0.039 (0.022)*	−0.027 (0.012)**	−0.050 (0.022)**
α_L	—	—	0.50	0.49
a	—	—	1,852	990
Observations	2,860	2,860	3,488	3,488

Standard errors of the Tobit model's estimates are in parentheses with '*' and '**' indicating statistical significance at the 10% and 5% levels, respectively.

ratio, the capital-output ratio, and the output share of firms with over 500 employees (as a proxy variable for the industry concentration ratio).

We do not report results from the first-stage empirical analysis that estimates endogenous variables and their non-linear transformation since they are not our focus in this chapter. Rather, we concentrate on the second-stage analysis described above. We include the residuals from the first-stage regression in the basic empirical Equation (1.2). The results demonstrate that the residual from the regression of the dependent variable of $I \times z/\varepsilon$ is statistically significant, but the residual from the regression of z/ε is insignificant. These results indicate that we can reject the null hypothesis that the variable of $I \times z/\varepsilon$ is exogenous, but we cannot reject the null hypothesis that the variable of z/ε is exogenous. Therefore, we treat the variable of $I \times z/\varepsilon$ as endogenous.

The Grossman and Helpman (1994) model predicts that β_1 (the coefficient on $I \times z/\varepsilon$) is positive, that β_2 (the coefficient on z/ε) is negative, and that $\beta_1 + \beta_2$ is positive. Table 5.9 reports our estimates for the model of determinants of Korea's anti-dumping: the β_1 values are positive but not significant in 2005, while they are positive and significant at the 5% level in 2009. Furthermore, the β_2 values are negative and significant at the 10% level in 2005 and 5% level in 2009. These results suggest that the Korean use of anti-dumping measures is consistent with the Grossman and Helpman (1994) theory that, during the global financial crisis of 2008–9, politically organised sectors receive more protection using anti-dumping duties than unorganised ones. From Equation (1.1) and the coefficients β_1 and β_2, we derive the fraction of the population owning a specific factor (α_L) and the weight that the government places on aggregate welfare relative to aggregate lobbying spending (a).

The fractions of the population owning a specific factor were around 0.5 and the social welfare weights were 1,852, much higher than in other studies, such as Bown and Tovar (2011), Bandyopadhyay and Gawande (2000), Goldberg and Maggi (1999) and Mitra (1999). These results provide evidence that Korean industries and the government employed anti-dumping measures to protect the commercial interests of domestic producers during the global financial crisis.

5 PRACTICAL USE OF SOUTH KOREA'S TEMPORARY TRADE BARRIERS

5.1 Previous Literature on Discretionary Practices

This section analyses potential changes in Korea's use of anti-dumping measures during the global crisis of 2008–9. In particular, we evaluate the impacts of the KTC's practices on firm-specific dumping margins. A number of previous studies have assessed the determination of the magnitude of US dumping margins. Baldwin and Moore (1991, pp 253–280) evaluated US dumping margin determinations in the 1980s and found that the US Department of Commerce's (USDOC) use of 'facts available' raised dumping margins to 38 percentage points higher than the average margin. However, they did not evaluate other discretionary practices. Lindsay (1999) evaluated USDOC's calculations of dumping margins from 1995 through 1998 and determined that the average dumping margin of 'facts available' was 95.58%, while the overall sample average amounted to 44.68%.[21] Blonigen (2006) examined the evolution of discretionary practices during 1980–2000 and found that USDOC discretionary practices such as 'facts available', 'adverse facts available' and cost tests significantly raised dumping margins.[22]

5.2 Background on Discretionary Practices

The extent of dumping is referred to as the 'dumping margin', which is calculated by subtracting the export price from the normal value and dividing the difference by the export price. According to Article 2 of the WTO Anti-Dumping Agreement, normal value can be defined as the price of the imported

[21]Lindsay (1999) also showed that dumping margins—primarily those using the foreign firm's prices in its domestic market or in another country's market to construct a normal value—were much lower than those generated using a constructed value, methods of non-market-economy status, or 'facts available'.

[22]In an effort to quantify the effects of methodological and practical distortions in specific cases, Ikenson and Lindsay (2002) analysed data on actual prices and costs used by USDOC to calculate dumping margins for foreign firms under investigation in 18 anti-dumping cases. They determined that many discretionary practices, including the use of zeroing, constructed value and sales below cost, resulted in substantial increases in dumping margins.

product in the ordinary course of trade in the country of origin. However, normal value can be calculated in various ways, as put forth in Article 2 of the WTO Anti-Dumping Agreement.

To calculate Korea's dumping margins, the KTC sends a questionnaire on the pricing and costs to the foreign exporter whose product is under investigation.[23] When the exporter's replies are deemed reliable, the KTC determines the normal value on the product by considering the home market price of the exporter, and costs associated with the production and sale of the relevant product including the respective shipping and transportation costs. However, there are many instances in which the KTC uses discretionary practices other than the home market price. In the process of determining normal values during 2000–2010, the KTC used three other discretionary practices: 'facts available', 'sales below costs' and 'non-market-economy status'.

When the exporter does not reply to the questionnaire or its replies are deemed unreliable, the KTC employs information provided by the domestic producer(s) or 'facts available' in order to determine the normal value.[24]

The second discretionary practice is a test of sales below costs. Although the normal value is calculated using the exporter's home market price, the KTC also assesses whether there are sales below production costs in its home market. If sales below production costs are more than 20%, then the KTC excludes these sales when determining the normal value.[25] This practice results in increases to the normal value and, thus, a higher dumping margin.

The final practice relies on the exporter's potential non-market-economy status and can be employed when the exporting firms are from countries such as China, Russia or Vietnam. The KTC frequently used the non-market-economy practice prior to 2000, considering the price in the domestic market of Indonesia as a third (reference) country for products from China, for example. In 2005, the Korean government ultimately decided to grant market-economy status to China.

Table 5.10 illustrates that the KTC has most frequently employed the 'facts available' clause when determining normal value, followed by the test of sales below costs, the home market price and non-market economy during 2000–2007. The use of 'facts available' increased in particular during the global financial crisis, resulting in declines in the shares of other practices. We develop an econometric analysis to assess whether the more frequent use of the 'facts available' approach leads to an increase in dumping margins.

---

[23] A questionnaire is sent to the domestic producer(s), importer and distributor(s) as well.

[24] Article 1 of Annex II of the WTO Anti-Dumping Agreement holds that if information is not supplied within a period of reasonable time, the authorities will be free to make determinations on the basis of the facts available, including those contained in the application for the initiation of the investigation by the domestic industry.

[25] This regulation is based on Article 2.2.1 and footnote 5 of the WTO Anti-Dumping Agreement.

Table 5.10: *The KTC's practices in determining normal prices (2000–2010).*

	Home market price	Facts available	Sales below costs	Non-market economy	Total
2000–2007					
Product	11	46	37	2	96
Share (%)	11.5	47.9	38.5	2.1	100.0
2008–10					
Product	4	46	10	0	60
Share (%)	6.7	76.7	16.7	0.0	100.0

Source: authors' calculations using KTC (2010).

Table 5.11: *Summary statistics.*

Variable	Number of observations	Mean	Standard deviation	Minimum	Maximum
Anti-dumping duty	156	29.39	21.65	2.80	129.84
Facts available	156	0.59	0.49	0.00	1.00
Test of sales below costs	156	0.30	0.46	0.00	1.00
Non-market economy	156	0.01	0.11	0.00	1.00
China	156	0.35	0.48	0.00	1.00
USA	156	0.08	0.28	0.00	1.00
Japan	156	0.10	0.30	0.00	1.00
Taiwan	156	0.14	0.35	0.00	1.00
Malaysia	156	0.09	0.29	0.00	1.00
Singapore	156	0.04	0.21	0.00	1.00
India	156	0.04	0.19	0.00	1.00
Indonesia	156	0.04	0.21	0.00	1.00

Source: authors' calculations using KTC (2010).

5.3 *Estimation Strategy and Data*

To estimate the impact of the KTC's discretionary practices in determining the normal price on dumping margins, we adopt an econometric model and regress firm-specific dumping margins on indicators for Korea's discretionary practices, including facts available, sales below costs, and non-market-economy approaches, in accordance with the work of Blonigen (2006). We consider whether the effects of these practices differ prior to and during the global financial crisis of 2008–9.

We constructed data on firm-specific dumping margins from the KTC's preliminary decisions during 2000–2010, using data available from the KTC. We include all cases, including those in which the final decision was negative, even though the preliminary decision was positive. We also include data regarding the KTC's discretionary practices, including facts available, the test of sales below costs, and the non-market-economy approaches. Each of these variables is a binary variable which takes the value 1 when dumping margins are calculated by that practice, and 0 otherwise. Additionally, in order to control for country-specific effects, we include country fixed effects for China, India, Indonesia, Japan, Malaysia, Taiwan and the USA.[26] Table 5.11 shows the descriptive statistics for the variables used in the analysis.

5.4 Empirical Results

Table 5.12 shows our empirical results. Column 1 indicates that 'facts available', 'test of sales below costs' and 'non-market economy' have significant impacts on dumping margins. The 'non-market economy' practice increases dumping margins by 35.3 percentage points, 'facts available' increases dumping margins by 34.5 percentage points, and 'test of sales below costs' increases dumping margins by 12.1 percentage points.

Column 2 of Table 5.12 provides the results after imposing additional controls for country-specific effects. The coefficients of Japan, Taiwan and Malaysia are statistically significant at the 1% level. The KTC's anti-dumping duties on Japanese exporters were 18.6 percentage points higher than those for the rest of the world, whereas those on Taiwanese and Malaysian exporters were lower, on average.

Columns 3 and 4 of Table 5.12 show the additional impact of these discretionary practices on dumping margins during the global financial crisis. Here, we introduce a binary variable of 'crisis' representing the 2008–10 period and construct interaction terms of discretionary practices and the crisis. The coefficients of these interaction terms show the additional effect of discretionary practices after the global financial crisis. Since the non-market-economy approach was not used by the KTC during the 2008–10 period, we exclude the interaction term of 'non-market economy' and 'crisis'.

The results shown in column 3 and 4 of Table 5.12 demonstrate that the coefficients of 'facts available' and 'non-market economy' are still statistically significant, whereas the interaction terms of 'crisis' and both 'facts available' and 'non-market economy' are not statistically significant. Therefore, we have no evidence to suggest that the discretionary practices of the KTC exerted an additional impact on dumping margins during the global financial crisis.

As indicated by Blonigen (2006), the specification model in Table 5.12 does not control for case-specific factors that may affect the calculation of firm-specific dumping margins. Additionally, certain macroeconomic variables, including the unemployment rate and exchange rates, may affect dumping margins as well. Furthermore, Kang *et al* (2010) determined that anti-dumping measures do not exert country-specific impacts but do exert industry-specific

[26]These countries were selected because they have more than 7 products out of the 156 total.

Table 5.12: *Impacts of anti-dumping practices and country characteristics on Korea's anti-dumping margins.*

	1	2	3	4
Facts available	34.47 (5.24)***	26.84 (3.90)***	39.28 (7.27)***	29.39 (5.27)***
Test of sales below costs	12.10 (5.24)**	4.00 (4.57)	15.08 (6.90)**	6.66 (5.87)
Non-market economy	35.31 (10.76)***	35.31 (10.25)***	38.95 (11.47)***	37.49 (10.67)***
Crisis	— —	— —	−41.21 (14.73)***	−36.67 (12.03)***
Facts available × Crisis	— —	— —	−14.75 (7.85)*	−8.51 (6.91)
Sales below costs × Crisis	— —	— —	−10.03 (7.66)	−9.97 (7.17)
China	— —	−3.19 (3.44)	— —	−3.18 (3.48)
USA	— —	4.84 (6.02)	— —	4.60 (6.00)
Japan	— —	18.58 (5.90)***	— —	17.97 (5.88)***
Taiwan	— —	−14.67 (4.00)***	— —	−14.90 (4.18)***
Malaysia	— —	−14.88 (5.20)***	— —	−16.02 (5.23)***
Singapore	— —	−8.39 (6.61)	— —	−9.65 (6.51)
India	— —	5.66 (4.94)	— —	5.68 (4.87)
Indonesia	— —	−8.13 (5.79)	— —	−7.86 (5.97)
Observations	156	156	156	156
R^2	0.58	0.71	0.59	0.71

In all specifications, year dummies were included. The constant term was included, but not reported. Robust standard errors are in parentheses, with '*', '**' and '***' indicating statistical significance at 10%, 5% and 1%, respectively.

effects. If industry-specific impacts are important for determining dumping margins, the omission of case-specific factors may introduce severe bias into the estimation.

A standard methodology used to control for case-specific factors is to include case-specific dummies. Since anti-dumping cases are product- and country-specific, one can no longer include country variables due to multicollinearity, as discussed by Blonigen (2006). Table 5.13 shows the case-specific fixed effects and suggests that they are not profoundly different from those in Table 5.12, even though the R^2 is improved. From Table 5.10, it is clear that the KTC has more frequently used 'facts available' than other discretionary practices during the global financial crisis. Nevertheless, Tables 5.12

Table 5.13: *Impacts of anti-dumping practices and country characteristics on Korea's anti-dumping margins: case-specific fixed effects.*

	1	2
Facts available	22.63	21.96
	(2.84)***	(4.47)***
Test of sales below costs	−2.58	−3.12
	(3.15)	(4.58)
Non-market economy	37.06	36.63
	(11.13)***	(10.93)***
Crisis	—	3.27
	—	(2.44)
Facts available × Crisis	—	1.70
	—	(5.08)
Sales below costs × Crisis	—	1.36
	—	(5.23)
Observations	156	156
Adjusted R^2	0.81	0.81

In all specifications, year dummies were included. The constant term was included, but not reported. Robust standard errors are in parentheses with '*', '**' and '***' indicating statistical significance at 10%, 5% and 1%, respectively.

Source: Bank of Korea (2010).

and 5.13 give no evidence to suggest that this discretionary practice increased dumping margins during the 2008–10 period.

6 CONCLUSION

This chapter examines Korea's use of TTBs, mainly anti-dumping measures, before and during the global financial crisis of 2008–9. Using the *Temporary Trade Barriers Database* (Bown 2010), we determined that the stock of imported products subject to anti-dumping duties in Korea has increased moderately over time.

Korea's initiations and final decisions in anti-dumping cases have been *counter-cyclical*, with evidence of a dramatic increase during the Asian financial crisis of 1997–8 and immediately before the recession of 2000. During the financial crisis of 2008–9, there was a relatively small number of initiations; however, we conclude that the KTC was active in imposing anti-dumping duties during the financial crisis. Additionally, it turns out that, among the products under the *review* process for possible removal during the 2008–9 crisis, no products were terminated and each product continued to be subject to anti-dumping measures (excluding the five anti-dumping measures that were expired without review). The stock of imports subject to anti-dumping measures also increased to 38 in 2008 and 37 in 2009, which is more than double their average during 1991–2007.

We conclude that anti-dumping measures have functioned as a substitute for tariff protection measures in Korea during this period, *ie* the continuing reduction of tariff rates has been accompanied by an increase in anti-dumping petitions and final measures. Furthermore, Korea exhibits a very high percentage of observations in which the anti-dumping margins exceed the tariff overhang.

We also conclude that anti-dumping duties imposed during the Asian financial crisis persisted for three or four years. The stock of import value subject to anti-dumping measures increased moderately, but it increased dramatically beginning in 2005, reaching a peak level of 0.37% in 2008. The sudden increase in this share since 2005 can be attributed primarily to a cumulative effect of the stock of anti-dumping measures. As the number of tariff lines subject to anti-dumping measures continues to increase, the import values subject to anti-dumping measures continue to accumulate, resulting in an increase in the share.

Prior to the global financial crisis of 2008–9, Korea's dominant user of anti-dumping measures was the wood and paper industry. Other frequent users of anti-dumping included the chemicals, machinery, metal, stone and glass, prepared food, and plastics and rubber industries. During the crisis of 2008–9, the most frequent user was again the wood and paper industry, and its relative share increased sharply.

Korea's use of anti-dumping has most frequently targeted China, with 50 products (24.4%) subject to anti-dumping, followed by Japan and the USA. Nevertheless, Korea's principal target has been high-income countries as a group—the OECD countries account for 91 products and the non-OECD high-income countries account for 19 products, for a total of 110 products (53.7%). This suggests that the majority of domestic producers in Korea that use anti-dumping compete with producers from high-income countries. We also find mixed results in terms of practical changes to Korea's use of anti-dumping before and after an FTA enters into force. Chile and the EFTA countries have never been targeted by Korean anti-dumping, but anti-dumping measures in Korea against imports from Singapore and ASEAN members have increased. We also note a slight increase in Korea's use of anti-dumping measures against its FTA partners during the financial crisis of 2008–9.

Moreover, Korean use of anti-dumping measures is consistent with the theory put forth by Grossman and Helpman (1994) that politically organised sectors tended to receive more protection than unorganised ones, especially in terms of anti-dumping duty use, during the global crisis of 2008–9. Therefore, taking into consideration the empirical analysis, we conclude that Korean industries and government did indeed use anti-dumping measures to protect domestic producers' commercial interests during the global crisis.

Finally, our analysis of the practical uses of Korea's determinants of dumping margins suggests that the KTC has more frequently used 'facts available' than any other discretionary practice during the global financial crisis. Nevertheless, we found no evidence to suggest that the use of facts available increased dumping margins during the 2008–10 period.

Moonsung Kang is an Associate Professor at Korea University.

Soonchan Park is an Associate Professor at Kongju National University.

REFERENCES

Ahn, D. (2008). Foe or friend of GATT Article XXIV: diversity in trade remedy rules. *Journal of International Economic Law* **11**(1), 107–133.

Amsden, A. H. (1989). *Asia's Next Giant: South Korea and Late Industrialization.* Oxford University Press.

Bank of Korea (2010). URL: www.bok.or.kr/.

Baldwin, R. E., and M. O. Moore (1991). Political aspects of the administration of the trade remedy laws. In *Down in the Dumps: Administration of the Unfair Trade Laws* (ed. R. Boltuck and R. E. Litan). Washington, DC: Brookings Institution.

Bandyopadhyay, U., and K. Gawande (2000). Is protection for sale? Evidence on the Grossman–Helpman theory of endogenous protection. *The Review of Economics and Statistics* **82**(1), 139–152.

Bischoff, I. (2003). Determinants of the increase in the number of interest groups in western democracies: theoretical considerations and evidence from 21 OECD countries. *Public Choice* **114**(1–2), 197–218.

Blonigen, B. A. (2006). Evolving discretionary practices of US anti-dumping activity. *Canadian Journal of Economics* **39**, 874–900.

Bown, C. P. (2011a). Introduction. In *The Great Recession and Import Protection: The Role of Temporary Trade Barriers* (ed. C. P. Bown). London: CEPR/World Bank. (Chapter 1 of this volume.)

Bown, C. P. (2011b). Taking stock of anti-dumping, safeguards, and countervailing duties, 1990–2009. *The World Economy*, forthcoming.

Bown, C. P. (2010). *Temporary Trade Barriers Database.* World Bank (July). URL: http://econ.worldbank.org/ttbd/.

Bown, C. P., and P. Tovar (2011). Trade liberalization, anti-dumping, and safeguards: evidence from India's tariff reform. *Journal of Development Economics* **96**(1), 115–125.

Coates, D., J. Heckelman, and B. Wilson (2007). Determinants of interest group formation. *Public Choice* **133**(3), 377–391.

G20 (2008). Declaration of summit on financial markets and the world economy. URL: www.g20.org/Documents/g20_summit_declaration.pdf.

Goldberg, P. K., and G. Maggi (1999). Protection for sale: an empirical investigation. *American Economic Review* **89**(5), 1135–1155.

Grossman, G. M., and E. Helpman (1994). Protection for sale. *American Economic Review* **84**(4), 833–850.

Ikenson, D. J., and B. Lindsay (2002). *Anti-Dumping 101: The Devilish Details of 'Unfair Trade' Law.* Washington, DC: Cato Institute.

Kang, M., H. Lee, and S. Park (2011). Industry-specific effects of anti-dumping activities: evidence from the US, the European Union and China. *Applied Economics*, forthcoming.

Kee, H. L., A. Nicita, and M. Olarreaga (2008). Import demand elasticities and trade distortions. *Review of Economics and Statistics* **90**(4), 666–682.

Kelejian, H. (1971). Two stage least squares and econometric systems linear in parameters but nonlinear in the endogenous variables. *Journal of the American Statistical Association* **66**, 373–374.

KTC (2010). Korea Trade Commission. URL: www.ktc.go.kr.

Lindsay, B. (1999). *The US Anti-Dumping Law: Rhetoric Versus Reality*. Washington, DC: Cato Institute.

Ministry of Foreign Affairs and Trade (2010). URL: www.fta.go.kr/new/index.asp.

Mitra, D. (1999). Endogenous lobby formation and endogenous protection: a long run model of trade policy determination. *American Economic Review* **89**(5), 1116–1134.

Murrell, P. (1984). An examination of the factors affecting the formation of interest groups in OECD countries. *Public Choice* **43**, 151–171.

Nicita, A., and M. Olarreaga (2007). Trade, production, and protection database, 1976–2004. *World Bank Economic Review* **21**(1), 165–171.

OECD (2010). *Trade and Economic Effects of Responses to the Economic Crisis*, OECD Trade Policy Studies. Paris: OECD.

The Statistics Korea (2010). Korean Statistical Information Service. URL: http://kosis.kr/.

Tovar, P. (2011). India: the use of temporary trade barriers. In *The Great Recession and Import Protection: The Role of Temporary Trade Barriers* (ed. C. P. Bown). London: CEPR/World Bank. (Chapter 7 of this volume.)

World Trade Organization (2010). *World Trade Developments in 2009, International Trade Statistics 2010*. Online Resource. URL: www.wto.org.

6

China: A Sleeping Giant of Temporary Trade Barriers?

PIYUSH CHANDRA[1]

1 INTRODUCTION

While tariff rates around the world have decreased during the last five decades, there has been an increase in other instruments of protectionism—in particular, anti-dumping, CVDs and global safeguards (collectively, TTBs). In this chapter, we examine China's use of these TTBs both before and during the 2008–9 crisis in order to identify underlying historical trends and to explore potential changes in their use over time.

It is important to understand China's use of TTBs given that it is one of the leading importers in the world. Figure 6.1(a) illustrates that, not only has China's economy been growing, its imports have also been expanding rapidly. China's real exports fell slightly during the 2008–9 crisis; however, its real imports continued to increase even during this period.[2] By the end of 2009, China was the world's third largest importer with merchandise imports of more than $1 trillion, following only the EU and USA with imports of $1.7 trillion and $1.6 trillion, respectively (WTO 2010). The scale of imports at stake is reason enough to study the frequency with which China uses these TTBs.

The 2008–9 crisis had much smaller macroeconomic effects on China than it did on many other countries. China's economy continued to grow and its unemployment rate has remained stable; however, Figure 6.1(b) illustrates how its growth rate did decrease during this period. China's real GDP growth rate had increased from 7.5% in 1998 to above 13% by 2007, only to fall to 9% in 2008.

[1]Department of Economics, Colgate University, 13 Oak Drive, Hamilton, NY 13346, USA. Email: pchandra@colgate.edu. I am grateful to Chad Bown for several helpful suggestions and guidance. Thanks to Rod Ludema, Anna Maria Mayda and Tom Prusa for comments and suggestions and to Aksel Erbahar for help in collecting the data. Any remaining errors and omissions are my own.

[2]Later, we show that China's non-oil merchandise imports, measured in nominal terms, fell during 2008–9. Throughout the rest of the chapter any discussion of imports refers to the non-oil nominal value unless otherwise noted.

(a)

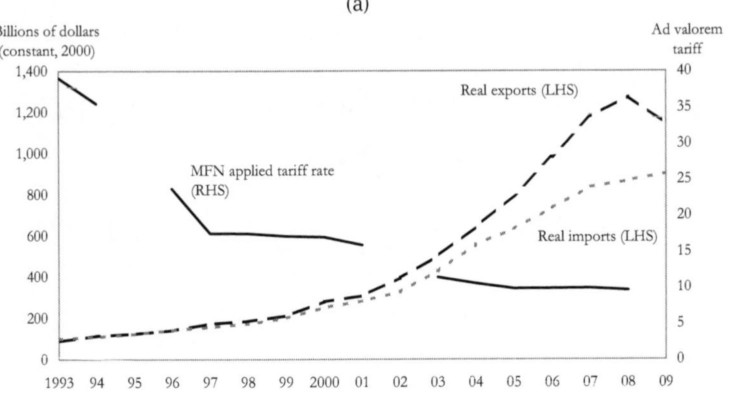

(b)

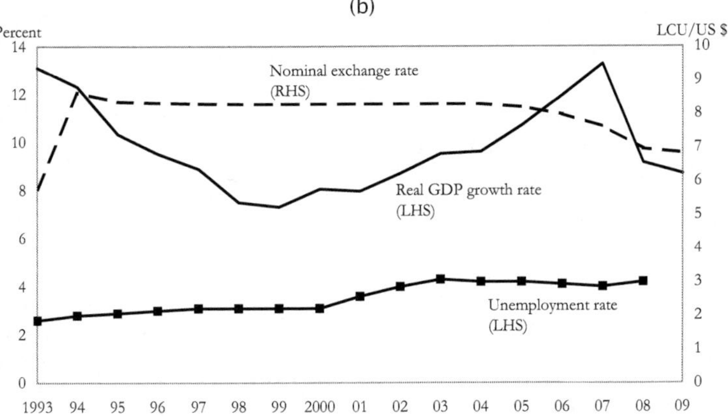

Figure 6.1: *Macroeconomic conditions in China, 1993–2009: (a) exports, imports and average tariffs; (b) growth rate of GDP, exchange rate and unemployment rate.*

Source: author's calculations using World Development Indicators (2010). In panel (a), the *ad valorem* tariff rate is defined as a simple average of applied MFN tariffs for all products. In panel (b), the exchange rate is the period average official exchange rate defined as yuan/$. The unemployment rate is a percentage of total employment.

Figure 6.1(a) also documents how a rapid reduction in China's average tariffs coincided with the dramatic increase in China's imports during 1995–2009. China's average applied MFN tariff decreased from roughly 40% in 1993 to 17% in 2000. China's accession to the WTO in December 2001 was associated with a further tariff reduction of roughly 6 percentage points. By the end of 2008, its average applied MFN tariff had decreased to 9.6%.

China began to use TTBs as an alternative form of protection while its tariffs were falling during this period (Messerlin 2004). China enacted its first anti-dumping law in March 1997, and it was investigating 20–30 cases per year in each of the first few years following its WTO accession (Bown 2010a). In this chapter, we extend the analysis of previous studies by examining China's use of all TTB policies up to 2009, examining both new initiations of investigations and instances in which China imposed new measures. Furthermore, as China's TTB use is dominated by anti-dumping, we explore China's use of anti-dumping in further detail. We examine its composition across sectors, the groups of foreign countries that China has targeted, and the time duration of the measures imposed.[3]

Our results indicate interesting patterns to China's anti-dumping investigations prior to and during the 2008–9 crisis. China initiated a large number of new anti-dumping investigations in 2002, immediately after its December 2001 entry to the WTO. Except in 2004, the number of new Chinese anti-dumping investigations decreased in each year during 2003–7. However, during 2008–9 the number of new anti-dumping investigations began to increase again. This pattern holds under a number of different metrics, whether we consider the number of anti-dumping cases, the share of HS-06 products involved in anti-dumping investigations, or the share of China's import value affected by anti-dumping investigations.

Despite this increase in the flow of new anti-dumping investigations during the 2008–9 crisis, the total stock of products under Chinese anti-dumping measures actually decreased during this period due to the removal of several previously imposed anti-dumping measures. For instance, 0.3% and 0.4% of China's HS-06 products were involved in new anti-dumping investigations in 2008 and 2009, respectively. However, during the same period, China's total stock of HS-06 products subject to anti-dumping measures decreased from 1.1% to 1.0%.

In terms of China's industries, chemicals, paper and pulp, plastics and rubber, steel, and textiles have been the main sectors petitioning for anti-dumping investigations during 1997–2009. The chemicals sector has dominated China's anti-dumping use with 104 of the 172 (60%) anti-dumping cases investigated during 1997–2009. However, in terms of the share of import value, only 8.6% of the imports in the chemicals sector were subject to anti-dumping measures at its within-period peak in 2008. Perhaps surprisingly, this figure is comparable to other sectors with many fewer investigations such as paper and pulp, plastics and rubber and steel, each of which had a stock of roughly 8% of industry imports subject to anti-dumping measures at their respective peaks.

Since the increase in the number of new Chinese anti-dumping investigations during the crisis coincided with a period that also saw a large number of

---

[3]We use the World Bank's *Temporary Trade Barriers Database* (Bown 2010b) for data on China's use of TTBs. In addition, we use imports data from Comtrade and tariff data from TRAINS via WITS. Further details on the data can be found in Chapter 1.

measures being removed, we also investigate whether the new investigations were filed largely in order to replace those being removed. The data quickly rule out such an explanation. While, in the years prior to the crisis, China's anti-dumping activity was dominated by relatively few sectors, a number of 'new' sectors that had never previously used anti-dumping sought initiations in 2008–9. At the same time, other traditional users of anti-dumping in China, such as paper and pulp and textiles, did not file any new anti-dumping investigations, even though several previously imposed anti-dumping measures on products from these sectors were removed.

Next, we provide evidence that China uses anti-dumping to target both developing and *developed* trading partners. The EU, Japan, South Korea and USA are four of the largest targets of China's anti-dumping activity, together accounting for 111 of the 172 (65%) anti-dumping cases that China filed during 1997–2009. These four economies also accounted for 62% of the total stock of HS-06 product–country combinations subject to Chinese anti-dumping measures by 2009. China's anti-dumping use exhibits other important differences depending on whether the anti-dumping targeted a developed or developing trading partner. For instance, while the total stock of HS-06 product–country combinations affected by anti-dumping measures decreased in 2009 compared with 2008 for both groups, the decline was much greater for developing economy exporters than the developed economy exporters.

An important question regarding China's anti-dumping use during the 2008–9 crisis is the extent to which it is motivated by retaliation. For example, China initiated anti-dumping investigations on imports of chicken parts and autos from the USA almost immediately after the USA imposed a safeguard on imports of Chinese tyres in September 2009.[4] Many interpreted the timing of the new Chinese investigations as a direct response to the US actions and raised the concern of a potential 'trade war'. Other Chinese anti-dumping cases with potential retaliatory motives include China imposing its own anti-dumping duty on steel fasteners from the EU within months of the EU initiating an anti-dumping investigation on steel fasteners from China (Bown 2010b).[5]

While these examples are suggestive of retaliation being a contributing motive to China's anti-dumping use, this evidence is merely anecdotal. Furthermore, while Bown (2011b) has found that a higher share of China's exports to *developing* countries are affected by their anti-dumping than its exports to

[4]China eventually imposed anti-dumping duties as high as 105% on chicken parts in September 2010. China also initiated and imposed CVD measures on chicken parts.

[5]EU producers initiated an anti-dumping investigation against imports of steel fasteners from China in November 2007. China responded by initiating an anti-dumping investigation against steel fasteners from the EU in December 2008. Both economies targeted imports of identical HS-06 products from each other's market (the most disaggregated level at which the classification is comparable across countries), though the varieties of the product produced by each country are likely to be different.

developed countries, we nevertheless find that the majority of China's anti-dumping measures targeted imports from *developed* countries. Even among the set of developed countries, one of China's main anti-dumping targets is Japan, a country that has not used anti-dumping actively against China.

We examine other features of China's anti-dumping use during 1997–2009, including the size of duties imposed, the relationship to changes in its applied tariffs, and the duration of imposed measures. China's average *ad valorem* anti-dumping duty in 2009 was roughly 20%, as opposed to the within-period peak of more than 95% in 2005. Furthermore, products that experienced a larger reduction in China's applied tariff during its WTO accession were more likely to be involved in a subsequent anti-dumping investigation. Finally, even though the modal duration of Chinese anti-dumping measures is five years (excluding anti-dumping measures in force as of end-2009), there are a number of products for which the ongoing anti-dumping measures have been in place for much longer. In fact, China's record in removing anti-dumping orders after the mandated *sunset review* within five years is very poor. Only 40% of the anti-dumping measures that China imposed during 1999–2004 were removed by the end of 2009.

The last issue that we explore is the Chinese firm-level involvement in anti-dumping investigations as petitioners, finding only a small number of participating firms. Excluding the 9 instances in which an industry association filed the anti-dumping petition, only 141 firms participated as petitioners in investigations during 1997–2009. Furthermore, many of the firms participated in only 1 anti-dumping case.

The rest of this chapter proceeds as follows. Section 2 constructs count- and value-based measures described in Chapter 1 by Bown and documents broad trends in China's use of TTBs. Section 3 investigates the sectoral composition of China's anti-dumping use, and Section 4 examines China's anti-dumping use across different groups of targeted countries. Section 5 highlights the relationship between China's tariff liberalisation and its subsequent anti-dumping use, trends in anti-dumping duties, and the average duration of Chinese anti-dumping measures. Section 6 illustrates the participation of Chinese firms as petitioners in anti-dumping investigations. Finally, Section 7 concludes.

2 CHINA'S USE OF TEMPORARY TRADE BARRIERS

2.1 Broad Trends in China's TTBs

Given that anti-dumping duty laws have been around for over a century, China is one of the more recent users of anti-dumping. While China established the principles of anti-dumping in its Foreign Trade Law of 1994, it only enacted its first anti-dumping law—the Anti-Dumping and Anti-Subsidy Regulation—in 1997 (Yu 2005). China initiated its first anti-dumping investigation in 1997, and by the end of 2009 it had investigated 172 separate anti-dumping cases.

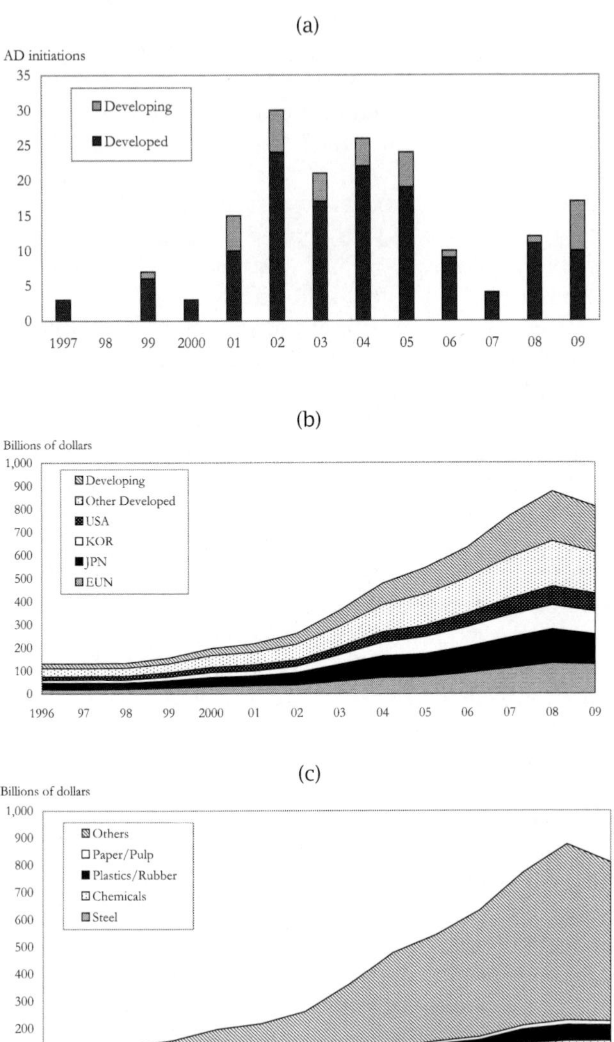

Figure 6.2: *China's anti-dumping investigations and aggregate imports, 1997–2009: (a) China's anti-dumping investigations; (b) China's total import value by major trading partners; (c) China's total import value by main sectors involved in anti-dumping.*

Source: author's calculations using data from Bown (2010b) and Comtrade. The EU is treated throughout as the set of 27 member countries. An anti-dumping case refers to the product-country pair from a given anti-dumping petition. Imports refer to China's non-oil imports.

Figure 6.2(a) shows the total number of China's anti-dumping investigations during this period by year.[6] While China initiated only three anti-dumping investigations in 1997, it gradually started increasing the number of anti-dumping investigations until 2002. China initiated 30 new anti-dumping cases in the year immediately following its entry into the WTO, twice as many as in 2001.

There could be several explanations for this increase in the number of anti-dumping cases in 2002. The first is the timing related to China's December 2001 WTO entry. Prior to 2001, China was free to use other measures of trade policy and thus there was no need to use anti-dumping. Because China's WTO accession was associated with a decrease in its applied import tariffs, this could have triggered an increase in demand for non-tariff barriers such as anti-dumping. A second contributing explanation could be China's adoption of a new set of anti-dumping regulations. China's first anti-dumping law in 1997 was far from complete, and a number of its administrative procedures led to confusion. For instance, the basis for calculating dumping margins for a preliminary affirmative determination was not disclosed to interested parties, and the determination of injury and causation was not based on an objective examination of sufficient evidence (Choi and Gao 2006). As part of its accession to the WTO, China enacted a more comprehensive and WTO-consistent set of rules guiding anti-dumping and CVDs.[7] Finally, a third possible explanation could be a potential slowdown in the growth rate of China's economy during 2001–2 (see again Figure 6.1(b)).

After the increase in China's anti-dumping filings in 2002, the number of new anti-dumping cases decreased each year until 2008 when the trend reversed.[8] That the increase in new anti-dumping cases coincided with the onset of the crisis is not necessarily evidence of a causal link. In fact, the

---

[6]In Figure 6.2, we treat the EU as a single economy and drop the duplicate cases in which two or more EU members are investigated. For instance, in December 2000, China initiated an anti-dumping investigation for dichloromethane (methylene chloride) against four members of the EU: France, Germany, the Netherlands and the UK. We count this as one case against the EU. For consistency, we define 'EU' as all 27 countries for the entire period even though some countries became members only midway through the period.

[7]The revision in 2002 was one of the main reforms to China's anti-dumping regulations, though a number of other smaller changes have taken place since. For instance, in July 2004, China revised its anti-dumping rules to make the newly constructed Ministry of Commerce of the People's Republic of China (MOFCOM) take anti-dumping responsibilities away from the Ministry of Foreign Trade and Economic Cooperation and The State Economic and Trade Commission. Another change during June 2004 was to include a clause directing MOFCOM to consider public interest in anti-dumping determinations.

[8]The only exception to the steady decline over the period 2003–7 was in 2004 when the total number of new anti-dumping cases increased to 26 after decreasing to 21 in 2003. Note that one might expect to see a decline in the following year given the large number of anti-dumping cases investigated in 2002. However, in 2003 the total number of cases was still higher than the 1997–2009 average.

average number of 14 investigations per year during the 2008–9 crisis period is similar to that of the pre-crisis period (1997–2007).

Figure 6.2(a) also illustrates that a large share of China's anti-dumping investigations targeted developed trading partners. Of the 172 anti-dumping cases initiated by China during 1997–2009, 138 (80%) were directed at developed economies. This is not surprising, since developed economies account for a large fraction of China's total imports. Figure 6.2(b) shows China's non-oil imports during this period broken down by developed and developing trading partners. Even in 2009, China's imports from developed countries totalled $612 billion as opposed to approximately $200 billion from developing countries.

Table 6.1 gives more details on Chinese anti-dumping investigations and their outcomes. Of the 166 anti-dumping cases that China initiated during 1997–2009 in which a final decision has been made, 135 (81%) cases ultimately resulted in the imposition of a final anti-dumping measure.[9] Furthermore, almost all Chinese anti-dumping measures were in the form of *ad valorem* duties; only eight cases resulted in a price undertaking. Moreover, each of the price undertakings resulted from anti-dumping cases initiated prior to the 2008–9 crisis and were directed at developed economies.

Table 6.1 also documents outcome variation both across years and targeted countries. China imposed a final anti-dumping measure in only 13 of the 24 anti-dumping cases (54%) filed in 2005, much lower than the period average of 81%. Of the 134 anti-dumping cases that China filed against developed countries, 110 (82%) resulted in the imposition of a final anti-dumping measure, compared with 25 out of 32 cases (78%) filed against developing countries. Finally, cases targeting developed countries had a higher average *ad valorem* anti-dumping duty rate during 1997–2009.

China has used other TTBs such as CVDs and global safeguards in addition to anti-dumping. However, it has used anti-dumping much more frequently than the other two policies. China initiated its first CVD case in June 2009, and by the end of 2009 it had already initiated three investigations over steel products, chicken parts and autos. All three CVD cases targeted US exporters and all three had a corresponding anti-dumping case.

China has been more restrained in its use of safeguards, having used this TTB only once since its WTO accession. China imposed a safeguard in 2002 over imports of a number of steel products, coinciding with similar safeguards that USA, the EU and a number of other countries imposed. China withdrew the safeguards in 2003 in response to a similar removal by the USA and the EU.

[9]Six of the 17 cases initiated during 2009 are still being investigated. Of the 31 cases initiated during 1997–2009 that did not result in the imposition of a final anti-dumping measure, 17 led to a negative injury determination, 5 were terminated and 9 were withdrawn.

Table 6.1: *China's anti-dumping initiations and outcomes: overall and by income group, 1997–2009.*

Year	Number of anti-dumping initiations	Number of cases that resulted in final anti-dumping measures (%)		Average minimum *ad valorem* anti-dumping duty	Average maximum *ad valorem* anti-dumping duty
		(a) All cases			
1997	3	3	(100)	48.0	70.3
1998	0	0	—	—	—
1999	7	7	(100)	25.8	58.3
2000	3	3	(100)	26.7	46.7
2001	15	9	(60)	8.6	32.1
2002	30	26	(86)	11.6	47.1
2003	21	20	(95)	63.5	105.5
2004	26	18	(69)	32.5	83.8
2005	24	13	(54)	13.8	42.7
2006	10	10	(100)	11.6	37.0
2007	4	4	(100)	6.3	51.6
2008	12	11	(91)	12.4	22.6
2009	11	11	(100)	11.9	39.4
Total	166	135	(81)	22.7	55.9
		(b) Developed countries			
1997	3	3	(100)	48.0	70.3
1998	0	0	—	—	—
1999	6	6	(100)	29.8	57.6
2000	3	3	(100)	26.7	46.7
2001	10	6	(66)	9.2	35.2
2002	24	20	(83)	10.5	50.0
2003	17	16	(94)	66.6	114.6
2004	22	15	(68)	37.5	80.8
2005	19	12	(63)	14.0	44.6
2006	9	9	(100)	11.8	37.0
2007	4	4	(100)	6.3	51.6
2008	11	10	(90)	13.1	22.6
2009	6	6	(100)	16.9	51.0
Total	134	110	(82)	24.4	58.7

2.2 The Share of China's Imports Subject to Anti-Dumping

We start the analysis by constructing stock and flow measures of the relevant TTBs based on Bown (2011b). In particular, we follow Equation (1.1) and Equation (1.2) of Chapter 1 and construct two separate measures of the use of TTBs: the first is based on the *count* of the HS-06 products affected by the

Table 6.1: *Continued.*

Year	Number of anti-dumping initiations	Number of cases that resulted in final anti-dumping measures (%)		Average minimum *ad valorem* anti-dumping duty	Average maximum *ad valorem* anti-dumping duty
(c) Developing countries					
1997	0	0	—	—	—
1998	0	0	—	—	—
1999	1	1	(100)	6.0	62.0
2000	0	0	—	—	—
2001	5	3	(60)	7.3	26.0
2002	6	6	(100)	15.2	37.3
2003	4	4	(100)	51.3	69.0
2004	4	3	(75)	7.2	98.6
2005	5	1	(20)	12.2	20.4
2006	1	1	(100)	10.1	37.7
2007	0	0	—	—	—
2008	1	1	(100)	5.4	21.8
2009	5	5	(100)	5.9	25.5
Total	32	25	(78)	15.0	46.5

The table does not include the six additional anti-dumping cases initiated in 2009 that are still ongoing.

Source: author's calculations using data from Bown (2010b).

TTBs as a share of the total number of products imported, and the second is a *value*-based measure that takes into account the share of China's value of imports affected by TTBs.

Prior to 2006, China used the HS-06 product classification to describe the products involved in TTB investigations.[10] Since 2006, China has started using the more disaggregated HS-08 classification.[11] Since a majority of cases (72%) are reported using the HS-06 classification, we conduct our analysis at that level. One caveat is that this approach can overstate the total share of imports subject to TTBs for cases initiated after 2006 if only a fraction of the HS-08 products within an HS-06 category is subject to the TTB investigation. In our case, all the underlying HS-08 products were involved in the investigations in only 55% of the HS-06 products investigated during 2006–9. However, in

[10]The only exception is the safeguard case initiated in 2002 in which China used the HS-08 classification.

[11]In two anti-dumping cases involving paper and catechol, originally investigated in 2002, China reclassified the products involved in a subsequent review using a finer HS-08 classification rather than the original HS-06 classification.

order for our comparison across years to be meaningful, we rely on the HS-06 classification.[12]

Figure 6.3 summarises our main results. Panels (a) and (b) refer to China's use of all TTB policies, while panels (c) and (d) report its use of anti-dumping only. We report the count measure in panels (a) and (c) and the value measure in panels (b) and (d). The count- and value-based measures have similar time series patterns over 1997–2009. The main difference is that the count measure provides a lower estimate of the share of imports affected by TTBs. For instance, at its within-period peak in 2003, around 2% of HS-06 products in China were under a TTB measure. However, these TTB measures affected 4% of the value of China's imports. This implies that China's TTBs disproportionately target relatively high import value products.

One of the most striking observations from panels (a) and (b) of Figure 6.3 is a spike in 2002. A large part of this increase is due to China's imposition of the previously mentioned global safeguard on steel products. With the withdrawal of the safeguard measure, China's total stock of products subject to TTB measures decreased to roughly 0.9% in 2004, less than half its level in 2003. Since 2004, the stock of products affected by TTBs remained roughly constant at 1.1% until it fell to 1.0% in 2009.

Panels (c) and (d) of Figure 6.3 focus on anti-dumping only and illustrate an upward trend in China's affected imports until 2005. Under the count measure, the stock of HS-06 products under anti-dumping more than tripled from 0.3% before China's accession to the WTO to 1.1% in 2005. The increase is even larger under the import-value measure, where the share of imports affected by anti-dumping more than quadrupled from 0.5% in 2001 to 2.2% in 2005.

The stock of products under anti-dumping measures remained roughly stable from 2005 until the beginning of the crisis in 2008, before falling in 2009. The decrease in the total *stock* of products under anti-dumping is especially notable given that a large number of new anti-dumping cases were initiated during 2008–9. The reduction in the stock is driven by the removal of several existing anti-dumping measures during this period. The new anti-dumping measures that were imposed during this period covered fewer HS-06 products and accounted for a smaller share of imports by value relative to the anti-dumping measures being removed.

The *flow* of new anti-dumping investigations reveals a similar pattern over 1997–2009 using either the count or the value of imports. The share of imports affected by new anti-dumping investigations increased in 2002, reaching the within-period peak. However, since the 2002 peak, the flow of new

[12]While using the HS-06 classification might overstate the share of imports affected by anti-dumping in terms of the value of imports, the direction of bias in terms of the share of *products* affected by anti-dumping could be the opposite. In fact, China initiated anti-dumping investigations in 0.8% of the HS-08 products with non-zero imports during 2006–9. When we use the HS-06 classification for the same period, the share of products affected by anti-dumping investigations was only 0.6%.

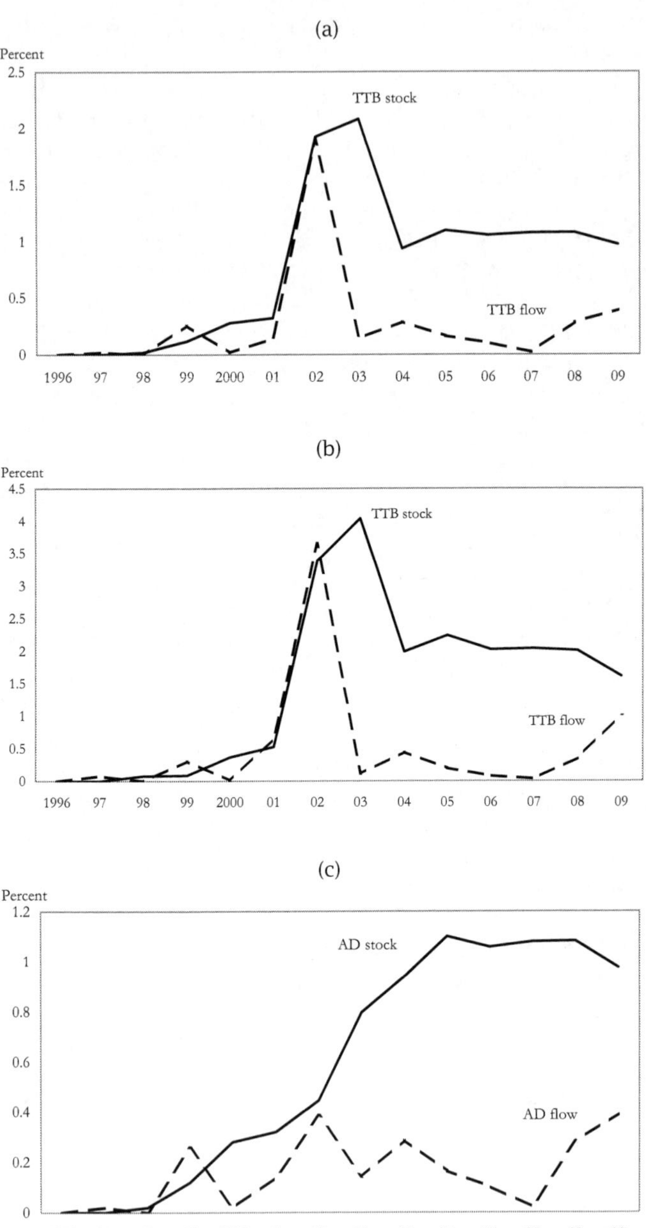

Figure 6.3: *China's TTB imports using count and value measures for the period 1997–2009: (a) all TTBs (count); (b) all TTBs (value); (c) anti-dumping only (count).*

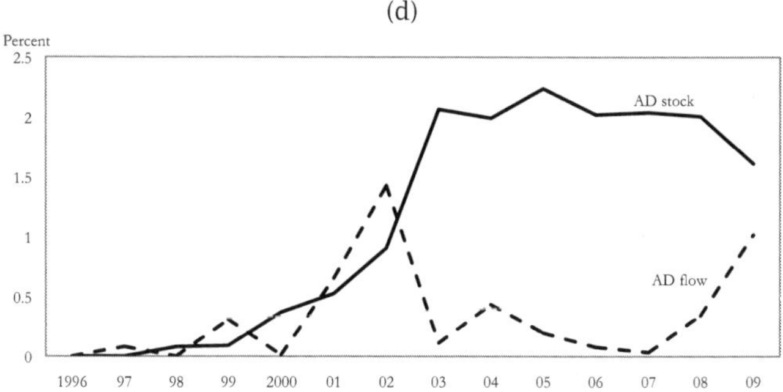

Figure 6.3: *Continued: (d) Anti-dumping only (value).*

Source: author's calculations using data from Bown (2010b) and Comtrade. The measures are based on Equations (1.1) and (1.2) from Chapter 1. The count measures report the percentage of HS-06 digit products affected by the relevant barrier. The value measures report the share of the imports affected by the corresponding measure. The stock measure corresponds to all measures currently in force (even if preliminary) and the flow measure corresponds to all new initiations.

anti-dumping investigations decreased steadily until 2007. With the onset of the crisis in 2008, the share of products subject to new anti-dumping investigations reversed trend and again started to increase.

3 SECTORAL TARGETS OF CHINA'S ANTI-DUMPING

The chemicals sector filed 104 (60%) of the 172 anti-dumping cases that China initiated during 1997–2009.[13] The other sectors that China targeted most heavily in its anti-dumping investigations are plastics and rubber (32 cases), paper and pulp (14 cases), steel (10 cases) and textiles (7 cases). Together these five sectors account for 97% of China's anti-dumping cases.

Nevertheless, there is no obvious trend in the value of industry-level imports to explain this anti-dumping pattern. Figure 6.2(c) shows China's total non-oil merchandise imports between 1997–2009 for chemicals, paper and pulp, plastics and rubber, and steel.[14] These sectors combined accounted for between 26-31% of China's total imports each year during 1997–2009, and China's total non-oil imports increased at an average annual rate of 14% during 1997–2009. However, except for the paper and pulp industry, where imports grew annually at only 10%, imports in each of the other three leading users

[13]The sectors are defined according to the 21 HS sections.

[14]Textiles imports are included in the 'others' category in Figure 6.2(c). Textiles imports decreased as a share of total imports from around 13% in 1996 to around 2% by 2009. Moreover, textiles imports grew only at an annual average rate of 0.8% during 1997–2009.

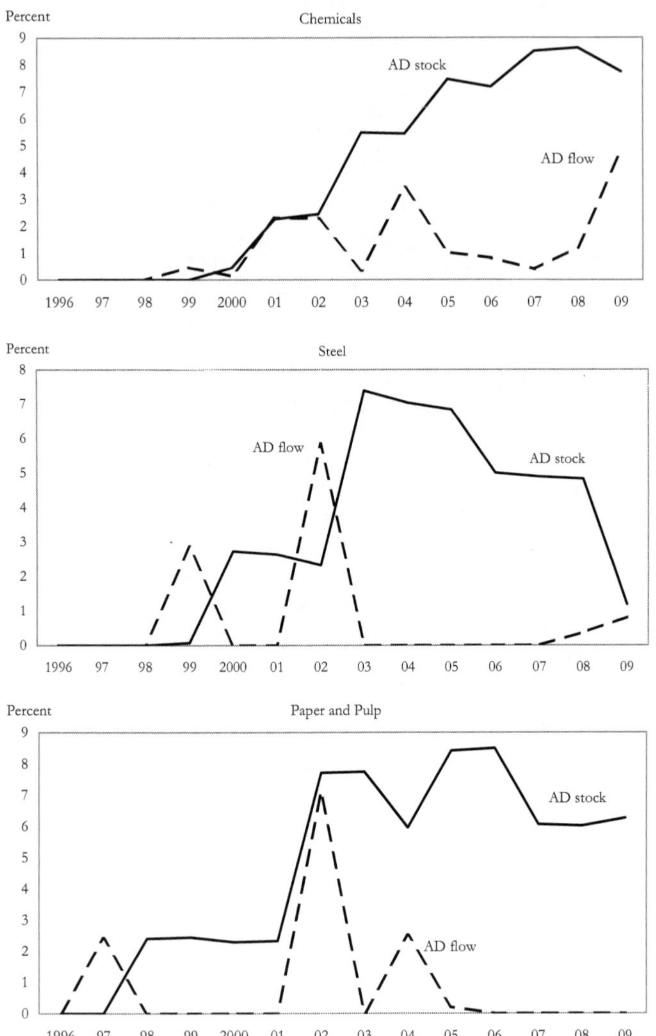

Figure 6.4: *Share of China's imports affected by anti-dumping by sector, 1997–2009.*

of anti-dumping (steel, chemicals, and plastics and rubber) grew at an annual rate of 13–15%.

Figure 6.4 presents the time series pattern of the share of imports affected by China's anti-dumping in each sector. The figure uses a slightly modified version of Equation (1.2) from Chapter 1; here we restrict analysis to only the sector in question. Despite accounting for the majority of China's anti-

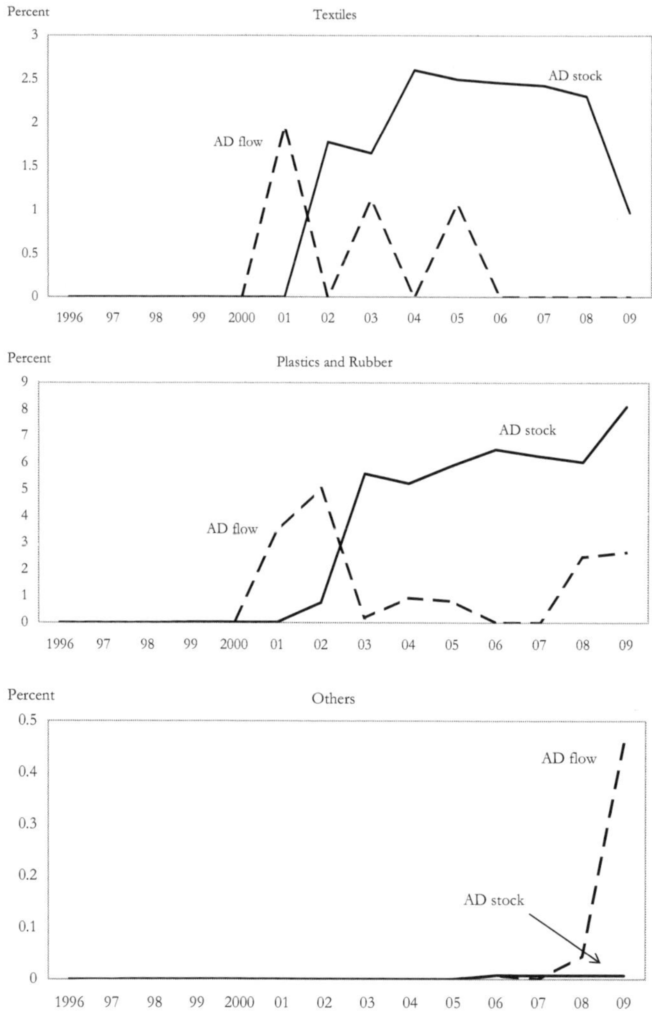

Figure 6.4: *Continued.*

Source: author's calculations using data from Bown (2010b) and Comtrade. These measures are based on Equation (1.2) from Chapter 1. The figure shows the share of import value in each sector affected by anti-dumping.

dumping cases, the share of *products* affected by anti-dumping in chemicals is comparable to the other leading sectors that initiated many fewer cases. At its within-period peak in 2008, about 8.6% of the total stock of imports in the chemicals sector were affected by China's anti-dumping. This is similar to the paper and pulp and plastics and rubber industries. And while the steel sector was involved in 10 times fewer anti-dumping cases (10 cases) than chemicals (104 cases), China's anti-dumping cases over steel products targeted almost as large a share of industry imports, with a peak of 7.4% in 2003.

There are substantial differences across sectors in the time series patterns of anti-dumping protection. China's accession to the WTO was accompanied by a flow of new anti-dumping investigations in 2002 that accounted for between 2% and 7% of the total imports in each sector. However, since 2002, sectors have had very different patterns to the flow of new anti-dumping investigations. China did not initiate any new anti-dumping investigation in the steel sector until the beginning of the crisis in 2008. On the other hand, China initiated new investigations in the chemicals sector each year since 2001. In 2009 alone, the chemicals sector had as much as 4.8% of imports under new anti-dumping investigations. Moreover, except for paper and pulp and textiles, the flow of new anti-dumping investigations increased during the 2008–9 crisis in all of China's leading sectoral users of anti-dumping.

Table 6.2 and 6.3 summarise and provide additional information on China's anti-dumping use across sectors. The second column of Table 6.2 reports the share of HS-06 products in a given sector that were involved in an anti-dumping investigation during 1997–2009. The next column reports a similar measure but only refers to those products in which an anti-dumping measure was imposed. Thus, differences between these two columns arise when an investigation results in termination or withdrawal or if the investigation is still pending. The fourth column reports the share of China's imports by value of the HS-06 products subject to anti-dumping measures at any point during 1997–2009.

Table 6.2 reveals that not all sectors in China have been involved in anti-dumping activity; in fact, some sectors that account for a large share of imports (*eg* machinery and electrical) had very little anti-dumping activity during 1997–2009. Nevertheless, some sectors that are heavy users of anti-dumping also account for a large share of China's total imports. Steel and chemicals accounted for 10% and 9% of China's total merchandise imports during this period, respectively. The products subject to China's anti-dumping also accounted for 12% and 13% of the value of steel and chemicals imports, respectively.

Table 6.3 further breaks down this information into the period before and during 2008–9. Though it is not reported in the table, China's imports fell in 16 of the 21 sectors during the crisis.[15] Some sectors that were heavy users of anti-dumping before the crisis did not start new anti-dumping investigations during 2008–9 (see again Figure 6.4). Table 6.3 identifies new sectors, *ie* those that initiated anti-dumping investigations during the crisis period, and reports the shares of HS-06 products under investigation. For example, China

[15] The five sectors in which imports continued to increase during this period were food and beverages, steel, transport equipment, arms and ammunition, and miscellaneous.

initiated new anti-dumping investigations on more than 4% of its HS-06 products in the transport equipment sector (autos). Other sectors such as animal products (chicken parts) and other instruments started new investigations covering 3.1% and 2% of each industry's imports, respectively.

4 THE COUNTRY TARGETS OF CHINA'S ANTI-DUMPING

4.1 Countries: Overall Trends

China initiated anti-dumping investigations against 19 different trading partners between 1997 and 2009. South Korea was targeted with 32 anti-dumping cases, followed by Japan (31), USA (28), the EU (20) and Taiwan (16). Combined, these five countries accounted for 74% of China's anti-dumping investigations.

Figure 6.5(a) shows the cumulative annual stock of HS-06 product-country combinations subject to China's anti-dumping measures by the targeted exporting economy.[16] Japan and South Korea together account for approximately 40% of China's annual stock of product-country combinations affected by anti-dumping measures. On average, 64–71% of China's stock of anti-dumping measures were targeted at developed countries in each year during 2003–8. While the stock of products subject to China's anti-dumping measures fell for both developed and developing trading partners in 2009, the decline was much greater for anti-dumping measures targeting developing countries.

The leading target countries are also among the major sources of China's imports. Panel (b) of Figure 6.2 shows the trend in the value of China's imports from its leading trade partners. Imports from the EU, Japan, South Korea and USA together accounted for 53–60% of China's total non-oil imports in each year during 1997–2009. During this period, imports from South Korea and the EU increased at an average annual rate of 16% and 15%, respectively, whereas imports from Japan and USA grew at an annual rate of 11% and 12%, respectively.

While the top five economies targeted by China are developed economies, China has also frequently targeted developing economies such as India, Indonesia, Malaysia, Thailand and Russia.[17] Although a much smaller share of China's imports during 1997–2009 were from developing countries, imports from developing countries grew at a faster rate (17.5%) than imports from developed economies (13%).

---

[16]Figure 6.5(a) uses a slightly modified version of the count measure, where we only use the numerator of Equation (1.2) of Chapter 1. Moreover, following Bown (2011b), we construct the measure using the count of combinations of HS-06 products and the target economy.

[17]We refer to all high-income countries according to the World Bank definition based on gross national income per capita as 'developed economies' and the rest as 'developing economies'.

Table 6.2: *Sectoral distribution of anti-dumping cases in China, 1997–2009.*

	HS section	Number of HS-06 products with non-zero imports	Share of HS-06 products within sector involved in anti-dumping investigations	Share of HS-06 products within sector subject to anti-dumping measure	Share of 1997–2009 imports within sector in HS-06 products subject to anti-dumping measure	Sectoral imports as a share of total imports (1997–2009)	Share of 1996 imports within sector in HS-06 products subject to anti-dumping measure	Sectoral imports as share of share of total 1996 imports
I	Live animals/ animal products	198	2.5	0.0	0.0	0.8	0.0	0.7
II	Vegetable products	269	0.4	0.4	0.1	2.3	0.2	2.6
III	Animal/vegetable fats, oils and waxes	46	0.0	0.0	0.0	0.9	0.0	1.3
IV	Prepared foodstuffs, beverages and tobacco	186	0.0	0.0	0.0	0.7	0.0	1.8
V	Mineral products	146	0.0	0.0	0.0	7.2	0.0	2.6
VI	Chemicals	786	3.7	3.1	12.1	8.8	9.9	7.9
VII	Plastics and rubber	198	5.1	4.5	12.0	7.1	10.3	7.7
VIII	Leather products	74	0.0	0.0	0.0	1.0	0.0	1.9
IX	Wood/bamboo products	81	0.0	0.0	0.0	1.1	0.0	1.2
X	Paper and pulp	151	6.6	6.6	9.7	2.2	18.6	3.2

Table 6.2: *Continued.*

	HS section	Number of HS-06 products with non-zero imports	Share of HS-06 products within sector involved in anti-dumping investigations	Share of HS-06 products within sector subject to anti-dumping measure	Share of 1997–2009 imports within sector in HS-06 products subject to anti-dumping measure	Sectoral imports as a share of total imports (1997–2009)	Share of 1996 imports within sector in HS-06 products subject to anti-dumping measure	Sectoral imports as share of share of total 1996 imports
XI	Textiles	822	0.7	0.7	4.7	4.2	3.9	12.6
XII	Footwear and umbrellas	55	0.0	0.0	0.0	0.1	0.0	0.3
XIII	Articles of stone/ plaster/cement	147	0.0	0.0	0.0	0.6	0.0	0.8
XIV	Precious stones and metals	50	0.0	0.0	0.0	0.7	0.0	0.3
XV	Steel	571	4.7	4.7	13.3	9.7	18.2	9.6
XVI	Machinery and electrical	804	0.0	0.0	0.0	40.7	0.0	37.1
XVII	Transport equipment	132	3.8	0.0	0.0	4.5	0.0	4.0
XVIII	Other instruments	238	1.7	0.0	0.0	7.0	0.0	3.5
XIX	Arms and ammunition	14	0.0	0.0	0.0	0.0	0.0	0.0
XX	Miscellaneous manufactured articles	130	0.0	0.0	0.0	0.4	0.0	0.8
XXI	Works of art	7	0.0	0.0	0.0	0.0	0.0	0.0
	Total	5,105	1.9	1.5	4.9	100.0	5.1	100.0

Source: author's calculations using data from Bown (2010b) and Comtrade.

Table 6.3: *Sectoral distribution of anti-dumping cases in China, before and during the crisis.*

	HS section	1997–2007			2008–2009		
		Share of HS-06 products within sector involved in anti-dumping investigations	Share of HS-06 products within sector subject to anti-dumping measure	Share of 1997–2007 imports within sector in HS-06 products subject to anti-dumping measure	Share of HS-06 products within sector involved in anti-dumping investigations	Share of HS-06 products within sector subject to anti-dumping measure	Share of 2008–2009 imports within sector in HS-06 products subject to anti-dumping measure
I	Live animals/ animal products	0.0	0.0	0.0	3.1	0.0	0.0
II	Vegetable products	0.4	0.4	0.2	0.0	0.4	0.0
III	Animal or vegetable fats, oils, and waxes	0.0	0.0	0.0	0.0	0.0	0.0
IV	Prepared foodstuffs, beverages and tobacco	0.0	0.0	0.0	0.0	0.0	0.0
V	Mineral products	0.0	0.0	0.0	0.0	0.0	0.0
VI	Chemicals	3.2	2.8	11.8	1.0	3.4	10.7
VII	Plastics and rubber	4.5	4.0	9.7	0.5	4.1	11.6
VIII	Leather products	0.0	0.0	0.0	0.0	0.0	0.0
IX	Wood/bamboo products	0.0	0.0	0.0	0.0	0.0	0.0
X	Paper and pulp	6.6	6.6	12.0	0.0	3.7	2.2

Table 6.3: *Continued.*

		1997–2007			2008–2009		
	HS section	Share of HS-06 products within sector involved in anti-dumping investigations	Share of HS-06 products within sector subject to anti-dumping measure	Share of 1997–2007 imports within sector in HS-06 products subject to anti-dumping measure	Share of HS-06 products within sector involved in anti-dumping investigations	Share of HS-06 products within sector subject to anti-dumping measure	Share of 2008–2009 imports within sector in HS-06 products subject to anti-dumping measure
XI	Textiles	0.7	0.7	5.0	0.0	0.5	1.8
XII	Footwear and umbrellas	0.0	0.0	0.0	0.0	0.0	0.0
XIII	Articles of stone /plaster/cement	0.0	0.0	0.0	0.0	0.0	0.0
XIV	Precious stones and metals	0.0	0.0	0.0	0.0	0.0	0.0
XV	Steel	3.9	3.9	13.5	1.3	3.3	7.0
XVI	Machinery and electrical	0.0	0.0	0.0	0.0	0.0	0.0
XVII	Transport equipment	0.0	0.0	0.0	4.1	0.0	0.0
XVIII	Other instruments	0.0	0.0	0.0	1.9	0.0	0.0
XIX	Arms and ammunition	0.0	0.0	0.0	0.0	0.0	0.0
XX	Miscellaneous manufactured articles	0.0	0.0	0.0	0.0	0.0	0.0
XXI	Works of art	0.0	0.0	0.0	0.0	0.0	0.0
	Total	1.4	1.4	4.9	1.6	1.3	3.3

Source: author's calculations using data from Bown (2010b) and Comtrade.

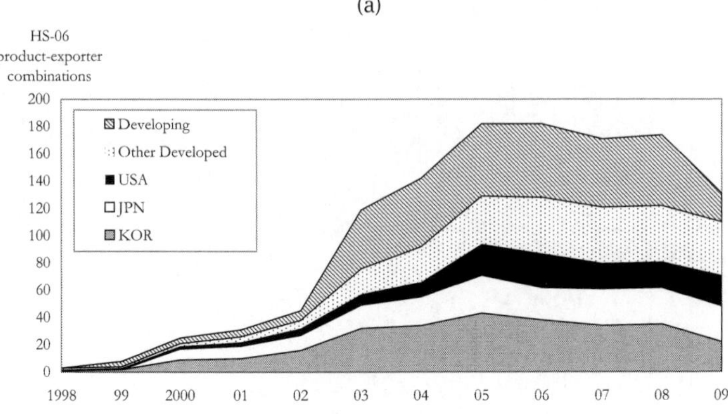

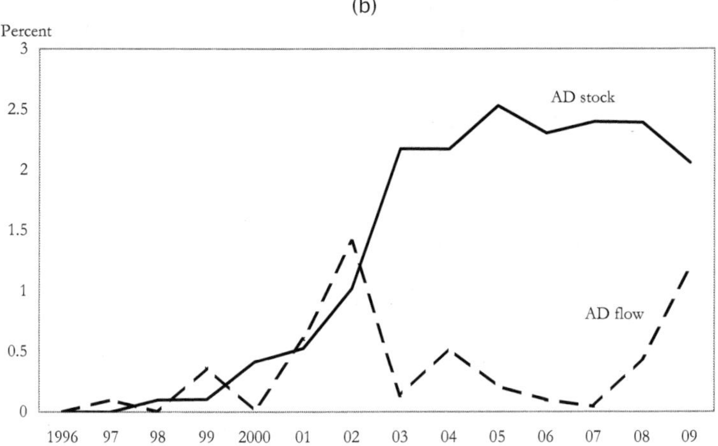

Figure 6.5: *China's imports affected by anti-dumping, by targeted trading partner, 1997–2009: (a) stock of products affected by anti-dumping measure, by trading partner; (b) share of imports from developed countries affected by anti-dumping.*

Panels (b) and (c) of Figure 6.5 focus on the share of China's imports subject to anti-dumping measures using the *value* measure. The figures rely on separately constructed measures for developed and developing trading partners using the stock and flow indicators based on Equation (1.2) of Chapter 1.[18] The pattern in China's flow of anti-dumping investigations is similar for both

[18]The denominator in each case refers to the imports from that group only. Therefore, if China imported very little from developing countries but all of its imports were subject to anti-dumping measures, the import share affected by anti-dumping would be 100%.

(c)

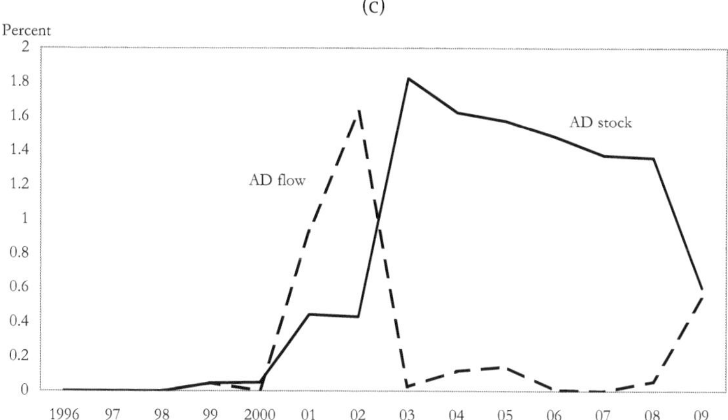

Figure 6.5: *Continued: (c) Share of imports from developing countries affected by anti-dumping.*

Source: author's calculations using data from Bown (2010b) and Comtrade. The measures in panel (a) are based on a slightly modified version of Equation (1.1) from Introduction (Bown, this volume) in which we drop the denominator. The measures illustrate the annual stock of product-exporting-target-country combinations affected by anti-dumping measures. The measures in panels (b) and (c) are based on Equation (1.2) from Chapter 1.

groups of countries; a large share of China's imports were affected by new anti-dumping investigations during 2002, followed by a gradual decline until 2007, with a reversal in trend during the crisis years. Despite the similarity in the pattern across both groups, the shares of imports affected by new anti-dumping investigations are very different. For instance, in 2009, 1.2% of China's imports from developed economies were subject to new anti-dumping investigations—almost as high as its within-period peak of 1.4% in 2002. On the other hand, roughly 0.4% of imports from developing countries were affected by new anti-dumping investigations in 2009, which was only one-fourth as much as the within-period peak of 1.6% in 2002. Thus, the flow of China's anti-dumping investigations during 2008–9 against developing countries was much smaller than the new cases against developed economies. Second, even within the set of developing country targets, the share of imports affected by new Chinese anti-dumping investigations during the crisis was much smaller than previous years.

Between 1997 and 2003, the total stock of Chinese imports subject to anti-dumping measures increased steadily, eventually affecting 1.8% of China's imports from developing countries and 2.2% of China's imports from developed countries. However, the two groups of countries show very different trends since 2003. While China's total stock of imports from developed economies subject to anti-dumping measures continued to increase until

2007, there was a dramatic decrease in its stock of imports from developing countries subject to anti-dumping measures.

4.2 Countries: Sectoral Composition of Anti-Dumping

Tables 6.4 and 6.5 explore potential sectoral differences in China's imports affected by anti-dumping depending on whether the targets were developed or developing economies. Table 6.4 examines the pre-crisis period (1997–2007) and Table 6.5 refers to 2008–9.

First consider Table 6.4. China has only targeted imports from developed countries in the textiles sector, whereas in each of the other leading anti-dumping sectors (chemicals, paper and pulp, plastics and rubber, and steel), China targeted imports from both groups of countries. Moreover, in each sector in which China has used anti-dumping, the products involved in the anti-dumping investigations form a much lower share of imports from developing trading partners than the share of imports from developed trading partners. For example, while 6.6% of the imported products from developed economies in the paper and pulp sector were involved in anti-dumping investigations, only 3.3% of paper and pulp products imported from developing countries were involved.

Two striking features arise when comparing the pre-crisis period with 2008–9. First, China initiated several new anti-dumping investigations against developed economies in sectors that had not previously participated in anti-dumping investigations prior to the crisis. For the developing economy targets, the entire increase during 2008–9 was due to increased product coverage in some of the traditional anti-dumping-using sectors. Second, the products involved in anti-dumping investigations in new sectors accounted for a much larger share of the value of imports. In the pre-crisis period, the largest share of imports for products involved in anti-dumping investigations accounted for only 14% of imports (plastics and rubber). During 2008–9, 35% of imports in the transport equipment sector became subject to China's anti-dumping investigations.

5 TARIFFS, ANTI-DUMPING DUTIES AND THE DURATION OF ANTI-DUMPING MEASURES

5.1 China's Anti-Dumping Duties

This section examines the magnitude of China's anti-dumping duties and explores whether China's anti-dumping has become more or less prohibitive over time. One of the features of anti-dumping is that it can be used to discriminate between different countries as well as between firms from the same target country. We focus on the *ad valorem* anti-dumping duty rates in Bown (2010b), which report the *minimum* and *maximum* firm-specific duties. We use these minimum and maximum rates to construct averages. Figure 6.6(a) reports the average over all HS-06 products subject to an anti-dumping measure imposed that year across all targeted countries.[19] The solid line in the figure is the average of the maximum *ad valorem* rate for a given product across all targeted countries, and the dashed line depicts the average of the corresponding minimum rate. Our first finding is that China's average *ad valorem* anti-dumping duty fell over the sample. At the end of 2009, the maximum rate for products with new anti-dumping measures was only 20%, which was significantly lower than 70% in 1999 when China first imposed an anti-dumping duty. This trend is particularly evident in the five years following the 2004 peak of the average rate.

Figure 6.6(b) reports the average maximum and minimum rates for the stock of products with an anti-dumping duty in place that year.[20] The average anti-dumping duty rate decreased over the sample period because of the addition of new anti-dumping measures that had lower average *ad valorem* anti-dumping rates than the existing measures. Nevertheless, the maximum *ad valorem* anti-dumping duty was 60% even as late as 2009. Average anti-dumping duties did not decrease at a faster rate despite the removal of previously imposed measures in 2008–9 because the measures being eliminated had lower *ad valorem* rates.

5.2 The Relationship between Average Tariff Rates and Anti-Dumping

There are a number of potential theories of the relationship between tariffs and anti-dumping. Sectors with more political power may be successful in both getting an anti-dumping measure imposed and lobbying for tariff protection in the first place. Alternatively, the prospect that protection through anti-dumping might act as an 'escape valve' for tariff liberalisation (Bagwell and Staiger 1990; Hoekman and Kostecki 2001) suggests a positive relationship between the extent of tariff liberalisation and subsequent anti-dumping use (see Bown and Tovar (2011) for evidence of this relationship in the case of India).

While we do not attempt a systematic exploration of these competing hypotheses, we explore potential differences between the average applied

[19] Figure 6.6 reports the average *ad valorem* rates based on HS-06 product–country combinations, whereas Table 6.1 reports average *ad valorem* anti-dumping duties at the anti-dumping case level. Figure 6.6 takes the average over all products in which the duty was *imposed* in that year, whereas Table 6.1 takes the average over all cases *initiated* in that year.

[20] In later years, the anti-dumping duty faced by a given firm could be higher or lower than the duty originally imposed because of *administrative* or *interim reviews*. However, constructing a measure based on data collected from interim reviews is beyond the scope of this study. Hence, for simplicity, we assume that the size of the anti-dumping duty rate remained unchanged over the duration of the measure.

Table 6.4: *Sectoral distribution of anti-dumping cases in China by income group, prior to crisis, 1997–2007.*

		Developed countries			Developing countries		
	HS section	Share of HS-06 products within sector involved in anti-dumping investigations	Share of imports within sector in HS-06 products involved in anti-dumping investigations	Sectoral imports as share of total imports (%)	Share of HS-06 products within sector involved in anti-dumping investigations	Share of imports within sector in HS-06 products involved in anti-dumping investigations	Sectoral imports as share of total imports (%)
I	Live animals/ animal products	0.0	0.0	0.7	0.0	0.0	1.6
II	Vegetable products	0.4	0.4	1.1	0.0	0.0	5.2
III	Animal/vegetable fats, oils and waxes	0.0	0.0	0.1	0.0	0.0	3.3
IV	Prepared foodstuffs, beverages and tobacco	0.0	0.0	0.4	0.0	0.0	2.0
V	Mineral products	0.0	0.0	2.8	0.0	0.0	16.0
VI	Chemicals	3.1	12.7	9.4	1.8	12.7	6.5
VII	Plastics and rubber	4.5	14.4	7.5	1.5	10.1	6.0
VIII	Leather products	0.0	0.0	1.1	0.0	0.0	1.0
IX	Wood/bamboo products	0.0	0.0	0.4	0.0	0.0	4.7
X	Paper and pulp	6.6	13.1	2.2	3.3	3.2	3.0

Table 6.4: *Continued.*

		Developed countries			Developing countries		
	HS section	Share of HS-06 products within sector involved in anti-dumping investigations	Share of imports within sector in HS-06 products involved in anti-dumping investigations	Sectoral imports as share of total imports (%)	Share of HS-06 products within sector involved in anti-dumping investigations	Share of imports within sector in HS-06 products involved in anti-dumping investigations	Sectoral imports as share of total imports (%)
XI	Textiles	0.7	5.2	5.3	0.0	0.0	3.8
XII	Footwear/umbrellas	0.0	0.0	0.1	0.0	0.0	0.1
XIII	Articles of stone/ plaster/cement	0.0	0.0	0.7	0.0	0.0	0.3
XIV	Precious stones/metals	0.0	0.0	0.5	0.0	0.0	1.1
XV	Steel	3.2	11.0	9.3	2.6	11.8	11.5
XVI	Machinery and electrical	0.0	0.0	44.5	0.0	0.0	31.6
XVII	Transport equipment	0.0	0.0	5.1	0.0	0.0	1.1
XVIII	Other instruments	0.0	0.0	8.3	0.0	0.0	0.9
XIX	Arms and ammunition	0.0	0.0	0.0	0.0	0.0	0.0
XX	Miscellaneous manufactured articles	0.0	0.0	0.4	0.0	0.0	0.1
XXI	Works of art	0.0	0.0	0.0	0.0	0.0	0.0
	Total	1.3	5.0	100	0.7	3.8	100

Source: author's calculations using data from Bown (2010b) and Comtrade.

Table 6.5: *Sectoral distribution of anti-dumping cases in China by income group, during crisis (2008–2009).*

	HS section	Developed countries			Developing countries		
		Share of HS-06 products within sector involved in anti-dumping investigations	Share of imports within sector in HS-06 products involved in anti-dumping investigations	Sectoral imports as share of total imports (%)	Share of HS-06 products within sector involved in anti-dumping investigations	Share of imports within sector in HS-06 products involved in anti-dumping investigations	Sectoral imports as share of total imports (%)
I	Live animals/ animal products	3.1	19.6	0.8	0.0	0.0	1.1
II	Vegetable products	0.0	0.0	1.8	0.0	0.0	6.9
III	Animal/vegetable fats, oils, and waxes	0.0	0.0	0.1	0.0	0.0	4.0
IV	Prepared foodstuffs, beverages and tobacco	0.0	0.0	0.5	0.0	0.0	1.4
V	Mineral products	0.0	0.0	6.0	0.0	0.0	27.7
VI	Chemicals	0.9	13.5	9.9	0.8	12.1	4.5
VII	Plastics/rubber	0.5	3.9	7.3	0.5	1.3	5.4
VIII	Leather products	0.0	0.0	0.7	0.0	0.0	0.8
IX	Wood/bamboo products	0.0	0.0	0.3	0.0	0.0	2.7
X	Paper and pulp	0.0	0.0	1.9	0.0	0.0	2.0

Table 6.5: *Continued.*

	HS section	Developed countries			Developing countries		
		Share of HS-06 products within sector involved in anti-dumping investigations	Share of imports within sector in HS-06 products involved in anti-dumping investigations	Sectoral imports as share of total imports (%)	Share of HS-06 products within sector involved in anti-dumping investigations	Share of imports within sector in HS-06 products involved in anti-dumping investigations	Sectoral imports as share of total imports (%)
XI	Textiles	0.0	0.0	2.5	0.0	0.0	2.1
XII	Footwear/umbrellas	0.0	0.0	0.1	0.0	0.0	0.2
XIII	Articles of stone/ plaster/cement	0.0	0.0	0.6	0.0	0.0	0.2
XIV	Precious stones/metals	0.0	0.0	0.7	0.0	0.0	1.2
XV	Steel	1.3	4.3	9.3	0.4	1.1	10.6
XVI	Machinery and electrical	0.0	0.0	40.9	0.0	0.0	27.8
XVII	Transport equipment	4.1	34.8	6.3	0.0	0.0	0.5
XVIII	Other instruments	1.9	3.7	9.9	0.0	0.0	0.7
XIX	Arms and ammunition	0.0	0.0	0.0	0.0	0.0	0.0
XX	Miscellaneous manufactured articles	0.0	0.0	0.4	0.0	0.0	0.2
XXI	Works of art	0.0	0.0	0.0	0.0	0.0	0.0
	Total	0.6	4.5	100	0.2	1.9	100

Source: author's calculations using data from Bown (2010b) and Comtrade.

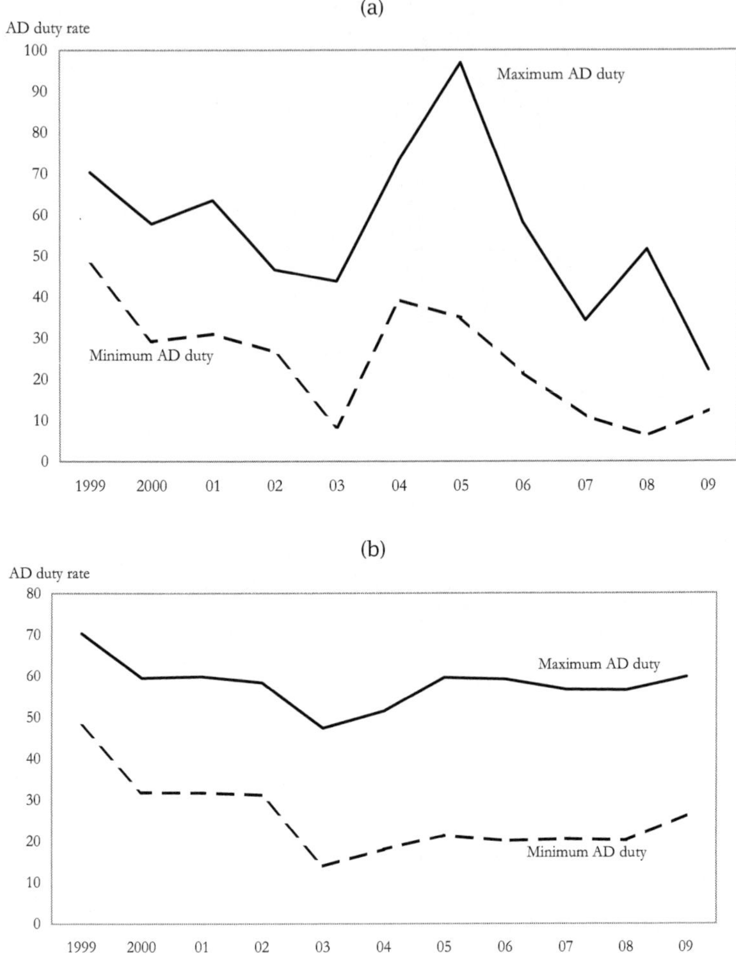

Figure 6.6: *China's average anti-dumping duties conditional on a final anti-dumping measure being imposed: (a) products with new anti-dumping measures only (flow); (b) all products with a final anti-dumping measure in force (stock).*

Source: author's calculations using data from Bown (2010b). Panel (a) reports the average *ad valorem* duty rate for all new measures conditional on a final anti-dumping measure being imposed. Panel (b) reports the same measure for all products that have a final anti-dumping measure in place.

tariff rates for products that were involved in anti-dumping investigations in China in comparison to products that were not. Figure 6.7 illustrates average tariffs for both groups of products during 1999–2009. The dashed line in the figure refers to the average applied MFN tariff rates for all HS-06 products involved in an anti-dumping investigation at any point during the period after China's WTO accession (2002–9). The solid line represents the average applied MFN tariff rates for all other HS-06 products that were never involved in Chinese anti-dumping investigations. Panel (a) of Figure 6.7 refers to all imported products; the other graphs report the same analysis for China's five leading anti-dumping sectors: chemicals, paper and pulp, plastics and rubber, steel, and textiles.[21]

The figure suggests a similar trend in the average tariff across all of China's leading anti-dumping users. China's average applied tariff decreased significantly during 2001–3 for both groups of products (those involved in anti-dumping investigations at any point during 2002–9 and those that were not). Furthermore, for many of the leading sectors, the average tariff for products that were subsequently involved in an anti-dumping investigation decreased at a faster rate and experienced a larger cut in absolute terms.[22] The larger decrease in absolute terms is noteworthy considering that, even prior to China's WTO accession, the average tariff for products subsequently involved in anti-dumping investigations was lower than the average tariff for other products. This suggests that products that experienced a larger tariff reduction during China's WTO accession were more likely to be involved in an anti-dumping investigation subsequently.

5.3 The Duration of China's Anti-Dumping Measures

According to WTO rules, members are required to conduct sunset reviews of all anti-dumping orders at the end of five years to determine whether the anti-dumping measure is still necessary. While WTO rules call for a mandatory sunset review, the members can extend the duration of the anti-dumping measure if they find a likely recurrence of dumping and injury.

As noted in Table 6.1, 135 of the 166 anti-dumping cases that China investigated during 1997–2009 resulted in the imposition of an anti-dumping measure.[23] Of these 135 measures, 105 (78%) were still 'in force' as of end 2009, *ie* China removed only 30 anti-dumping measures during 1999–2009. China

---

[21]We use data on China's applied MFN *ad valorem* tariff at the HS-06 level from TRAINS through WITS. There is no tariff data for China for 2002.

[22]The only exceptions to this were plastics and rubber and steel in which average tariffs decreased at a similar rate. The average tariff in the steel sector decreased from 9.6% in 2000 to 7.9% in 2003 for the products that were never investigated with anti-dumping, and the average tariff for the products involved in anti-dumping decreased from 8.5% in 2001 to 6.9% in 2003—a decrease of 18% in each case. Similarly, the average tariffs for the plastics and rubber sector decreased by 33% and 36% during 2001–3, for products that were in subsequent anti-dumping investigations and those that were not, respectively.

[23]Six additional anti-dumping investigations in 2009 are still ongoing.

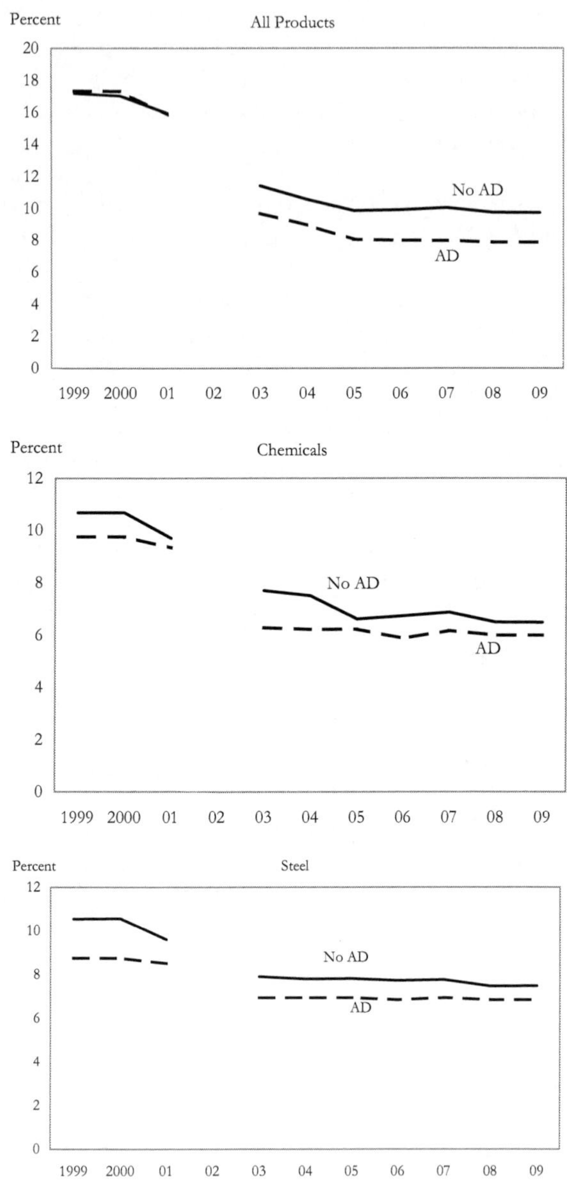

Figure 6.7: *China's average applied tariffs for products affected by anti-dumping, overall and by sector (1999–2009).*

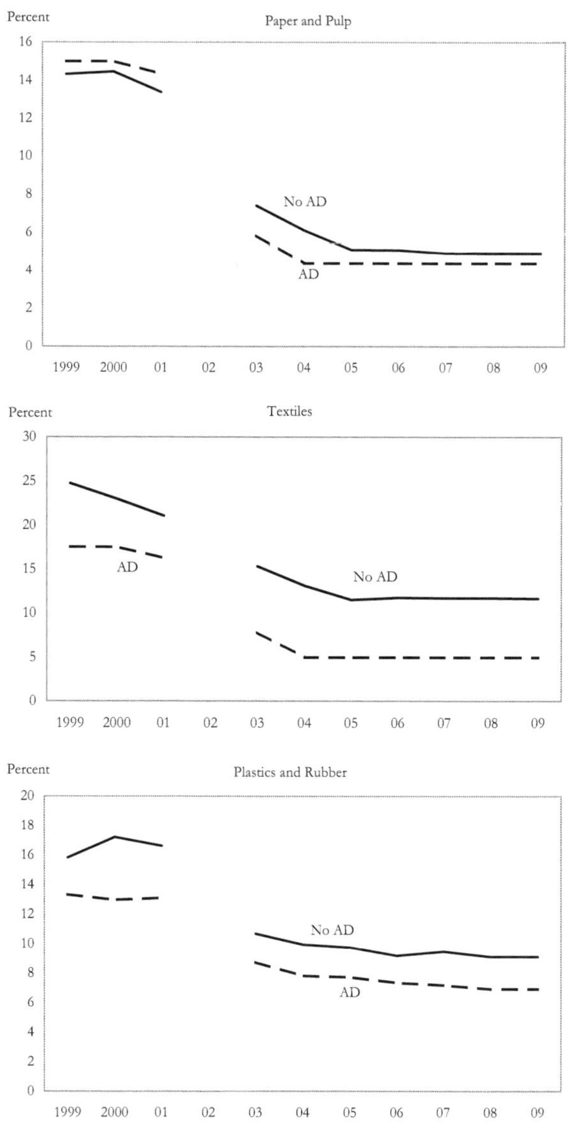

Figure 6.7: *Continued.*

Source: author's calculations using data from Bown (2010b) and TRAINS using WITS. Applied tariff rates are simple averages with data from TRAINS at the HS-06 level. Products are classified as anti-dumping if they were involved in an anti-dumping investigation in China at any time during 2002–9, *ie* the period after China's WTO accession.

removed 20 of these 30 anti-dumping measures during the 2008–9 crisis. On the one hand, it is not surprising that China removed so many anti-dumping measures during the crisis given that a large number of cases had been imposed in 2002–3; *ie* many cases were scheduled for a sunset review in 2008. Nevertheless, this is not meant to suggest that China is successful at removing its anti-dumping measures 'on time', *ie* after five years. In 2008–9, China removed only 11 of the 34 (32%) anti-dumping measures imposed during 2002–3.

Figure 6.8(a) shows the duration (in years) of all Chinese anti-dumping measures imposed during 1997–2009 categorised by whether the anti-dumping measure has been removed. First focus on the anti-dumping measures that have been removed by 2009. Of the 30 removed measures, 15 (50%) were removed after five years. Adding the number of measures that were removed in the fourth and sixth years, and given that we are using annual figures rather than the exact date at which the anti-dumping measure was imposed or removed, this number increases to 22 cases (73%).[24] Thus, a large share of anti-dumping measures that *have been* removed were removed around the sunset review period of five years. However, if we include the measures that have not yet been removed as of end 2009, a very different picture emerges. Many Chinese anti-dumping measures that were in force as of 2009 were imposed more than five years earlier.

Panels (b) and (c) of Figure 6.8 focus on the Chinese anti-dumping measures that were imposed prior to 2005 and that already completed the five-year period required for the initial sunset review. Figure 6.8(b) shows the number of anti-dumping measures based on whether they have been removed, further subdividing the removed cases according to whether they were removed at, before, or after the expected five-year term. With the exception of 1999, a large share of the measures imposed *before* China's accession to the WTO have been removed on time. However, this is not the case for anti-dumping measures that China imposed *after* it entered the WTO.

Figure 6.8(c) provides data by year that examine the percentage of anti-dumping measures imposed more than five years earlier that have not been removed. Between 2005 and 2009, the share of anti-dumping measures that were not removed but that were imposed five or more years earlier varied between 40% to 60%. The exception is 2004, when none of the three anti-dumping measures (originally imposed in 1999) were removed. Figure 6.8(c) also shows that the share of anti-dumping measures not removed on time increased slightly during the crisis.

---

[24] The sunset review investigations could also last for several months, thus the measures removed in six years were presumably removed after the completion of the sunset review.

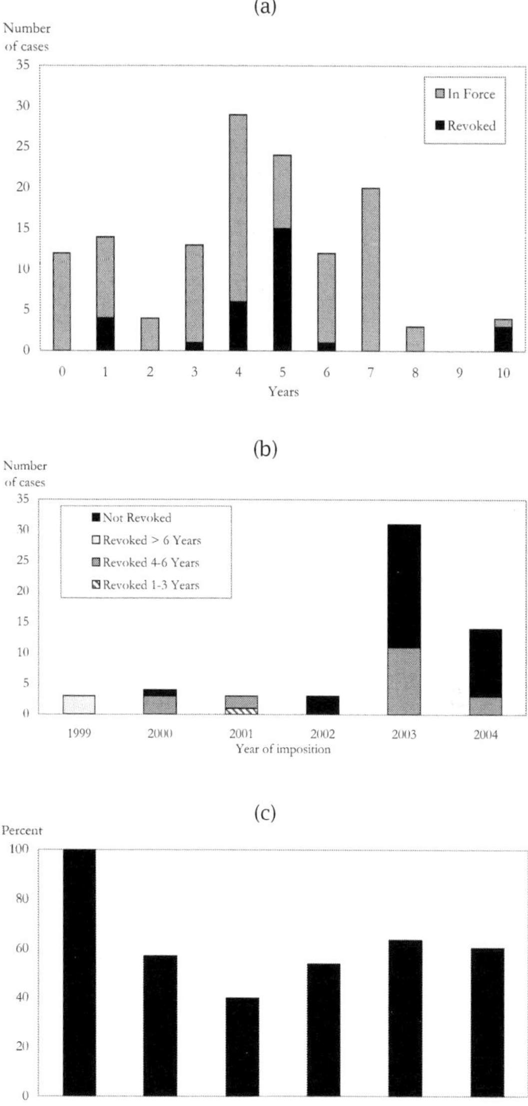

Figure 6.8: *Duration of China's anti-dumping measures: (a) all anti-dumping cases conditional on a final anti-dumping measure being imposed, 1999–2009; (b) all anti-dumping cases conditional on a final anti-dumping measure being imposed, 1999–2004; (c) percentage of anti-dumping measures imposed five or more years earlier that have not been removed.*

Source: author's calculations using data from Bown (2010b).

6 THE PARTICIPATION OF CHINESE FIRMS IN ANTI-DUMPING CASES AS PETITIONERS

According to China's anti-dumping regulations, the government can initiate an anti-dumping investigation after a petition is submitted by or on behalf of the domestic industry. While the government authority concerned (Ministry of Commerce People's Republic of China) could also self-initiate a petition, a group of firms representing the industry has initiated almost all of the anti-dumping cases in China until 2009.[25]

We pause at this stage to make three clarifications. First, anti-dumping petitions filed against the imports of a given product may be directed towards more than one country. Thus, here we refer to each product–country combination as a separate anti-dumping case. Second, there are nine instances during 1997–2009 in which an industry association (and not individual firms) filed the anti-dumping petition. We drop these cases from our analysis since the number of firms within the association that support the petition is unknown.[26] Third, on occasion, subsidiaries of the same corporation participate in filing the petition. For example, in 2007 China initiated an anti-dumping investigation on imports of acetone from Japan, South Korea, Singapore and Taiwan. Two of the petitioners were Beijing Yanshan Branch Sinopec and Shanghai Gaoqiao Branch Sinopec. In our analysis, we treat these as two distinct firms even though both are subsidiaries of the same corporation. We justify this under the assumption that subsidiaries of the same corporation may engage in very different operations.

During 1997–2009, only 141 Chinese firms participated in the anti-dumping proceedings as petitioners. Furthermore, the average number of firms involved in a given anti-dumping case is also very small. Figure 6.9(a) shows the distribution of Chinese firms involved in an anti-dumping case as petitioners during 1997–2009. Three or fewer petitioning firms were involved in 128 of the 163 anti-dumping cases (80%). While 14 firms were listed as petitioners in 1 case, 37 anti-dumping cases (23%) listed only 1 petitioning firm.

Table 6.6 shows the average number of firms participating as petitioners for each year during 1997–2009. There is little difference in how many firms

---

[25] According to Chinese anti-dumping regulations, the domestic industry constitutes the firms producing *like* products. In addition, for the government authority to initiate the anti-dumping case, the anti-dumping petition should be supported by a majority of the industry, *ie* firms representing at least 50% of the output (Wang and Yu 2002).

[26] Through 2009, only five 'associations' were petitioners in anti-dumping investigations: China's Industrial Association of Mechanical General Parts, China Methanol Association, China Animal Agricultural Association, China Association of Automobile Manufacturers, and Chemical Fiber Industry Association of China. Together, these five associations accounted for nine separate anti-dumping cases.

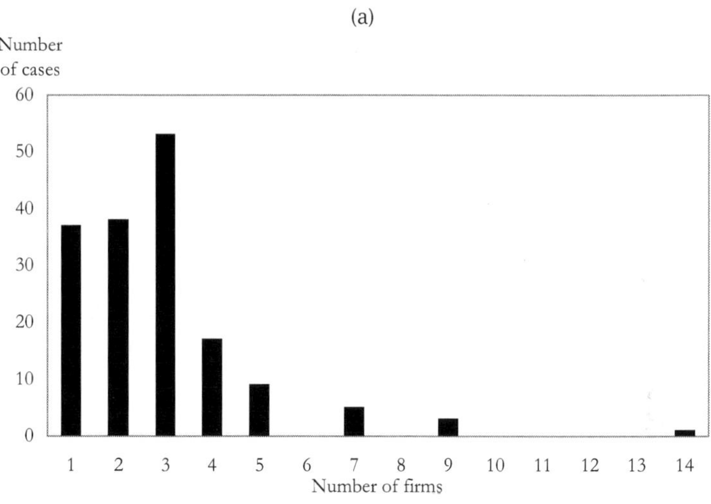

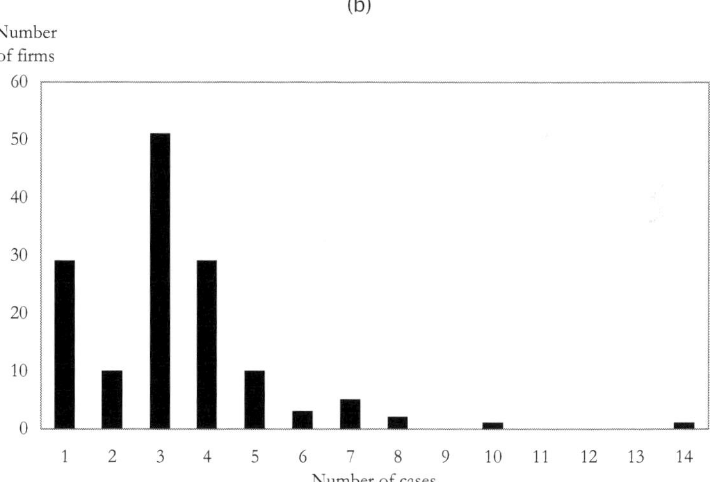

Figure 6.9: *Chinese anti-dumping petitioning firms, 1997–2009: (a) Chinese firms involved in an anti-dumping case as petitioners; (b) anti-dumping cases filed by petitioning Chinese firms.*

Source: author's calculation. Each unique petitioner identified separately in the anti-dumping petition is defined as a separate firm even if they are subsidiaries of a single corporation. We exclude cases where the petition was filed by an industry association. Each anti-dumping case is defined as a separate product-country anti-dumping investigation.

Table 6.6: *Participation of Chinese firms as petitioners in anti-dumping cases between 1997 and 2009: number of firms.*

Year	Average number of firms listed as petitioners in an anti-dumping case	Total number of anti-dumping cases	Average number of firms listed as petitioners in an anti-dumping petition	Total number of anti-dumping petitions
1997	9.0	3	9.0	1
1998	—	0	—	0
1999	3.0	7	3.0	4
2000	2.0	3	2.0	1
2001	3.2	13	3.3	4
2002	3.8	30	3.6	9
2003	2.6	21	4.0	6
2004	2.0	26	2.0	8
2005	2.3	24	1.9	7
2006	2.5	10	2.8	5
2007	3.0	4	3.0	1
2008	1.2	11	1.2	5
2009	3.7	11	2.8	5
Total	2.8	163	2.8	56

A single anti-dumping petition for a product may be directed against more than one country. We treat each product-country combination as a separate anti-dumping case. In addition, we drop the nine cases where the anti-dumping petition was filed by an industry association during this period.

Source: author's calculations using data from Bown (2010b).

participated in an anti-dumping investigation before and during the 2008–9 crisis. Except for 1997, the average number of petitioners varied between two and four until 2007. Though the anti-dumping cases filed during 2008 had relatively fewer firms listed as petitioners, it increased again in 2009.

We next explore the average number of anti-dumping cases in which each firm participates. Figure 6.9(b) reports that the modal number of anti-dumping cases in which a firm participates is three, with more than 50 firms participating in three anti-dumping cases during 1997–2009. One firm, Jilin Chemical Co. Ltd., was involved in 14 separate anti-dumping cases and was listed as a petitioner in 4 separate anti-dumping petitions during 1997–2009 (Table 6.7). Of the 141 firms that have participated in Chinese anti-dumping investigations, 128 (91%) were involved in only one anti-dumping petition each up until 2009.

Although a number of firms participated in multiple anti-dumping cases, Figure 6.9(b) shows that, of the 141 firms, 29 (21%) participated in just one anti-dumping case. These firms were involved in anti-dumping petitions that targeted imports from only one trading partner.

Table 6.7: *Participation of Chinese firms as petitioners in anti-dumping cases, 1997–2009: anti-dumping cases and outcomes for Chinese firms involved in more than one anti-dumping petition.*

Name of firm	Product under investigation	Countries (ISO 3)	Year of initiation	Final anti-dumping imposed	Year revoked	Average *ad valorem* rate	
						Minimum	Maximum
Beijing Oriental Chemical No. 4 Plant	Spendex	KOR, SGP, TWN, JPN, USA	2005	AVD	In force	18.0	61.0
Beijing Oriental Chemical No. 4 Plant	Glassine/other glazed transparent or translucent papers	USA, EUN	2005	AVD	In force	7.1	42.8
Daxinanling Lixue Potato Starch Co. Ltd.	Butan-1-Ol (N-Butyl Alcohol)	RUS, JPN, EUN, ZAF, USA, MYS	2005	Negative injury	—	—	—
Daxinanling Lixue Potato Starch Co. Ltd.	Potato starch	EUN	2006	AVD	In force	17.0	35.0
Gansu Xinda Potato Starch Co. Ltd.	Octylphenol Nonylphenol and their isomers and salts thereof	TWN, IND	2005	AVD	In force	8.2	20.4
Gansu Xinda Potato Starch Co. Ltd.	Potato starch	EUN	2006	AVD	In force	17.0	35.0
Guangdong Xinhui Meida Nylon Co. Ltd.	Polycaprolactam/ Polyamide-6 (PA6)/Nylon 6	TWN, RUS, EUN, USA	2009	AVD	In force	11.8	37.2
Guangdong Xinhui Meida Nylon Co. Ltd.	Chloroform (Trichloromethane)	KOR, IND, EUN, USA	2003	AVD	In force[1]	80.0	96.0
Guangdong Zhaoqing Xinhu Biotech Co. Ltd.	Disodium 5'-Inosinate/ Disodium 5'-Guanylate	THA, IDN	2009	AVD	In force	5.6	29.7
Guangdong Zhaoqing Xinhu Biotech Co. Ltd.	Dimethyl Cyclosiloxane or Cyclic Dimethyl Siloxane	EUN, JPN, USA	2004	AVD	In force	14.8	22.0

Table 6.7: *Continued.*

Name of firm	Product under investigation	Countries (ISO 3)	Year of initiation	Final anti-dumping imposed	Year revoked	Average *ad valorem* rate	
						Minimum	Maximum
Jilin Chemical Co. Ltd.	Spendex	KOR, SGP, TWN, JPN, USA	2005	AVD	In force	18.0	61.0
Jilin Chemical Co. Ltd.	Polybutylene Terephthalate Resin (PBT)	JPN, TWN	2005	AVD	In force	6.2	17.3
Jilin Chemical Co. Ltd.	Trichloroethylene	RUS, JPN	2004	AVD	In force	81.0	159.0
Jilin Chemical Co. Ltd.	Bisphenol-A (BPA)	RUS, SGP, TWN, JPN, KOR	2004	Withdrawn	—	—	—
Lianyungang Sanjili Chemical Industry Co. Ltd.	Disodium 5'-Inosinate Disodium 5'-Guanylate	JPN, KOR	2004	AVD	In force	25.0	119.0
Lianyungang Sanjili Chemical Industry Co. Ltd.	Catechol	EUN	2002	AVD	In force	20.0	79.0
Oriental Chemical (BOCIG)	Esters of acrylic acid	JPN, EUN, USA	1999	AVD	2005[2]	31.0	63.5
Oriental Chemical (BOCIG)	Esters of acrylic acid	IDN, SGP, MYS, KOR	2001	AVD	In force[3]	11.8	32.8
Qilu Chemical (Sinopec)	Spendex	KOR, SGP, TWN, JPN, USA	2005	AVD	In force	18.0	61.0
Qilu Chemical (Sinopec)	O-Dihydroxybenzene (Catechol Pyrocatechol)	USA, JPN	2005	AVD	In force	23.4	44.8
Qilu Chemical (Sinopec)	Dimethyl Cyclosiloxane or Cyclic Dimethyl Siloxane	EUN, JPN, USA	2004	AVD	In force	14.8	22.0

Table 6.7: *Continued.*

Name of firm	Product under investigation	Countries (ISO 3)	Year of initiation	Final anti-dumping imposed	Year revoked	Average *ad valorem* rate	
						Minimum	Maximum
Qinghai Weisidun Biotech Co. Ltd.	Butan-1-Ol (N-Butyl alcohol)	RUS, JPN, EUN, ZAF, USA, MYS	2005	Negative injury	—	—	—
Qinghai Weisidun Biotech Co. Ltd.	Potato starch	EUN	2006	AVD	In force	17.0	35.0
Shanghai Baosan Steel Group	Grain oriented flat-rolled electrical steel	RUS, USA	2009	AVD	In force	7.1	44.4
Shanghai Baosan Steel Group	Cold-rolled steel products	RUS, UKR, TWN, KOR, KAZ	2002	AVD	2008	7.2	44.2
Wuhan Steel Group	Grain oriented flat-rolled electrical steel	RUS, USA	2009	AVD	In force	7.1	44.4
Wuhan Steel Group	Grain oriented other	RUS	1999	AVD	2004	6.0	62.0
Wuhan Steel Group	Cold-rolled steel products	RUS, UKR, TWN, KOR, KAZ	2002	AVD	2008	7.2	44.2
Zhejiang Xin'an Chemical Co. Ltd.	Dimethyl Cyclosiloxane or Cyclic Dimethyl Siloxane	THA, KOR	2008	AVD	In force	15.3	23.5
Zhejiang Xin'an Chemical Co. Ltd.	Trichloroethylene	RUS, JPN	2004	AVD	In force	81.0	159.0

'AVD' stands for *ad valorem* duty. [1]China removed the anti-dumping measure against India in 2009; anti-dumping against other countries is still in force. [2]China removed the anti-dumping measure against EU in 2004; anti-dumping against other countries was removed in 2005. [3] China removed the anti-dumping measure against South Korea in 2009; anti-dumping against other countries is still in force.

Source: author's calculations using data from Bown (2010b).

7 CONCLUSIONS

This chapter examines the underlying trends in China's use of a particular set of non-tariff barriers (collectively referred to as TTBs). We focus on historical patterns in China's use of TTBs and examine whether this pattern changed during the 2008–9 crisis. The share of China's imports subject to TTB measures during 2008–9 was not very different from previous years, and in fact had declined compared with 2007. Nevertheless, a more detailed exploration of the data reveals a number of potential changes to this trend.

Although China's total stock of imports subject to anti-dumping measures decreased during the crisis, China initiated a number of new investigations. This increase in new anti-dumping investigations was a reversal of the existing pattern, as the flow of China's anti-dumping investigations had generally been decreasing since 2003. Furthermore, a number of Chinese anti-dumping investigations over sizeable amounts of imports are still pending. Finally, another notable feature of 2008–9 was the new industries for which China initiated an anti-dumping investigation for the first time, including transport equipment and animal products.

Furthermore, although China removed a number of anti-dumping measures during the crisis period, there were many cases in which the duration of previously imposed anti-dumping measures surpassed five years without removal. Turning TTBs into quasi-permanent protection is potentially troubling.

Our analysis also revealed a number of other interesting patterns in China's use of TTBs. We find that, during 1997–2009, a much larger share of China's TTBs targeted developed countries than developing countries. Even at its peak, only 1.5% of China's total imports from developing countries were subject to anti-dumping measures, much lower than the respective within-period peak of 2.5% for the developed countries. Moreover, during the crisis, China's stock of imports subject to anti-dumping measures decreased at a much faster rate for developing countries as compared with developed countries. This stands in contrast to many other developing countries in which the pattern of anti-dumping has increasingly become more 'south–south'.

We also explore participation by Chinese firms as petitioners in the anti-dumping proceedings and find it to be surprisingly small. Only 141 Chinese firms were involved in anti-dumping activities as petitioners during 1997–2009, and 128 (91%) of these firms have filed only one petition. In a large number of anti-dumping cases, the anti-dumping petitions were filed by only one Chinese firm.

We conclude with one final caveat. While this chapter focused on instruments of contingent protection (anti-dumping, CVDs and global safeguards), these TTBs are not the only instruments of import protection. During the crisis, many countries, including China, resorted to protectionism through indirect and often disguised means such as bailouts, local content requirements, and subsidies (Global Trade Alert 2009). For instance, in June 2009, the Chinese government made more stringent 'buy Chinese' provisions in its new stimulus program. Similarly, in May 2009, China's National Development and Reform Commission and a number of Chinese Ministries signed a notification to give priority to the local content in government contracts. A more complete picture of the policy responses during the crisis would therefore require accounting for many other instruments of protectionism beyond TTBs.

Piyush Chandra is Assistant Professor of Economics at Colgate University.

REFERENCES

Bagwell, K., and R. W. Staiger (1990). A theory of managed trade. *American Economic Review* **80**(4), 779–795.

Bown, C. P. (2011a). Introduction. In *The Great Recession and Import Protection: The Role of Temporary Trade Barriers* (ed. C. P. Bown). London: CEPR/World Bank. (Chapter 1 of this volume.)

Bown, C. P. (2011b). Taking stock of antidumping, safeguards, and countervailing duties, 1990–2009. *The World Economy*, forthcoming.

Bown, C. P. (2010a). China's WTO entry: antidumping, safeguards, and dispute settlement. In *China's Growing Role in World Trade* (ed. R. Feenstra and S. J. Wei). Chicago, IL: University of Chicago Press/NBER.

Bown, C. P. (2010b). *Temporary Trade Barriers Database*. World Bank (July). URL: http://econ.worldbank.org/ttbd/.

Bown, C. P., and P. Tovar (2011). Trade liberalization, antidumping, and safeguards: evidence from India's tariff reform. *Journal of Development Economics* **96**(1), 115–125.

Choi, W. M., and H. S. Gao (2006). Procedural issues in the anti-dumping regulations of China: a critical review under the WTO rules. *Chinese Journal of International Law* **5**(3), 663–682.

Global Trade Alert (2009). URL: www.globaltradealert.org/measure.

Hoekman, B. M., and M. M. Kostecki (2001). *The Political Economy of the World Trading System: The WTO and Beyond*, 2nd edn. Oxford University Press.

Messerlin, P. A. (2004). China in the World Trade Organization: antidumping and safeguards. *World Bank Economic Review* **18**(1), 105–130.

Wang, L., and S. Yu (2002). China's new anti-dumping regulations: improvements to comply with the World Trade Organization rules. *Journal of World Trade* **36**(5), 903–920.

World Development Indicators (2010). World Bank reference data. URL: http://data.worldbank.org/data-catalog/world-development-indicators.

World Trade Organization (2010). *International Trade Statistics 2010*. Geneva: World Trade Organization.

Yu, T. (2005). The 10 major problems with the anti-dumping instrument in the People's Republic of China. *Journal of World Trade* **39**(1), 97–103.

7

India: The Use of Temporary Trade Barriers

PATRICIA TOVAR[1]

1 INTRODUCTION

India implemented a significant unilateral trade liberalisation reform as part of an arrangement requested from the IMF in 1991 following a balance-of-payments crisis. With the reform, the import-weighted average tariff decreased from 87.0% in 1990–1 to 24.6% in 1996–7. The sharpest tariff reductions took place from 1991 to 1992, and while India had not used the WTO-permitted 'contingent' forms of import protection such as anti-dumping, safeguards or countervailing measures before, it initiated its first anti-dumping investigation in 1992 and went on to become the WTO system's foremost user of anti-dumping policies by 2001. India also initiated its first safeguard investigation in 1997.

In this chapter we examine India's use of anti-dumping, safeguards and countervailing measures—collectively referred to as TTBs—from 1992 to 2009, making use of detailed product-level data from the World Bank's *Temporary Trade Barriers Database* (Bown 2010a). We also study the use of such policies during the global recession years of 2008–9 and compare it with trends from previous years. We focus on whether there have been important changes not only regarding India's aggregate use of TTBs, but also their incidence across products, sectors and targeted countries, the amount of time that these 'temporary' measures stay in place, and the relationship between their use and India's WTO commitments regarding applied tariffs.

Although India's financial sector was not overexposed to subprime lending and was thus able to avoid the direct effects of the global financial crisis, its economy was severely affected by the worldwide recession (see, for example, Bajpai 2010). As shown in Figure 7.1, India's growth in GDP per capita decreased from 8.2% in 2007 to 3.7% in 2008. Moreover, exports and imports

[1]Department of Economics, MS021, Brandeis University, PO Box 549110, Waltham, MA 02454- 9110, USA. Email: tovar@brandeis.edu. I would like to thank Chad Bown, Baybars Karacaovali, Michael Moore and Raymond Robertson for helpful comments. I also thank Aksel Erbahar for his help with providing the data.

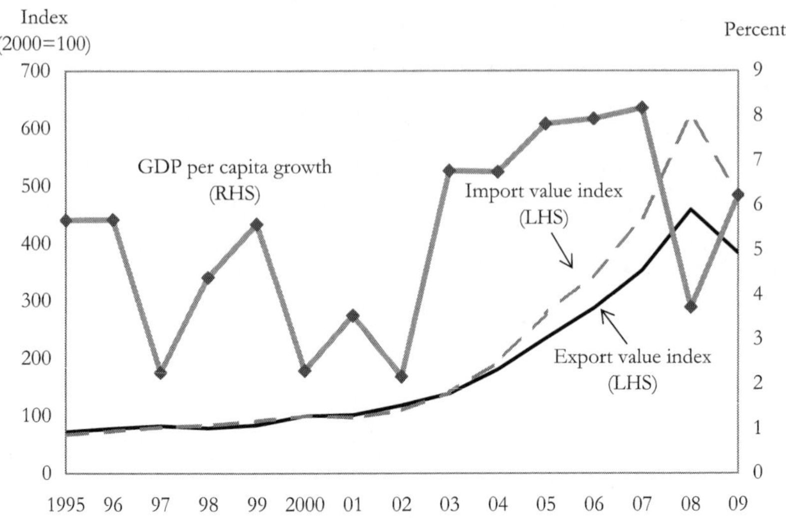

Figure 7.1: *India's exports, imports and growth in GDP per capita, 1995–2009.* *Source:* World Bank (2010).

decreased sharply in 2009, in contrast to previous periods of economic contraction such as 1997 and the early 2000s. During the recent recession there was also considerable discussion in the media about a potential trade war with China due to India's extension of its ban on imports of Chinese dairy products and the imposition of a temporary ban on imports of Chinese toys in 2009, as well as the large number of anti-dumping investigations initiated against China over a variety of products (including steel and textiles) in 2008–9 (see, for example, *Times of India* 2009a,b; *Hindustan Times* 2009). This raises the question of whether India's 'protectionism' changed during the global economic crisis.

We first provide information on the behaviour of India's aggregate and product-level use of anti-dumping—both the 'flow' of new investigations as well as the 'stock' of measures in place—over time. While the flow data indicate that the annual share of eight-digit Harmonized System (HS) products subject to a new anti-dumping investigation reached a peak of 2.10% in 2007, the stock measure in particular allows us to infer that the product coverage of anti-dumping policies increased from 1992 through 2009. Moreover, the percentage of products affected by anti-dumping measures as well as the percentage of India's import value with anti-dumping measures in place experienced a sizeable increase during the recession years of 2008 and 2009. Using data at the tariff line (eight-digit HS) product level, we find that the percentage of products subject to anti-dumping measures increased from 1.82% in 2007 to 4.03% in 2009, and that this increase is larger than what the pre-crisis trend would predict.

Our next contribution is to examine the use of anti-dumping policy by sector. Almost half of India's anti-dumping investigations were initiated by the chemicals sector, and the other main users of anti-dumping have been plastics/rubber, machinery/electrical, metals and textiles. Those sectors also have the largest number of anti-dumping initiations worldwide. Furthermore, those sectors were the top five users of anti-dumping in India during the global recession of 2008–9, and most of them have displayed an increasing trend in the percentage of sectoral import value affected by anti-dumping measures since 1992. Finally, those main users of anti-dumping also account for an important fraction of India's import value—37% for the 1992–2009 period—which indicates that anti-dumping policy may have economically important effects in India.

We then study the countries that are affected by India's anti-dumping policies. China was the most frequent target of Indian anti-dumping (in terms of both investigations and measures imposed), and the average size of the anti-dumping import restriction against China is also the highest of any targeted country. This bias in the incidence of anti-dumping policy against China accelerated during 2008–9. More broadly, the share of investigations targeting developing countries increased from 48% in 1992–2007 to 71% in 2008–9, while the share of imports from those countries remained fairly stable.[2] The shift in incidence towards China and other developing countries over time is also observed with regard to the stock of product-exporter combinations that are affected by an anti-dumping measure. In 1997, 53% of India's stock of anti-dumping measures affected developed countries, 22% affected China, and 24% affected other developing countries. In contrast, by 2009, only 25% of the stock of measures was imposed against developed countries, while 39% was imposed against China and 36% was imposed against other developing countries. This result is consistent with Bown's (2011b) argument that anti-dumping is increasingly a 'south–south' phenomenon.[3]

We also find that there are several instances in which, having imposed an anti-dumping measure in a previous year, India imposed new anti-dumping measures against different exporters of the same product in subsequent years. We also provide some evidence (subject to the available data) that, in an important number of those cases, the newly affected exporting countries had not exported the product to India in the years preceding the initial investigation. These results suggest that *trade diversion* has played an important role leading to additional use of anti-dumping policy. The results might also mean

[2]The share of imports from China did exhibit a substantial increase, as we detail in Section 3.3.

[3]Bown (2011b) performs a cross-country examination of the use of TTBs over time and uses product data at the six-digit HS level. We use more disaggregated tariff-line data at the eight-digit HS product level for India.

that India is using anti-dumping policy as a form of import protection not conditional on the actual presence of dumping.

We then examine the actual duration of India's anti-dumping measures. According to the WTO's Anti-Dumping Agreement, a 'sunset review' process should take place after five years of the imposition of a measure, and the measure should be removed unless it is determined that its removal would be likely to generate injury due to renewed dumping. We find that 60% of the measures imposed were removed after no more than five years. Moreover, anti-dumping measures in the chemical sector and measures against China both tend to last longer than the average. In addition, we find that another dimension through which anti-dumping protection increased during the global economic crisis of 2008–9 was the failure to remove policies imposed prior to the crisis that were supposed to be terminated during the crisis under the five-year limit.

Another issue that we consider is potential evidence that India used anti-dumping to increase import restrictions to levels that would otherwise violate the rules of the WTO system. For example, if India were to have increased its applied tariff rate instead, how often would that result in a violation of its WTO commitments? We find some evidence consistent with that argument, and we also provide additional evidence of a shift in India's anti-dumping protection towards developing countries during the recent global recession.

Although anti-dumping has been the dominant TTB in India, we also examine other relatively substitutable forms of temporary import protection. We begin by characterising India's use of global safeguards over time and find that, although the largest number of safeguard investigations was initiated during the global economic crisis of 2008–9, most of them did not result in the imposition of a final safeguard measure. We also provide information regarding the sectors with higher safeguard activity as well as the number of products affected. The chemical sector is, again, the main user of safeguard measures in India. Next, we describe India's use of China-specific safeguards as well as countervailing measures. There was an increase in the use of China-specific safeguards during the recent global economic crisis that affected various imported products. India has only initiated one countervailing measure investigation so far, which took place in 2009 and also targeted China.

Our final contribution is to study whether the alternative forms of TTBs have been used across similar products and/or sectors. Overall, we find that, while there is not much overlap of different TTBs over the same (eight-digit HS) products, there is substantial overlap regarding the sectors that use those policies. Furthermore, those features of the use of TTBs have not changed much during the global recession years. We also examine the interaction between the use of TTBs and applied import tariffs. Moreover, we relate our results to those of Bown and Tovar (2011), who study the link between India's tariff liberalisation reform and its subsequent use of anti-dumping and safeguard policies in 2000–2002.

The rest of the chapter is organised as follows. In the next section we provide an overview of India's trade liberalisation experience. Section 3 examines India's use of anti-dumping. Section 4 describes the use of other TTBs by India, including global safeguards, China-specific safeguards and countervailing measures. In Section 5 we examine the interaction among alternative TTBs, as well as their interaction with MFN applied tariffs. We conclude in Section 6.

2 INDIA'S UNILATERAL TRADE LIBERALISATION

India was one of the initial 23 contracting parties to the 1947 General Agreement on Tariffs and Trade that laid the groundwork for the post-World War II, rules-based trading system (Irwin *et al* 2008). India was one of the main protagonists in the effort to obtain major exceptions to basic WTO rules that limited the use of quantitative restrictions and tariffs.

Between 1947 and the late 1980s, India followed an inwards-orientated development strategy. It was characterised by import protection, complex industrial licensing requirements, significant intervention in financial markets, and government ownership of heavy industry (Cerra and Saxena 2002). International trade was significantly restricted by high tariffs and non-tariff barriers, which included import licensing, state monopoly of some imports and exports ('canalisation'), government purchases that favoured domestic producers, and restrictions on imports by intermediaries.

A combination of external shocks in the late 1980s and early 1990s led to larger macroeconomic imbalances. Increased import costs due to high oil prices, a decrease in remittances from Indian workers because of the conflict in the Middle East, weak demand in export markets, a deterioration of the fiscal position and the current account deficit, high external debt, and rising political uncertainty led to a loss of confidence by investors and capital outflows. The loss of international reserves continued and ended in a severe balance-of-payments crisis (see Cerra and Saxena (2002) for a discussion of the factors that led to the crisis).

In August 1991, India requested a standby arrangement from the IMF. One of the conditions for the arrangement was that India had to implement major structural reforms, including trade liberalisation, financial sector reform and tax reform.

Before the reform, in 1990–1, the import-weighted average of tariffs was 87%, the simple average was 128% and some tariffs were over 300%. Moreover, non-tariff barriers (especially quantitative restrictions) affected imports of 65% of all products and 90% of manufactures (Srinivasan 2001). The subsequent reform package included a significant reduction in the average level as well as the dispersion of tariffs. The maximum tariff fell from 355% in 1990–1 to 150% in 1991–2, and to 30.8% by 2002–3. The weighted average tariff decreased from 87% in 1990–1 to 24.6% in 1996–7, although it then gradually increased to 38.5% in 2001–2. The increase coincided with a significant lifting of quantitative restrictions (Narayanan 2006) and was possible because India's tariff bindings from the Uruguay Round were set at much higher levels than the applied rates (Srinivasan 2001).[4] The simple average tariff rate fell from 128% in 1990–1 to 34.4% in 1997–8. It then increased to 40.2% in 1998–9 but continued to decrease after that. In 2002–3, the simple and weighted averages of tariffs were 29% (Narayanan 2006).

As reported by Topalova (2004), there was a sharp decrease in tariffs in most industries from 1991 to 1992—the sharpest reduction in average tariffs and their dispersion took place from 1991 to 1992. Quantitative restrictions on most imports have been eliminated. In 1991, most quantitative restrictions on intermediate and capital goods were removed and the list of goods subject to quantitative restrictions was reduced significantly (although it was still long) to include mainly consumer goods and agricultural products.[5] The Uruguay Round agreement, signed in 1994, required the elimination of quantitative restrictions and India's quantitative restrictions expired on 1 April 2001.[6]

As a result of the reforms, total trade as a percentage of GDP increased from an average of 13% in the 1980s to almost 19% in 1999–2000. The volume of exports and imports has also increased significantly since the early 1990s (Topalova 2004). Lastly, and importantly, the first anti-dumping case was initiated in 1992.

3 INDIA'S USE OF ANTI-DUMPING

India introduced legislation on anti-dumping in 1985, and it was subsequently reformed to conform with obligations after 1995. In 1998, a separate division—the Directorate-General of Anti-Dumping and Allied Duties—was created within the Department of Commerce, which had more staff and dedicated resources to manage anti-dumping complaints and recommend anti-dumping duties. Narayanan (2006) also reports that, in the 1990s, the government frequently and publicly informed the domestic industries about the

[4]India imposed bindings on 62% of the tariff lines of industrial products. Before the Uruguay Round, only 3% of tariff lines had bindings (National Board of Trade 2005).

[5]According to estimates by the World Bank, the share of imports from all sectors included in their study and covered by non-tariff barriers decreased from 95% in 1988–9 to 62% in 1998–9, and to 24% in 1999–2000 (Srinivasan 2001).

[6]A small number of quantitative restrictions permitted under Articles XX and XXI of the GATT remain on grounds of health, safety and moral conduct (Narayanan 2006).

availability of anti-dumping (and safeguard) measures. Duties are levied by the Ministry of Finance.[7]

3.1 Anti-Dumping Investigations and Measures

Table 7.1 documents the year-by-year data on India's anti-dumping use between its first case, initiated in 1992 just after the 1991 commencement of the trade liberalisation reforms, through 2009.[8] As India started the process of trade liberalisation, the use of anti-dumping took off, and presented an increasing trend until 2002. There is a decrease in the number of initiations in 2003 and 2004, but an increase thereafter until 2008. In conjunction with the spread of the global economic crisis, India initiated 54 anti-dumping cases in 2008 and another 32 during 2009.[9]

In addition to the data on new industry demands for anti-dumping protection, Table 7.1 also presents a breakdown over time of the number of investigations begun each year that resulted in the imposition of new import restrictions. Of the 588 investigations started in the period 1992–2009, 420, or 71%, have resulted in the imposition of new definitive trade barriers. Excluding 2009, for which some data on final measures are not yet available, that share increases to 74%. A lack of evidence of dumping was found in only 26 cases and no injury was found in 42 cases. Only 16 cases were withdrawn or terminated. The main implication of these figures is that not only is the number of Indian anti-dumping initiations high, but the vast majority of cases result in the imposition of new trade barriers.

The combined information on the large number of Indian anti-dumping cases and the high frequency with which they result in new and definitive import restrictions raises a number of basic questions about the economic scale of this particular form of import protection. For example, despite the 2003–6 relative drop in frequency of newly initiated investigations, by other measures the scope of anti-dumping protection steadily increased throughout the *entire* 1992–2009 period. Consider Figure 7.2(a), which, instead of

---

[7]On the requirements to initiate an investigation as well as a timeline for the findings and imposition of duties, see, for example, Aggarwal (2002) and National Board of Trade (2005).

[8]Indian anti-dumping data are taken from the *Temporary Trade Barriers Database* (Bown 2010a). The working paper accompanying the database describes the detailed data, but, in short, the data for India were taken directly from what the Directorate General of Anti-Dumping and Allied Duties in the Ministry of Commerce publicly reported in *Gazette of India* (http://commerce.nic.in/ad_cases.htm).

[9]During the period between 1995 and 2009, India was the top initiator of anti-dumping cases, followed by the USA, the EU, Argentina and South Africa. India also had the highest number of anti-dumping measures imposed. As we discuss in more detail below, in 2009 India started to use more aggressively other substitutable forms of contingent protection aside from anti-dumping, including global safeguards (see also Table 7.1), China-specific safeguards and even countervailing ('anti-subsidy') measures.

Table 7.1: *India's anti-dumping and global safeguard initiations and outcomes, 1992–2009.*

	Anti-dumping							Global safeguards			
	Initiations	Prelim. measure	Final measure	No dumping	No injury	Terminated or withdrawn	Missing	Initiations	Final measure	No injury	Terminated or withdrawn
1992	5	5	5	0	0	0	0	0	0	0	0
1993	0	0	0	0	0	0	0	0	0	0	0
1994	7	1	7	0	0	0	0	0	0	0	0
1995	6	6	5	0	0	1	0	0	0	0	0
1996	21	21	18	0	0	0	0	0	0	0	0
1997	13	12	13	0	0	0	0	1	1	0	0
1998	28	19	18	3	5	2	1	5	3	0	1
1999	63	51	49	9	9	2	3	3	2	0	0
2000	41	29	32	0	0	0	4	2	1	0	0
2001	77	62	62	4	6	1	0	0	0	0	0
2002	77	67	56	3	4	1	8	2	1	1	0
2003	45	12	26	7	14	4	1	1	0	0	0
2004	20	9	9	0	4	1	4	1	1	0	0
2005	25	18	19	0	0	1	5	0	0	0	0
2006	30	15	30	0	0	0	0	0	0	0	0
2007	44	23	32	0	0	0	0	0	0	0	0
2008	54	33	32	0	0	3	0	2	1	0	0
2009*	32	31	7	0	0	0	24	9	1	0	4
Total	588	414	420	26	42	16	50	26	11	1	5

* Information on *final* decisions and measures for some of the anti-dumping initiations and one global safeguard initiation in 2009 is still not available.

Source: author's calculations using data from Bown (2010a).

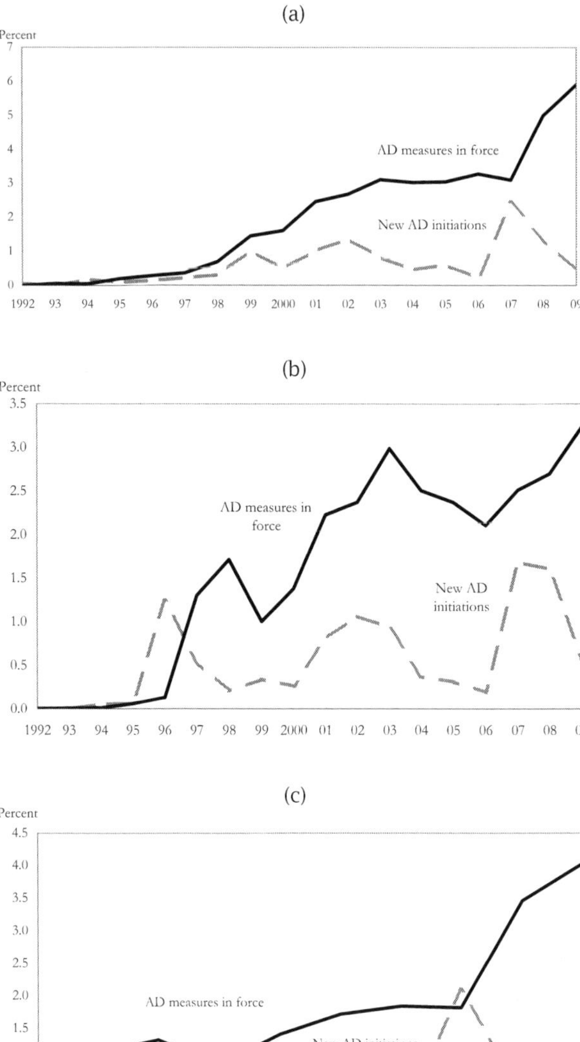

Figure 7.2: *India's use of anti-dumping: (a) percentage of imported six-digit HS products with new anti-dumping initiations and measures; (b) percentage of import value with new anti-dumping initiations and measures (using data at the six-digit HS level); (c) percentage of imported eight-digit HS products with new anti-dumping initiations and measures.*

Source: author's calculations using data from Bown (2010a).

simply using the number of investigations as its unit of observations, measures anti-dumping use by the percentage of imported six-digit HS products affected. Figure 7.2(a) uses this share of imported six-digit HS products subject to anti-dumping to plot the flow of new investigations over time and the stock of imposed anti-dumping measures.[10] It is clear that, even though there was a decline in the number of new investigations over the 2003–6 period, a likely contributor to this was the stock of anti-dumping measures already in place resulting from earlier (pre-2003) investigations, which continued to climb through 2009. If imports are already being restricted by trade barriers, there is a reduced need for new anti-dumping investigations.

The figure also shows a significant increase in the percentage of six-digit HS products affected by anti-dumping measures in the recession years of 2008 and 2009, which almost doubled from 3.10% in 2007 to 5.91% in 2009. We can ask whether this observed increase could have been predicted by the trend observed in previous years. Consistent with the results of Bown (2011b), we find that if we regress the 1992–2007 data on the percentage of six-digit products affected by an anti-dumping measure on a linear time trend and use the estimated coefficient to predict such a percentage for 2009, the difference between the actual and predicted values (5.91% versus 5.00%) is not large enough to conclude that there was a substantial shift away from the previous trend in 2008–9.

Since the effect of anti-dumping protection on a given product depends on the level of Indian imports that are affected by it, we also use another measure that exploits data at the bilateral level on whether imports of a given product from a certain exporting country are affected by anti-dumping. Figure 7.2(b) thus shows the percentage of non-oil import value with new anti-dumping initiations and anti-dumping measures in force. This measure is based on Equation (1.2) of the Introduction (Bown, this volume). Again, there is an increasing trend in the stock of products affected by anti-dumping measures, which reaches its peak covering 3.24% of India's import value in 2009. In this case we also find that the predicted share for 2009 based on a linear time trend (3.66) does not differ much from the observed one (3.24).

In Figure 7.2(c) we exploit import data at the tariff-line level (available since 2000) to report the percentage of imported eight-digit HS products subject to new anti-dumping initiations and measures in force from 2000 to 2009. The pattern is very similar to that shown in Figure 7.2(a): in both cases the *flow* of initiations reaches its peak in 2007 but the *stock* of products affected by measures continues to increase through 2009. In 2009, 4.03% of India's eight-digit HS imported products were affected by anti-dumping measures.[11] Moreover,

---

[10]We use the year in which the first measure was imposed, even if it was a preliminary measure.

[11]India has imported approximately 10,000 products at the eight-digit HS level annually in the last five years of our data (2005–9).

we find that the percentage of eight-digit HS products affected by an anti-dumping measure in 2009 predicted by the linear time trend is substantially lower than the actual one (2.46% versus 4.03%, respectively). Thus, using the more disaggregated data we *do* find some evidence that India's observed pattern of protectionism in 2009 was larger than predicted by historical trends.[12] The difference in the results relative to those using the data at the six-digit HS product level is likely to be due to the increase over time in the number of eight-digit HS products within a six-digit HS product that are affected by anti-dumping.[13]

3.2 The Use of Anti-Dumping by Sector

Table 7.2 details the incidence of India's anti-dumping use by taking a different approach, reporting the number of initiations by each two-digit HS sector. The most frequent user of anti-dumping has been the chemicals industry, with almost half of all Indian initiations during this time period. Put differently, India's chemicals sector alone initiated more anti-dumping cases during this period than the combined sectors of any other individual WTO member apart from the USA, the EU and Argentina. Not surprisingly, the decline in new anti-dumping initiations in India during the period 2003–6 is partly explained by a decrease in the number of initiations by the chemicals sector, which fell by more than 60%, from an average of 31 new cases per year between 1999 and 2002 to an average of only 12 new cases per year between 2003 and 2006. Other sizeable users of Indian anti-dumping include plastics/rubbers, machinery/electrical, metals and textiles; combined with chemicals, they are also the five sectors with most anti-dumping initiations worldwide (WTO 2010a). (This is also true if Indian initiations are excluded from the world total.) Textiles had 13 initiations in 2005 alone, coinciding with a restructuring of the global textile and apparel market with a phase-out of the Multi Fibre Arrangement and the end of textile quotas under the WTO's transitional Agreement on Textiles and Clothing. The 24 initiations in the metals sector in 2008 (after almost no new anti-dumping activity in the previous five years) correspond to steel products and took place in November and December, coinciding with the heightening of the global recession. Finally, we note

[12]This also holds if we increase the number of observations by using the average ratio of the percentage of eight-digit HS products affected by an anti-dumping measure to the corresponding percentage of six-digit HS products affected (from 2000 to 2007) as a proxy for the percentage of eight-digit HS products affected by an anti-dumping measure from 1992–9 (by applying such a ratio to the corresponding percentage at the six-digit HS level). In that case, the predicted percentage for 2009 is 2.36.

[13]We do not report the analogue of Figure 7.2(b) at the eight-digit HS level since import data at that level are only available since 2000, which implies that we do not have the value of imports before the earliest initiation affecting each product, and we would have to use import values that have already been affected by anti-dumping and would therefore provide a less accurate assessment.

Table 7.2: *India's anti-dumping initiations by sector and year: 1992–2009.*

Sector	'92	'93	'94	'95	'96	'97	'98	'99	'00	'01	'02	'03	'04	'05	'06	'07	'08	'09	Total	% of total initiations '92–'09	% of imports '92–'09
Animal/ animal products	0	0	0	0	0	0	0	0	0	0	1	0	0	0	0	0	0	0	1	0.16	0.05
Vegetable products	0	0	0	0	0	0	0	0	0	0	0	0	0	0	0	0	0	0	0	0.00	3.44
Foodstuffs	0	0	0	0	0	0	0	0	2	5	1	0	0	0	0	0	0	0	8	1.32	0.44
Mineral products	0	0	0	1	0	2	0	0	2	0	3	1	0	0	0	3	0	2	14	2.31	35.06
Chemicals and allied industries	1	0	6	2	5	3	7	29	26	28	41	24	10	4	11	24	10	14	245	40.36	9.50
Plastics/rubbers	4	0	2	0	2	5	8	9	3	13	0	10	4	8	8	0	4	10	90	14.83	2.34
Raw hides, skins, leather and furs	0	0	0	0	0	0	0	0	0	0	0	0	0	0	0	0	0	0	0	0.00	0.26
Wood and wood products	0	0	0	0	3	0	0	4	0	1	1	5	0	1	0	0	5	0	20	3.29	2.09
Textiles	0	0	0	0	3	0	5	9	4	12	1	2	2	13	0	0	6	2	59	9.72	1.78
Footwear/ headgear	0	0	0	0	0	0	0	0	1	0	0	0	0	0	0	0	0	0	1	0.16	0.07
Stone/glass	0	0	0	0	0	0	0	0	0	2	2	3	2	0	0	0	1	0	10	1.65	15.24
Metals	0	0	0	3	0	4	3	11	3	5	17	0	0	0	1	0	24	0	71	11.70	6.57
Machinery/ electrical	0	0	0	0	8	0	5	0	1	11	10	0	6	0	9	20	4	6	80	13.18	16.65
Transportation	0	0	0	0	0	0	0	0	0	0	0	0	0	0	1	0	2	0	3	0.49	4.29
Miscellaneous	0	0	0	0	0	0	0	1	0	0	4	0	0	0	0	0	0	0	5	0.82	2.22
Total	5	0	8	6	21	14	28	63	42	77	81	45	24	26	30	47	56	34	607	100.00	100.00

Source: author's calculations using data from Bown (2010a).

that the top users of anti-dumping during the global economic crisis of 2008–9 are also the same five sectors that constitute the main anti-dumping users in India since 1992. Bown and Tovar (2011) provide evidence that the variation in India's use of anti-dumping across sectors (in the early 2000s) is related to the tariff liberalisation reform that India implemented in the 1990s, and that it also responds to motives of political economy according to the predictions of the Grossman and Helpman (1994) model.

How sizeable are imports in these manufacturing sectors that populate India's use of anti-dumping? Over the period 1992–2009, the dominant anti-dumping user, chemicals, accounted for 10% of all Indian imports, reaching almost 15% in some years. Other major users of anti-dumping are also large importers, including machinery (17%) and metals (7%). Note that the importance to the Indian economy of imports in these sectors is likely to be underestimated if the level of imports in those sectors is lower than it would be under the counterfactual that India had not used anti-dumping. Figure 7.3 shows the number of initiations by year for each of the five main anti-dumping-user sectors, as well as the value of imports and the percentage of India's imports that they represent in 2000–2009. Some of those sectors (chemicals, textiles and metals) experienced a decrease in imports in 2009 (Figure 7.3(b)), and India's total imports also fell due to the recession. Figure 7.3(c) shows that the *percentage* of imports of metal products increased significantly from 2003 to 2007 (from 4.7% to 7.8%) despite the use of anti-dumping in the preceding years, which may also help to explain the large number of initiations in this sector in 2008 that we mentioned previously.

We also examine the share of four-digit HS products that were affected by an anti-dumping initiation *within* each of the two-digit HS sectors that are the main anti-dumping users. Between 1992 and 2009, 34% of the four-digit HS products in the chemical sector were affected by an anti-dumping initiation at some point. Similarly, 30% of the four-digit HS products in the plastics/rubbers sector and 14% of the four-digit HS products in the machinery/electrical sector were affected. Metals and textiles exhibit smaller shares—8% and 6%, respectively—of affected products. This pattern in terms of the two-digit HS sectors with more/fewer four-digit products affected by anti-dumping is broadly similar during the 2008–9 recession period.

To examine the potential impact of anti-dumping protection across sectors in more detail, Figure 7.4 shows the percentage of India's non-oil import value affected by anti-dumping in each of the five main-user sectors, including both the flow of new investigations over time and the stock of imposed anti-dumping measures, computed using bilateral import data at the six-digit HS level as described in the previous section. Each sector presents an increasing trend in the stock of imports affected by anti-dumping protection, except metals. As already mentioned, metals experienced a decrease in anti-dumping initiations from 2003 to 2007, but due to the spike in initiations in 2008, there was a subsequent large increase in the stock of affected imports of metal prod-

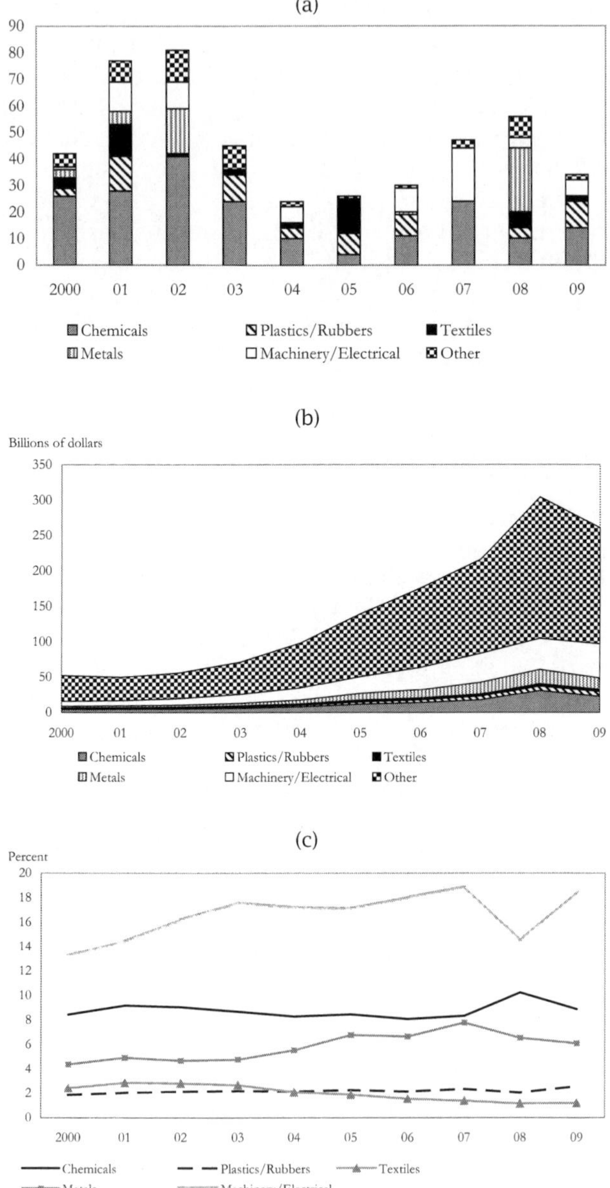

Figure 7.3: *India's use of anti-dumping and imports by sector for the period 2000–2009: (a) anti-dumping initiations by sector; (b) import value by sector; (c) percentage of import value by sector.*

Source: author's calculations using data from Bown (2010a) and WITS.

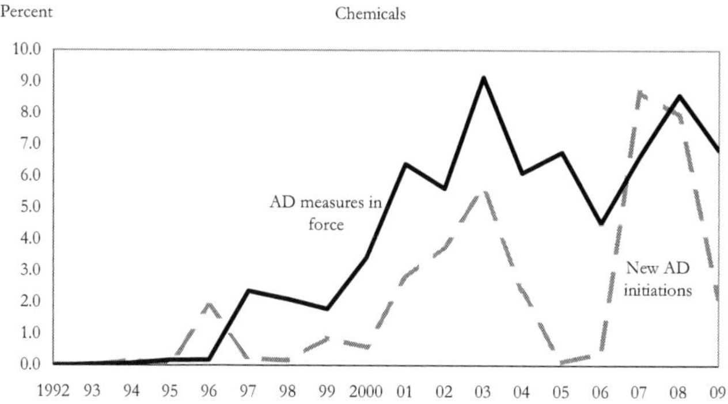

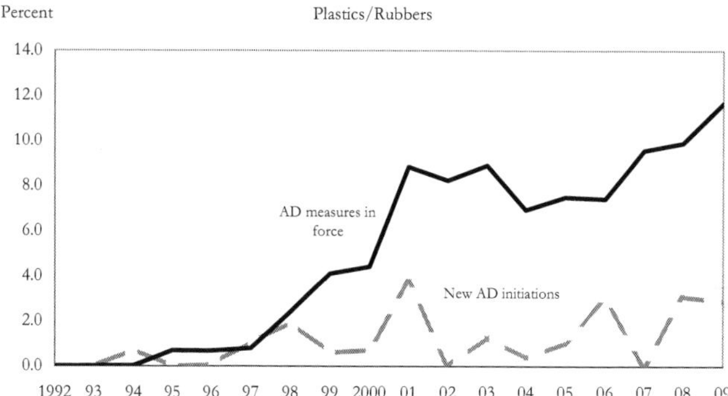

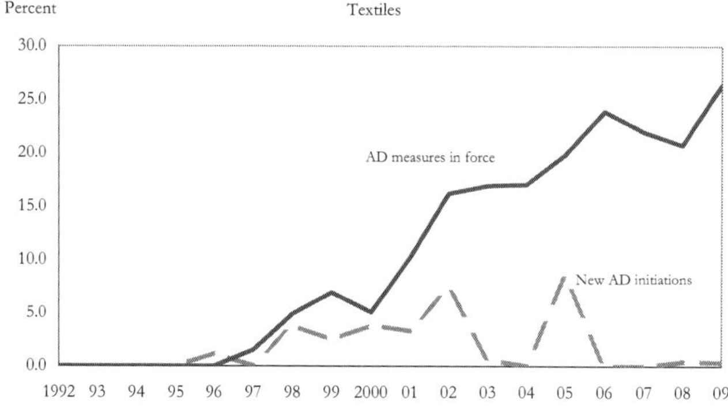

Figure 7.4: *Percentage of India's import value affected by anti-dumping by sector, 1992–2009.*

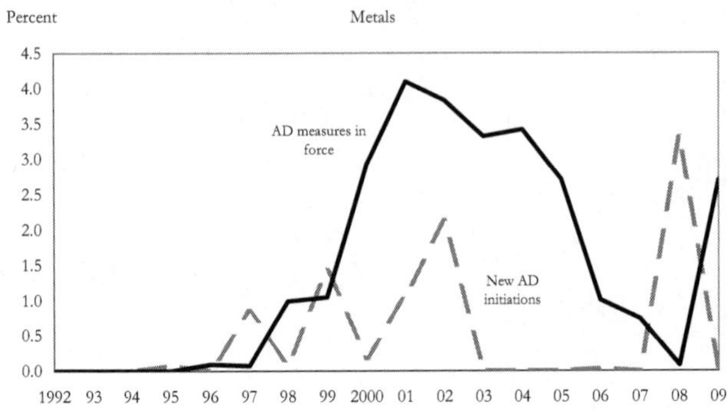

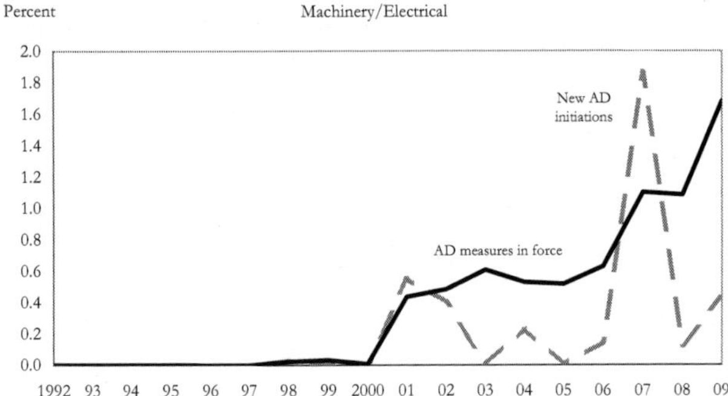

Figure 7.4: *Continued.*

Source: author's calculations using data from Bown (2010a) and WITS. This figure uses data at the six-digit HS level.

ucts in 2009. The other sectors—with the exception of chemicals—also show a sizeable increase in the percentage of affected imports in 2009, which may be related to the global recession.

3.3 Countries Affected by India's Use of Anti-Dumping

In this section we study how India's use of anti-dumping varies across its trading partners. Are some exporting countries more likely to be targeted with anti-dumping than others? Table 7.3 illustrates the Indian use of anti-dumping by its 20 most frequently named foreign targets, with these targets broken down into developing versus developed country categories. The table also breaks down the sample period into two subperiods: 1992–2007 and 2008–9.

India has named 40 countries (counting all of the EU members as only one country). As shown in Table 7.3, the country most frequently named was China

Table 7.3: *India's use of anti-dumping by targeted exporting country, 1992–2009: (a) developing/transition economies.*

Rank[c]	Exporting country target	Anti-dumping investigations (share of total)		Investigations resulting in measures (share of target country's investigations)[a]		Only country named in investigation (share of target country's investigations)		Share of India's import market (rank)		Mean anti-dumping margin[b]
	1992–2009									
1	China	130	(0.22)	109	(0.89)	65	(0.50)	0.08	(2)	114.41
6	Thailand	32	(0.05)	22	(0.76)	0	(0.00)	0.01	(24)	64.53
8	Indonesia	23	(0.04)	18	(0.78)	2	(0.09)	0.02	(16)	61.56
10	Malaysia	19	(0.03)	13	(0.72)	0	(0.00)	0.02	(13)	37.83
11	Russia	19	(0.03)	13	(0.72)	1	(0.05)	0.01	(20)	76.90
13	Iran	10	(0.02)	6	(0.60)	1	(0.10)	0.03	(10)	97.01
14	Brazil	9	(0.02)	9	(1.00)	0	(0.00)	0.01	(26)	68.56
15	South Africa	9	(0.02)	6	(0.67)	0	(0.00)	0.02	(17)	65.63
16	Ukraine	9	(0.02)	3	(0.33)	1	(0.11)	0.00	(28)	70.87
18	UAE	7	(0.01)	5	(0.71)	1	(0.14)	0.05	(5)	97.03
19	Turkey	6	(0.01)	5	(0.83)	0	(0.00)	0.00	(36)	47.84
	Other developing	27	(0.05)	20	(0.80)	5	(0.19)	0.21	—	46.17
	Total developing	300	(0.51)	229	(0.80)	76	(0.25)	0.46	—	86.47

Table 7.3: *Continued.*

Rank[c]	Exporting country target	Anti-dumping investigations (share of total)		Investigations resulting in measures (share of target country's investigations)[a]		Only country named in investigation (share of target country's investigations)		Share of India's import market (rank)		Mean anti-dumping margin[b]
	1992–2007									
1	China	104	(0.21)	94	(0.90)	53	(0.51)	0.06	(3)	—
6	Thailand	22	(0.04)	16	(0.73)	0	(0.00)	0.01	(23)	—
8	Indonesia	20	(0.04)	16	(0.80)	1	(0.05)	0.02	(14)	—
10	Malaysia	14	(0.03)	11	(0.79)	0	(0.00)	0.02	(12)	—
11	Russia	16	(0.03)	12	(0.75)	1	(0.06)	0.01	(19)	—
13	Iran	8	(0.02)	6	(0.75)	1	(0.13)	0.02	(15)	—
14	Brazil	9	(0.02)	9	(1.00)	0	(0.00)	0.01	(26)	—
15	South Africa	7	(0.01)	5	(0.71)	0	(0.00)	0.02	(16)	—
16	Ukraine	8	(0.02)	3	(0.38)	1	(0.13)	0.00	(31)	—
18	UAE	7	(0.01)	5	(0.71)	1	(0.14)	0.04	(6)	—
19	Turkey	5	(0.01)	5	(1.00)	0	(0.00)	0.00	(39)	—
	Other developing	19	(0.04)	16	(0.84)	4	(0.21)	0.24	—	—
	Total developing	239	(0.48)	198	(0.83)	62	(0.26)	0.46	—	—

Table 7.3: *Continued.*

Rank[c]	Exporting country target	Anti-dumping investigations (share of total)		Investigations resulting in measures (share of target country's investigations)[a]		Only country named in investigation (share of target country's investigations)		Share of India's import market (rank)		Mean anti-dumping margin[b]
	2008–9									
1	China	26	(0.30)	15	(0.83)	12	(0.46)	0.11	(2)	—
6	Thailand	10	(0.12)	6	(0.86)	0	(0.00)	0.01	(23)	—
8	Indonesia	3	(0.03)	2	(0.67)	1	(0.33)	0.02	(15)	—
10	Malaysia	5	(0.06)	2	(0.50)	0	(0.00)	0.02	(16)	—
11	Russia	3	(0.03)	1	(0.50)	0	(0.00)	0.01	(20)	—
13	Iran	2	(0.02)	0	(0.00)	0	(0.00)	0.04	(6)	—
14	Brazil	0	(0.00)	0	—	0	—	0.01	(27)	—
15	South Africa	2	(0.02)	1	(0.50)	0	(0.00)	0.02	(18)	—
16	Ukraine	1	(0.01)	0	(0.00)	0	(0.00)	0.00	(32)	—
18	UAE	0	(0.00)	0	—	0	—	0.07	(4)	—
19	Turkey	1	(0.01)	0	(0.00)	0	(0.00)	0.01	(31)	—
	Other developing	8	(0.09)	4	(0.67)	1	(0.13)	0.15	—	—
	Total developing	61	(0.71)	31	(0.67)	14	(0.23)	0.47	—	—

Table 7.3: *Continued: (b) Developed economies.*

Rank[c]	Exporting country target	Anti-dumping investigations (share of total)		Investigations resulting in measures (share of target country's investigations)[a]		Only country named in investigation (share of target country's investigations)		Share of India's import market (rank)		Mean anti-dumping margin[b]
	1992–2009									
2	European Union	88	(0.15)	70	(0.80)	7	(0.08)	0.15	(1)	72.81
3	South Korea	45	(0.08)	37	(0.84)	4	(0.09)	0.03	(9)	46.54
4	Taiwan	42	(0.07)	34	(0.83)	5	(0.12)	0.01	(21)	73.73
5	Japan	32	(0.05)	19	(0.68)	5	(0.16)	0.03	(8)	84.23
7	USA	28	(0.05)	22	(0.79)	1	(0.04)	0.07	(3)	74.71
9	Singapore	23	(0.04)	17	(0.77)	0	(0.00)	0.03	(12)	62.71
12	Hong Kong	10	(0.02)	8	(0.80)	0	(0.00)	0.02	(18)	84.92
17	Saudi Arabia	7	(0.01)	3	(0.50)	0	(0.00)	0.05	(4)	62.03
20	Canada	5	(0.01)	3	(0.60)	0	(0.00)	0.01	(22)	74.68
	Other developed	8	(0.01)	4	(0.57)	2	(0.25)	0.15	—	36.25
	Total developed	288	(0.49)	217	(0.78)	24	(0.08)	0.54	—	64.69

Table 7.3: *Continued.*

Rank[c]	Exporting country target	Anti-dumping investigations (share of total)		Investigations resulting in measures (share of target country's investigations)[a]		Only country named in investigation (share of target country's investigations)		Share of India's import market (rank)		Mean anti-dumping margin[b]
	1992–2007									
2	European Union	84	(0.17)	69	(0.82)	6	(0.07)	0.16	(1)	—
3	South Korea	41	(0.08)	35	(0.85)	3	(0.07)	0.03	(11)	—
4	Taiwan	39	(0.08)	32	(0.82)	5	(0.13)	0.01	(20)	—
5	Japan	26	(0.05)	19	(0.73)	5	(0.19)	0.04	(7)	—
7	USA	27	(0.05)	21	(0.78)	1	(0.04)	0.07	(2)	—
9	Singapore	22	(0.04)	17	(0.77)	0	(0.00)	0.03	(10)	—
12	Hong Kong	9	(0.02)	7	(0.78)	0	(0.00)	0.01	(18)	—
17	Saudi Arabia	5	(0.01)	3	(0.60)	0	(0.00)	0.04	(5)	—
20	Canada	5	(0.01)	3	(0.60)	0	(0.00)	0.01	(22)	—
	Other developed	5	(0.01)	3	(0.60)	2	(0.40)	0.15	—	—
	Total developed	263	(0.52)	209	(0.79)	22	(0.08)	0.54	—	—

Table 7.3: *Continued.*

Rank[c]	Exporting country target	Anti-dumping investigations (share of total)		Investigations resulting in measures (share of target country's investigations)[a]		Only country named in investigation (share of target country's investigations)		Share of India's import market (rank)		Mean anti-dumping margin[b]
	2008–9									
2	European Union	4	(0.05)	1	(0.25)	1	(0.25)	0.12	(1)	—
3	South Korea	4	(0.05)	2	(0.67)	1	(0.25)	0.03	(10)	—
4	Taiwan	3	(0.03)	2	(1.00)	0	(0.00)	0.01	(24)	—
5	Japan	6	(0.07)	0	(0.00)	0	(0.00)	0.02	(13)	—
7	USA	1	(0.01)	1	(1.00)	0	(0.00)	0.07	(3)	—
9	Singapore	1	(0.01)	0	—	0	(0.00)	0.02	(14)	—
12	Hong Kong	1	(0.01)	1	(1.00)	0	(0.00)	0.02	(19)	—
17	Saudi Arabia	2	(0.02)	0	(0.00)	0	(0.00)	0.06	(5)	—
20	Canada	0	(0.00)	0	—	0	—	0.01	(26)	—
	Other developed	3	(0.03)	1	(0.50)	0	(0.00)	0.16	—	—
	Total developed	25	(0.29)	8	(0.50)	2	(0.08)	0.53	—	—

[a] Excludes cases initiated in 2009 that have not ended yet (and thus information on final measures is still not available). [b] Mean anti-dumping margin only shown for 1992–2009 since there are not enough observations per country in the data for the 2008–9 period to make any meaningful comparisons or inferences. [c] Targeted country's rank in the total number of initiations over 1992–2009. For consistency, this table only allows for one 'EU' entry for each product-specific investigation.

Source: author's calculations using data from Bown (2010a) and Comtrade.

(130 times), followed by the EU (88 times), South Korea (45 times), Taiwan (42 times) and Thailand and Japan (32 times each).

The investigations against China represented more than one-fifth of the total number of India's anti-dumping investigations, and China was also the country targeted with the highest number of measures (109). In addition, in almost all (89%) of the investigations against China, a measure was imposed. Furthermore, in 50% of the investigations against China, it was the only country named in the investigation. That share is much larger than for the other main targeted countries. Put differently, although this is not shown in the table, in 53% of all product-level investigations, one of the named countries was China. These trends of targeting China in particular during the post-2001 period especially are quite typical to almost all of the countries using anti-dumping in the WTO system (Bown 2010b; Prusa 2010).[14] In addition, the last column in Table 7.3 shows the mean anti-dumping margin by country, which suggests that the mean *size* of the anti-dumping import restriction is highest against China as well.[15] Moreover, the share of investigations against China increased from 21% in 1992–2007 to 30% in the global recession years of 2008–9. The share of product-level investigations involving China also increased, from 50% in 1992–2007 to 76% in 2008–9.

Among the main targeted countries, the share of investigations against China, Thailand, Malaysia and Japan show a particularly important increase in 2008–9. The share of measures imposed against Thailand and Taiwan also increased during those two years. Are these increases associated with increases in imports coming from those countries in particular? Table 7.3 shows that the share of imports from China almost doubled in 2008–9 relative to the previous period; however, the share of imports from the other countries mentioned remained stable or even fell. In addition, the share of investigations targeting developing countries increased from 48% in 1992–2007 to 71% in 2008–9, while the share of imports from those countries stayed roughly the same.

Figure 7.5(a) shows the number of eight-digit HS product–exporter combinations that are affected by an anti-dumping initiation over time. We divide the

[14]Although India considers China to be a non-market-economy country, it has adopted a policy whereby if it is shown that market conditions prevail for some firms subject to an investigation, the authorities are able to grant market-economy treatment. However, Kumaran (2005) notes that only in very few cases was such market-economy treatment granted to individual exporters from China.

[15]The computation of the mean anti-dumping margin uses data on the final dumping margin calculations, which are reported in *ad valorem* terms. The mean is taken over the minimum and maximum final dumping margin levels that are reported and correspond to different targeted exporting firms of a given product (and country). We describe this in more detail in Section 3.5. Although there is a requirement that the anti-dumping duty should not exceed the dumping margin, Kumaran (2005) explains how, under certain circumstances, the anti-dumping duty may end up being higher than the dumping margin in India.

(a)

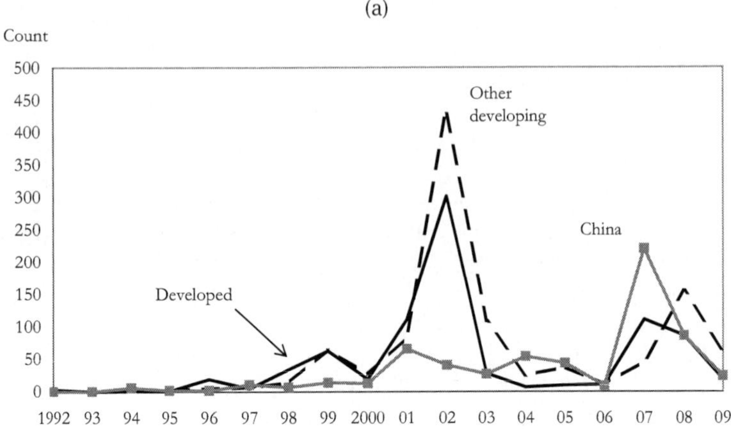

(b)

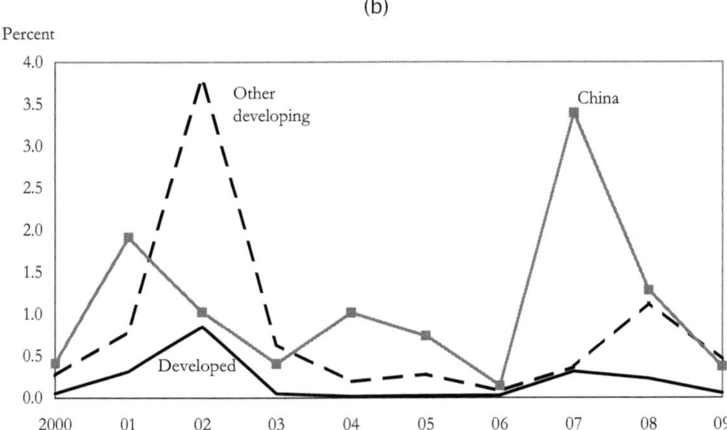

Figure 7.5: *India's anti-dumping investigations by targeted country: (a) number of eight-digit HS product-exporter combinations with anti-dumping initiations; (b) percentage of imported eight-digit HS product-exporter combinations with anti-dumping initiations.*

Source: author's calculations using data from Bown (2010a) and WITS.

affected exporting countries into three groups: developed countries, China, and other developing countries. As shown, the number of product-exporter combinations targeted by new Indian anti-dumping initiations more than tripled in 2008 relative to 2007 in the case of other developing countries—while it fell in the case of China and developed countries—and although it decreased in 2009, it was still higher than in 2007.

In Figure 7.5(b), we show the *percentage* of eight-digit HS product–exporter combinations imported from developed countries, China, and other developing countries that are affected by a new anti-dumping initiation over time.[16] The increase in the number of combinations of eight-digit HS products and other developing country exporters targeted by new anti-dumping initiations in 2008 from Figure 7.5(a) was associated with an increase in the percentage of product–exporter combinations imported from the same group of countries that are affected by Indian anti-dumping in the same year.

It is also important to examine the stock of eight-digit HS product–exporter combinations that are affected by an Indian anti-dumping measure for each exporting country category. Figure 7.6(a) presents the number of such combinations while Figure 7.6(b) displays the percentage of imported combinations from each country category subject to Indian anti-dumping protection. Regarding the former, there has been a shift in the incidence of anti-dumping protection towards China and other developing countries in recent years. In 2006, the number of products imported from China and affected by an anti-dumping measure started to exceed the number of product–exporter combinations that are imported from anti-dumping-affected *developed* countries. Analogously, in 2002, the number of product–exporter combinations imported from other developing countries and affected by an anti-dumping measure began exceeding the corresponding number of combinations with a developed exporter source. In 1997, for example, 53% of India's stock of anti-dumping measures affected developed countries, 22% affected China, and 24% affected other developing countries. By 2009, only 25% of India's stock of anti-dumping measures was imposed against developed countries, whereas 39% was imposed against China and 36% against other developing countries.

A similar trend can be observed regarding the percentage of the stock of product–exporter combinations subject to an anti-dumping measure affecting each country category in Figure 7.6(b). In particular, the percentage of products imported from China subject to an anti-dumping measure presents a significant increase in 2008–9.[17] While, in 2007, 3.65% of products imported from China were affected by an Indian anti-dumping measure, by 2009 that had risen to 7.45%. The percentage of combinations of products and other developing country exporters affected reached a peak of 3.21% in 2009. Although the percentage of analogous combinations with a developed exporter source also reached its peak in 2009, it remained below 1%.

[16]When counting the total number of eight-digit HS product–exporter combinations, we exclude suppliers that account for less than 1% of a given eight-digit HS product's imports per year.

[17]A sizeable increase is also found by comparing the prediction for that percentage based on a linear time-trend regression with the observed one, either at the six-digit or eight-digit HS product level.

(a)

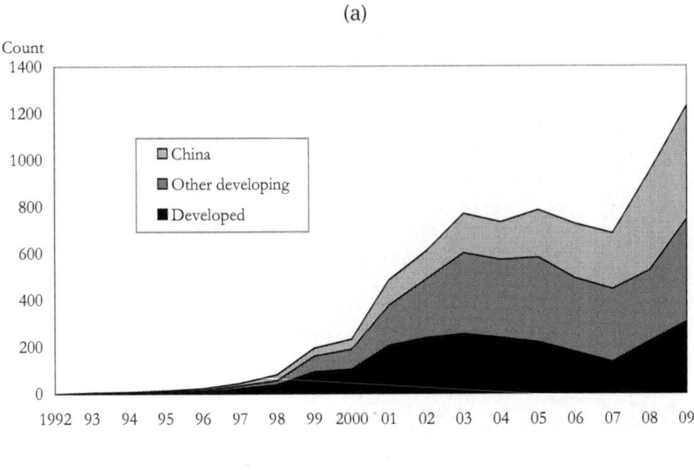

(b)

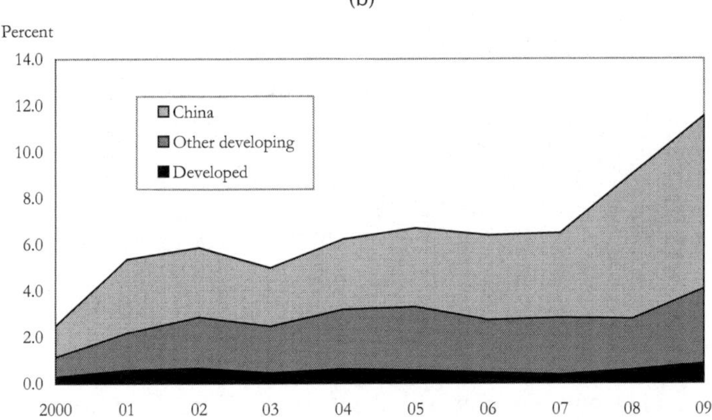

Figure 7.6: *India's anti-dumping measures by targeted country: (a) total number of eight-digit HS product-exporter combinations with anti-dumping measures in force; (b) percentage of imported eight-digit HS product-exporter combinations with anti-dumping measures in force.*

Source: author's calculations using data from Bown (2010a) and WITS.

Using the information from Table 7.3 we can calculate the percentage of Indian imports coming from each of the previous country categories. From 1992-2007, 54% of India's imports came from developed countries, 6% came from China and 39% came from other developing countries. In 2008-9, 53% of India's imports were exported by developed countries, 11% by China and 37% by other developing countries. Therefore, while an increase in the share of imports from China is associated with the increasing incidence of anti-dumping protection against that country, the share of imports from other developing countries actually decreased slightly, whereas the incidence of Indian anti-dumping increasingly concentrated on those countries.

The economic issue of trade diversion is another issue that arises because of India's use of anti-dumping and non-MFN treatment. Can it help us to understand the multitude of occasions in which India has imposed new anti-dumping measures against different sources of the same product, year after year? There are 129 different eight-digit HS products for which, having initiated an anti-dumping investigation in a previous year, India initiated a new investigation in the same product against different exporting countries. These products represent 14% of the total number of products with anti-dumping initiations. Moreover, in 84 (65%) of those cases a final measure was imposed. Since import data at the eight-digit HS product level are only available for the period since 2000, we cannot determine which exporting countries were new entrants into India's market for a given affected product. We can only say that, in 72 out of those 129 (eight-digit HS) products for which India initiated a subsequent anti-dumping investigation in the same product against a different exporting country, the newly affected exporting country had not previously exported to India since 2000.[18] Gulati *et al* (2005) study anti-dumping policy in the vitamin-C industry in India and find that, although anti-dumping effectively restricted imports from the countries named to be dumping, new countries started exporting the product to India after the petition was filed, and this trade diversion in turn led to new anti-dumping investigations and measures. Our results also suggest that trade diversion has played an important role leading to additional use of anti-dumping policies.

This result suggests that anti-dumping measures may be used as a form of protection regardless of whether dumping is actually taking place, and it could help to explain the large-scale use of anti-dumping by India. It also raises the question of why India did not use global safeguards that could be imposed on an MFN basis instead of anti-dumping in those cases, since safeguards can apply to all countries and thus would help to prevent surges in imports from new exporters. On the other hand, this could help to explain why India has begun to increase its use of global safeguard measures in 2008–9, which we discuss in Section 4.

3.4 The Duration of Anti-Dumping Measures

In this section we examine the actual duration of Indian anti-dumping policy's temporary acts of import protection. The WTO's Anti-Dumping Agreement mandates a 'sunset review' process under which countries are supposed to investigate whether removal of the anti-dumping measures after five years

[18]We cannot rule out that the country could potentially have exported that product to India before 2000.

will be likely to lead to a recurrence of injury caused by renewed dumping; if not, the imposed anti-dumping measures should then be removed.

Consider how India's actions relate to the spirit of the WTO rules in this area. We focus on anti-dumping measures imposed *prior* to 2005, so that the five-year period has elapsed sufficiently for the 'sunset review' process to be potentially meaningful. First, we find that 60% of the imposed measures had their import restrictions removed within the basic five-year limit stipulated by the 'sunset review' process. For all measures that have subsequently had the import restrictions removed, the average period for which measures stay in force is 4.3 years.

As Figure 7.7(a) illustrates, the most common (modal) duration period is five years (with 58 cases), followed by four years (56 cases), three years (24 cases) and six years (17 cases). Overall, 98 cases had measures revoked *before* five years, while in 21 cases *with measures already revoked* they lasted more than five years. The minimum duration of measures was one year (4 cases) and the maximum for cases that have been removed is 12 years. In addition to the cases included in Figure 7.7(a), there are 83 cases with measures imposed before 2005 that have not yet been removed, and thus have lasted *more than* five years but for which we do not know exactly how many years they will be in place.[19]

Figure 7.7(a) also allows us to break out the typical duration of measures imposed in the chemicals sector, the most frequent user of anti-dumping in India. There we find that 52% of all measures are removed within five years, lower than the corresponding percentage over all measures. Moreover, for the measures imposed before 2005 that have subsequently been removed, the mean duration of measures in that sector is 4.4 years, which is slightly above the average over all measures. There were 26 measures lasting five years, 37 measures stayed in place for less than five years, and 13 measures lasted more than five years. There have been 45 measures imposed before 2005 that have lasted longer than five years and that have yet to be removed. These are not pictured. Combined, this evidence indicates that anti-dumping measures in the chemicals sector are more likely to become 'quasi-permanent' protection.

While not pictured in Figure 7.7(a), we can also examine whether there is a differential treatment with respect to measures imposed against China, the country most targeted by India's anti-dumping. Here we find that the average duration of measures is 4.9 years, which is also higher than the overall average. Of the measures imposed prior to 2005 that have subsequently been removed, there were 12 measures against China that stayed in force less than five years, 15 lasted five years, and 4 remained in force more than five years. In addition, 21 measures were imposed before 2005 that have lasted longer

[19]We measure the duration for all cases in years; that is, we do not consider in which month of a given year a measure was revoked. In that sense our figures are approximations.

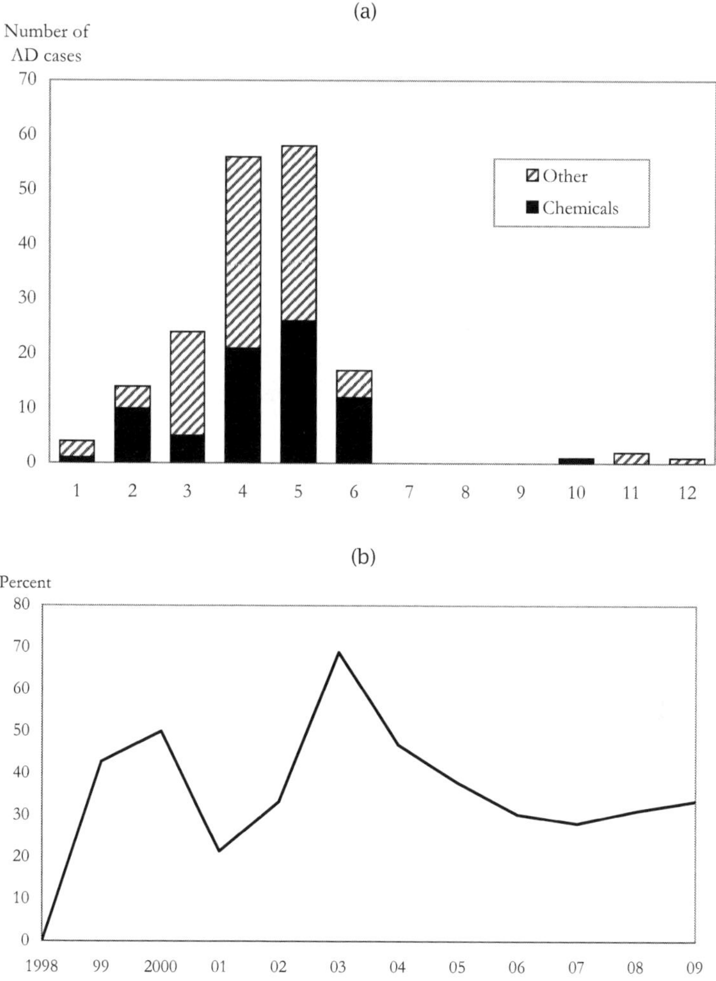

Figure 7.7: *Duration of anti-dumping measures in India: (a) duration of measures (in years); (b) percentage of measures imposed five or more years ago that have not yet been removed.*

Source: author's calculations using data from Bown (2010a).

than five years and have yet to be removed. Overall, there is some evidence that Indian anti-dumping measures imposed against China tend to last longer.

Next, we examine whether, over time, the measures that were imposed five or more years ago have been removed. Figure 7.7(b) displays the yearly behaviour of the percentage of measures imposed five or more years ago that are not removed *even though the five-year limit of the 'sunset review' process has elapsed.* Interestingly, after a decrease in this percentage taking place each year between 2003 and 2007, there was an increase in 2008 and 2009. This suggests that another dimension through which anti-dumping protection increased during the global recession is via the failure to *remove* policies that were imposed prior to the crisis and were supposed to be terminated during the crisis under the five-year-period limit.

We also calculated the percentage of measures that were imposed *exactly* five years ago (and thus came up for sunset review) and were removed each year. [20] This percentage actually shows a decreasing trend since 2005, and although it increased in 2008, it fell again in 2009. Therefore, even though India was less likely to remove previously imposed anti-dumping measures that came up for sunset review in 2009, this seems consistent with previous trends and might not be directly related to the global economic crisis.

3.5 Imposed Anti-Dumping Measures and WTO Tariff Bindings

For most economists, anti-dumping is not a policy that is well grounded in economic theory. Because the main legal definitions of dumping—whether it be international price discriminatory or pricing below average costs, even temporarily—can be rational, profit-maximising behaviour for a firm without necessarily having any predatory intent (and there is no required evidence for predation found in anti-dumping laws), the policy itself may be viewed as little more than import protection that governments offer to industries on a contingent basis. Therefore, suppose that we adopt the view of treating anti-dumping as merely one of many potential forms of import protection. Then, a basic question is, do governments use anti-dumping to raise import barriers to levels that would not otherwise be possible under the rules of the WTO system? More precisely, if India did not implement the new protection in the form of anti-dumping measures but instead simply raised its applied tariff rate by the same amount, how frequently would doing so result in a violation of its commitments?[21] The counterfactual that we adopt in this particular application of examining whether India is complying with WTO rules is to imagine that it would otherwise impose the same level of protection that it is currently imposing via anti-dumping, but simply by raising its applied tariff by that amount instead of using an anti-dumping measure.

---

[20]Cadot *et al* (2008) provide a rigorous analysis of the effect that the introduction of sunset reviews into the WTO system has had on the duration of anti-dumping measures in several countries.

[21]An alternative and more legalistic approach to evaluating whether a country is following the basic rules on anti-dumping would be to evaluate whether there was sufficient economic evidence of injury caused by dumping, and whether the size of the imposed measures was based on the size of evidence of the dumping margin. Such an approach requires access to data well beyond the scope of this study.

Since it is best to use data at the tariff-line (eight-digit HS) level to examine this question, we focus on the 2004–9 period, given that data on applied tariffs at such level of disaggregation are only available for the period since 2004. Although most Indian anti-dumping measures are imposed as specific duties while applied tariffs and tariff bindings are *ad valorem*, we have data on the final dumping margin calculations, which are reported in *ad valorem* terms. In some cases the margin is reported at the level of the exporting firm within an investigated country, but in other cases it is only reported as a *range* of values of new trade barriers facing the exporters of that product in a given investigated country. Therefore, for each anti-dumping case we report both the lowest and highest firm-specific anti-dumping margins corresponding to a given targeted country. While this is admittedly a very facile approach, when viewed from the perspective of this particular counterfactual, there is some evidence that India is indeed following the rules of the WTO system. As Table 7.4 indicates, if we use the highest anti-dumping margin, then in 420 of the 529 instances (79%) in which India imposed anti-dumping measures on a foreign firm's exports of a given product, the size of the new import restriction was larger than the difference between the product's applied tariff and the product's tariff binding—also referred to as the 'tariff overhang'. A tariff binding is the limit over which India has agreed under the WTO not to raise its tariff. If we use the lowest anti-dumping margin, the number of instances in which the imposed anti-dumping measure was larger than the tariff overhang is lower but still sizeable.[22] The table breaks this down further into two subperiods, 2004–7 and 2008–9, and shows that there has been a decrease in the percentage of cases in which the anti-dumping measure exceeds the tariff overhang. However, considering the highest anti-dumping margins, the percentage of cases in which the imposition of a tariff of equal size would have led to a violation of India's WTO commitments is still high in the later subperiod.

Table 7.4 also shows similar information for the subset of anti-dumping measures imposed against developing countries only. During 2004–9, in 93% of the cases in which India imposed anti-dumping measures on a developing country's exports of a given product, the size of the new import restriction was larger than the tariff overhang corresponding to the same product (using the highest anti-dumping margin), which is higher than for the whole sample over the same period. Moreover, while this percentage between 2004 and 2007 was similar to the percentage for the whole sample (90% in both cases), in 2008–9 the percentage of cases in which the anti-dumping measure exceeded the tariff overhang was much larger for developing countries (97%)

[22]Of course, this is conditional on the size of the Indian anti-dumping measure being exogenous, and it also ignores the fact that the anti-dumping measure can be foreign-firm specific and thus is not equivalent to raising an applied tariff, which must be done on an MFN basis.

Table 7.4: *India's anti-dumping measures and WTO tariff bindings, 2004–9.*

	2004–9		2004–7		2008–9	
	Lowest firm-specific anti-dumping margin	Highest firm-specific anti-dumping margin	Lowest firm-specific anti-dumping margin	Highest firm-specific anti-dumping margin	Lowest firm-specific anti-dumping margin	Highest firm-specific anti-dumping margin
All observations						
Total number of eight-digit HS product observations	524	529	245	245	279	284
Number of observations with anti-dumping margin greater than tariff overhang	223 (0.43)	420 (0.79)	204 (0.83)	221 (0.90)	19 (0.07)	199 (0.70)
Number of observations with anti-dumping margin less than or equal to tariff overhang	301 (0.57)	109 (0.21)	41 (0.17)	24 (0.10)	260 (0.93)	85 (0.30)
Developing countries						
Total number of eight-digit HS product observations	378	383	187	187	191	196
Number of observations with anti-dumping margin greater than tariff overhang	172 (0.46)	358 (0.93)	159 (0.85)	168 (0.90)	13 (0.07)	190 (0.97)
Number of observations with anti-dumping margin less than or equal to tariff overhang	206 (0.54)	25 (0.07)	28 (0.15)	19 (0.10)	178 (0.93)	6 (0.03)

Table 7.4: *Continued.*

	2004–9		2004–7		2008–9	
	Lowest firm-specific anti-dumping margin	Highest firm-specific anti-dumping margin	Lowest firm-specific anti-dumping margin	Highest firm-specific anti-dumping margin	Lowest firm-specific anti-dumping margin	Highest firm-specific anti-dumping margin
Chemicals						
Total number of eight-digit HS product observations	353	353	91	91	262	262
Number of observations with anti-dumping margin greater than tariff overhang	92 (0.26)	268 (0.76)	78 (0.86)	88 (0.97)	14 (0.05)	180 (0.69)
Number of observations with anti-dumping margin less than or equal to tariff overhang	261 (0.74)	85 (0.24)	13 (0.14)	3 (0.03)	248 (0.95)	82 (0.31)

Based on observations with non-missing anti-dumping margin and tariff overhang; observations are exporting country-product pairs. Numbers in parentheses represent the share of the total. Tariff overhang calculated as the difference between the country's bound tariff rate and its MFN applied tariff rate at the eight-digit HS level the year of the imposition of the anti-dumping measure, computed from India's tariff data available in WITS.

Source: author's calculations using data from Bown (2010a).

than for all countries combined (70%). This is consistent with the finding in Section 3.3 that the incidence of India's anti-dumping protection has shifted towards developing countries during the 2008–9 global recession. Although we do not report similar information corresponding to anti-dumping measures applied against imports from China only, we find that, in essentially *all* instances, the highest anti-dumping margin exceeded the tariff overhang in both 2004–7 and 2008–9.[23]

Finally, Table 7.4 also reports equivalent information for the chemicals sector. In 2004–7, the percentage of cases in which the anti-dumping margin on chemical products was larger than the corresponding tariff overhang was higher than the total for all sectors; nonetheless, that percentage fell in 2008–9 and became fairly similar to the one for the whole sample of products. Thus, along this dimension there does not seem to be a shift in the incidence of anti-dumping protection towards chemicals in the latter period.

4 INDIA'S USE OF SAFEGUARDS AND COUNTERVAILING MEASURES

While anti-dumping is India's most frequently utilised TTB, there are other relatively substitutable forms of import protection in use. In this section we examine three other examples that India has resorted to, including global safeguards, transitional China-specific safeguards associated with China's 2001 WTO accession, and countervailing measures for anti-subsidy policies.

4.1 Global Safeguards

India's domestic law concerning the implementation of the Agreement of Safeguards was enacted under Section 8B and Section 8C of the Customs Tariff Act, 1975. The procedures were outlined in the Customs Tariff (Identification and Assessment of Safeguard Duty) Rules, 1997, and Customs Tariff (Transitional Products Specific Safeguard Duty) Rules, 2002.[24] A director-general of Safeguards under the Department of Revenue of the Ministry of Finance was appointed to receive the petitions and conduct the investigations required for the imposition of a safeguard duty. The director-general of Safeguards should then submit the findings to the central government.[25]

---

[23]The percentage of cases in which the lowest anti-dumping margin imposed against Chinese firms exceeded India's tariff overhang decreased in 2008–9 relative to 2004–7, however.

[24]Section 8C regulates the imposition of safeguard duties on any product imported from China for which increased imports are causing or threatening to cause 'market disruption' to the domestic industry.

[25]For more details about the applications, investigations and timelines, see the website of the Directorate General of Safeguards: http://dgsafeguards.gov.in.

India initiated its first safeguard investigation in 1997. Between 1995 and 31 October 2010, India initiated the most (26) safeguard investigations of the entire WTO membership.[26] As Table 7.1 again illustrates, 11 of the 26 investigations taking place between 1997 and 2009 resulted in the imposition of definitive safeguard import restrictions. No injury was found in only 1 case during that period, and 5 cases were terminated. Interestingly, 11 out of the 26 investigations were initiated between 2008 and 2009 in the midst of the global economic crisis (2 in 2008 and 9 in 2009), but 8 of those did not result in the imposition of a final safeguard measure. Furthermore, in 5 out of the 26 cases, most or all developing countries were exempt from the application of safeguards.

The most frequent sectoral user of safeguards has been chemicals, with 14 initiations. As noted before, the chemicals sector was also India's most frequent user of anti-dumping. Moreover, the WTO reports that, since 1995, chemical products were the most frequent subject of safeguards (investigations and measures) in the world (WTO 2010b). The second most active sector in India was wood and wood products (4 safeguard initiations), and a handful of other industries have also initiated investigations, including vegetable products, foodstuffs, plastics/rubbers, textiles and metals. Each of these industries, with the exception of vegetable products, also initiated anti-dumping cases. Overall, 198 different eight-digit HS codes have been investigated under India's global safeguard activity between 1997 and 2009.

4.2 China-Specific Safeguards

As part of China's terms of accession to the WTO in 2001, the existing members of the WTO were granted access to an additional 'Chinese safeguard' policy instrument that could be used to implement new and discriminatory import restrictions against China without any evidence of unfair trade (dumping or illegal subsidies), but only a surge in Chinese imports, and would last during a transitional period until 2014.

Before 2009, India initiated an investigation under this policy only once—a 2002 investigation of 'industrial sewing machine needles' that did not result in the imposition of final import restrictions. Amidst the global economic crisis, however, as Table 7.5 illustrates, India initiated five China-specific safeguard investigations in 2009 over a variety of imported products. In two cases a final measure was imposed, in one case no injury was found, and two cases were withdrawn. Overall, 35 different eight-digit HS products have been the subject of a China-specific safeguard investigation by India.

---

[26]It was followed by Jordan (15), Turkey (15), Chile (12), Indonesia (12) and the USA (10). Moreover, India imposed the most safeguard measures during the same period (along with Turkey).

Table 7.5: *India's use of China-specific safeguards and countervailing measures, 2002–2009.*

	Policy	Product and investigated country	Number of eight-digit HS products	Year of initiation of investigation	Outcome of investigation
1	China safeguard	Industrial sewing machine needles from China	1	2002	Despite affirmative final injury determination, no final measure imposed
2	China safeguard	Soda ash from China	3	2009	Final measures imposed in November 2009
3	China safeguard	Aluminum flat-rolled products and aluminum foil from China	19	2009	Final measures imposed in June 2009
4	China safeguard	Nylon tyre cord fabric from China	2	2009	Withdrawn by industry
5	China safeguard	Front axle beam/steering knuckle and crankshaft of medium and heavy commercial vehicles from China	8	2009	Negative injury decision
6	China safeguard	Passenger car tyres from China	2	2009	Withdrawn by industry
7	Countervailing measures	Sodium nitrite from China	1	2009	Withdrawn by industry

Source: Temporary Trade Barriers Database (Bown 2010a).

4.3 Countervailing Measures

In January 2009, India initiated its first (and only, as of December 2010) countervailing measure investigation to deal with foreign use of WTO-inconsistent subsidies. As Table 7.5 illustrates, somewhat unsurprisingly, it was a case initiated against China and over a product in the chemicals sector (sodium nitrite). The case was withdrawn.

5 THE INTERACTION OF TEMPORARY TRADE BARRIERS

In this section we describe whether and how the alternative TTBs interact, both with one another and with India's applied tariffs.

We begin by asking whether the products that were the subject of safeguard initiations between 1992 and 2009 were also subject to anti-dumping investigations at some point during the same period. We find that 39% of the eight-digit HS products that initiated a safeguard investigation had also been subject to an initiated anti-dumping investigation at some point. Thus, although there is some degree of overlap between both types of policies across products, there is also a substantial percentage (61%) of cases in which safeguard investigations were used in products never affected by anti-dumping. Are there instances in which a product is subject to both an anti-dumping and a safeguard measure *at the same time*? This turns out to be very uncommon. There was only one eight-digit HS product subject to both types of measures in 1999 and one in 2000, as well as four products affected by both measures in 2004. These findings would seem more consistent with a relationship of 'substitutability' between both types of policies.

Regarding China-specific safeguards, the product with the investigation initiated in 2002 was also subject to an anti-dumping investigation initiated in 1998 against China and three other countries, but after a preliminary anti-dumping measure was imposed, the final decision was negative. Six out of the 34 (8-digit HS) products that were subject to a China-specific safeguard investigation in 2009 also had anti-dumping initiations, and anti-dumping measures were imposed against China (and two other countries) in 2004 and 2008. These cases suggest some examples of industries attempting to obtain *additional* protection on the same products; however, in each of those instances, the China-specific safeguard investigation was either withdrawn or there was a negative decision.

Finally, the product subject to the (subsequently withdrawn) countervailing measure investigation was not subject to any anti-dumping or global safeguard initiation. Overall, and particularly on the basis of India's actual imposition of measures, these findings again seem consistent with the previous statement that the TTBs exhibit more of a relationship of substitutability, and that they are typically not used on the same products.

Although there does not seem to be substantial overlap of different TTBs over the same eight-digit HS products, we can also examine whether there is overlap over the same *sectors*. Are the same sectors the main users of all types of policies (with different products within a sector generally using different policies as previously found)? Table 7.6 presents information on the use of the most commonly utilised policies—anti-dumping, global safeguards and tariffs—across two-digit HS sectors.

First consider the use of anti-dumping and safeguards. There is substantial overlap in terms of the sectors that use those policies. For example, there are 12 sectors that initiated an anti-dumping investigation at some point between 1992 and 2009, and 7 sectors with a safeguard investigation over the same period. Of the 7 safeguard-user sectors, 6 *also* used anti-dumping. We also find that this relationship has not changed much during the global recession years. In 2008–9, 8 sectors initiated an anti-dumping investigation and 4 sectors initiated a safeguard investigation. All of those 4 sectors were also users of anti-dumping over the same period. In addition, overall, the chemicals sector was the main user of both policies.

The last two columns of Table 7.6 show the average applied tariffs at the eight-digit HS level (available since 2004, as noted earlier) by sector, with the mean applied tariff over all products reported at the bottom of the table.[27] As shown, the five sectors that were the main users of anti-dumping and safeguards (chemicals, plastics/rubbers, textiles, metals, and machinery/electric) did *not* have tariffs higher than the overall mean across all products. This is true across the whole sample period (1992–2009) as well as during the global economic crisis (2008–9). Similarly, the sectors with average tariffs above the overall mean were not major anti-dumping users and did not use safeguards at all. In order to interpret these findings it is important to take into account India's tariff liberalisation reform. Bown and Tovar (2011) study the relationship between India's reductions in applied tariffs associated with its unilateral trade liberalisation (described in Section 2) and the subsequent reapplication of anti-dumping (and safeguard) import restrictions. They show that the products that Indian industries demanded and received new anti-dumping import restrictions on during the period 2000–2002 were those that had (pre-1991 liberalisation) higher tariffs and that had undergone larger tariff reductions (see Bown and Tovar (2011, Figure 2)). They also provide a formal set of regression-based approaches and present significant, product-level evidence that the tariff reform itself is associated with subsequent resort to Indian use of anti-dumping.[28] Finally, Table 7.6 also shows that the lower average tariffs

[27] Since tariff data are not available for 2006, we use the average of the applied tariffs in 2005 and 2007 for that year.

[28] Vandenbussche and Zanardi (2010) estimate a gravity model for a group of countries and find that the trade decrease resulting from India's anti-dumping policy is of the same magnitude as the trade increase that resulted from its earlier trade liberalisation.

Table 7.6: *India's TTBs and tariffs by sector, 1992–2009.*

Sector	1992–2009		2008–9		2004–9 average applied tariff	2008–9 average applied tariff
	Anti-dumping initiations	Safeguard initiations	Anti-dumping initiations	Safeguard initiations		
Animal and animal products	4	0	0	0	30.8	30.5
Vegetable products	0	2	0	0	42.9	36.1
Foodstuffs	7	1	0	0	48.5	45.3
Mineral products	10	0	0	0	11.0	5.6
Chemicals and allied industries	235	14	24	5	14.9	8.8
Plastics/rubbers	82	2	14	0	15.2	9.6
Raw hides, skins, leather and furs	0	0	0	0	12.0	7.5
Wood and wood products	19	4	5	3	13.8	9.2
Textiles	59	1	8	1	14.8	9.7
Footwear/headgear	0	0	0	0	15.2	10.0
Stone/glass	9	0	1	0	14.9	9.4
Metals	70	2	24	2	15.7	7.0
Machinery/electrical	66	0	9	0	12.7	7.2
Transportation	2	0	1	0	33.8	29.7
Miscellaneous	5	0	0	0	14.0	8.8
Total	568	26	86	11	18.8	13.3

Source: author's calculations using data from Bown (2010a) and WITS.

for 2008–9 relative to the previous years suggest that India was able to continue with its process of tariff liberalisation even in the midst of the global economic crisis.[29] It is possible that the use of TTBs may have helped India to continue along such a path.[30]

We therefore conclude that the alternative forms of import restrictions were mostly used by similar sectors, with some substitutability across the policies (formally examined by Bown and Tovar (2011)) and with different products within a sector generally making use of different TTBs.

6 CONCLUSION

In this chapter we first examine the behaviour of India's use of TTBs (anti-dumping, safeguards and countervailing measures) over time. We then study any changes regarding their use that may have occurred during the global economic crisis of 2008–9. We rely on detailed product-level data from 1992 to 2009 from the World Bank's *Temporary Trade Barriers Database* (Bown 2010a).

We find that the stock of products subject to an anti-dumping measure increased from 1992 through 2009. Furthermore, the percentage of tariff-line (eight-digit HS) level products subject to an anti-dumping measure increased significantly during the crisis, from 1.82% in 2007 to 4.03% by 2009, and such an increase exceeds what would be predicted based on the observed trends from previous (pre-crisis) years.

We also find that the sectors that are the main users of anti-dumping policy in India—chemicals, plastics/rubber, machinery/electrical, metals and textiles—are also the major anti-dumping user sectors worldwide. This pattern regarding the sectoral use of anti-dumping also prevailed during the global recession of 2008–9. Moreover, those sectors account for an important share of India's import value, which suggests that the effects of the use of anti-dumping protection in India may be economically important.

Regarding the exporter incidence of the use of anti-dumping by India, China was the most frequent target of Indian anti-dumping as well as the recipient of the highest average anti-dumping barriers. During 2008–9, this bias in the incidence of anti-dumping policy against China increased. The share of investigations affecting developing countries more generally also increased from 48% in 1992–2007 to 71% in 2008–9, even though the share of imports from those countries stayed roughly the same. This increasing incidence in India's anti-dumping use against China and other developing countries over time is also seen with respect to the stock of product–exporter combinations that are

---

[29]The tariffs also fell relative to 2007.

[30]However, there are other possible explanations for those findings as well that we do not rule out here, and further research would be needed to distinguish among them.

affected by an anti-dumping measure. These results are consistent with the findings of Bown (2011b) and suggest a pattern of substantial discrimination that may be important to examine further in light of the WTO's MFN principle.

Furthermore, we find that an additional dimension through which India's anti-dumping protectionism increased during the global economic crisis of 2008–9 was via the failure to remove policies imposed in the years preceding the crisis that were supposed to be terminated during the crisis under the five-year 'sunset review' limit.

We also provide some evidence consistent with the possibility that India may have used anti-dumping policy to increase import restrictions to levels that would otherwise violate the rules of the WTO system, and consistent with the possibility that the use of TTBs might have helped India continue its process of tariff liberalisation in the midst of the global economic crisis. However, those are only a few of a number of possible alternative explanations behind the observed patterns, and further research is needed to draw definitive conclusions.

Although anti-dumping is the major TTB used by India, we also examine India's use of other forms of temporary import protection. We find an increase in the number of global safeguard investigations initiated during the 2008–9 global economic crisis, as well as in India's use of China-specific safeguards.

Finally, we find that, although there is not much overlap in terms of different TTBs being used over the same (eight-digit HS) products, there is substantial overlap regarding the sectors that use such barriers, both before and during the global recession years of 2008–9.

Even though our focus in this chapter has been on TTBs, it is possible that India may have used other forms of trade barriers during the global economic crisis. For example, in November 2008, some steel products were placed into the 'restricted' list of imported goods, and in 2009 the government imposed a licensing requirement on imports of electrical energy as well as an increase in the minimum support prices for several cereals. There were also some increases in applied tariffs (although the average applied tariffs fell, as reported earlier). For instance, in November 2008, a 20% tariff was imposed on imports of soybean oils, as well as a 5% tariff on several iron and steel products (see Global Trade Alert (2010)).[31] Therefore, further research is needed in order to examine the use of other forms of import restrictions in more detail and to establish any changes that may have occurred in the crisis years.

Patricia Tovar is Assistant Professor at the Department of Economics and International Business School at Brandeis University.

---

[31] The restrictions on imports of steel products were lifted in January 2010 and the tariff on soybean oils was removed in April 2009.

REFERENCES

Aggarwal, A. (2002). Anti dumping law and practice: an Indian perspective. Indian Council for Research on International Economic Relations Working Paper 85 (April).

Bajpai, N. (2010). Global financial crisis, its impact on India and the policy response. Mimeo, Asian Development Bank. URL: http://aric.adb.org/grs/papers/Bajpai.pdf.

Bown, C. P. (2011a). Introduction. In *The Great Recession and Import Protection: The Role of Temporary Trade Barriers* (ed. C. P. Bown). London: CEPR/World Bank. (Chapter 1 of this volume.)

Bown, C. P. (2011b). Taking stock of anti-dumping, safeguards, and countervailing duties, 1990–2009. *The World Economy*, forthcoming.

Bown, C. P. (2010a). *Temporary Trade Barriers Database*. World Bank (July). URL: http://econ.worldbank.org/ttbd/.

Bown, C. P. (2010b). China's WTO entry: anti-dumping, safeguards, and dispute settlement. In *China's Growing Role in World Trade* (ed. R. Feenstra and S. Wei). Chicago, IL: University of Chicago Press for NBER.

Bown, C. P., and P. Tovar (2011). Trade liberalization, anti-dumping, and safeguards: evidence from India's tariff reform. *Journal of Development Economics* **96**(1), 115–125.

Cadot, O., J. de Melo, and B. Tumurchudur (2008). Anti-dumping sunset reviews: the uneven reach of WTO disciplines. CEPR Discussion Paper 6502 (October).

Cerra, V., and S. C. Saxena (2002). What caused the 1991 currency crisis in India? *IMF Staff Papers* **49**(3), 395–425.

Global Trade Alert (2010). URL: www.globaltradealert.org.

Grossman, G. M., and E. Helpman (1994). Protection for sale. *American Economic Review* **84**(4), 833–850.

Gulati, S., N. Malhotra, and S. Malhotra (2005). Extent of protection via anti-dumping law: a case study of the vitamin C industry in India. *Journal of World Trade* **39**(5), 925–36.

Hindustan Times (2009). China warns India to lift ban on dairy products (27 July). URL: www.hindustantimes.com.

Irwin, D. A., P. C. Mavroidis, and A. O. Sykes (2008). *The Genesis of the GATT*. Cambridge University Press.

Kumaran, L. A. (2005). The 10 major problems with the anti-dumping instrument in India. *Journal of World Trade* **39**(1), 115–24.

Narayanan, P. (2006). Anti-dumping in India: present state and future prospects. *Journal of World Trade* **40**(6), 1081–97.

National Board of Trade (2005). The use of anti-dumping in Brazil, China, India and South Africa: rules, trends and causes. Report 2005-02-10, Stockholm.

Prusa, T. J. (2010). Comments on 'China's WTO entry: anti-dumping, safeguards, and dispute settlement', by C. P. Bown. In *China's Growing Role in World Trade* (ed. R. Feenstra and S. Wei). Chicago, IL: University of Chicago Press for NBER.

Srinivasan, T. N. (2001). India's reform of external sector policies and future multilateral trade negotiations. Economic Growth Center Discussion Paper 830. Yale University.

Times of India (2009a). China warns of tit-for-tat over dairy ban (1 July). URL: http://timesofindia.indiatimes.com.

Times of India (2009b). India imposes anti-dumping duties on stainless steel (23 April). URL: http://timesofindia.indiatimes.com.

Topalova, P. (2004). Trade liberalisation and firm productivity: the case of India. IMF Working Paper 04/28.

Vandenbussche, H., and M. Zanardi (2010). The chilling trade effects of anti-dumping proliferation. *European Economic Review* **54**(6), 760–77.

World Bank (2010). *World Development Indicators.* URL: data.worldbank.org/data-catalog/world-development-indicators.

World Trade Organization (2010a). Anti-dumping initiations: by sector. URL: http://www.wto.org/english/tratop_e/adp_e/adp_e.htm.

World Trade Organization (2010b). Safeguard measures. URL: http://www.wto.org/english/tratop_e/safeg_e/safeg_e.htm.

8

Brazil: Micro- and Macrodeterminants of Temporary Trade Barriers

MARCELO OLARREAGA AND MARCEL VAILLANT[1]

1 INTRODUCTION

Temporary trade barriers such as anti-dumping, CVDs and global safeguards affect an increasingly large share of emerging-economy imports. Bown (2011a) finds that, in countries such as Argentina, Brazil, China, India and Turkey, 1.5% to 4.5% of their (non-oil) annual imports are affected by TTBs.[2] Perhaps surprisingly, the increase in the use of TTBs occurred while most of these emerging countries were engaging in a process of broad trade reforms. Brazil is an interesting illustration. At the end of the 1980s, Brazil had a simple average tariff of 45%, but there were no TTBs. By 2010, the simple average tariff had fallen to 14%, but more than 100 products at the six-digit HS (HS-06) level were affected by some form of TTB with a simple *ad valorem* average of 60%.[3]

The objective of this chapter is to provide a description of the evolution in Brazil's use of TTBs. What types of TTBs are most frequently used: anti-dumping duties, safeguards or countervailing measures? Which sectors are

---

[1]Marcelo Olarreaga: Department of Economics, University of Geneva, 40 Blv. du Pont d'Arve, 1211 Geneva 4, Switzerland. Email: marcelo.olarreaga@unige.ch. Marcel Vaillant: Departamento de Economía, Facultad de Ciencias Sociales, Constituyente 1502 6to Piso, Montevideo CP11200, Uruguay. Email: marcel@decon.edu.uy. We are grateful to Chad Bown, Lawrence Edwards and Hylke Vandenbussche for their comments and suggestions on an earlier draft, to Honorio Kume for many fruitful discussions on Brazil's trade policy and Aksel Erbahar for providing us with most of the data used.

[2]In more developed economies (*eg* the USA and the EU), the share of imports affected by TTBs has been declining over the last decade. While 3.5–5% of more developed countries' imports were affected by TTBs during the 1997–2005 period, this has fallen to 1.5–3% of their annual imports during the 2006–9 period (Bown 2011a).

[3]Note that the average TTB duty cannot be readily compared with the MFN tariff that is imposed (in principle) on all import sources, whereas the most common TTB (*eg* anti-dumping) is often only imposed on a few exporters from a few exporting countries.

TTBs most likely to be imposed upon, and which partners are more likely to be affected by Brazil's TTBs?

Brazil experienced a significant degree of macroeconomic volatility over the 1990–2009 period. Figure 8.1 illustrates the evolution over the period 1995–2009 of Brazil's imports to GDP ratio, GNP per capita, real exchange rate and the number of new TTB measures imposed each year. The values of the four variables are set at 100 in 1995. Interestingly, the number of TTBs imposed each year seems to follow the ups and downs of Brazil's economic activity and the real exchange rate. However, contrary to what might be expected, the correlation between the number of TTBs imposed each year and GNP per capita is positive, suggesting that more TTBs are imposed when Brazil's economy is booming. This is somewhat counterintuitive and contradicts some of the early literature on macroeconomic determinants of TTBs, which tended to suggest that TTBs were more likely to be used in the presence of domestic macroeconomic weakness (Takacs 1981). See also Feigenbaum *et al* (1985), Feigenbaum and Willett (1985), Salvatore (1987), Coughlin *et al* (1989) and Leidy (1997).

As is also illustrated in Figure 8.1, Brazil's real exchange rate shows a negative correlation with the number of new TTB measures. While there exists a small amount of literature on exchange-rate determinants of TTB use, there is no consensus on the impact that exchange-rate changes have on TTBs.[4] As explained by Knetter and Prusa (2003), an appreciation of the domestic currency makes it less likely to be able to find sales below the price at which partners sell to other markets, but it makes it much easier to find injury to domestic firms. Whether the first or the second effect is more important in Brazil is an open question.

Results reported in Section 3 suggest that Brazil's TTBs affect a relatively small share of its imports (around 5%), but within sensitive sectors, 18% of imports are affected by some form of a TTB, and this figure reached 100% of imports in the footwear sector in 2009. Brazil's main TTB instrument is anti-dumping, which is responsible for 94% of the total value of imports affected by some form of Brazilian TTB. The main targets of Brazil's TTBs are high-income and upper-middle-income countries. However, the share targeted towards imports from China and lower-middle-income countries has been growing over the 2000s. Sectors affected by TTB investigations have consistently higher MFN tariffs than sectors where there have been no TTB investigations. Furthermore, sectors where the investigations end up with imposed measures have even higher MFN tariffs. This may suggest that MFN tariffs and

[4] A very interesting discussion on exchange rates and TTBs can be found in Leidy and Hoekman (1990). They do not focus on the determinants of TTBs, but rather their impact on trade in the presence of exchange-rate risk. They consider an exporting firm facing random exchange-rate shocks. The firm must decide how much to export to an importing country that can impose anti-dumping duties as a reaction to an important exchange-rate shock. They find that the mere presence of an anti-dumping mechanism reduces exports.

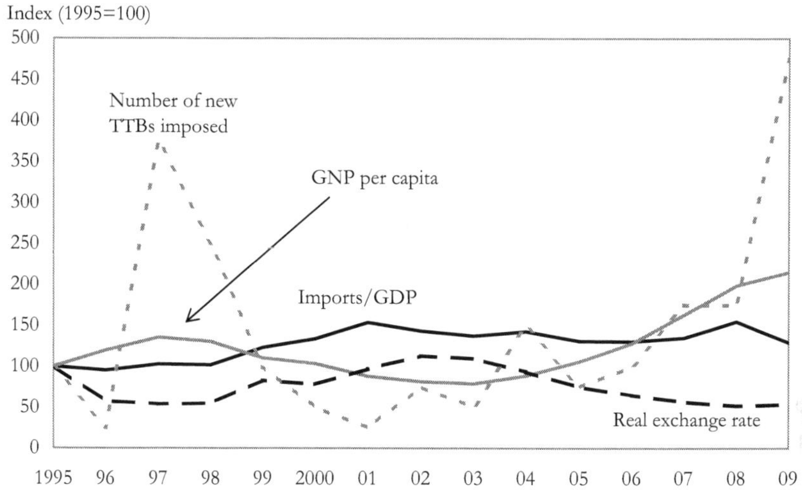

Figure 8.1: *Macroeconomic variables and TTBs in Brazil, 1995–2009.*
Source: authors' calculations from World Bank World Development Indicators (2010) and Bown (2010).

TTBs are complements, but it can also simply signal that these are sectors that are politically strong. Finally, even though there is a significant amount of 'water' (protection in excess) in Brazil's MFN tariff structure, the levels of protection reached through TTBs are twice as large as that which would be permitted by the water in the existing tariff structure.

Interestingly, any acceleration of Brazilian TTBs during the international financial crisis of 2008–9 appears unrelated to the performance of Brazilian real economy. Although GDP per capita growth slowed during the crisis, Brazil continued to grow quite significantly. It is likely that an important force driving the increase in Brazil's TTB activity the appreciation of the Brazilian currency (real) with respect to the currency of Brazil's trading partners. Indeed, Brazil experienced a significant strengthening of its currency that has reduced the international competitiveness of its firms. There were numerous calls for trade policy to limit the rapid increase in imports, and one of the mechanisms employed were TTBs, in particular anti-dumping procedures.[5]

[5]By early 2011, protectionist pressure had strengthened with demands to generalise the use of import licences and some arguing for the re-establishment of a mechanism of import controls. These recent calls led Jose Tavares, a well-known Brazilian economist from CINDES (Rio de Janeiro) with academic and governmental background, to write in the press that it is not feasible to re-establish imports control in Brazil, partly because of its international commitments (Tavares 2011). See Barral and Brogini (2010) for similar arguments.

Thus, one response from Brazil's policymakers to a strong and wide increase in protectionist demands caused by the strong appreciation of the Brazilian currency has been an increase in the use of TTBs. Nevertheless, the import coverage of these TTBs remained limited. Furthermore, TTBs are arguably more consistent than other forms of import protection under the rules of Brazil's international obligations within Mercosur, the WTO and other trade agreements. Seen through this light, the rapid increase in the use of TTBs may be a very moderate response to a very large increase in protectionist demand during this period.

2 TRADE LIBERALISATION IN BRAZIL

Like many other Latin American countries, Brazil adopted import substitution policies in the 1960s and had a very restrictive trade policy regime for the following two decades. At the end of the 1980s, there was a gradual move towards a more open trade policy regime that was triggered by two complementary factors: the presence of very large economic distortions that required reform, and, more importantly, exogenous changes in the political economy preferences of policymakers away from a view that development could flourish under import substitution policies.

This change in policy preferences led to two reforms during the Sarney Administration. These reforms were later extended during the 1990s by the Collor de Mello government through four scheduled stages (1991–3).[6] The Sarney Administration's reforms focused mainly on liberalising imports of intermediate goods. The Collor de Mello Administration then pursued an important media campaign in favour of trade openness that led to an erosion of public support for protectionist policies. It also extended the Sarney Administration reforms to include capital goods. The economic rationale for these reforms was based on the idea that Brazil was lagging behind the technological frontier due to the high rate of protection in intermediate and capital goods.

Brazil's unilateral tariff reforms led to drastic reductions in protection levels, as illustrated in Table 8.1. The nominal average MFN tariff was reduced

[6]The Sarney Administration implemented two reforms, in June 1988 and September 1989. The first was a generalised reduction of import tariffs and the second was concentrated on intermediate and capital goods. Both reforms reduced redundant protection. The average tariff fell by 26 percentage points between 1987 and 1989, but the structure of protection did not change significantly; the correlation between the tariff structure across sectors was 0.72 between 1987 and 1989. The government of Collor de Mello staged four tariff reductions: February 1992, January 1992, January 1993 and January 1994. After the first reduction, superfluous protection persisted. This was almost completely absent after the second adjustment, though with the exception of some consumption goods. The projected targets were fully achieved. Between 1990 and 1993, the average tariff declined from 27.2% to 12.5%, the standard deviation fell from 14.9% to 6.7%, the minimum value from 3.3% to 0% and the maximum from 78.7% to 34% (Kume *et al* 2003).

Table 8.1: *Tariff trade policy in Brazil weighted by value added in free trade by sector, 1987–98 (in percent).*

	1987	1988	1989	1990	1991	1992	1993	1994	1995	1996	1997	1998
(a) Nominal MFN tariff												
Simple average	57.5	39.6	32.1	30.5	23.6	15.7	13.5	11.2	12.8	13.0	15.6	15.5
Weighted average	54.9	37.7	29.4	27.2	20.9	14.1	12.5	10.2	10.8	10.8	13.4	13.4
Standard deviation	21.3	14.6	15.8	14.9	12.7	8.2	6.7	5.9	7.4	8.7	7.6	6.6
Maximum	102.7	76.0	75.0	78.7	58.7	39.0	34.0	23.5	41.0	52.4	47.1	38.1
Minimum	15.6	5.6	1.9	3.3	1.7	0.6	0.0	0.0	0.0	0.0	0.0	0.0
(b) Effective protection												
Simple average	77.1	52.1	46.5	47.7	34.8	20.3	16.7	13.6	17.1	19.9	21.6	20.2
Weighted average	67.8	46.8	38.8	37.0	28.6	17.7	15.2	12.3	10.4	14.3	16.6	16.2
Standard deviation	53.8	36.6	44.5	60.6	36.5	17.2	13.5	8.4	19.5	37.2	29.6	21.3
Maximum	308.1	201.3	244.3	351.1	198.3	93.5	76.5	27.7	113.8	217.5	177.0	129.2
Minimum	8.3	−2.9	−5.4	−3.4	−4.0	−4.0	−5.0	−4.9	−2.4	−1.8	−2.2	−2.2

Source: Kume *et al* (2003).

from 32% in 1990 to 11% in 1994, and the effective rate of protection also fell from 45% to 14% during that period (Kume *et al* 2003).

Nevertheless, Brazil's large tariff reductions did not lead to a substantial increase in imports. Imports did not respond to these tariff cuts because most of the very high levels of protection had already been eroded by the end of the 1980s through the existence of a multitude of special regimes that allowed producers to import at much lower levels of protection. The 'apparent' drastic liberalisation was therefore not one that had a real impact on the costs faced by importers. The unilateral reduction of these MFN tariffs was combined with a simplification or elimination of many special trade regimes. The redundancy of the MFN tariffs also explains why the private sector did not oppose the trade reforms. The reforms simply led to a consolidation of trade legislation towards a similar level of protection within a much simpler regime. Thus, what seems to be a very large reduction in protection levels (66% reduction in nominal tariffs, 69% reduction in effective rates) during 1990–1994 was, in fact, less dramatic due to the large number of special regimes in existence *prior* to the reforms.

With the implementation of the Real Plan during the Itamar Franco Administration, Brazil's policy of trade openness was deepened, though it later experienced a setback.[7] During this period there was both a misalignment of relative prices and a resurgence of domestic demand that led to a large increase in imports. By 1994, Mexico's peso crisis had triggered a reduction in foreign financing, and in 1995 trade policy was used to help this adjustment, leading to a reversal of the movement towards lower tariffs.[8] However, this reversal was not large enough to counteract the earlier tariff reductions so that average tariffs at the end of the 1990s were much lower than in the late 1980s. Figure 8.2 indicates that there was not much change in average tariff protection after 1993; *ie* the trend is a slow but relatively permanent reduction in the average MFN tariff. The exception is the small increase in average MFN tariffs observed during the crisis period of 2008–9.

2.1 Mercosur and the South–South Reciprocal Liberalisation Strategy

From the late 1990s, Brazil's trade reforms were undertaken through a series of discriminatory 'south–south' trade agreements. The most important objective of these agreements was to facilitate the access to foreign markets for Brazilian producers, but contrary to the reforms of the early 1990s, they were less likely to increase the competitive pressure on import-competing and inefficient Brazilian producers. Of all the PTAs that Brazil signed, Mercosur, which

---

[7] In July 1994, during the Itamar Franco Administration and under the framework of the stabilisation plan known as Plan Real, all tariffs above 20% were reduced to this level.

[8] In 1995, Brazil increased tariffs for some sectors: cars, consumption goods, *etc.* In 1996, non-automatic import licences were reactivated, and there was limitation for the long-run financing of imports.

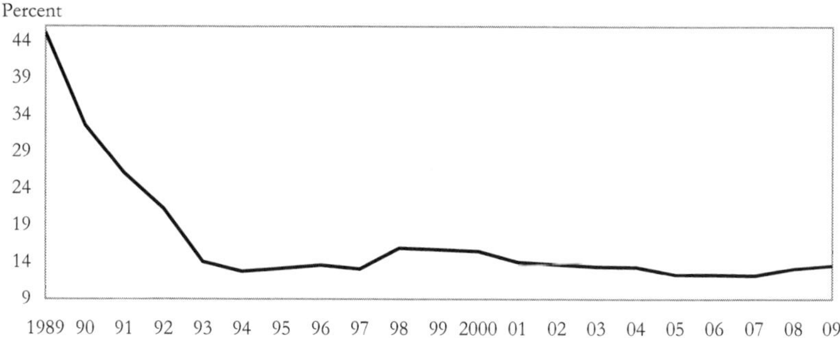

Figure 8.2: *Brazil's MFN ad valorem tariff, 1989–2009.*
Source: authors' calculations with data from TRAINS at the six-digit HS level.

was signed in 1991, is by far the most important, both politically and economically. This bloc stands out as an ambitious agreement by four developing countries (Argentina, Brazil, Paraguay and Uruguay) aiming towards deep economic integration.

The integration agreement was formulated around two major timelines: the Trade Liberalisation Program (TLP) and the Regime of Adaptation to Mercosur (RAM). These two instruments governed the process of trade integration and formed the linchpin of the agreement. The TLP dates back to the initial treaty of 1991 and was the basis for creating a 'free-trade area' (FTA). Intra-regional tariffs were gradually eliminated using a linear and automatic reduction scheme. This liberalisation scheme was announced in advance by the member countries' governments and then carried out twice a year on a regular basis, as envisaged at the outset.

The second instrument, the RAM, emerged from the Ouro Preto summit of December 1994. It was established to finalise the FTA as the TLP was reaching completion. However, this new instrument broadened the terms of liberalisation, slowed down the construction process of the 'free-trade zone' and defined a new list of products excluded from intra-regional free trade. After the schedule laid down for these RAM lists had been fulfilled, the integration agreement could be described as a universal, non-tariff, 'free-trade zone' with some harmonisation of external trade policies *vis-à-vis* third parties.

Despite Brazil's broad regional trade agenda, just a few PTAs are actually in force (see Table A8.1 in the Statistical Appendix). Most of these agreements were signed by the four Mercosur members. Since only the agreements with Chile and Bolivia are to be harmonised with the other three Mercosur members, this presents a challenge to a *common* external trade policy. With the Andean countries, each Mercosur member follows its own bilateral framework. Most of Brazil's trade agreements have the objective of reaching free-trade area status within ten years; the exceptions are the agreements with

Mexico and Cuba. As a result, the existing degree of trade liberalisation varies across agreements. Mercosur is the oldest agreement and the one with the highest preference given and obtained by Brazil. Another interesting characteristic of Mercosur is that the four members share a common external tariff (CET), and the level of preference is therefore partly determined jointly by the four members as they have to agree on the CET.[9]

The evidence from the 2000s suggests that trade policy preferences of both the private sector and the government in Brasília are moving towards a more open trade regime once again. For example, the position adopted by the Brazilian government in the non-agricultural market access negotiations held in Geneva within the Doha Round is aligned with a clear pro-trade orientation.[10] Traditionally, Brazil has maintained a protectionist position in favour of its own industry in its trade agreements, partly owing to its strong import substitution policies of the 1960s and 1970s. Since 2008, Brazil has adopted a different strategy in the most important forum for international trade negotiations.[11]

3 TEMPORARY TRADE BARRIERS IN BRAZIL

When Brazil began its process of trade liberalisation at the end of the 1980s, it simultaneously introduced a domestic law for the use of TTBs. As the country engaged in a deep process of trade liberalisation, Brazil put a buffer mechanism in place to subsequently manage strong economic and political reactions to these policy changes.[12]

---

[9]Note that there are limits to this type of argument for Mercosur as the CET is not always 'common', given its numerous exceptions. There are sector exceptions (investment goods, informatics and telecommunications, automotive sector, and sensitive goods), and national exceptions lists. Also, countries' trade regimes and trade preferences have not been fully harmonised. The CET is the same as the collected tariffs (tariff revenues over imports) in a third of Mercosur imports from third parties. However, two-thirds of these imports are subject to a zero CET.

[10]As was established in a Chairman Stephenson document (WTO NAMA negotiations, July 2008), the key element in non-agricultural market access is the well-known Swiss formula of tariff reductions. This trade liberalisation schedule has very important properties in terms of the way it affects the tariff structure. It reduces tariff escalation, eliminates tariff peaks, and has a consequent reduction in tariff dispersion.

[11]Brazil announced another important change in early 2011 by initiating bilateral negotiations with Mexico with the objective of signing an FTA.

[12]Nelson (2006) points out that the academic literature on anti-dumping recognises that anti-dumping law is often adopted as part of a strategy of tariff reduction or to resist protectionist pressures. Such policies may also serve as insurance for uncertain trade policy negotiators that allow them to take on deeper commitments in a trade agreement than they might otherwise undertake without access to such 'exceptions' (Fischer and Prusa 2003).

Table 8.2: *2009 imports of Brazil's sensitive industries with TTB investigations, 1989–2009.*

Three-digit ISIC industry	Total imports (millions of dollars)	Imports covered by TTBs (millions of dollars)	Imports covered by anti-dumping only (millions of dollars)	Anti-dumping/ TTB (%)	TTB/ total (%)
Footwear	157	157	157	100.0	100.0
Plastic	1,307	550	550	100.0	42.1
Other manufacturing	1,138	324	56	17.2	28.5
Rubber	1,521	527	511	96.9	34.7
Food	2,678	168	168	100.0	6.3
Chemicals	18,600	3,927	3,927	100.0	21.1
Textiles	2,516	574	472	82.1	22.8
Agriculture	3,861	144	125	86.4	3.7
Steel	3,357	251	226	90.3	7.5
Glass	423	47	47	100.0	11.0
Metal products	2,630	308	308	100.0	11.7
Paper	1,355	81	63	78.2	6.0
Sensitive sectors (a)	39,545	7,058	6,610	93.6	17.8
Total (b)	127,348	7,637	7,189	94.1	6.0
Percentage share (a)/(b) × 100	31.1	92.4	91.9		

Note: columns 2, 3 and 4 defined in (8.4), (8.5) and (8.6), respectively. Anti-dumping/TTB defined as column 4/column 3 × 100. TTB/total defined as column 3/column 2 × 100.

Source: authors' calculations using *Temporary Trade Barriers Database* (Bown 2010).

As expected, Brazil's trade liberalisation was accompanied by an increase in the use of TTBs. We begin with a discussion of TTB use by focusing on Brazil's sensitive industries and targeted markets. We then distinguish between different types of TTBs, starting with anti-dumping, which is by far the most frequently used TTB in Brazil. We then turn to CVDs and safeguard measures.

3.1 *Sensitive Industries and Target Markets*

Some sectors and some origins of Brazil's imports are more likely to be affected by Brazil's use of TTBs. In this section we use different indicators to measure how likely TTB measures are to be imposed on certain sectors and countries. The formal definitions of the indicators are described in Appendix 5.

Temporary trade barriers are concentrated in 12 industries: footwear, plastics, rubber, food, other manufactures, chemicals, textiles, agriculture, steel, glass, metal products and paper.[13] In these sectors, an average of 18% of imports were covered by at least one investigation. The equivalent figure for

[13]These sectors have a share of imports affected by TTBs greater than the global average for 1989–2009.

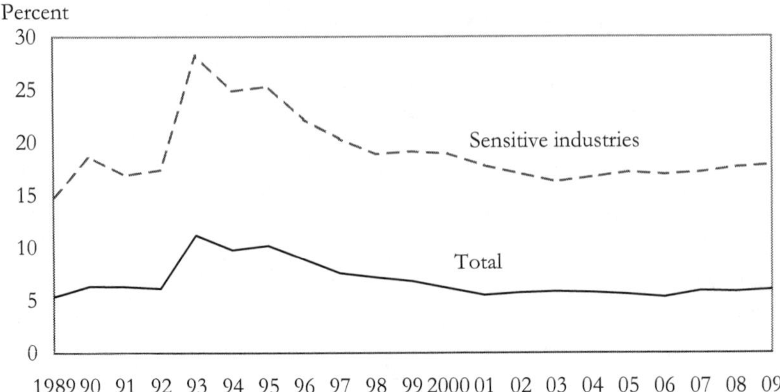

Figure 8.3: *Brazil's coverage of imports with TTB investigations, 1989–2009.*
Source: authors' calculations using *Temporary Trade Barriers Database* (Bown 2010). See definition of both variables in (8.1) and (8.3).

overall imports is around 6% (see Table 8.2 and Figure 8.3). The evolution of this magnitude for sensitive sectors increases during the first episode of unilateral trade liberalisation (1989–1993). The trend then begins to decline until 2003 when it slowly and permanently increases until the end of the period.

Table 8.2 reports that only 6% of Brazil's imports are affected by some form of TTB. However, for these most sensitive sectors, *ie* defined as a sector with an above average share of imports affected by TTBs, 18% of of sectoral imports are affected by some form of TTB. These sensitive sectors are also listed in Table 8.2. sensitive sectors represent 31% of Brazil's imports, they represent 92% of imports affected by some form of TTB. TTB. Thus, these sectors are by far the main drivers of the 6% figure reported at the end of Table 8.2. The sectors with more exposure to TTB measures are: footwear, plastics, other manufactures and rubber, where the share of imports affected by some form of TTB reaches 100%, 42%, 29% and 35%, respectively (see the last column of Table 8.2).

The most commonly used TTB in Brazil is anti-dumping, as 94% of imports affected by some form of TTB are subject to anti-dumping (see the fourth column in Table 8.2). In six sectors (footwear, plastics, food, chemicals, glass and metal products) this share reaches 100%. Take, for example, the case of footwear. In 2009 the amount of imports was $157 million, all the HS-06 products imported in 2009 had some type of TTB investigations during 1989–2009, and each of the TTB investigations took place under anti-dumping.

Among sensitive sectors, the sector where anti-dumping seems to affect the smallest share of imports is 'other manufacturing', indicating that CVDs and safeguard measures play a more important role in this sector. Taken together, these sensitive sectors represent 92% of Brazil's imports affected by some form of TTB.

Trading partners affected by Brazil's TTBs tend to be high-income or upper-middle-income countries, as well as China. Figure 8.4 shows the value of imports from different types of countries affected by a TTB during 1989–2009. Countries are divided into the four World Bank categories: high income, upper-middle income, lower-middle income and low income. We consider China separately from the lower-middle-income group given its importance as a source of imports affected by Brazil's TTBs. The share of high-income countries and upper-middle-income countries slowly decreases during the period, while lower-middle-income countries, in particular China, have an increasing share of Brazil's imports that are affected by TTBs. This phenomenon is magnified as we shift towards a more restrictive definition of products affected by TTBs from panel (a) to panel (c) of Figure 8.4.

Products that have been under a TTB investigation tend to be highly protected goods. Figure 8.5 illustrates that the average MFN tariff for products under TTB investigations is always greater than the average MFN tariff. Also, among the products subject to TTB investigations, those with an imposed measure tend to have a higher MFN average tariff than the set of products for which there has been a TTB investigation, but no measure imposed. Interestingly, in 2009, for the set of products that have been investigated but which have no TTB in place, the increase in MFN tariffs has been stronger than for other products. This suggests that there exists some degree of substitution between trade protection obtained through MFN tariffs and trade protection obtained through TTBs.

It is important to distinguish products with TTB investigations and products where a TTB measure is in place. There are 212 products (at the six-digit HS level) where some type of TTB investigation has taken place, which we refer to as products with TTB investigations.[14] Brazil imposed a TTB in 48% of these products (102) during 1989–2009. Figure 8.6 presents the evolution of new products with TTB measures in Brazil. The last year of the series established a record with the largest number of new products affected by a TTB measure (19).

Figure 8.7(a) illustrates the number of products affected by a TTB measure in any given year and the average *ad valorem* duty associated with these TTBs. As a share of total imports or the total number of products, TTBs have been relatively stable since the end of the 1990s, but there has been a sharp increase in their importance since the beginning of the international crisis in 2008–9. Figure 8.7 shows an increase in the proportion of the number of products and the share of total imports affected by TTBs, which is additional evidence of acceleration during the international crisis. However, whether in terms of

[14]In terms of cases, the number is larger because some products appear in several cases.

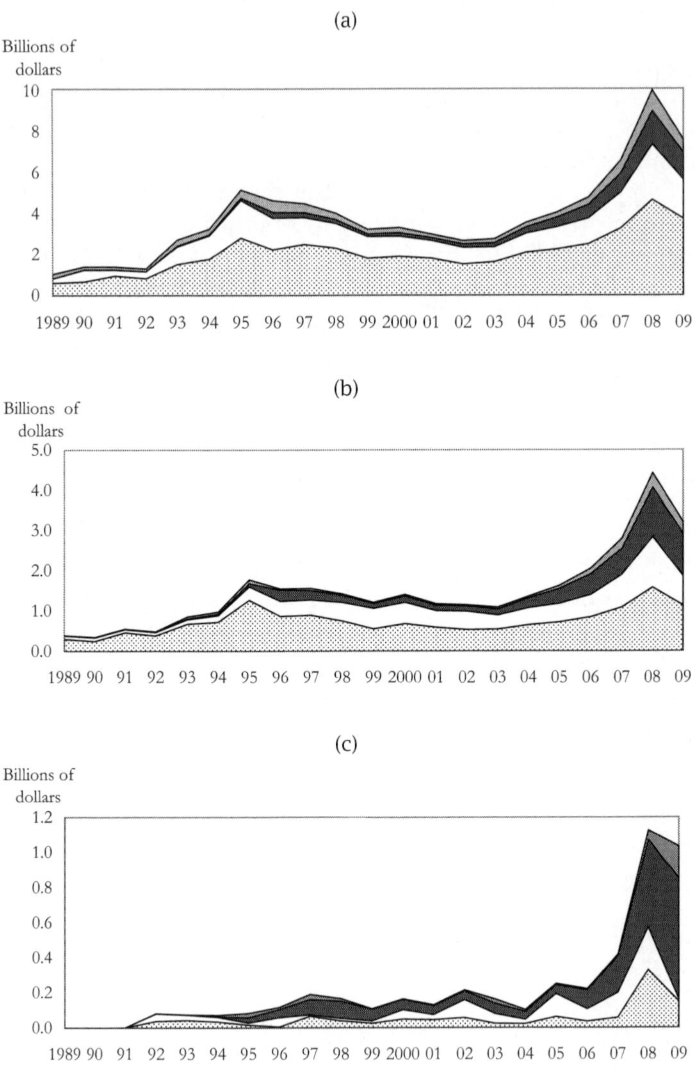

Figure 8.4: *Brazil's imports affected by TTB investigations in 1989–2009, by country type: (a) entire sample, products under investigation during the period; (b) imports of products with TTB measure during the period; (c) imports of products with measure in the current year.*

Source: authors' calculations using *Temporary Trade Barriers Database* (Bown 2010). See definition of variables in (8.7), (8.8) and (8.9).

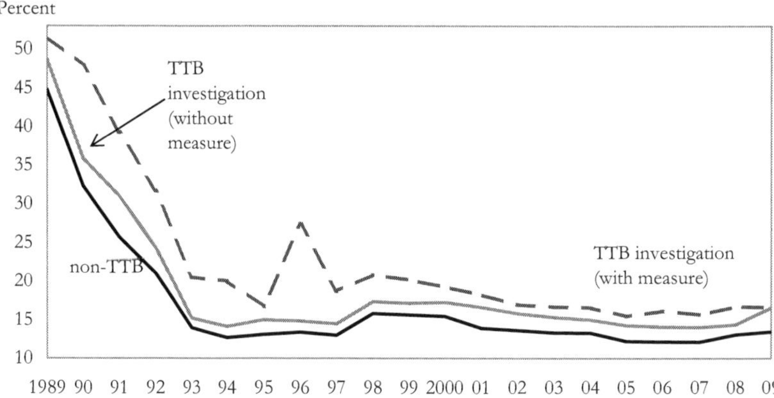

Figure 8.5: *Brazil's MFN tariffs in products with TTB investigation (with and without measures) and without TTBs, 1989-2009.*

Source: authors' calculations using TRAINS and *Temporary Trade Barriers Database* (Bown 2010). See definition of variables in (8.10)-(8.12).

total imports or total number of products, TTBs only represent around 1% of the total by 2009.

According to Global Trade Alert project (Evenett 2009), Brazil implemented other adjustments in trade protection during the crisis through changes in MFN tariffs—both increases and reductions. In fact, MFN tariff changes represent 55% of the total number of policy changes that Global Trade Alert reports for Brazil. Temporary trade barriers are the second most frequent type of policy change, representing around one-third of the total number.

The frequent increases in MFN tariffs to respond to stronger demands for protectionism are consistent with Brazil's obligations in the WTO due to the large amount of 'water' in its tariff structure.[15] According to estimates by Foletti *et al* (2011), on average, Brazil could double its MFN tariffs without violating its WTO commitments.[16] Half of this potential increase is what is called 'smoke' in the tariff water, as it would be impossible for Brazil to raise tariffs by that amount due to its preferential tariff commitments, notably within Mercosur, or due to the fact that the WTO tariff binding is above the prohibitive level and therefore irrelevant.[17] Nevertheless, their results imply that

[15]Tariff water refers to the fact that WTO bound tariffs are above the MFN applied tariffs in Brazil, and therefore provide (in principle) some policy space for tariff increases.

[16]The fact that MFN tariffs could be doubled before reaching the level of bound tariffs corresponds to what is observed, on average, across all countries in Foletti *et al* (2011).

[17]The average share of smoke in the tariff water across countries is 28%, so Brazil is a country with a significant share of smoke in its tariff structure.

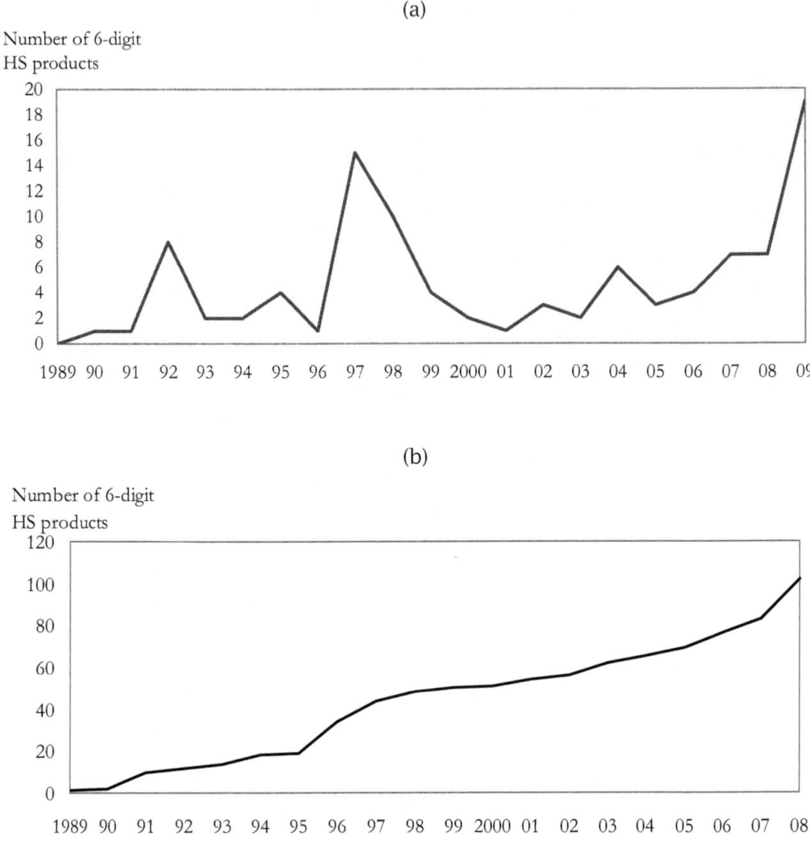

Figure 8.6: *New HS-06 products with TTB measures, 1989–2009: (a) new products with TTB measures by year; (b) accumulated series of new products.*

Source: authors' calculations using *Temporary Trade Barriers Database* (Bown 2010). See definition of variables (8.13) and (8.14).

Brazil could increase its average MFN tariff by 50% without violating its WTO commitments.

Table 8.3 illustrates how similar increases in MFN tariffs are possible for products that have been under a TTB investigation, regardless of whether a measure was applied. MFN tariffs on these products could almost double on average without violating the average WTO commitment. However, a doubling of MFN tariffs may not be enough in some sensitive sectors, where the *ad valorem* duty imposed through TTBs reaches on average 60%, *ie* four times the MFN level.

(a)

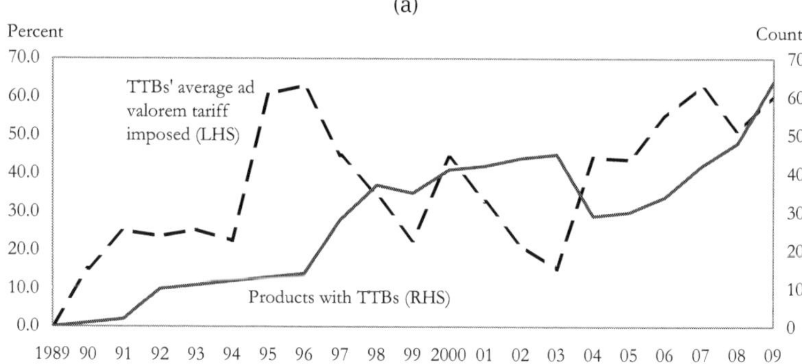

(b)

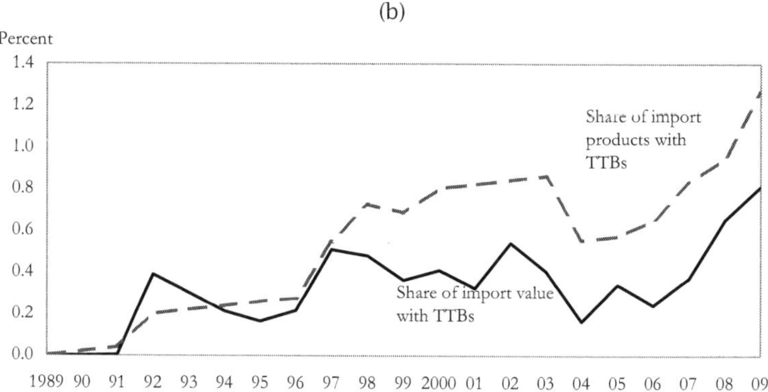

Figure 8.7: *TTB with measure, ad valorem tariff, products and imports coverage, 1989–2009: (a) ad valorem TTB measure (%) and number of products (HS-06); (b) shares of imports subject to TTBs.*

Source: authors' calculations using *Temporary Trade Barriers Database* (Bown 2010). See definition of variables (8.15)–(8.18).

3.2 Anti-Dumping, CVDs and Safeguards

There are two stages in an anti-dumping procedure: preliminary and final. In each stage it is necessary to establish evidence of dumping and injury to the domestic sector. It is also necessary to establish causality from dumping to injury to be able to apply anti-dumping measures. In the preliminary stage, the observed values of the decisions (dumping and injury) are the following: accepted (A), bypassed to the final decision (B) or denied (N). In the final stage, the observed values for the final decisions are the following: accepted (A), interrupted (withdrawn by private sector (W) or terminated by public authorities (T)) or denied (N). Table 8.4 presents results for Brazil (see also Table A8.2).

Table 8.3: *MFN tariffs and WTO bindings for products with TTB investigations, 2006–9.*

Type of TTB product	Average tariff	2006 (%)	2007 (%)	2008 (%)	2009 (%)	Total (%)
With measures	WTO binding	31.8	31.7	31.6	31.7	31.7
	MFN applied	16.2	15.7	16.8	16.7	16.3
Without measures	WTO binding	30.5	30.3	30.3	30.6	30.4
	MFN applied	14.1	14.1	14.4	16.7	14.9
All products	WTO binding	31.3	31.3	31.1	31.0	31.2
	MFN applied	15.3	15.0	15.7	16.7	15.7

Source: authors' calculations using TRAINS, WTO and *Temporary Trade Barriers Database* (Bown 2010).

Table 8.4: *Typology of anti-dumping cases in Brazil, 1988–2010 (cases and products at HS-06 level).*

	Cases	Products
Without anti-dumping measures	90	147
With anti-dumping measure	140	273
- in preliminary stage	11	56
- in final stage	75	98
- in two stages	54	119
Anti-dumping in process	13	21
Total	243	441

Source: authors' calculations using Table A8.2.

The cases are divided in three main categories: without anti-dumping measures, with anti-dumping measures, and in process.

Approximately 58% of Brazil's 243 cases during 1988–2010 ended up with anti-dumping measures. Almost half of those cases had an anti-dumping duty imposed in the preliminary stage. In terms of products, there were 441 HS-06 products affected, of which 63% ended up with an anti-dumping measure. More than 60% of those had an anti-dumping duty imposed in the preliminary stage.

Figure 8.8 presents the evolution in the number of anti-dumping cases initiated over 1988–2010. The figure distinguishes between cases that resulted in the imposition of an anti-dumping duty and those without anti-dumping duties, similarly to Table 8.4 (see also Tables A8.2 and A8.3).

An important observation is that the number of anti-dumping measures, whether measured in terms of cases or products, tends to spike in the early 1990s, then the late 1990s, as well as the late 2000s. This coincides with periods when Brazil's real exchange rate was undergoing a significant appreciation. This is consistent with the finding of Knetter and Prusa (2003) that exchange-rate appreciation leads to increases in the number of anti-dumping

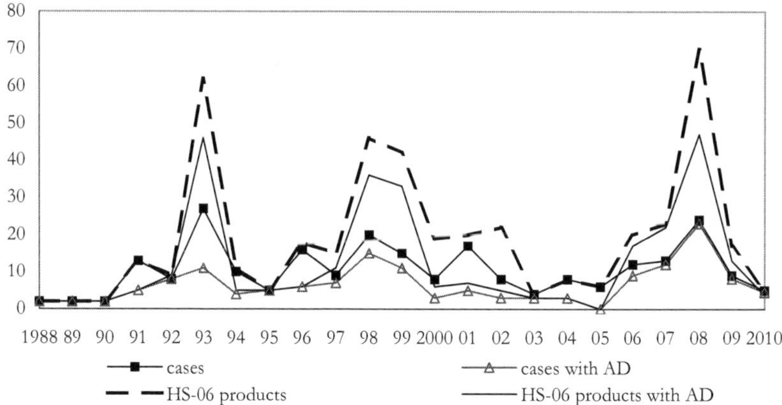

Figure 8.8: *Evolution of anti-dumping initiated cases and anti-dumping measures in Brazil, 1988–2010.*

Source: authors' calculations using *Temporary Trade Barriers Database* (Bown 2010). For the last two years the cases in process are divided between 'failed' and 'not failed' using the average success of the last three years with complete information (2006–8). See definition of variables (8.19)–(8.22).

cases. While the number of cases initiated each year oscillates, the number of anti-dumping cases in force in any given year has been systematically increasing throughout the period, except during the late 1990s. The rapid increase in the number of measures in place corresponds to the peaks in the number of cases initiated.

In terms of sector coverage there are clearly some industries that are more likely to benefit from anti-dumping duties than others. Table 8.5 shows the number of anti-dumping cases initiated by sector, and it disaggregates into those with and without anti-dumping duties, by case and by HS-06 product. Chemicals, textiles, and iron and steel represent more than 50% of cases initiated (or products covered in those cases) during 1988–2010. The footwear and food sectors follow. Agriculture and sectors intensive in natural resources, such as minerals or wood, are less likely to be subject to anti-dumping. Figure 8.9 presents imports affected by anti-dumping investigations and applied measures. Chemicals, plastics and textiles covered more than the 60% of imports with imposed measures by 2009. These results partly reflect the comparative advantage of Brazil but also the relative political strength of these sectors in Brazil's internal politics.

The average duration of Brazil's imposed anti-dumping measures is not necessarily correlated with the number of cases brought by a sector. This is partly natural, because a sector may bring a large number of cases without much of a legal base to intimidate foreign exporters in order to reduce their share of the domestic market (see Leidy and Hoekman (1990)). As shown in Table 8.6,

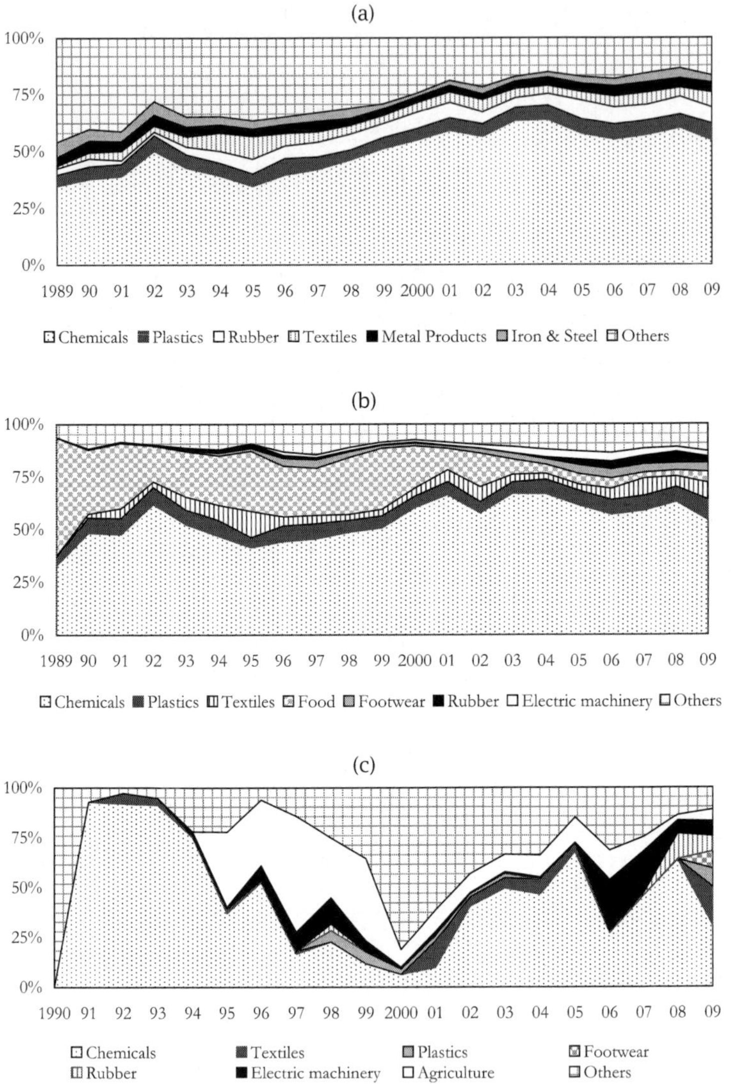

Figure 8.9: *Evolution of the structure of imports in products affected by Brazil's anti-dumping by industry for the period 1989–2009: (a) whole sample products under anti-dumping investigation; (b) structure of imports of products with anti-dumping measure; (c) imports of products with anti-dumping measure in the current year.*

Source: authors' calculations using *Temporary Trade Barriers Database* (Bown 2010). See definition of variables in (8.23)–(8.25).

Table 8.5: *Stock of anti-dumping initiated cases, with and without anti-dumping measures in Brazil by industry using ISIÇ 3, 1988–2010 (cases and products at HS-06 level).*

Sectors		Cases			HS-06 products		
Name	ISIC3	Without anti-dumping	With anti-dumping	Total	Without anti-dumping	With anti-dumping	Total
Agriculture	111	0	5	5	0	6	6
Agriculture	111-311/12	0	1	1	0	2	2
Minerals	200	1	0	1	1	0	1
Food	311/12	1	7	8	6	30	36
Textiles	321	7	13	20	13	48	61
Footwear	324-356	1	1	2	23	23	46
Wood	331	1	0	1	1	0	1
Paper	341	4	3	7	4	5	9
Chemicals	351	45	46	91	61	56	117
Other chemicals	352	2	4	6	2	6	8
Rubber	355	1	6	7	1	6	7
Plastics	356	2	0	2	2	0	2
Glass	362	4	1	5	4	1	5
Glass	362-351	0	1	1	0	2	2
Glass	362-351-356	5	2	7	15	6	21
Other non-metallic	369	2	4	6	2	6	8
Iron and steel	371	9	19	28	15	37	52
Nonferrous metal	372	10	1	11	10	1	11
Metal products	381	2	11	13	2	11	13
Metal products	381-371	0	2	2	0	5	5
Machinery	382	0	2	2	0	3	3
Electric machinery	383	0	3	3	0	5	5
Electric machinery	383-351	0	1	1	0	2	2
Transport	384	0	2	2	0	2	2
Professional/ scientific	385	2	2	4	2	7	9
Other manufactured	390	4	3	7	4	3	7
Total		103	140	243	168	273	441

Some sectors appear twice because some cases cover several sectors simultaneously.

Source: authors' calculations using *Temporary Trade Barriers Database* (Bown 2010).

sectors with the largest average duration of measures are the machinery and electric machinery sector and the glass sector. Chemicals and footwear, which were the sectors with the largest number of cases, have an average duration that tends to be below the mean.

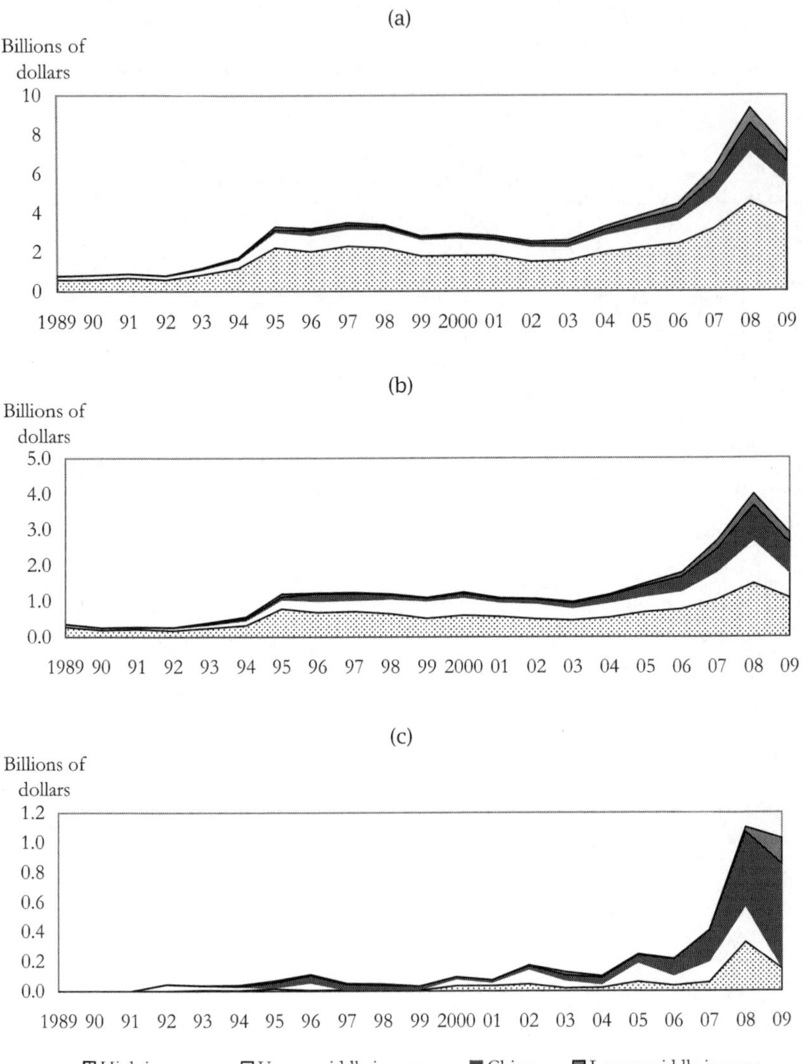

Figure 8.10: *Imports in products affected by Brazil's anti-dumping investigations, by partner, 1989–2009: (a) whole sample products under anti-dumping investigation during the period; (b) imports of products with anti-dumping measure during the period; (c) imports of products with anti-dumping measure in the current year.*

Source: authors' calculations using *Temporary Trade Barriers Database* (Bown 2010). See definition of variables in (8.26)–(8.28).

Table 8.6: *Average duration of anti-dumping measures in Brazil by industry using ISIC 3, 1988–2010.*

Sectors		Average duration (years)	
Name	ISIC3	With anti-dumping	Total
Agriculture	111	4.6	4.6
Agriculture	111-311/12	2.0	2.0
Minerals	200	N/A	N/A
Food	311/12	7.6	6.6
Textiles	321	4.0	2.6
Footwear	324-356	1.0	0.5
Wood	331	0.0	0.0
Paper	341	7.6	3.3
Chemicals	351	5.2	2.6
Chemicals	352	5.3	3.5
Rubber	355	5.8	5.0
Plastics	356	0.0	0.0
Glass	362	30.0	6.0
Glass	362-351	5.3	5.3
Glass	362-351-356	5.0	1.4
Other non-metallic	369	7.5	5.0
Iron and steel	371	7.1	4.8
Nonferrous metal	372	6.0	0.5
Metal products	381	7.7	6.5
Metal products	381-371	5.0	5.0
Machinery	382	7.5	7.5
Electric machinery	383	7.7	7.7
Electric machinery	383-351	1.0	1.0
Transport	384	3.5	3.5
Professional and scientific equipment	385	2.0	1.0
Other manufactured products	390	6.0	2.6
Total		5.9	3.4

'N/A' means that no data were available.

Source: authors' calculations using *Temporary Trade Barriers Database* (Bown 2010).

Figure 8.10 illustrates the value of imports and the share in the total value of imports by trading partner affected by Brazil's anti-dumping cases. The USA, the EU and Argentina are the principal targets of Brazil's anti-dumping measures. They jointly represent around 75% of Brazil's affected imports. They are followed by South Korea, Taiwan, Colombia and Russia, but these four countries only represent around 10% of the value of imports affected by anti-dumping duties.

Brazil has used countervailing measures much less frequently than anti-dumping. Brazil had 16 CVD cases during the period 1989–2010, and it applied measures in only 10 of the 16 cases. These measures generally took the form of *ad valorem* tariffs. For one of these ten cases ('latex yarn' from Malaysia), we have no information regarding the type of duty applied. In the Statistical Appendix, Table A8.4 summarises the number of cases and products affected by countervailing measures with and without duties.

Safeguard measures are even less commonly used in Brazil. During the period 1989–2010, Brazil initiated three safeguard investigations: one each in 1996, 2001 and 2008. In two of these cases (toys and coconuts), Brazil applied measures. For toys, Brazil applied the same *ad valorem* measures from 1997 until 2003 in 15 HS-06 products. For coconuts, which started in 2002 and lasted until 2006, Brazil imposed quantitative restrictions. The last case resulted in a negative finding in 2009.

4 CONCLUSION

As Brazil's trade liberalisation intensified in the late 1980s and early 1990s, it put in place a regime of temporary trade protection. This chapter describes the Brazilian authority's use of TTBs in the period 1990–2009. Brazil's TTBs have been highly concentrated in a few sectors (chemicals, plastics and textiles). When the whole set of TTB investigations are considered, Brazilian TTBs mainly target high-income and middle-income trading partners. If the sample of imports is restricted to products where TTBs are imposed, the likelihood of observing a middle-and-low-income country being affected by Brazil's TTB increases considerably, with China becoming more important in the late 2000s.

The vast majority of Brazil's TTBs are in anti-dumping. Over the period between 1990 and 2009, Brazil had only 3 safeguard cases and 16 countervailing cases, compared with 243 anti-dumping cases. The number of imposed anti-dumping measures accelerated in the early 1990s, again in the late 1990s and once more in the late 2000s. This coincides with periods when Brazil's real exchange rate was significantly appreciating. This is consistent with the finding of Knetter and Prusa (2003) that exchange-rate appreciations lead to increases in the number of anti-dumping cases when it becomes easier to find evidence of injury.

Brazil's use of TTBs is consistent with its concern regarding changes in international competitiveness and it is in reaction to some of the constraints imposed on Brazil by its multilateral and regional commitments. One economic concern with using TTBs to address such concerns is that it is highly inefficient and it does not target the source of the problem.

Marcelo Olarreaga is Professor of Economics at the University of Geneva and research fellow at CEPR, London.

Marcel Vaillant is Professor of International Trade at the Universidad de la República (Uruguay) and research fellow at Mercosur Economic Research Network.

REFERENCES

Barral, W., and G. Brogini (2010). Defesa da indústria e defesa comercial. *Revista Brasileira de Comercio Exterior* **105**, 53–62.

Bown, C. P. (2011a). Taking stock of anti-dumping, safeguards, and countervailing duties, 1990–2009. *The World Economy*, forthcoming.

Bown, C. P. (2011b). Introduction. In *The Great Recession and Import Protection: The Role of Temporary Trade Barriers* (ed. C. P. Bown). London: CEPR/World Bank. (Chapter 1 of this volume.)

Bown, C. P. (2010). *Temporary Trade Barriers Database*. World Bank (July). URL: http://econ.worldbank.org/ttbd/.

Coughlin, C., J. Terza, and N. Kahlifah (1989). The determinants of escape clause petitions. *Review of Economics and Statistics* **71**(2), 341–347.

Evenett, S. (2009). Global trade alert: motivation and launch. *World Trade Review* **8**(4), 607–609.

Feigenbaum, S., H. Ortiz, and T. Willett (1985). Protectionist pressures and aggregate economic conditions: comment on Takacs. *Economic Inquiry* **23**(1), 175–182.

Feigenbaum, S., and T. Willett (1985). Domestic versus international influences on protectionist pressures in the US. In *Exchange Rates, Trade and the US Economy* (ed. S. Arndt, R. Sweeney and T. Willett). Cambridge, MA: Ballinger.

Fischer, R., and T. Prusa (2003). Contingent protection as better insurance. *Review of International Economics* **11**(5), 745–757.

Foletti, L., M. Fugazza, A. Nicita, and M. Olarreaga (2011). Smoke in the (tariff) water. *The World Economy*, forthcoming.

Knetter, M., and T. Prusa (2003). Macroeconomic factors and anti-dumping filings: evidence from four countries. *Journal of International Economics* **61**(1), 1–17.

Kume, H., G. Piani, and C. Souza (2003). A política Brasileira de importação no período 1987–98: descrição e avaliação. In *A Abertura Comercial nos Anos 1990: Impactos sobre Emprego e Salários* (ed. C. H. Corseuil and H. Kume). Brasília: Ministério do Trabalho e Emprego, e IPEA.

Leidy, M. (1997). Macroeconomic conditions and pressures for protection under anti-dumping and countervailing duty laws: empirical evidence from the US. *IMF Staff Papers* **44**(1), 132–144.

Leidy, M., and B. Hoekman (1990). Production effects of price- and cost-based anti-dumping laws under flexible exchange rates. *Canadian Journal of Economics* **23**(4), 873–895.

Moncarz, P., M. Olarreaga, and M. Vaillant (2010). Regionalismo y política industrial en los países en desarrollo: el caso del Mercosur. In *Integración Regional en América Latina: Desafíos y Oportunidades*, Monografía de la RED del Instituto Virtual de la UNCTAD. Geneva: United Nations.

Nelson, D. (2006). The political economy of anti-dumping: a survey. *European Journal of Political Economy* **22**(3), 554–590.

Salvatore, D. (1987). Import penetration, exchange rates, and protectionism in the United States. *Journal of Policy Modeling* **9**, 125–141.

Takacs, W. (1981). Pressures for protectionism: an empirical analysis. *Economic Inquiry* **19**(4), 687–693.

Tavares, J. (2011). A inviável volta do controle de importacoes. *Newspaper O Estado do Sao Paulo* (10 February).

5 METHODOLOGICAL APPENDIX

In Figure 8.3 we define coverage of imports using the following definitions:

$$\mathrm{co}_t^{\mathrm{TTB}} = \frac{\sum_i b_i \, \mathrm{vm}_{it}}{\sum_i \mathrm{vm}_{it}}, \tag{8.1}$$

with $b_i = 1$ if i has a TTB investigation in $t \in [1989, 2009]$, and $b_i = 0$ otherwise; vm_{it} denotes the value of imports of product i (HS-06) in period t, $i \in I$ such that $\mathrm{vm}_{it} > 0$ in some $t \in [1989, 2009]$.

By analogy, we define import coverage by sector as follows:

$$\mathrm{co}_{st}^{\mathrm{TTB}} = \frac{\sum_{i_s} b_{i_s} \, \mathrm{vm}_{i_s t}}{\sum_{i_s} \mathrm{vm}_{i_s t}}. \tag{8.2}$$

We choose the set of products in sectors where coverage of imports under investigation is higher than average coverage. If $\mathrm{co}_{st}^{\mathrm{TTB}} > \mathrm{co}_t^{\mathrm{TTB}}$, then, for $s \in \bar{S}$ (sensitive sectors),

$$\mathrm{co}_{\bar{S}t}^{\mathrm{TTB}} = \frac{\sum_{i \in \bar{S}} b_i \, \mathrm{vm}_{it}}{\sum_{i \in \bar{S}} \mathrm{vm}_{it}}. \tag{8.3}$$

In column 1 of Table 8.2 we compute

$$\mathrm{vm}_{st} = \sum_{i_s} \mathrm{vm}_{i_s t} \quad \text{if } s \in \bar{S}, \tag{8.4}$$

in column 2 of Table 8.2 we have

$$\mathrm{vm}_{st}^{\mathrm{TTB}} = \sum_{i_s} b_{i_s} \, \mathrm{vm}_{i_s t} \quad \text{if } s \in \bar{S}, \tag{8.5}$$

and in column 3 of Table 8.2 we have

$$\mathrm{vm}_{st}^{\text{anti-dumping}} = \sum_{i_s} a_{i_s} \, \mathrm{vm}_{i_s t} \quad \text{if } s \in \bar{S}, \tag{8.6}$$

with $a_i = 1$ if i has an anti-dumping investigation in $t \in [1989, 2009]$, and $a_i = 0$ otherwise.

In Figure 8.4 the magnitudes computed are

$$\mathrm{vm}_{jt}^{\mathrm{TTB}} = \sum_i b_i \, \mathrm{vm}_{ijt}, \tag{8.7}$$

$$\mathrm{vm}_{jt}^{\mathrm{TTB\,m}} = \sum_i b_i^{\mathrm{m}} \, \mathrm{vm}_{ijt}, \tag{8.8}$$

$$\mathrm{vm}_{jt}^{\mathrm{TTB\,mf}} = \sum_i b_i^{\mathrm{mf}} \, \mathrm{vm}_{ijt}, \tag{8.9}$$

where j denotes high income, lower income, lower middle income, China and upper middle income; where $b_i^{\mathrm{m}} = 1$ if i has a TTB measure in $t \in [1989, 2009]$, and $b_i^{\mathrm{m}} = 0$ otherwise; and where $b_{it}^{\mathrm{mf}} = 1$ if i has a TTB measure in force in the current period, and $b_{it}^{\mathrm{m}} = 0$ otherwise.

In Figure 8.5, three different averages of MFN tariff are presented:

$$t_{it}^{\text{mfn,NOTTB}} = \frac{\sum_i (1 - b_i) t_{it}^{\text{mfn}}}{\sum_i (1 - b_i)}, \tag{8.10}$$

$$t_{it}^{\text{mfn,TTB wm}} = \frac{\sum_i b_i^{\text{wm}} t_{it}^{\text{mfn}}}{\sum_i b_i^{\text{wm}}}, \tag{8.11}$$

$$t_{it}^{\text{mfn,TTB m}} = \frac{\sum_i b_i^{\text{m}} t_{it}^{\text{mfn}}}{\sum_i b_i^{\text{m}}}, \tag{8.12}$$

where $b_i^{\text{wm}} = 1$ if i has a TTB investigation but without a measure in $t \in [1989, 2009]$, and $b_i^{\text{wm}} = 0$ otherwise. Note that $b_i^{\text{wm}} = b_i - b_i^{\text{m}}$.

In Figure 8.6 the evolution of the number of new products with TTB measures are computed as

$$n_t^{\text{TTBnm}} = \sum_i b_{it}^{\text{nm}}, \tag{8.13}$$

$$an_t^{\text{TTBnm}} = \sum_{z=0}^{t} \sum_i b_{iz}^{\text{nm}}, \tag{8.14}$$

where $b_{it}^{\text{nm}} = 1$ if i has a TTB measure in the current period t and not in any period $t - z$, and $b_{it}^{\text{nm}} = 0$ otherwise.

In Figure 8.7(a) products with TTB measure and the average level of the measure by year are computed as

$$n_t^{\text{TTB mf}} = \sum_i b_{it}^{\text{mf}}, \tag{8.15}$$

$$\text{ttb}_t = \frac{\sum_i b_{it}^{\text{mf}} \text{ttb}_{it}}{\sum_i b_{it}^{\text{mf}}}, \tag{8.16}$$

where ttb_{it} is the TTB measure in *ad valorem* terms.

In Figure 8.7(b) the shares of the count of products and imports with measures in the current year are computed as

$$\text{sh}_t^{\text{pro}} = \frac{\sum_i b_{it}^{\text{m}}}{I_t}, \tag{8.17}$$

$$\text{sh}_t^{\text{vm}} = \frac{\sum_i b_{it}^{\text{m}} \text{vm}_{it}}{\sum_i \text{vm}_{it}}, \tag{8.18}$$

where I_t is the number of products such that imports are greater than zero in the current year t.

These last two measures are similar to those computed in Bown (2011b); see equations (1.1) and (1.2). In the shares of imports we did not correct for the effect of the TTB measure on the level of imports as it is done in Equation (1.2).

In Figure 8.8 the flow of cases and products with anti-dumping initiated investigations and measures by year are computed as

$$nc_t^{\text{anti-dumping}} = \sum_c b_{ct}^{\text{anti-dumping}}, \tag{8.19}$$

$$np_t^{\text{anti-dumping}} = \sum_i b_{it}^{\text{anti-dumping}}, \tag{8.20}$$

$$nc_t^{\text{anti-dumping m}} = \sum_c b_{ct}^{\text{anti-dumping m}}, \tag{8.21}$$

$$np_t^{\text{anti-dumping m}} = \sum_i b_{it}^{\text{anti-dumping m}}, \tag{8.22}$$

where $b_{ct}^{\text{anti-dumping}} = 1$ if the case c has initiated an anti-dumping investigation in the current period, and $b_{ct}^{\text{anti-dumping}} = 0$ otherwise; with $b_{it}^{\text{anti-dumping}} = 1$ if the product i is in an anti-dumping investigation initiated in the current period, and $b_{it}^{\text{anti-dumping}} = 0$ otherwise; with $b_{ct}^{\text{anti-dumping m}} = 1$ if the case c has an anti-dumping measure in the current period, and $b_{ct}^{\text{anti-dumping m}} = 0$ otherwise; with $b_{it}^{\text{anti-dumping m}} = 1$ if the product i has an anti-dumping measure in the current period, and $b_{it}^{\text{anti-dumping m}} = 0$ otherwise.

In Figure 8.9 the structure of imports by sector with some anti-dumping investigations during the period is presented:

$$\text{vm}_{st}^{\text{anti-dumping}} = \sum_{i_s} b_i^{\text{anti-dumping}} \text{vm}_{i_s t}, \tag{8.23}$$

$$\text{vm}_{st}^{\text{anti-dumping m}} = \sum_{i_s} b_i^{\text{anti-dumping m}} \text{vm}_{i_s t}, \tag{8.24}$$

$$\text{vm}_{st}^{\text{anti-dumping mf}} = \sum_{i_s} b_{i_s}^{\text{anti-dumping mf}} \text{vm}_{i_s t}, \tag{8.25}$$

where definitions of dummies are similar to (8.7)–(8.9), but restricted to anti-dumping.

In Figure 8.10 the structure of imports by country with some anti-dumping investigations during the period is presented:

$$\text{vm}_{jt}^{\text{anti-dumping}} = \sum_i b_i^{\text{anti-dumping}} \text{vm}_{ijt}, \tag{8.26}$$

$$\text{vm}_{jt}^{\text{anti-dumping m}} = \sum_i b_i^{\text{anti-dumping m}} \text{vm}_{ijt}, \tag{8.27}$$

$$\text{vm}_{jt}^{\text{anti-dumping mf}} = \sum_i b_i^{\text{anti-dumping mf}} \text{vm}_{ijt}, \tag{8.28}$$

where definitions of dummies are similar to (8.7)–(8.9) but restricted to anti-dumping.

6 STATISTICAL APPENDIX

Table A8.1: *Brazil's PTAs in force with third countries, 1991–2008.*

Partner	Year	Type of agreement	
Argentina, Paraguay and Uruguay (ACE, 18)	1991	Plurilateral	FTA (2001) and CU (in construction)
Chile (ACE, 35)	1996	Common with Mercosur countries	FTA in goods
Bolivia	1997	Common with Mercosur countries	FTA in goods
Mexico (ACE 53 and 55)	2003	Bilateral	Trade rules and automotive sector
Cuba	2000	Bilateral	Partial preference
Peru (ACE, 58)	2005	Common with Mercosur but different bilateral preference	FTA in goods (2014)
Ecuador, Colombia and Venezuela (ACE, 59)	2005	Common with Mercosur but different bilateral preference	FTA in goods (2018)

'ACE' stands for Acuerdo de Complementación Económica (Economic Complementation Agreement).
Source: Moncarz *et al* (2010).

Table A8.2: *Typology of anti-dumping cases in Brazil for 1988–2010, combinations of decisions at the preliminary and final stages of the procedure (cases and products at HS-06).*

	Cases	Products	Calculation of interval period of anti-dumping measures	Average interval (years)
Without anti-dumping	*90*	*147*	—	*0.0*
· · · · ·	1	23	—	0.0
AA- ·N	1	1	—	0.0
BB- ·N	1	1	—	0.0
BB-AN	19	25	—	0.0
BB-NN	49	63	—	0.0
BB-TT	10	16	Revoke-Final	0.8*
BB-WW	8	12	—	0.0
NN-NN	1	6	—	0.0
Anti-dumping in process of study	*13*	*21*	—	*0.0*
MIMI-MIMI	13	21	—	0.0
Anti-dumping in preliminary stage	*11*	*56*	—	—
AA-NN	8	46	Final–Preliminary	1.5
AA-TT	2	9	Final–Preliminary	8.5
AA-WW	1	1	Final–Preliminary	1.0
Anti-dumping in final stage	*75*	*98*	—	—
BB-AA	66	89	Revoke-Final	5.3**
BB-OTHOTH	2	2	Revoke-Final	5.0
MIMI-AA	5	5	Revoke-Final	6.2
NN-AA	2	2	Revoke-Final	1.0
Anti-dumping in two stages	*54*	*119*	Revoke-Preliminary	—
AA-AA	54	119	Revoke-Preliminary	6.4
Total	243	441	—	3.4

A denotes 'accepted'; N denotes 'denied'; B denotes 'bypassed'; T denotes 'terminated'; W denotes 'withdrawn'; MI denotes 'missing'; and OTH denotes 'other'. Thus, an investigation with bypassed preliminary stage and final affirmative dumping but final negative injury finding will show up as BB-AN. '*' denotes cases where the final decisions are T but the revoke year is not immediate. '**' denotes cases where we do not have information about the revoke year and thus we use the average to perform calculations.

Source: authors' calculations using *Temporary Trade Barriers Database* (Bown 2010).

Table A8.3: *Brazil's anti-dumping initiations with and without anti-dumping measures, 1988–2010.*

	Cases			Products (HS-06)		
	Total	Without anti-dumping	With anti-dumping	Total	Without anti-dumping	With anti-dumping
1988	2	0	2	2	0	2
1989	2	0	2	2	0	2
1990	2	0	2	2	0	2
1991	13	8	5	13	8	5
1992	8	0	8	9	0	9
1993	27	16	11	62	16	46
1994	10	6	4	11	6	5
1995	5	0	5	5	0	5
1996	16	10	6	18	12	6
1997	9	2	7	15	4	11
1998	20	5	15	46	10	36
1999	15	4	11	42	9	33
2000	8	5	3	19	13	6
2001	17	12	5	20	13	7
2002	8	5	3	22	17	5
2003	4	1	3	4	1	3
2004	8	5	3	8	5	3
2005	6	6	0	6	6	0
2006	12	3	9	20	3	17
2007	13	1	12	23	1	22
2008	24	1	23	70	23	47
2009	9	1	8	17	4	13
2010	5	1	4	5	1	4
Stock	243	91	152	441	152	289

In 2009 and 2010, cases and products with anti-dumping measures are estimated due to lack of information. The observed figures for both cases and products with anti-dumping measure in 2009 are 1 and 0 in 2010.

Source: authors' calculations using *Temporary Trade Barriers Database* (Bown 2010).

Table A8.4: *Brazil's CVDs.*

		Dates			Measure	
Country	Products	Initiation year of the investigation	Start of measure	Duration in years	Type	Level
Argentina	Disposable diapers	1991	—	0	—	—
Malaysia	Latex yarn	1991	1991	6	Missing	Missing
European Union	Milk products	1992	1992	3	*Ad valorem*	20.7
USA	Wheat	1992	—	—	—	—
Pakistan	Cotton yarn	1993	—	0	—	—
Canada	Wheat	1993	—	0	—	—
Côte d'Ivoire	Grated coconut (dehydrated)	1994	1995	7	*Ad valorem*	87.9
Indonesia	Grated coconut (dehydrated)	1994	1995	7	*Ad valorem*	155.7
Malaysia	Grated coconut (dehydrated)	1994	1995	7	*Ad valorem*	196.5
Philippines	Grated coconut (dehydrated)	1994	1995	7	*Ad valorem*	121.5
Sri Lanka	Grated coconut (dehydrated)	1994	1995	7	*Ad valorem*	81.4
Sri Lanka	Coconut milk (powdered)	1994	1995	7	*Ad valorem*	175.8
USA	Cotton (not carded or combed)	1994	—	0	—	—
India	Polyethylene terephthalate films (PET Films)	2001	—	0	—	—
India	Stainless steel bars	2003	2004	6	Specific duty	$172.00/t
India	Polyethylene terephthalate films (PET Films)	2007	2008	3	Specific duty	$165.08/t

Source: authors' calculations using *Temporary Trade Barriers Database* (Bown 2010).

9

Argentina: There and Back Again?

MICHAEL O. MOORE[1]

1 INTRODUCTION

Argentina's economy came under considerable stress in 2008 as the global financial crisis swept the world. Argentine economic growth stumbled as exports fell dramatically and credit markets dried up worldwide. This economic distress raised the spectre of a renewed inward protectionist approach that Argentina has followed so frequently in times of severe downturn. In the event, there is evidence that the Argentine government began to use TTBs more intensely from 2008 until the first half of 2010. One estimate suggests that, taking into account the suppression of trade associated with the import restrictions, over 5% of Argentine imports were affected by such contingent protection measures in 2009, which is far in excess of any earlier period. Temporary trade barriers have been particularly commonly used against Chinese exports to Argentina. However, there is less evidence of a systematically more protectionist approach by Argentina in the post-crisis period using transparent trade restrictions such as increased MFN tariffs. There has been a greater use of opaque measures such as non-automatic import licences and reference prices, though the broader impact of such policies remains unclear.

Argentina's experience can provide important insights into the use of WTO-consistent trade restrictions in times of turmoil. Argentina has a long and complicated relationship with trade protection and with the use of contingent protection measures from the early 1990s until the first decade of the 2000s. In the last 25 years, Argentina has whipsawed back and forth from a highly protected economy with a reliance on import substitution through the early 1980s to a dramatically more open model in the late 1980s due to unilateral trade liberalisation, and then back again to a more inwards-focused approach

[1]Department of Economics, Elliott School of International Affairs, and Institute for International Economic Policy, George Washington University, 1957 E Street, NW, Washington, DC 20052, USA. Email: mom@gwu.edu. I would like to thank Maggie Chen, Maurizio Zanardi and Aksel Erbahar for their help on this project as well as Sungil Kwak and Urvi Thanki for their excellent research assistance. The project, of course, would have been impossible without the hard work and vision of Chad Bown.

in the early years of the 2000s. During that time, it has faced economic shocks from both international and domestic sources. This includes a severe balance-of-payments crisis and subsequent devaluation of the peso in the 2001–2 period as well as the consequences of the international crisis that began in 2008.

In the post-2008 crisis period, economic disruptions grew in Argentina, as was the case across the rest of the world. Annual Argentine GDP growth fell significantly from 6.8% in 2008 to 0.9% in 2009 as the crisis that began in developed countries moved towards developing countries.[2] Official unemployment rose from 7.3% in 2008 to 8.4% in 2009. The pressures on the trade side were evident as well. Argentine merchandise exports fell 20% from $70 billion in 2008 to $55.7 billion in 2009. Slower Argentine economic growth resulted in an even more dramatic 29% drop in imports from $54.3 billion in 2008 to $38.3 billion in 2009. Given the sharp drop in economic growth and the contemporaneous Argentine government's scepticism towards *laissez-faire* policies, one might expect a strong reaction in trade policy.

The following analysis will show two important features. The first is that the total amount of trade affected by ongoing TTBs in Argentina rose significantly in the post-crisis period. Second, Argentine TTBs have become less and less about industries traditionally targeted by such measures (such as steel) and more and more about restrictions on Chinese exports in a variety of industries. Such data patterns mean that it is difficult to know with certainty whether this increased use of contingent protection is a move against China or a more general reaction to the broader economic crisis.

This chapter includes a section on the broad trade policy context in Argentina in Section 2, followed by a discussion in Section 3 of basic descriptive statistics on anti-dumping and safeguard use.[3] Section 4 includes a more detailed analysis of the amount of trade affected by the measures, Section 5 has a more detailed discussion of Argentina's experience with China, and Section 6 contains a brief discussion of other trade policy measures such as import licences and adjustments of applied tariffs. Section 7 contains some concluding remarks.

---

[2]World Bank World Development Indicators are the source for all macroeconomic data while the United Nations Comtrade is the source for trade data.

[3]Argentina has also intervened frequently in its export markets, primarily through export taxes and quotas, in order to moderate domestic price increases. This tendency has been particularly acute in agricultural markets such as beef and wine. While important in understanding the broader story about trade policy, this chapter is focused on interventions in the import side alone. See Rossi *et al* (2009) for an analysis of Argentine export policies and Global Trade Alert (2010a,b) for a catalogue of actions in the crisis period.

2 BROAD TRADE OVERVIEW

Argentina was one of the most consistent practitioners of import substitution policies in Latin America during the mid-1980s. For example, Nogues and Baracat (2006) report that average Argentine applied *ad valorem* tariffs reached 39% in 1987, with about 50% of tariff lines subject to import licences. Starting in 1988, Argentina began a remarkable unilateral trade liberalisation package that subsequently resulted in average applied tariffs of only 12% with no products being subject to import licences.

Argentina has long had a system of TTBs, even prior to the liberalisation period of the 1980s. It adopted an anti-dumping system in 1972 (Zanardi 2004) that would allow for individual industries to file for temporary protection through this administered protection system. It also instituted systems that allow CVDs in the event of subsidised exports for narrowly defined product areas as well as broad industry-level restrictions from all sources in the event of import surges that result in 'serious' injury (safeguards).[4] The Argentine system included a central role by Comisión Nacional de Comercio Exterio (CNCE), which is the administrative body responsible for investigating dumping and injury allegations filed by domestic industries.

Argentina certainly has one of the longest histories of intense use of potentially WTO-consistent contingent protection measures among developing countries. This has been primarily through the use of anti-dumping. Prusa (2001) shows that Argentina was the second most frequent new user of anti-dumping in the 1990s. On the other hand, Argentina's authorities used safeguards and CVD actions against importers very infrequently. Thus, while this chapter will include an analysis of safeguard actions, the focus will be on anti-dumping as the primary example of Argentina's TTBs.[5]

Based on what took place after the peso crisis of 2001–2, one might have expected there to be a marked increase in protectionist measures in Argentina after the economic crisis that began in late 2008. There was indeed an uptick in the use of new contingent protection measures during the global economic crisis, though there were no new CVDs or safeguard actions. There is strong evidence that the overall impact of anti-dumping actions, measured by the share of trade affected by *ongoing* anti-dumping orders, grew substantially in Argentina in 2008 and 2009. As discussed below, this shows that Argentine

---

[4]See Nogues and Baracat (2006) for details on the anti-dumping, CVD and safeguard systems in Argentina.

[5]Argentina, like the vast majority of WTO members, has initiated only a handful of CVD investigations (*ie* actions taken against potentially injurious imports that have received subsidies from a government). In particular, there have been a total of only six CVD investigations undertaken by the Argentine government, all but one of which involved agricultural goods. These cases also represent a very small percentage of trade affected by TTBs; the greatest percentage was in 1997 when only 6% of trade affected by contingent protection, or only 0.02% of total trade, involved CVD measures.

Table 9.1: *Argentina's economy, 1991–2009.*

Year	GDP growth (annual %)	Unemployment rate	Exchange rate	Current account (% of GDP)	Anti-dumping initiations
1991	12.7	6.5	1.43	−0.2	1
1992	11.9	7.1	1.36	−2.8	14
1993	5.9	11.7	1.37	−3.4	28
1994	5.8	14.4	1.46	−4.3	18
1995	−2.8	18.9	1.49	−2.0	25
1996	5.5	19.1	1.44	−2.5	24
1997	8.1	15.9	1.35	−4.0	13
1998	3.9	14.7	1.41	−4.8	6
1999	−3.4	16.2	1.37	−4.2	21
2000	−0.8	17.4	1.30	−3.1	26
2001	−4.4	20.7	1.26	−1.4	33
2002	−10.9	20.8	4.51	8.5	10
2003	8.8	14.5	4.32	6.3	1
2004	9.0	12.1	4.60	1.7	12
2005	9.2	10.1	4.31	2.6	8
2006	8.5	8.7	4.58	3.2	10
2007	8.7	7.5	4.94	2.3	8
2008	6.8	7.3	5.29	1.5	20
2009	0.9	8.4	5.93	2.0	28

Exchange rate (nominal) = peso per IMF special drawing right. Anti-dumping initiations are at investigation level (*eg* footwear from China).

Source: GDP growth and exchange rate taken from World Development Indicators; unemployment rate and current account taken from IMF World Economic Outlook; and anti-dumping initiations taken from Bown (2010) and Moore and Zanardi (2009).

authorities have become much more likely to impose an anti-dumping order after an initiation and are far less likely to remove them after the five-year period as envisioned by international anti-dumping agreements negotiated in the Uruguay Round.

However, there was relatively little broad new retrenchment against imports during the 2008–9 period, including only a modest increase in applied tariffs that Argentina could have raised significantly given its tariff overhang. This, of course, reflects Argentina's membership in Mercosur, which makes unilateral increases in applied MFN tariffs potentially problematic.[6] There has been an increase of other types of tariff barriers, including non-automatic import licences. However, one difficulty with import licences is their opaque nature—they have uncertain effects on trade flows since they vary depending on how bureaucracies implement the restrictions.

[6]Argentina, Brazil, Paraguay and Uruguay are the members of Mercosur, a customs union that in principle requires common tariffs on non-members and zero tariffs among member nations.

Table 9.1 displays some basic information about the Argentine economy from 1991 to 2009, including data on the annual GDP growth rate, the exchange rate (pesos per IMF 'special drawing rights'), and the current account as a share of GDP. Argentina's economic growth has been highly volatile during the period. Economic growth was quite strong during the early 1990s as the country embarked on its remarkable economic liberalisation program. This was followed by a sharp contraction in 1999 during the aftermath of the Brazilian and Russian crises, and an even greater decline in 2001 and 2002 during the peso crisis. The nominal exchange rate reflects this currency turmoil with a dramatic devaluation in 2002 followed by a slowly depreciating peso thereafter. The current account as a percentage of GDP has been in surplus for the entire period subsequent to the devaluation. The 2008–9 global financial crisis period reflects a sharp slowdown in growth (from 6.8% in 2008 to 0.9% in 2009) but with a retained current account surplus and a depreciating exchange rate.

Table 9.1 also includes the number of newly initiated anti-dumping investigations in each year, *ie* the number of country-product petitions filed by the Argentine industry. Thus, an anti-dumping petition against Swiss 'laminated floors', which might involve myriad individual tariff lines, is counted as one 'investigation', which is the standard method of counting anti-dumping activity in the literature.

There are two clear patterns for anti-dumping activity. The first is the increased use of anti-dumping in the years immediately prior to the balance-of-payments crisis in 2001–2. The Argentine peso became significantly overvalued in the late 1990s and early 2000s as Argentina experienced a large and persistent current account deficit. Argentine use of anti-dumping rose to its highest rate (measured by the number of investigations initiated) in this period; industries effectively used the anti-dumping system to decrease imports. Anti-dumping initiations fell dramatically in 2002 to fewer than half of the 2000 total, which coincided with a massive 10.9% contraction of the economy.

The experience in the post-devaluation period shows that a sharp slowdown in macroeconomic growth has not been enough to trigger anti-dumping use in Argentina. The main mitigating factor was the dramatic 56% fall in imports that occurred in the post-devaluation period, which normally makes proving that imports have caused material injury more difficult for petitioning domestic industries.

The post-2007 period provides a slightly different lesson. Anti-dumping use rose three-fold from 2007 and 2009 in terms of initiated investigations, even as the peso continued to depreciate and imports fell. During this period, and in contrast to the years immediately following the peso devaluation, the dramatic reduction in economic activity coincided with a rise in anti-dumping use (the data for 1991–1994 come from Moore and Zanardi (2009); the balance is from Bown (2010)). Table 9.2 includes a list of initiated anti-dumping inves-

Table 9.2: *Argentina's initiated anti-dumping investigations, January 2008–March 2010.*

Target country	Product	Initiation date
Thailand	Air conditioners	1/10/2008
Brazil, Indonesia	Acrylic yarns	25/3/2008
Brazil, China	Stainless steel cutlery	25/4/2008
China	Large chains	28/4/2008
China, Peru, Taiwan	Zippers	5/5/2008
China, Romania	Oil rigs	22/5/2008
China	Cooling liquid or water for engines	28/7/2008
China, India	Dyes	29/7/2008
China	Dishware	31/7/2008
China	Steel pipe accessories	23/10/2008
China, India, Indonesia, Taiwan	Polyester fibre and yarn	17/11/2008
Brazil, China	Certain taffeta ligament weft and warp fabrics	6/1/2009
Brazil, China	Electric food processors	14/1/2009
China, Germany, Switzerland	Laminated floors	23/1/2009
China	Footwear	2/3/2009
China	Steel wheels	9/3/2009
Brazil, China	Stainless steel knives with plastic handles	20/3/2009
China	Denim	25/3/2009
Paraguay	Recordable compact discs	25/3/2009
Brazil, China	Iron pipe accessories	14/5/2009
China	Elevator and forklift engines	29/5/2009
China	Lighters used in kitchens	7/7/2009
Brazil	Printing ink	14/7/2009
India	Connectors for metal conductors	16/7/2009
Brazil	Gas compressors (except air)	9/9/2009
China	Electric centrifugal pump	9/9/2009
China	Syringes	9/9/2009
China	Methane chloride	24/9/2009
China	Electric heaters	19/10/2009
China	Starting and regulator devices for motorcycles	29/10/2009
China	Steel tubes	2/11/2009
China	Electric fans	24/11/2009
China	Rubber tyres	17/12/2009
Brazil	Polypropylene fabric	11/2/2010
China	Suits and jackets	13/2/2010
Korea, Malaysia, Thailand, Vietnam	Air conditioners	13/2/2010
China	Chain saw blades	3/3/2010

Source: Temporary Trade Barriers Database (Bown 2010).

tigations from January 2008 to March 2010. As illustrated by the table, China was clearly the prominent target, a pattern discussed in more detail below.

It will be useful to consider how applied tariffs in sectors affected by all types of TTBs compare with tariffs in sectors that are free from these types of

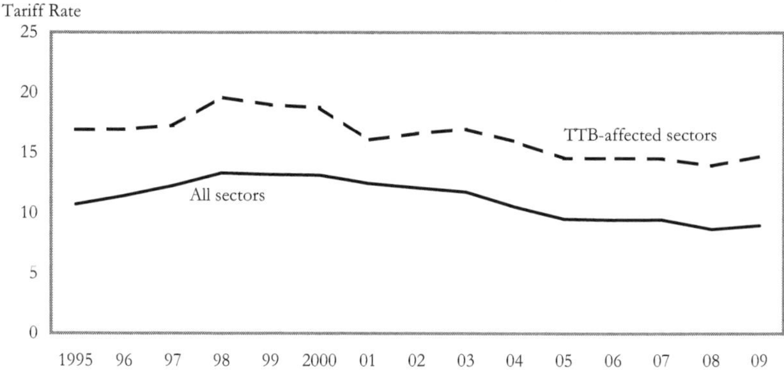

Figure 9.1: *Argentina's unweighted average applied MFN tariffs.*
Source: TRAINS database.

restrictions. Figure 9.1 shows that the average (unweighted) applied MFN tariffs in sectors that were subject to TTBs in any year of the sample always exceed the average tariffs of all sectors for 1995–2009.[7] In other words, those sectors that use contingent protection already have higher-than-average tariffs for all years in the data. This suggests that sectors that have been subject to less dramatic tariff reductions have also been the most active in seeking additional protection. One interpretation of these data is that, in Argentina, TTBs and MFN tariffs could be considered complements rather than substitutes.

Another important trade policy change was Argentina's 1991 decision to join Mercosur, a customs union, along with Brazil, Paraguay and Uruguay. Membership of Mercosur entailed a common external tariff that was completed by the end of 1994. Four aspects of this agreement are particularly important. First, the customs union means that imports from other Mercosur countries would normally enter Argentina without restrictions.[8] Second, the common external tariff means that Argentina would be limited in its ability to increase its MFN tariffs on non-Mercosur countries. While Argentina might have other methods (*eg* non-automatic import licences, regulatory practices, internal taxation and contingent protection measures) to reduce imports, their impact would be more limited than what Argentina might otherwise impose. Third, the Treaty of Asunción and the subsequent trade policy arrangement among Mercosur countries had important implications for the use of contingent measures such as TTBs. For example, the treaty did not allow for a

[7]Note that the average tariffs in TTB sectors do not reflect any additional trade restrictions from contingent protection.

[8]The applied MFN tariffs in Figure 9.1 do not reflect lower tariffs for Mercosur countries or other countries with which Argentina now has preferential tariffs such as Colombia.

safeguard for intra-Mercosur trade, unlike the 'snapback' provisions of the NAFTA. The treaty also permitted the continued use of anti-dumping and CVD actions against Mercosur partners. Finally, all three contingent protection measures are administered by Argentina alone for its imports—there are no formal Mercosur-level anti-dumping, CVD or safeguard measures.

3 DESCRIPTIVE STATISTICS ON TEMPORARY TRADE BARRIERS (1991–2010)

Table 9.3 shows the simple count of anti-dumping actions (both those initiated and those resulting in measures) for the period from 1991 to 2010.[9] Note that since anti-dumping authorities may take more than a year to complete an anti-dumping investigation, most of the investigations initiated in 2009 and 2010 had not been finalised by the time this study was completed. The unit of observation for these counts is the number of cases at the HS-08 level.[10]

Counting anti-dumping frequency is complicated. Each instance involves a specific exporting country and a 'product' under investigation. However, each 'product' may include literally dozens of HS-08 tariff-line codes for each target country's exporters under investigation. Going forward, 'investigation' will refer to a particular country and group of products investigated by the authorities, *eg* 'hot-rolled steel products' from Slovakia. A 'case' will refer to each country–tariff-line combination, *eg* 7208.27.10 and 7208.27.90 from Slovakia will be considered as two cases even if they are part of the same investigation. Since anti-dumping analysis has traditionally taken place at the 'investigation' level but most of the analysis in this chapter will be at the 'case' level, one should be careful when making comparisons of anti-dumping statistics across this and other studies. The current data set, for example, has 317 initiated investigations with 933 individual exporter–HS-08 code pairs. Table 9.1 includes investigation-level data, while Table 9.3 is at the case level.

Table 9.3 shows jurisdictions most involved in Argentina's anti-dumping actions in the data set. China, Brazil and the European Union alone are the targets in 435 out of 933 cases. Exports from China have been the single most frequent target of anti-dumping actions, with 188 individual products facing anti-dumping actions, or 20% of all cases. Exports from Brazil are just behind, with 167 cases. The EU15 countries as a group have the third largest number of anti-dumping cases with 80 anti-dumping cases initiated by Argentine authorities.[11] More disaggregated data show that Argentina has focused

[9]Information about TTB actions used in this study end in July 2010, when the database developed by Bown (2010) was updated as of January 2011.

[10]HS refers to the harmonized tariff classification system. 'HS-02' and 'HS-08' refer to the two-digit and eight-digit categories.

[11]EU15 nations are used instead of the current 27 member states of the EU for consistency across the years analysed in the study.

Table 9.3: *Argentina's anti-dumping initiations and measures imposed.*

	1991-1994	1995-2001	2002-2007	2008-2010	1991-2010 total
			(a) Initiations		
China	7	46	23	112	188
Brazil	56	82	12	17	167
Other Mercosur	3	12	3	1	19
EU15	19	44	8	9	80
USA	5	10	1	0	16
Japan	3	4	0	0	7
South Africa	0	46	8	0	54
Korea	6	26	13	3	48
Russia	0	33	8	0	41
Kazakhstan	0	37	0	0	37
Others	54	127	58	37	276
Total	153	467	134	179	933
			(b) Final measures imposed		
China	7	38	20	57	122
Brazil	24	59	9	6	98
Other Mercosur	3	9	3	0	15
EU15	4	23	6	0	33
USA	2	6	0	0	8
Japan	3	4	0	0	7
South Africa	0	42	8	0	50
Korea	5	17	12	0	34
Russia	0	33	0	0	33
Kazakhstan	0	37	0	0	37
Others	37	107	44	17	205
Total	85	375	102	80	642

Data taken at the case level (HS-08-country pairs). Note that many cases filed in 2009-10 were not yet finalised as of July 2010.

Source: author's calculations using *Temporary Trade Barriers Database* (Bown 2010).

primarily on developing country exports for the entire period: only 151 of the 940 cases involve exports from high-income countries such as the EU15, Australia, the USA, Switzerland, Japan, Canada and New Zealand.

Panel (b) of Table 9.3 contains the outcomes for cases adjudicated to the final stage. Almost 69% of initiated petitions (642 out of 933) have ended with a final measure imposed. Clearly, most Argentine anti-dumping cases end in final 'orders' (*ie* anti-dumping measures restricting imports). The rest have been concluded without final measures—either by the withdrawal of the petitioning industry, the termination by the anti-dumping authorities, or decisions not yet rendered. Note that the totals for 2008–10 should be treated with caution since many cases filed in 2009 and 2010 were not yet finalised at the time this study was completed. For these cases, there is strong evidence to suggest that nearly all petitions will likely result in final measures, in large part because Argentina has begun to impose restrictions on essentially all anti-dumping cases that involve imports from China.

The simple count of anti-dumping petitions and actions does not take into account the 'intensity' of anti-dumping use. In particular, it is useful to compare the percentage of anti-dumping petitions with the share of total imports from particular jurisdictions. For example, US products represented an average of 18.3% of total Argentine imports for 1991–2009 but only 1.6% of the total number of anti-dumping petitions at the case level (16 out of 933).[12] EU15 trade was also targeted less (8.5% of total anti-dumping petitions) than expected given its overall import share (22.5%). Brazil is slightly unrepresented as well, with 17.9% of anti-dumping petitions compared with an average of 27.3% of annual total imports for the period. China stands out as its annual average import share was only 5.4% for the entire period, but it faced 20% of the anti-dumping complaints. However, Chinese exports to Argentina were increasing dramatically during this time period.

3.1 Argentine Anti-Dumping Use Over Time: Country Patterns

One striking aspect of Argentina's use of anti-dumping shown in Table 9.3 is how the pattern of countries targeted evolves over time. During 1991–4, Argentina initiated 153 cases on HS-08 product lines, and 85 of those cases ended in final anti-dumping orders. In other words, during this period of economic and trade liberalisation, Argentine authorities were quite stringent in their administration of the anti-dumping laws, with high standards before a final anti-dumping order would be imposed.

Brazil was by far the single most frequent target with 56 total cases, representing one-third of all initiations in 1991–4. US exports, in contrast, were involved in only 5 cases. The EU15 countries lag far behind as well with only 19 cases. East Asian imports were only lightly touched: the numbers for Japan (3), South Korea (6), and Taiwan (2) are much smaller than in traditional anti-dumping users such as the USA during the 1990s. Strikingly, China only had 7 HS-08 codes involved in the Argentine anti-dumping system during this early period. Argentine authorities targeted developing countries with just over one-third of anti-dumping petitions in this period, with the balance focused on high-income countries.

Argentina's use of anti-dumping surged in the next period (1995–2001). A combination of Argentina's liberal economic regime and integration within

---

[12]Trade data for 2010 were not available at the time this study was completed.

WTO bound tariffs, Mercosur membership, a fixed peg to the US dollar, and the Brazilian devaluation put enormous pressure on import-competing industries, as reflected in the current account deficits displayed in Table 9.1. As Nogues and Baracat (2006) point out, these industries turned frequently to anti-dumping as a means of limiting foreign sales, since their traditional means of protection (*eg* import licence regimes and high MFN tariffs) were unavailable. In particular, there were 467 individual HS-08 codes from various countries involved in the anti-dumping cases that Argentina initiated during this period, and final anti-dumping orders covered 377 of these products.

Argentina's anti-dumping cases became even more focused on developing countries during the 1995–2001 period, with twice as many initiated against this group than against high-income countries. This period also saw particular pressures on Brazilian exports that faced 82 initiated cases. The period also begins the intense focus on China with 46 petitions. The emergence of China as a target for Argentina is consistent with other case studies in this volume, though the focus on Brazil is far more unusual. US exporters continue to be rare targets of anti-dumping in Argentina, despite the large share of its imports in the Argentine market.

There was another dramatic change in anti-dumping use during 2002–7 (after the peso crisis and before the international financial crisis that begin in 2008). Even though the Argentine government took a number of steps to reduce its integration into the world economy during this period, the number of Argentine anti-dumping case initiations dropped from an average of almost 60 HS-08 products per year in 1995–2001 to just over 20 products per year in 2002–7. Cases brought against its Mercosur partner Brazil, an upper-middle-income country, dropped from 82 in the earlier period to only 12 in the latter period. Cases brought against China fell by a much smaller margin from 46 to 23 in the latter period. Actions taken against higher-income-country exports faded into insignificance; only 1 case was brought against the USA (which did not result in a final measure) and only 8 against all EU15 countries. On the other hand, developing countries were now targeted in 60% of all Argentine anti-dumping actions. In short, Argentine anti-dumping activities in this period increasingly turned against developing and emerging market economies, with special attention to China.

Recall from Table 9.1 that the 2002–7 period was one of significant economic volatility for Argentina. Imports and economic growth fell dramatically in 2002 while anti-dumping activity was reduced to a near standstill. In other words, an economic slowdown, even a dramatic one, was not a sufficient condition for anti-dumping use to increase. Perhaps most importantly, the relieved pressure on importers due to the devaluation of the peso meant that Argentina's import-competing industries did not turn to administered protection methods such as anti-dumping to deal with their economic problems. Of course, the concurrent convulsions related to Argentina's domestic economic problems meant that firms had few resources with which to take on the legal costs of filing an anti-dumping case, regardless of the likelihood of final success, and firms were often fighting for mere survival during the crisis.

Does Argentina's experience with the earlier 2001–2 economic crisis serve as a useful predictor of anti-dumping use in the post-2007 period? There was a marked increase in anti-dumping during the pre-peso crisis period and then a sharp decline afterwards, even as the economy contracted and imports fell. In general, the period of the recent global financial crisis suggests broad economic patterns similar to the peso crisis period, but on a much less dramatic scale. There was a significant slowdown in Argentina's GDP growth from 2008 (6.8%) to 2009 (0.9%) and a 30% fall in imports from 2008 ($54.3 billion) to 2009 ($38.3 billion).

Nevertheless, the pattern of reduced anti-dumping activity observed in the post-2002 period is not matched by the post-2007 period. Argentina initiated 179 cases from 2008 to July 2010. This translates into just under 72 cases per year (counting 2010 as half a year). This is greater than the pre-peso crisis period of 1995–2001 and far above the rate of initiation that Argentina experienced after the 2002 devaluation.

There are, however, two important differences between these two periods of economic contraction. First, the position of the Argentine currency was quite different in the two recessions. The spectacular devaluation in 2002 was not repeated in the 2008–9 period. Moreover, the real exchange-rate appreciation that was so disruptive in the lead-up to 2002 is absent in the 2008–9 crisis. In fact, Table 9.1 shows that there was an increase in the Argentine current account surplus in 2008 and 2009, indicating that broad import pressures were falling. Second, the rise of China as a major source of Argentine imports does not have an analogue in the earlier period.

There is also a continued tendency for Argentina to focus less of its anti-dumping activities on high-income countries. In fact, there were only nine cases brought against a member of the EU15 and only three cases brought against South Korea for 2008 until the middle of 2010. There have been no cases filed against the USA in the 2008–10 period and only one since 2002, and that particular case did not result in a final anti-dumping order. Similarly, Japan has escaped attention from Argentine anti-dumping authorities after 2002. Instead, Argentina has continued to concentrate on other developing countries in 2008–10, with 90% of total initiations directed against such countries and 72% against China and Brazil alone.

Chinese exports to Argentina, as in so many other countries, rose dramatically in the 2000s. China's sales in Argentina became more than 38 times greater from 1991 to its historic high in 2008, compared with a 12-fold increase for Brazil and 7-fold increase in imports overall (all in nominal terms). This alone explains some of the newfound focus on China within the Argen-

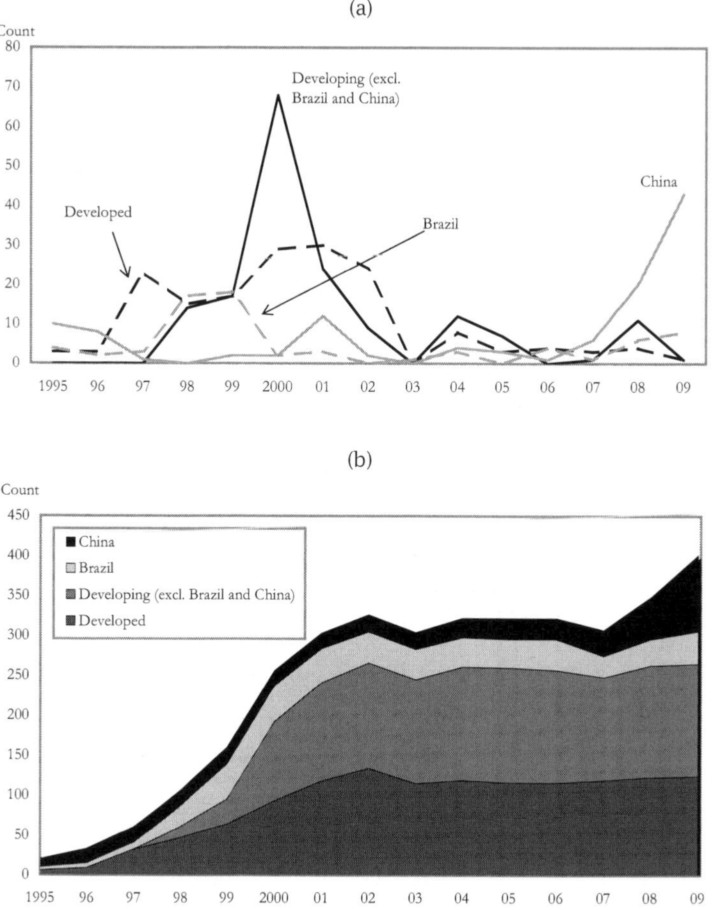

Figure 9.2: *Argentine anti-dumping actions: (a) initiations, by target-country group; (b) orders in place (count of country–HS-08 pairs).*

Source: author's calculations using *Temporary Trade Barriers Database* (Bown 2010).

tine anti-dumping system.[13] The increased competition has almost certainly resulted in increased focus on using administered protection to limit Chinese imports.

Figure 9.2(a) shows the count of anti-dumping initiations at the HS-08-country level for different country groups, including developed countries,

[13]Even during the 2008–9 crisis, Chinese exports fell 24% compared with a 30% overall reduction from all sources.

Brazil, China, and developing countries (excluding China and Brazil).[14] Developed countries played a more important role earlier in the data, including spikes in 1997 and the 2000–2002 periods. After this time, there was little Argentine anti-dumping activity that targeted developed country exports. Developing countries excluding Brazil and China were targeted especially in 2000, which reflects a handful of steel cases involving numerous HS-08 tariff lines (discussed in more detail below). The most striking feature of the figure, of course, is the dramatic increase in cases involving China in 2008 and 2009. This focus on China is also clear in Table 9.2; the overwhelming majority of Argentina's anti-dumping initiations from January 2008 until March 2010 targeted Chinese imports.

Figure 9.2(b) shows the count of anti-dumping orders in place based on the same country breakdown. There have been a very steady number of continued orders against developed countries beginning in 2003. The number of anti-dumping orders against developing countries (excluding China and Brazil) is also fairly steady. Most notable is the rapid growth of orders against China that begins in 2007. Not only have there been more investigations targeting Chinese exports, but they also represent a much larger share of orders that continue to restrict trade.

3.2 Targeted Product Sectors

Table 9.4 contains information about the most important sectors targeted under Argentine anti-dumping procedures. We include only the new petitions filed at the case level; success rates for petitions do not vary significantly across sectors. These sectors represent 67% of all Argentine anti-dumping cases for the 1991–2010 period.

The dominant sectoral users of Argentine anti-dumping in the 1991–2010 period are basic iron and steel (HS-02 sector 72) and articles of iron and steel (HS-02 sector 73). Over 44% of all Argentine cases were in these two sectors, with the vast majority in HS-02 sector 72. The next largest sector is electrical machinery (HS-02 sector 85) with only 75 product–country pairs.

Argentina is not unusual in that the steel industry (both basic steel and articles of steel) has traditionally been the single biggest category targeted in anti-dumping. However, there is very little Argentine targeting of chemicals (organic and inorganic) industry imports, which has traditionally been the second largest category worldwide (Moore and Zanardi 2009).

There is a dramatic change in Argentina's sectoral focus over time. The focus on iron and steel occurs in two periods. The first is the 1992–3 period, in which there was a global steel crisis. This spike in cases took place in spite of the booming Argentine economy during that period. The second is in the late 1990s, subsequent to the steel sector turmoil in Asia, Russia and

[14]Developed and developing country categories are based on World Bank definitions.

Table 9.4: *Argentina's anti-dumping initiations by HS-08–country pairs.*

Year	Articles of wood (HS-02 44)	Articles of clothing (HS-02 62)	Footwear (HS-02 64)	Basic iron and steel (HS-02 72)	Articles of iron and steel (HS-02 73)	Tools of base metals (HS-02 82)	Mechanical machinery (HS-02 84)	Electrical machinery (HS-02 85)	Optical and photographic instruments (HS-02 90)
1991	0	0	0	0	0	0	0	0	1
1992	0	0	0	62	0	0	1	4	0
1993	2	0	0	27	0	2	0	12	3
1994	0	6	0	5	0	0	0	11	0
1995	0	0	0	0	5	8	1	5	0
1996	0	0	0	0	1	0	5	14	1
1997	9	0	0	0	1	6	2	6	4
1998	0	0	0	57	0	0	0	0	0
1999	1	0	0	28	0	3	0	2	0
2000	6	0	0	109	3	2	4	1	0
2001	0	0	0	48	8	1	12	1	4
2002	0	0	0	48	0	0	0	0	0
2003	0	0	0	0	0	0	0	0	0
2004	0	0	0	0	0	0	0	1	5
2005	0	0	0	0	2	2	0	0	1
2006	0	0	0	0	0	4	2	3	3
2007	0	0	0	0	1	0	0	7	0
2008	0	0	0	0	3	8	7	0	0
2009	29	0	30	0	9	2	8	8	3
2010	0	11	0	0	0	2	12	0	0
Total	47	17	30	384	33	40	54	75	25

Source: Temporary Trade Barriers Database (Bown 2010).

Brazil. This relatively large number of cases should be interpreted with care. Steel cases typically involve many individual HS-08 categories. Domestic steel industries often file these cases against multiple steel-exporting countries simultaneously. For example, almost all of the 109 anti-dumping cases initiated in 2000 represent only four countries (Kazakhstan, Romania, Slovakia and South Africa) for only one product ('hot-rolled steel products') with 20 individual HS-08 codes. While 20 separate HS-08 lines certainly represents a wide range of steel products, this can have very different effects from cases against 40 different products from 2 different countries (these trade effects will be taken into account in Sections 4 and 5).

The number of separate HS-02 sectors involved in anti-dumping has increased in the 2003–9 period. Basic iron and steel has dropped out of the picture completely in Argentina, with no petitions filed since 2002. Not only have the number of new anti-dumping orders in the Argentine steel sector fallen dramatically in recent years, but the orders put in place during the late 1990s and early 2000s have largely lapsed. Instead, there is a wide variety of different HS categories now affected by Argentina's anti-dumping, including footwear and electrical and mechanical machinery. This sectoral broadening also reflects the increasing range of products imported from China.

3.3 Argentine Administration of Anti-Dumping

Argentine Injury and Dumping Decisions

Broadly speaking, Argentina is like many other countries—the vast majority of investigations end with a positive dumping margin while a slightly lower majority results in a positive determination on injury.[15] Nevertheless, there has been a dramatic change in the administration of anti-dumping in Argentina over time.

In the early 1990s, Argentine authorities were quite strict in their application of anti-dumping, which is consistent with the open economy approach adopted by Argentina during this period. As noted above, Nogues and Baracat (2006) argue that Argentina's trade policymakers were able to use the anti-dumping system to effectively diffuse the pressures for broader protection in the early years of liberalisation.[16] For example, about one-third of all anti-dumping initiations from 1991 to 1994 resulted in a final anti-dumping duty.[17]

---

[15]Note that this discussion necessarily takes place at the investigation level, *ie* all HS-08 subject to the petition from the particular country.

[16]Miranda (2007) argues instead that the ability of Argentina to withstand pressures to use TTBs, especially anti-dumping, for protectionist purposes has been much more limited.

[17]Author's calculations based on Argentine anti-dumping authorities' annual reports.

Table 9.5: *Argentina's dumping and material injury decisions.*

Year of initiation	Initiated investigations	Positive dumping decision	Affirmative dumping decisions (%)	Positive injury decision	Affirmative material injury decision (%)
1995	25	15	60	10	40
1996	23	14	61	7	30
1997	13	12	92	10	77
1998	6	5	83	5	83
1999	21	20	95	20	95
2000	33	28	85	23	70
2001	26	24	92	21	81
2002	10	9	90	7	70
2003	1	1	100	1	100
2004	12	12	100	9	75
2005	8	8	100	7	88
2006	10	10	100	6	60
2007	7	7	100	7	100
2008	19	19	100	18	95
1995–2008	214	184	86	151	71

Dumping and injury decisions are usually rendered in a year subsequent to the initiation. All decisions are at the investigation level (*eg* footwear from China); withdrawn and terminated investigations are not included.

Source: Temporary Trade Barriers Database (Bown 2010).

Table 9.5 shows a breakdown of the decisions for the 1995–2008 sample.[18] The table includes the number of initiations in each year as well as the number that ended in either a positive dumping or material injury decision in a subsequent year. Note that these are based on the investigation level (*eg* hot-rolled steel sheet from Kazakhstan) rather than the individual HS-08 product level (*eg* 20 different tariff lines for each hot-rolled steel investigation for Kazakhstan) used in many of the tables above. This level of aggregation is appropriate because the decisions about injury and dumping are made at the investigation level.

Argentina's authorities exhibited a continued reluctance to approve anti-dumping petitions filed in 1995 and 1996, as only 60% and 61% of investigations, respectively, resulted in a positive dumping decision. Positive injury decisions were even less likely with only a 40% and 30% affirmative rate for investigations filed in these two years. Argentine firms could certainly not presume that they would win an anti-dumping case during this period.

[18]The 1991–4 investigation data from Moore and Zanardi (2009) do not include a breakdown of dumping and injury investigations, so this information is not reported here. Any investigations for which there is not yet a final decision by the time this study was completed are not included.

This trend changes in subsequent years as Argentine authorities became increasingly likely to approve petitions. Argentine authorities made a positive determination of dumping in 86% of all investigations initiated between 1995 and 2008. Almost 72% also resulted in a final positive injury decision. There is clearly a very high probability that dumping orders will be imposed. Moreover, there is an upward trend. For investigations begun in 2000, 85% resulted in a positive dumping margin and 70% in a positive injury decision. By 2003, these percentages rose to 100% for dumping and remained so for the rest of the sample. A finding of injury became much more likely as well; 85% of investigations resulted in an affirmative injury decision for investigations initiated in the 2003–8 period, with some year-to-year variation. It is too early to ascertain what the patterns are in the post-crisis stage. However, there is little reason to expect that the percentage of affirmative investigations would decrease relative to the pre-crisis experience.

It is also necessary to take into account how long an anti-dumping measure stays in place, not simply the counts of new investigations. This is examined in more detail, especially with regard to the percentage of trade affected through ongoing TTB measures. Figure 9.3(a) depicts the duration of Argentina's anti-dumping orders at the investigation level, measured from the year in which the order was first imposed to the date it was revoked. Note that the duration for orders that remain in place as of June 2010 is included; for those instances, duration is measured up to 2010. The mean duration for the entire sample is 4.7 years, *ie* just below the 5 years suggested by the sunset review procedures in the Uruguay Round Anti-Dumping Agreement. There are, however, many cases that extend far beyond the 5 years, including three steel orders of 11 years and two others of 12 years.

Once again, there is strong evidence of important changes in the administration of Argentina's anti-dumping system over time. For cases that were initiated in 1995, the average duration for imposed measures was 2.6 years. No order from that year remained in place after 2001. Thus, anti-dumping was very much a short-term trade restriction in the early days of Argentina's intensive anti-dumping use. This also means that Argentine anti-dumping cases did not generally last long enough even to be subject to a five-year sunset review process mandated by the Uruguay Round Anti-Dumping Agreement. This places early Argentine anti-dumping use into sharp contrast with the US experience; Moore (2006) demonstrates that the USA almost always renewed its anti-dumping orders after five years during this period.

The duration of Argentina's anti-dumping orders has changed significantly during the 2000s. Only 6 of the cases initiated in 2001 that resulted in final dumping orders had been terminated as of June 2010; 13 remained in place 9 years later. Only 5 investigations that were initiated *after* 2001 were revoked by June 2010. In other words, it is not only more likely in the first decade of the 2000s that an anti-dumping investigation will result in an imposed restriction in place, but anti-dumping orders are also more likely to remain

(a)

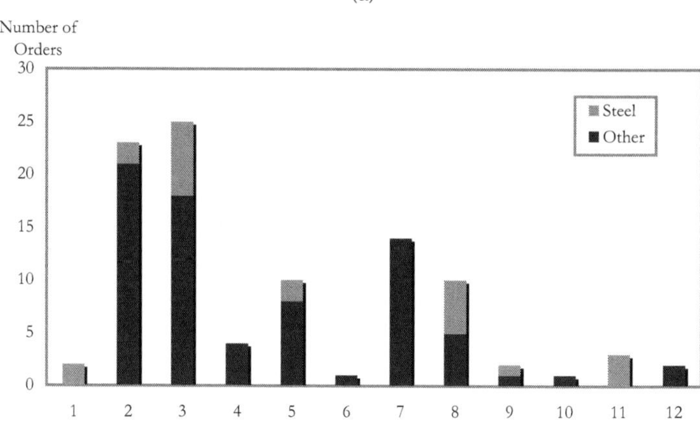

(b)

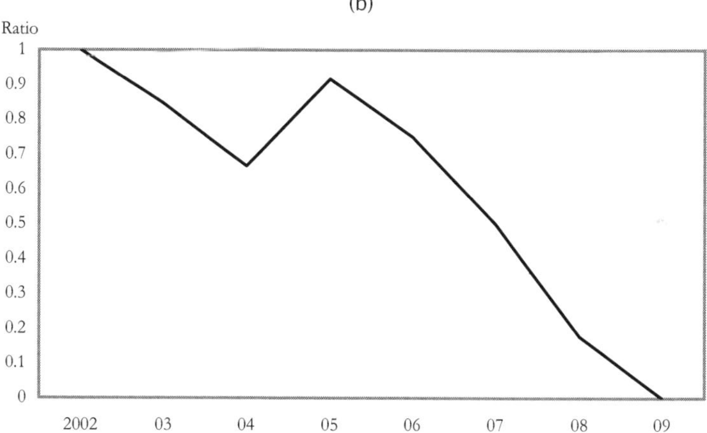

Figure 9.3: *Duration of Argentine anti-dumping orders (in years): (a) number of anti-dumping orders in effect by length of years; (b) share of anti-dumping orders removed in five years.*

Source: author's calculations using *Temporary Trade Barriers Database* (Bown 2010). In (a), duration is the difference between the year when the measure is imposed and the year when it is revoked. For orders remaining in place in 2010, duration is measured by 2010 minus the year when the measure is invoked. In (b), year is five years subsequent to the imposition of the original anti-dumping order.

in place for longer periods of time. Argentina has become much more like the USA and other countries regarding the *ongoing* nature of anti-dumping import protection (see Cadot *et al* (2008) for a systematic analysis of many countries' experience with anti-dumping duration for the 1979–2005 period).

Figure 9.3(b) shows this dynamic. One hundred percent of orders that came into force in 1997 were terminated within five years (denoted by the year '2002'). Subsequent to 2005, there has been a steady decrease in the number of Argentine anti-dumping orders removed within five years of their initial imposition. By 2009 (*ie* cases put in place in 2004), all orders exceed the five-year sunset review threshold.

In short, there is strong evidence that Argentine anti-dumping orders in the 2000s last longer than five years; nevertheless, this tendency *preceded* the 2008–9 international economic crisis.

Anti-Dumping Duty Level

The basis for the level of restrictions in anti-dumping actions is the dumping margin calculated as part of the investigation. Under the Anti-Dumping Agreement, this represents the upper bound of anti-dumping duties. Calculating the average dumping margin is difficult because this margin varies across firms within an investigation, *ie* it might differ across individual Chinese footwear exporters involved in the same investigation. In order to get some sense of the average margin calculated by Argentine authorities, the average of the high and low margins within an investigation as reported in Bown (2010) is used.

The average maximum dumping margin on this basis for Argentina's anti-dumping cases is 167% for the entire available data set, compared with a minimum of 96%. This means that individual foreign firms faced minimum possible anti-dumping duties of almost 100% on average, with much higher rates possible. The average maximum dumping margin for Chinese firms is much higher at 456%, with two notably high calculations: playing cards (2550%) and stainless steel cutlery (1450%).

Assessing the level of anti-dumping duty in place is even more complicated for Argentina. First, Argentina uses a 'lesser duty' rule, which means the anti-dumping margin may not exceed the amount that is necessary to eliminate injury to the domestic industry. This assessment is further obscured by an unusual aspect of the Argentine anti-dumping process, *ie* the frequent use of minimum prices for imported goods subject to an anti-dumping order instead of *ad valorem* duties as is more typical across countries. If the 'freight on board' price of imports is above this reference price, then no duty is imposed; if it is below the reference price, then a tariff (often a specific tariff) is imposed to eliminate this gap (Nogues and Baracat 2006, p 64).

The data at the investigation level include information on the type of final dumping measure in 152 instances. Just fewer than 60% (91 out of 152) of those investigations concluded with a minimum price target. An additional 8 cases were covered by a 'price undertaking', which is a similar means by which foreign firms agree to a target price in order to avoid duties. Only 53 cases had measures imposed as anti-dumping duties; 46 were *ad valorem* duties and 7 were specific duties.

Table 9.6: *Argentina's countervailing duty and safeguard actions (since 1995).*

	Targeted country	Measure	Initiation year	Revocation year
CVD measures				
Peaches in syrup	European Union	Yes	1995	N/A
Vital wheat gluten	European Union	Yes	1996	2006
Virgin and refined olive oil	European Union	Yes	1997	2006
Safeguard measures				
Footwear	N/A	Yes	1997	2000
Toys	N/A	Terminated	1998	N/A
Footwear	N/A	Yes	2000	2003
Motorcycles	N/A	Yes	2000	2004
Peaches	N/A	Yes	2001	2004
Coloured television sets	N/A	Yes	2004	2007
Recordable compact discs	N/A	Yes	2006	2010

Source: Temporary Trade Barriers Database (Bown 2010).

This pattern has changed somewhat over time. In the pre-2008 period, the percentage of price undertakings and minimum prices reached almost 70% (90 out of 129 investigations). In 2008–9, only 9 investigations resulted in minimum prices while 14 were standard anti-dumping duties. This change could reflect a more aggressive stance towards imports; foreign firms will face duties regardless of their own pricing behaviour as long as the anti-dumping order remains in place. In addition, a minimum price has effects similar to a quota; foreign firms are allowed to raise the price with the potential to benefit from an increase in quota rents.[19]

3.4 Safeguard Actions

World Trade Organization member countries can also restrict broad categories of imports, including those deemed traded 'fairly', under the safeguard provisions. Safeguards can be directed at a broad industry category (*eg* 'steel') from all import sources rather than a particular product as in anti-dumping or CVD cases (*eg* 'hot-rolled steel' of certain dimensions) from particular firms within a specific country. Safeguards therefore have the potential to affect a much wider range of imports than anti-dumping or CVD actions.

For various reasons, including the high standards for WTO compliance as determined by the Dispute Settlement Body especially with regard to 'serious injury' and the possible need for compensation to exporting countries, safeguard use has been very infrequent relative to anti-dumping. Argentina is

[19]Moore (2005) argues however that minimum price regimes may increase the ability of domestic and foreign oligopolists to raise prices at the expense of domestic consumers.

no exception to this characterisation. From 1995 to 2010, Argentina investigated only seven petitions for relief under its safeguard system, a list of which appears in Table 9.6. The list includes footwear (an original case initiated in 1997 plus an additional revised petition initiated in 2000), toys, motorcycles and mopeds, peaches, colour television sets and recordable compact discs. All but the safeguard investigation on toys resulted in import restrictions on the broad category named in the petition. This table also lists the small number of Argentine CVD cases since 1995.

Argentina does not follow the pattern sometimes seen in other nations whereby an industry files a safeguard and anti-dumping in the same industry category. For example, a common occurrence in the USA is for the steel industry to file many anti-dumping petitions simultaneously with a safeguard and/or CVD action. In Argentina, there is only one instance (footwear) where the same product is targeted across multiple TTB procedures, and even in this instance the overlap in HS-08 codes is not complete. The Argentine industry filed safeguard cases in 1997 and 2000 *in seriatum* and then followed up with an anti-dumping investigation against Chinese footwear covering many of the same product lines in 2009. Nevertheless, the anti-dumping investigation was initiated six years after the last footwear safeguard was terminated.

One particularly striking aspect of Argentina's safeguard use is that there were no such petitions filed in the 2008–9 financial crisis period, contrary to what would be expected from a period of economic distress *and* increased anti-dumping activity. Overall, imports fell quite markedly from 2008 to 2009, and one result is that it may have become difficult to find sufficient evidence to win a safeguard case. Also, Argentina did not initiate a China-specific safeguard, which is permitted under the provisions of China's WTO accession. Instead, China's exports have been affected almost exclusively by the use of anti-dumping measures during 2008–10. The bottom line is that Argentina's use of traditional administered protection (*ie* anti-dumping, CVD and safeguards) is dominated by the use of anti-dumping. This was true before the crisis and has continued through the global economic crisis that started in 2008.

4 VALUE OF TRADE AFFECTED BY ARGENTINA'S TEMPORARY TRADE BARRIERS

The discussion thus far examines the simple counts of cases (initiations and measures imposed). This has the distinct disadvantage that one case involving millions of dollars of imports is counted similarly to one with only very limited trade value. We turn, therefore, to a trade-weighted version of these measures in order to get a sense of the broader economic impact of TTBs. These are 'temporary' barriers and, consequently, are removed at a later date, at least in principle. Thus, we use an alternative measure that takes import values into account when assessing the 'stock' of measures that varies over time as new measures are imposed and older measures are removed.

4.1 Methodology

We adopt a modified version of the technique discussed in the Introduction (Bown, this volume) to measure the ongoing impact of contingent protection in Argentina. One version, presented below, contains the observed values of trade under an anti-dumping or safeguard measure as a share of total observed Argentine imports. The other version attempts to account for 'predicted' values in the absence of the restriction.[20] This analysis will take place at the HS-06 level rather than HS-08 because of data limitations.

As Bown (2011b) points out, the suppression of imports by trade restrictions means that using observed values of imports as a weight can be misleading, especially given the high level of restrictions found in many anti-dumping petitions. Thus, it is necessary to calculate an appropriate 'counterfactual' to approximate what imports might have been in the absence of any import restriction. In an ideal world, one would calculate the 'normal' level of imports for each individual product by considering past import levels, world supply and demand elasticities, and Argentina's domestic economic conditions, *ie* when no TTB is in place. However, this is a very problematic undertaking at the detailed HS-06 level used in this study.

In what follows, we calculate a 'predicted' import value for each year in which a TTB is in place using a simplistic rule. The counterfactual for the first year t in which a TTB is in place is based on the previous year's level of unrestricted imports. In particular, imports at the HS-06 level subject to a TTB in year $t-1$ are multiplied by g_{it}, the percentage change in overall 'normal' import growth from year $t-1$ to t. The predicted level of HS-06 level imports for each industry is the maximum of the observed level in year t or the previous year, scaled up by the overall import growth rate. Using the maximum of the two ensures that the realities of the market take precedence over any prediction based on overall import growth. In subsequent years of the restriction's operation, we once again use the maximum of the previous year's predicted imports multiplied by g_{it} or the observed import levels.[21]

[20]Vandenbussche and Zanardi (2010) use a gravity equation approach to try to ascertain the overall trade effects of anti-dumping among intensive (or 'heavy') users of anti-dumping among developing countries.

[21]This approach may be clearer if we use a simple example. Suppose that observed Chinese imports for a particular HS-06 product subject to a TTB are \$100 in 2000, \$120 in 2001, \$50 in 2002 and \$50 in 2003. Import restrictions are in place for 2001 through 2003. Furthermore, suppose that non-restricted import growth rates are 10% for all years. Consequently, the import level used would be \$100 in 2000, \$120 in 2001, \$132 in 2002 and \$145.2 in 2003.

The 'normal' growth rate is calculated based on Bown (2011b). This is the simple percentage change for each year in 'non-restricted' import flows, *ie* all HS-06 categories not covered in anti-dumping, CVD or safeguard cases in *any* year during 1995–2010 for *any* country exporting to Argentina. These categories are ones in which there are no direct effects of TTBs; their growth rate is taken to reflect the 'normal' rate at which imports have changed in Argentina. This growth rate may be higher or lower than what might be expected for an individual product subject to a TTB. However, it might also be expected that those sectors faced with extraordinary restrictions might have grown even more than those for the economy as a whole, so this is probably a conservative approach.

When calculating the predicted share of imports affected by TTBs, the following procedure is used. The numerator is the predicted value for each year for all anti-dumping and safeguard measures. The denominator is the sum of the imports not affected by a TTB in that year plus the predicted value for those sectors under a TTB for that same year. For the observed values, we simply use the total value of trade in sectors for which there is an ongoing anti-dumping action, divided by the observed value of trade. Naturally, the former measure will always exceed the latter measure, since trade restrictions reduce the flow of goods across borders.

4.2 Aggregate Effects of TTB Use

Figure 9.4 includes the combined import coverage of the stock of Argentina's anti-dumping, safeguard and CVD actions. Note that this is not just the effect of new measures imposed in any particular year, but also reflects the continued presence as well as the eventual revocation of the measure. One series is the ratio of observed import values of sectors subject to a TTB to the observed values of imports into Argentina. The other series is the predicted values of TTB imports as a share of predicted total imports.

The observed values reflect some of the patterns noted above using descriptive statistics. In particular, TTBs had very little impact from 1995 to 1999; only 1.5% of total observed imports were affected by anti-dumping and safeguards by 1999. This rose to 2.6% by 2001, *ie* the year of maximum stress associated with the overvalued peso. Affected imports remained below 2% for Argentina up until 2008. Through the global economic crisis period, the observed share of imports affected by TTBs rose to 2.8% by 2008 and then 2.7% by 2009.

However, there are indications that these simple statistics may significantly underestimate the effect of TTBs because of the suppression of imports. The counterfactual procedure described above results in a time series that has broadly similar patterns to the observed values through 2001 but diverges sharply thereafter. The predicted share of affected imports rises to an early peak during the disruptions of the peso crisis, then falls, and then rises again

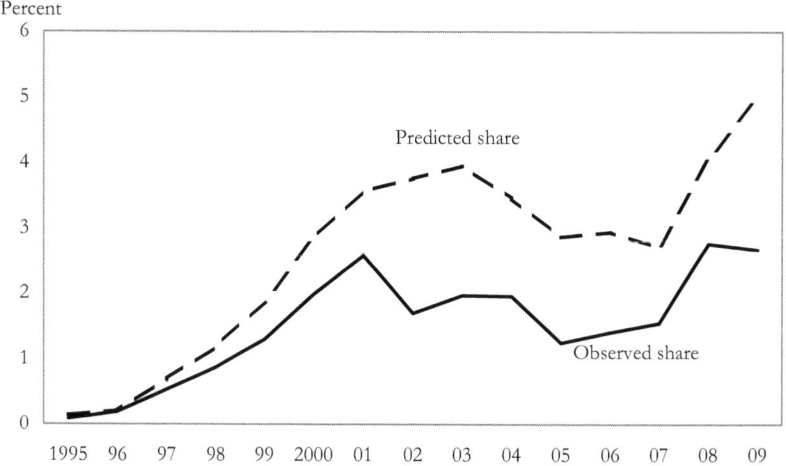

Figure 9.4: *Argentine imports (observed and predicted) affected by anti-dumping, CVD and safeguards.*

Source: author's calculations using Comtrade and *Temporary Trade Barriers Database* (Bown 2010). Share based on stock of restrictions in place.

in the post-global-crisis period. However, the level is much higher than the observed value. For example, the predicted share of affected imports rises to 4.0% in 2003 compared with 2.0% in the observed data. After the surge of contingent protection measures in the 1999–2000 period, the estimated levels in subsequent years are nearly double the observed values. This growth reflects the effects of the greater likelihood that new petitions will result in new measures (see Table 9.5) but also that existing measures are more likely to remain in place (see Figure 9.3(b)).

Perhaps most strikingly, there is a dramatic increase in the share of imports affected by TTBs in the post-crisis period. In 2008, the predicted share was 4.1% and it had reached 5.0% by 2009. This estimate suggests that Argentina was imposing TTBs in 2009 that involved almost twice as many imports as those affected in the immediate run-up to the peso crisis in 2002.

However, note that there are a number of investigations initiated in 2009 that were not yet completed by July 2010. We assumed that all investigations filed in 2009 in fact resulted in anti-dumping measures.[22] This is justifiable for two reasons. First, as demonstrated in Table 9.5, there is a very strong likelihood that such measures will result in an anti-dumping duty. This is especially true for investigations involving China, where the affirmative rate

[22]Recall that the 2010 import data were not available at the time of this study, so the 2010 shares cannot be computed.

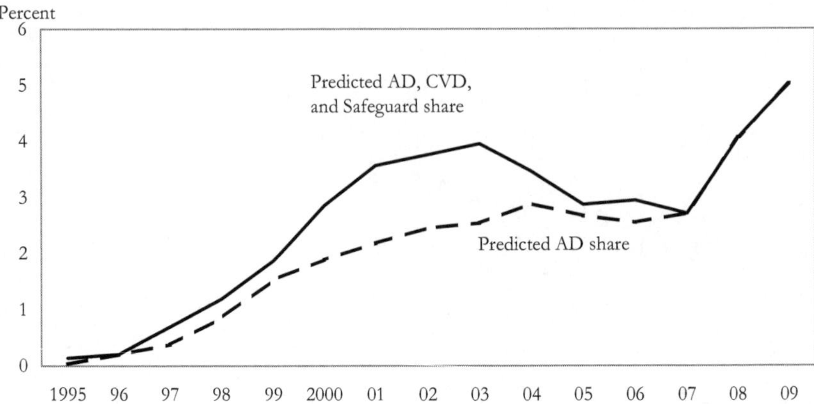

Figure 9.5: *Argentine anti-dumping, CVD and safeguard predicted share of total imports.*

Source: author's calculations using Comtrade and *Temporary Trade Barriers Database* (Bown 2010). Share based on stock of restrictions in place. The two lines coincide in 2007–9.

has essentially reached 100% in the crisis years, as detailed below. Second, there are likely to be trade effects even before the investigation is completed, as noted by Staiger and Wolak (1994), so that petitions filed in 2009 are likely to have real trade effects in the short term even if they are not subject to a final anti-dumping restriction.

These results are consistent with the view that Argentina's use of TTBs may have begun to play a much larger role through the global economic crisis. It can be argued that this is clear evidence that Argentina was using anti-dumping measures to deal with the crisis. However, as noted above and discussed in more detail below, this change coincided with much more aggressive action with respect to China, which may have happened even in the absence of the economic crisis.

Figure 9.5 compares the predicted value of imports affected by anti-dumping and other TTBs. Anti-dumping has generally dominated the relative economic importance among TTBs, especially in the late 2000s. There is, however, a surge of imports affected by safeguards that began in 1997, rose to a peak in 2002 and subsequently faded. This reflects the effects of three safeguard actions. The first two are temporary restrictions on imports of footwear described above, and the third is on motorcycles. There is no evidence that this pattern of safeguards affecting large amounts of imports has continued; Argentina's new TTB use through the 2000s has become focused even more on anti-dumping. Countervailing duty actions had only a trivial effect throughout the period.

5 ARGENTINE USE OF ANTI-DUMPING AGAINST CHINA AND BRAZIL

The number of Argentine anti-dumping petitions against China has risen steadily. This complicates the process of ascertaining how much of the recent rise in anti-dumping actions is a consequence of the economic crisis and how much is due to growing concern about increased Chinese exports to Argentina. Table 9.7 includes a simple count of unique HS-08 product line imports from China affected by Argentina's anti-dumping actions during 1995–2010. Cases brought against Brazil, which had earlier been the focus of Argentine anti-dumping actions, are included for comparison. The table also includes the sectors (with counts aggregated up to the HS-02 level) most frequently involved in anti-dumping for each country. Brazilian exporters have been involved in 111 total initiations at the case level, compared with 181 for China. However, there are many more Chinese investigations that had not yet been completed at the time of this study, compared with Brazil, which reflects the rash of cases brought against China in 2009–10.

Brazilian cases are concentrated in the 1995–2001 period soon after the implementation of Mercosur obligations. In addition, Argentina focused on basic iron and steel (HS-02 sector 72), with 35 cases initiated during this period, 34 of which ended in a final anti-dumping measure. The vast majority of these cases were in only two steel sector investigations: 'hot-rolled steel' initiated in 1998 and 'cold-rolled steel' initiated in 1999, each of which involved multiple individual HS lines combined into a single anti-dumping investigation. In subsequent periods, anti-dumping actions against Brazil were scattered across various HS sectors with no particular pattern. Furthermore, Argentine investigations against its primary Mercosur partner had slowed to a trickle by the end of the 2000s.

Perhaps most striking is that Argentine authorities imposed anti-dumping orders on Chinese exporters in 87% of the cases during 2002–7 and 100% of the cases in 2008–10 for which there is a final anti-dumping decision (a handful of cases were withdrawn by the domestic industry). Some of the cases in the latter period have not yet reached the final stage, but 100% of the preliminary decisions during this time frame have resulted in at least temporary restrictions. In short, the 2002–10 period shows that Chinese firms always lose anti-dumping petitions in Argentina.

Another notable comparison *vis-à-vis* Brazil is that there is a wide distribution of sectors involved in Chinese anti-dumping cases, and no particular sector stands out as with Brazilian steel imports. The largest single group of cases (30) is in footwear but this simply reflects the large number of product lines in one particular anti-dumping investigation in 2009. Moreover, there is not a single case against Chinese exports of basic iron and steel (HS-02 sector 72) but numerous cases involving electrical and mechanical machinery. The implication seems clear: Argentine industries and authorities have concerns about a wide variety of Chinese products.

Table 9.7: *Argentina's anti-dumping cases brought against China and Brazil.*

	1995–2010	1995–2001		2002–2007		2008–10 (completed decisions)	
	All initiations	Initiations	New measures	Initiations	New measures	Initiations	New measures
China							
Articles of clothing (62)	11	0	0	0	0	0	0
Footwear (64)	30	0	0	0	0	30	30
Articles of iron and steel (73)	18	5	5	3	3	3	3
Tools (82)	15	8	8	0	0	4	4
Mechanical machinery (84)	18	10	9	0	0	2	2
Electrical machinery (85)	16	6	4	5	4	0	0
Optical and surgical equipment (90)	11	2	0	6	6	—	—
Others	62	15	12	9	7	12	12
Total	181	46	38	23	20	51	51

Table 9.7: *Continued.*

	1995–2010	1995–2001		2002–2007		2008–10 (completed decisions)	
	All initiations	Initiations	New measures	Initiations	New measures	Initiations	New measures
Brazil							
Meat (2)	5	5	2	0	0	0	0
Articles of wood (44)	6	6	0	0	0	0	0
Basic iron and steel (72)	35	35	34	0	0	0	0
Articles of iron and steel (73)	8	6	6	0	0	0	0
Tools (82)	11	4	4	2	0	4	4
Mechanical machinery (84)	9	7	0	0	0	0	0
Electrical machinery (85)	12	8	6	3	3	0	0
Others	25	11	7	7	6	2	2
Total	111	82	59	12	9	6	6

Based on HS-08-country pairs. HS-02 codes are shown in parentheses. Note that many petitions filed in 2009 and 2010 have not yet reached a final decision.

Source: Temporary Trade Barriers Database (Bown 2010).

Table 9.8: *Argentine merchandise imports (billions of dollars).*

Year	Overall	USA	Brazil	China	Japan	EU15	High income OECD	Low and upper middle income
1995	19.8	4.2	4.2	0.6	0.7	5.7	11.8	6.9
1996	23.3	4.7	5.3	0.7	0.7	6.6	13.4	8.5
1997	29.6	6.1	6.9	1.0	1.1	7.9	16.9	10.9
1998	31.1	6.2	7.1	1.2	1.5	8.5	17.9	11.5
1999	25.3	5.0	5.6	1.0	1.1	7.3	14.9	9.3
2000	24.6	4.8	6.5	1.2	1.0	5.7	12.9	10.4
2001	19.9	3.8	5.3	1.1	0.8	4.5	10.1	8.6
2002	8.7	1.8	2.5	0.3	0.3	2.0	4.5	3.7
2003	13.4	2.3	4.7	0.7	0.4	2.7	6.0	6.7
2004	21.4	3.4	7.6	1.4	0.6	4.0	9.0	11.3
2005	28.4	4.5	10.6	1.5	0.6	5.3	11.3	15.4
2006	32.7	4.3	11.9	3.1	0.9	5.5	12.1	18.8
2007	42.5	5.3	14.7	5.1	1.2	6.9	15.1	24.6
2008	54.3	7.0	18.0	7.1	1.4	8.3	18.8	31.3
2009	38.3	5.4	11.8	5.4	0.9	6.4	14.7	21.3

Source: Comtrade.

The increasingly intense focus on China reflects its growing importance in Argentina's international trade. Table 9.8 shows that overall manufacturing imports from China increased nearly 12-fold, from $0.6 billion in 1995 to a high of $7.1 billion in 2008. This compares with about a three-fold increase in Argentina's imports from all sources, from $19.8 billion to $54 billion for the same time period, which closely matches that sourced from Brazil, Argentina's largest import source throughout the period of analysis. In sharp contrast, US and EU15 exports to Argentina rose only slightly in nominal terms. In short, China's share of Argentina's imports grew dramatically, both in terms of absolute levels and as a share of overall imports (from 3.1% in 1995 to over 13% in 2009). China was on the radar screen of those in Argentina concerned about import protection even before the global economic turmoil began in 2008.

Even the increase in Chinese imports described above underestimates the increased potential importance of Chinese market penetration given Argentina's already widespread anti-dumping use against them. The observed share of Chinese products subject to Argentine anti-dumping actions went from $3.5 million in 1995 to over $348 million in 2010 (though this latter figure reflects cases for which no final decisions have been made). In the absence of such anti-dumping actions, Chinese exports to Argentina would undoubtedly have been larger.

Figure 9.6 shows the dramatic increase in Chinese exports to Argentina as well as the ramped up use of anti-dumping by Argentine authorities. Total Argentine imports from China remained relatively flat through most of the

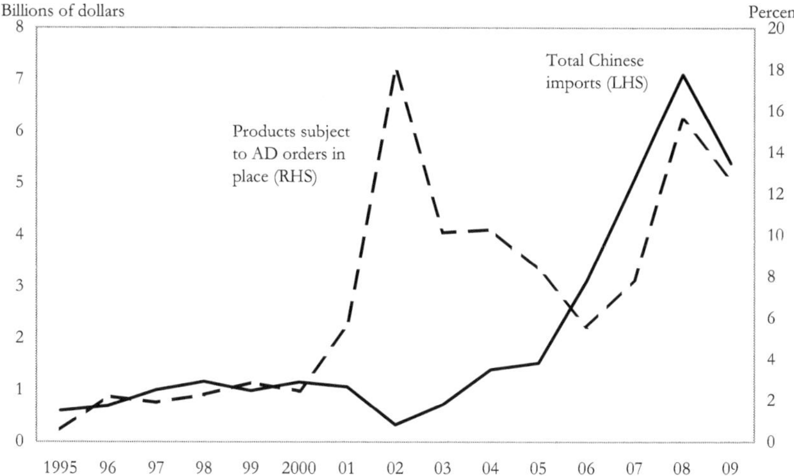

Figure 9.6: *Chinese imports (observed and share subject to anti-dumping).*
Source: author's calculations using Comtrade and *Temporary Trade Barriers Database* (Bown 2010).

1990s, with a notable decrease after the economic trauma following the peso devaluation of 2002. Subsequently, imports from China have risen steadily before falling again in 2009, though to an even higher level than they had been in 2007.

The share of Chinese imports subject to Argentine anti-dumping measures closely follows the overall import pattern, with the notable exception of 2003 when over 18% of Chinese products sold in Argentina involved anti-dumping actions. While the total percentage fell in the latter part of that decade, Chinese imports subject to anti-dumping orders once again reached over 12% during the post-financial-crisis period.

6 OTHER MEASURES OF RECENT ARGENTINE TRADE POLICY

Argentina may also restrict imports through other means. We first briefly consider the average applied tariffs across sectors in Argentina. Naturally, this gives an indication of how imports are affected through traditional tariffs rather than temporary measures that are the focus of this chapter.

Recall that Figure 9.1 included the annual average (unweighted) applied MFN tariffs for all sectors, which rose from 11.5% in 1995–7 to 13% in 1998–2001. This corresponds to the pressures associated with real exchange-rate appreciation during the period in which the peso was pegged to the dollar. Subsequently, average tariffs fell consistently from 2003 (11.8%) until 2008. There was a small uptick in 2009 when it reached 9%, but this is still lower than in any year other than 2008. Thus, the Argentine government may have increased its imposition of anti-dumping measures in 2007–10, but this has not been accompanied by broad increases in applied MFN duties. This is despite the fact that Argentina's tariffs remain far below their bound rates, so there is significant tariff overhang.

However, given the provisions of Mercosur, it is important to note that Argentina's tariffs are not set in a vacuum. In particular, any changes to Argentina's applied tariffs in principle should be coordinated with movements in the CET as laid out by the customs union's rules. Argentina might have preferred to have higher tariffs than allowed in the CET, or even lower. Thus, an analysis of the CET only allows for an imperfect interpretation of Argentina's particular preferences for MFN tariffs. In addition, the increase in the number of Mercosur PTAs (such as with Colombia) means that the effective average tariff is below the one calculated here.

Argentina restricted imports during 2008–10 in other ways, though with a much less certain trade effect. For example, the US Department of Commerce has compiled a list of Argentina's public notifications of new non-automatic import licences and noted an important increase after October 2008. In 2009, there were at least 200 such notifications at the HS-08 level, 93 of which were in the textiles sector (HS-02 sectors 50 to 63) and in electrical and mechanical machinery sectors (HS-02 sectors 84 and 85). Other opaque measures catalogued by Global Trade Alert include, for example, reference prices for imports (see Global Trade Alert (2010a,b)).

Unfortunately, it is very difficult to ascertain how restrictive these import licence regimes and reference prices are since they depend on the bureaucratic implementation of each licence. At the very least, this increases the uncertainty under which importers operate in Argentina, which in turn is likely to decrease trade.

7 CONCLUSIONS

Argentina has gone back and forth in its commitment to having an economy that is open to international competition. For decades, Argentina pursued import substitution policies. Its government became a star example of economic liberalisation in the 1990s when it reduced tariffs and generally embraced the strictures of the 'Washington Consensus'. After the trauma of the peso crisis in 2001 and 2002, Argentina's traditional scepticism about openness to the global economy regained its prominence and the government began to undertake strong interventions in the economy. This ultimately shallow commitment to a liberal trade regime raised the question of how Argentina would respond to the economic pressures associated with the global economic crisis that began in 2008.

This chapter makes clear that Argentina has relied heavily on anti-dumping as a means of limiting imports since the mid-1990s, with only very limited reliance on CVD and safeguards throughout the period (and no use at all since 2007). As Nogues and Baracat (2006) point out, the Argentine government used anti-dumping only in a very limited fashion during the early 1990s. This ability to withstand the intense pressures for protection has broken down in the 2000s, as is evidenced by the case of anti-dumping. In particular, anti-dumping petitions have been approved more frequently by the government and the imposed measures have longer lives. While roughly 50% of petitions were 'approved' in the 1990s, this rate ratcheted up steadily to 85% in the 2006–8 period. This caused 2.7% of all observed Argentine imports to be affected by anti-dumping by 2009. Once the suppressed trade that occurs because of the highly restrictive actions is taken into account, trade in these sectors might have been twice as much in the absence of anti-dumping actions.

The most notable change in Argentina has been the dramatically larger role that imports from China have played in its application of TTBs. Chinese exports are far more likely to be subject to Argentine anti-dumping actions than their overall import share would suggest. In 2007–10, Chinese exporters targeted by Argentine anti-dumping were virtually guaranteed to face significant trade barriers as a result. Indeed, the estimate provided here suggests that, by 2009, over 13% of all Chinese exports to Argentina were affected by anti-dumping, either by new petitions or the ongoing effects of orders that were imposed in earlier years.

This increased focus on China has occurred simultaneously with the economic crisis. It is therefore difficult to determine whether this more intense targeting of China would have happened in the absence of the global financial meltdown. Because the increased Argentine targeting of China in TTB cases began before the crisis, there is no reason to believe that it will change even after the Argentine and world economies have regained their footing. Nonetheless, there is relatively little evidence that Argentina has responded to the global financial crisis by dramatically increasing import barriers across the board.

Michael Moore is Professor of Economics and International Affairs at the Department of Economics, Elliott School of International Affairs, and Institute for International Economic Policy at George Washington University.

REFERENCES

Bown, C. P. (2011a). Introduction. In *The Great Recession and Import Protection: The Role of Temporary Trade Barriers* (ed. C. P. Bown). London: CEPR/World Bank. (Chapter 1 of this volume.)

Bown, C. P. (2011b). Taking stock of anti-dumping, safeguards, and countervailing duties 1990–2009. *The World Economy*, forthcoming.

Bown, C. P. (2010). *Temporary Trade Barriers Database*. World Bank (July). URL: http://econ.worldbank.org/ttbd.

Cadot, O., J. de Melo, and B. Tumurchudur (2008). Anti-dumping sunset reviews: the uneven reach of WTO disciplines. Mimeo, University of Lausanne.

Global Trade Alert (2010a). Argentina: reference prices for designated imports (May). Reference data. URL: www.globaltradealert.org/measure/argentina-reference-prices-designated-imports.

Global Trade Alert (2010b). Argentina: reference prices for drinking glasses (December). Reference data. URL: www.globaltradealert.org/measure/argentina-reference-prices-drinking-glasses.

IMF World Economic Outlook (2010). IMF and statistics. Reference data. URL: www.imf.org/external/data.htm.

Miranda, J. (2007). Fighting fire with fire and getting burnt: a review of safeguards and anti-dumping in Latin American trade liberalization: review essay. *World Trade Review* **6**(2), 311–312.

Moore, M. O. (2006). An econometric analysis of US anti-dumping sunset review decisions. *Review of World Economics* **142**(1), 122–150.

Moore, M. O. (2005). VERs and price undertakings under the WTO. *Review of International Economics* **13**(2), 298–310.

Moore, M. O., and M. Zanardi (2009). Does anti-dumping use contribute to trade liberalization in developing countries? *Canadian Journal of Economics* **42**(2), 469–495.

Nogues, J. J., and E. Baracat (2006). Political economy of anti-dumping and safeguards in Argentina; safeguards and anti-dumping. In *Latin American Trade Liberalization: Fighting Fire with Fire* (ed. J. M. Finger and J. J. Nogues). New York: Palgrave Macmillan.

Prusa, T. (2001). On the spread and impact of anti-dumping. *Canadian Journal of Economics* **34**(3), 591–611.

Rossi, P., M. Kagatsume, and M. Prosperi (2009). Impact of export control policy measures in an attempt to tame Argentina's inflation. In *International Marketing and Trade of Quality Food Products* (ed. M. Canavari, N. Cantore, A. Castellini, E. Pignatti and R. Spadoni). Wageningen: Wageningen Academic Publishers.

Staiger, R. W., and F. A. Wolak (1994). Measuring industry specific protection: anti-dumping in the United States. *Brookings Papers on Economic Activity: Microeconomics* **1** 51–118.

Vandenbussche, H., and M. Zanardi (2010). The chilling trade effects of anti-dumping proliferation. *European Economic Review* **54**(6), 760–777.

World Development Indicators (2010). Reference data, World Bank. URL: http://data.worldbank.org/data-catalog/world-development-indicators.

Zanardi, M. (2004). Anti-dumping: what are the numbers to discuss at Doha? *World Economy* **27**(3), 403–433.

10

Mexico: A Liberalisation Leader?

RAYMOND ROBERTSON[1]

1 INTRODUCTION

The goal of this chapter is to illustrate how Mexico's use of TTBs has evolved since their inception, with a particular focus on the 2008–10 financial crisis. Mexico is an important case to consider for several reasons. First, as an early liberaliser, Mexico is considered to be a leader among developing countries. In examining the early development of Mexico's anti-dumping policies, Niels and Ten Kate (2004) describe Mexico as an 'aggressive' user of anti-dumping policies and suggest that Mexico may be an indicator of how other emerging countries may employ anti-dumping policies. Vandenbussche and Zanardi (2010) include Mexico among the developing countries that significantly employed anti-dumping measures (their analysis covered 1980–2003). Niels and Ten Kate (2006) suggest that the spread of anti-dumping activity to developing countries, including Mexico, may be an obstacle to free trade.

Second, Mexico holds a unique 'intermediate' position in the world economy. Its GDP per capita in 2009 was $13,200 (down from $14,300 in 2008), ranking 84th in the world.[2] At the same time, Mexico was one of the first to enter into a free-trade agreement with a developed country—the NAFTA with the USA and Canada—and, as such, experiences the extremely strong influence of the USA in many areas (see Weintraub (2010) for a discussion of key issues of the US-Mexican relationship). In particular, Mexico's trade is dominated by the USA.

Although Mexico's trade is dominated by the USA, the rise of China has played a particularly important role in shaping Mexico's TTBs. Several studies have remarked on the surge of anti-dumping duty initiations against China in the early 1990s, but few studies have focused on the lingering effect that these initiations have had—an effect that emerges starkly when studying the stock of anti-dumping activity.

[1]Department of Economics; Macalester College, 1600 Grand Ave., St. Paul, MN 55105, USA. Email: robertson@macalester.edu.

[2]Data taken from CIA World Factbook.

The significance of the US relationship and the early activity against China brought Mexico to the attention of many researchers. Several studies analyse the determinants of Mexico's anti-dumping initiations, with a particular focus on macroeconomic determinants. Niels and Ten Kate (2004), Francois and Niels (2006), and Bianchi and Sanguinetti (2006) suggest that, when macroeconomic conditions, such as GDP, exchange rates, and the current account balance deteriorate, Mexico is more likely to initiate anti-dumping claims. The 2008–10 financial crisis provides yet another unfortunate opportunity in which to evaluate the role of macroeconomic fluctuations.

These and other papers also identify the sectors that have attracted the most anti-dumping initiations. Francois and Niels (2006), for example, note that 62.8% of investigations between 1987 and 2000 fall into just three categories: steel (and steel products), chemicals, and textiles (and textile products). In the last ten years, however, the economic landscape has shifted. Several well-known anti-dumping cases have emerged that have changed the mix of sectors affected by anti-dumping measures. For example, Mexican antidumpings against US beef that were eliminated on 11 August 2010 covered a significant share of Mexican beef imports from the USA for the previous ten years.

This chapter therefore makes several contributions to the growing literature on Mexico's use of TTBs. First, this chapter focuses mostly on the stock, rather than the flow, of anti-dumping coverage. As with the other chapters in this volume, this shift in focus gives a more complete and accurate picture of anti-dumping coverage. Second, we update recent findings in terms of both geography (the countries that Mexico targets) and products, revealing important shifts in how Mexico has been applying anti-dumping measures over time. Third, this chapter also employs a probit analysis of determinants of affirmative decisions that reveals how Mexico's policy has changed over time. Together, these three contributions help to explain Mexico's anti-dumping behaviour during the 2008–10 economic crisis.

The findings of this chapter contrast sharply with previous research in several ways. First, as noted above, previous work that has looked at the relationship between macroeconomic variables and Mexico's anti-dumping initiations might suggest that the 2008 crisis would have been accompanied by an increase in anti-dumping activity. In practice, the results suggest the opposite. Far from being 'aggressive' with its anti-dumping policies, in 2008, 2009 and 2010, Mexico was at or near the bottom of the list of countries initiating new anti-dumping investigations. The stock of covered industries and covered trade volume also fell dramatically in 2008, though for reasons that seem unrelated to the economic crisis. Second, although Mexico has significantly diversified its trade over the last decade, anti-dumping measures remain concentrated on two countries: the USA and China. While other countries are increasingly involved, their share of trade, and, therefore, their role in Mexico's larger anti-dumping picture, remains small. Third, the probit results suggest that the probability of an initial affirmative dumping decision has fallen over time. Together, these results might be consistent with an explanation that Mexico's use of anti-dumping policies has shifted from political to economic and, in any case, may signal a move away from an aggressive use of TTBs.

This chapter describes Mexico's anti-dumping policies in five additional sections. The first presents an overview of Mexico's trade policies and trade volumes during the 1990–2010 period to provide context for the evolution of TTB policies. Section 3 describes the three foundations necessary for understanding Mexico's TTB activity: the birth and development of the TTB regime, China, and the USA. Section 4 describes Mexico's implementation and use of anti-dumping duties. Section 5 discusses CVDs and safeguard measures. The final section concludes by summarising and providing directions for future research.

2 CONTEXT: TRADE POLICY, TRADE, AND MACROECONOMIC FLUCTUATIONS

The 'great trade collapse' that came with the financial crisis was especially acute for Mexico (Robertson 2009). It is almost a cliché to say that Mexico's economy is closely tied to the US economy. Nevertheless, context plays an important part in understanding Mexico's trade policy response to the crisis, especially with respect to TTBs. In this section we briefly review the evolution of Mexico's trade policy, recent trade patterns, and some of the specific implications of the crisis.

2.1 Mexico's Trade Policy: A Brief Review

For much of the 20th century, Mexico was a leader in the 'import substitution industrialisation' model that was largely characterised by very high tariffs and little emphasis on exports. As is well known to students of the Mexican economy, Mexico's debt default in 1982 triggered the beginning of the 'lost decade' of low GDP growth and the end of the import substitution industrialisation era. Mexico began to liberalise in 1983 through revisions to the *maquiladora* policies that governed investment and production along Mexico's US border region. Possibly the next most important step in liberalisation was the 1985 decision to join the GATT—a move that included significant revisions to tariffs and import restrictions domestically but also brought Mexico into the international community and the rules that govern all members of the GATT.

When Mexico joined the GATT in 1986, the drop in tariffs was significant. The maximum tariff fell from 100% in 1985 to 20% by 1992.[3] At the same

[3]The drop in tariffs was widespread but apparently concentrated in less-skill-intensive industries, contributing to a rise in the relative price of skill-intensive goods that helps to explain the subsequent rise in income inequality (see Hanson and Harrison (1999) and Robertson (2004)).

Table 10.1: *Mexico's free-trade agreements and tariffs.*

Partner(s)	Date of signature	Tariffs 1991	Tariffs 2008
NAFTA: USA	17/12/1992	13.70	1.32
NAFTA: Canada	17/12/1992	13.85	1.56
Costa Rica	5/4/1994	14.00	1.35
G3: Colombia	13/6/1994	15.49	4.56
Bolivia	10/9/1994	14.60	3.28
Nicaragua	18/12/1997	10.47	1.61
Chile	17/4/1998	15.73	4.34
Israel	10/4/2000	14.56	3.26
El Salvador	29/6/2000	14.12	1.89
Honduras	29/6/2000	14.27	2.62
Guatemala	29/6/2000	14.74	1.72
EFTA: Iceland	27/11/2000	13.49	2.98
EFTA: Norway	27/11/2000	13.55	2.94
EFTA: Switzerland/ Liechtenstein	27/11/2000	12.76	2.97
Uruguay	15/11/2003	15.62	5.16
Japan	17/9/2004	14.10	8.52
Non-FTA countries			
Argentina	—	13.98	11.03
Brazil	—	13.67	10.56
Panama	—	16.02	14.67
Paraguay	—	13.09	10.26
Peru	—	15.73	12.22

G3 represents Mexico, Colombia and Venezuela. In May 2006, Venezuelan president Hugo Chavez announced that Venezuela would withdraw from the agreement. EFTA stands for the European Free Trade Association, which was established in 1960 and today consists of Iceland, Norway, Switzerland and Liechtenstein. Tariff data for Switzerland and Liechtenstein are pooled in the tariff database. Tariff rates are the simple averages of *ad valorem* taken across all HS-06 products available in the WITS database.

Source: author's calculations from Foreign Trade Information System (2011).

time, Mexico fixed the value of the peso and initiated macroeconomic initiatives (the *pactos*) to control inflation. In 1991 the government liberalised the capital accounts and in 1992 it signed the NAFTA. At the time, the domestic manufacturing sector was quite disconcerted about the rate of change in policies and the loss of protection from import competition (Poitras and Robertson 1994).

One of the goals of the NAFTA was to codify this relationship and to mitigate the variance that had characterised Mexican trade and economic policy in the previous 50 years. The agreement's main goal was to increase both trade and investment and, while the NAFTA's influence has been debated, it is clear that both trade and investment increased after the NAFTA was implemented in 1994.

The NAFTA was significant because Mexico's situation in the global economy is unique. There are few, if any, developing countries that share such a close economic relationship with a developed country. Not only does Mexico share a 2,000-mile border with the USA, but trade, immigration and capital flows—factors that often define globalisation—are overwhelmingly dominated by the relationship with the USA.

Realising the overwhelming influence of the USA may have been concentrating risk, Mexico subsequently pursued free-trade agreements with partners all over the world. Table 10.1 lists Mexico's free-trade agreements and illustrates the change in tariffs for countries with and without trade agreements in 1991 and 2008. Mexico started with Latin American countries and then signed agreements with the European Union, Israel and Japan. While tariffs fall for every country in the table, it is clear that those countries engaged in free-trade agreements with Mexico had much larger reductions in average tariffs facing their exports. Not surprisingly, these agreements coincided with dramatic reductions in the overall trade-weighted average tariffs. Figure 10.1 shows the evolution of the trade-weighted average tariff between 1991 and 2008. There is little evidence to suggest that Mexico has not aggressively embraced trade liberalisation.

One important note is that these tariff data come from the WITS database, which is considered to be the most comprehensive and authoritative tariff database, and yet there is not a single separate tariff entry for China. The lack of a separate line for China in any year of the database is the result of at least two possible explanations. First, either the database is missing tariffs that Mexico actually applied against China, or Mexico did not impose separate tariffs against China before China joined the WTO in 2001. While the first explanation is possible, it seems more likely that Mexico did not impose separate tariffs against China before China joined the WTO. The lack of separate tariffs assigned to China plays an important part in understanding Mexico's pattern of anti-dumping duties.

2.2 *Recent Patterns in Mexican Trade*

To describe the changes in Mexico's imports, we use data from the UN's Comtrade database, one of the common sources used in the chapters in this volume. There are several versions of the trade data. Since the 1990s are particularly important for the Mexican case, we use data coded by the six-digit 1992 Harmonized System unless noted otherwise. These data include annual imports from each of Mexico's trade partners in nominal US dollars. For the purposes of this chapter, we convert all trade values to real using the US Consumer Price Index, with 2000 as the base year.

Figure 10.2 shows the evolution of the real value of Mexican imports decomposed into the contributions of the main trading partners from 1990 to 2009.

Figure 10.1: *Mexican average tariff rates.*

Source: trade-weighted tariff calculated using country and HS-06 product trade shares as weights using available tariff and trade data from WITS and Comtrade.

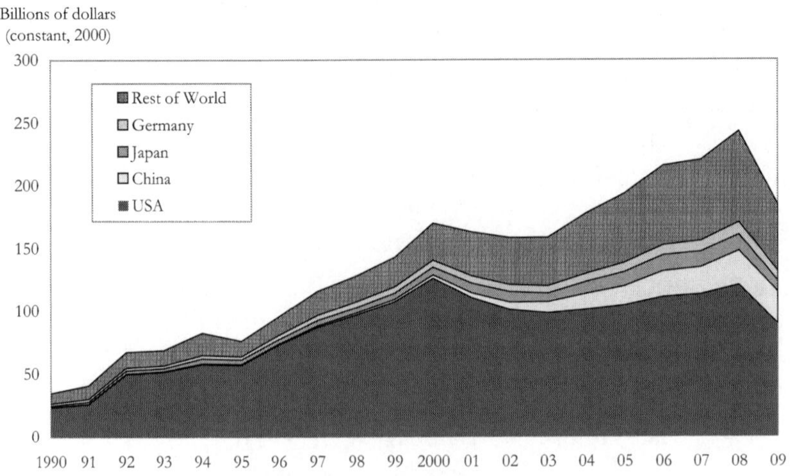

Figure 10.2: *Total Mexican imports.*

Source: WITS and Comtrade.

The combined area (represented by the top border of the data) represents total imports. Figure 10.2 reveals that Mexico's trade patterns are quite different in the 2000s when compared with the 1990s. First, real imports increased by nearly a factor of five over this period, but not consistently. The drops in imports coincide with the recession that accompanied the Mexican peso crisis (at the end of 1994) and the US recessions in 2001 and 2008. Similarly, sharp increases are evident in both 1995 (following both the NAFTA and Mexico's recovery from the peso crisis) and again in 2003 during the recovery of the US economy after the 2001 recession.

Figure 10.2 also shows that the USA is Mexico's most important source of imports by far. One of the most dramatic changes in Mexico's trade pattern over the last ten years has been the sharp decline in the share of imports that come from the USA. This fall is evident in Figure 10.2, as the US share of total Mexican imports declines from over 70% in 1990 to less than 50% in 2009. The fall in the US share of Mexican imports is due to a rising contribution from non-traditional trading partners. Mexico's traditional second and third most significant sources of imports—Japan and Germany—also fall as a share of the total.

Figure 10.2 also illustrates that China's share in total imports rises significantly, especially after 2000, but remains a relatively small fraction. The majority of the loss of US share is made up by increases in the rest of the world—most of which individually remain very small suppliers to the Mexican market, but, when taken together, represent a significant diversification of total imports.[4] This diversification is probably largely due to the increase in the number of free-trade agreements Mexico has signed.

Understanding Mexico's overall changing trade and trade policy is important for understanding Mexico's pattern of anti-dumping for several reasons. First, the fact that the USA makes up such a large share of Mexican imports suggests that if anti-dumping measures are applied in proportion to trade, we would expect a majority of anti-dumping measures to be applied against the USA, and that this share should be falling over time. Second, following the same reasoning, the rise of China after 2000 suggests that we might expect China to become an increasing target of anti-dumping measures, especially after 2000. Third, the rise in trade shares of the rest of the world suggests that Mexico might follow the pattern of the rest of the developing world in increasing the application of anti-dumping measures against other developing countries. In the next section, we will see that only one of these predictions holds, and weakly at that.

---

[4]Mexico's Hirschman-Hirfindahl Index (HHI), which is a traditional measure of economic concentration, changed for trade partners from 0.459 in 1990 to 0.260 in 2009. Figures over 0.180 are considered highly concentrated, but the fall in concentration is significant according to both the HHI and Figure 10.2.

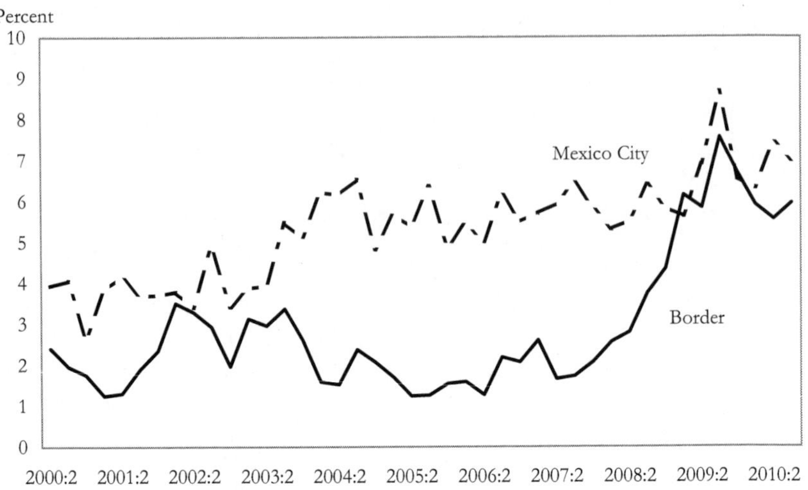

Figure 10.3: *Mexican unemployment.*

Source: quarterly unemployment data from INEGI. Encuesta Nacional de Ocupación y Empleo (ENOE) Indicadores Estratégicos. 'Border' represents the state of Baja California Norte, which is the Mexican state that borders California near San Diego, includes Tijuana, and historically has had the largest number of maquiladora plants. 'Mexico City' is Mexico's Federal District (the capital of Mexico).

2.3 Macroeconomic Effects of the Crisis

It is clear that the financial crisis was accompanied by a sharp drop in trade flows. As the trade shock spread through the rest of the Mexican economy, it had macroeconomic implications as well (Kaplan *et al* 2011). The shock was clearly transmitted to Mexico from the USA through trade channels. In an examination of Mexico's anti-dumping use between 1990 and 2001, Lederman *et al* (2005) show that the unemployment rate is one of the few macroeconomic variables that significantly affect anti-dumping filings. Figure 10.3 shows the quarterly unemployment rate for two regions of Mexico: the US–Mexico border region (represented by Baja California Norte) and Central Mexico (represented by the Federal District). The border region is the most integrated with the USA. This integration is characterised by vertical integration into the North American production chain that has intensified since the NAFTA (Robertson 2007). The unemployment rate is generally lower in the more integrated and dynamic border region than in the interior, but the effects of the trade shock are immediately apparent as the unemployment for the border region jumps sharply during the crisis. This is consistent with the labour markets of the two countries being closely integrated, with the degree of integration being higher in the border region (Robertson 2000).

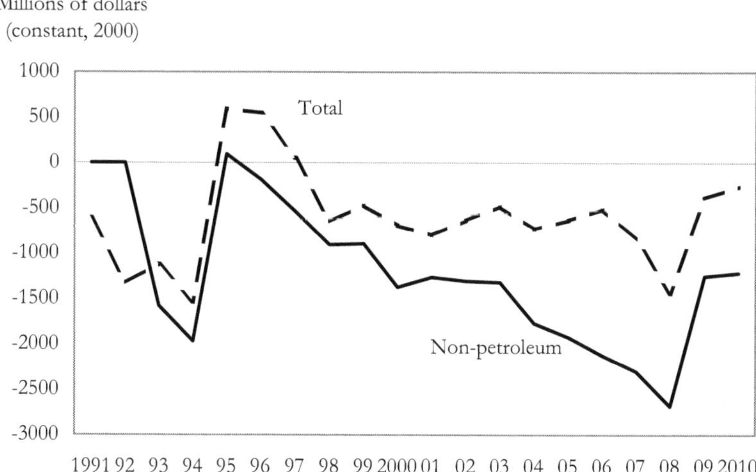

Figure 10.4: *Mexican trade balance.*
Source: Banco de Información de INEGI.

The fact that the shock was primarily a trade shock and therefore mainly affected the border region may help to explain the response in terms of anti-dumping policy. Furthermore, the fact that the Mexican economy is increasingly integrated with the USA reverses the traditional assumption that increased imports pose a threat to employment. In fact, Kaplan *et al* (2011) find that the contrary holds for the border region: imports are positively correlated with employment. Therefore, increasing tariffs through anti-dumping measures may not necessarily offer the same kind of protection that might be possible in an environment in which imports are substitutes for, rather than complements with, domestic production.

In order to illustrate the possibly unique nature of Mexico's trade relationships, Figure 10.4 shows Mexico's aggregate trade balance (total, petroleum, and non-petroleum products). Mexico is obviously a net oil exporter. Mexico's non-oil balance was positive following the peso crisis, but then continued to fall until the 2008 financial crisis. The crisis represents a nadir for the non-oil products trade balance, with the trade balance becoming less negative during and following the crisis. To the extent that anti-dumping activity is tied to a negative change in the trade balance, the pattern that Mexico exhibits would suggest that the crisis reduced political pressure for anti-dumping measures.[5]

[5] It is also interesting to point out that the total trade balance falls sharply between 1991 and the end of 1992, which may have contributed to Mexico's anti-dumping policy at the time. This is discussed in subsequent sections.

It is also important to mention that the crisis coincided with several other negative shocks. The H1N1 influenza virus (also known as the 'swine flu') pandemic in 2009 started in Veracruz, Mexico. The outbreak adversely affected tourism, which is one of Mexico's most significant foreign-exchange-earning sectors. In addition, narcotics-related violence increased sharply, capturing much of the attention of both the public and policymakers. Remittances from the USA to Mexico fell 36% between October 2008 and October 2009 as employment opportunities for Mexicans became more difficult to find in the USA (Iliff 2009).

3 FUNDAMENTALS: THE BIRTH OF THE ANTI-DUMPING REGIME, CHINA AND THE USA

To understand Mexico's TTB policies, three key elements stand out: the conditions in which the TTB policies were first formed, the role of China and the relationship that Mexico shares with the USA.

3.1 The Birth of Mexico's Modern Anti-Dumping Policy Structure

Mexico's anti-dumping policies came of age at the end of the 1980s as part of Mexico's liberalising reforms. To address the political concerns about liberalisation and to help harmonise its trade policies with the rest of the countries in the GATT, Mexico felt the need to have viable and credible anti-dumping mechanisms. Gonzàlez and Reyes de la Torre (2006) present what is possibly the most thorough description of the birth and early evolution of Mexico's anti-dumping policies, suggesting that they were 'born only to protect the liberalisation process'.[6]

Mexico's anti-dumping legislation was enacted in January 1986 and Mexico initiated its first anti-dumping case in 1987. Mexico signed the Tokyo Round Anti-Dumping Code in 1988, the year president Carlos Salinas de Gortari was elected. Over the next several years, Mexico developed an administrative infrastructure necessary to successfully implement anti-dumping policies. Specifically, Mexico published the new Foreign Trade Law and its Regulations in the *Diario Oficial* in July and December of 1993 (Leycegui and Reyes de la Torre 2005). (See also Giesze (1994) for additional legal background of the formation of Mexico's anti-dumping policies.) It was also during this period that Mexico's anti-dumping initiation activity reached its peak (for more details, see Gonzàlez and Reyes de la Torre (2006)).

To illustrate the evolution of Mexico's anti-dumping activity over time, Table 10.2 contains four variables constructed from the World Bank's *Temporary Trade Barriers Database* (Bown 2010), with data broken down by year:

[6]Francois and Niels (2004) also explore the political dimensions of Mexico's anti-dumping regime.

Table 10.2: *Flow and stock of Mexico's anti-dumping cases.*

	Flow		Stock	
Year	New cases	HS-08 categories	Cases	HS-08 categories
1987	18	23	6	7
1988	11	134	8	9
1989	7	8	12	14
1990	11	13	18	20
1991	9	16	26	34
1992	26	1,156	36	69
1993	60	2,206	54	2,176
1994	9	18	60	2,188
1995	4	5	62	2,191
1996	4	6	65	2,193
1997	6	7	68	2,193
1998	10	20	75	2,209
1999	10	23	79	2,225
2000	5	11	73	2,202
2001	5	9	71	2,193
2002	12	17	67	2,169
2003	13	25	72	2,182
2004	5	6	72	2,178
2005	7	21	71	2,176
2006	6	12	70	2,175
2007	3	6	68	2,173
2008	1	1	66	2,170
2009	2	6	45	85
2010	1	4	39	79

Bown (2010) contains four-digit categories for some cases. For these categories, the number of HS-08 categories included in each four-digit HS category was counted for the HS-08 column. Full data for 2010 were not available at the time of writing.

the number of initiated anti-dumping cases, the number of HS-04 and HS-08 categories covered by the cases, the number of cases with anti-dumping measures imposed and the number of HS-08 categories covered by imposed anti-dumping measures.[7]

The spike in 1992 and 1993 is immediately obvious in terms of cases. Of the 245 cases in the anti-dumping database, 10.6% (26/245) were initiated in 1992. Another 25% (60/245) were initiated in 1993. The spike in these two years (1992 and 1993) is even more stark if we consider the number of HS products covered by these cases, as shown in the second column. Not only did the number of HS-08 categories increase, but the average number of HS-08

[7]Most of the cases have an eight-digit HS category associated with them, but not all. The rest have four-digit HS categories assigned to them. Columns 2 and 4 follow a modified version of counting products as described in the Introduction (this volume, Equation (1.1)).

categories covered per case increased from 1.14 in 1989 to 36.77 in 1993. That is, Mexico significantly expanded the scope of coverage.

The spike in 1992 and 1993 attracted the most attention in terms of initiations, but the stock of coverage has received much less attention. To describe the stock, we again rely on the data in Bown (2010) and define a binary 'stock' variable equal to one (and zero otherwise) for initiated cases that had an affirmative final dumping decision and had not yet been revoked. Summing the stock variable by year gives us the number of cases with anti-dumping measures imposed, shown in the third column of data in Table 10.2. The anti-dumping database also includes the HS-08 categories associated with each case, and the count of these is shown in the final column.

Taking the stock of cases into account is extremely important, as shown in the fourth column of Table 10.2. The 'flow' measure documenting the number of new cases drops in 1994 and remains relatively low (less than 14) through 2010. Aside from 2002 and 2003 (with 12 and 13 new cases respectively), the number of new cases never rises above 10 for the entire 1994–2010 period. One possible explanation for this is shown in column 4: products covered by anti-dumping measures imposed during the 1992–3 period remained extensive and lasted until 2008. That is, it is possible that the 1992–3 cases provided a cover that obviated the need for future anti-dumping measures.

Therefore, examining the policies specific to the 1992 and 1993 period is very important for understanding the stock and the vast majority of Mexican anti-dumping coverage. Figure 10.5 breaks down the cases by country over the entire sample period and shows that the country with the largest share of anti-dumping-case initiations is the USA. This is fairly consistent with Figure 10.2 in the sense that the USA is Mexico's largest source of imports. Figure 10.5 also shows that China is the second most significant target of new anti-dumping cases. Brazil, Spain, South Korea and Germany make up the next largest portions. Interestingly, although Japan is one of the largest trade partners by volume, it does not appear as a significant target of anti-dumping case initiations. The remaining cases are divided up in small percentages among the remaining countries.

Figure 10.5 may give the impression that anti-dumping cases are relatively dispersed among trading partners. In terms of trade covered by the stock of anti-dumping measures, however, a very different picture emerges. Figure 10.6 shows the composition of the total trade volume covered by imposed anti-dumping measures (the stock of cases). Two important facts are immediately obvious from Figure 10.6. First, the total trade volume covered by imposed anti-dumping measures increases dramatically in the 2000–2009 period. Second, the composition of the trade covered by imposed anti-dumping measures changes dramatically. In the 1990s, the vast majority of the trade volume covered by anti-dumping comes from the USA. Very little is left for either China or all other countries targeted by anti-dumping measures. After 2000, however, the picture changes dramatically. The US share falls as

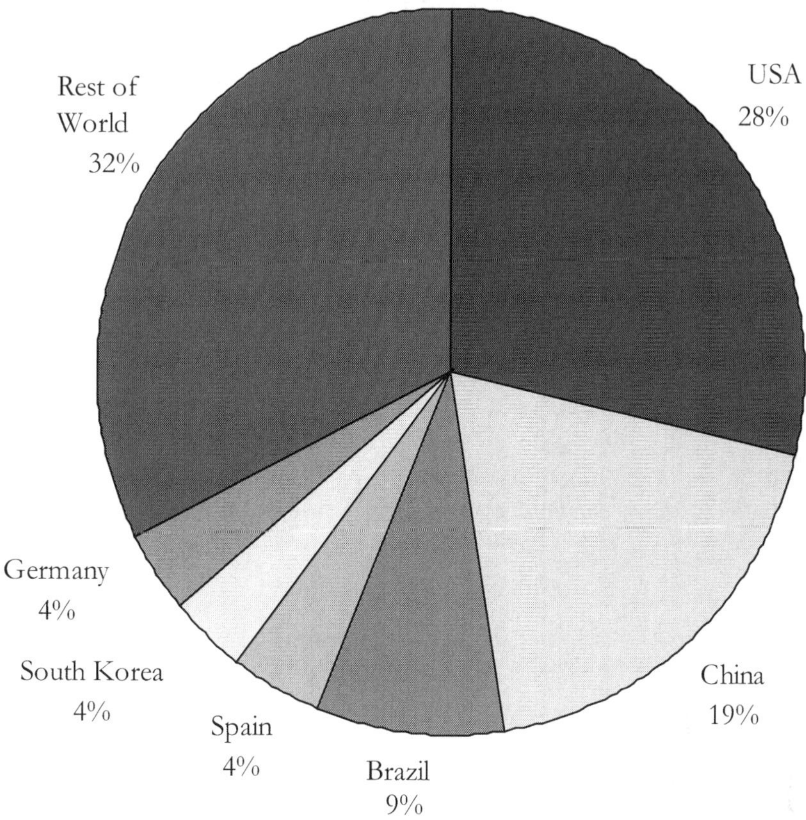

Figure 10.5: *Number of Mexican anti-dumping cases by target country. Source: Temporary Trade Barriers Database* (Bown 2010).

the Chinese share swells. The most likely explanation for this is implied by Figure 10.2 and Table 10.3. Chinese trade was covered preemptively. As Chinese trade grew, so did the volume that was covered by active measures. As a result, recognising the 'China Package' of the 1992–3 measures in Mexico is critical for understanding Mexican anti-dumping activity during the 1990–2010 period.

3.2 The 'China Package'

As Gonzàlez and Reyes de la Torre (2006) explain, the 1992–3 spike mainly (but not entirely) consisted of two components. The first was the 'China Package' and the second was a group representing the 'multiproduct/multicountry steel cases'. The 'China Package' turned out to be especially relevant for

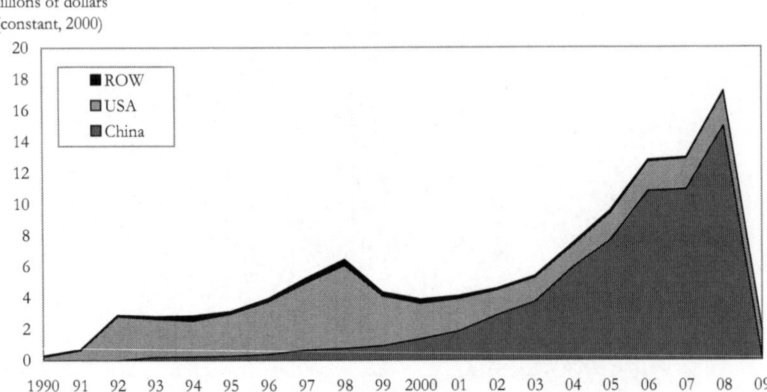

Figure 10.6: *Mexican anti-dumping covered trade by country.*

Source: WITS, Comtrade and the *Temporary Trade Barriers Database* (Bown 2010). Covered trade calculated at the four-digit HS level using a binary indicator if any of the HS-08 sectors within a given four-digit sector had an active anti-dumping measure in place. The sum of China, the USA and the rest of the world represents the total value of trade affected by all anti-dumping cases in each year across all countries. China's value in 2009 appears as zero in the graph because the actual value (in billion constant US dollars) is 0.094, which excludes the exceptions for 'sensitive industries'.

Mexico's stock of anti-dumping measures documented in Table 10.2. Mexico initiated a very wide range of anti-dumping cases brought against China. Nearly 27% of the cases were against China in 1992, and 21.7% were against China in 1993, making China the primary target for these measures in these years. The second most targeted country during these years was the USA, with 23% and 18%, respectively. No other country comes close to these two in terms of the number of cases.

The number of cases and covered industries is especially curious because many of them applied to industries in which Mexico had very little, if any, trade. Rather than being economic, however, these measures seemed to play an important political function. At the time, the Mexican business community was uneasy about the pace and extent of Mexican liberalisation. The anti-dumping mechanism offered the promise of protection if necessary. Imposing the measures against China sent the signal to the business community that these measures would offer protection that might compensate for the loss of coverage that took place during Mexico's GATT-focused unilateral liberalisation. These cases helped to solidify political support for Mexico's early anti-dumping program.

Targeting China and goods with relatively little imports seems to have been a successful strategy for two reasons. First, targeting industries that had little trade at the time meant that the measures would impose minimal distortions

Table 10.3: *Average anti-dumping duties imposed by Mexico.*

Country	Number of HS-08 categories covered	Earliest final dumping decision date	Latest final dumping decision date	Average *ad valorem* duty
China	1,098	25/5/1992	16/4/2009	212.7
Germany	4	19/12/1995	19/12/1995	185.8
Indonesia	1	4/7/2003	4/7/2003	182.1
India	1	7/12/1995	7/12/1995	116.0
Japan	4	25/5/1996	30/10/2000	97.7
Bulgaria	2	29/6/1999	29/6/1999	88.0
Romania	5	2/4/2004	8/9/2005	62.5
Brazil	30	7/9/1992	24/1/2006	55.2
EU	5	3/6/1994	23/8/1999	50.9
Ukraine	13	13/11/1998	8/9/2005	49.8
Netherlands	5	25/5/1992	19/12/1995	48.4
Canada	6	19/12/1995	28/12/1995	41.2
USA	51	5/6/1991	18/7/2005	40.4
Russia	16	7/6/1996	8/9/2005	39.7
Kazakhstan	2	29/6/1999	29/6/1999	34.0
Spain	2	25/5/1992	8/12/1992	32.0
South Korea	5	19/8/1993	30/5/2001	28.8
Guatemala	2	13/1/2003	13/1/2003	25.9
Denmark	2	28/3/2000	28/3/2000	25.0
Taiwan	3	27/6/1997	30/5/2001	20.7
United Kingdom	1	23/12/2009	23/12/2009	5.9
Ecuador	1	4/7/2003	4/7/2003	3.8
Hong Kong	1	9/9/1991	9/9/1991	0.5

The average duty is calculated as the simple average across all cases for each country. Cases here only include those that applied an *ad valorem* dumping duty; 94.60% of the final anti-dumping measures are *ad valorem* duties.

on the domestic economy. Bown (2011a), for example, notes that the Mexican tariffs covered only 0.8% of Mexico's total imports in 1992. Second, targeting China seemed to be either the result of a goal of imposing minimal distortions on Mexico's new GATT relationships or remarkable foresight (or both). China was not a member of the GATT at the time, and therefore may have seemed like a reasonable country to target to demonstrate to the domestic producers that the authorities were willing and able to impose anti-dumping measures. As Figures 10.2 and 10.6 show, however, China's importance in Mexican imports surged ten years later—both in terms of total trade (Figure 10.2) and especially in terms of trade covered by anti-dumping measures (Figure 10.6).

Note that in Figure 10.6 we do not apply Bown's (2011a) approach of using the growth rate of imports that are not affected by TTBs to estimate the counterfactual growth rate of imports that might have occurred in the absence of TTBs (for a discussion, see Bown (2011b, Equation (1.2))). That approach is appropriate when one expects a strong discouraging effect from TTBs that would make the TTB-affected sectors grow more slowly relative to sectors not covered by TTBs. In the Mexican case, however, using actual imports is perhaps more accurate for two reasons. First, to the extent that the TTBs slowed Chinese imports, the import growth would have been even greater, which makes the rise presented in Figure 10.6 even more dramatic. Second, using the growth rate of imports from other countries to represent the import growth that might have occurred without TTBs would understate the true counterfactual growth in Chinese imports, especially in the early 2000s (see Figure 10.6) if the discouraging effect was greater than the rate of import growth from other countries (which seems possible given the scope of coverage).

In addition to covering a large number of HS-08 products, Chinese cases involved much higher average tariffs than those imposed in other cases. Table 10.3 provides information about the tariff levels applied across the different cases. Using the application of a final anti-dumping measure as a selection criterion, Table 10.3 includes the number of HS-08 products, the dates for the earliest and latest final dumping decision, and the simple average of the *ad valorem* duties (not including specific or other duties) applied to each country across all applicable HS-08 categories and cases. Again, the dominance of China is immediately apparent—not only in terms of the number of covered HS-08 products, which has already been discussed, but by the span of time covered by final anti-dumping decisions (1992–2009) and the average applied *ad valorem* duty (212.7%). Germany spans a similar length of time, but has many fewer covered HS-08 products (five) and an average *ad valorem* tariff about 14% below China. (the log difference is 0.136). The country with the next highest applied tariff—Indonesia—includes only one HS-08 product and one date.

As is evident from Figure 10.6, the anti-dumping provisions against China were removed nearly as suddenly as they were imposed. When China joined the WTO in 2001, its accession protocol specified that measures against China that were not consistent with WTO regulations were to be phased out, but the 'Peace Clause' allowed a six-year delay before WTO principles would be applied to the provisions (Bravo *et al* 2010).

In late December 2007, Mexico attempted to extend the delay, but on 1 June 2008, Mexico and China signed the 'Transitional Agreement on Trade Remedies' that resulted in the dramatic drop in the number of anti-dumping-covered industries. This agreement was published on 14 October 2008 in the *Diaro Oficial* and explains that Mexico agreed to eliminate duties on 749 tariff-line (HS-08) items and phase out protection for another 204. The reductions would begin on 15 October 2008 and the rest would be eliminated by 11 December 2011. The agreement allows Mexico to employ transitional measures for the duties scheduled to be removed in 2011, although these transitional measures may also be challenged by China and Mexican importers (Bravo *et al* 2010).

One could reasonably argue that the June 2008 agreement with China was expected, possibly even before China entered the WTO. If countries successfully rely on anti-dumping protection during periods of recession or economic crisis, then the timing of the agreement was simply unfortunate for Mexico to the extent that the 2008 financial crisis was unexpected. In terms of empirical analysis, therefore, it is clearly inaccurate to attribute the significant reduction in Mexico's anti-dumping coverage to macroeconomic conditions.

3.3 The United States of America

As Weintraub (2010) argues, understanding Mexican economics in general or trade policy in particular requires significant attention to be devoted to Mexico's relationship with the USA. In terms of anti-dumping, it is important to examine the NAFTA, Mexican tariff preferences granted towards the USA, and the product areas that are most affected by Mexican anti-dumping activity directed towards the USA.

Chapter 19 of the NAFTA addresses anti-dumping duties and was modelled on Chapter 19 of the Canadian–US Free Trade Agreement. One critical provision of Chapter 19 was the creation of binational review panels. Lederman *et al* (2005) suggest that, while imports surged following the NAFTA, the benefits to Mexico from the provisions of Chapter 19 were not immediately apparent and, in fact, the review panels had no way to enforce their decisions. Esquivel and Solis (2002) argue that the NAFTA reduced US vulnerability to Mexican anti-dumping provisions, even though the USA remained a significant target (which might be driven by the significant share the USA commands of total Mexican trade). Interestingly, they also suggest that the NAFTA did not reduce Mexican vulnerability to US anti-dumping action, raising the possibility that at least Mexican anti-dumping activity might be responsive to US action in the sense of Blonigen and Bown (2003).

The NAFTA also included an eventual elimination of Mexican tariffs against Canada and the USA. Figure 10.7 shows the pattern of average (non-anti-dumping) Mexican tariffs (both simple average and trade-weighted average) imposed against the USA versus those imposed against all other countries that had matching data for trade volumes (from the trade database) and tariffs (from the tariff database). The top line represents Mexico's simple average tariff for all non-US countries and contrasts sharply with the trade-weighted average tariff for non-US countries. The time series pattern of these two lines, however, is similar in that they both show a falling trend over the entire sample period. The non-trade-weighted average tariff rises in the late 1990s, but then continues to fall through 2009.

The trade-weighted and unweighted Mexican tariffs towards the USA are very similar because most of the trade observed in both data sets is with the USA. The effect of the NAFTA is immediately apparent in that, in 1994, the simple average tariff rate for the USA was very similar to the rest of the

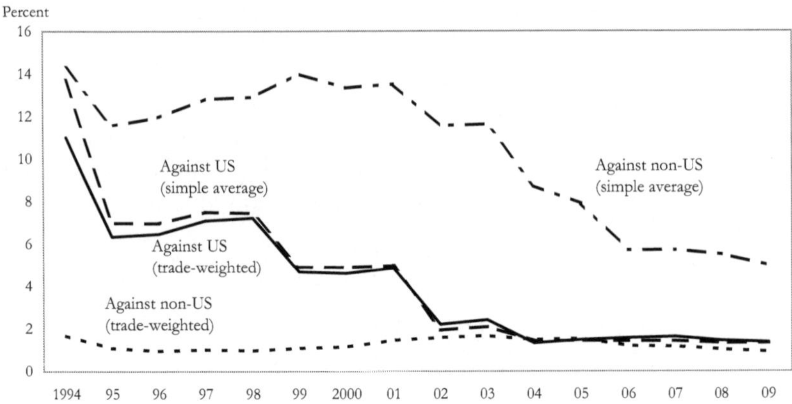

Figure 10.7: *Mexico's tariffs after the NAFTA.*
Source: WITS and TRAINS database.

world. Following the NAFTA, however, Mexican tariffs towards the USA drop sharply. They continue to drop in a stepwise fashion as the NAFTA provisions are phased in and approach zero by the end of the sample period.

Figure 10.7 shows that there was a benefit to the USA in terms of tariff reduction. While overall tariffs were falling in Mexico, the USA did receive preferential treatment after the NAFTA, which is not surprising. What might be surprising is that Mexico continued to diversify its trade away from the USA even while giving the USA lower and lower tariffs. Furthermore, the falling tariffs eventually covered all goods. The pattern for the five product groups mainly targeted by anti-dumping measures is very similar to the other goods that had fewer anti-dumping cases. Tariff levels were comparable prior to NAFTA but dropped sharply for the USA relative to others. One possibility is that these were particularly sensitive and that sensitivity was revealed post-NAFTA, resulting in anti-dumping duties.

Mexican anti-dumping measures tend to cover a small fraction of total trade with the USA and the initiations tend to be concentrated in relatively few product categories. Figure 10.8 shows the HS-02 categories with more than 5% of the total anti-dumping cases (not HS categories covered) initiated against the USA. Measures against the USA include both areas that have received media attention (*eg* beef and steel) and those that are economically important but may have received less attention (*eg* plastics and inorganic chemicals).

The trade volume covered by the stock of anti-dumping cases follows a somewhat different pattern. Figure 10.9 shows the time series of the volume of trade covered by some anti-dumping measures within each HS-02 sector. The cases brought against US beef (shown in the 'meat' category in Figure 10.9) arise in the late 1990s, while the other main sectors fell in significance. Com-

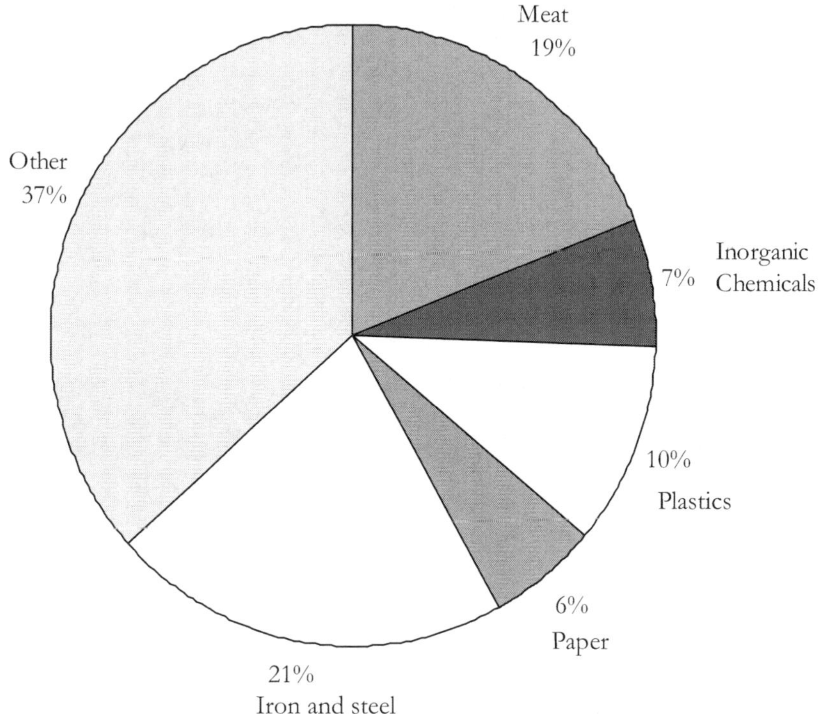

Figure 10.8: *Mexico's case initiations against the USA by sector.*

Source: Temporary Trade Barriers Database (Bown 2010). The 'Other' category contains all two-digit sectors with less than 5% of total filings.

pared with the late 1990s, there is much less trade covered by Mexican anti-dumping measures. Interestingly, however, Figure 10.9 also shows that there is a general increase in the share of anti-dumping-covered trade following 2004. This increase is most likely explained by an increase in trade during the recovery from the 2001 recession. The drop in trade following the 2008–9 trade collapse shows again that there was a decrease, rather than an increase, in trade covered by anti-dumping measures during the crisis.

4 IMPLEMENTATION

In this section we examine four key features of Mexico's implementation of anti-dumping measures: duration, products, tariffs and affirmative decisions. Each subsection reveals important patterns about Mexico's anti-dumping policies in light of the crisis.

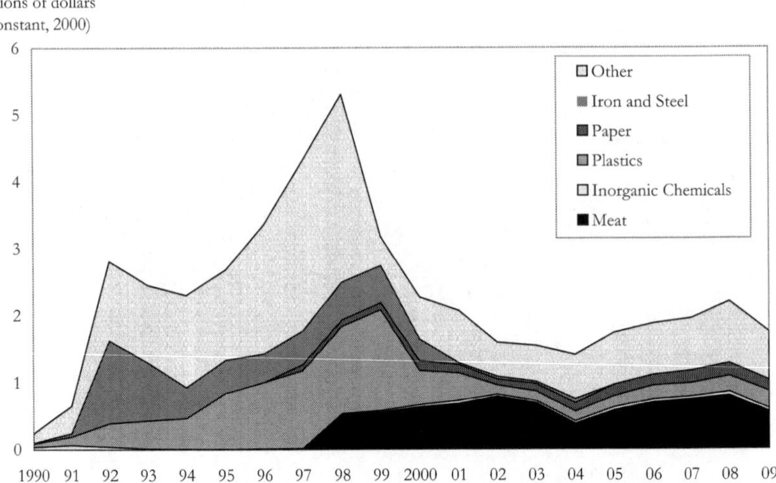

Figure 10.9: *Mexico's anti-dumping covered trade volume (US trade only).*

Source: WITS, Comtrade and *Temporary Trade Barriers Database* (Bown 2010). The sum of trade in these industries is equal to the US trade shown in Figure 10.6.

4.1 Duration

One potential reason that the stock of anti-dumping measures remains high is that measures are not revoked within the five-year timeframe suggested by the Uruguay Round's sunset review provisions. The China case clearly ran contrary to those provisions, but, considering the duration of measures applied to other countries, it is also informative.

Table 10.4 presents the average duration of anti-dumping provisions by country. Several interesting points are immediately evident from Table 10.4.[8] First, China is not the country with the longest duration of anti-dumping measures. That distinction goes to France, whose anti-dumping measure applied to Sorbitol on 28 September 1990 is listed as still in force in the anti-dumping database with an applied specific duty of $0.24/kg. Nineteen of the 27 countries listed in Table 10.4 have average durations greater than five years.[9] The USA falls above the five-year mark with an average duration of 6.81 years.

There is no clear relationship between provisions that were implemented more recently and their duration other than the obvious frontier issue imposed by treating in-force provisions as having a revocation date of 1 Jan-

[8]Here we assume that all 'in force' measures are revoked on 1/1/2011 to calculate length. Such a strategy grants a lower bound for duration.

[9]In Table 6, the European Union enters as a single country.

Table 10.4: *Average duration of anti-dumping measures by country (years).*

Country	Mean	Standard deviation	Frequency
France	20.3	0.0	1
Hong Kong	19.3	0.0	1
South Korea	14.9	5.5	5
China	13.8	1.2	1,108
Bulgaria	11.5	0.0	2
Kazakhstan	11.5	0.0	2
Russia	10.7	3.6	12
Japan	10.2	0.0	3
Ukraine	9.0	2.9	10
Denmark	8.3	0.0	2
Taiwan	7.7	3.2	4
Netherlands	7.3	5.0	5
USA	6.8	3.3	66
Brazil	6.3	3.4	32
India	6.3	5.3	2
Venezuela	5.8	2.1	12
Germany	5.1	0.0	4
Guatemala	5.0	0.0	2
EU	5.0	0.0	2
Ecuador	5.0	0.0	1
Indonesia	5.0	0.0	1
Romania	5.0	0.0	1
Chile	4.6	0.0	1
Spain	4.3	2.8	4
West Germany	2.0	0.0	1
Canada	1.8	2.5	6
United Kingdom	1.0	0.0	1
Total	12.9	3.0	1,291

Average duration is calculated as the number of days between the final anti-dumping date and the revocation date. For measures still in force (*eg* the French case), 1/1/2011 was used as the revocation date.

uary 2011. Therefore, there is no evidence that the duration of anti-dumping provisions is falling over time.

Table 10.5 shows the cases that were eligible to have been removed during the crisis. Eligibility is based on having an initiation date after 2000 such that the final anti-dumping decision date fell in 2003 or later (five years before the crisis hit). There is little evidence from Table 10.5 that the probability of being revoked fell during the crisis, given the average durations for other cases shown in Table 10.4. For example, the Ukraine case remained in force, although it began in 2003. But this is just one of the ten cases for Ukraine as shown in Table 10.4, in which the average duration for cases brought against Ukraine is nearly nine years. For the USA, the duration for most of those cases falls short of the average duration of cases brought against the USA in Table 10.5. The one exception seems to be Venezuela, in which the out-

Table 10.5: *Potential crisis-affected anti-dumping cases in Mexico.*

Final anti-dumping date	Country	Revocation date	Duration (1/1/2011)
17/7/2003	Ecuador	16/7/2008	5.0
17/7/2003	Indonesia	16/7/2008	5.0
26/9/2003	China	In force	7.3
18/7/2003	China	In force	7.5
25/9/2003	Ukraine	In force	7.3
22/4/2004	Russia	22/4/2009	5.0
22/4/2004	Romania	22/4/2009	5.0
14/5/2004	Venezuela	In force	6.6
5/8/2004	China	In force	6.4
8/4/2005	USA	In force	5.7
9/4/2005	USA	In force	5.7
9/4/2005	USA	In force	5.7
28/5/2005	USA	In force	5.6
28/5/2005	USA	In force	5.6
26/1/2006	Brazil	In force	4.9
18/5/2006	China	In force	4.6
18/5/2006	Chile	In force	4.6
13/6/2006	China	In force	4.6
21/4/2009	China	In force	1.7
6/1/2010	United Kingdom	In force	1.0

The duration measure, in years, is calculated by applying 1/1/2011 as the revocation date for all measures currently in force.

standing case has lasted longer than the average shown in Table 10.4, but the duration in Table 10.5 is still less than the sum of the average duration and standard deviation shown in Table 10.4. Therefore, at first pass, it does not seem that Mexico increased its propensity to 'hold on' to anti-dumping measures during the crisis as compared with previous years.

4.2 Products

Much of the previous literature focuses on the specific industries covered by anti-dumping measures. In particular, the steel cases stand out. One of the main differences between the China package and the steel cases lies in applied anti-dumping duties. As Gonzàlez and Reyes de la Torre (2006) explain, cases in the 'Chinese Package' were quite likely to have preliminary anti-dumping duties applied. None of the steel cases, in contrast, applied preliminary anti-dumping duties. The approach was clearly different from the steel cases in terms of treatment and national coverage, and readers are again referred to Gonzàlez and Reyes de la Torre (2006) for more details.

Table 10.6: *Top ten two-digit HS industries sorted by anti-dumping coverage of total trade.*

HS-02	Description	HS-02 share of total (%)	Anti-dumping coverage of total (%)	Within HS-02 coverage (%)
85	Electrical machinery/equipment/parts, telecommunications equipment, sound recorders, television recorders	21.5	1.7	8.0
72	Iron and steel	3.1	0.4	13.3
39	Plastics/plastic articles	6.2	0.4	6.6
02	Meat and edible meat offal	1.9	0.2	12.0
95	Toys	0.6	0.2	31.8
29	Organic chemicals	2.8	0.1	4.9
90	Optical, photographic, cinematographic, measuring, checking, precision, medical or surgical instruments and accessories	3.2	0.1	2.9
08	Fruits and nuts	0.3	0.1	22.8
48	Paper and paperboard, articles of paper pulp	2.3	0.0	2.3
55	Man-made staple fibres, including yarns, *etc*	0.4	0.0	11.2

Anti-dumping coverage is calculated using a binary indicator for whether or not a given country-HS-04 industry had any anti-dumping coverage multiplied by the real (in constant 2000 US dollars) trade value for that country-HS-04 observation and then summing that product over all countries (for each HS-04 industry) and dividing that sum by the total trade in each HS-04 industry.

Table 10.6 presents the top ten HS-02 industries covered by anti-dumping measures, sorted by anti-dumping covered trade as a share of total trade within each HS-04 industry.[10] This value (called 'anti-dumping coverage' in Table 10.6) is accompanied by the share of each two-digit industry in total trade (HS-02 share of total) in the first data column and the share of trade within each HS-02 industry covered by anti-dumping measures in the last data column. These three measures reveal different aspects of Mexico's anti-dumping application. For example, the industry with the highest share of within-HS-02 coverage (HS-02 sector 95, labelled 'toys' in Table 10.6) has a very small share of total trade largely because this sector makes up a very small share of total trade. On the other hand, electrical machinery (HS-02 sector 85) has the highest share of total trade covered because this sector makes up 21.5% of all of Mexico's imports and achieves this rank in spite of the fact that it has one of the lowest within-sector coverage ratios.

[10]Specifically, this measure ('anti-dumping coverage' in Table 10.6) is calculated using a binary indicator for whether or not a given country-HS-04 industry had any anti-dumping coverage multiplied by the trade value for that country-HS-04 observation and then summing that product over all countries (for each HS-02 industry) and dividing that sum by the total trade in each HS-04 industry.

Several additional results are evident from Table 10.6. First, the overall coverage (in terms of trade volume) of anti-dumping measures is relatively small—less than 2% on average in all cases and less than 0.5% in all but one. The relatively small share of covered trade has been noted by other authors (Leycegui and Reyes de la Torre 2005), but the small coverage suggests that Mexico might not be a good example of a significant deterrent effect on trade such as that found elsewhere (Vandenbussche and Zanardi 2010). Second, formal tests reveal that the amount of trade covered within an industry and that industry's share of total trade are not significantly correlated, suggesting that the industries with the most imports are not disproportionately targeted. The third data column shows a wide range of within-industry coverage, even among the top ten industries. Finally, within-industry anti-dumping coverage is not greater than one-third, consistent with the usual notion that anti-dumping cases are generally narrowly focused on specific products.[11] The values in Table 10.6 are calculated over all years. Separating out the same values by year for the top four categories listed in Table 10.6 reveals significant heterogeneity over time. Table 10.7 contains the within-industry anti-dumping coverage for 1990–2009. The well-known beef dispute emerges in 1998 and initially covers just over 27% of the two-digit HS sector. But the coverage falls over time as individual cases get resolved. By 2009, the coverage is less than half of the 1998 value.

Analysing the stock for other products reveals a similar wave pattern. For example, plastics (HS-02 39) starts low and gradually rises, cresting at the end of the 1990s before dropping off in 2000. A similar pattern emerges for steel. As part of the steel package in 1992–3, coverage rises significantly in those years but is followed by a gradual decay through the rest of the sample, reaching less than 0.5% by 2009. Electric machinery, on the other hand, shows a very different pattern of gradually increasing coverage over the sample period (until 2009, which may be an anomaly due to missing data). Taken together, these patterns illustrate the importance of focusing on the stock of anti-dumping coverage rather than new cases. They also seem to suggest a gradual shift towards a more trade-based criterion of anti-dumping application, since the rising share in electric machinery coincides with that industry's relative importance in Mexico's total imports.

4.3 *Tariffs*

Anti-dumping duties may be complements with, substitutes for, or have no relationship with, other forms of tariffs. In particular, it is possible that sectors receive anti-dumping protection with tariffs that are otherwise too low to provide the desired protection. On the other hand, a particularly sensitive

[11]One concern about Table 10.6 is that it may miss some relatively high-profile cases, such as sweeteners (see Moss *et al* (2005) for a discussion of the Mexico's high fructose corn syrup dispute with the USA).

Table 10.7: *Within-industry anti-dumping coverage (top four two-digit HS industries).*

	HS-02			
	02	39	72	85
Year	Meat (%)	Plastics (%)	Iron and steel (%)	Electric machinery (%)
1990	0.0	3.7	2.1	0.0
1991	0.0	7.9	2.1	3.8
1992	0.0	8.5	40.2	6.3
1993	0.0	9.2	39.9	6.9
1994	0.0	8.6	26.7	6.5
1995	0.0	14.6	27.4	6.4
1996	0.0	14.6	22.2	7.6
1997	0.0	14.0	23.2	8.4
1998	27.2	14.7	25.5	8.4
1999	27.1	14.8	24.0	1.6
2000	22.6	4.6	12.3	1.9
2001	21.4	4.0	4.6	3.1
2002	24.7	1.3	3.2	5.6
2003	21.8	1.3	2.8	8.0
2004	11.7	1.2	4.0	11.5
2005	15.8	1.3	3.5	14.1
2006	17.9	1.4	1.2	18.1
2007	18.4	1.4	0.6	19.9
2008	17.6	1.7	0.7	22.7
2009	13.9	2.4	0.4	N/A

sector may be characterised by high tariffs and this underlying sensitivity may drive affected parties to seek anti-dumping protection.

To investigate the possible correlation between anti-dumping activity and tariff levels, we turn to the WITS database. The tariff data are not available every year, so we interpolate missing tariff values when the tariff values are the same in the most recent available year and in the next available year. When the values of tariffs are different on either side of the tariff value, we use the previous value of tariffs. When the tariff data are missing for all earlier years, we leave the missing values alone.

To compare the average tariffs in anti-dumping sectors and non-anti-dumping sectors, we merge the eight-digit product data from the TTB database with the eight-digit tariff data from WITS. Comparing the average values of tariffs between these two groups, both by two-digit HS sector or by year, reveals that the average tariff levels are very similar (with significant overlap of 95% confidence intervals, and with an overall average (standard deviation) of 9.96% (9.46%) for non-anti-dumping sectors and 9.49% (6.14%) for anti-dumping sectors). Interesting exceptions seem to be HS-02 categories 34 (soaps, waxes, *etc*), 29 (organic chemicals), 76 (aluminium), 90 (optical and measuring instruments) and 01 (live animals) with log differences at least 30% higher for the anti-dumping sectors.

One point that is important to reiterate is that the main source of tariff data, the WITS database, does not include separate tariff lines for China. As mentioned earlier, this may be either because the WITS data are incomplete, or because Mexico did not impose separate tariffs against China. The more likely option seems to be that Mexico did not impose separate tariffs against China at that time because the levels of trade were so low and there were very few, if any, countries that had separate tariff lines.

4.4 A Probit Analysis of Affirmative Decisions

Leycegui and Reyes de la Torre (2005) describe ten major problems with Mexico's anti-dumping administration. While recognising that Mexico has set up 'strong and professional institutions to conduct anti-dumping procedures', it is clear that the system has been evolving over time. One area of particular concern is the determination of dumping and injury. Reynolds (2007) has indicated the possibility of bias in anti-dumping investigations with regards to agricultural products, which suggests that understanding anti-dumping decisions is important.

To analyse the factors affecting these decisions and the evolution of these decisions over time, we employ a probit analysis of determinants of affirmative decisions during the 1990–2009 period. As is well known, there are at least four key decision points involved in anti-dumping cases: preliminary dumping, final dumping, preliminary injury and final injury. The share of affirmative decisions for each of these categories, as well as the number of cases, for the 1987–2010 period are shown in Table 10.8. Table 10.8 shows that the preliminary and final decisions are very similar. This is an artefact of Mexico's reporting; it is often difficult to determine exact dates for separate decisions. It is also difficult to separate the dumping and injury decisions. Table 10.8 does not seem to suggest any clear change or trend over time. The relatively small number of cases means that each case is highly influential in the overall percentages.

When carrying out the probit analysis of the affirmative decisions, we add trade data (aggregated to the HS-04 level) to the case data, which effectively expands the case data to include all of the affected four-digit industries. This allows us to include proxies for trade volumes in the estimation. Other variables included are those suggested by the discussion above, including a time trend (or individual year controls), a dummy variable for China, and another for the USA.

Table 10.9 contains the probit estimation for preliminary (column 1) and final (column 2) affirmative dumping decisions, including a time trend. Columns 3 and 4 include an interaction between the time trend and China, the USA, and trade volume variables. All of the probit coefficients have been

Table 10.8: *Share of affirmative decisions by year.*

Initiation year	Cases	Preliminary dumping (%)	Final dumping (%)	Preliminary injury (%)	Final injury (%)
1987	18	78	33	78	33
1988	11	91	27	91	27
1989	7	71	57	71	57
1990	11	100	55	100	55
1991	9	100	89	100	89
1992	26	69	46	69	46
1993	60	63	43	63	43
1994	9	89	67	89	67
1995	4	100	100	100	100
1996	4	100	100	100	100
1997	6	100	83	100	83
1998	10	100	70	100	70
1999	10	100	70	100	70
2000	5	40	20	40	20
2001	5	100	100	100	100
2002	12	100	83	100	83
2003	13	92	92	92	92
2004	5	80	60	60	60
2005	7	57	57	57	43
2006	6	100	17	100	0
2007	3	67	33	67	33
2008	1	100	100	100	100
2009	2	50	0	100	0
2010	1	0	0	0	0

The share of affirmative decisions is the simple average across cases of a binary variable equal to one (and zero otherwise) if the decision in the case is affirmative. Other decisions (represented by a zero value of the binary affirmative indicator) include bypassed, withdrawn, terminated, negative, partial, other, and missing. Full 2010 data were not available at the time of writing.

converted to represent marginal probabilities, and the test statistics are based on the underlying coefficients.

The estimated negative sign on the year variable suggests that the probability of affirmative decisions, controlling for other factors, falls over time. The coefficient is statistically significant, but very small. The effect of trade volume is not statistically significant, which is consistent with the discussion earlier suggesting that Mexican anti-dumping policies, especially in the early years, do not seem focused on trade volumes. The fact that China is included and that anti-dumping measures in the 'China Package' were targeted at areas with very small amounts of trade explain this result. The 'China Package' also helps to explain the very large magnitude (and significance) of the China dummy variable. It is interesting that the USA also has significantly higher probability of affirmative dumping decisions.

Table 10.9: *Probit dumping analysis affirmative decisions.*

	(1) Preliminary	(2) Final	(3) Preliminary	(4) Final
Year	-1.441×10^{-4}	-1.024×10^{-4}	-1.413×10^{-4}	-9.499×10^{-5}
	(10.09)**	(9.06)**	(7.16)**	(5.85)**
Trade (billions)	0.006	0.004	0.008	0.004
	(15.74)**	(12.35)**	(4.69)**	(3.25)**
China	0.244	0.231	0.274	0.258
	(146.47)**	(143.16)**	(55.49)**	(54.16)**
USA	0.056	0.031	0.044	0.024
	(69.80)**	(50.27)**	(24.40)**	(17.49)**
China × Year	—	—	-9.096×10^{-5}	-6.001×10^{-5}
	—	—	(2.69)**	(2.37)*
USA × year	—	—	1.149×10^{-4}	7.480×10^{-5}
	—	—	(3.04)**	(2.35)*
Trade × year	—	—	-9.307×10^{-5}	-2.758×10^{-5}
	—	—	(0.97)	(0.37)
Observations	536,267	536,267	536,267	536,267

Absolute value of z-statistics in parentheses. Coefficients are transformed to represent marginal effects, including for dummy variables. '*' denotes significance at 5%; '**' denotes significance at 1%.

When the time trends are interacted with the trade and country dummy variables, the magnitude of the Chinese variable increases significantly, but the time interaction is negative, which is again consistent with the effects of the 'China Package'. Over time, the probability of an affirmative action against China falls. In contrast, the probability of a positive finding against the USA rises over time. In neither case is the volume of trade found to be statistically significant.

The effects of time may not be linear. In a separate estimation, we replaced the continuous time-trend variables with dummy variables for each year and interacted them with trade, China and USA variables. The sum of the main country effects and the marginal yearly effects are shown in Figure 10.10. The differences through time are statistically significant, but very small. Nevertheless, the trends seem clear. China starts from a high value and falls. As the probability of an end to anti-dumping protection against China increased in the mid-2000s, the probability of an affirmative decision against China also increases slightly. On the other hand, the USA starts from a relatively low value and rises—especially after the provisions of the NAFTA are phased in. There is also a jump in the US value during the financial crisis, which is consistent with other studies that suggest more aggressive use of TTBs during difficult economic periods.

One of the main implications of this section is that Mexico started out as a 'very aggressive' user of anti-dumping measures, but then reduced its use over

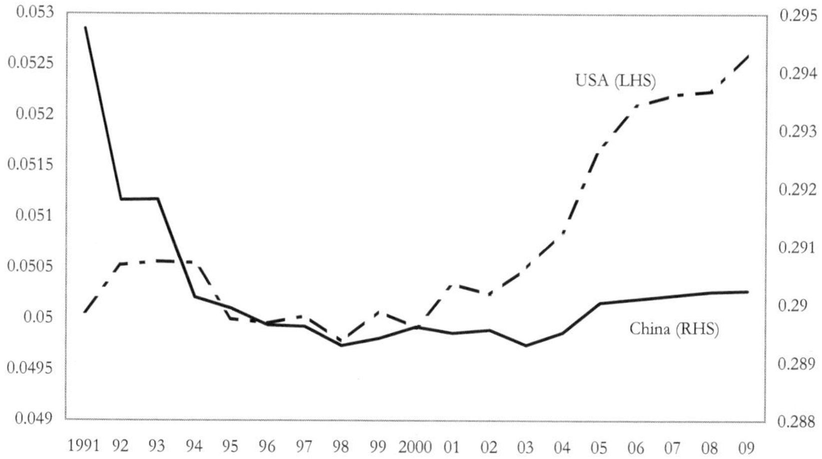

Figure 10.10: *Annual probit results (China and the US).*

Source: author's calculations. Lines represent the marginal plus main effects from a probit estimation using an affirmative preliminary dumping decision as the dependent variable.

time. This is clear from both the number of cases and the falling probability of affirmative decisions over time. Several other papers (Niels and Ten Kate 2004; Francois and Niels 2006; Bianchi and Sanguinetti 2006) suggest that economic crises lead to an increased use of anti-dumping measures. To evaluate this hypothesis, Figure 10.11 plots the (transformed) annual dummy variable coefficients from the probit estimation described above for Figure 10.10. Figure 10.11 marks three key economic downturns in the last 20 years: the Mexican peso crisis (1994–5), the US recession of 2001 and the financial crisis of 2008–9. Supporting the hypothesis advanced by these papers, there is a clear uptick of the probability of preliminary affirmative dumping decisions in each of these cases when controlling for China, the USA and total (real) trade volume. Of course, these upticks are temporary and relatively small compared with the overall declining trend of the line. The results suggest that Mexico is clearly becoming less 'aggressive' over time and the 2008–9 financial crisis has not had a large enough effect to reverse this trend.

One possibility is that Mexico has moved away from anti-dumping duties as a form of administrative protection and moved towards CVDs and safeguards. Nearly every other paper that has analysed Mexico's anti-dumping policies has noted that Mexico's use of these instruments has been quite limited, but we examine these policies in depth in the next section (papers that examine global trends, most notably Bown (2011a), also make this point).

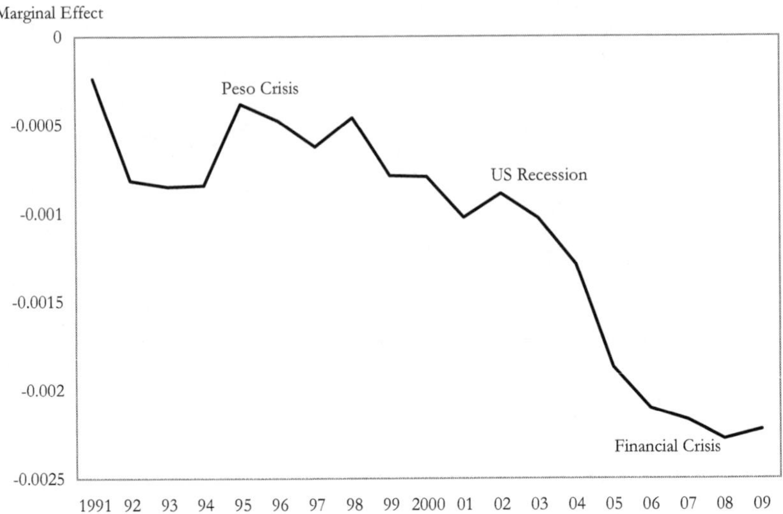

Figure 10.11: *Annual probit results (year coefficient estimates).*

Source: author's calculations. Line represents the (transformed) coefficients on the annual dummy variables in a probit estimation of the preliminary dumping decision being affirmative. Other controls include total (real) trade volume, a China and US dummy variable alone, and interacted with annual dummy variables. The unit of observation was country-HS-04 cells for years 1990–2009. 1990 is the omitted category.

5 COUNTERVAILING DUTIES AND SAFEGUARDS

5.1 *Countervailing Duties*

There are 19 Mexican CVD cases included in Bown (2010), and they are listed in Table 10.10. Table 10.10 includes the country, product, preliminary injury decision, final injury decision date and final injury decision. It is clear from Table 10.10 that Mexico has not moved to offset its decline in anti-dumping activity with an increase in CVD activity. If anything, the two have moved together through time in the sense that both fall. The majority of CVD use was during the mid-1990s, and nearly all of the cases at that time centred on steel. There is only one case with a final injury decision date after 2000, and that was the case of olive oil from the European Union (see Bown and Meagher (2010) for a discussion of Mexico's olive oil case). Aside from the crest of activity in 1995, which coincides with the peso crisis, there is little evidence that CVD use increases during recessions. There are no cases during the 2001 recession and, at least through 2009, there are no cases that correspond to the financial crisis of 2008. The papers that discuss Mexico's past anti-dumping activity that have also discussed CVD activity (see, for example, González and Reyes

Table 10.10: *Mexican countervailing duty cases.*

Case	Country	Product	Preliminary injury decision	Final injury decision date	Final injury decision
1	Venezuela	Aluminum ingots	Affirmative	5/9/1991	Negative
2	EU	Frozen beef	Affirmative	6/3/1994	Affirmative
3	USA	Steel	Negative	—	—
4	Brazil	Hot-rolled steel	—	19/12/1995	Affirmative
5	Venezuela	Hot-rolled steel	—	19/12/1995	Affirmative
6	Brazil	Steel sheets	—	29/12/1995	Affirmative
7	USA	Steel sheets	—	29/12/1995	Negative
8	Brazil	Cold-rolled steel	—	19/12/1995	Affirmative
9	Venezuela	Cold-rolled steel	—	19/12/1995	Affirmative
10	USA	Cold-rolled steel	—	19/12/1995	Negative
11	Brazil	Steel plates in rolls	Affirmative	28/12/1995	Affirmative
12	Venezuela	Steel plates in rolls	Affirmative	28/12/1995	Affirmative
13	USA	Steel plates in rolls	Affirmative	28/12/1995	Negative
14	Indonesia	Wood	Affirmative	12/7/1995	Negative
15	Canada	Wheat	Negative	—	—
16	USA	Wheat	Negative	—	—
17	Denmark	Pork	Affirmative	2/10/1996	Negative
18	Greece	Tinned sliced peaches in syrup	Affirmative	25/11/1998	Negative
19	EU	Olive oil	Affirmative	11/5/2005	Affirmative

Source: trade-weighted tariff calculated using country and HS-06 product trade shares as weights using available tariff and trade data from WITS and Comtrade.

de la Torre 2006) remain excellent resources given the lack of CVD activity since their publication.

5.2 Safeguards

Mexico has only had two safeguard petitions between 1995 and 2010. The first involves plywood panels and was initiated on 15 August 2002. It was subsequently withdrawn on 2 July 2005. The second case involves steel tubes and was initiated on 3 July 2010. Given that the second investigation is still pending, there is little information about this case. What is perhaps more telling is the lack of cases: one observation does not make a trend, so it is difficult to argue that there has been a clear shift towards using safeguard protections. It is interesting, of course, that steel remains a sensitive industry and therefore it is a case that certainly merits continued attention (see Crowley and Howse (2010) for a discussion of the US–Mexican stainless steel dispute).

6 CONCLUSIONS

For nearly 30 years, Mexico has been considered a leader among developing countries with respect to economic policy. Mexico was one of the first liberalisers and has been cited as a country that may be a bellwether for international trade policy in developing countries. In the case of TTBs, Mexico captured the world's attention early as an aggressive user of anti-dumping measures.

The analysis in this chapter highlights the importance of focusing on the stock of anti-dumping protection. Focusing on the stock of anti-dumping coverage reveals a dramatic change in effective anti-dumping coverage in 2008. Rather than revealing a dramatic change in policy, however, the analysis in this paper suggests that the dramatic drop in anti-dumping coverage was primarily due to the unsustainability of Mexico's early aggressive anti-dumping efforts. Specifically, Mexico's imposition of measures against China predated China's entrance to the WTO and, upon entering, China was able to successfully negotiate the removal of Mexico's extensive anti-dumping coverage.

It is also interesting that Mexico has not replaced the fall in coverage with a surge of new anti-dumping duties. In fact, Mexico's anti-dumping initiations have been relatively modest—even in the face of the global financial crisis. In addition to fewer initiations, a probit analysis of affirmative decisions shows a declining probability of affirmative findings over time, suggesting a moderation of Mexico's early enthusiasm. Therefore, to the extent that Mexico might be a bellwether for the developing countries, it may be that the current surge in anti-dumping activity among other developing countries is also temporary.

Raymond Robertson is Professor of Economics at Macalester College, a nonresident fellow at the Center for Global Development, and a member of the Advisory Committee on International Economic Policy at the US State Department.

REFERENCES

Banco de Informaciòn de INEGI (2011). Online resource. URL: http://dgcnesyp.inegi.org.mx.

Bianchi, E., and P. Sanguinetti (2006). Trade liberalization, macroeconomic fluctuations, and contingent protection in Latin America. *Economia: Journal of the Latin American and Caribbean Economic Association* **6**(2), 147–177.

Blonigen, B., and C. P. Bown (2003). Anti-dumping and retaliation threats. *Journal of International Economics* **60**, 249–273.

Bown, C. P. (2011a). Taking stock of anti-dumping, safeguards, and countervailing duties, 1990–2009. *The World Economy*, forthcoming.

Bown, C. P. (2011b). Introduction. In *The Great Recession and Import Protection: The Role of Temporary Trade Barriers* (ed. C. P. Bown). London: CEPR/World Bank. (Chapter 1 of this volume.)

Bown, C. P. (2010). *Temporary Trade Barriers Database*. World Bank (July). URL: http://econ.worldbank.org/ttbd/.

Bown, C. P., and N. Meagher (2010). Mexico olive oil: remedy without a cause? *World Trade Review* **9**(1), 85–116.

Bravo, V. V., H. López-Portillo, and A. Vázquez (2008). Anti-dumping duty agreement marks new dawn for trade with China. International Law Office Newsletter (October). URL: www.internationallawoffice.com/newsletters/detail.aspx?g=64a54f5d-aec1-4f02-ac93-9828f0b9d461.

Central Intelligence Agency (2011) *CIA World Factbook*. URL: www.cia.gov/library/publications/the-world-factbook/geos/mx.html.

Crowley, M., and R. Howse, R. (2010). US stainless steel (Mexico). *World Trade Review* **9**(1), 117–150.

Esquivel, G., and M. Solis (2002). Anti-dumping processes in Mexico. Unpublished Paper, Office of the Chief Economist for Latin America and the Caribbean, World Bank.

Foreign Trade Information System (2011). Organization of American States. Online Resource. URL: www.sice.oas.org/ctyindex/MEX/MEXAgreements_e.asp.

Francois, J., and G. Niels (2006). Business cycles, the exchange rate, and demand for anti-dumping protection in Mexico. *Review of Development Economics* **10**(3), 388–399.

Francois, J., and G. Niels (2004). Political influence in a new anti-dumping regime: evidence from Mexico. CEPR Discussion Paper 4297.

Giesze, C. R. (1994). Mexico's new anti-dumping and countervailing duty system: policy and legal implications, as well as practical business risks and realities, for United States exporters to Mexico in the era of the North American Free Trade Agreement. *St. Mary's Law Journal* **25**, 885–1040.

Gonzàlez, J., and L. E. Reyes de la Torre (2006). Anti-dumping and safeguard measures in the political economy of liberalization: the Mexican case. In *Safeguards and Anti-dumping in Latin American Trade Liberalization* (ed. J. M. Finger and J. J. Nogués), pp 205–246. Washington, DC: World Bank/Palgrave Macmillan.

Hanson, G., and A. Harrison (1999). Trade, technology, and wage inequality in Mexico. *Industrial and Labor Relations Review* **52**(2), 271–288.

Iliff, L. (2009). Remittances to Mexico fall 36%. *Wall Street Journal* (December). URL: http://online.wsj.com/article/SB125968197266271325.html.

INEGI, Encuesta Nacional de Ocupación y Empleo (2011). Indicadores Estratégicos (ENOE). URL: http://dgcnesyp.inegi.gob.mx/.

Kaplan, D. S., D. Lederman, and R. Robertson (2011). Formal labor markets in northern Mexico during the United States recession of 2008–2009. Working Paper, Macalester College.

Lederman, D., W. F. Maloney, and L. Servèn (2005). *Lessons from NAFTA for Latin America and the Caribbean*. Washington, DC: World Bank/Stanford University Press.

Leycegui, B., and L. E. Reyes de la Torre (2005). The 10 major problems with the anti-dumping instrument in Mexico. *Journal of World Trade* **39**(1), 137–146.

Moss, C. B., A. Schmitz, T. Spreen, and D. Orden (2005). Mexico's anti-dumping regime against high fructose corn syrup from the United States. In *International Agricultural Trade Disputes: Case Studies in North America* (ed. A. Schmitz *et al*), pp 207–223. University of Calgary Press.

Niels, G., and A. Ten Kate (2006). Anti-dumping policy in developing countries: safety valve or obstacle to free trade? *European Journal of Political Economy* **22**(3), 618–638.

Niels, G., and A. Ten Kate (2004). Anti-dumping protection in a liberalising country: Mexico's anti-dumping policy and practice. *World Economy* **27**(7), 967–983.

Poitras, G., and R. Robertson (1994). The politics of NAFTA in Mexico. *Journal of Inter-american Studies and World Affairs* **36**(1), 1–36.

Reynolds, K. M. (2007). Dumping on agriculture: are there biases in anti-dumping regulations? *Journal of International Agricultural Trade and Development* **3**(2), 135–153.

Robertson, R. (2009). Mexico and the great trade collapse. In *The Great Trade Collapse: Causes, Consequences and Prospects* (ed. R. Baldwin). VoxEU.org e-book. URL: http://voxeu.org/index.php?q=node/4297.

Robertson, R. (2007). Trade and wages: two puzzles from Mexico. *World Economy* **30**(9), 1347–1489.

Robertson, R. (2004). Relative prices and wage inequality: evidence from Mexico. *Journal of International Economics* **64**(2), 387–409.

Robertson, R. (2000). Wage shocks and North American labor market integration. *American Economic Review* **90**(4), 742–764.

Vandenbussche, H., and M. Zanardi (2010). The chilling trade effects of anti-dumping proliferation. *European Economic Review* **54**(6), 760–777.

Weintraub, S. (2010). *Unequal Partners: The United States and Mexico.* University of Pittsburgh Press.

11

Turkey: Temporary Trade Barriers as Resistance to Trade Liberalisation with the European Union?

BAYBARS KARACAOVALI[1]

1 INTRODUCTION

This chapter examines Turkey's use of TTBs—in the form of anti-dumping, safeguards and CVDs—from 1990 to 2009. We rely on detailed product-level data to analyse the structure of Turkey's TTBs across industries and target countries over time.

Turkey, as a major emerging economy, started to use anti-dumping policies in 1989 and has been one of its more active users ever since. It has adopted other measures of TTBs—namely, global safeguards, China-specific safeguards and CVDs—and its total use of TTBs has increased, especially over the second half of the 2000s.

Turkey went through significant trade liberalisation as it fully formed a customs union with the EU in January 1996. Based on the customs union decision, Turkey has abolished all trade barriers in the manufacturing sector *vis-à-vis* the EU, and it has considerably reduced barriers against third countries by adopting the EU's common external tariff. Turkey has also gradually taken on an array of EU preferential trading relationships, such as the Euro-Mediterranean partnership and Generalised System of Preferences. Turkey formed free-trade areas with the EFTA in 1992 and then with the prospective EU candidate countries in Central and Eastern Europe since joining the customs union.[2]

[1]Department of Economics, University of Hawaii at Manoa, Saunders Hall Room 542, 2424 Maile Way, Honolulu, HI 96822, USA. Email: baybars@hawaii.edu. Website: www2.hawaii.edu/~baybars. I gratefully acknowledge Chad Bown for very helpful comments and Aksel Erbahar for the fact checks and corrections. I also thank Michael Moore, Raymond Robertson and Patricia Tovar for their comments. The views expressed in this paper and any errors are solely my own.

[2]The members of the EFTA in 1992 were Austria, Finland, Iceland, Liechtenstein, Norway, Sweden and Switzerland. Austria, Finland and Sweden left the EFTA and joined the EU in 1995.

Turkey's predominant use of TTBs took the form of anti-dumping throughout the 1990–2009 period, with an increasing rate of import coverage. However, Turkey also started to use global safeguard measures beginning in 2005, and this policy quickly became a significant temporary barrier as a complement to anti-dumping. Moreover, in addition to an increase in the number of TTB initiations over the 2000s, the higher rate of initiated investigations resulting in new imposed measures also contributed to Turkey's expanding stock of imported products subject to TTBs. There is also some evidence of sluggishness in terms of Turkey's removal of TTBs over time.

Turkey has been significantly affected by the 2008–9 global economic crisis, with especially negative effects in 2009. After six years of positive growth, Turkish real GDP per capita contracted by 0.6% in 2008 and by 6% in 2009 (see Figure 11.1(a)). The unemployment rate increased to 10.9% in 2008 only to be surpassed by an increase to 14% in 2009 (see Figure 11.1(a)). The 2008–9 crisis proved to be as severe as Turkey's two previous major economic crises. In 1994, real GDP per capita had declined by 6.3%, and in 2001 it fell by 7.1%. However, unlike the earlier crises, both Turkey's imports and exports declined in 2009 (Figure 11.1(b)), an experience shared by the rest of the world (WTO 2010). The 1994 and 2001 crises were financial in nature as the Turkish lira depreciated sharply: by 36% in 1994 and by 31% in 2001 in real terms (Figure 11.1(b)).[3] Consequently, Turkey's exports kept increasing while its imports declined during those periods. In 2009, Turkey's exports also declined despite the 14% real depreciation of the lira.

During 2008–9, Turkey considerably increased its use of TTBs. Nevertheless, apart from the significant emergence of global safeguard measures, it is hard to argue that the 2008–9 increase was not part of a pre-existent upward trend. However, the full response to the crisis may be felt with a lag; Turkey's use of TTBs may continue to expand even after the crisis. The drastic intra- and extra-group trade liberalisation brought on by the adoption of the EU's common external tariff and its preferential agreements seems to have particularly contributed to the rise in Turkey's use of TTBs over the 2000s. Due to various trade policy commitments with the EU, TTBs offer one of the few channels through which Turkey retains some control over its trade policy.

Turkey's use of TTBs has become more widespread across sectors over time. The products that Turkey has covered with TTBs coincide with the list of goods that were deemed 'sensitive' in its initial agreement with the EU. These products had higher rates of import protection that were phased out by 2001. Turkey has increasingly targeted textiles with TTBs, especially after

[3]The real exchange rate is calculated by multiplying Turkish lira per US dollar nominal exchange rate with the ratio of US to Turkish GDP deflators. Therefore, a rise in the real exchange rate indicates a real depreciation of the Turkish currency.

(a)

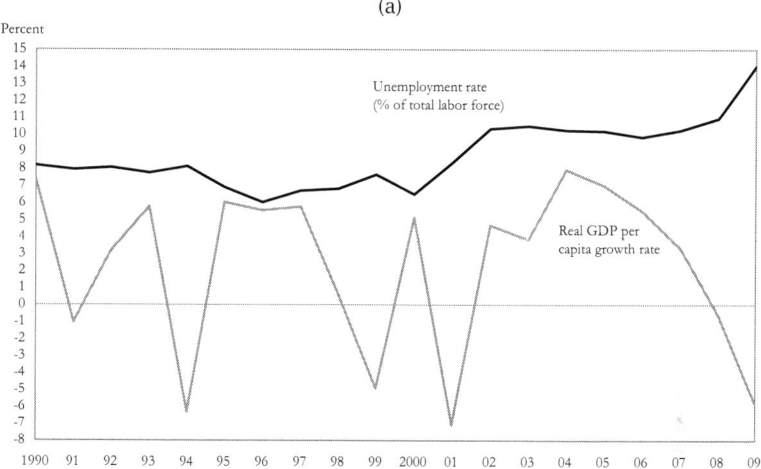

(b)

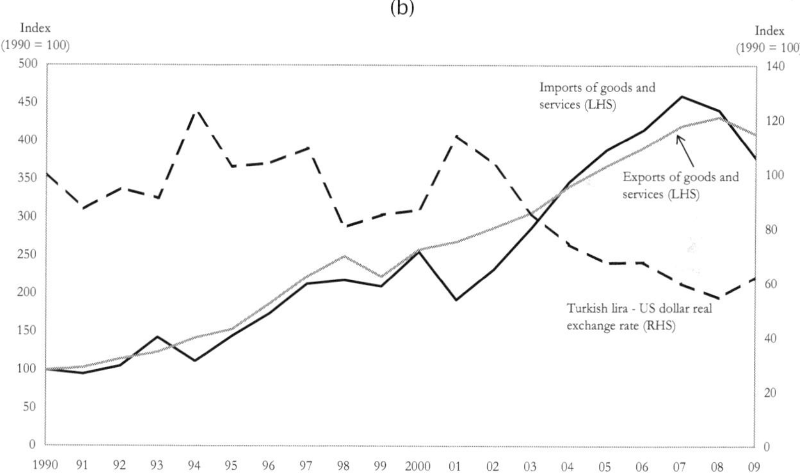

Figure 11.1: *Turkish macroeconomic indicators, 1990–2009.*
Source: author's calculations using WDI and IMF International Financial Statistics. Increase in the real exchange rate indicates depreciation of the Turkish lira.

the expiration of the WTO Agreement on Textiles and Clothing that allowed Turkey to use import quotas despite the customs union agreement.[4]

[4]Furthermore, under the Doha Round of WTO negotiations, in 2006, Turkey demanded 'sectoral' treatment for textiles. Their request that textile tariffs should be negotiated separately was backed by the USA but opposed by the EU, thereby creating some controversy (Beattie 2006).

We also find that, on average, the products that Turkey subjected to TTBs had higher tariff rates and preference margins. The political economy forces that lead to higher tariff protection and more preferential access seem also to affect Turkey's use of TTBs. In general, Turkey does not target established EU members with TTBs, although there is no legal prohibition against doing so. Turkey mainly targets developing countries, and China especially, at rates that are disproportionate to their import market shares. On the other hand, apart from South Korea, the high-income countries are underrepresented relative to their shares of the Turkish import market.

The rest of this chapter is organised as follows. In Section 2 we introduce the measurement strategy, examine the use of different kinds of TTBs by Turkey over time, and discuss the effects of economic crises. In Section 3 we examine the relationship between tariffs, imports, PTAs and the use of TTBs. In Section 4 we analyse the cross-industry variation, and in Section 5 we investigate the foreign-exporter incidence in Turkey's use of TTBs between 1990 and 2009. Section 6 concludes.

2 THE USE OF TEMPORARY TRADE BARRIERS OVER TIME

Turkey has been an active user of TTBs, mainly anti-dumping, since the early 1990s. Beginning in the mid-2000s, Turkey has also started to use global safeguards, China-specific safeguards and CVDs. In the next subsection, we introduce the main measurement strategies and briefly discuss the data before moving on to the analysis.

2.1 Data and Measurement

Detailed TTB data are obtained from the *Temporary Trade Barriers Database* (Bown 2010a). The imports at the six-digit Harmonized System level are from Comtrade, UN Statistics Division, through World Bank's WITS software.

The *Temporary Trade Barriers Database* lists the original product names in the investigations. Furthermore, the database identifies the corresponding products at various levels of aggregation; investigations range from the HS 4-digit to HS 12-digit levels. Given the lack of import data at the 12-digit level dating back to the 1990s, the analysis is kept at the 6-digit level. Given the nature of the products for Turkey, this does not seem to bias the results.[5]

[5] For example, for the anti-dumping case against Finland over paper, which was in effect between 1990 and 2000, the TTB database identifies the following two product codes: '480252201000' and '480252801000'. Both are defined as 'printing and writing paper' in the WTO's consolidated tariff schedules for Turkey. The definition for the HS six-digit code we use, '480252' (which covers both products), in the Comtrade imports data is 'Paper...(excluding mechanical fibres), weighing $\geqslant$ [4]'. As illustrated in this example, the six-digit code is sufficiently detailed as compared with the 12-digit code and should not introduce a sizeable bias for the Turkish data.

We consider both stock and flow measures of TTBs. The stock measure refers to the TTBs in force in a given year, whereas the flow measure refers to the newly initiated TTB investigations that may or may not eventually result in newly imposed barriers. Following Bown (2011b), we employ two basic approaches to measure both stocks and flows. The first approach relies on counts of products subject to TTBs as a share of all products imported in a given year and is captured by Equation (1.1) in Bown (2011a).

The second approach introduces trade weights by product and import source country. In this respect, it takes into account the economic importance of the product subject to a TTB and also allows for variation across targeted countries. For instance, some of Turkey's TTBs involve only one country, while others involve several countries. Furthermore, new TTB measures may be introduced on the same product before an earlier one expires, potentially introducing new target countries in a given year. When trade-weighting the new TTB indicator (which is now target-country specific), we have to account for the trade dampening effect of the barrier in the first place. In this respect, imports by source country subject to TTBs are imputed by allowing the pre-barrier import values to 'grow' at the same rate as the non-TTB products in the economy for as long as the TTB for the target-country–product combination is in force. This approach also provides consistent figures across target countries over time. We calculate the second measure following Equation (1.2) of Chapter 1. Note that, in the case of global safeguards, the target country is 'world', hence we take into account the total imports from all sources for a product under safeguards. Finally, in all estimates of Equation (1.2), we only consider non-oil imports to avoid volatility in oil prices affecting the consistency of the measures over time.

2.2 General Trends in the Use of Different Types of TTBs

Turkey has actively used anti-dumping since 1989. Since 2004, it has adopted other TTB measures as well. In Figure 11.2(a) we present the stock and flow estimates based on Equation (1.1), and in Figure 11.2(b) we present estimates based on Equation (1.2) for anti-dumping and combined TTB measures at the HS-06 product level. Figure 11.2(a) illustrates that Turkey's anti-dumping policy use (stock) was relatively steady, covering around 0.7% of the HS-06 imported products between 1992 and 2000. After a rise in coverage in 2001 to 1.5%, the use of anti-dumping measures surged, reaching a 4.4% coverage rate by 2009.

In Table 11.1 we present the underlying stock and flow numbers used in Figure 11.2 and further break down the TTBs into four categories: anti-dumping, safeguards, China-specific safeguards and CVDs. We also show counts of products subject to TTB measures, and thus employ the numerator of Equation (1.1) only.

In 2004, Turkey initiated safeguard investigations for the first time. These covered 13 different HS-06 products, and 2 resulted in imposed safeguards in

Table 11.1: *Turkey's use of TTBs at the HS-06 product level, 1990–2009.*

	1990–1993 average	1994	1995–99 average	2000	2001	2002	2003	2004	2005	2006	2007	2008	2009
(a) Stock (in force)													
Counts of HS-06 products													
Anti-dumping	29.5	28	34.0	36	69	99	114	119	152	163	155	164	192
Safeguard	—	—	—	—	—	—	—	—	2	23	24	84	82
China-specific safeguard		—	—	—	—	—	—	—	—	4	4	4	4
Countervailing duty		—	—	—	—	—	—	—	—	—	—	—	3
Import share (%) by count													
Anti-dumping	0.657	0.649	0.739	0.784	1.534	2.216	2.544	2.630	3.339	3.581	3.569	3.769	4.428
Safeguard	—	—	—	—	—	—	—	—	0.044	0.505	0.553	1.931	1.891
China-specific safeguard		—	—	—	—	—	—	—	—	0.088	0.092	0.092	0.092
Countervailing duty		—	—	—	—	—	—	—	—	—	—	—	0.069
Import share (%) by value													
Anti-dumping	0.368	0.253	1.476	1.494	1.170	1.627	2.043	2.100	2.362	2.638	2.779	3.234	2.155
Safeguard	—	—	—	—	—	—	—	—	0.026	0.571	0.822	1.630	1.640
China-specific safeguard		—	—	—	—	—	—	—	—	0.022	0.023	0.022	0.022
Countervailing duty		—	—	—	—	—	—	—	—	—	—	—	0.004

Table 11.1: *Continued.*

	1990–1993 average	1994	1995–99 average	2000	2001	2002	2003	2004	2005	2006	2007	2008	2009
(b) Flow (new investigations)													
Counts of HS-06 products													
Anti-dumping	30.5	144	2.3	86	5	9	15	37	9	11	6	43	40
Safeguard	—	—	—	—	—	—	—	13	—	24	21	40	1
China-specific safeguard		—	—	—	—	—	—	—	4	5	—	—	—
Countervailing duty		—	—	—	—	—	—	—	—	—	—	3	—
Import share (%) by count													
Anti-dumping	0.692	3.222	0.030	1.874	0.111	0.201	0.335	0.818	0.198	0.242	0.138	0.988	0.923
Safeguard	—	—	—	—	—	—	—	0.287	—	0.527	0.484	0.919	0.023
China-specific safeguard		—	—	—	—	—	—	—	0.088	0.110	—	—	—
Countervailing duty		—	—	—	—	—	—	—	—	—	—	0.069	—
Import share (%) by value													
Anti-dumping	0.306	1.847	0.033	0.439	0.291	0.108	0.062	0.291	0.248	0.142	0.164	0.451	0.157
Safeguard	—	—	—	—	—	—	—	0.164	—	0.811	0.434	0.369	0.002
China-specific safeguard		—	—	—	—	—	—	—	0.023	0.137	—	—	—
Countervailing duty		—	—	—	—	—	—	—	—	—	—	0.004	—

Source: author's calculations using *Temporary Trade Barriers Database* (Bown 2010a) and Comtrade.

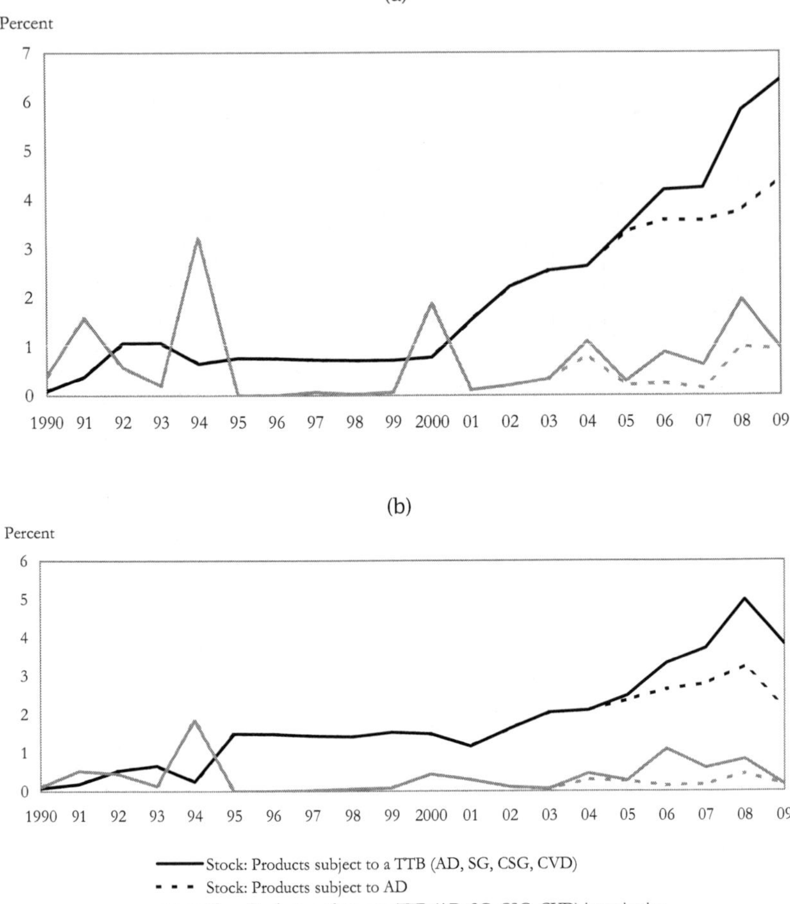

Figure 11.2: *Turkey's use of TTBs, 1990–2009: (a) share of TTB-impacted HS-06 products by count; (b) share of TTB-impacted HS-06 products by import value.*

Source: author's calculations using *Temporary Trade Barriers Database* (Bown 2010a) and Comtrade (UN Statistics Division).

2005. In Figure 11.2 these turning points are illustrated by the dashed lines (measuring anti-dumping only) and solid lines (measuring all TTBs) starting to branch out in 2004 (for the flow figures) and 2005 (for the stock figures). Table 11.1 again documents how safeguard coverage expanded drastically from 0.07% (2 HS-06 products) of the imported products initially in 2005 to 1.9% (83 HS-06 products) by 2008.

In 2006, Turkey imposed China-specific safeguards over four HS-06 imported products and initiated investigations covering five other products that did not subsequently turn into China-specific safeguard measures. The imposed China-specific safeguard measures were expired in 2009. There were three HS-06 products (from India) investigated for CVDs that were eventually imposed in 2009; these covered 0.07% of the imported products at the HS-06 level (Table 11.1).

Figure 11.2 illustrates intermittent jumps in the flow of TTBs (grey solid lines in panels (a) and (b)), *ie* in the newly initiated TTB investigations at the product level. There was a big jump in 1994 when the number of products investigated hit 144, which covered 3.2% of the imported product lines and 1.8% of the imports by value (Figure 11.2 and Table 11.1). The WTO's subsequent Trade Policy Review of Turkey indicated that '...the large build-up of cases initiated through 1994 may be explained by the overvalued domestic currency, which, as in a number of other countries, might have caused domestic industries to seek protection through anti-dumping measures...' (WTO 1998, p 59). Turkey did experience a drastic currency crisis in 1994 as its currency depreciated by 36% in real terms against the US dollar (see again Figure 11.1(b)) and real GDP per capita contracted by about 6.3% (see again Figure 11.1(a)). The surge in the number of products investigated in 1994 was mostly due to the new investigations in the textiles sector. These did not subsequently result in anti-dumping measures so there was not a corresponding jump in the stock of anti-dumping measures in Figure 11.2(a).

In Figure 11.2(b) we present the stock and flow estimates based on Equation (1.2) and thus trade-weight the indicators to better account for the economic importance of the TTBs.[6] When we consider the share of import value of each target-country-product combination, there was actually a sudden increase in the value of products subject to anti-dumping in 1995 (after a small drop in 1994 due to the crisis), although the number of anti-dumping-products did not change noticeably (see again Figure 11.2(a)). This difference is due to the fact that a few new products in the metals and plastics/rubbers industries were added to the stock of products already under anti-dumping. Similarly, the jump in 1994 in the flow of anti-dumping investigations is not as pronounced when we consider their share in total imports by value as opposed to counts of products. This jump is completely due to the 138 newly investigated HS-06 products in the textiles (excluding silk and wool) sector. In terms of trade value, they do not amount to much when compared with other sectors like metals. The cross-industry variation in the use of TTBs is further explored in Section 4.

A second jump in anti-dumping investigated products occurred in 2000 (see Figure 11.2 and Table 11.1). Several of the earlier anti-dumping measures were

[6]Note that only non-oil total imports are used for the denominator in Equation (1.2) to avoid price volatility and hence to ensure consistency in the estimates over time.

revoked during this year, and this was also one year prior to the requirement that Turkey, as part of the EU customs union, would have to completely phase out all remaining protection on 'sensitive sectors' and adopt the EU's PTAs (Togan 2000). Moreover, in late 2000, Turkey experienced a liquidity crisis that turned into a major financial crisis in early 2001 (Onis 2009), as real GDP per capita contracted by 7.1% (see again Figure 11.1(a)). This macroeconomic shock is also a likely contributor to the demands for additional import protection. Given the lag between the initiation of anti-dumping investigations and the imposition of anti-dumping measures, Turkey's anti-dumping stock gradually increased from 2001 onwards (Figure 11.2(a) and Table 11.1). Again due to the liquidity crisis, the import value of the goods covered by TTBs first fell in 2001, before increasing until 2009 when the next crisis hit (Figure 11.2(b)). In 2009, the total (non-oil) imports were significantly contracted by 36% due to the global economic crisis. We discuss the effects of this crisis on the use of TTBs and make comparisons with earlier crises in Section 2.4.

There was a steady stream of new anti-dumping investigations beginning in 2002 with significant jumps again in 2004, 2008 and 2009 (the grey dashed line in Figure 11.2(a)). The increase in other TTB investigations—first in 2006 and then through 2008—led to some divergence in the flow of anti-dumping versus the other TTBs. This is shown by the gaps between the solid and dashed grey lines in Figure 11.2(a).

Table 11.2 presents information on the TTB investigation cases and their outcomes.[7] Some anti-dumping investigations involve just one country, while others involve several. Each anti-dumping case in Table 11.2 refers to unique country-investigation combinations. In Section 5 we further break down the anti-dumping investigation cases by target country and examine cross-target-country differences. Between 1990 and 1999, Turkey initiated a total of 62 anti-dumping cases and 64.5% resulted in a final measure (Table 11.2). However, between 2000 and 2009, the anti-dumping investigations were decisively more likely to end in new barriers as 95.1% of the 143 cases resulted in final measures.

Turkey initiated its first five global safeguard investigations in 2004, and 40% of them resulted in the imposition of final measures.[8] Between 2006 and 2009, all of Turkey's ten safeguard investigations resulted in measures. In 2005, Turkey initiated its first China-specific safeguard investigation, which resulted in a new trade barrier, whereas the other two investigations initiated in 2006 had negative outcomes. Finally, Turkey initiated only one CVD investigation (against India) during the period (in 2008) and that resulted in a final measure.

---

[7]Investigations that have missing initiation and final decision information are not included in the calculations.

[8]Notice the difference between anti-dumping cases that are target-country specific and safeguard investigations that apply to 'world' as the target country.

Table 11.2: *Turkey's TTB initiations and outcomes.*

	Anti-dumping			Global safeguards			China-specific safeguards			Countervailing duties		
Year	Number of initiations	Final measure	% resulting in measures	Number of initiations	Final measure	% resulting in measures	Number of initiations	Final measure	% resulting in measures	Number of initiations	Final measure	% resulting in measures
1990	10	8	80.0	—	—	—	—	—	—	—	—	—
1991	5	5	100.0	—	—	—	—	—	—	—	—	—
1992	4	4	100.0	—	—	—	—	—	—	—	—	—
1993	8	6	75.0	—	—	—	—	—	—	—	—	—
1994	21	8	38.1	—	—	—	—	—	—	—	—	—
1995	—	—	—	—	—	—	—	—	—	—	—	—
1996	—	—	—	—	—	—	—	—	—	—	—	—
1997	5	1	20.0	—	—	—	—	—	—	—	—	—
1998	1	1	100.0	—	—	—	—	—	—	—	—	—
1999	8	7	87.5	—	—	—	—	—	—	—	—	—
2000	7	7	100.0	—	—	—	—	—	—	—	—	—
2001	15	14	93.3	—	—	—	—	—	—	—	—	—
2002	17	17	100.0	—	—	—	—	—	—	—	—	—
2003	17	17	100.0	—	—	—	—	—	—	—	—	—
2004	32	32	100.0	5	2	40.0	—	—	—	—	—	—
2005	12	12	100.0	—	—	—	1	1	100.0	—	—	—
2006	8	8	100.0	5	5	100.0	2	0	0.0	—	—	—
2007	6	6	100.0	3	3	100.0	—	—	—	—	—	—
2008	23	18	78.3	1	1	100.0	—	—	—	1	1	100.0
2009	6	5	83.3	1	1	100.0	—	—	—	—	—	—
Total	205	176	85.9	15	12	80.0	3	1	33.3	1	1	100.0

Source: author's calculations using *Temporary Trade Barriers Database* (Bown 2010a).

In addition to Turkey's increase in its initiations over the 2000s, the higher rate of initiations finding support also played a role in expanding the stock of its TTBs. In the next subsection we analyse the duration of TTB measures and examine whether there was sluggishness in their removal, potentially adding to the recent build-up.

2.3 Duration of TTBs

The Uruguay Round made sunset reviews after five years a requirement for anti-dumping measures. Nevertheless, enforcement is lax and WTO's Anti-Dumping Agreement 'allows WTO members great latitude in their determination of the likelihood of dumping and injury resumption' (Cadot *et al* 2007). Turkey officially adopted the Anti-Dumping Agreement in 1999 (*Official Gazette* 1999), agreeing to limit definitive anti-dumping measures to five years. Nevertheless, according to Turkey's legislation on the Prevention of Unfair Competition in Imports, a 'definitive anti-dumping duty may remain in force as long as and to the extent necessary to counteract dumping which is causing injury' (Undersecretariat of the Prime Ministry for Foreign Trade 2010, p 3). In Table 11.3 we present information on the duration of anti-dumping measures in Turkey at the investigation level. Using the available Turkish data in the *Temporary Trade Barriers Database* (Bown 2010a), we find that 45 anti-dumping measures have been revoked with an average duration of 7.09 years; 36% of measures were revoked in 5 years, and 60% were revoked in 6 to 10 years. One anti-dumping measure lasted for 15 years (against Belarus in the textiles sector for 'polyster synthetic staple fibers (not processed)' from 1994 to 2009) and one lasted for 4 years.

Anti-dumping measures in the textiles sector had an average duration of 9 years, which is above Turkey's overall anti-dumping average. However, anti-dumping measures against China had an average duration of 7.4 years, which is roughly the same as Turkey's anti-dumping measures against other countries. As will be discussed below, Turkey uses TTBs frequently in the textiles sector and to target China. We analyse cross-industry variation in Turkish use of TTBs in Section 4 and we explore foreign-exporter incidence in Section 5.

While Turkey has revoked 45 anti-dumping measures, 128 measures were still in effect as of June 2010. Although these barriers have not yet been removed, 55% of them are already beyond 5 years in duration. On average, the overall duration for all cases is 5.4 years thus far, with a similar average figure for textiles and China.

In panel (b) of Table 11.3, starting from 1995 (five years beyond which the first anti-dumping measures were imposed), we present the annual data for the percentage of anti-dumping measures imposed five or more years ago that have still not been revoked. Until 1999, as might be expected, in the absence of a sunset review legislation, almost all cases remained in effect beyond five years. However, beginning in 2000 (the year after the Turkish anti-dumping legislation), all but two anti-dumping measures that were imposed

Table 11.3: *Duration of Turkey's anti-dumping measures.*

(a) Duration

Number of years	Number of anti-dumping cases (already revoked)	Number of anti-dumping cases (still in force as of June 2010)
1	0	9
2	0	11
3	0	6
4	1	20
5	16	12
6	4	25
7	7	24
8	3	11
9	7	2
10	6	7
11	0	1
12	0	0
13	0	0
14	0	0
15	1	0
Total	45	128
Average duration	7.09 years	5.4 years
Average duration (textiles)	9 years	5.7 years
Average duration (China)	7.4 years	5.4 years

(b) Percentage of anti-dumping measures imposed five or more years ago but still not revoked

	1995	1996	1997	1998	1999	2000	2001	2002
%	100.0	100.0	89.5	83.3	84.6	2.9	2.9	2.9

	2003	2004	2005	2006	2007	2008	2009	2010
%	2.9	5.7	20.9	29.2	42.4	51.1	60.9	64.6

Source: author's calculations using *Temporary Trade Barriers Database* (Bown 2010a).

prior to 2000 were revoked. Therefore, the percentage of anti-dumping measures imposed five or more years ago but still not revoked remained in single digits between 2000 and 2004. Of the 147 anti-dumping measures that Turkey imposed since 2000, 5% were retired within five years, 3% were retired in seven years and the remaining 92% were still in force as of June 2010. Consequently, the percentage of measures that linger beyond five years has increased consistently from 2005, reaching 64.6% by 2010.

Turkey enacted its legislation on safeguards in 2004 according to which 'the duration of safeguard measures shall not exceed 4 (four) years, including the duration of any provisional measure unless it is extended...in accordance with the results of a new investigation to be initiated...[and] the total period of application of a safeguard measure shall not exceed 10 years' (*Official Gazette* 2004). Of the 12 global safeguard measures imposed since 2005, 2 expired in 2008, 5 had not expired as of 2010, 4 were supposed to expire in 2009 but were extended until 2012, and 1 was supposed to expire in 2009 but was revoked in 2010. Therefore, there is some evidence of tardiness in Turkey's removal of global safeguard measures as well.

There was only one China-specific safeguard measure that was imposed in 2006 and it expired in 2009. Finally, there was only one CVD case that came into force in 2009 and was still in effect as of 2010.

2.4 The 2008–9 Global Economic Crisis and the Use of TTBs

In 2008 and 2009, Turkey experienced a significant increase in the number of products subject to TTBs (Table 11.1 and Figure 11.2, stock figures). Throughout the period from 1990 to 2009, Turkey's predominant TTB policy was anti-dumping with an increasingly upward trend in the coverage of products. However, since first turning to their use in 2005, safeguard measures quickly became an important TTB for Turkey, complementing its use of anti-dumping measures.

While the share of Turkey's products subject to anti-dumping in its total number of imported products (Equation (1.1) estimate) increased from 3.3% in 2005 to 4.4% in 2009, the share of products covered under global safeguards increased even more dramatically—from 0.04% in 2005 to 1.9% in 2009 (see Table 11.1, stock figures). Turkey's anti-dumping coverage steadily increased, beginning in 2001. In that respect, the global safeguards, China-specific safeguards and CVDs that Turkey has subsequently introduced has not replaced the anti-dumping measures that it has in force.

During the 1994 currency crisis in Turkey, there was an explosion in the number of anti-dumping investigations, as illustrated by the jump in the solid grey line in Figure 11.2(a), even though the stock figures did not change visibly (solid black line). However, as indicated above, due to the compositional change in products subject to anti-dumping, their import value increased in 1995 (Figure 11.2(b)).

In late 2000, Turkey suffered a liquidity crisis, followed by a financial crisis in early 2001. Having been almost absent between 1995 and 1999, new anti-dumping investigations re-emerged in 2000. However, it is hard to disentangle the effect of the crisis from the fact that earlier anti-dumping measures were revoked in 2000 and also because Turkey was expected to complete trade liberalisation with the EU and to adopt an array of EU-related bilateral agreements during this period.

Apart from the significant emergence of global safeguard measures, it is hard to argue that Turkey's considerable increase in TTB use during 2008–9 was not part of an already existing upward trend in contingent protection. In 2009, only one product was under global safeguard investigation and all the existing safeguard measures were set to expire by 2012. The China-specific safeguard measure that was in force against one product expired in 2009. Turkey introduced CVDs for the first time in 2009. If new global safeguards, China-specific safeguards or CVD measures do not rise in the post-crisis period, it might be possible to partly attribute the 2008–9 increase in non-anti-dumping TTB measures to the global economic crisis.

A more formal analysis is required to determine whether crises entail more protection through TTBs. What is clear, however, is that the number of new investigations (flow) increased in crisis periods, as can be observed by the significant jumps in the solid grey line in Figure 11.2(a) in 1994, 2000 and 2008.

Although the decisiveness in turning anti-dumping investigations into final measures seems to be stronger over the 2000s, this was moderated slightly during the 2008–9 crisis. The percentage of initiated investigations resulting in measures actually declined to 78.3% (of 23 investigations) in 2008 before rising slightly to 83.3% (of 6 investigations) in 2009. This contrasts with the 2002–7 period, in which 100% of the 92 investigations resulted in imposed TTBs (Table 11.2).

The duration of anti-dumping measures not being revoked at the five-year mark (as required by sunset reviews) also increased after 2005, as discussed in the previous subsection. While the 2008–9 crisis may make it easier to justify the extension of TTBs, any delay in their removal seems to be in line with pre-crisis trends.

Turkey did not resort to other policy changes such as tariff increases in the crisis period, with the exception of a tariff increase in 'beam fish' in 2010 (Global Trade Alert 2010).[9] However, this product is already excluded from the EU agreement, and thus the restriction on Turkey changing its tariff policy due to the customs union with the EU may be preventing other plausible increases in its applied tariffs—many of which are way below their bound rates given the significant trade liberalisation in Turkey since the Uruguay Round.

In the next section, we explore the relationship between tariffs, imports, PTAs and Turkey's use of TTBs.

---

[9]Global Trade Alert also identifies a public procurement legislation in December 2008 (measure no. 1098) allowing a 15% price preference for domestic suppliers. However, given the lack of information about this policy prior to 2008, it is hard to compare the crisis era with earlier periods.

3 TARIFFS, IMPORTS, PREFERENTIAL TRADE AGREEMENTS AND TEMPORARY TRADE BARRIERS

Turkey has a complex structure of tariffs including specific, *ad valorem* and compound components as well as a mass housing fund levy on imports. The internal taxes, namely special consumption tax, value-added tax and stamp duty apply in a cascading manner on top of each other, creating yet another differential for imported goods. For instance, value-added tax applies to imports inclusive of tariffs, levies and special consumption tax. Yet the average protection levels are fairly low (apart from agricultural goods and food items). Togan (2010) computes *ad valorem* equivalents of nominal protection rates in Turkey, taking into account the complexities of the Turkish customs procedures and finds that the simple average nominal protection rate against the EU was 9.12% in 2009. However, it was actually 0% in all sectors except agriculture (52.2%) and chemicals (0.08%). The MFN protection rate averaged 13.86% with 56.5% in agriculture, 8.93% in textiles and 8.03% in footwear and miscellaneous manufactures. When only tariffs plus the mass housing fund levy are considered, the WTO (1998) estimates that average MFN tariffs declined from 26.7% in 1993 to 12.7% in 1998.

The drastic intra-group and extra-group trade liberalisation—brought on by the adoption of the common external tariff of the EU and its preferential agreements, as well as the requirement to finalise the liberalisation of sensitive sectors—are potential contributing factors to the rise in Turkey's use of TTBs. Due to various trade policy commitments with the EU, TTBs offer some of the few outlets where Turkey enjoys a certain level of trade policy independence.

In this section we examine how Turkey's imports, tariffs and PTAs interact with its use of TTBs. Using the available UNCTAD TRAINS data on applied MFN and preferential tariffs, we first look at the trends in tariffs for all products that have been subjected to a TTB, versus the remainder, with the exception of agricultural goods. As indicated above, the tariff rates in the agricultural sector are very high and they are excluded from the Turkey–EU agreement. Consequently, Turkey does not impose any TTBs in this sector. We also exclude oil industry products that are solely imported, not comparable with other imports, and also subject to price volatility. Figure 11.3(a) shows that average MFN tariffs for TTB products were always higher than the tariffs for non-TTB products during the 1990–2009 period. The gap ranged between 2% (in 1993) and 4% (in 1997). This suggests that Turkey used TTBs for products that were already more protected through tariffs, and hints at a complementarity between the two forms of protection. Therefore, it is plausible to argue that tariff liberalisation might have accelerated the use of TTBs, especially after 2000. Nevertheless, a suggestion of causality requires a more formal analysis that would necessitate controlling for the effects of various other factors.[10]

In addition to trade liberalisation concerning the EU, Turkey also entered agreements to completely eliminate tariffs in industrial goods with Israel by 2000; with Hungary, Czech Republic, Slovak Republic and Lithuania by 2001; with Romania, Bulgaria and Poland by 2002; with Estonia and Latvia by entry into force of agreement in 2004; with Croatia and Bosnia-Herzegovina by 2007; and with Macedonia by 2008 (WTO 2003). Computing preference margins as the difference between MFN tariffs and the lowest available preferential tariff by product, Figure 11.3(b) illustrates that preference margins were higher for TTB products over time. One interpretation of this is that products with a larger preference margin were more likely to be protected by TTBs. Given that preferential tariffs for the products involved were either duty-free or very low, preferential margins also directly reflect the cross-product variation in MFN tariffs in a similar way to Figure 11.3(a). Therefore, it is not possible to disentangle the importance of the two channels affecting the use of TTBs without a formal econometric analysis.

Figure 11.3(c) illustrates Turkey's import values for TTB versus non-TTB products, normalising their 1990 figures to 100. Imports of TTB products have expanded more rapidly, suggesting once more the import-competing nature and hence political sensitivity of these products for policymakers.

In addition to the independence from the EU in the use of TTBs against third countries, there is no restriction on TTB use between the EU and Turkey. In Figure 11.3(d), we report the percentage share of HS-06-product–target-country combinations subject to a TTB by Turkey's PTA partners versus non-partners. This calculation is similar in spirit to Equation (1.1) (discussed in Section 2.1) in terms of being a count measure. It is computed as the number of distinct HS-06-product–TTB-country combinations as a share of all export-country–HS-06-product combinations, dropping observations for countries supplying less than 1% of the imports for a given product. In Figure 11.3(e) we present the percentage share of the *import value* of HS-06 products subject to a TTB by PTA partner, which is an application of Equation (1.2) (discussed in Section 2.1).

Figures 11.3(d) and 11.3(e) describe results for four different target groups: 'EU15' includes the 15 EU members as of 1996, the year Turkey formed the

[10]Another point to check would be to compare the anti-dumping margins with the tariff overhang (bound MFN tariff rates minus applied tariffs) but this cannot be performed for Turkey given the incompatibility of product codes (and lack of correspondence) in the *Temporary Trade Barriers Database* (Bown 2010a) with WTO's consolidated tariff schedules and four different versions of the HS code (8 to 12 digit) in the TRAINS data set. Given that MFN tariffs are actually determined in tandem with the EU, Turkey does not have the ability to raise its applied tariffs that are not bound instead of introducing new TTBs. Otherwise, the question of whether anti-dumping margins exceed the tariff overhang could be used to investigate whether Turkey is using TTBs 'unfairly'.

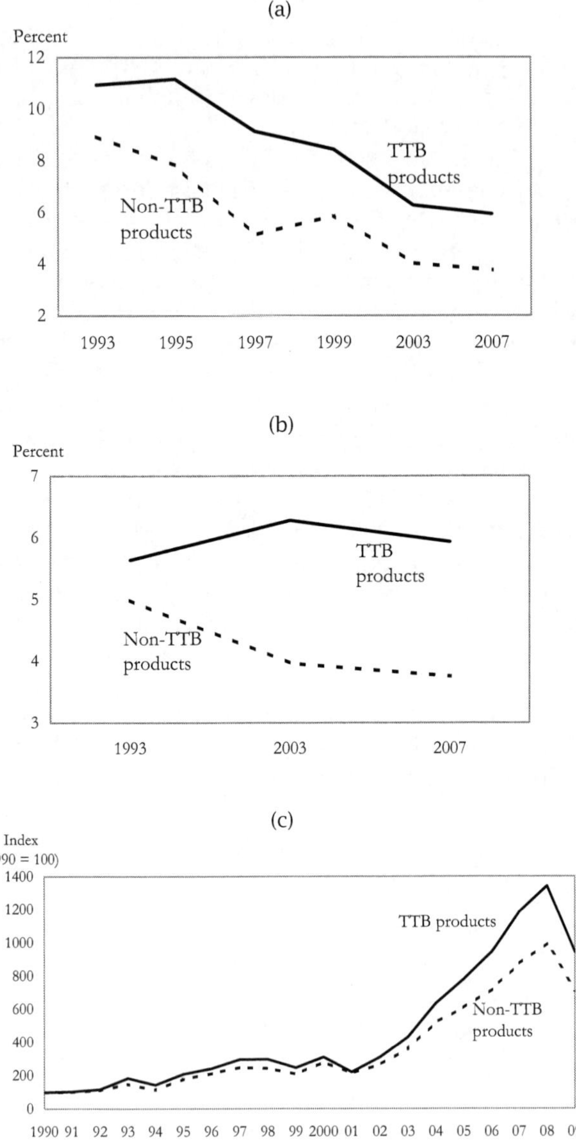

Figure 11.3: *Turkey's tariffs, PTAs, preference margins, imports and TTBs. (a) Average tariffs for TTB versus non-TTB products. (b) Preference margins for TTB versus non-TTB products. (c) Import values for TTB versus non-TTB products.*

(d)

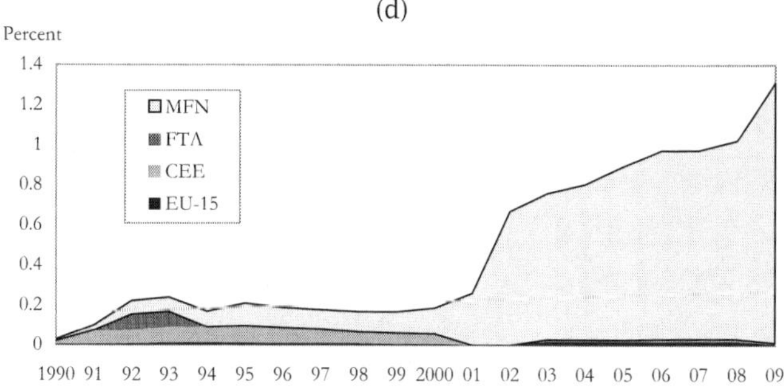

(e)

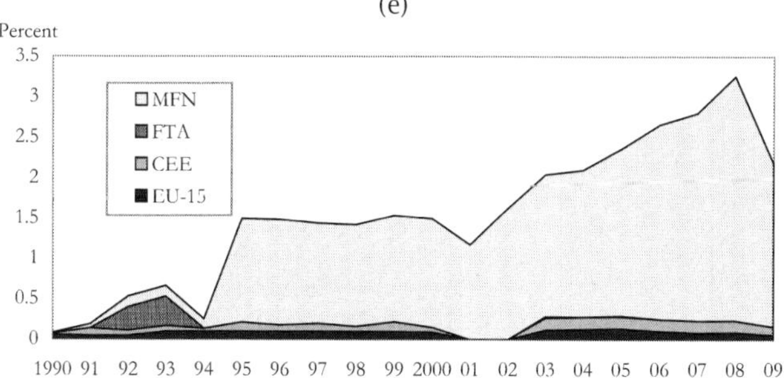

Figure 11.3: *Continued: (d) Share of HS-06 product-target-country combinations subject to a TTB by PTA partner (stock); (e) share of the import value of HS-06 products subject to a TTB by PTA partner (stock).*

Source: (a) author's calculations using TRAINS, UNCTAD and *Temporary Trade Barriers Database* (Bown 2010a). (b) Author's calculations using TRAINS and *Temporary Trade Barriers Database* (Bown 2010a). (c) Author's calculations using *Temporary Trade Barriers Database* (Bown 2010a) and Comtrade.

customs union with the EU; 'CEE' includes the Central and Eastern European countries with which Turkey initially signed an FTA and which joined (or are in process of joining) the EU after 1996 (namely, Bulgaria, former Czechoslovakia, Hungary, Poland, Romania and former Yugoslavia); 'FTA' includes two other countries with which Turkey has an FTA (Israel and Pakistan); and 'MFN' includes the remainder of the target countries subject to a TTB.

Until 2003, the number of HS-06 products from EU15 that Turkey subjected to TTBs was minimal, averaging 2.4 between 1990 and 2000, none in 2001 and 2002, 6 between 2003 and 2008, and finally 2 in 2009. Temporary trade barrier products from CEE countries averaged 17.9 between 1990 and 2000, none in 2001 and 2002, and averaged only 2.4 between 2003 and 2009. For the FTA group, there were 20 HS-06 products from Pakistan subject to TTBs in 1992 and 1993, and 1 HS-06 product from Israel under TTBs between 2003 and

2008. The rest of the MFN countries shouldered the burden of TTBs with a significant upward trend beginning in 2002 (Figure 11.3(d)).

Figure 11.3(e) presents the import values of TTB products by target country as a share of total imports. Again, non-PTA countries (identified as MFN) constitute the highest share of TTB imports with the exception of Pakistan (FTA group) in 1992 and 1993. As might be expected, although the share of TTB-products is small for EU15, their incidence is higher in terms of import value. The import value of TTB products for CEE countries was initially small but increased to more than EU15 values by 2003. However, PTA imports subject to TTBs are relatively negligible as compared with non-PTA imports starting from 1995. The cross-target-country distribution of TTBs is examined further in Section 5.

4 CROSS-INDUSTRY VARIATION IN THE USE OF TEMPORARY TRADE BARRIERS OVER TIME

4.1 General Trends

The use of contingent protection is frequently concentrated in only a few sectors. In Figure 11.4(a) we present the stock estimates across a selected subset of HS-02 industries/sections based on a variant of Equation (1.1). In Figure 11.4(b) we present stock estimates based on import value as defined by Equation (1.2) discussed in Section 2.1. Finally, in panels (c) and (d) of Figure 11.4, we present flow versions of Equation (1.1) and Equation (1.2) estimates across a selected subset of HS-02 industries/sections.

Table 11.4(a) documents the stock versions of Equation (1.1) and Equation (1.2) estimates across all HS-02 industries/sections and, wherever applicable, at the HS-02 or HS-04 level if the products subject to TTBs refer to specific two-digit or four-digit industries within the HS-02 section rather than covering several subsectors. For example, rather than considering the mineral products sector, which spans chapters 25–27 at the HS-02 level, we report the salt category, whose HS code is 25 because this is the only subcategory in which a Turkish TTB (namely, a global safeguard) applies. Similarly, rather than the 'raw hides, skins, leather and furs' sector covering HS-02 chapters 41–43, we report HS-04 level sector 4202, '[Leather] travel goods, handbags, wallets, jewelry cases *etc*'. Then, in Table 11.4(b), we present the flow versions of Equation (1.1) and Equation (1.2) estimates (*ie* based on new investigations) across the same HS-02 industries/sections.

Until the end of 2000, stone/ceramics/glass consistently had the highest number of products subject to TTBs.[11] In 1992 and 1993, textiles (excluding silk and wool) exceeded stone/ceramics/glass, which was followed by

[11]Note that the only TTB measure used by Turkey until 2005 was anti-dumping.

Table 11.4: *Cross-industry distribution of Turkey's TTBs at the HS-06 product level: (a) TTBs in force (stock).*

	HS code	1990–1993 average	1994	1995–1999 average	2000	2001	2002	2003	2004	2005	2006	2007	2008	2009
Counts of products														
Salt	25	—	—	—	—	—	—	—	—	—	1	1	1	1
Chemicals	29-38	0.50	1	1.80	1	—	—	1	1	2	2	2	3	3
Plastics/rubbers	39-40	—	—	2.00	2	—	—	6	6	16	17	19	20	23
Leather handbags, *etc*	4202	—	—	—	—	—	—	—	—	—	—	—	12	12
Wood and paper products	44,48	1.00	1	1.00	1	—	—	—	—	—	7	4	9	9
Textiles (excl. silk and wool)	52-63	11.25	2	2.20	4	63	90	91	91	106	106	97	139	167
Footwear	64	—	—	—	—	—	—	—	—	—	18	16	15	15
Stone/ceramics/glass	68-70	10.00	16	16.00	16	—	—	1	1	1	7	9	9	8
Metals	72-83	3.25	4	5.20	6	4	4	8	12	16	15	15	15	14
Machinery/electrical	84-85	1.75	3	3.00	3	—	—	—	—	3	7	7	14	13
Automotive	87	1.00	1	0.40	—	—	—	—	1	1	1	4	4	4
Miscellaneous manufactures	90,96	0.75	1	2.40	3	2	5	7	7	10	10	10	12	11

Table 11.4: *Continued.*

	HS code	1990–1993 average	1994	1995–1999 average	2000	2001	2002	2003	2004	2005	2006	2007	2008	2009
Import share by value														
Salt	25	—	—	—	—	—	—	—	—	—	0.009	0.009	0.009	0.009
Chemicals	29–38	0.001	0.003	0.013	0.012	—	—	0.001	0.001	0.010	0.010	0.010	0.021	0.015
Plastics/ rubbers	39–40	—	—	0.171	0.150	—	—	0.317	0.334	0.384	0.408	0.428	0.432	0.421
Leather handbags, *etc*	4202	—	—	—	—	—	—	—	—	—	—	—	0.266	0.266
Wood and paper products	44,48	0.055	0.046	0.046	0.044	—	—	—	—	—	0.038	0.022	0.037	0.033
Textiles (excl. silk and wool)	52–63	0.196	0.096	0.107	0.191	0.217	0.654	0.728	0.733	0.800	0.785	0.842	1.363	1.629
Footwear	64	—	—	—	—	—	—	—	—	—	0.413	0.399	0.397	0.431
Stone/ ceramics/ glass	68–70	0.040	0.041	0.065	0.075	—	—	0.005	0.004	0.004	0.090	0.073	0.066	0.078
Metals	72–83	0.039	0.009	1.016	0.974	0.945	0.960	0.959	0.989	1.075	1.126	1.222	1.503	0.160
Machinery/ electrical	84–85	0.018	0.034	0.041	0.032	—	—	—	—	0.141	0.379	0.382	0.513	0.433
Automotive	87	0.009	0.011	0.003	—	—	—	—	0.008	0.008	0.008	0.274	0.269	0.272
Miscellaneous manufactures	90,96	0.008	0.011	0.014	0.016	0.008	0.013	0.033	0.032	0.060	0.059	0.057	0.101	0.074

Table 11.4: *Continued: (b) New TTB investigations (flow).*

	HS code	1990–1993 average	1994	1995–1999 average	2000	2001	2002	2003	2004	2005	2006	2007	2008	2009
Counts of products														
Salt	25	—	—	—	—	—	—	—	—	—	1	—	—	—
Chemicals	29–38	0.25	1	—	—	—	—	1	1	1	—	—	2	1
Plastics/rubbers	39–40	0.25	1	0.20	—	1	4	1	15	—	4	—	8	—
Leather handbags, *etc*	4202	—	—	—	—	—	—	—	—	—	—	12	—	—
Wood and paper products	44,48	0.25	1	—	—	—	—	—	—	4	3	4	1	—
Textiles (excl. silk and wool)	52–63	26.33	138	0.60	85	—	4	—	16	—	1	2	74	33
Footwear	64	—	—	—	—	—	—	—	—	—	18	—	—	—
Stone/ceramics/ glass	68–70	6.25	—	—	—	—	—	1	9	4	8	—	1	—
Metals	72–83	1.25	2	0.20	1	—	—	9	2	2	—	—	—	6
Machinery/ electrical	84–85	1.25	—	0.20	—	—	—	—	3	2	2	7	—	1
Automotive	87	0.50	—	—	—	—	—	1	—	—	3	—	—	—
Miscellaneous manufactures	90,96	0.75	1	0.20	—	4	1	2	4	—	—	2	—	—

Table 11.4: *Continued.*

	HS code	1990–1993 average	1994	1995–1999 average	2000	2001	2002	2003	2004	2005	2006	2007	2008	2009
Import share by value														
Salt	25	—	—	—	—	—	—	—	—	—	0.009	—	—	—
Chemicals	29–38	0.001	0.015	—	—	—	—	0.001	0.009	0.002	—	—	0.101	0.002
Plastics/ rubbers	39–40	0.016	0.124	0.002	—	0.281	0.009	0.007	0.141	—	0.102	—	0.023	—
Leather handbags, *etc*	4202	—	—	—	—	—	—	—	—	—	—	0.264	—	—
Wood and paper products	44,48	0.014	0.070	—	—	—	—	—	—	0.015	0.023	0.005	0.015	—
Textiles (excl. silk and wool)	52–63	0.187	0.562	0.027	0.434	—	0.097	—	0.096	—	0.043	0.158	0.684	0.141
Footwear	64	—	—	—	—	—	—	—	—	—	0.413	—	—	—
Stone/ ceramics/ glass	68–70	0.021	—	—	—	—	—	0.005	0.042	0.023	0.111	—	0.001	—
Metals	72–83	0.019	1.075	0.002	0.005	—	—	0.019	0.008	0.104	—	—	—	0.011
Machinery/ electrical	84–85	0.014	—	0.001	—	—	—	—	0.133	0.128	0.124	0.138	—	0.005
Automotive	87	0.030	—	—	—	—	—	0.008	—	—	0.266	—	—	—
Miscellaneous manufactures	90,96	0.003	0.001	0.001	—	0.010	0.003	0.021	0.027	—	—	0.033	—	—

Temporary trade barriers include anti-dumping, CVDs, safeguards and China-specific safeguards.

Source: author's calculations using *Temporary Trade Barriers Database* (Bown 2010a) and Comtrade.

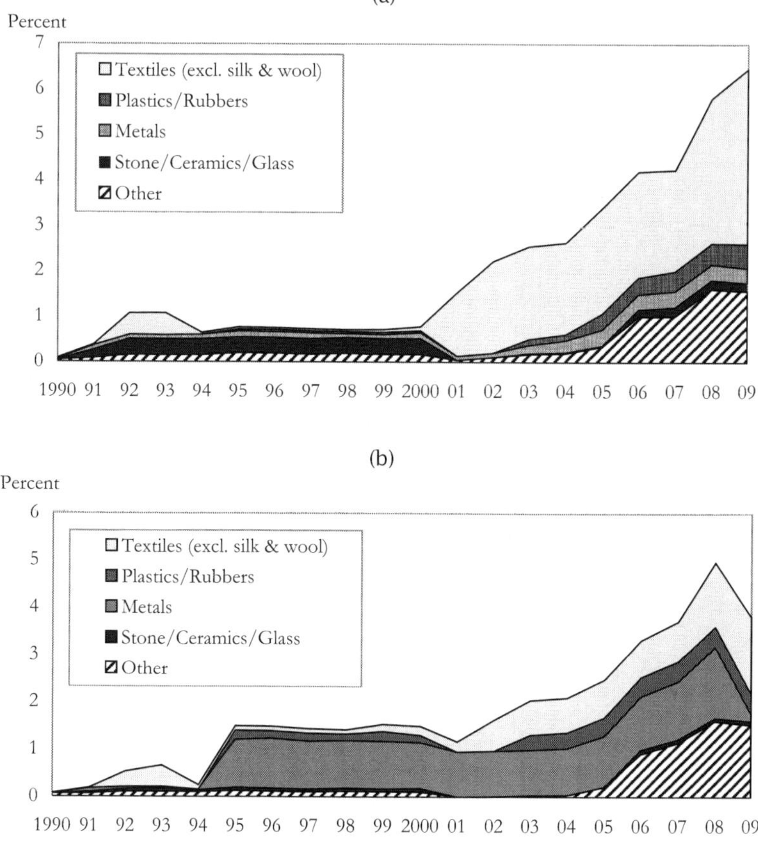

Figure 11.4: *Cross-industry variation in Turkey's use of TTBs: (a) share of HS-06 products subject to a TTB by industry (stock); (b) share of the value of HS-06 imports subject to a TTB by industry (stock).*

metals as the next biggest TTB target between 1990 and 2000 (see Figure 11.4(a) and Table 11.4(a)). However, when we consider the import shares using import values of target-country-product combinations subject to TTBs (*ie* a Equation (1.2) variant) in the 1990–1994 period, textiles is the most important economically sizeable sector covered, followed by wood/paper and stone/ceramics/glass (see Figure 11.4(b) and Table 11.4(a)). Beginning in 1995, import value share of metals is first (1% of all non-oil imports), followed by plastics/rubbers (0.17%) and textiles (0.11%).

Consider next the measure of new TTB investigations (flow) between 1990 and 1994. A majority of new TTBs were in textiles followed by stone/ceramics/glass. In textiles, 56 different HS-06 products were investigated in 1991, 21 in

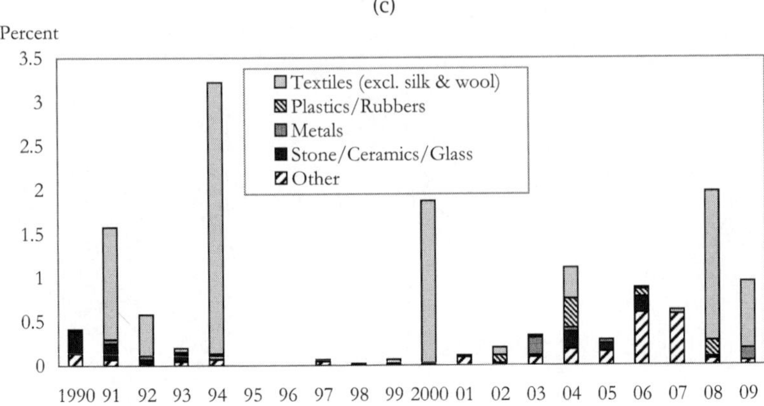

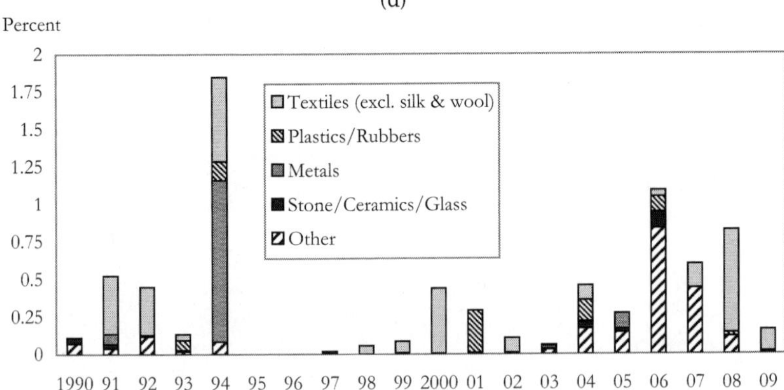

Figure 11.4: *Continued: (c) Share of HS-06 products under new TTB investigation by industry (flow); (d) share of the value of HS-06 imports under new TTB investigation by industry (flow).*

Source: author's calculations using using *Temporary Trade Barriers Database* (Bown 2010a) and Comtrade.

1992 and 138 in 1994 (see again Figure 11.4(c) and Table 11.4(b)). Yet when we rank TTB coverage for new investigations by value of imports, metals is first in 1994 and textiles second (Figure 11.4(d) and Table 11.4(b)).

Starting in 2001, the highest stock of products subject to TTBs by count was clearly textiles, with notable shares of plastics/rubbers and metals (Figure 11.4(a) and Table 11.4(a)). Beginning in 2006, other sectors became prominent users: footwear, machinery/electrical, and wood/paper, and later leather handbags in 2008 and 2009 (Table 11.4(a)). Between 1995 and 2008, metals had the largest share of TTB-covered imports by value, closely followed by textiles from 2002 to 2008 (Figure 11.4(b) and Table 11.4(a)). However, textiles commanded the highest share by import value in the crisis year of 2009. The share of plastics/rubbers by import value was sizeable, beginning in 2003, joined by footwear and machinery/electrical in 2006 and leather handbags in 2009. Figure 11.4 (panels (a) and (b)) also illustrates this as the 'other' category expanded during 2003–9.

An important implication from these observations is that the incidence of TTBs has become more widespread across sectors as Turkey's overall coverage has increased over time. In 2008–9, most new investigations (flow) were again in textiles, followed by plastics/rubbers and metals (see panels (c) and (d) of Figure 11.4, and panel (b) of Table 11.4). A few other sectors had investigations that were small in terms of import value. One exception is the CVD case against India in chemicals in 2008 (Table 11.4(b)). Overall, it is not clear whether the late 2000s trend of diversification of industries subject to TTBs will continue in the post-crisis era.

In Figure 11.5 we separate the stock and flow figures by share of import value within selected sectors over time (a variant of Equation (1.2) estimates) in order to more clearly assess within-industry trends.

There is a clear upward trend in TTBs against textiles after 2002, with a significant jump in 2008 due to new investigations (Figure 11.5(a)). The share of the import value of HS-06 products subject to TTBs relative to all textiles imports expanded from an average of only 4% prior to 2002 to 36% in 2009.

Plastics/rubber imports were first subjected to TTBs in 1995 following investigations in 1993 and 1994 (Figure 11.5(b)). After dipping in 2001 and 2002, there was a dramatic increase in the import share associated with new investigations in 2001. Turkey implemented the additional TTBs in this sector, beginning in 2003, with notable new initiations in 2004 and 2006 resulting in an average of 12% of plastics/rubbers imports (by value) being covered by TTBs.

The metals sector initiated investigations covering only two HS-06 products (namely, steel billets) in 1994. Nevertheless, these products commanded a remarkable 1.1% of total imports by value and were not revoked until 2008. The share of metals dropped from 1.5% to 0.16% of imports by value in 2009 (Figure 11.4(b) and Figure 11.4(d)). The within-sector coverage rate by import value of metals was also substantial, averaging 50% between 1995 and 2008 (Figure 11.5(c)).

The stone/ceramic/glass sector (HS 68–70) had a small but robust share of total imports by value between 1992 and 2000. Temporary trade barriers in this sector largely disappeared between 2001 and 2005, only to return, beginning in 2006 (Figure 11.4(b)). The within-sector share of imports subject to TTBs relative to the more general stone/glass sector (HS 68–71) was noteworthy, with an average above 10% during the period, except between 2001 and 2005 (Figure 11.5(d)).

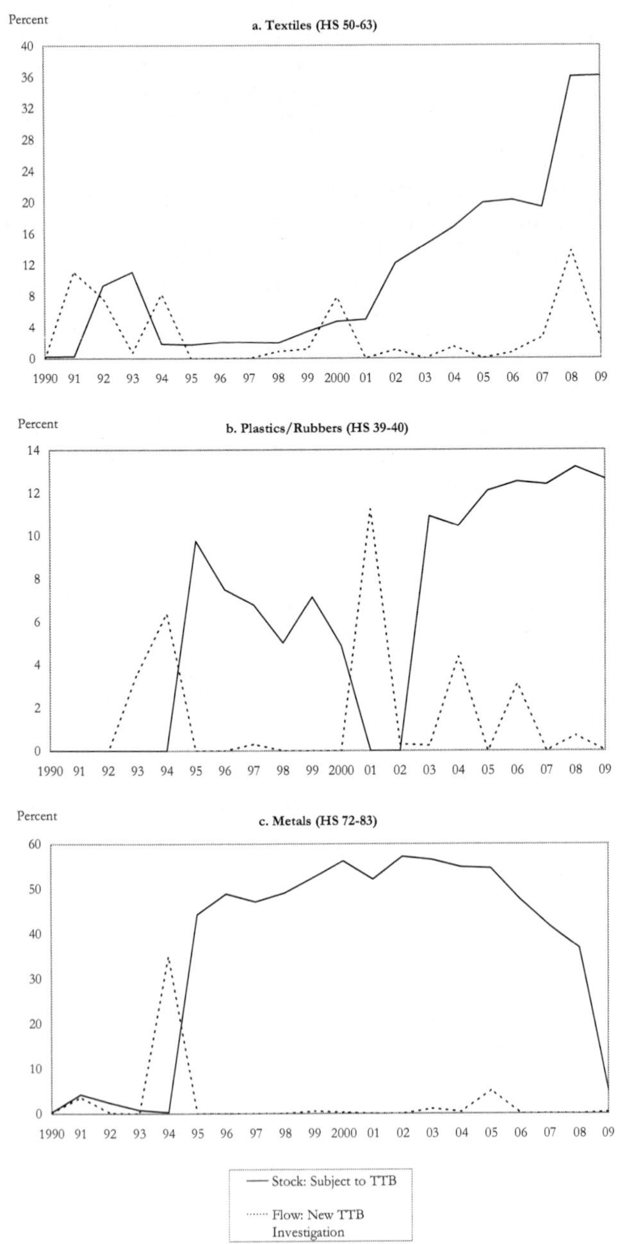

Figure 11.5: *Turkey's use of TTBs by share of import value within industries.*

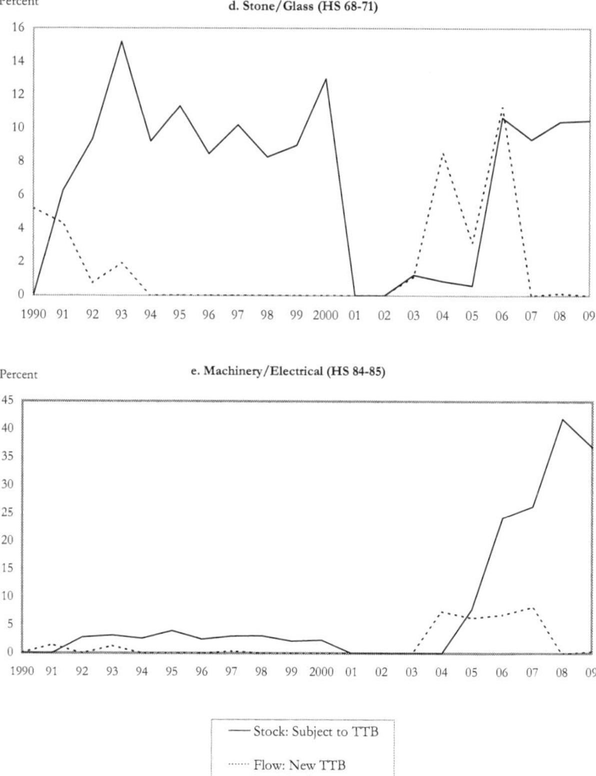

Figure 11.5: *Continued.*

Source: author's calculations using *Temporary Trade Barriers Database* (Bown 2010a) and Comtrade. Temporary trade barriers include anti-dumping, CVDs, safeguards and China-specific safeguards.

Finally, machinery/electrical had a small share of TTB coverage by import value through the 1990s. New investigations from 2004 until 2007 allowed TTBs to reach a considerable share of imports beginning in 2005. By 2008, 42% of imports within the sector were covered by TTBs (Figure 11.5(d)).

4.2 Contributing Factors to TTB Use across Industries

Turkey experienced significant trade liberalisation both bilaterally and against third countries by forming a customs union with the EU in 1996. It also signed several of the EU's pre-existing preferential agreements under the expectation that Turkey would eventually become a member of the EU.

Although the industrial goods originating from the EU were already receiving a duty-free status as of 1996, Turkey was granted exceptions for some 'sensitive' products until 2001. These included 'motor vehicles with an engine capacity smaller than 2,000cc, bicycles, leather cases and bags, footwear and their parts, furniture, chinaware and ceramic ware, iron and steel wires and ropes not electrically insulated, and paper or paperboard sacks and bags for cement or fertilisers' (WTO 1998, p 35). The TTBs that Turkey introduced over the 1990–2009 period directly include these 'sensitive' products.

In the case of textiles/clothing, which is Turkey's largest export sector, quotas were still in effect in the 1990s, as was permitted under the WTO Agreement on Textiles and Clothing and as part of the trade policy harmonisation requirement with the EU. The expiration of this agreement in January 2005, accompanied by China's accession to the WTO in late 2001, were likely contributors to the expanding set of products in this sector being targeted by Turkish TTBs beginning in 2002.

5 FOREIGN EXPORTER INCIDENCE OF TEMPORARY TRADE BARRIERS OVER TIME

5.1 By Country Group

Using the World Bank classification of countries by income, we divide the set of exporters subject to Turkey's TTBs into four groups: China, South Korea (OECD high income), non-China (includes low-income, lower-middle-income and upper-middle-income countries) and high income (includes both OECD and non-OECD high-income countries). In Figure 11.6(a) we present the stock estimates of a variant of Equation (1.1), that is, we analyse the variation in the use of TTBs across country groups by counts of product-target-country combinations for measures in force.[12] Similarly, in Figure 11.6(b) we present stock estimates based on Equation (1.2) by country group, using import values of each country-product combination subject to TTBs.[13] In panels (c) and (d) of Figure 11.6 we depict the flow versions of Equation (1.1) and Equation (1.2) estimates. This part of the analysis excludes global safeguards, which typically apply to all countries, as opposed to the other three TTB measures, which are country specific.

Since the early 1990s, Turkey has used TTBs predominantly against developing countries, *ie* countries in the non-China group and China itself. Applying Equation (1.1) on a country-group basis, the percentage share of HS-06 products subject to TTBs between 1990 and 2000 averaged 0.020% for the

[12]Recall that this is computed as the share of distinct HS-06-product–TTB-country combinations as a share of all export-country-HS-06-product combinations, dropping the observations for countries supplying less than 1% of imports for a given product.

[13]Again, only non-oil imports are considered for consistency.

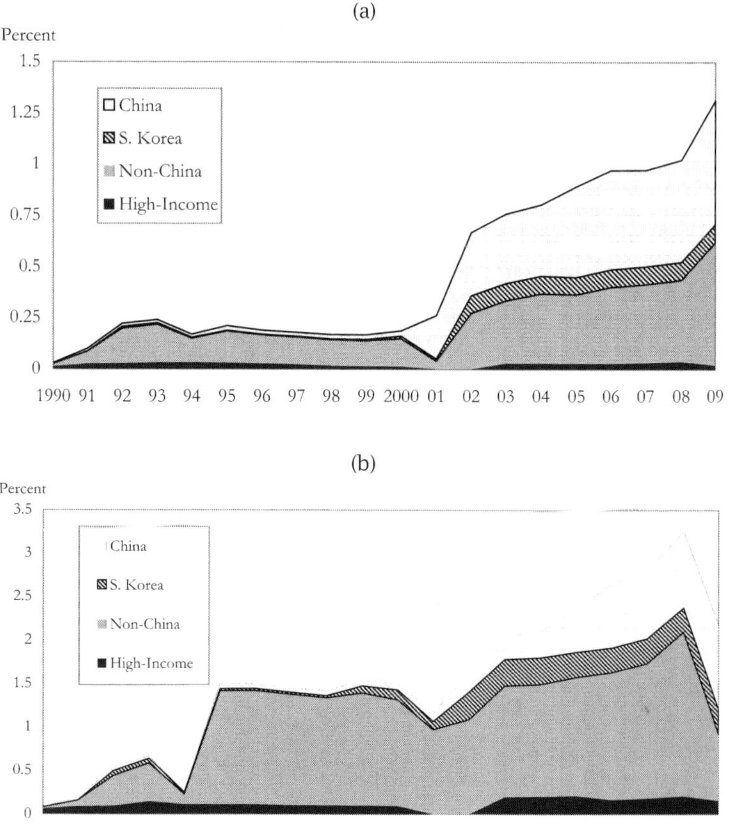

Figure 11.6: *Cross-country variation in Turkey's use of TTBs: (a) share of HS-06 product-target-country combinations subject to a TTB by country group (stock); (b) share of the import value of HS-06 products subject to a TTB by country group (stock).*

high-income group, 0.005% for South Korea, 0.018% for China, and 0.120% for the rest of the developing countries (Figure 11.6(a)). After a drop in coverage for all groups except China in 2001, it increased again for all groups in 2002 as compared with the 1990–2000 period. The percentage of imported goods subject to TTBs from high-inome exporters was 0% for 2001 and 2002, and averaged 0.025% between 2002 and 2009. For South Korea, the share of products under TTBs had a stable average of 0.086% between 2002 and 2009. In the case of China, there was a dramatic increase in the share of imported products subject to TTBs. The average was 0.44% for the 2002–9 period, starting at 0.31% in 2002 and reaching 0.61% in 2009. For the non-China developing country group, the average coverage rate of HS-06-product-target-country

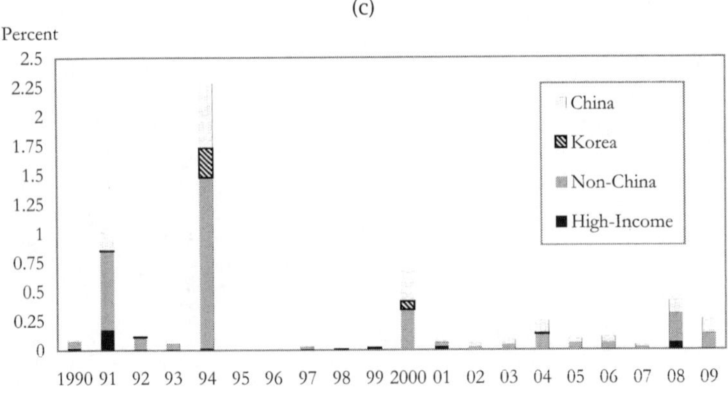

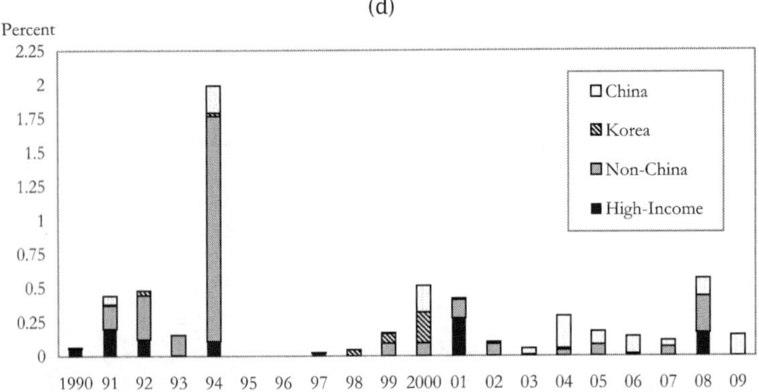

Figure 11.6: *Continued: (c) Share of HS-06 product-target-country combinations under new TTB investigation by country group (flow); (d) share of the import value of HS-06 products under new TTB investigation by country group (flow).*
Source: author's calculations using *Temporary Trade Barriers Database* (Bown 2010a) and Comtrade. Temporary trade barriers include anti-dumping, CVDs, safeguards and China-specific safeguards.

combinations was 0.38%, steadily increasing from 0.27% in 2002 to 0.40% in 2008, and significantly rising to 0.60% in 2009 (Figure 11.6(a)).

Consider next the value of imports from target exporting countries as a share of total imports (*ie* employing Equation (1.2) by country group). For products subject to TTBs, the import share by value in high-income and non-China developing countries were initially quite similar (Figure 11.6(b)). The import-value shares of China and South Korea also began at relatively low levels. Between 1995 and 2000, the import-value share of non-China developing countries increased significantly to an average of 1.27%, while high-income economies averaged 0.10%. China and South Korea's shares remained small at an average of 0.06% and 0.05%, respectively.

For the high-income group, import-value share of their products subject to TTBs dropped to 0% in 2001 and 2002, then averaged 0.20% between 2003 and 2008, and finally decreased to 0.16% by 2009 with the global economic crisis. South Korea, as a high-income emerging market, had an average import-value share of 0.30% from 2002 to 2008, surpassing all other high-income economies subject to TTBs. For the non-China group, the import share started at 1.09% in 2002, increased to 1.89% in 2008, and fell to 0.77% in 2009. Therefore, non-China developing countries continued to have the highest import-value share of products subject to TTBs until 2008. China started with an import share of 0.22% in 2002, steadily increasing through 2009 to 0.98% (Figure 11.6(b)).

These figures show that Turkey's use of TTBs is mainly a developing country/emerging market phenomenon and is increasingly applied towards China. In terms of the counts of products, most TTB investigations were also predominantly against developing countries (Figure 11.6(c)). When import values are considered, the largest share of investigations in the late 2000s has been against China, followed by non-China developing countries (Figure 11.6(d)).

Figure 11.7(a) focuses on the share of anti-dumping investigation cases (as opposed to anti-dumping products at the HS-06 level) across the same four country groups. The number of measures against China in force (stock) as a share of total number of anti-dumping cases started at 14% in 1990, consistently averaging around 14% until 2000. Later on, China's share rose to 25% in 2001, to 39% in 2002, and finally reached 46% in 2009. Non-China developing and high-income countries both started at 43% in 1990. While the non-China group averaged 62% between 1991 and 2001, its share then decreased to an average of 45% between 2002 and 2009. The high-income group averaged 27% between 1992 and 1994 before its share gradually decreased to 10% by 2000, 0% in 2001 and 2002, increasing to an average of 9% between 2003 and 2009. While South Korea faced no investigations in 1990 and 1991, its exporters faced, on average, 5% of investigations between 1992 and 2000. Its share rose to an average of 17% in the 2001–2 period, when other high-income countries did not face any anti-dumping measures, and decreased to an average of 5% between 2003 and 2009. In terms of the number of anti-dumping investigations, China alone became as large a target as the entire non-China developing economies by the late 2000s (Figure 11.7(a)).

Figure 11.7(b) presents Turkey's import market shares by country group subject to anti-dumping measures. Among the group of countries subject to anti-dumping measures, China's import market share averaged 7% from 1990 to 1999, and 12.7% from 2000 to 2009. Comparing panels (a) and (b) of Figure 11.7, China's anti-dumping burden was disproportional to its import market share. Non-China developing countries made up, on average, 38% of Turkey's import market between 1990 and 1999 and 41% between 2000 and

(a)

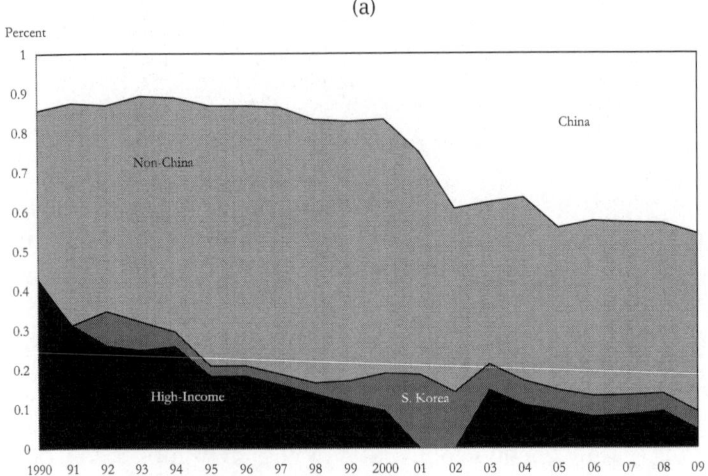

(b)

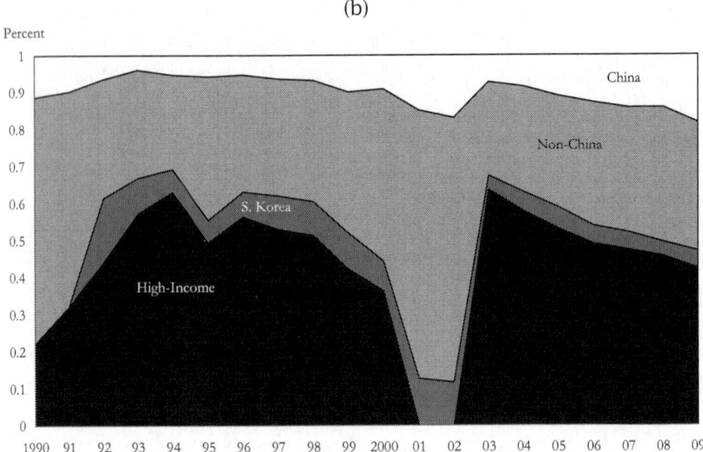

Figure 11.7: *Cross-country variation in Turkey's anti-dumping investigations: (a) share of anti-dumping cases among target-country groups (stock); (b) import market share of target-country groups subject to anti-dumping.*

Source: author's calculations using *Temporary Trade Barriers Database* (Bown 2010a) and Comtrade.

2009. The anti-dumping burden on non-China developing countries was also slightly disproportional to their import market share. South Korea had an import market share of 7% for 1990–1999 and 6% for 2000–2009, therefore, its anti-dumping burden was roughly proportional to its market share. Finally, high-income countries had an average market share of 47% for the 1990–1999 period and 40% for 2000–2009. In terms of market share, high-income countries were underrepresented as targets for anti-dumping.

5.2 By Country

Table 11.5 details the countries frequently targeted by Turkey's TTBs. Between 1990 and 2000, Romania was targeted the most, followed by Indonesia and China in terms of the number of HS-06 products subject to anti-dumping measures (Table 11.5(a)). This group was followed by Taiwan and South Korea. The second part of Table 11.5(a) considers the import-value share of target-country–product combinations. South Korea had a higher share than the other individual countries between 1990 and 1994 and in 2000, although it had fewer products subject to anti-dumping measures. This is due to the fact that South Korea is the only country classified as 'high income' within the group of target countries displayed.

China became Turkey's largest target of TTBs in 2001, facing TTBs in 63 HS-06 products (Table 11.5(a)). The rest of Turkey's trading partners faced TTBs over a total of only 15 products. Turkey increased the number of HS-06 products subject to TTBs from China from 93 in 2002 to 190 products in 2009 (Table 11.5(a)) as it initiated new investigations every year (Table 11.5(b)). South Korea, Taiwan, Malaysia and Thailand were the next most targeted countries, holding a relatively stable stock of about 25–30 products subject to TTBs between 2002 and 2009 (Table 11.5(a)). India emerged as an important target in 2009 with 40 TTB-covered products mostly due to Turkey's imposition of a CVD measure. Indonesia and Vietnam also emerged as targets with 37 and 8 products, respectively, covered by TTBs by 2009. Romania (which joined the EU in 2007) had only one product subject to an anti-dumping imposed initially in 2003 that was part of a multicountry anti-dumping measure—a rare occasion that included other EU members such as Germany and the Netherlands. In general, Turkey has not targeted established EU members, even though there is no restriction on the use of anti-dumping measures between the EU and Turkey.

Table 11.5(b) presents flow figures regarding newly initiated investigations across target countries. There were a large number of products investigated in 1994 and almost none between 1995 and 1999. Turkey targeted China with the most new investigations (140 products), followed by Indonesia (138), India (74) and South Korea (64) in 1994. The second spike in new investigations came in 2000 when China was the most frequently targeted (85 products), followed by Taiwan, Thailand, South Korea and Malaysia. Finally, the rise in the stock of products subject to TTBs imported from India and Indonesia (Table 11.5(a)) was foreshadowed by the surge in investigations against them in 2008 (Table 11.5(b)).

The second part of Table 11.5(b) illustrates the import-value shares of these same countries' products subject to TTB investigations as a share of total

Table 11.5: *Cross-country distribution of Turkey's TTBs at the HS-06 product level: (a) TTBs in force (stock).*

	1990–1993 average	1994	1995–1999 average	2000	2001	2002	2003	2004	2005	2006	2007	2008	2009
Counts of products													
China	3.00	4	6.40	8	63	93	105	110	143	159	152	161	190
South Korea	1.00	1	1.20	4	3	26	26	27	27	28	28	28	28
Taiwan	2.50	3	3.00	5	2	26	27	32	32	32	32	32	32
Malaysia	—	—	—	—	—	23	24	24	24	25	25	26	30
Thailand	—	—	—	—	—	23	28	28	28	30	30	31	31
India	—	—	—	1	1	1	4	5	5	7	9	9	40
Indonesia	4.00	8	8.00	9	1	1	1	1	1	7	4	5	37
Romania	7.75	10	11.20	9	—	—	1	1	1	1	1	1	1
Vietnam	—	—	—	—	—	—	—	4	4	4	6	8	8
Other (high income)	6.00	8	6.40	4	—	—	9	9	9	9	10	12	6
Other (non-high income)	13.00	9	18.80	19	8	8	9	12	13	16	16	16	9

Table 11.5: *Continued.*

	1990–1993 average	1994	1995–1999 average	2000	2001	2002	2003	2004	2005	2006	2007	2008	2009
Import share by value													
China	0.024	0.001	0.056	0.069	0.103	0.220	0.260	0.297	0.494	0.744	0.780	0.881	0.976
South Korea	0.028	0.023	0.035	0.113	0.095	0.317	0.311	0.314	0.295	0.286	0.284	0.277	0.283
Taiwan	0.014	0.018	0.016	0.033	0.012	0.059	0.079	0.080	0.078	0.081	0.080	0.078	0.080
Malaysia	—	—	—	—	—	0.039	0.054	0.061	0.067	0.058	0.056	0.076	0.076
Thailand	—	—	—	—	—	0.014	0.040	0.013	0.015	0.016	0.019	0.034	0.045
India	—	—	—	0.020	0.015	0.016	0.046	0.045	0.044	0.077	0.079	0.077	0.220
Indonesia	0.014	0.026	0.024	0.036	0.012	0.012	0.012	0.012	0.012	0.037	0.035	0.059	0.134
Romania	0.017	0.008	0.034	0.012	—	—	0.106	0.107	0.104	0.102	0.102	0.100	0.101
Vietnam	—	—	—	—	—	—	—	0.005	0.005	0.005	0.002	0.007	0.001
Other (high income)	0.096	0.113	0.103	0.093	—	—	0.195	0.205	0.211	0.166	0.183	0.209	0.157
Other (non-high income)	0.175	0.064	1.208	1.117	0.933	0.949	0.941	0.961	1.038	1.089	1.181	1.459	0.109

Table 11.5: *Continued: (b) New TTB investigations (flow).*

	1990–1993 average	1994	1995–1999 average	2000	2001	2002	2003	2004	2005	2006	2007	2008	2009
Counts of products													
China	10.25	140	0.60	85	4	8	13	33	11	16	6	36	40
South Korea	0.50	64	0.60	23	—	—	—	2	—	—	—	—	—
Taiwan	10.25	—	0.20	24	—	2	—	6	—	—	—	—	—
Malaysia	—	—	—	23	—	—	1	1	—	—	1	4	—
Thailand	—	—	0.20	23	—	5	—	1	1	—	1	—	—
India	13.75	74	0.20	—	—	3	—	2	1	3	—	31	—
Indonesia	2.00	138	0.20	—	—	—	—	1	5	—	1	33	—
Romania	3.50	1	—	—	1	—	—	—	—	—	—	—	—
Vietnam	—	—	—	—	—	—	—	4	—	3	—	2	—
Other (high income)	12.00	4	0.60	—	9	—	—	—	—	1	—	20	1
Other (non-high income)	22.75	157	0.20	—	1	—	1	3	4	—	—	6	—

Table 11.5: *Continued.*

	1990–1993 average	1994	1995–1999 average	2000	2001	2002	2003	2004	2005	2006	2007	2008	2009
Import share by value													
China	0.016	0.204	0.002	0.195	0.009	0.015	0.047	0.238	0.099	0.129	0.046	0.130	0.152
South Korea	0.010	0.024	0.024	0.226	—	—	—	0.013	—	—	—	—	—
Taiwan	0.007	—	0.005	0.038	—	0.017	—	0.015	—	—	—	—	—
Malaysia	—	—	—	0.035	—	—	0.007	0.004	—	—	0.032	0.001	—
Thailand	—	—	—	0.022	—	0.035	—	0.001	0.002	—	0.015	—	—
India	0.007	0.017	0.007	—	—	0.036	—	0.007	0.000	0.002	—	0.150	—
Indonesia	0.001	0.035	0.004	—	—	—	—	0.009	0.009	—	0.019	0.089	—
Romania	0.010	0.013	—	—	0.066	—	—	—	—	—	—	—	—
Vietnam	—	—	—	—	—	—	—	0.005	—	0.001	—	0.005	—
Other (high income)	0.095	0.110	0.004	—	0.276	—	—	—	—	0.012	—	0.169	0.000
Other (non-high income)	0.139	1.589	0.001	—	0.070	—	0.001	0.002	0.070	—	—	0.024	—

Temporary trade barriers include anti-dumping, CVDs, safeguards and China-specific safeguards.

Source: author's calculations using *Temporary Trade Barriers Database* (Bown 2010a) and Comtrade.

Table 11.6: *Cross-country distribution of Turkey's anti-dumping investigations.*

Exporting country target	Total number of target country cases of anti-dumping investigations (share of total number of cases)		Share of involvement in distinct number of investigations	Import market share of target country (rank)		Only country named in investigation (share of target country's cases)		Cases resulting in measures (share of target country's investigations)		Average anti-dumping margin
1990–1999										
China	12	(0.14)	0.27	0.021	(10)	4	(0.33)	6	(0.50)	278
Romania	8	(0.09)	0.18	0.013	(12)	1	(0.13)	7	(0.88)	39
Russia	7	(0.08)	0.16	0.042	(7)	0	(0.00)	5	(0.71)	77
South Korea	6	(0.07)	0.13	0.029	(8)	2	(0.33)	5	(0.83)	21
Taiwan	6	(0.07)	0.13	0.015	(11)	4	(0.67)	3	(0.50)	19
India	4	(0.05)	0.09	0.008	(18)	0	(0.00)	1	(0.25)	14
Indonesia	4	(0.05)	0.09	0.005	(24)	1	(0.25)	2	(0.50)	22
Bulgaria	4	(0.05)	0.09	0.010	(15)	2	(0.50)	3	(0.75)	111
Hungary (high income)	3	(0.04)	0.07	0.005	(25)	1	(0.33)	2	(0.67)	N/A
Other (high income)	15	(0.18)	0.33	0.782	—	3	(0.20)	5	(0.33)	N/A
Other (non-high income)	15	(0.18)	0.33	0.070	—	3	(0.20)	6	(0.40)	38
Total	84	(1.00)	—	1.000	—	21	(0.25)	45	(0.54)	—

Table 11.6: *Continued.*

Exporting country target	Total number of target country cases of anti-dumping investigations (share of total number of cases)		Share of involvement in distinct number of investigations	Import market share of target country (rank)		Only country named in investigation (share of target country's cases)		Cases resulting in measures (share of target country's investigations)		Average anti-dumping margin
2000–2009										
China	62	(0.43)	0.82	0.098	(3)	40	(0.65)	60	(0.97)	91
Taiwan	10	(0.07)	0.13	0.017	(14)	1	(0.10)	10	(1.00)	35
Thailand	9	(0.06)	0.12	0.010	(23)	0	(0.00)	9	(1.00)	59
India	8	(0.06)	0.11	0.018	(13)	0	(0.00)	8	(1.00)	28
Indonesia	8	(0.06)	0.11	0.011	(20)	0	(0.00)	8	(1.00)	18
Malaysia	6	(0.04)	0.08	0.010	(21)	1	(0.17)	6	(1.00)	17
Vietnam	6	(0.04)	0.08	0.002	(31)	0	(0.00)	6	(1.00)	38
South Korea	3	(0.02)	0.04	0.037	(7)	0	(0.00)	3	(1.00)	14
Russia	3	(0.02)	0.04	0.112	(2)	1	(0.33)	2	(0.67)	3
Other (high income)	19	(0.13)	0.25	0.576	—	0	(0.00)	15	(0.79)	22
Other (non-high income)	9	(0.06)	0.12	0.110	—	2	(0.22)	8	(0.89)	30
Total	143	(1.00)	—	1.000	—	45	(0.31)	135	(0.94)	—

Source: author's calculations using *Temporary Trade Barriers Database* (Bown 2010a) and Comtrade.

imports (Equation (1.2) estimate). China was the most targeted exporter until 1994. Between 1995 and 2000, South Korea was the most targeted country before this shifted to Romania in 2001. In 2002, Thailand and India's anti-dumping investigations had the highest import-value share despite covering fewer products than China's. However, beginning in 2003, China again became the country with the highest share of Turkey's import value subject to TTB flows (Table 11.5(b)).

Finally, in Table 11.6, following Bown (2010b) and Prusa (2010), we present the cross-country distribution of anti-dumping investigations (rather than HS-06 products). We divide the sample into two eras: 1990–1999 and 2000–2009. We then rank the target countries based on the total number of anti-dumping investigations against them and report the highest nine countries along with totals of the remaining countries separated into two groups: high income and non-high income.

Between 1990 and 1999, China faced 14% of Turkey's anti-dumping cases, followed by Romania (9%) and Russia (8%). China was involved in 27% of all distinct investigations, followed by Romania (18%) and Russia (16%). When we compare the ranking based on involvement rates with import market share relative to all target countries, each of the top nine countries were disproportionately represented in anti-dumping investigations. For example, China was investigated at the highest rate but it ranked only tenth in terms of its share of Turkish imports (Table 11.6).

Between 1990 and 1999, Taiwan was most frequently named as the only country in its respective anti-dumping investigations with a 67% rate, whereas China was investigated as the only country in 33% of its anti-dumping cases. Romania had the highest share of its investigations resulting in measures with an 88% rate. Russia had a 71% rate, while China had a 50% rate.

Between 2000 and 2009, China clearly became the single biggest target with involvement in 43% of all anti-dumping cases and 82% of distinct anti-dumping investigations. This figure becomes even starker when comparing China with the next countries in line: Taiwan and Thailand faced only 7% (13%) and 6% (12%) of the anti-dumping cases (distinct anti-dumping investigations), respectively. Moreover, in 65% of the anti-dumping cases brought against China, it was the only country named in the investigations (a significant increase from its 33% rate between 1990 and 1999). China was trailed by Russia with a 33% rate of being named as the only country in its anti-dumping cases, for the same period.

For the 2000–2009 period, China's share of Turkey's imports increased substantially. This contrasts with, for example, Russia, which had Turkey's second largest share of imports, but was the ninth highest anti-dumping target. Finally, when compared with the 1990–1999 period, the rate at which Turkey's cases resulted in measures was significantly higher. It was 97% for China (60 of the 62 cases) and 100% for countries ranked second to eighth place. This might be an indication that investigations were carried out more decisively and may be a further contributing factor to the rise in Turkey's TTB use.

The last column of Table 11.6 reports the mean firm level anti-dumping margins by country for the two eras. These rates are expressed in *ad valorem* terms, and we focus on the average of the minimum and maximum margins. In the 1990–1999 period, China faced an average anti-dumping margin of 278%, followed by Bulgaria at 111%, whereas the rest faced a 33% rate on average. In the 2000–2009 period, China again stayed in front with an anti-dumping margin of 91%, followed by Thailand at 59%, while the remainder had a 23% rate on average.

6 CONCLUSION

Turkey has been an active user of TTBs, and especially anti-dumping measures, since the early 1990s. At the same time, it has significantly liberalised its foreign trade through WTO commitments and through formation of a customs union with the EU in 1996. As part of the harmonisation efforts with the EU, Turkey has signed several free-trade agreements and has also started to grant unilateral preferences through the Generalised System of Preferences.

Over the 2000s, Turkey's use of TTBs increased both in terms of the number of products covered and in terms of their economic importance, as evidenced by the rise in the value of imports subject to TTBs. There is also evidence that TTB initiations more frequently result in imposed measures and there is some tardiness in the removal of existing barriers. Each of these factors contributes to the build-up of Turkey's stock of barriers. While Turkey was significantly affected by the 2008–9 global economic crisis, it is difficult to argue that the crisis was the main factor in the surge of TTB protection, given that this increase is part of a pre-existing upward trend. Yet the response to the crisis may come with a few years' lag, and thus a more definitive analysis requires observations beyond 2009.

Turkey's TTB coverage has spread over a larger number of industries over time. Furthermore, Turkey has begun to complement its anti-dumping policy by introducing global safeguards, China-specific safeguards and CVDs. The products targeted with TTBs overlap with Turkey's list of 'sensitive' products omitted from the 1996 agreement with the EU and for which tariffs were phased out by 2001. The forces of political economy and import competition that keep tariffs high in these sectors also seem to make them potential targets for TTBs.

Turkey's TTBs mainly aim at developing countries and emerging markets and are imposed at rates that are disproportional to their import market shares. Nevertheless, China increasingly bears the brunt of Turkey's TTB protection over the 2000s, as compared with any other nation or country group.

Baybars Karacaovali is Assistant Professor at the Department of Economics at University of Hawaii at Manoa.

REFERENCES

Beattie, A. (2006). Trade talks hit by US–EU split on textiles. *Financial Times*, June 20.

Bown, C. P. (2011a). Introduction. In *The Great Recession and Import Protection: The Role of Temporary Trade Barriers* (ed. C. P. Bown). London: CEPR/World Bank. (Chapter 1 of this volume.)

Bown, C. P. (2011b). Taking stock of anti-dumping, safeguards, and countervailing duties, 1990–2009. *The World Economy*, forthcoming.

Bown, C. P. (2010a). *Temporary Trade Barriers Database*. World Bank (July). URL: http://econ.worldbank.org/ttbd/.

Bown, C. P. (2010b). China's WTO entry: anti-dumping, safeguards, and dispute settlement. In *China's Growing Role in World Trade* (ed. R. C. Feenstra and S.-J. Wei), pp 281–337. University of Chicago Press.

Cadot, O., J. de Melo, and B. Tumurchudur (2007). Anti-dumping sunset reviews: the uneven reach of WTO disciplines. CEPR Discussion Paper 6502.

Global Trade Alert (2010). Turkey: increase of tariff on bream fish: measure #1237. URL: www.globaltradealert.org/measure?tid=All&tid_1=485&tid_3=All.

International Financial Statistics (2010). IMF Statistics. URL: www.imfstatistics.org/imf/.

Official Gazette (2004). Regulation on the safeguard measures for imports, no. 25486 (June 8).

Official Gazette (1999). Regulation on the prevention of unfair competition, no. 23861 (October 30).

Onis, Z. (2009). Beyond the 2001 financial crisis: the political economy of the new phase of neo-liberal restructuring in Turkey. *Review of International Political Economy* **16**(3), 409–432.

Prusa, T. J. (2010). Comments on 'China's WTO entry: anti-dumping, safeguards, and dispute settlement' by Chad P. Bown. In *China's Growing Role in World Trade* (ed. R. C. Feenstra and S.-J. Wei). University of Chicago Press.

Togan, S. (2000). Effects of Turkey–European Union customs union and prospects for the future. *Russian and East European Finance and Trade* **36**(4), 5–25.

Togan, S. (2010). Turkey: trade policy review, 2007. *World Economy* **33**(11), 1339–1389.

Undersecretariat of the Prime Ministry for Foreign Trade, Republic of Turkey (2010). Brief note on Turkey's implementation of WTO dumping and subsidy agreements. URL: www.dtm.gov.tr/dtmweb/index.cfm?action=detayrk&yayinID=1246&icerikID=1357&dil=EN.

World Bank (2010). World Development Indicators. URL: http://data.worldbank.org/data-catalog/world-development-indicators.

World Trade Organization (2010). *International Trade Statistics 2010*. Geneva, Switzerland: WTO.

World Trade Organization (2003). Trade policy review Turkey: report by the secretariat, no. WT/TPR/S/125. Geneva, Switzerland: WTO.

World Trade Organization (1998). Trade policy review Turkey: report by the secretariat, no. WT/TPR/S/44. Geneva, Switzerland: WTO.

12

South Africa: From Proliferation to Moderation

LAWRENCE EDWARDS[1]

1 INTRODUCTION

Like many other middle-income economies in the 1990s, South Africa reduced import tariffs in accordance with the offer made during the Uruguay Round of the GATT/WTO. However, there were important differences in the subsequent reform process. First, the period coincided with the demise of apartheid and the transition towards a democratically elected government. This led to the inclusion into the policy space of previously unrepresented interests, which, it is argued, impacted powerfully on the substance of industrial policy (Lewis *et al* 2004).

Second, South Africa became a prolific user of anti-dumping measures during the second half of the 1990s, making it the fifth-largest user of these measures (after the USA, the EU, India and Argentina) in this period (WTO 2003, p 34).

However, South Africa responded differently to the financial crisis in its initiation and use of anti-dumping measures to offset the adverse effects of the recession (Bown 2011b). Whereas the stock of product lines subject to TTBs increased in many developing countries, in South Africa the stock of TTBs fell.

This chapter explores the dimensions of South Africa's use of TTBs in more detail, drawing on the product-level *Temporary Trade Barriers Database* of Bown (2010). Its objective is fourfold. First, the chapter documents the evolution of the flow and stock of imported products subject to TTBs in South Africa. Second, it explores whether South Africa's use of TTBs changed during the financial crisis. Third, the chapter investigates whether the prolific use of anti-dumping measures by South Africa during the 1990s reflects a 'reversal' of the multilateral tariff liberalisation that took place during the period. The effect of the various PTAs on South Africa's use of anti-dumping measures

[1]School of Economics, University of Cape Town, Rondebosch 7701, South Africa. Email: lawrence.edwards@uct.ac.za.

after 2000 is also explored. Finally, the chapter seeks to establish whether the industrial characteristics that correlate with the stock of products subject to anti-dumping measures have changed over time.

The focus of the chapter is primarily on anti-dumping measures. South Africa has made very little use of safeguards (one case in 2007) and CVDs (only four affirmative final decisions). These CVDs largely apply to the same products affected by anti-dumping measures, and thus the analysis and conclusions are unlikely to be affected by their exclusion.

The key findings of the analysis are as follows. South Africa's use of TTBs is characterised by two distinct periods. During the 1990s, South Africa used anti-dumping duties widely as an instrument to protect domestic industries from disruptive price competition. This process reversed after 2001 and the stock of imported products subject to anti-dumping measures fell. For example, by 2009, the number of partner specific product lines at the HS-06 level affected by anti-dumping measures had declined to 83 from a peak of 201 in 2002. The share of imports affected by anti-dumping measures declined from 1% to 0.63% over the same period. This period also corresponds to a shift in the incidence of anti-dumping measures towards developing countries, with China and India targeted in particular.

Unlike other emerging economies surveyed by Bown (2011b) and described elsewhere in this volume, South Africa did not increase its use of anti-dumping measures in response to the financial crisis. The stock of imported products affected by anti-dumping measures actually declined. A key reason for this was the decision by the High Court that the five-year window period for the implementation of anti-dumping-duties would commence from the date that preliminary, and *not* final, duties were imposed. The implication was that various sunset reviews in process or soon to be initiated were terminated. A particular characteristic of the anti-dumping measures affected by this ruling was that many of them had already been in place for ten years or more.

While this is the dominant source of the decline in the stock of anti-dumping measures, there is also no evidence of an increase in industry petitions for anti-dumping investigations in response to the crisis. The response by South Africa during the crisis therefore stands in contrast to that of many other developing countries.

The chapter also explores whether the prolific use of anti-dumping measures during the 1990s served to insulate domestic industries from the effects of tariff liberalisation after 1995. The evidence suggests that anti-dumping duties were not used as a substitute for tariff protection. Products on which anti-dumping duties were imposed faced smaller tariff reductions than other products. In addition, the probability of imposing anti-dumping measures on EU members declined after the South Africa–EU free-trade agreement was implemented, despite the reduction in tariffs.

Finally, the chapter uses econometric estimates to identify conditional relationships that help to explain the sectoral composition of anti-dumping measures. These are used for descriptive purposes rather than as tests of theory-based hypotheses. Products that faced high tariffs, high import penetration and that were produced by concentrated industries were more likely to be protected by anti-dumping measures. This relationship did not change significantly over the period. One interpretation of this outcome is that the political economy of tariff policy may not have changed, despite the political transition to democracy. This opens an area of future research.

The remainder of the chapter is structured as follows. Section 2 documents the changes in South Africa's stock and flow of TTBs from 1992 to 2009, with particular emphasis placed on its response to the economic crisis of 2008–9. Section 3 explores whether anti-dumping measures were used to offset or reverse the process of multilateral liberalisation from the mid-1990s. Section 4 then focuses on the industries targeted by anti-dumping measures and presents various estimates to identify the industrial characteristics that may explain these patterns.

2 THE STOCK AND FLOW OF TEMPORARY TRADE BARRIERS

2.1 A Brief History of Anti-Dumping Institutions in South Africa

South Africa's use of TTBs has a long history. In 1914, it became the fourth country after Canada, Australia and New Zealand to promulgate anti-dumping legislation (Brink 2008, p 256). This was followed by a period of relatively intensive use of anti-dumping and countervailing measures with over 90 investigations undertaken between 1921 and 1947 (Joubert 2005). By 1958, 21 of 37 anti-dumping decrees in force were in South Africa (Finger 1993).

The 1970s led to a shift in South Africa's trade policy as concerns mounted about the continued dependence on gold as a source of foreign currency and the diminishing contribution of import substitution towards growth (Fallon and de Silva 1994; Edwards *et al* 2009). This gave rise to a relaxation of quantitative restrictions as well as to the introduction of an export incentive scheme. South Africa's policy of using TTBs to protect local industries also changed as it was considered that the high tariffs at the time provided sufficient protection to domestic companies. In 1978, all anti-dumping duties were removed and disruptive competition was treated through the use of *formula* duties that maintained import prices above set floors. If international prices fell below the reference price, additional duties were imposed.[2]

[2] The amount of duty payable (Dc) if the import price (Pm) fell below the reference price (Pz) was calculated as $Dc = Pm - (1 - \theta)Pz$. The *ad valorem* equivalent rate therefore increases as the 'freight on board' price declines (WTO 1998).

This system essentially continued until 1992, when a specialist unit was established in the Department of Trade and Industry to deal with anti-dumping and countervailing investigations. Various guides to the policy and procedure for actions against disruptive competition were published at this time, but it was South Africa's joining the WTO in 1994 and the requirement that it conform to the Agreement on Implementation of Article VI of GATT 1994 (the Anti-Dumping Agreement) that defined how subsequent anti-dumping investigations would be conducted (Joubert 2005). Nevertheless, it took until 2003, with the help of some pressure from the other WTO members, for the South African government to amend legislation on anti-dumping, countervailing and safeguard actions to comply with the requirements of the WTO agreements. An outcome of this process was the establishment of a new body, the International Trade Administration Committee (ITAC), to administer trade remedies and tariff changes within South Africa (Joubert 2005; WTO 2003).[3]

There was one further important development. South Africa, together with Lesotho, Swaziland, Botswana and Namibia, formed the Southern African Customs Union (SACU). Under the 1969 SACU Agreement, members applied the customs, excise, sales, anti-dumping, countervailing and safeguard duties set by South Africa (WTO 2003). This agreement was replaced with the 2002 SACU Agreement that came into force on 15 July 2004. The 2002 agreement introduced, *inter alia*, new institutional structures to deal with the formulation of policies of SACU and the approval of customs tariffs, rebates, refunds or drawbacks and trade-related remedies (WTO 2003). An objective of these new institutional structures was to democratise the decision-making process within the customs union (Joubert 2005).

For example, in terms of the SACU Agreement, national bodies such as the ITAC for South Africa are to forward recommendations on customs, anti-dumping, countervailing and safeguard duties to a centralised Tariff Board, which is constituted by an even number of members from each member state (Brink 2005; WTO 2003). The Tariff Board in turn makes a recommendation to the Council of Ministers—the supreme decision-making institution—which is constituted by the Ministers (or Secretaries) of Trade of the member states. Decision making in this body is to be made by consensus.

As of 2010, the SACU Tariff Board has not yet been constituted and ITAC continues to make decisions on behalf of the SACU members. Nevertheless, the proposed establishment of these institutions is expected to fundamentally alter the way in which SACU tariff policies are implemented in the future.

---

[3]The International Trade Administration (ITA) Act was promulgated on 22 January 2003. Anti-dumping regulations to guide ITAC in conducting its anti-dumping investigations were promulgated in November 2003.

2.2 Tariffs and TTBs Since the 1990s

The early 1990s signalled a dramatic shift in South Africa's trade policy.[4] Although some effort had been made to liberalise prior to 1994, trade policy in essence remained protectionist (Edwards 2005; Edwards *et al* 2009). In its offer to the GATT/WTO during the Uruguay Round, South Africa committed to bind 98% of its tariffs, rationalise the over 12,000 tariff lines and replace the quantitative restrictions with tariffs on agricultural products. In addition, South Africa participated as a 'developed' country and hence was required to make more substantive reductions in its bound rates than developing countries.

The outcome was a simplification of the tariff book and a decline in nominal and effective protection that was comparable with other middle-income countries (Edwards 2005). Table 12.1 summarises the tariff reform from 1994 to 2009. The number of tariff lines fell from over 11,000 in 1994 to 6,701 in 2009. Transparency was improved with the share of product lines subject to *ad valorem* rates rising from 68.6% in 1994 to over 97% in 2009. There were also considerable reductions in the number of international tariff spikes (tariffs in excess of 15%), but less progress was made in reducing the number of different tariff rates, which, at over 100 in 2009, still far exceeds the 6 proposed during the Uruguay negotiations.[5]

The bulk of the MFN reform took place prior to 2000; very little additional progress was made subsequently in the 2000s (Edwards *et al* 2009). For example, the weighted-average import tariff fell from 21.4% (inclusive of import surcharges) in 1994 to 12.8% in 1999, but then to only 8.1% in 2009. The average 2009 MFN tariff is almost identical to its 2000 value. Further progress in tariff reduction was achieved through PTAs: from 2000 for the EU and the Southern African Development Community (SADC), and from 2007 for EFTA. By 2009, average protection on imports from SADC countries was 0.5%, and it was 2.3% and 5.4% on imports from EFTA and the EU, respectively.

The decline in average levels of protection coincided with an increased use of anti-dumping measures. Table 12.2 documents the initiation of anti-dumping investigations after requests by South African industries over the 1992–2009 period. Most of the investigations covered multiple products at the HS-08 level and targeted multiple countries. The number of newly initiated investigations averaged just over ten during the 1990s, with a relatively high number occurring during the period of tariff reform after 1995. In addition, applications for anti-dumping measures were increasingly successful, rising from 56% on average during the first half of the 1990s to 81% in the

---

[4]I refer to South Africa, not SACU, as SACU tariff policy was defined by South Africa under the 1969 SACU Agreement.

[5]Domestic tariff spikes are defined as those exceeding three times the overall simple average applied rate. International tariff spikes are defined as those exceeding 15% and nuisance rates are those greater than zero, but less than or equal to 2%.

Table 12.1: *Structure of Southern African Customs Union tariffs, 1994–2009.*

				2009			
		1994	1999	EFTA	EU	MFN	SADC
1	Number of tariff lines	11,231	7,694	6,701	6,701	6,701	6,701
2	Share *ad valorem* (%)	68.6	74.3	97.7	97.4	96.8	98.6
3	Share formula (%)	8.9	0.3	0.1	0.1	0.1	0.0
4	Number of distinct tariff rates	773	272	111	108	100	43
	- *Ad valorem*	31	42	54	52	40	3
	- Other	742	230	57	56	60	40
5	Duty-free lines (% all lines)	26.1	42.7	61.4	65.0	54.0	98.4
6	Domestic tariff 'spikes' (% all lines)	43.6	43.4	37.0	29.7	44.3	0.8
7	International tariff 'spikes' (% all lines)	50.4	43.0	17.5	7.4	31.5	0.6
8	Nuisance' applied rates (% all lines)	1.8	1.6	0.7	1.6	1.2	0.6
9	Simple average						
	- Tariff	17.9	12.8	5.5	3.3	8.1	0.2
	- Import surcharge	3.4	0.0	0.0	0.0	0.0	0.0
	- Tariff incl. surcharge	21.4	12.8	5.5	3.3	8.1	0.2
10	Import weighted average						
	- Tariff	15.5	8.2	2.3	5.4	6.8	0.5
	- Import surcharge	1.9	0.0	0.0	0.0	0.0	0.0
	- Tariff incl. surcharge	17.4	8.2	2.3	5.4	6.8	0.5
	- Agriculture	7.8	10.9	7.6	1.0	2.8	10.6
	- Mining	0.3	0.0	0.0	0.0	0.0	0.0
	- Manufacturing	19.2	9.2	2.3	5.5	8.8	0.1
11	Effective protection	36.3	17.5			11.6	

Calculations are based on the published South African tariff schedules including *ad valorem* equivalents. Effective protection rates include import surcharges imposed in the early 1990s and are calculated using the 2002 supply–use table provided by Statistics South Africa. 'SADC' stands for Southern African Development Community.

Source: Edwards (2005), updated with the 2009 tariff schedule obtained from South African Revenue Services.

second half of the 1990s. The increased proportion of anti-dumping investigations receiving affirmative decisions corresponds with a similar increase in the support of applications for tariff increases (Casale and Holden 2002).

After 2001, the number of newly initiated investigations declined and, with the exception of 2005, there were fewer than six cases initiated each year. The proportion of investigations leading to imposed anti-dumping measures also fell. The use of anti-dumping measures in South Africa is therefore characterised by two distinct periods: a rise in use during the 1990s, and a decline from 2001.

These trends are also reflected in Figure 12.1, which plots two indicators of the stock and flow of anti-dumping measures and investigations using

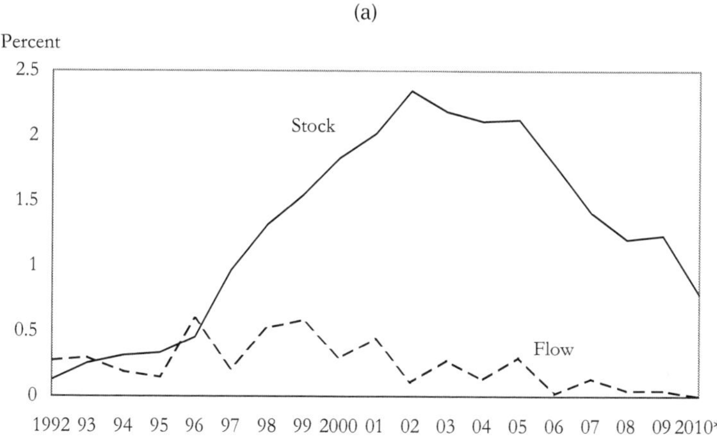

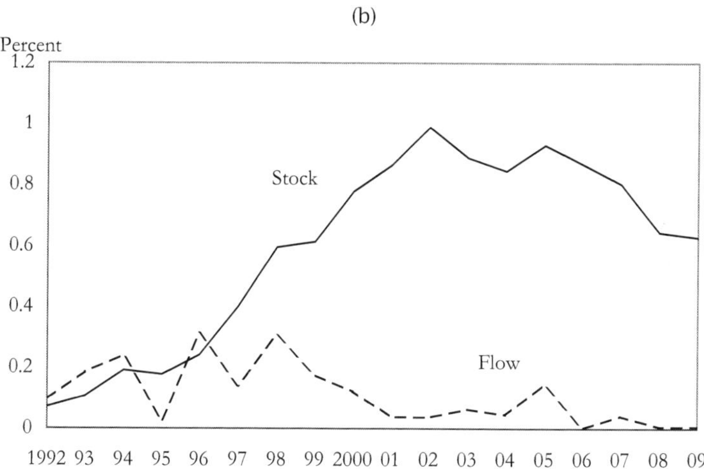

Figure 12.1: *South Africa's use of TTBs, 1992–2009: (a) imported HS-06 products affected by anti-dumping measures (calculated using Equation (1.1)), by count; and (b) import value affected by anti-dumping measures (calculated using Equation (1.2)).*

Source: author's calculations. An HS-06 product is classified as having an anti-dumping measure A rise in the realif an anti-dumping measure is imposed on at least one subproduct. In five cases, the date when the anti-dumping measure was revoked was missing. In these instances it was assumed that the measure was revoked five years after the date of final imposition. The stock in each year includes products revoked in that year. Revoked products only affect stock in the subsequent year; 2010 reflects the stock in the beginning of the year and uses 2009 import values as weights.

Table 12.2: *South Africa's TTB initiations and outcomes.*

	Number of anti-dumping initiations	Number of initiations with final anti-dumping measure	Percentage resulting in imposed measures	Number of CVD initiations	Number of CVD initiations with final measure
1992	9	7	77.8	—	—
1993	11	7	63.6	—	—
1994	9	1	11.1	—	—
1995	8	6	75.0	—	—
1996	19	12	63.2	—	—
1997	5	4	80.0	1	0
1998	13	12	92.3	1	0
1999	10	10	100.0	2	0
2000	8	5	62.5	6	3, 1(p)
2001	3	3	100.0	1	1
2002	4	2	50.0	—	—
2003	5	1	20.0	—	—
2004	4	1	25.0	—	—
2005	11	5	45.5	—	—
2006	3	0	0.0	—	—
2007	5	3	60.0	—	—
2008	2	2	100.0	2	1(p)
2009	2	1	50.0	—	—
Total	131	82	62.6	—	—

Preliminary decisions on anti-dumping duties are used in two cases: one for 2007 and one for 2009. Each anti-dumping and CVD investigation may cover imports of a particular product over multiple countries; '(p)' denotes preliminary.

Source: author's calculations using data from Bown (2010).

the methodology presented in the Introduction. The anti-dumping data are obtained from the *Temporary Trade Barriers Database* (Bown 2010) and updated using various South African Gazettes (this primarily involved updating the list of products affected by anti-dumping measures). Anti-dumping duties in South Africa are often applied at the HS-08 level. However, the analysis here is conducted at the HS-06 level (revision 1988/92) as there is no concordance map that links the various revisions of the HS at the eight-digit level.

The solid lines in Figure 12.1 reflect the stock of products under anti-dumping duties, while the dashed lines reflect the flow of products that are subject to newly initiated anti-dumping investigations. Panel (a) presents a simple measure of the *product coverage* calculated as the count of distinct HS-06 products facing anti-dumping duties (either preliminary or final) or investigations as a proportion of the number of HS-06 product lines with positive import values. Panel (b) presents the share of imports affected by anti-dumping measures or investigations. The calculation is based on Equation (1.2) from the Introduction and uses counterfactual import values for products affected by anti-dumping investigations or anti-dumping measures.

An important consideration when analysing the figures is that the stock in each year includes products revoked in that year. Revoked products therefore only decrease the stock in the subsequent year.

Looking first at the count of products (panel (a)), there was a dramatic increase in the proportion of imported HS-06 products facing anti-dumping duties from 0.25% (12 products) in 1993 to 2.35% (110 products) in 2002. What drove this increase was a persistently high number of products covered in new investigations; these averaged around 17 for each year from 1993 to 2001 (0.37% of product lines). The share of imports affected by anti-dumping measures reveals similar increases (panel (b)). In 1993, only 0.11% of imports by value were affected by anti-dumping measures. By 2002, this had increased to 0.99%.

South Africa's use of anti-dumping measures at this time was high compared with its international peers, and the country was estimated to be the fifth largest user of these measures (after the USA, the EU, India and Argentina) by the end of the 1990s (WTO 2003).

The increase through 2002 is contrasted by the subsequent decline in the stock of anti-dumping measures. The number of HS-06 products facing at least one anti-dumping measure fell from 110 to 55 (1.23% of product lines) in 2009. Much of the decline occurred from 2006 to 2008 as the five-year window period for anti-dumping duties imposed during the late 1990s lapsed. By the beginning of 2010, only 35 HS-06 product lines, or less than 1% of product lines, were targeted by anti-dumping measures. The number of products covered by new investigations also fell and averaged only 6 per year from 2002, much less than the average of 17 for the prior period.

Similar trends are evident when considering the share of imports affected by anti-dumping measures (panel (b)). The share of imports affected by anti-dumping measures rose to 1% in 2002 and then fell to 0.49% by the beginning of 2010. An interesting difference from the count of products (panel (a)) is that the decline in the share of import value targeted was more moderate, suggesting that anti-dumping duties were more likely to remain on product-country combinations in which import values were relatively large.[6]

Table 12.2 illustrates a similar trend in South Africa's use of CVDs. South Africa initiated a total of 13 CVD investigations, with all but two of these occurring in the period 1997–2001. Many of the products covered by CVDs are similar to those of the anti-dumping investigations. Many of these investigations were terminated and a total of 6 cases led to the imposition of preliminary or final CVDs (see Table 12.3). At most 3 of these remained in place by 2009.

The period since the 1990s is therefore characterised by a change in South Africa's use of TTBs: from relatively intensive use in the 1990s to a shift away

[6]Or, more precisely, predicted to be large, as the import weights are based on counterfactual estimates of import values of products facing anti-dumping measures.

Table 12.3: *South Africa's use of CVDs.*

Country	Product	Initiation date	Final decision date	Final decision	Final margin	Revocation date
India	Porcelain insulators	7/4/1997	—	W	—	—
India	Paper insulated lead covered electric cable	21/8/1998	5/11/1999	Terminated	—	—
India	Acetaminophenol	26/2/1999	29/6/2001	Terminated	—	—
India	Overhead aluminium steel reinforced conductor cable	30/4/1999	25/5/2001	Negative	—	—
India	Suspension PVC	24/3/2000	15/6/2001	Affirmative	21.77	3/11/2006
Pakistan	Bedlinen	24/3/2000	28/12/2001	Affirmative	Missing	4/5/2007
India	PVC rolled goods	25/8/2000	28/6/2002	Terminated	—	—
India	Footwear	15/9/2000	Missing	Missing, A(p)	Missing	—
India	Wire ropes	22/9/2000	28/8/2002	Affirmative	17.00	Still in force (as of end 2009)
South Korea	Wire ropes	22/9/2000	28/8/2002	Terminated	—	—
India	Welded galvanized steel pipe	16/3/2001	14/6/2002	Affirmative	7.30	14/6/2007
China	Stainless steel kitchen sinks	25/7/2008	—	W	—	
Malaysia	Stainless steel kitchen sinks	25/7/2008	Missing	Missing, A (p)	Missing	Missing

'(p)' denotes preliminary; 'A' denotes affirmative; 'W' denotes withdrawn prior to ruling by petitioning industry.

Source: author's calculations using data from Bown (2010).

from TTB protection after 2000. The factors that may explain these trends will be explored more thoroughly in the following sections. There is also an additional characteristic of South Africa's use of TTBs: namely, the decline in coverage during the financial crisis of 2008–9. The following section explores the reasoning behind this in more detail.

2.3 Temporary Trade Barriers and the 2008–9 Recession

Like the rest of the world, the Great Recession had a sharp negative impact on the South African economy. Capital controls and tight banking regulations implied that the South African banking and financial sector were well capitalised and not highly exposed to high-risk, foreign-currency-denominated assets (South African Reserve Bank 2009). The banking sector was therefore mostly protected against the direct effects of the global financial crisis. The real economy, however, was not immune to changes brought about by the collapse of world trade and the decline of world economic growth. South African exports and import volumes declined sharply (Figure 12.2) in the third quarter of 2008 and had not recovered to pre-crisis levels by the end of 2010. Manufacturing output also fell by close to 15% in 2009. Unemployment, which had been declining, rose from 23.2% in the third quarter of 2008 to 25.3% in the third quarter of 2010 with over 500,000 jobs lost (Statistics South Africa 2010).[7]

Historically, periods of weak economic growth have been associated with increased lobbying for protection. This was evident in the late 1980s, when the Board of Trade and Tariffs (BTT) received an increased number of applications from businesses for protection in the form of *ad valorem* and formula duties (Bell 1992). During the 1990s, firms were also more likely to file an anti-dumping petition in response to declines in employment and the BTT was more likely to grant an affirmative decision during periods of weak economic growth (Drope 2007).[8]

Yet an analysis of Figure 12.1 reveals a decline in the initiation of anti-dumping investigations and the stock of product lines subject to anti-dumping measures. For example, the number of HS-06 product lines on which at least one anti-dumping duty is imposed declined from 61 in 2007 to 54 in 2008. The share of imports facing anti-dumping measures also hardly changed during the crisis. In total, only four new anti-dumping investigations were initiated in 2008 and 2009 (Table 12.4). Affirmative dumping decisions (preliminary or final) were granted in a total of 6 cases in this period. The

[7]According to Statistics South Africa's Quarterly Labour Force Survey (P0211), total employment fell from 13.65 million in September 2008 to 13.06 million in September 2010.

[8]However, Casale and Holden (2002), for tariff changes, and Drope (2007), for anti-dumping duties, find that an affirmative decision was more likely if the firm had experienced positive employment growth during the prior period.

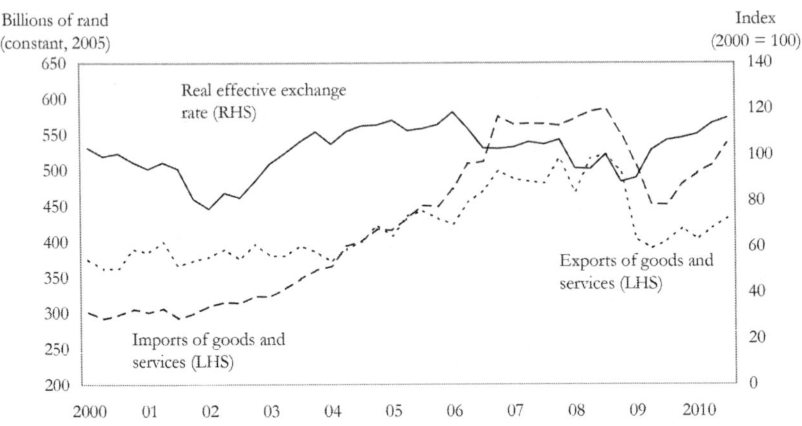

Figure 12.2: *South African quarterly exports, imports and the real effective exchange rate.*

Source: South African Reserve Bank (2010). A rise in the real effective exchange rate reflects a real appreciation of the South African rand.

decline in the stock of products subject to anti-dumping measures can therefore primarily be attributed to the removal of anti-dumping duties imposed previous to the crisis. In 8 of the 12 cases where anti-dumping duties were terminated, these duties had been applied for more than five years (Table 12.4). The decline in the stock of products subject to anti-dumping measures contrasts with the international evidence presented in Bown (2011b). He finds, for example, that, on average, countries increased the stock of product lines subject to TTBs by 25% during the crisis, with developing countries increasing their stock of product coverage by 40%.

There are a number of explanations for the trends during the crisis, the most important of which relates to the Supreme Court of Appeal ruling on anti-dumping sunset reviews in September 2007. This ruling determined that the five-year period over which anti-dumping duties could be applied unless extended after a sunset review commences at the 'date of imposition of the *provisional* payments where such provisional payments were imposed and not the date of the *final* decision to impose definitive anti-dumping duties' (own italics) (ITAC 2008).[9]

[9]See also Brink (2007b). In a later ruling, the March 2010 case of the ITAC versus SCAW South Africa, the Constitutional Court determined that the five-year period may be extended by ITAC for a maximum of 18 months to allow for a review of existing anti-dumping duties and to make appropriate recommendations to the Minister. If a decision is not made within this period, the anti-dumping duty must automatically lapse at the end of the five years (Shepstone & Wylie Attorneys 2010).

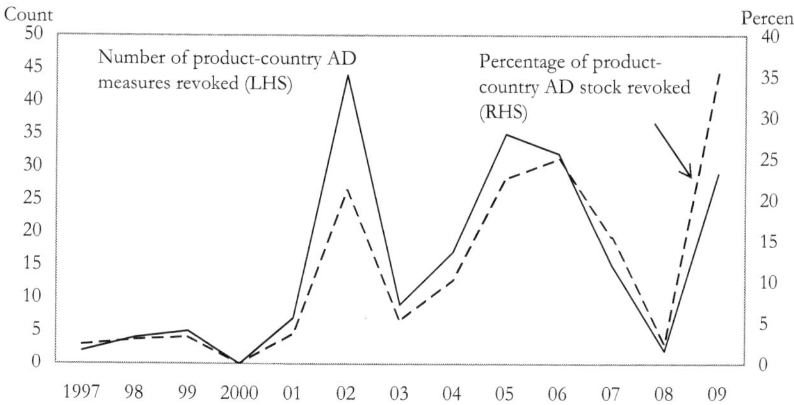

Figure 12.3: *South Africa's revocations of anti-dumping measures, by product-country combination.*

Source: author's calculations using data from Bown (2010). Stock in each year includes products revoked in that year. Revoked products only affect stock in subsequent year.

This ruling had wide ramifications for industries where current and imminent anti-dumping sunset reviews were not finalised or initiated prior to the ending of the five-year term. Duties in these cases (cut paper (A4), carbon black, welded and galvanized pipes, aluminium hollowware) had to be terminated (ITAC 2008) (see Table 12.4). These made up a third of the cases where anti-dumping duties were terminated in 2008 and 2009.[10]

The effect of the decision is also reflected in Figure 12.3, which presents the number and proportion of the stock of product–country anti-dumping measures revoked in each year. Consistent with the trends presented in Figure 12.1, the post-2000 period is characterised by a rise in the number of anti-dumping measures being revoked. The share of the stock affected, however, is greatest in 2009 when 35% of all country–product anti-dumping measures were revoked. This decline is not reflected in the 2009 value for the share of HS-06 products facing an anti-dumping measure in Figure 12.1, as the stock of products in the diagram includes products revoked in that year. However, the sharp decline in the stock of products subject to anti-dumping measures is revealed in the year 2010 of Figure 12.1(a), where the HS-06 product coverage, excluding new measures imposed in 2010, fell to 0.8% (35 product lines).

[10]In the case of cut paper and carbon black, ITAC had already completed sunset reviews and had recommended that duties be terminated. However, ITAC was interdicted from sending its recommendation to the Minister until after its recommendation could be reviewed in the High Court. Duties were then terminated as a result of the ruling by the Appellate Court.

Table 12.4: *South Africa's TTBs in 2008–9: investigations, dumping decisions and revoked duties.*

Product	Initiation year	Country	Final dumping decision	Final dumping decision year	Year revoked
New investigations					
Tall oil fatty acid	2008	Sweden	A	2009	—
Stainless steel sinks	2008	China, Malaysia	A	2009	—
Staple polyester fibre	2009	China	A	2009	—
Picks	2009	India	A (p)	2010 (p)	—
Pre-recession investigations					
Welded link steel chain	2007	China	A	2008	—
Citric acid	2007	China	T	—	—
Plates/sheets/film/foil and strip of polymers of vinyl chloride (PVC)	2007	Taiwan, China	A	2008	—
Extruded aluminium profiles	2007	China	A (p)	2008 (p)	—
Revoked duties					
Cut paper (A4)	1998	Brazil, Indonesia	A	1999	2008
Picks	1995	India	A	1996	2009
Aluminium hollowware	1995	China, Egypt	A	1997	2009
Circuit breakers	1996	France, Italy	A	1997	2009
Uncoated wood-free paper	1996	Brazil, Poland	A	1998	2009
Suspension PVC	1996	Brazil, France, UK, USA	A	1997	2009
Stainless steel tubes and pipes	1998	South Korea, Malaysia, Taiwan	A	1999	2009
Carbon black	1998	Egypt, India	A	1999	2009
Welded and galvanized tubes/pipes and hollow profiles	2001	India	A	2002	2009
Colour coated steel plate	2002	Australia	A	2004	2009
Acrylic fabrics	2003	China	Missing	—	2009
Acrylic fabrics	2003	Turkey	A	2004	2009

'(p)' denotes preliminary decision. In the column 'Final dumping decision', 'T' denotes terminated, and 'A' denotes affirmative decision made.

Source: author's calculations using data from Bown (2010).

One implication of the High Court decision is that we are unable to observe the outcomes of the internal deliberation by ITAC on whether to extend or terminate the dumping duties relating to these sunset reviews. Yet the High Court decision affected only half of the cases in which anti-dumping measures were revoked (Table 12.4). The decision to revoke the remaining anti-dumping measures during this period therefore suggests that ITAC did not become more lenient in its extension of anti-dumping measures in response to the financial crisis.

The High Court decision helps explain to why existing duties were terminated during the crisis, but an important additional characteristic of 2008–9 is that the number of new investigations did not rise relative to prior levels. A possible explanation is that the macroeconomic conditions in South Africa prior to the crisis were not favourable for a determination of injury in the anti-dumping investigation. Anti-dumping determinations are based on data covering the three years prior to the initiation of the investigation. South Africa was experiencing above average economic growth rates prior to the financial crisis: 5% per annum compared with the 2–3% of the 1990s. The local currency had also gradually depreciated in real terms from early 2006 (see Figure 12.2), which helped insulate domestic industries from international price competition.[11] Finally, the rand depreciated sharply (from R6.76 to the US dollar in the fourth quarter of 2007 to R9.95 to the US dollar in the first quarter of 2009) and import volumes dropped during the first few months of the crisis (Figure 12.2), further insulating domestic producers from injury associated with foreign price competition. An appreciation of the rand associated with an inflow of foreign currency in subsequent months has more than offset the initial depreciation. The effect that this may have on anti-dumping filings by industries and the decisions by ITAC is yet to be seen.

2.4 Duration

The stock of products subject to TTBs is an outcome of new anti-dumping measures imposed as well as the continuation or removal of anti-dumping measures in response to the sunset reviews that are mandated by the WTO's anti-dumping agreement. Anti-dumping measures can be retained for a further five-year cycle if the investigation finds that the removal of the anti-dumping measure will lead to a recurrence of injury caused by renewed dumping. This section analyses the duration of South Africa's anti-dumping measures and explores whether changes in the duration may account for shifts in the trend of the stock of products subject to TTBs.

Figure 12.4 plots the number of product-country anti-dumping measures according to the duration over which the measure is applied. The duration is calculated in years from date of final anti-dumping measure imposed to year revoked. Only cases in which anti-dumping measures are imposed prior to

---

[11] Empirical evidence provided by Casale and Holden (2002) and Drope (2007) indicates that the BTT (now ITAC) has been less likely to impose higher tariffs or anti-dumping duties if the currency depreciated prior to the initiation of the investigation.

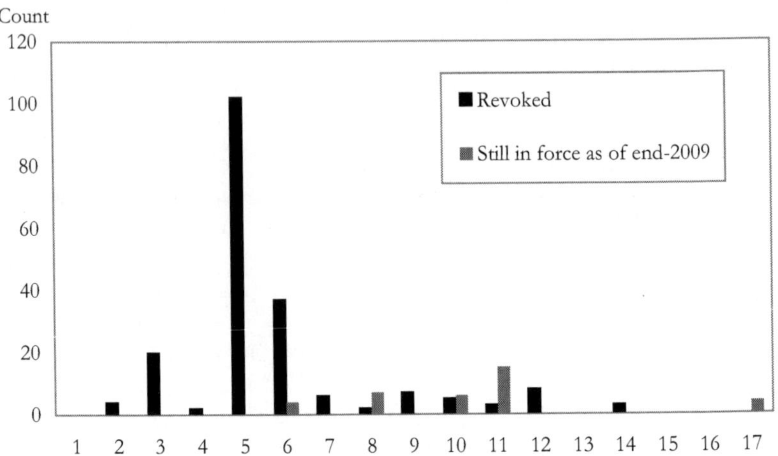

Figure 12.4: *Duration of anti-dumping measures in South Africa that were imposed prior to 2005.*

Source: author's calculations using data from Bown (2010). Only includes anti-dumping measures for which final affirmative decisions were made in years up to 2004. Revoked anti-dumping measures for which the date of revocation is missing are excluded.

2005 are included to allow for the completion of the five-year anti-dumping cycle by the end of 2009. The actual duration over which an anti-dumping measure is applied may be longer as preliminary barriers are not included. Furthermore, the actual duration also depends on the month that the anti-dumping measure is imposed and revoked.[12] Figure 12.4 also plots the average duration of product–country anti-dumping measures still enforced as of the end of 2009.

Most product–country anti-dumping measures are revoked within the mandated five-year cycle. In total, 64% of all anti-dumping measures were revoked within this period. The modal duration is five years, as found by Tovar for the case of India (this volume), but there are three cases in which product-country anti-dumping measures were revoked after 14 years. There are also 36 product–country anti-dumping measures imposed prior to 2005 that were still in force as of the end of 2009. Four of these were imposed towards the end of 1993, resulting in a duration of more than 16 years. These products covered

[12]One caveat to the approach followed here is that anti-dumping measures are implemented and revoked in different months of the year. The approach followed here assumes that the date of enforcement and revocation is mid-year. For example, the duration of a product subject to an anti-dumping measure from 2000 to 2005 is calculated as five years. The actual duration could range from four years (31 December 2000 to 1 January 2005) to six years (1 January 2000 to 31 December 2005).

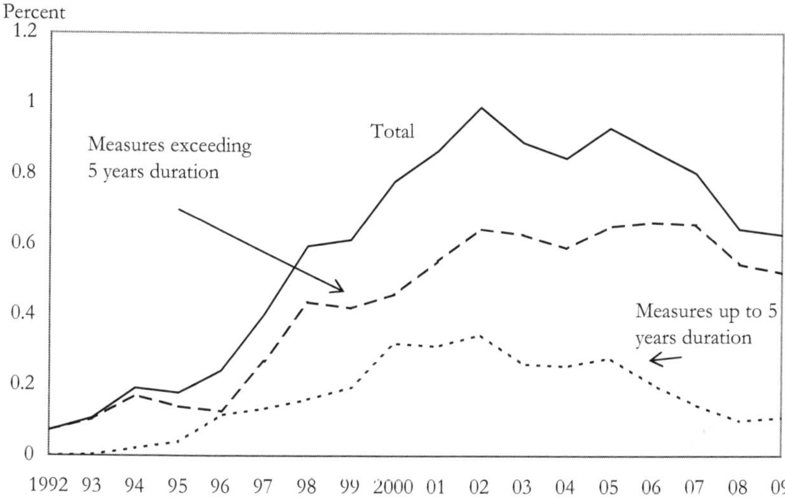

Figure 12.5: *Percentage of import value affected by South Africa's anti-dumping measures, by duration categories.*

Source: author's calculations using data from Bown (2010). Excludes product-country combinations for which the year of revocation is missing. Categories cover products according to whether anti-dumping measures were imposed for more than or up to five years.

imports of shovels, picks, forks, rakes and acetaminophenol from China.[13] While South Africa revoked most of the product-country anti-dumping measures within the five-year window, those that extended beyond five years disproportionately affected import values. This is shown in Figure 12.5, which decomposes the share of South Africa's import value affected by anti-dumping measures according to whether the product-country anti-dumping barrier was applied for up to five years or for more than five years. Products affected by anti-dumping measures for less than five years accounted for a peak of 0.32% of South Africa's import value in 2002, whereas the share of imports affected by products on which anti-dumping measures exceeded five years rose steadily to 0.64% in 2002, and remained at these levels until 2007 before beginning to fall.

Figure 12.5 also reveals that the decline in the share of South Africa's import value targeted by anti-dumping measures from 2002 to 2007 can primarily be

[13]In the case of garden picks, the SACU industry indicated that it would prefer a new investigation to extend the scope of the product to prevent circumvention of the anti-dumping measure. The ITAC therefore decided not to initiate the sunset review and, as a result, the duties were withdrawn. The preliminary investigations in 2010 found evidence of dumping but not of injury.

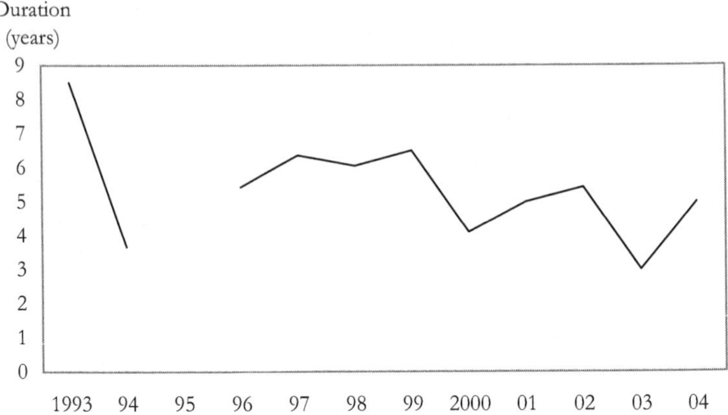

Figure 12.6: *Mean duration of South Africa's product-country final anti-dumping measures, by year of implementation.*

Source: author's calculations using data from Bown (2010). Duration is calculated from year of final anti-dumping measure imposed to year revoked. One caveat is that anti-dumping measures are implemented and revoked during different months of the year. The approach followed here assumes that the date of enforcement and revocation is mid-year. The duration of a product subject to an anti-dumping measure from 2000 to 2005 is therefore calculated as five years. The actual duration could range from four (31 December 2000–1 January 2005) to six years (1 January 2000–31 December 2005). There are no observations for 1995 as no final anti-dumping measures were imposed in that year, although various provisional anti-dumping measures were imposed.

attributed to the revocation of anti-dumping measures on products that faced at most five years of anti-dumping barriers. It is only from 2007 that anti-dumping measures that had been in place for more than five years began to be revoked on a significant scale. For example, the average duration of product-country anti-dumping measures revoked in 2001–6 was 5.1 years. This rose to an average of 7.2 years in 2007, 9 years in 2008 and 8.4 years in 2009. The average duration of anti-dumping measures that were still applied as of the end of 2009 was 7.9 years. Most of the anti-dumping barriers currently applied have therefore been in place for a relatively long time period.

In conclusion, the composition of stock of products facing anti-dumping measures has shifted strongly towards those products on which anti-dumping measures have been imposed for some time. This is an outcome of two effects. First is the failure to revoke anti-dumping measures on products that account for a relatively high share of South Africa's import value. The second contributing factor is a decline in the average duration of anti-dumping barriers initiated after 2000. Figure 12.6 plots the mean duration of product-country anti-dumping measures by year of imposition of the final anti-dumping measure. The average duration of anti-dumping measures initiated in the 1990s was 6.1 years. This declined to an average of 4.5 years from 2000 through 2004.

These trends are consistent with those found for India, Argentina, Turkey, China and the EU by Cadot *et al* (2007). Their explanation is that, in part, this reflects the compliance by these countries to the introduction of mandatory sunset reviews during the Uruguay Round. Practitioners in South Africa have also argued that the requirements to have an anti-dumping duty maintained following a sunset review have become more onerous than those required to have the duty imposed in the first instance (Brink 2005, 2007a).[14] The ITAC argues that the decline in duration reflects a more rigorous process of evaluating evidence of dumping and the effects that anti-dumping measures have on downstream industries, including the public.[15]

2.5 The Geographic Composition of Anti-Dumping Measures

The geographic composition of imported products facing South Africa's anti-dumping measures has also changed. South African industries have requested anti-dumping investigations against a wide range of countries. In total, anti-dumping investigations were initiated against 47 countries over the period from 1992 to 2009. Table 12.5 presents a list of all the countries against which three or more anti-dumping investigations were initiated over the period, ranked according to the number of initiations. China tops the rankings with 45 anti-dumping initiations, 25 of which resulted in imposed measures. This is followed by India with 26 initiations and then a number of high-income countries such as Germany, Hong Kong, USA, Taiwan, South Korea and the United Kingdom, all of which faced more than 10 investigations from 1992 to 2009.

This table belies a change in South African industries' targeting of anti-dumping against imports from developing countries. Figure 12.7 decomposes the stock of product-country anti-dumping barriers according to the region or country that is being targeted. The figure illustrates the total count of HS-06 product—trading partner combinations on which anti-dumping measures are imposed. Trading partners are categorised as China, Taiwan, Hong Kong, India, other emerging economies and high-income economies.[16] Hong

[14]The industry, for example, is required to obtain *prima facie* evidence that dumping is likely to continue or recur. In many cases, the good is no longer imported from the country on which anti-dumping duties have been applied. It is also difficult to obtain normal value information from exporters who are also aware of the impending lapse of the duties (Brink 2005). Finally, the notification of the impending lapse of an anti-dumping duty has been irregular and places a considerable burden on firms who have only 30 days from the date of publication to indicate whether they would require the anti-dumping duties to be maintained.

[15]Interview with Siyabulela Tsengiwe: ITAC Chief Commissioner (Tsengiwe 2011).

[16]The classification of high-income and emerging economies is based on the World Bank's classification of countries according to 2009 gross national income per capita.

Table 12.5: *South Africa's anti-dumping initiations and outcomes by country.*

	Number of anti-dumping initiations	Number of initiations with final anti-dumping measure	% resulted in imposed measures	Income group
China	45	25	55.6	Lower middle income
India	26	19	73.1	Lower middle income
Germany	17	9	52.9	High income: OECD
Hong Kong	16	11	68.8	High income: non-OECD
USA	16	8	50.0	High income: OECD
Taiwan	15	8	53.3	High income: non-OECD
South Korea	14	13	92.9	High income: OECD
United Kingdom	11	5	45.5	High income: OECD
Spain	10	3	30.0	High income: OECD
Indonesia	10	6	60.0	Lower middle income
Belgium	9	4	44.4	High income: OECD
France	9	5	55.6	High income: OECD
Thailand	8	5	62.5	Lower middle income
Brazil	8	4	50.0	Upper middle income
Australia	7	5	71.4	High income: OECD
Netherlands	7	3	42.9	High income: OECD
Malaysia	7	3	42.9	Upper middle income
Italy	4	2	50.0	High income: OECD
Turkey	4	2	50.0	Upper middle income
Saudi Arabia	3	0	0.0	High income: non-OECD
Singapore	3	2	66.7	High income: non-OECD
Austria	3	1	33.3	High income: OECD
Canada	3	2	66.7	High income: OECD
Ireland	3	2	66.7	High income: OECD
Sweden	3	2	66.7	High income: OECD
Egypt	3	3	100.0	Lower middle income

Anti-dumping investigations were initiated against 47 countries over the period 1992–2009.
Source: author's calculations using data from Bown (2010).

Kong is treated separately as the BTT tended to treat imports from Hong Kong as originating in China as re-exports (Holden 2002).

During the early 1990s, South Africa's anti-dumping duties were predominantly applied on imports from high-income economies. However, as the stock of HS-06-partner coverage increased from 1996, there was a shift towards targeting products imported from developing countries. This shift continued even after 2002 as the stock of imported products subject to anti-dumping measures declined. By 2009, high-income countries (including Taiwan and Hong Kong) made up just over one out of every three (28 of 83) anti-dumping

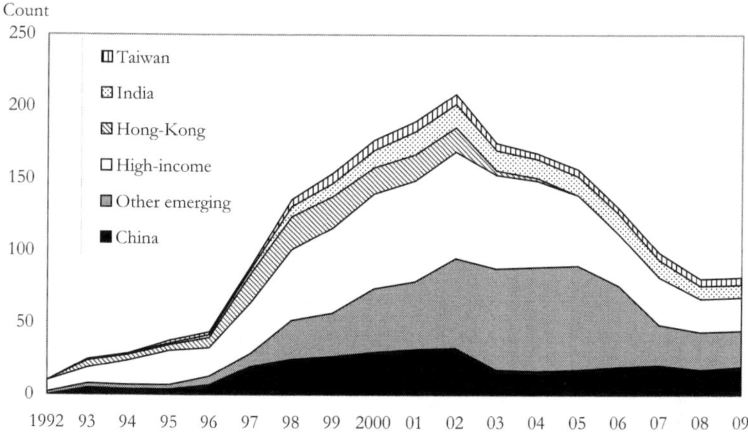

Figure 12.7: *South Africa's anti-dumping stock imposed on developing and developed countries and regions.*

Source: author's calculations using data from Bown (2010). Figure reflects the total count of HS-06 product-by-partner combinations facing anti-dumping measures.

duties imposed on product–partner combinations. This is substantially lower than in the 1990s, when 50–80% of all anti-dumping duties were imposed on high-income countries.

To get a sense of how restrictive these anti-dumping measures were, Figure 12.8 decomposes the stock of anti-dumping duties according to the region or country targeted. Panel (a) presents the percentage of product (HS-06)–trading partner combinations affected by anti-dumping measures, while panel (b) presents the share (stock) of import value from each country that faced anti-dumping duties in each year.

Like other emerging economies (Bown 2011b), there has been a shift in the targeting of anti-dumping measures towards developing economy exporters. A relatively high and growing proportion of products imported from China, India and Hong Kong faced anti-dumping measures up until 2002. Furthermore, up to 2002, South African industries targeted the same products imported from both China and Hong Kong when they initiated anti-dumping investigations. This reflected the concern that Chinese exports were being rerouted via Hong Kong (Holden 2002). After China joined the WTO, the anti-dumping duties on imports from Hong Kong were revoked, and by 2006 no anti-dumping duties were imposed on imports from this country.

The shift towards targeting developing countries is most evident in Figure 12.8(b), which plots the share of import value from each country or region affected by anti-dumping measures. There was a general rise in the value of imports targeted by anti-dumping measures for both developed and developing regions, but there was a sharp divergence towards the targeting of China,

(a)

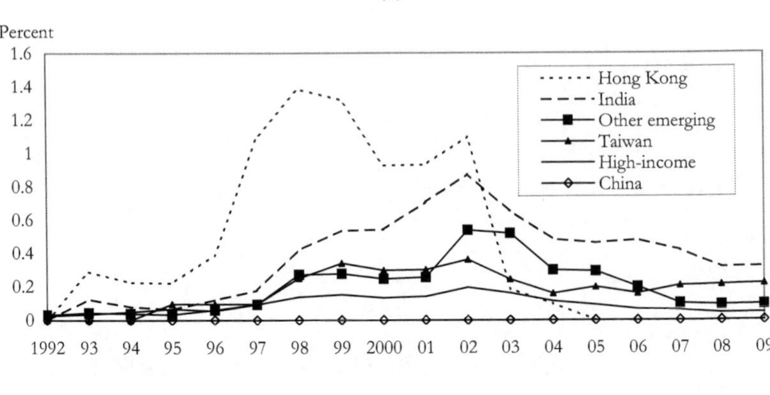

(b)

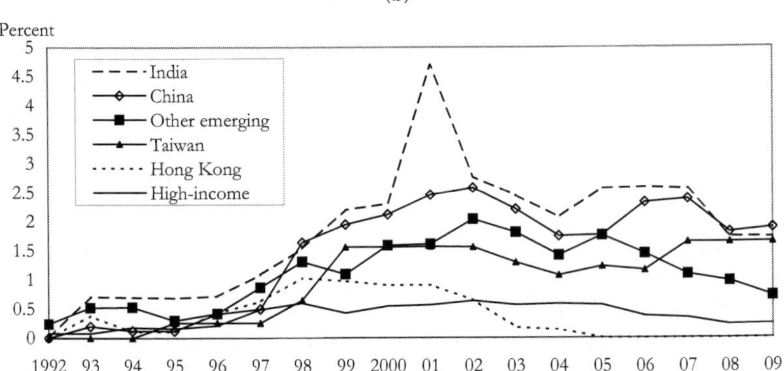

Figure 12.8: *South Africa's anti-dumping stock imposed on developed and emerging countries and regions.*

Source: author's calculations using data from Bown (2010). Panel (a) is calculated using a modified version of Equation (1.1) (Bown, this volume). The numerator is the count of HS-06 product-partner combinations facing anti-dumping measures. The denominator is the number of HS-06 product-partner combinations with positive trade values. Panel (b) is constructed following Equation (1.2) (Bown, this volume). Import weights include counterfactual estimates of the import value of products facing anti-dumping measures following the approach presented in Chapter 1 by Bown.

India and other emerging economies beginning in 1997. Imports from Taiwan and Hong Kong were also targeted, but for the remaining high-income economies the share of imports affected by anti-dumping measures remained stable at around 0.5% up to 2005, after which it declined.

For China, India and other emerging economies, the share of imports affected by South Africa's anti-dumping measures rose to 2–2.5% by 2002. After 2002, the share of developing country imports affected by anti-dumping measures fell, but the decline was sharper for other emerging economies (fell to less than 1% of import values) than for China and India, which remained close to 2%. For Taiwan, there was a slight increase (to 1.65%) in the share of the value of imports affected by anti-dumping measures.

In summary, South Africa's use of anti-dumping measures has evolved considerably throughout the post-1990 period. The 1990s were a period of widespread use of anti-dumping measures with a relatively strong focus on high-income countries. Beginning in 2000, South Africa reduced its use of anti-dumping measures, although the composition of the stock of products targeted shifted towards products on which anti-dumping measures have been imposed for some time. Further, developing countries (and China and India in particular) were increasingly targeted.

What explains these shifts? The following two sections explore two possible explanations for some of the trends.[17] Section 3 examines a possible association with tariff liberalisation, while Section 4 explores various industrial determinants of anti-dumping measures.

3 ANTI-DUMPING MEASURES AS A SUBSTITUTE FOR TARIFF PROTECTION

As has been noted, South Africa became a prolific user of anti-dumping measures during the 1990s. One possible explanation is that, like their Indian counterpart (see Bown and Tovar 2011), the Board of Trade and Tariffs (which was replaced by ITAC after 2003) used anti-dumping measures to offset the WTO-negotiated decline in tariff protection. This possibility has been raised, but not tested, by a number of authors who have studied South Africa's use of anti-dumping measures (Holden 2002; Joubert 2005; Brink 2005; National Board of Trade 2005).

This view is also consistent with the evidence on tariff changes during the 1990s. For example, Casale and Holden (2002) find that applications for tariff increases were more likely to be accepted in the post-1995 period even after conditioning on various deterministic variables including concentration, employment changes, capital stock and the real exchange rate. Although the tariff increases did not reverse the decline in protection, they argue that they softened the adjustment process.

This section uses product-level data to examine whether South Africa used anti-dumping exceptions to reverse or offset its commitments to lower tar-

[17] An explanation not dealt with here is the change in the institutional and policy regime following the creation of ITAC to administer trade remedies in South Africa. South Africa also granted China market economy status in 2004, which may have reduced the number of requests filed by businesses for anti-dumping measures against Chinese imports as well as the likelihood that evidence of dumping and injury are found. More recently, the emphasis in the Department of Trade and Industry's National Industrial Policy Framework placed on reducing the costs of inputs may have deterred industries within the base metals and chemicals sectors from filing anti-dumping requests.

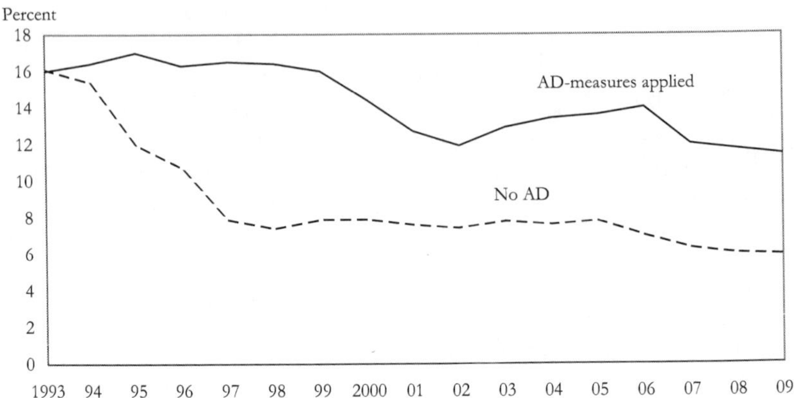

Figure 12.9: *South Africa's average tariffs on anti-dumping-protected HS-06 products and non-anti-dumping-protected products.*

Source: author's calculations. HS-08-level tariffs including *ad valorem* equivalents of non-*ad valorem* rates are aggregated up using unadjusted import values as weights. A product at the HS-06 level is defined as an anti-dumping-protected product if it faced at least one anti-dumping measure during 1992–2009.

iffs under the WTO agreement. It also examines whether South Africa's anti-dumping behaviour altered once it entered into free-trade agreements with the EU, SADC and EFTA in the post-2000 period.

3.1 Multilateral Liberalisation

Figure 12.9 plots South Africa's import-weighted average tariff imposed on HS-06 products that faced or did not face an anti-dumping measure over the period 1992–2009. The average import tariff on both these categories was just above 16% in 1993. Subsequently, there was a divergence with the average tariff on products that never faced an anti-dumping measure, falling by half by 1999. In contrast, the average tariff on the anti-dumping-protected category of products did not change at all over this period. It is only after 2000 that the average tariff on the anti-dumping-protected goods fell, but even then the average tariff remained substantially higher than on other goods' tariff levels.

This relationship does not show causation, though it suggests common underlying political economy determinants of anti-dumping measures and tariffs in South Africa. To investigate this more thoroughly, we exploit the country, product and time variation of the database and estimate the association between past changes in tariffs and the probability of an investigation being initiated. The specification of the equation is as follows:

$$\begin{aligned} AD_{ic,t} = {} & \beta_1 \, DADexist_{i,c,t} + \beta_2 \ln(1 + tariff_{i,c,t}) \\ & + \beta_3 \ln(uv_{i,c,t-1}) + \beta_4 \ln(m_{i,c,t-1}) \\ & + \beta_5 \ln(rer_{c,t}) + \beta_6 \, Dformula_{i,t} \\ & + cntry_c \, /product_i + \lambda_t + \varepsilon_{i,c,t} \end{aligned}$$

where the dependent variable $AD_{ic,t}$ is a binary variable and equals 1 if an anti-dumping investigation is initiated on a partner-product (denoted by c and i, respectively) combination in year t. The data used vary by time, country and product. DADexist is a dummy variable that equals 1 if an anti-dumping measure is already imposed on a product-country combination in year t. The inclusion of this variable deals with the issue that an investigation is unlikely to be initiated on product-country combinations already facing anti-dumping measures.

To capture the effect of tariff reform on anti-dumping investigations, the equation includes the log-applied tariff rate and a dummy variable for whether the HS-06 product line contains a formula duty. Formula duties had been used in place of anti-dumping measures prior to the 1990s and this variable is included in order to identify whether their removal is associated with an increased use of anti-dumping measures. Also included are lagged import values and import unit values to account for the probability of a determination of injury and dumping (Blonigen and Prusa 2003). These variables are lagged to address concurrent effects that the investigation may have on unit values and imports of the product from the targeted country.

Macroeconomic effects are captured through the inclusion of the log bilateral real exchange rate (a rise reflects an appreciation) and a time-fixed effect for changes in aggregate GDP. Knetter and Prusa (2003), for example, find that a depreciation of the currency reduces the probability of anti-dumping petition filings (see also Casale and Holden (2002) for South Africa). We do not have data over time for industrial characteristics such as concentration, capital intensity, employment, *etc* that have been shown to be important determinants of anti-dumping petitions (Blonigen and Prusa 2003). However, we include country by product fixed effects that capture time-invariant political economy influences on anti-dumping petitioning at the country-product level. The equations are estimated using ordinary least-squares estimations. The results are presented in Table 12.6.

The first column presents the results for the full 1993–2009 period. The coefficients reflect the change in the probability of a product-country specific anti-dumping investigation being initiated in response to a change (1% change in the case of the log variables) of the explanatory variable. The coefficients are small, reflecting the large number of imported product-country combinations relative to anti-dumping investigations.

As found in the international empirical literature, anti-dumping investigations are more likely to occur against products that experienced increasing

Table 12.6: *Tariff liberalisation and the initiation of investigations.*

	1993–2009 1	1993–2000 2	2001–9 3
ADexists_t	−0.04768*** (0.01234)	−0.06390** (0.03195)	−0.03413* (0.01748)
$\ln(\text{uv})_{t-1}$	−0.00006*** (0.00001)	0.00002 (0.00004)	−0.00004*** (0.00001)
$\ln(\text{tariff})_t$	0.00061 (0.00066)	0.00313** (0.00155)	−0.00404** (0.00178)
$\ln(\text{rer})_t$	0.00013 (0.00021)	0.00141 (0.00095)	0.00039*** (0.00012)
Dformula_t	0.00466*** (0.00112)	0.00265** (0.00135)	−0.00023** (0.00012)
$\ln(\text{imports})_{t-1}$	0.00012*** (0.00002)	0.00024*** (0.00006)	0.00009*** (0.00002)
N	763,602	264,916	498,686
F	10.5	5.73	3.54
Fixed effects	Country/ product year	Country/ product year	Country/ product year

Robust t-statistics are in parentheses below the coefficients. '*' denotes $p < 0.1$; '**' denotes $p < 0.05$; '***' denotes $p < 0.01$'.

import values and decreasing import unit values. However, we find no association between the bilateral real exchange rate and anti-dumping petitions. The coefficient on average tariff is also not significant, although the probability of an investigation on a particular product rises if a formula duty is imposed.

Given trends in the stock of products facing anti-dumping measures in South Africa, it makes sense to split the period into years before and after 2000. Column 2 presents the results for the period from 1993 to 2000. This was the period during which the extensive reductions in MFN tariff rates took place. The coefficient on the tariff variable is now significant, but it is positive, implying that a *rise* in protection during this period was associated with a *rise* in the probability of an anti-dumping investigation being initiated. Furthermore, anti-dumping investigations continued to be positively associated with the presence of a formula duty, despite their earlier use as a substitute for anti-dumping measures. These results suggest that anti-dumping measures were not used to offset the effects of tariff reductions and the removal of formula duties. Rather, those industries that were successful in negotiating more moderate reductions in MFN rates in the early 1990s and the continued use of formula duties were also those that were more active in initiating anti-dumping investigations.

This relationship changed in the post-2000 period (column 3) and reductions in tariffs and removal of formula duties are associated with a rise in the probability of an anti-dumping investigation. This result suggests that anti-dumping was used by industries to offset the effect of tariff reform in the post-2000 period. The economic impact, however, is likely to be small. Most-favoured-nation reform in South Africa progressed very slowly from 2000, which helps to explain why the number of anti-dumping investigations declined, despite the reductions in tariffs. South Africa engaged in various PTAs beginning in 2000. We address the impact of these on anti-dumping investigations and anti-dumping measures in the following section.

A further contributing factor was the exchange rate. After 2000, anti-dumping investigations were more likely to be initiated against countries whose bilateral real exchange rate depreciated *vis-à-vis* South Africa. This helps to explain the relatively low number of investigations in 2002 when the rand depreciated, the slight increase afterwards through 2005 as the rand appreciated, and the subsequent decline as the rand once again depreciated. Finally, throughout each period, anti-dumping investigations were more likely to be initiated against products from countries where import values rose and unit values fell.

3.2 Preferential Trade Agreements

Liberalisation under South Africa's various PTAs provides additional insight into the relationship between trade policy and the use of anti-dumping measures. Each preferential agreement contains provisions on anti-dumping, countervailing and safeguard measures (Joubert 2005). Yet the effect on the use of anti-dumping measures is potentially ambiguous. First, firms with lobbying power may already have negotiated exceptions or a phase down of tariffs that insulate them from increased price competition under the PTA. Second, the tariff board may be less willing to impose duties on countries with which trade agreements have been negotiated. Both of these cases would lead to a decline in the initiation and success of anti-dumping investigations. In contrast, lower tariffs and increased price competition in response to preferential access may induce industries to initiate anti-dumping investigations, particularly if the scope to apply for tariff increases is restricted by the agreement.

Figure 12.10 decomposes the flow of investigations and the stock of anti-dumping measures according to South Africa's three preferential partners. Panel (a) presents the count of imported partner–product (HS-06 level) combinations subject to anti-dumping investigations (flow), while panel (b) presents the share of value of imports affected by anti-dumping measures (stock). The EU grouping in each diagram includes all current EU members, *ie* the sample of countries in the diagram does not change in accordance with the change in EU membership over time. South Africa's free-trade agreements with the EU and SADC started in 2000 while the EFTA FTA commenced in 2007. We are interested in identifying changes in the stock and flow of imported products subject to anti-dumping measures or investigations that correlate with the commencement of the FTAs.

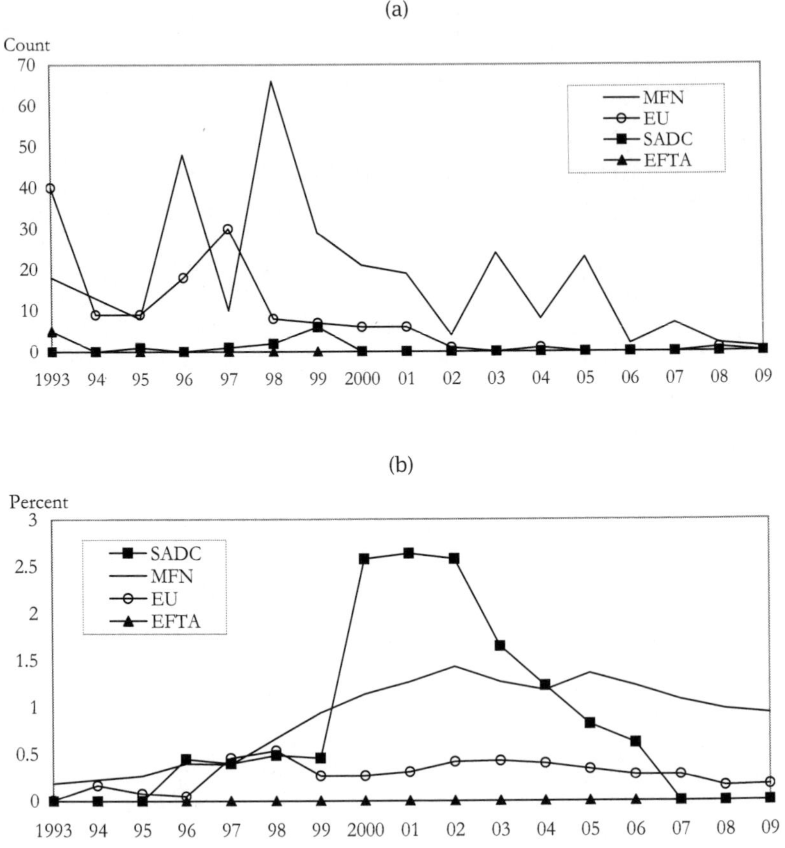

Figure 12.10: *South Africa's use of anti-dumping measures by preferential trading partner.*

Source: author's calculations using data from Bown (2010). 'EU' denotes all EU members as of 2009. Products are defined at the HS-06 level. Import weights include counterfactual estimates of the import value of products facing anti-dumping measures following the approach described in Chapter 1 by Bown.

No anti-dumping measures were imposed on EFTA countries in any year, so this FTA is ignored. The remaining groupings experienced similar increases in the share of value of imports affected by anti-dumping measures up to 1997 (panel (b)), although the anti-dumping duties on SADC members is entirely attributed to aluminium hollowware imported from Zimbabwe. After 1997, negotiations on the EU and SADC FTA commenced. As is shown in panel (a), the number of initiations against future EU FTA partners declined, falling to at most one per year by 2002. As a consequence, the stock of imported products from EU countries affected by anti-dumping measures (panel (b)) remained less than 0.5% of the value of imports for the remainder of the period. This is contrasted by the continued increase in South Africa's share of imports from non-PTA countries (MFNs) facing anti-dumping measures.

For SADC members, there was a spike in product-level initiations in 1999 that is attributable to imports of bedlinen from Malawi. These goods accounted for a high share of South Africa's total imports from SADC members, which helps to explain the dramatic increase in the share of SADC imports affected by the imposition of preliminary anti-dumping duties in 2000. In 2003, the anti-dumping duties on aluminium hollowware from Zimbabwe were revoked and this was followed by the removal of anti-dumping duties on bedlinen from Malawi in 2006.

The figures suggest that, at least in the case of the EU FTA, the negotiation and implementation of a FTA may be associated with a decline in the flow of new investigations and the stock of anti-dumping measures imposed against partner countries. To test this more rigorously, we estimate the following equation using ordinary least squares:

$$\mathrm{AD}_{ict} = \beta_{\mathrm{efta}}\,\mathrm{Defta}_{ct} + \beta_{\mathrm{eu}}\,\mathrm{Deu}_{ct} + \beta_{\mathrm{sadc}}\,\mathrm{Dsadc}_{ct} + \mathrm{cntry}_c\,/\,\mathrm{product}_i + \lambda_t + \varepsilon_{\mathrm{ict}}$$

The dependent variable AD_{ict} is a binary variable for the stock of products subject to anti-dumping measures and equals 1 for all partner-product (denoted by c and i, respectively) combinations subject to an anti-dumping measure in year t. The dummy variables for each preferential agreement equal 1 over the years in which the PTAs are active for that member (*ie* the variable varies over time according to when the country becomes a member of the EU). The control group in the estimation are MFN countries. The equation is a less restrictive version of a simple difference-in-difference specification.[18] The beta coefficients can therefore be interpreted as the change in probability of an imported product facing an anti-dumping measure in response to the PTA.

---

[18]Assume, for simplicity, that the only preferential agreement that South Africa joined with was SADC in 2001. A simple difference-in-difference specification to measure the effect of the FTA on the stock of products affected by anti-dumping duties is the following:

$$\mathrm{AD}_{ict} = (\alpha + \beta_1\,\mathrm{D2001}) \times \mathrm{Dsadc}_{ct} + \beta_2\,\mathrm{D2001} + \varepsilon_{ict}$$

where Dsadc is a dummy variable for SADC members and D2001 equals 1 for the period over which the FTA operates (and 0 otherwise). β_1, the coefficient on the double-interaction term, measures the change in the stock of products affected by anti-dumping measures that can be attributed to the FTA. Intuitively, the specification compares the change in the stock of anti-dumping measures imposed on SADC members after the FTA is formed (first difference) with the change in the stock of anti-dumping measures imposed on non-SADC after the FTA is formed (second difference). The specification estimated replaces the region and FTA dummy variables with country-by-product fixed effects and time-fixed effects. This is a less restrictive specification as it allows for heterogeneity across countries and products in base level of the stock of anti-dumping measures.

Estimates explaining the flow of anti-dumping initiations were also conducted, but these did not yield any significant relationships. The focus of these estimates is therefore on the stock of products affected by anti-dumping measures.

The results[19] are as follows:

$$\begin{aligned}&\text{AD}_{ict} = -0.009\text{Defta}_{ct} - 0.067\text{Deu}_{ct} + 0.040\text{Dsadc}_{ct},\\ &t\text{-statistic:}\quad (0.64), \qquad (2.92)^{***}, \qquad (0.57),\\ &\text{Obs} = 1{,}297{,}422, \qquad F\text{-statistic} = 7.32^{***}, \qquad \text{R}^2\text{-within} = 0.0007.\end{aligned}$$

The results suggest that formation of the FTA with the EU was associated with a statistically significant decline in the number of imported products from EU members subject to anti-dumping measures. No association is found for SADC or EFTA countries.

In sum, the empirical evidence suggests that anti-dumping measures were not used to directly offset the decline in protection associated with multilateral tariff liberalisation in the 1990s. Furthermore, the conclusion of PTAs, particularly with the EU, appears to be associated with a decline in the stock of imported products subject to anti-dumping measures. The relationship between tariff reform and use of anti-dumping measures for South Africa therefore differs from other countries such as India (Moore and Zanardi 2008; Bown and Tovar 2011).

4 THE INDUSTRIAL DETERMINANTS OF ANTI-DUMPING POLICY

This section briefly documents the changing sectoral patterns of South African anti-dumping initiations. It also presents a descriptive regression analysis to identify the various industrial correlates of the stock of products subject to anti-dumping measures.

Table 12.7 decomposes South Africa's use of anti-dumping initiations and measures by industry. Industries are aggregated according to the section headings of the Harmonized System. The average values for the entire 1992–2009 period are presented.

The dominant users of anti-dumping duties are base metals with 53 investigations and textiles and clothing with 35 investigations. As a proportion of HS-06 product lines, however, non-metallic minerals, base metals, plastic products, paper products and footwear requested to initiate the most investigations with over 7% of all product lines affected. These are also typically the industries in which anti-dumping duties were imposed, whether measured as the count of distinct HS-06 products affected (column 2) or the share of

[19] Robust t-statistics are in parentheses below the coefficients. All coefficients are multiplied by 100. The estimates include country-by-product and time-fixed effects. '***' denotes $p < 0.01$.

import value affected (column 1). These sectors, however, were not the dominant import sectors—none made up more than 5% of the total value of South Africa's imports from 1992 to 2009.

Figure 12.11 presents a visual decomposition of the importance of anti-dumping measures within the four dominant industry users. The figures illustrate heterogeneity across industries in the evolution of the stock of products targeted by anti-dumping measures. A key difference in these sectors compared with the trends for the overall economy (Figure 12.1) is that the share of import value targeted by anti-dumping measures remained high or continued to rise after 2002. The share of paper imports affected more than halved from 2007 to 2009 as existing anti-dumping measures were revoked and then fell to under 0.5% by the end of 2009 as duties on cut paper (Brazil and Indonesia) and uncoated wood-free paper (Brazil and Poland) were removed in accordance with the High Court ruling on sunset reviews.

The share of imports of textiles and clothing also fell from 2008, first in response to changes in the composition of import values and then in response to the revocation of 9 of the 13 product–country anti-dumping measures that were placed in response to the High Court ruling. Similarly, in the base metals sector, 10 of the 24 product–country anti-dumping measures were revoked, but the effect on the share of imports by the beginning of 2010 (see 2010*) was small as new anti-dumping measures were imposed in 2009 on stainless steel sinks from China (see Table 12.4). In contrast, there was a rise in the share of imports of non-metallic minerals affected by anti-dumping measures, but this reflects changes in the composition of imports rather than new anti-dumping measures.

The industrial composition of anti-dumping initiations bears some resemblance to the industrial composition in the rest of the world. Bekker (2006), for example, notes that the top six industries targeted by anti-dumping investigations by 29 countries from 1987 to 2004 include base metals, chemicals, plastics and rubber, machinery equipment, textiles and clothing, and pulp and paper. Other than machinery equipment, these are also amongst the most targeted industries by South African firms.

However, there are unique South African interests that have helped shape its tariff policy (Drope 2007). South Africa has a long history of using tariffs in the pursuit of industrial development (Bell 1997; Edwards 2005; National Board of Trade 2005). In the early stages of import substitution industrialisation prior to the Second World War, tariff policy was used to encourage substitution of imports of consumer goods by local manufacturers (Fallon and de Silva 1994). In addition, it focused on creating employment opportunities for white labour (Zarenda 1977). From the 1950s, tariff and industrial policy shifted towards deepening import replacement in upstream industries including the basic metals and chemicals subsectors. A characteristic of the trade regime during this period was the extreme specificity of protection. Tariffs were designed on a case-by-case basis (Fallon and de Silva 1994).

Table 12.7: *South Africa's anti-dumping initiations and imports by industry.*

	Stock: percentage of imported products affected by anti-dumping, by value (1)	Stock percentage of imported HS-06 products affected by anti-dumping, by count (2) (= (5)/(4))	Flow: percentage of imported HS-06 products affected by anti-dumping investigations, by count (3) (= (6)/(4))	Number of HS-06 lines (4)	Number of HS-06 lines with anti-dumping measures (5)	Number of HS-06 lines with anti-dumping investigations (6)	Percentage imports, 1992–2009 (7)
Live animals, animal products	2.7	6.3	6.3	190	12	12	0.8
Vegetable products	0.5	0.7	3.0	269	2	8	1.9
Animal or vegetable fats and oils	0.1	1.9	3.8	53	1	2	0.9
Food, beverages and tobacco	0.1	1.1	1.1	181	2	2	2.1
Mineral products	0.0	0.0	0.6	159	0	1	15.4
Chemical products	0.8	1.6	2.1	760	12	16	9.5
Plastic products	1.6	6.9	7.4	189	13	14	3.8
Raw hides	0.0	0.0	0.0	72	0	0	0.5
Wood products	0.0	1.3	2.5	79	1	2	0.6
Paper products	3.2	4.7	7.3	150	7	11	1.9
Textiles and clothing	3.8	4.2	4.3	808	34	35	3.2

Table 12.7: *Continued.*

	Stock: percentage of imported products affected by anti-dumping, by value (1)	Stock percentage of imported HS-06 products affected by anti-dumping, by count (2) (= (5)/(4))	Flow: percentage of imported HS-06 products affected by anti-dumping investigations, by count (3) (= (6)/(4))	Number of HS-06 lines (4)	Number of HS-06 lines with anti-dumping measures (5)	Number of HS-06 lines with anti-dumping investigations (6)	Percentage imports, 1992–2009 (7)
Footwear	0.1	3.6	7.3	55	2	4	0.8
Non-metallic minerals	4.0	7.2	10.1	138	10	14	1.3
Precious stones and metals	0.0	0.0	0.0	50	0	0	1.6
Base metals	3.4	7.7	9.0	586	45	53	4.6
Machinery	0.3	0.8	0.9	762	6	7	27.7
Transport equipment	0.0	0.0	0.8	132	0	1	10.7
Specialised equipment	0.2	1.3	1.3	230	3	3	3.4
Miscellaneous manufactures	0.0	0.0	1.4	148	0	2	1.5
Collectors' pieces and antiques	0.0	0.0	0.0	7	0	0	0.1
Other unclassified goods	0.0	0.0	0.0	2	0	0	7.7
Total	0.7	3.0	3.7	5,020	150	187	100.0

Source: author's calculations using data from Bown (2010).

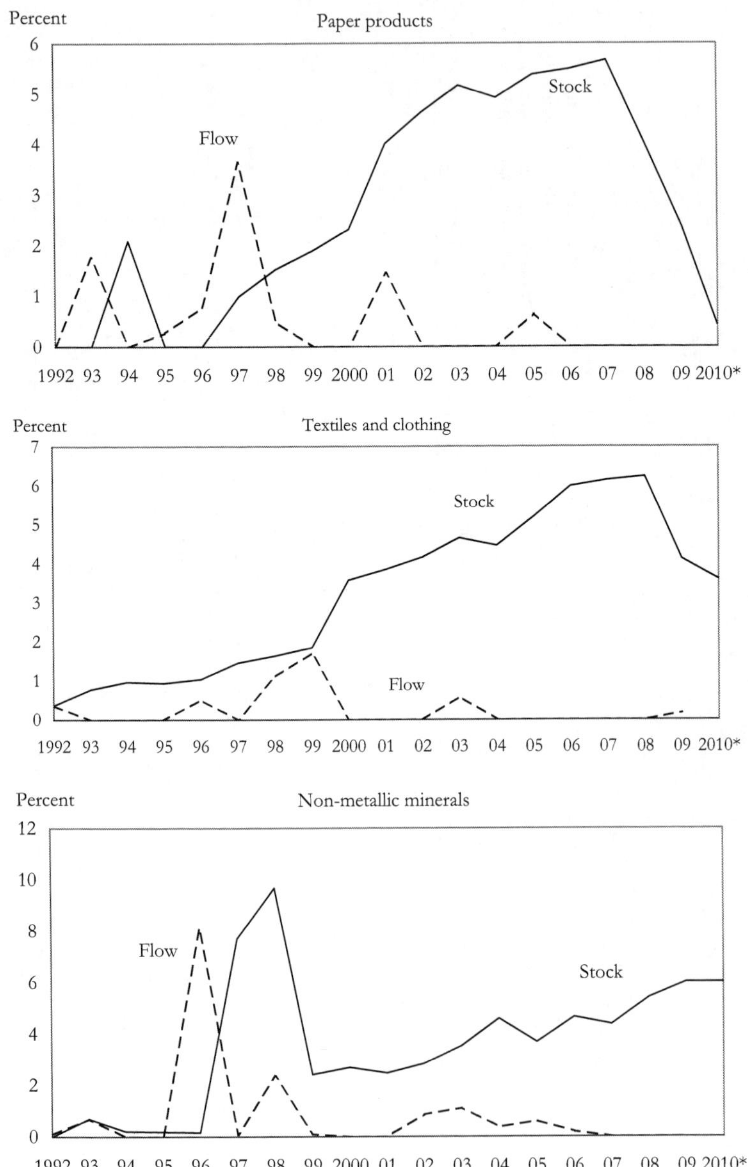

Figure 12.11: *Share of South Africa's import value affected by anti-dumping measures, by sector.*

Source: author's calculations using data from Bown (2010). 2010 reflects the stock at the beginning of the year and uses 2009 import values as weights.

The implication was that, by the late 1980s, South Africa had an extremely complex tariff structure, despite attempts to simplify the structure from the 1970s (Belli *et al* 1993). An additional outcome was that there was considerable scope for industries to lobby for protection in the face of international competition. This was evident in the late 1980s, when a wide range of industries responded to the recession by applying for (and being awarded) tariff increases. Finally, the industrial policy incentives led to a highly concentrated industrial structure and powerful business sectors that wielded influence over the government (Drope 2007).

The democratic election of the new government in 1994 coincided with a shift in South Africa's development strategy from export promotion with import controls to greater openness through tariff liberalisation (Edwards *et al* 2009). It also led to the inclusion of previously unrepresented interests into the policy space. It is argued that this impacted powerfully on the substance of industrial policy (Lewis *et al* 2004) as the state attempted to strike a balance between addressing the needs of existing business sectors, new black-owned enterprises, vocal unions and the previously disenfranchised majority.

The application of anti-dumping duties in the post-1994 period provides a unique opportunity to test the outcomes of these interactions (see also Drope 2007).[20] This requires a more comprehensive analysis than is possible in this chapter. As an alternative, this section presents preliminary estimates that identify the industrial characteristics that correlate with the stock of products subject to anti-dumping measures in South Africa. It then looks at whether these have changed over time.

Table 12.8 presents various estimates explaining the initiation of investigations and the stock of products targeted by anti-dumping measures *in manufacturing*. The aim of these regressions is primarily descriptive and they do not explicitly test any theoretically based hypothesis. The dependent variable varies by product (HS-06) and time, and equals 1 if any investigation or anti-dumping measure is targeted against a country in that year. The independent variables include various indicators commonly used in the political economy literature of trade barriers. Trade-related variables at the HS-06 level include the log import value (lagged), log tariffs, log unit values (lagged) and a dummy if a formula duty was imposed on any HS eight-digit product within the HS-06 product line. Variables for industry characteristics include concentration (share employment of four largest firms), unskilled wage share, share of white workers, and value added per worker (a proxy for efficiency). All these variables are defined at the four-digit level of the South African Standardized Industrial Classification and are obtained from the 1996 manufacturing cen-

[20]South Africa's GATT offer was also the outcome of negotiations between the apartheid government, businesses and the African National Congress (ANC) and its partners. However, the ANC was not yet in power and needed to appeal to international investors as well as to make compromises to the existing state (see Bell 1997).

Table 12.8: *Estimates of the industrial determinants of anti-dumping investigations and the stock of anti-dumping measures in manufacturing.*

	HS-06 products affected by investigations				Stock of HS-06 products affected by anti-dumping measures			
	All years 1	1992–2000 2	2001–9 3	2008–9 4	All years 5	1992–2000 6	2001–9 7	2008–9 8
$\ln(\text{uv})_{t-1}$	−0.092***	−0.074***	−0.141***	−0.212***	−0.095***	−0.062***	−0.116***	−0.153***
	(0.020)	(0.022)	(0.029)	(0.046)	(0.018)	(0.021)	(0.021)	(0.036)
ln(1 + tariff)	0.978***	1.132***	0.459	3.802***	1.117***	1.158***	1.351***	1.297**
	(0.235)	(0.255)	(0.508)	(0.904)	(0.299)	(0.352)	(0.383)	(0.647)
Dformula*	0.287	0.354*	—	—	0.132	0.284*	—	—
	(0.180)	(0.184)	—	—	(0.150)	(0.158)	—	—
$\ln(\text{imports})_{t-1}$	0.120***	0.137***	0.093***	0.078	0.100***	0.118***	0.090***	0.125***
	(0.018)	(0.024)	(0.024)	(0.060)	(0.020)	(0.025)	(0.022)	(0.032)
Concentration	0.625*	0.525	0.848	1.138	0.37	−0.275	0.679	0.053
	(0.356)	(0.410)	(0.562)	(2.026)	(0.438)	(0.534)	(0.465)	(0.657)
ln(number firms)	0.062	0.052	0.1	0.619**	−0.007	−0.113	0.043	0.004
	(0.065)	(0.082)	(0.085)	(0.310)	(0.079)	(0.097)	(0.085)	(0.122)
ln(employment)	0.074*	0.059	0.085	−0.306**	0.136**	0.129*	0.132**	0.119
	(0.043)	(0.055)	(0.057)	(0.133)	(0.061)	(0.073)	(0.064)	(0.083)
Share white employment	−0.749**	−0.662	−1.046*	2.391	0.278	0.216	0.315	−0.229
	(0.354)	(0.426)	(0.576)	(1.566)	(0.437)	(0.519)	(0.454)	(0.674)
Share unskilled	0.247	−0.039	0.759	−0.349	0.442	−0.141	0.798**	0.804
	(0.292)	(0.336)	(0.491)	(1.135)	(0.332)	(0.369)	(0.362)	(0.511)
ln(efficiency)	0.196***	0.147*	0.264***	0.345**	0.033	0.062	0.04	0.202
	(0.065)	(0.079)	(0.095)	(0.156)	(0.097)	(0.133)	(0.101)	(0.131)

Table 12.8: *Continued.*

	HS-06 products affected by investigations				Stock of HS-06 products affected by anti-dumping measures			
	All years 1	1992–2000 2	2001–9 3	2008–9 4	All years 5	1992–2000 6	2001–9 7	2008–9 8
N	66,939	30,610	36,196	7,822	66,939	30,610	36,196	7,822
R_p^2	0.126	0.11	0.141	0.174	0.0967	0.0975	0.0962	0.106
N_{clust}	4,364	4,249	4,279	3,935	4,364	4,249	4,279	3,935
Chi-squared	375	216	183	198	170	122	166	98.3
Fixed effects	Years	Years	Years	Years	Years	Years	Years	Years

Coefficients reflect the marginal change in the probability of an investigation or anti-dumping measure in response to a marginal change in the explanatory variable. Robust standard errors are in brackets below the coefficients. Standard errors are adjusted for clustering at the HS-06 level. * dF/dx is for discrete change of dummy variable from zero to one. The dummy variable for existence of formula duty is dropped in the post-2000 estimates as they perfectly predict the existence of an investigation or anti-dumping measure. Efficiency is calculated as value added per worker. Share of unskilled in the sector is calculated as the production worker share of the wage bill. '*' denotes $p < 0.1$; '**' denotes $p < 0.05$; '***' denotes $p < 0.01$.

sus. Unfortunately, data at this level of disaggregation are not available over time.[21]

The relationships are estimated using a probit model.[22] The presented coefficients reflect the marginal change in the probability of an investigation or anti-dumping measure in response to a marginal change in the explanatory variable.

The first column of Table 12.8 presents the results for the anti-dumping investigations based on the full sample of data. The signs of the coefficients are mostly consistent with the earlier estimates presented in Table 12.6. A new insight gained from these regressions, which exploit the cross-product variation (as opposed to the within-country–product variation in Table 12.6), is that the investigations are more likely to occur in industries with relatively high value added per worker. Surprisingly, concentration is only weakly related to anti-dumping investigations. Except for tariffs, which lose significance in 2001–9, there is no change in the relationship for the pre-2000 (column 2) and post-2000 (column 3) periods. The results for investigations over the financial crisis period are also similar to those of the full sample, although there were too few investigations in this period for any meaningful interpretation.

Columns 5–8 present results for the estimates predicting the probability of a product being subject to an anti-dumping measure. The results for tariffs, unit values and import values are equivalent to those for the anti-dumping investigations and remain significant in all periods, including during the financial crisis. A product is more likely to face an anti-dumping measure if the unit price is relatively low, tariffs are high, and import values are large. Employment numbers are a significant determinant of anti-dumping measures, with industries that employ relatively large numbers of workers more likely to be protected. This relationship is strongest in the post-2000 period. In addition, industries that intensively use unskilled workers were also more likely to be protected through anti-dumping measures in the post-2000 period. These results may reflect the concern by the state about the persistently high unemployment rates. The finding is also similar to that of Casale and Holden (2002) for tariff changes in South Africa.

Overall, the variables explaining anti-dumping investigations and the use of anti-dumping measures appear to be consistent over the full 1992–2009 period. There is some evidence that the BTT and ITAC increasingly targeted employment-intensive sectors with anti-dumping measures. Nevertheless, the results do not suggest a major structural shift in the initiation of anti-dumping investigations or the use of anti-dumping measures to protect industries. One interpretation is that the institutional structures governing tariff policy have

---

[21] There are data at the SIC three-digit level, but they cover less than 40 industries. The four-digit data cover 112 industries.

[22] The probit model is defined as $\Pr(AD_{it} = 1) = \Phi(x_{it}\beta)$, where Φ is the standard cumulative normal distribution.

not changed significantly despite the political transition in 1994. A more rigorous analysis is required to ascertain the validity of this interpretation.

5 CONCLUSION

This chapter explores South Africa's use of TTBs from the early 1990s through the global financial crisis of 2008–9. South Africa is found to have been a prolific user of anti-dumping measures during the 1990s, but to have made considerable progress in reducing the number of products and share of import value subject to these measures after 2001. By early 2010, the share of imports affected by anti-dumping measures had fallen to 0.49%, less than half the peak of 1% in 2000. Another insight from the background review is that the incidence of anti-dumping measures in South Africa has shifted towards developing countries, in particular China and India. This corresponds with shifts in other emerging economies. The chapter also reveals a decline in the average duration of anti-dumping measures that corresponds with the decline in stock of products targeted by anti-dumping measures beginning in 2000.

A second focus of the chapter is South Africa's response to the global financial crisis. South Africa did not increase its use of anti-dumping measures in response to the financial crisis and therefore differs from some other emerging economies. However, the decline in the use of anti-dumping measures can largely be attributed to a High Court ruling regarding when the five-year cycle for anti-dumping measures commences (from the date of the first decision to impose anti-dumping duties, whether preliminary or final). As a consequence, numerous sunset reviews were terminated and the anti-dumping measures revoked. Therefore, the decline in anti-dumping stock from 2008 to end-2009 did not reflect an active response by the ITAC to the financial crisis.

The remainder of the chapter looks at the various correlates of anti-dumping measures in South Africa. We find that South Africa's prolific use of anti-dumping measures in the 1990s does not reflect a reversal of multilateral or preferential tariff liberalisation. Rather, protection through tariffs and anti-dumping measures appear to have common political economy determinants. The formation of the SA–EU free-trade agreement has also reduced the probability of products imported from the EU facing anti-dumping measures. Finally, we find that the industrial characteristics that correlate with the stock of products subject to anti-dumping measures have remained largely unchanged, although there appears to be an increased targeting of high employment sectors that use unskilled labour relatively intensively.

Lawrence Edwards is Associate Professor in the School of Economics at the University of Cape Town, South Africa.

REFERENCES

Bekker, D. (2006). The strategic use of anti-dumping in international trade. *South African Journal of Economics* **74**(3), 501–521.

Bell, T. (1997). Trade policy. In *The Political Economy of South Africa's Transition* (ed. J. Michie and V. Padayachee). London: Dryden Press.

Bell, T. (1992). Should South Africa further liberalise its foreign trade? Economic Trends Research Group Working Paper 16, Cape Town.

Belli, P., J. M. Finger, and A. Ballivan (1993). South Africa: a review of trade policies. World Bank Informal Discussion Papers on Aspects of the Economy of South Africa no. 4.

Blonigen, B. A., and T. J. Prusa (2003). Anti-dumping. In *Handbook of International Trade* (ed. E. K. Choi and J. Harrigan). Malden, MA: Blackwell Publishing.

Bown, C. P. (2011a). Introduction. In *The Great Recession and Import Protection: The Role of Temporary Trade Barriers* (ed. C. P. Bown). London: CEPR/World Bank. (Chapter 1 of this volume.)

Bown, C. P. (2011b). Taking stock of antidumping, safeguards, and countervailing duties, 1990–2009. *The World Economy*, forthcoming.

Bown, C. P. (2010). *Temporary Trade Barriers Database*. World Bank (July). URL: http://econ.worldbank.org/ttbd/.

Bown, C. P., and P. Tovar (2011). Trade liberalization, anti-dumping, and safeguards: evidence from India's tariff reform. *Journal of Development Economics* **96**(1), 115–125.

Brink, G. (2008). A nutshell guide to anti-dumping action. *Journal of Contemporary Roman Dutch Law* **71**, 255–271.

Brink, G. (2007a). Sunset reviews in South Africa: new directions given by the High Court. Tralac Trade Brief no. 05/2007.

Brink, G. (2007b). Sunset reviews in South Africa: how long is five years? Tralac Trade Brief no. 07/2007.

Brink, G. (2005). The 10 major problems with the anti-dumping instrument in South Africa. *Journal of World Trade* **39**(1), 147–157.

Cadot, O., J. de Melo, and B. Tumurchudur (2007). Anti-dumping sunset reviews: the uneven reach of WTO disciplines. CEPR Discussion Paper 6502.

Casale, D., and M. Holden (2002). Endogenous protection in a trade liberalizing economy: the case of South Africa. *Contemporary Economic Policy* **20**(4), 479–489.

Drope, J. M. (2007). The political economy of nontariff trade barriers in emerging economies. *Political Research Quarterly* **60**(3), 401–414.

Edwards, L. (2005). Has South Africa liberalised its trade? *South African Journal of Economics* **73**(4), 754–775.

Edwards, L., R. Cassim, and D. Van Seventer (2009). Trade policy since democracy. In *South African Economic Policy Under Democracy* (ed. J. Aron, B. Kahn, and G. Kingdon). Oxford University Press.

Fallon, P., and L. A. P. de Silva (1994). South Africa: economic performance and policies. World Bank Discussion Paper 7.

Finger, J. M. (ed.) (1993). *Anti-Dumping: How It Works and Who Gets Hurt*. Ann Arbor, MI: University of Michigan Press.

Holden, M. (2002). Anti-dumping: a reaction to trade liberalisation or anti-competitive? *South African Journal of Economics* **70**(5) 912–931.

International Trade Administration Commission of South Africa (2008). Ramifications of the court ruling on anti-dumping sunset reviews. Media statement prepared by the International Trade Administration Commission of South Africa (28 July).

Joubert, N. (2005). The reform of South Africa's anti-dumping regime. In *Managing the Challenges of WTO Participation: 45 Case Studies* (ed. P. Gallagher, P. Low, and A. L. Stoler). Geneva: World Trade Organization.

Knetter, M. M., and T. J. Prusa (2003). Macroeconomic factors and anti-dumping filings: evidence from four countries. *Journal of International Economics* **61**(1), 1–17.

Lewis, D., K. Reed, and E. Teljeur (2004). South Africa: economic policy-making and implementation in Africa: a study of strategic trade and selective industrial policies. In *The Politics of Trade and Industrial Policy in Africa: Forced Consensus?* (ed. C. Soludo, O. Ogbu, and H. Chang). Africa World Press/IDRC, Trenton, NJ.

Moore, M., and M. Zanardi (2008). Trade liberalization and antidumping: is there a substitution effect? ECARES Working Paper 2008-024, Université Libre de Bruxelles.

National Board of Trade (2005). The use of anti-dumping in Brazil, China, India and South Africa: rules, trends and causes. Report (2005–2010) prepared for the National Board of Trade, Sweden.

Shepstone & Wylie Attorneys (2010). Constitutional court finds that anti-dumping duties are punitive. Online Article (3 August). URL: http://www.moneyweb.co.za/mw/view/mw/en/page292681?oid=499470&sn=2009+Detail+no+image&pid=292520.

South African Reserve Bank (2010). *Quarterly Bulletin*, no. 258. Pretoria: South African Reserve Bank.

South African Reserve Bank (2009). *Financial Stability Review*. Pretoria: South African Reserve Bank.

Statistics South Africa (2010). *P0211: Quarterly Labour Force Survey*. Pretoria: South African Government Printers.

Tovar, P. (2011). India: the use of temporary trade barriers. In *The Great Recession and Import Protection: The Role of Temporary Trade Barriers* (ed. C. P. Bown). London: CEPR/World Bank. (Chapter 7 of this volume.)

Tsengiwe, S. (2011). Personal interview (31 March).

World Trade Organization (2003). Trade policy review: Republic of South Africa, WT/TPR/S/114. Geneva: World Trade Organization.

World Trade Organization (1998). Trade policy review: Republic of South Africa, WT/TPR/S/34. Geneva: World Trade Organization.

Zarenda, H. (1977). The policy of state intervention in the establishment and development of manufacturing industry in South Africa. Unpublished Master's Thesis, Department of Economics at the University of the Witwatersrand, Johannesburg.